MW00768449

Computer Concepts: Systems, Applications, and

James F. Clark, Ph.D.
Clark Systems Corporation

Dale H. Klooster, Ed.D.

Warren W. Allen, M.A.

3d Edition

JOIN US ON THE INTERNET
WWW: http://www.thomson.com
EMAIL: findit@kiosk.thomson.com A service of I(T)P®

South-Western Educational Publishing
an International Thomson Publishing company I(T)P®

Cincinnati • Albany, NY • Belmont, CA • Bonn • Boston • Detroit • Johannesburg • London • Madrid
Melbourne • Mexico City • New York • Paris • Singapore • Tokyo • Toronto • Washington

ISBN: 0-538-67607-8

Library of Congress Catalog Card Number: 96-70605

2 3 4 5 6 7 VH 03 02 01 00 99 98

Managing Editor: *Janie F. Schwark*
Editor: *Cheryl Beck*
Photography Coordinator: *Ann Small*
Photo Research: *Meyers Photo-Art, Connie Springer*
Internal Design: *Ann Small*
Internal Illustrations: *Fox Art*
Cover Design: *Ross Design*
Cover Photo: *Guildhaus Photographics*
Marketing Manager: *John Wills*
Production Services: *York Production Services*

I(T)P®
International Thomson Publishing

South-Western Educational Publishing is a division of International Thomson Publishing, Inc. The ITP logo is a registered trademark used herein under license by South-Western Educational Publishing.

Preface

Over the years, each edition of this text has reflected advances in the computer industry that have been brought about by the ever-increasing changes in both computer hardware and software. This edition is no exception. As a matter of fact, this edition incorporates more extensive change than all previous editions combined. The reason for such a major revision can be directly contributed to the exponential rate at which the computer industry is progressing and growing. This rate of expansion has had a profound affect on our society and has provided an indication of the ever-increasing role that the computer will have in our personal and working lives in the future.

The tremendous increase in the use of computers in our homes, businesses, and industries is a result of (1) decreasing cost of equipment due to new and more efficient methods of manufacturing; (2) small-scale, yet very powerful, inexpensive microcomputers that now make it financially possible for small (as well as very large) businesses to use the technology; (3) explosive growth in the home/personal computer area, thus contributing to the general public's better understanding of computer capability and use; (4) increased utilization of the computer for communication; and (5) many other additional uses that take advantage of the computer's potential and capabilities.

The goal of this text is to prepare students to function in an environment—educational, personal, and work—in which computer confidence has become the expected norm. It seeks to develop an understanding of the entire area of computers and information processing, while at the same time developing precise knowledge in using common software applications. These applications include word processing, spreadsheet and database programs, as well as applications in a wide array of different subjects (e.g., math, science, English, business), graphing, telecommunications, operating systems, and many others.

For the student who is college bound, preparing for post-secondary technical education, or planning to enter the work force upon leaving high school, this text is ideal for developing basic computer knowledge and skills. For those continuing their education, it provides the foundation for further study. For those beginning employment, it develops the basic skills required for successful computer use in many jobs.

Few would disagree that we are living in a complex society with complex informational needs. Many businesses and industries have turned to the computer as a means of staying competitive, helping control costs, and managing their resources. If students are to be effective employees in these businesses and industries, it is essential that they have an understanding of the uses and functions of computers.

Text Organization

The *Computer Concepts: Systems, Applications, and Design, 3d Edition* text consists of 14 self-contained modules. This means that the presentation of the material can be sequenced by the instructor to meet the specific needs of students depending upon their level of computer literacy. Each module follows a carefully thought-out pedagogy that uses the same format, features, and generic approach to concepts and software, enabling students to become involved in the learning processes. The 14 modules are Introduction to the Computer System; Input, Processing, and Output; Operating Systems; Networks; Telecommunications; Word Processing; Spreadsheets; Publishing; Graphics and Presentations; Multimedia and Hypermedia; Databases; Additional Applications; Systems Analysis and Design; and Software Design, Development, and Implementation.

Features That Enhance Learning

This text includes many special features designed to stimulate and enhance learning and to actually include students in the learning process. Among them are the following:

- *Overview:* Each module begins with an overview of the topics that will be covered. Specific learning objectives are listed with each overview.
- *Trends:* Subjects dealing with new, innovative, or unique uses for technology or software.
- *Issues in Technology:* Short discussions of new or unique computer applications that provide interesting starting points for additional classroom discussion or research.
- *Ethics:* Issues addressing computer crime, ethics, copyright, etc., are presented in short vignettes that offer information, or present circumstances designed for classroom discussion and individual opinion.
- *Profiles:* Individuals who have made significant contributions to the computer industry are profiled in each module.
- *Careers:* A vignette describing a job and/or career opportunity in the computer industry is presented in each module. The type of work, educational requirements, career path, etc., are also presented.
- *Do It! Activities:* Do It! activities are short hands-on or participative activities placed strategically throughout each module that ask students to demonstrate or apply what has been learned in a practical application.
- *Summary:* Detailed summaries at the end of each module provide a convenient way for students to review the key concepts presented.
- *Key Terms:* Selected key terms are presented at the end of each module in a matching exercise to reinforce understanding and to practice using the term in the proper context.
- *Review Questions:* Review questions at the end of each module are designed to evaluate student understanding of the material presented.
- *Activities:* These end-of-module activities are designed to reinforce important concepts, encourage students to complete additional research, and enable students to make practical use of the material presented. While many of the activities are hands-on, they go far beyond merely using the computer and encourage students to think and make logical decisions.

Supplementary Materials

Several supplementary items have been developed to enhance student learning and to assist in lesson preparation, instruction, and testing.

- *Reteaching and Enrichment Activities.* This student workbook contains various types of study guides and exercises designed to reinforce students' understanding of the material presented in each module of the student text.

- *Template Disk.* Generic template files are provided on disk that can be used to complete activities in the *Reteaching and Enrichment Activities.* These template files are formatted for many of the most popular computer application software packages (e.g., word processors, spreadsheets, etc.) for the IBM PC, IBM PC compatibles, and Macintosh computers.
- *Manual.* The manual is available to all instructors who adopt the text for classroom use. The manual includes detailed outlines and teaching suggestions for each module. The manual contains solutions to all questions and activities in the textbook and in the *Reteaching and Enrichment Activities.*
- *CD-ROM.* An interactive, stand-alone CD-ROM entitled *Computer Concepts: Systems, Applications, and Design* for IBM PC, IBM PC compatibles, and Macintosh computers is available as an enhancement to the student text. The CD-ROM allows for individual exploration and discovery of computer technology.
- *Presentation Disks.* Disks containing a graphic presentation of the major illustrations and important subject matter in each module are provided to all instructors who adopt this text for classroom use. The presentation disks are available for the IBM PC, IBM PC compatibles, and Macintosh computers.
- *Pass! Performance Assessment Software System.* A computerized test bank is available for the IBM PC, IBM PC compatibles, and Macintosh computers.

Acknowledgments

The authors acknowledge the contributions of thoughtful reviewers and users of the previous editions. John Steffe, R. E. Lee High School; Julie Davis, Nacogdoches High School, Evelyn Warner, Bel Air High School; and Karen Rhodes, Cypress Creek High School, provided comprehensive reviews of this new edition.

Closing Comments

Few people would argue that the information age has been brought upon us through technological advances. Perhaps the most significant contribution has come from the computer industry. Increased research and development, coupled with a growing need for more sophistication, have contributed to an accelerated pace of technological improvement and accumulation of human knowledge. One only needs to look around the environment to see the many changes brought about by technology over the past few years. Rapid advances in technology have also affected the way businesses and industries function, causing them to become more complex and dependent upon more information to be competitive.

It has become crucial that students learn about computers and the characteristics, procedures, and techniques that enable them to have such a profound impact upon our environment, businesses, and industries. Students need to learn how computer systems are developed and how these systems must also change in order to keep pace with their surroundings. Upon completion of this text, students will have a strong foundation upon which to build as they begin their journey along today's information superhighway.

James F. Clark
Warren W. Allen
Dale H. Klooster

Table of Contents

Input, Processing, and Output IP

Operating Systems OS

Networks NT

Telecommunications TE

Word Processing WP

Spreadsheets SP

Publishing PB

Graphics & Presentations GP

Multimedia & Hypermedia MH

Databases DB

Table of Contents

Additional Applications AP

Systems Analysis & Design SA

Software Design, Development & Implementation SD

Glossary G

Photo Acknowledgments P

Index I

Introduction to The Computer System

Overview

Some people compare the advent of the computer to the discovery of the wheel or the invention of the printing press. Others say that its effects on society are more important than those of the Industrial Revolution.

A *computer* is an electronic device that accepts data, performs computations, and makes logical decisions according to instructions and data that have been given to it, and it produces meaningful information in a form that is useful to humans. Computers are complex and powerful tools that enable us to perform tasks. Many of these tasks can be completed in a fraction of the time it would take a human being to perform them. Some of the tasks a human could not possibly perform at all.

Computers can be found everywhere from space vehicles to our own homes. Their use affects society in general as well as each of us individually in our everyday lives. The varied and widespread use of computers continues to be fueled by an ever-changing, technologic growth. As technology finds more efficient ways of building more powerful computers, the users of these computers find more efficient ways to use technologic innovations.

This module describes the distinctive characteristics of computers; examines how a computer system functions in an information processing environment; identifies the various types, sizes, and shapes of computers; and recognizes several ways that its use has impacted on our society.

Objectives

1. Identify several characteristics of computers that have made them such powerful and popular tools.
2. Describe a computer system.
3. Recognize and describe the difference between hardware and software.
4. Explain the basic information processing cycle of input, processing, and output.
5. Identify and explain the differences between microcomputers, minicomputers, mainframe, and special-purpose computers.
6. Recognize the impact of the computer on society.

Distinctive Characteristics of Computers

Why are computers used? Why have they become so popular? These questions can be answered by examining the characteristics of a computer, which include its tremendous speed, accuracy, capacity, durability and reliability, versatility, cost-effectiveness, and technical growth.

Speed

Computers are electronic devices and, like all such devices, are exceptionally fast. Even the smallest, slowest computers are fast compared with human standards. Today, most computers operate at speeds recorded in **microseconds** (one millionth of a second, or 1/1,000,000). These devices can perform 1 million instructions in just 1 second. Newer, high-speed supercomputers can operate at speeds approaching the **nanosecond** range (one billionth of a second, or 1/1,000,000,000).

All processing that the computer performs is regulated by a clock that delivers regular impulses. The concept of how a computer clock works is somewhat similar to a bass drum in a band; the regular beat of the drum keeps the rest of the band following the proper tempo. Likewise, the computer clock's pulses keep the processor functioning in the proper tempo. Clock speeds for microprocessors are measured in megahertz. A **megahertz** (MHz) is 1 million cycles, or pulses, per second. For example, a particular processor running at a clock speed of 100 MHz can perform 100 million actions in 1 second. Because most processing operations require more than one action—one clock cycle—to be completed, however, fewer than 100 million operations per second can actually be performed. Completing a simple arithmetic calculation, for example, may require several clock cycles. Generally speaking, the greater the computer's megahertz cycle time, the greater the number of tasks it can perform in any given time span.

Because computers are so fast, they can perform tasks in a matter of seconds that would take humans weeks, months, years, or even a lifetime to complete (figure 1). In some instances, computers can perform within a matter of seconds or minutes tasks that would be impossible for a person to complete by hand in a lifetime. Also, unlike humans, computers operate at a steady, untiring pace. They do not need to take a break or to sleep 8 hours a night. The ability of computers to carry out their instructions in such a short period of time is one of the main reasons computers are used today. It is also a contributing factor to their increased popularity.

Accuracy

When a computer fails to function correctly, it is often because a mechanical device has worn out or an electronic component burned out. When a failure like this occurs, a computer engineer or technician must replace the faulty mechanism in the computer.

Computers have proven so accurate that they are trusted in virtually every application, even those involving life-and-death situations (figure 2). For example, jet pilots and flight crews rely on computer computations for guidance and navigation of their craft. Hospitals rely on patient-monitoring systems in critical-care units. Businesses and industries rely on the accuracy of the information provided by computers to keep track of their resources and to make decisions that often involve large sums of money. Computers,

figure 1

During the time it takes this drop of water to reach the ground, a computer operating at microsecond speeds could perform all of the following tasks and more:

- *Compute the grade point averages for 2500 students.*
- *Calculate the total value of all books used by students in a large school or university.*
- *Figure the electric utility bills for 1500 customers.*
- *Compute the fare for 1000 passengers' airline flights.*

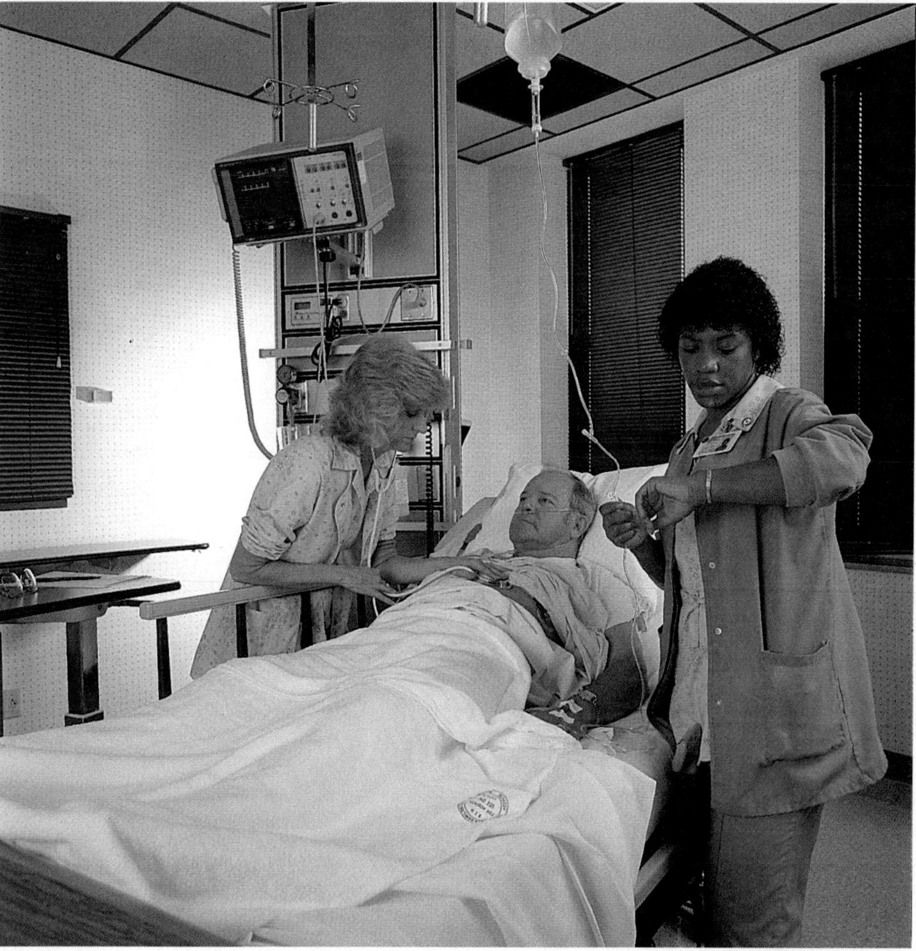

figure 2

Computers are so accurate that they are trusted in life-and-death situations, such as monitoring patients in critical-care units in hospitals.

Profile

Steve Jobs and Steve Wozniak

Who helped launch the personal computer to stardom? Credit two guys, friends since high school, named Steve—Steve Jobs and Steve Wozniak. In the late 1970s, using parts they had obtained from Atari and Hewlett-Packard, they built their own computer in Jobs' parents' garage. That first computer was the Apple I.

Soon, they were assembling computers for their friends, a local computer club, and even a computer store for sale to the general public. To finance their new computer venture, Jobs sold his Volkswagen bus, and Wozniak parted with his two Hewlett-Packard scientific calculators. In 1977, they officially launched Apple Computer Company and located its offices in Cupertino, CA, just two miles from their old high school. Their first production computer—the Apple II—was the first shot fired in the personal computer revolution. It weighed just 12 pounds, was easy to use, and was relatively inexpensive. Just as important, it inspired many established computer manufacturers (including industry giant IBM) to produce smaller, more user-friendly machines, changing the computer market forever.

Leading the way in this new market, the two Steve's company enjoyed explosive growth. In its first year of operation, Apple Computer Company registered sales of $800,000. In its eighth year, 1984, sales hit $1.5 billion.

however, are only as accurate as the instuctions and data that humans provide them. Software "bugs" and incorrect input can cause serious output errors.

Capacity

The ability of computers to store vast amounts of data both internally and externally continues to mushroom. For example, in 1978, the microprocessor used in a typical personal computer contained 29,000 transistors, was able to store 4000 characters of data in its internal memory, and could access 160,000 characters of data stored externally on disk or tape. By 1996, such a microprocessor contained over 5.5 million transistors, could store over 128 million characters of data internally, and could access billions of characters stored on external devices.

New computer architecture facilitates more efficient ways of utilizing this increased capacity. For example, today's computers can execute multiple operations during each clock cycle; in some cases, as many as five operations can be performed during a single cycle. In addition, more data can be moved at one time from one location to another. A computer operating at 166–200 MHz can move data from one location to another at a rate in excess of 1.2 billion characters per second.

Durability and Reliability

Computers are durable and extremely reliable devices. They can operate error-free over long periods of time, and they have become more reliable and more durable with technical enhancements. Today's computers have fewer mechanical parts that can physically wear out. Improved materials that are more resistant to wear, heat, and other elements of the external environment contribute to computer durability and reliability. The development of tiny circuit boards with mind-boggling capabilities has also enabled computers to be more durable and less sensitive to their environments. The technologic developments built into today's computers enable them to be installed and used in many and varied environments. They can be used as stationary devices or jostled about and still retain their ability to perform error-free over prolonged periods of time.

Versatility

Early computers were designed and developed for specific purposes. Generally, these early machines were used for one of two specific types of applications: mathematic computation, or business data processing. The computers designed to handle mathematic computations had high-speed computational abilities but minimal input and output capabilities. The computers designed for business data processing had high-speed input/output devices to handle high-volume input and output applications but minimal computational capabilities. Therefore, users who needed a computer to perform engineering or design tasks involving a lot of mathematic problem-solving chose to use the type of computer designed to handle those types of applications. Conversely, those users who needed a computer for business applications chose the type of computer specifically designed for that type of processing.

Because of technologic advancements in the computer industry, most computers today are considered to be **general-purpose computers**. That is, both their computation and input/output processing capabilities are such that they can be used for almost any type of application. For example, the same computer that is used to handle an engineering company's mathematic and design computations can also be efficiently used by the company to track inventory, process payroll, project earnings, and fulfill all its reporting needs. Today's computers are very versatile in what they can do.

Because of recent advances in computer technology and the miniaturization of computer components, computers and their component parts are being used in applications never before envisioned (figure 3). For example, computer components are being used in home appliances (washing machines, ovens), home entertainment centers, traffic lights, automobiles, banking, assembly plants, space probes, art, music, education, hospitals, sports, and agriculture, to name a few. The versatility of the computer and its use in a wide array of applications are limited only by the imagination of the human mind.

Cost-Effectiveness

Early computers were huge and very expensive. It was not uncommon for a computer to occupy the floor space of a regulation-size basketball floor and cost several million dollars. More recently, a computer that fit inside a

figure 3

(a) This homemaker is using a microwave/convection oven that is controlled by a computer to prepare a meal.
(b) These youngsters are using a specially designed computer to play a video game.
(c) This scientist is using a computer containing a special math processor to conduct an experiment.
(d) This businessperson is using a general-purpose computer to keep track of inventory.

a

b

c

d

figure 4

IBM's first computer filled an entire room. A recent typical notebook computer fit inside a small briefcase, weighed 15 ounces to 15 pounds, cost less than $3000, and had 100 times the processing power.

briefcase weighed 15 ounces to 15 pounds, cost less than $3000, and had 100 times the processing power of its early predecessors (figure 4).

The development of computer technology has been truly phenomenal. Consider what has happened to the costs and capabilities of other electronic devices such as calculators and watches. Their costs have dramatically decreased over the years, but their capabilities have dramatically increased. Figure 5 illustrates how computer costs and sizes have decreased, while at the same time, computer speed, capacity, reliability, durability and accuracy, versatility, and capability have increased.

figure 5

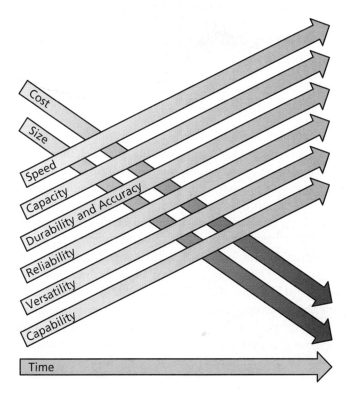

The speed, capacity, durability, accuracy, reliability, versatility, and capabilities of computers have increased as their size and cost have decreased.

Do It!

1 Find out the speed (in MHz) of one of the computers you have access to, and explain what it means.

2 Prepare a list of devices (other than those mentioned here) you come in contact with during an average day that contain computer components.

3 Prepare a chart contrasting the cost, speed, size, capacity, and other characteristics of a modern computer to an older computer (still used in your school, at home, at an office, and so on).

The cost of modern computers, weighed against the varied tasks they can perform, makes them truly cost-effective devices. Based on this industry's short history, one can expect that their costs will continue to decline while their capabilities will continue to rise.

Technical Growth

The computer is a unique device in that it actually fuels its own growth. In other words, its use in research because of its computational, logic, and decision-making capabilities allows it to participate in its own development. As computers become more sophisticated, other computers must be used to help design and build complex and intricate parts.

Another contributing factor in the popularity and growth of the computer is the never-ending thrust for new knowledge. Not only are computers being used in areas never before envisioned, current users want their computers to do even more. This thrust is creating a demand for new, more powerful devices to meet an ever-growing need for more information and new knowledge. Again, the computer is actually fueling its own growth and proliferation.

What Is a Computer System?

A **system** is a combination of related elements that work together to achieve a common goal. In a corporation, for example, many elements or departments, such as personnel, production, quality assurance, and administration, must work together as a whole unit to make the corporation successful. People from these various departments must interact with one another. A **computer system** is made up of hardware and software working together to accomplish a common goal. Hardware is the tangible, physical equipment that can be seen and touched; software is the intangible instructions that tell the computer what to do (figure 6). The software and hardware interact with each other.

A computer contains several hardware devices of various sizes, shapes, and functions that must work together as one system. These hardware devices enable the computer to accept data, process it into meaningful information, store it, and report it in a form that humans can understand. A

figure 6

The keyboard, mouse, printer, monitor, and processor of this modern personal computer work together with the software to form a computer system.

hardware device that enables the computer to accept data is called an **input device**; an example of an input device is a keyboard. A hardware device that processes the data into meaningful information is called the **processor**. A hardware device that permits data storage is called a **storage device**, and one example is a disk drive. A hardware device that reports the information in a form we can understand is called an **output device**. An example of an output device is a monitor.

A computer system is also composed of several software programs that control the hardware devices and in turn tell the computer what to do. A **program** can be defined as a series of detailed, step-by-step instructions that tell the computer precisely what actions to perform. Just as there are several hardware devices that must all work together, there are several software programs that must also work together as one system. For example, a **system program** controls the computer's circuitry and hardware devices, while an **application program** instructs the computer to perform a specific, user-defined task. Later, you will learn much more about system and application programs.

In summary, input, processing, storage, and output devices work together with system and application software programs as a whole toward the completion of a common goal or task. This is a computer system.

How a Computer System Functions

Data consists of facts in the form of numbers, alphabetic characters, special symbols, or words. Data that is manipulated into a form that humans can use or learn new knowledge from is called information. **Information** can be defined as knowledge of some fact or circumstance that is given or

Careers

Careers in the Hardware Industry

If one word could sum up careers in the computer hardware industry, that word would be "great." The research and design of computer hardware continues to be a great career area in terms of great importance, great opportunity, and great challenge.

Persons working in computer design may be involved in any of these areas: basic research; development of a new computer hardware system; or development of component parts, such as a processor chip or communications circuits. Not surprisingly, those who design computers and their components use existing computers as a tool in their work. For example, a computer may be used to help design the layout of a new processor chip.

To design a successful career in the computer hardware industry, a college degree is essential. While some individuals with little or no college experience have made important contributions to the computer industry, they are rare exceptions. Most professionals involved in basic research have advanced degrees in their area of study; those who apply research findings in new computer designs usually have engineering or science degrees.

Design is not the only career opportunity in the computer hardware industry. New designs must be documented, which calls for the skills of technical writers. Manufacturing expertise is needed to plan production, and actual product production is controlled by production personnel. Once the product comes off the line, marketing and advertising professionals must sell it. In addition, if the product breaks new ground, attorneys, lobbyists, and other resources may be needed to change the laws or regulations relating to the new product.

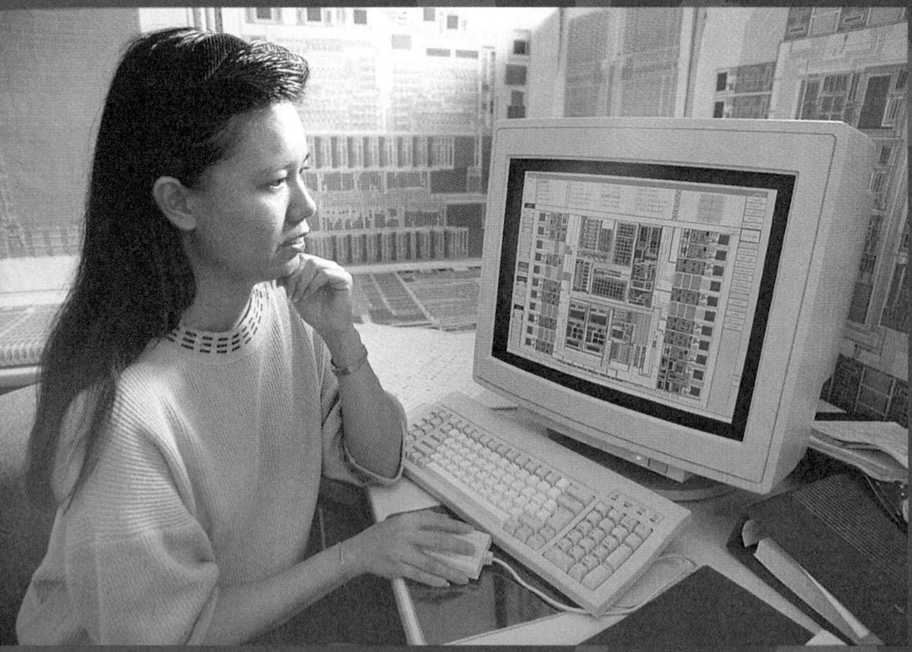

received. Humans share information with each other through spoken words, written communication, and a variety of other methods. Humans can also share information with and receive information from computers. This process of sharing information between humans and computers can be referred to as **information processing** (also called **data processing**).

In an information processing system, data is created or collected and fed into the system. Data that enters the system (via an input or storage device) are referred to as **input**. Useful information that leaves the system (via an output or storage device) is referred to as **output**, or processed information. In between the input and output stages, the data is processed. **Processing** takes place in the computer's processor, where detailed instructions (called software programs) tell the computer what should be done to the data to produce the desired information. Figure 7 illustrates this basic cycle of input, processing, and output.

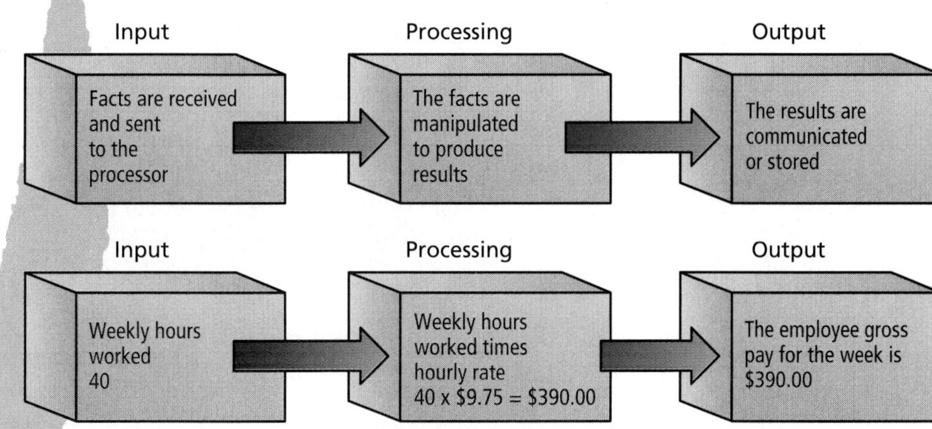

figure 7

The basic information-processing cycle consists of input, processing, and output.

Input

Data that is input to an information system comes from many sources and takes many different forms. Regardless of where the data comes from or the format in which the data exists (handwritten memos, invoices, payroll checks, and so on), all data must be verified for accuracy before entering the computer. This will help to guard against errors in the output. Once the data has been verified and entered, the computer can make further checks for validity and completeness.

Data about student performance comes from test scores, grade transcripts, and similar sources. Data regarding hours worked by an employee is taken from forms or time-clock cards. Data fed into the computer for processing is commonly referred to as **raw data** or **original data**. If raw data is first recorded on forms, these forms are known as **source documents**, because the forms become the source of the data entered into the computer's input device. Many applications do not use source documents. Instead, data is fed directly into the computer as the data is originated. Frequently, some of the input may be data that has already been collected and processed earlier. Figure 8 shows an application of this type.

figure 8

Both raw data and previously processed data may be used as input to a system.

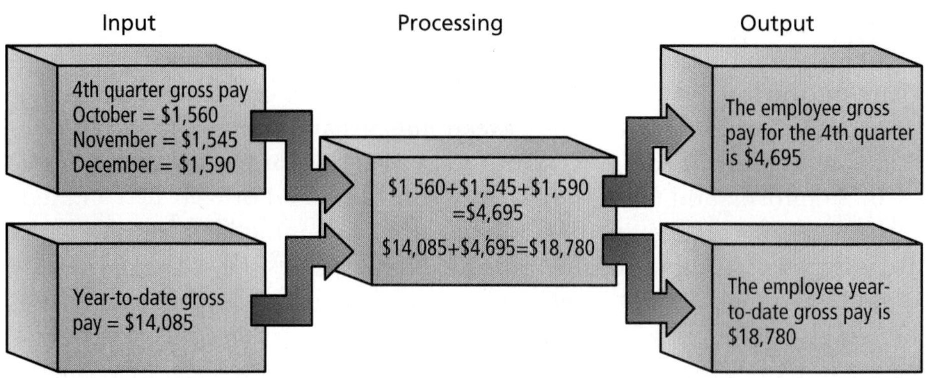

Processing

Whether the data is raw, previously processed, or a combination of the two, data must go into the computer's processor to be processed. Processing includes such tasks as performing mathematic calculations, making comparisons, classifying, summarizing, and arranging data into a desired order. Computers follow processing steps provided by software programs in much the same way that humans follow commands provided by the brain. For both, each step leading to the desired result must be included in the processing plan, and these steps must be in logical order. When steps are left out, are out of order, or when logic is not followed in finding the solution to a problem, neither a human nor a computer will produce the desired result.

Output

When the processing of data is completed, output takes place. Output is the process of storing the processed information for later recall or of communicating it to a user immediately. This can be done via a printed report, graphic representation, screen display, audio or spoken output, transmission to a remote location, or a storage device (figure 9). If stored, the informa-

figure 9

Output allows the user to access information that is stored in the computer.

Do It!

1 List the hardware (keyboard, processor, monitor) and software (system software such as DOS or Windows; application software such as word processors, spreadsheets, and so on) installed on a computer system to which you have access.

2 Review a listing of a computer program (from a textbook, technical manual, computer magazine, and so on), and describe your observations (amount of detailed instructions, number of instructions required to perform a task, and so on).

3 Make a list of the raw data that a computer would need to prepare your grade transcript.

tion is available whenever it is needed by the user. In any of these examples, the information will eventually reach the user, who may be a human or even the same or another computer system.

The steps of input, processing, and output are essential in an information-processing system. Regardless of the kind of information being produced or whether the system is manual or computerized, the processing of data uses these same three functions. Data enters the processing system, various operations are performed on the data to convert it to useful information, and the useful information leaves the system. For example, the names of students are data. Arranging the names in alphabetic order so that a certain name can be found quickly is a form of information processing. Using a computer system to record the test scores of students, prepare electric bills for customers, design a new automobile, or control a steel mill are also examples of information processing.

Types, Sizes, and Shapes of Computers

Computers come in a variety of types, sizes, and shapes, with varying capabilities and speeds. Initially, all computers were large in size and called **mainframes**. As computer technology grew, smaller, less powerful computers, called **minicomputers,** were developed. Later, technology developed the "computer on a chip," called a **microprocessor** (figure 10). The microprocessor led to the creation of yet another category of computers, which were even smaller and less powerful than the minicomputer and called the **microcomputer**.

Technology has now caused the evolutionary scale of computers to move "upward." Today's microcomputers have become more powerful than minicomputers used to be, and today's minicomputers have become more powerful than many mainframes used to be. Today's mainframes are also more powerful than ever before. This is primarily because of the microminiaturization of the computer processor. **Microminiaturization** is the technologic process that enables an entire microprocessor to occupy the space of a tiny chip no larger than the size of your fingertip.

Trends

The Evolution of Computers—ENIAC to PDA

Computers have come a long way in 50 years. In 1946, the first electronic computer went into operation. Known as ENIAC (the Electronic Numerical Integrator and Calculator), it was designed by Drs. John W. Mauchly and J. Presper Eckert under a contract from the U.S. Army. ENIAC was no desktop computer; it took up as much space as a regulation-size basketball court, weighed about 30 tons, and contained approximately 18,000 vacuum tubes. It was used to perform mathematic calculations. Programming ENIAC was no easy task, either. It required changes to thousands of wires and switches.

Compare ENIAC to its great-grandchild—and the latest example of computer technology—the PDA (Personal Digital Assistant). The PDA is small enough to fit in a suit pocket or purse, weighs just 15 ounces, and costs less than $1,000. Perhaps most amazing: the PDA is hundreds of times more powerful than the giant ENIAC. The PDA is easy to use, too; simply use the PDA's pen stylus to write, print, or draw write on the screen, or touch the on-screen keyboard to input information. And it offers its user a host of other practical capabilities, including:

- A date book with alarm.
- An address book.
- A notebook for writing memos and drawing sketches or diagrams.
- A full-function calculator, which can also be used to convert currencies and measurements.
- A world time clock for over 200 cities.
- A dictionary of over 50,000 words.
- A thesaurus of over 600,000 synonyms.
- A translation dictionary for 26 languages.
- Information on U.S. holidays, states, and cities.
- Information on foreign countries and cities.
- Access to electronic mail, online, and fax services.
- Sound capabilities.
- Mass storage.

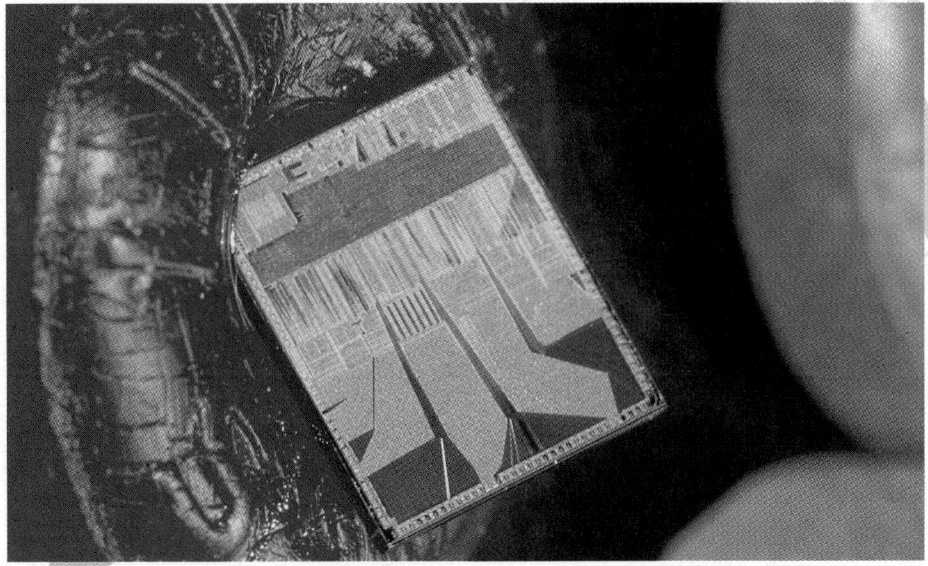

figure 10

A microprocessor provides tremendous amounts of power and occupies a space smaller than a piece of candy.

Not only has this technology caused computers to become increasingly smaller in size, it has also caused them to become increasingly more powerful. Today, computer capabilities range all the way from very limited to very powerful. In size, today's computers range from a hand-held unit to one that occupies a large room.

Technologic advances have also enabled computers of all sizes and shapes to become increasingly important in the area of communications. It is now possible for a computer to communicate with another computer sitting next to it on the same desk or to other computers located anywhere in the world. This means that data and information that would otherwise have been impossible or very time-consuming to acquire can be quickly accessed and shared.

Computers communicate with other computers via communication networks called **local area networks**, or **LANs**, and **remote networks** (also called **wide area networks**). Local area networks are those limited to small geographic areas, such as a school or an office building. Computers on local area networks are often connected together with cables. Remote networks, however, are not limited by geographic area. Computers using this type of communication network use a variety of transmission carriers, such as telephone lines, satellites, and microwave stations, to carry data.

Microcomputers

A computer used in the home, when traveling, or in a small or large business and that generally has less power and speed than a minicomputer or mainframe can be classified as a microcomputer. A microcomputer contains one or more microprocessors that can follow the instructions of a software program in a manner similar to its larger minicomputer and mainframe counterparts. Microcomputers have found their way into virtually every aspect of everyday life. For the purpose of discussion, microcomputers are classified into two subcategories: personal computers, and portable computers.

Personal computers A **personal computer** is a small, desk-size microcomputer designed for and used primarily in small and large businesses. In addition to businesses, personal computers have found their way into homes, schools,

figure 11

These students are using personal computers in a computer lab.

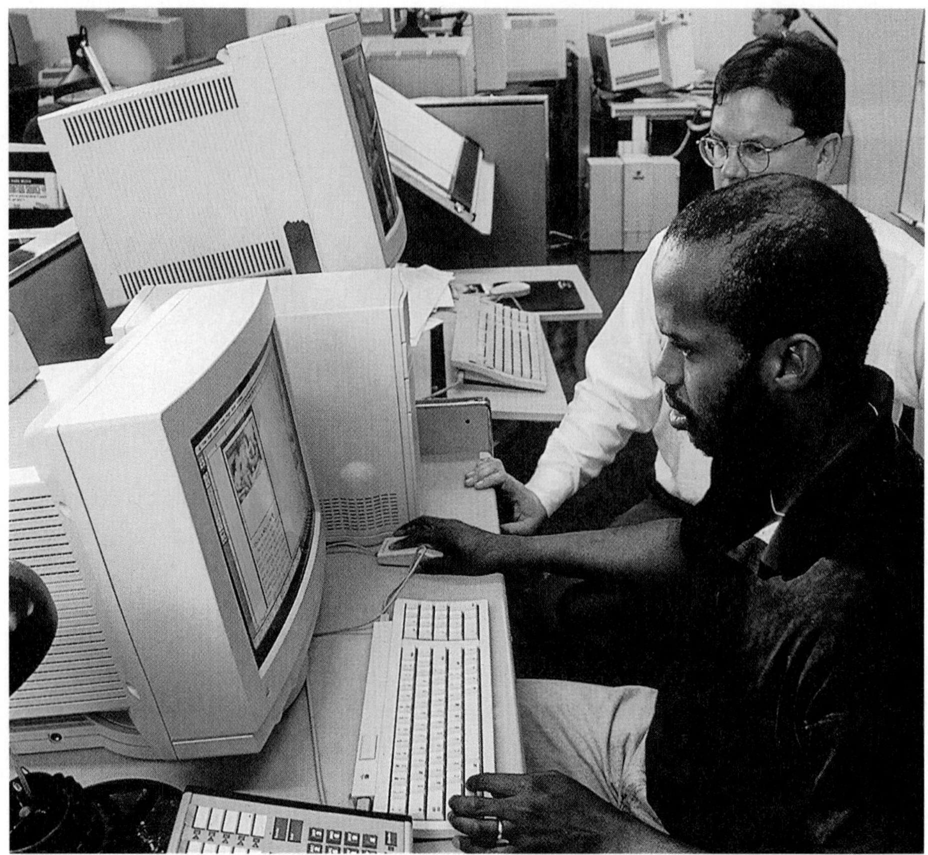

government, and industry (figure 11). Many different input, storage, and output devices can be connected to these computers, and coupled with its powerful processing capabilities, this enables the personal computer to perform many and varied tasks, which has made it the most popular computer in use today. Small and large businesses and industries use these machines to perform individual processing tasks as well as to communicate with larger minicomputers and mainframes.

As a result of this popularity, many software programs are available from which the user may choose. Examples of common software include programs in entertainment, accounting, customer billing, communication, spreadsheets, word processing, and database applications.

Network computers The network computer (not to be confused with a file server, workstation, or personal computer on a network) is a stripped-down version of a personal computer. It is geared toward Internet access, including downloading of software and programs from various networks. Because it focuses on Internet access for the source of its programs and data, the network computer does not require as much memory or storage capacity as a modern personal computer. This helps keep the cost of a network computer well below that of a personal computer.

Portable computers Portable computers (also called notebooks, laptops, powerbooks, or PDAs [Personal Digital Assistants]) have features and performance very similar to their personal-computer counterparts. The primary differ-

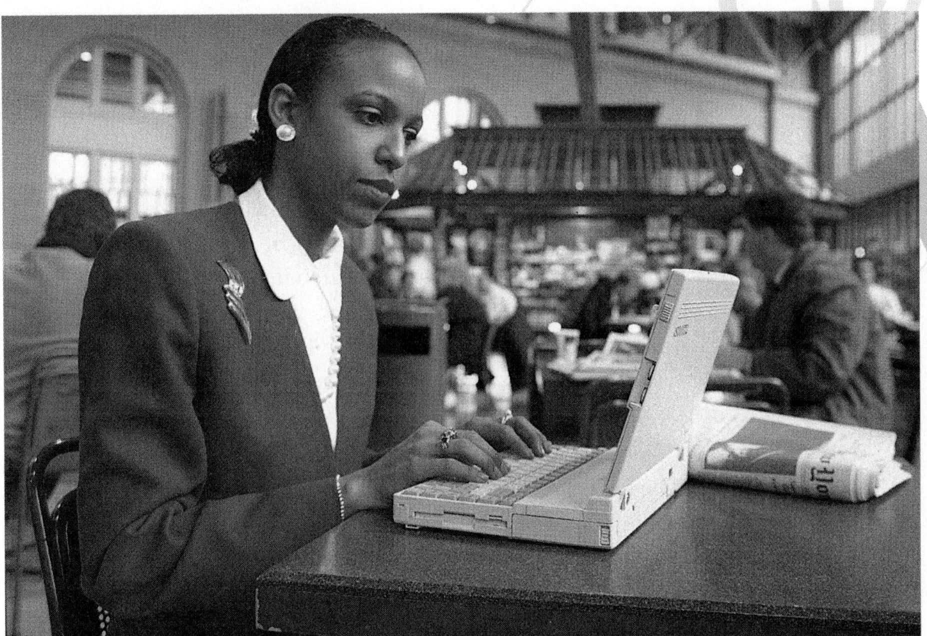

figure 12

This businessperson is using a notebook computer in an airport lounge while waiting to board a plane.

ence is that **portable computers** are lightweight (15 ounces to 15 pounds), transportable, and have the ability to connect several input, output, and storage devices. Because of their light weight, they can easily be moved from one location to another. Most portable computers can be folded and placed into a single carrying case for easy transportation. These computers are convenient tools for use in remote locations or when traveling (figure 12). Also, most portable computers are battery powered, can be used when away from an electrical power source, and can communicate with other computers.

Minicomputers

A minicomputer is defined as a computer with less power and speed than a mainframe but that is capable of storing and processing large volumes of data. Today's minicomputer is characterized by its ease of installation and operation. Because it is smaller than its predecessors, a minicomputer takes up less floor space and does not require special environmental-control systems or power supplies. Its ability to handle a full line of input, storage, and output devices provides a great deal of flexibility. In addition, its processing power lends itself to use by multiple users in many different areas. For example, it can be used as a multistation word processor linked to several other micro- or minicomputers, all working together to support remote geographic locations.

Another feature of a minicomputer is its ability to expand and be tailored to the growing needs of the user. As an organization grows, its processing needs also grow. Additional input, storage, and output devices may be added to an existing minicomputer to accommodate such growth. When the processing requirements of one minicomputer are exceeded, another can be installed and linked to the first to meet the new needs. It is also common to find one or more minicomputers located in remote offices or plants linked to a mainframe computer at an organization's main headquarters.

Mainframe Computers

A mainframe is a large computer with more processing power and speed than a minicomputer and is capable of quickly processing very large volumes of data. The mainframe computer is the foundation of the computer industry from which much technologic innovation stems.

A mainframe can store millions of characters and support many high-speed input, storage, and output devices. Organizations that require the processing capabilities of mainframe computers are usually very large, with a need for storing and accessing large amounts of data in a very short period of time. Examples of mainframe users include the federal government for processing of tax forms, state governments for driver vehicle registration, insurance corporations with huge policyholder databases, large banks and investment houses, large research and science industries, and other types of corporations.

Mainframe computers require special environmental controls, such as special power supplies as well as heating and cooling systems. Cables and wires that connect all of its component parts must be housed under a raised flooring platform on which the computer sits. Very sophisticated software programs control the operation of all devices that comprise the system and often require the operator to have special training to operate the system effectively.

The largest, fastest, and most expensive computers in existence are special mainframe computers called **supercomputers** (figure 13). Few supercomputers are built each year because the cost is so high and the applications for which they are used are so limited. Supercomputers represent the most advanced computer technology in the world today. They are used for advanced research and mathematic calculations in such areas as the space program, weather forecasting, and nuclear-weapons research and development. Because of their lightning speed and tremendous power, they can perform complex tasks that cannot be accomplished by other computers.

figure 13

Supercomputers are the most powerful computers in existence.

figure 14

This specially designed computer is used to check equipment and prescribe needed repairs.

Specially Designed and Equipped Computers

The microcomputers, minicomputers, and mainframes discussed previously are referred to as general-purpose computers because they can perform many different tasks depending on the software program they are using. Special-purpose computers, however, have been designed to perform specific, specialized tasks. These specially designed and equipped computers vary in size and power from a tiny microchip used in a microwave oven to a large, automatic machine-tooling system. Other examples and uses of special-purpose computers include the digital instrumentation and ignition systems in automobiles, the monitoring and control systems of space vehicles, the functioning of home appliances (washing machines, refrigerators, ovens), and the controls of traffic lights and assembly lines (figure 14). Recent use of computers in robotics has also led to an increased use of robot machines. With the technologic ability to develop these special-purpose machines, many mundane tasks that require monitoring and control will soon be done by computers.

Societal Impact of Computers

The use of computers in society has affected everyone. Some ways in which computers affect daily living may be evident, while others are more indirect. This section briefly looks at some common uses of computers in everyday living and their benefits to individuals and business.

Learning Aids

Computerized learning aids come in many varieties, the most common of which are learning toys. There are also literally hundreds of computer-assisted learning programs, dealing with a vast array of subjects, available for use on personal computers. These programs range from simple arithmetic to calculus, from English grammar to creative writing and foreign languages, and from basic graphics to engineering design models, to name a few.

Entertainment Computer games are available for all kinds of computers—from small, hand-held microprocessor units to large, mainframe systems. Computer games can be found in homes, schools, arcade centers in shopping malls, and at the local pizza parlor. They range from action games found in arcades to fantasy and adventure games to simulations to games of chance.

Game designers are always looking for ways to make a game seem more realistic. Designers are working to use the human senses in conjunction with visual images. For example, an exciting new type of gaming software, called virtual reality, is now becoming available. This type of technology uses three-dimensional display that is so real the user actually believes he or she is in the game itself (figure 15).

figure 15

This person is using a gaming helmet to play a virtual-reality game.

Benefits to Business

Computers are needed to perform business operations that require handling large amounts of data. Fortunately, several computer applications are available to assist businesses in working with large volumes of data. For example, with the help of word-processing software, business documents can be produced with speed and accuracy. Electronic spreadsheets allow businesses to make projections and forecasts that can be valuable in making decisions concerning activities such as expansion and investment. Databases created on the computer allow companies to organize large collections of related data that are easy to access and maintain. In almost every aspect, computers help businesses increase their efficiency and productivity.

Information Utilities

Businesses known as **information utilities** use large computers that store huge amounts of information about many different subjects. These computer systems and their vast amounts of data are available for personal use. For example, information utilities can allow a computer user to read the daily news, research published works, send a letter to a friend, play games, make airline reservations, obtain the latest stock market quotations, and perform many other activities. Ambitious plans are under way to link computers and information utilities all over the world, creating a huge **Information Superhighway**. The Information Superhighway of the future will provide digital, voice, and video communication access through computer-controlled telephones and televisions to any information resource anywhere in the world.

A small computer (with communication capabilities) attached to a phone line can be used to access an information utility's services. A fee is often charged by the utility based either on the amount of time the individual's computer is connected or on the services rendered. Examples of popular information utilities include America Online, CompuServe, and Prodigy.

The world's largest information network is called the **Internet**—a physically structured network of computers around the world. Access is commonly obtained through software known as a Web browser. Examples of Web browsers include Netscape Navigator and Internet Explorer.

A variation of the Internet is the Intranet, which is an interconnection scheme between the computers in a particular company. Only people who work for the company can access its Intranet, even though the same Web browsers that can tap into the Internet are used. Internal company documentation is often included on a company's Intranet. Outside access to these sites is blocked via "fire walls," which is a term for security coding methods.

Electronic Banking and Services

Banks have used computers for years. Nearly every bank offers an electronic teller that is in service 24 hours a day, and many banks have issued their customers cards that permit them to use other banks' teller machines nationwide. A growing number of customers prefer the machine to a human teller, even during hours when the bank is open.

One service that connects personal computers to a bank's main computers is called online banking. Through a modem and special software, a bank customer can use his or her home computer to check account balances, transfer funds, and pay bills. Some banks even offer access to stock prices through their online service. As with the use of a bank card, a personal identification number (PIN) is used as the first level of security for the customer.

Another service becoming popular through the banking industry is the bill-payment-by-phone service. To use this service, a customer tells the bank the name and address of each business to be paid on a regular basis along with his or her account number at each business. Payments that are the same every month, such as rent or mortgage payments, can be scheduled for automatic payment. Items that vary in amount, such as the phone or electric bill, are paid when the customer instructs the computer to do so. To pay a bill, a customer dials the computer's phone number and uses the phone's keypad to enter the bank-card number and secret password, the codes for the transfer of payment to the business from either the checking or savings account, the business code number (provided by the bank), the amount of money to be paid, and the date on which the payment should be made.

Another banking service involves the use of debit cards. A **debit card** is a small plastic card that looks just like a credit card, but it causes the amounts of purchases to be immediately deducted from the user's checking account rather than appearing on a bill days or weeks later.

Shopping from Home

In addition to the use of debit cards, computers are changing the way that people shop. Many stores have joined forces with both the information utilities discussed earlier and cable-television stations to provide shopping services. After "browsing" through a list of items, and perhaps watching animated demonstrations of products on television, a person may immediately place an order. Consequently, individuals may now shop by computer in the comfort of their homes.

Household Control

Surprisingly, a growing number of the newer household devices are computer controlled. For example, security systems, refrigerators, ranges, microwave ovens, washers and dryers, stereos, televisions, videodisk players, and thermostats contain small computers. Some homes, however, have all aspects of their operation supervised by computers (figure 16). The air-conditioning and heating system is under computer control to produce the most comfort at the lowest cost. Lawn sprinklers are turned on automatically whenever they are needed, and fire and burglar alarms keep constant watch. Some control units can automatically call the fire or police department if an emergency develops.

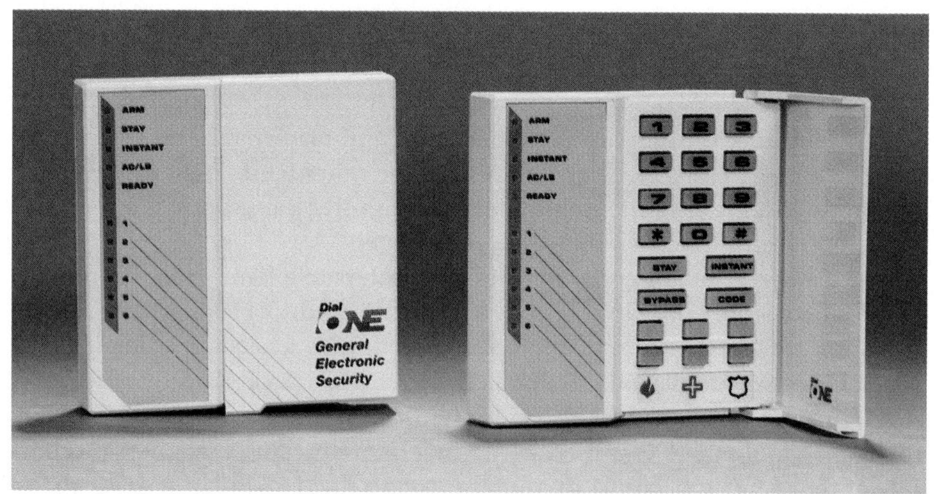

figure 16

This computer-controlled home-security system monitors movement, broken glass, unlawful entry without a security code, and so on, and it alerts the local police department.

Weather and Environment

Probably every commercial television station in the country uses some form of computerized presentation equipment on its weather show. This equipment may show temperature ranges, precipitation levels, and wind flow. Computer-enhanced, animated weather-satellite data can show the position and direction of storms and issue warnings for those in their paths. Computers are also used extensively in weather forecasting (figure 17).

In addition to weather forecasting, other environmental successes are possible because of computers. Tracking the flow of oil spills and other pollutants in streams, for example, has helped us to overcome environmental hazards. This is because the path that water currents will take, changes in the wind, and changes in the water temperature affect the direction in which

figure 17

A meteorologist is using computer-generated models to forecast weather.

pollutants will travel. When computers predict their direction of travel, action can be quickly taken to conduct clean-up operations and to minimize damage.

Transportation

Almost every kind of transportation has been affected by computers. Rapid-transit trains operate with no crew members. Many aircraft can fly to their destinations and land under the control of the computer, making the flight safer and more efficient; in this situation, the captain simply serves as a manager by telling the computer what to do. For a number of years, computers have provided functional controls such as spark and fuel control in cars. Another system reduces the car's wind resistance by changing its height and altitude toward the wind by using air bags that inflate or deflate at each corner of the car.

Community Services

Firefighting and the saving of lives are also aided by the computer. Computerized mapping systems can quickly point out the location of a problem and identify the emergency crew closest to the scene. Computers can help decide where to place equipment and personnel to ensure the shortest response time. In some communities, computers can keep firefighters updated with the floor plans of buildings in which they may need to fight a fire.

Crime Control

Crime control is another area in which computers help to organize vast amounts of information. For example, states have agreed to share drivers' license records for persons whose licenses have been taken away. This means that those individuals cannot go to a neighboring state and obtain a license. Other records of crimes that have been committed are kept by the FBI's National Crime Information Center; this information has been used to find stolen cars driven across state lines. In other cases, computers have been used to analyze the details of a series of crimes that seemed to be committed by the same person, eventually leading to the arrest of that criminal. Law-enforcement officers may have small computers in their cars for immediate access to information stored in these huge computer information sources. An officer may use such a computer to check if a suspect car has been stolen.

Medical and Health Care

Computers have long been used by hospitals for routine record-keeping. Today, however, many people owe their lives to the computer. A modern hospital is a showplace of computerized equipment. Sensors (devices that detect changes) can be attached to patients to tell when there are changes in temperature, heart rate, blood pressure, or other vital signs. If there is a negative change, the hospital staff is alerted immediately, in many cases saving lives. Medical tests that were once very time-consuming or impossible are now completed quickly by computer. A machine can scan the body and provide three-dimensional views never before thought possible. New technology is even providing computers with the ability to replicate the workings of specific internal organs of a patient. This information can be enhanced, magnified, and animated in three-dimensions, providing doctors with valuable information in diagnosing problems or preparing for surgery (figure 18).

figure 18

Computers help this surgeon to provide more effective treatment.

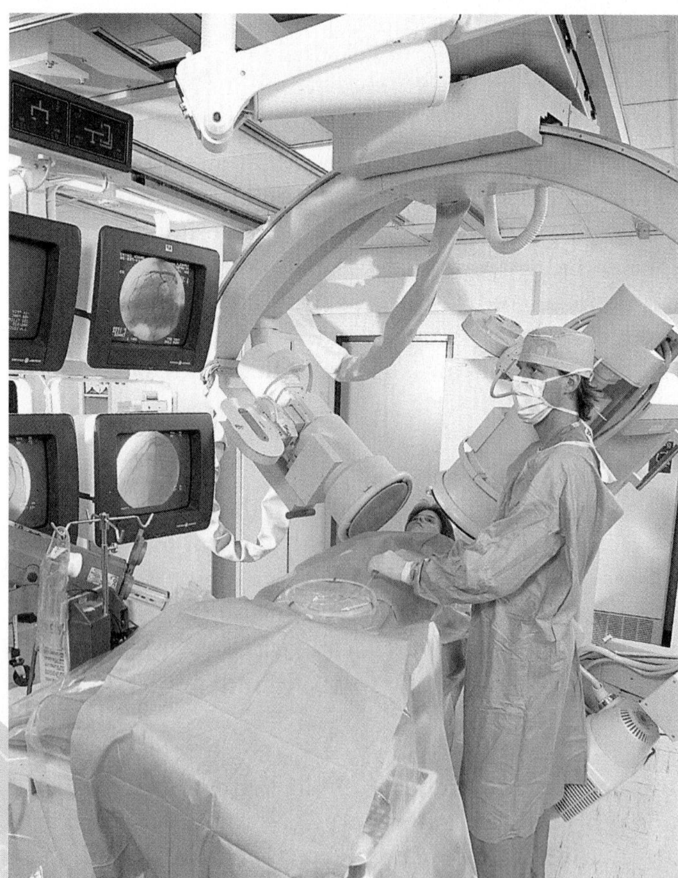

An equally exciting area for computers in the medical/health field is patient treatment. Computer-controlled pumps can be used to inject drugs into the bloodstream. Technology is being developed so that the computer not only injects the drug but also performs the full-time measurement of chemicals within the body, with the computer making second-by-second decisions on how much of the drug is required. Such uses of the computer should provide much better treatment of illnesses such as diabetes.

Routine and Dangerous Tasks

A major impact on business employees has been the use of the computer for routine tasks. When the computer is put to work doing routine, boring tasks, the employees who previously performed these tasks can be freed to do more interesting work. Office jobs that require the same calculations to be repeated frequently and assembly line work that requires the same recurring tasks to be performed are examples of situations in which the computer can be put to good use. Computers are also used to handle hazardous materials and perform tasks that are dangerous to humans (figure 19).

figure 19

Computers can perform tasks in environments too dangerous for human workers.

Issues In Technology

Lookalike Icons Cause Confusion

To save a document or perform other computer functions in a Macintosh or Windows environment, simply "click" on the appropriate icon—the little picture that represents an individual computer action. These icons are usually self-explanatory. For example, a wastebasket may represent the action of deleting a document, or a folder may represent the action to file a document.

These icons have made computing easier for everyone by portraying complex functions in a simple, graphic, obvious way. However, software designers are running out of "obvious" graphic devices. The more icons that are already in use, the more difficult it is to come up with new ones that work. A new icon must be clearly different than existing ones, or there will be confusion on the part of users.

In the past, designers have used the traffic safety field as a model for their icons. For example, symbols on traffic signs for "do not enter," "caution," and "merge" have been modified and used as computer icons. When icons are clear, they can make using a computer almost instinctive; however, when icons are abstract and meaningless, they are no better than the words they were designed to replace. See for yourself; try to match the appropriate icon to its intended computer action from the list provided below. (The answers are provided below the function list.)

Icons were first used on computers by Xerox Corporation in 1981. In 1984, the Apple Computer Company's Macintosh computer expanded the use of icons. Microsoft Corporation further expanded the popularity of icons with its Windows operating system, bringing the symbols to IBM and compatible computers.

With the widespread use of icons comes the potential for confusing or unclear symbols. To combat this problem, iconographers (people who design icons) are using new technologies to design animation icons, sound icons, and three-dimensional–looking icons. Other software developers are even adding words to their icons.

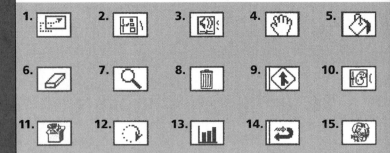

Identify the Icon

Match the icon with its function

1. 2. 3. 4. 5.

6. 7. 8. 9. 10.

11. 12. 13. 14. 15.

a. Rotate image
b. Change screen set-up
c. Dr. Watson
d. Enlarge or reduce object
e. Delete file
f. Merge document
g. Change sound
h. Undo
i. Object packager
j. Move through document
k. Enlarge/reduce view
l. Draw chart
m. Fill with color
n. Adjust color
o. Erase image

Answers:

1-d, 2-b, 3-g, 4-j, 5-m, 6-o, 7-k, 8-e, 9-f, 10-n, 11-i, 12-a, 13-l, 14-h, 15-c.

Do It!

1 Categorize the computers used in your school, college, or university as mainframes, minicomputers, and microcomputers.

2 Give an example of how the microminiaturization of computer components has affected our everyday lives.

3 Do you think that the popularity and use of mainframe and minicomputers have decreased or increased during the past few years? Justify your answer.

4 Have you used a computer device today? Explain.

Summary

A computer can generally be defined as an electronic device that performs computations and makes logical decisions according to instructions and data that has been given to it. If the instructions and data are accurate, the computations and logical decisions that the computer makes will also be accurate.

- Computers are electronic devices and, like all electronic devices, are exceptionally fast. Even the smallest, slowest computers are fast compared with human standards. All processing performed by the computer is regulated by a clock that delivers regular impulses; these impulses are measured in megahertz (1 MHz equals 1 million cycles).

- Computers are remarkably accurate devices. More often than not, they are blamed for errors that in reality are caused by humans.

- The ability of computers to store vast amounts of data both internally and externally continues to mushroom. New computer architecture enables multiple operations to be executed during a single clock cycle and data to be moved from location to location much more efficiently.

- Computers have become more reliable and more durable with technical enhancements. In addition, improved materials that are more resistant to wear, heat, and other elements of the external environment contribute to their durability and reliability.

- Because of technologic advancements in the computer industry, most computers today are considered to be general-purpose devices. In other words, both their computation and input/output processing capabilities are such that they can be used for nearly any type of application.

- Computers are truly cost-effective devices. Their costs have dramatically decreased over the years, but their capabilities have dramatically increased.

- The computer is a unique device in that it actually fuels its own growth. Its use in research for its computation and logic decision-making capabilities allows it to participate in its own development.

- Computer systems can be defined as a combination of related elements (called hardware and software) working together as a whole to achieve a common goal.

- Hardware is the tangible, physical computer equipment that can be seen and touched, whereas software is the intangible instructions (software programs) that tell the computer what to do.

- Hardware devices are used to input data, process raw data into meaningful information, store data, and output information in a form that humans can understand.

- A program is a series of detailed, step-by-step instructions that tell the computer what to do.

- Data that is manipulated into a form that humans can use or learn new knowledge from is called information. The process of sharing information between humans and computers can be referred to as information processing (also called data processing).

- Data that is input into the computer must be verified to ensure accuracy.

Summary

- Processing data includes sorting, classifying, calculating, summarizing, and comparing the data.

- Output is the process of storing processed information for later recall or of communicating it to a user immediately.

- The basic information-processing cycle consists of input, processing, and output. All computer systems have this same basic processing cycle in common.

- Computers come in a wide variety of sizes, capabilities, and speeds. With the advent of the "computer on a chip" also came a blurring of the categories in which various sizes and shapes of computers could be classified. Not only has this technology caused computers to become increasingly smaller in size, they have become increasingly more powerful.

- Computers communicate with other computers via communication networks called local area networks (LANs) or remote networks (also called wide area networks).

- Microcomputers are a category of computers that can be used in the home, when traveling, and in small and large businesses. Microcomputers have less power and speed than a minicomputer or mainframe.

- Minicomputers are a category of computers with less power and speed than a mainframe but that are capable of storing and processing large volumes of data.

- Mainframe computers are large computers with more processing power and speed than a minicomputer and that are capable of quickly processing very large volumes of data. The largest, fastest, and most expensive computers in existence are special mainframe computers called supercomputers.

- Special-purpose computers have been designed and equipped to perform specific, specialized tasks. These specially designed and equipped computers vary in size and power from a tiny microchip used in a microwave oven to a large, automatic machine-tooling system.

- Businesses known as information utilities have large computers that store huge amounts of information that can be accessed. Information highways of the future will provide digital, voice, and video communication access through computer-controlled telephones and televisions to any information resource anywhere in the world.

- Some common uses of computers in our everyday lives include electronic banking and services, shopping from home, household control, learning aids, weather forecasting and environmental preservation, transportation, community service, crime control, medical and health care, and both routine and dangerous tasks.

The following key terms were defined in this module. For each of the following terms, write on a separate piece of paper the number of the definition followed by the letter of the appropriate term.

Terms

A. computer

B. general-purpose computers

C. information

D. information/data processing

E. information utilities

F. application program

G. computer system

H. hardware

I. input

J. input device

K. microminiaturization

L. output

M. output device

N. processing

O. processor

P. program

Q. raw data/original data

R. software

S. source documents

T. storage device

U. system program

V. Information Superhighway

W. megahertz

X. local area network (LAN)

Y. Internet

Definitions

1 a combination of related elements (hardware and software) working together to achieve a common goal

2 tangible, physical equipment that can be seen and touched

3 the intangible instructions that tell the computer what to do

4 a hardware device which enables the computer to accept data

5 an electronic device that accepts data, performs computations, and makes logical decisions according to instructions and data that have been given to it and that produces meaningful information in a form useful to humans

6 a hardware device that processes data into meaningful information

7 a hardware device that permits the storage of data

8 a hardware device that reports processed information in a form that humans can understand

9 a series of detailed, step-by-step instructions that tell the computer precisely what actions to perform

10 a program that controls the computer's circuitry and hardware devices

11 a program that instructs the computer to perform a specific, user-defined task

Matching

12 data that enters the computer

13 useful information that leaves the computer

14 activity that takes place in the computer's processor, where detailed instructions tell the computer what should be done to the data to produce the desired information

15 data from a source document that is fed into the computer for processing

16 forms that become the source of the data entered into the computer's input device

17 knowledge of some fact or circumstance that is given or received

18 the process of sharing information between humans and computers

19 the technologic process that enables an entire microprocessor to occupy the space of a tiny chip no larger than the size of your fingertip

20 term(s) used to identify computers in which their computation and input/output processing capabilities are such that they can be used for almost any type of application

21 digital, voice, and video communication access through computer-controlled telephones and televisions to any information resource anywhere in the world

22 the internal clock speed of a computer measured in millionths of a second

23 businesses that use computers to store huge amounts of information, then make access to these computers and the stored information available for personal use

24 a communications network that covers a limited geographic area

25 a physically structured network of computers around the world

Review

1. What fractional part of a second is a microsecond? A nanosecond? (Obj. 1)
2. Why are computers considered to be extremely accurate devices? (Obj. 1)
3. What factors have contributed to the modern computer's increased durability and reliability? (Obj. 1)
4. What is a general-purpose computer? (Obj. 5)
5. Why are modern computers considered (for the most part) to be cost-effective devices? (Obj. 1)
6. How have computers participated in their own development? (Obj. 1)
7. Why should data be verified both before and after being entered into the computer? (Obj. 4)
8. Identify the basic functions of the information-processing cycle. (Obj. 4)
9. What are the most important characteristics of computer-generated output? (Obj. 4)
10. Explain the difference between computer hardware and computer software. (Obj. 3)
11. Explain the difference between an input device, a processor, a storage device, and an output device. (Obj. 4)
12. Explain the difference between a system program and an application program. (Obj. 2)
13. Briefly explain how a computer system works. (Obj. 4)
14. Describe the differences between a microcomputer, a minicomputer, a mainframe computer, and a special-purpose computer. (Obj. 4)
15. Describe the differences between a personal computer and a portable computer. (Obj. 5)
16. Identify at least three uses of special-purpose computers (other than those given in this text). (Obj. 5)
17. What is an information utility service? (Obj. 6)

18 Describe how computers can provide better service for bank customers. (Obj. 6)

19 How may computers be used in the home? (Obj. 6)

20 What are some ways the computer is used in dealing with the weather and environment? (Obj. 6)

21 How have computers affected transportation? (Obj. 6)

22 How have computers contributed to improved community services? (Obj. 6)

23 Describe ways in which computers improve medical and health care as well as the quality of life for those who are ill or disabled. (Obj. 6)

24 What are the advantages to humans of having computers perform routine and dangerous tasks? (Obj. 6)

25 Identify at least six uses of computers (other than those given in the text) in our society or everyday living. (Obj. 1, 6)

Activities

1 *Speaking* Divide into teams based on your major discipline of interest. For example, those interested in business would be on one team, those interested in math would be on another, and so on. As a team, research and find a software application for your discipline, then present the team's findings to the class. Include a visual aid (transparency, poster, or computer presentation) describing the purpose of the software, how much it costs, and the minimum hardware and software requirements. Prepare a handout for your classmates. (Hint: visit a local computer store, read a computer magazine, or check the software used in your school.)

2 *Writing* Prepare a written report describing the characteristics of a computer system that you would like to purchase. Consult a computer magazine, visit a computer store, or check with your library or other sources to obtain information. Include information about the speed, accuracy, durability and reliability, versatility, and cost-effectiveness in your findings. Also include information such as hard-disk size, memory size, and whether the computer would be easy to upgrade.

3 *Teamwork* With other classmates, organize into four or five teams. Each team should select a local business or industry. Visit your selected business or industry, and find out the different ways that they use computers. As a team, prepare a short (5 minutes) presentation to share your findings with the other teams.

4 *Science* Research the ways that computers are being used in medicine and health care. Possible topics include:

- Persons who have lost the use of their legs through spinal-cord injuries are now walking with the aid of computer stimulation of their leg muscles.
- Important steps made toward artificial vision for the blind.
- Computer-controlled wheelchairs and robot arms that respond to spoken words are proving to be of tremendous value to the disabled.

5 *Math* Most modern computer systems have an online calculator that can be used at any time. Find out how to access the calculator on the computer you are using. (Hint: refer to your computer's online help or user manuals.) Use it to calculate the number of computer cycles per second a computer operating at 15, 33, and 66 MHz performs.

6 *Ethics* Find someone who uses a computer in his or her job. Ask this person what he or she considers to be the greatest threat to the security and safety of their computers and the data stored within them. Find out what safety measures or procedures are used to protect these assets.

7 *Global* Information utilities have enabled computer users to communicate with other users anywhere in the world. Consult a computer magazine, your local newspaper, a computer store, or other sources to obtain information about an information utility (Internet, America Online, CompuServe, and so on) that is used to link computer users here in the United States or anywhere around the world.

8 *Internet* If you have access to the Internet, use your Web software to find information about the internal memory speed of the newest personal computers. Find out how the newest computers are designed to efficiently move more than one character of data or execute more than one instruction during each clock cycle. Use terms such as CPU, MEMORY, SPEED, MEGAHERTZ, NANOSECOND, and so on to help narrow your search. Report your findings.

Input, Processing, & Output

II

Overview

We now learn about the types of input devices used to enter software instructions (programs) and data into a computer's memory. Following a discussion of input devices, we examine how memory and processor components of the central processing unit function. Next, we learn about the most commonly used output devices and the kinds of applications for which they are best suited. Finally, commonly used auxiliary storage devices that record data for later access or processing will be discussed.

Today's need to use computers for multimedia presentations and graphic image integration has led to new, more powerful, and faster input, processing, output, and auxiliary storage devices. For example, new input devices can scan color photographs and drawings in one, two, or three dimensions and enter them directly into the computer. Fast processors with large amounts of memory are capable of rotating, flipping, enhancing, reducing, enlarging, and animating these graphic images. High-resolution output devices can display and print high-quality graphic images in thousands of different colors. High-density auxiliary storage devices are capable of holding mind-boggling amounts of data and graphic images that are accessible in thousandths of a second. Many of the animated graphics you see on television announcing sporting events, movies, sitcoms, or advertising a product use this type of computer hardware to produce the desired effect. Another form of computer input is through downloading graphic and text files from the Internet. Most Web browser software includes methods for downloading a file from the Web right onto your computer's hard disk.

Objectives

1. Identify and explain usage of the most common input devices.
2. Describe how the processor directs the computer's actions, performs arithmetic operations, and makes logical comparisons.
3. Identify and explain usage of the most common output devices.
4. Identify and describe the various types and characteristics of auxiliary storage devices.

Input Devices

Input devices come in many sizes and shapes, operate at different speeds, and have different capacities and capabilities. Many computers have more than one input device attached. The task to be accomplished determines the best device to use.

Keyboard

The most common way to enter data into the computer is by using the computer **keyboard**. When you press a key, the computer converts the alphabetic, numeric, or special symbol into a code and stores it in the memory.

The computer keyboard is similar to a typewriter keyboard. Figure 1 shows a typical computer keyboard divided into four sections: function keys, typewriter keyboard, numeric pad, and directional keys. The arrangement of these keys and the tasks that they perform vary from keyboard to keyboard.

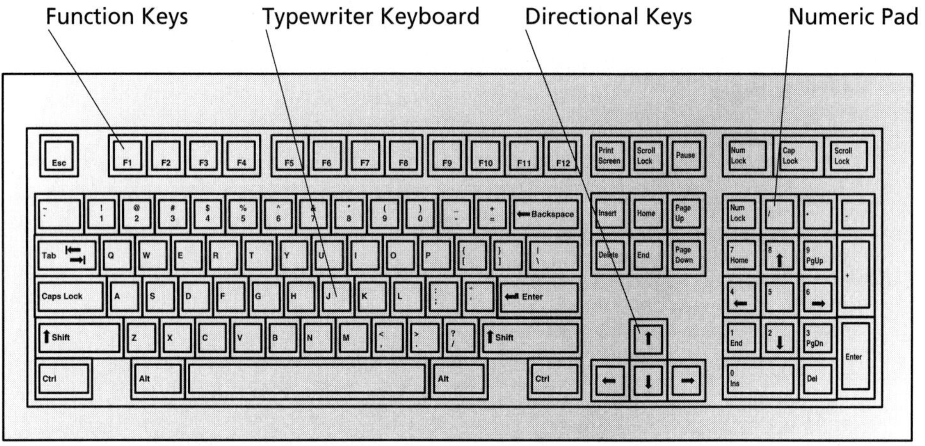

figure 1

Function keys are designed to work in conjunction with the instructions in a stored program. A software program will detect when a designated function key is pressed and then instruct the computer to perform a specific task. The typewriter keyboard section is very similar to the key arrangement of a typewriter. The key labeled Enter (on some computers, this key is labeled Return) is commonly used to tell the computer to accept data as it appears on the display screen for processing or storage. Other keys, such as the Esc, Ctrl, PrtScn, Alt, Num Lock, Home, PgUp, End, PgDn, Del, and so on, are active only if the program running in the computer at any given time is designed and written to use them. (Note that not all of these keys are available on all keyboards.) The numeric pad is commonly used to key numeric data into the computer quickly, because the arrangement of the numeric keys are the same as that on a standard calculator keyboard. Directional keys enable the user to work with various areas on the display screen; each arrow points in the direction that will be taken by the cursor every time the corresponding key is struck. The cursor serves as a marker and is often depicted as a flashing insertion point (|), an underline (_), or a square (■) symbol on the display screen.

One specialized type of keyboard is called a touch-sensitive, keyless, or **membrane keyboard** (figure 2). It is covered with a seamless material to protect it and is designed to withstand a hazardous environment.

figure 2

Membrane keyboards are used in locations where liquid may be splashed on them or where workers operating them have grease on their hands.

When different areas (called buttons or blisters) representing keys of the membrane are pressed, the characters represented are transmitted to the computer in the same way as they are with a standard keyboard. A keystroke on a membrane keyboard requires more pressure than the same keystroke on a traditional keyboard. The membrane keyboard therefore is better suited for situations where simple, low-volume inputting is required.

Joystick

A **joystick** (also called a controller) consists of a plastic or metal rod that is mounted on a base. The rod (joystick) can be moved in any direction. As the rod is moved, an *x* (horizontal) direction and a *y* (vertical) direction can be input to the computer. In turn, the computer uses these coordinates (sets of numbers) to determine a specific location on the display screen, which is denoted by a cursor. A **cursor** is a marker that is depicted on the screen as a flashing insertion point (I) , an underline (_) , or a square (■) symbol on the display screen. Most joysticks also have one or more simple switches or buttons that can input data in a simple on/off response.

Mouse

Like the joystick, the **mouse** is also a pointing device that is used with a video display screen (figure 3a). The body of the mouse is palm size, has a ball housed in the undercarriage, and contains one or more push buttons. As the body of the mouse is moved over a hard, flat surface, the ball rotates. Moving the mouse moves the cursor on the display screen in the same direction. Once the cursor has been positioned in the desired location, pressing a button on the mouse causes an action to be taken. The type of action depends on the computer program in use at the time.

A device known as a **trackball** is designed to perform the same functions as a mouse (figure 3b). A trackball can be thought of as a stationary mouse (or a mouse on its back), and it consists of a ball in a stationary housing. Some trackballs are designed as extensions of standard keyboards.

a

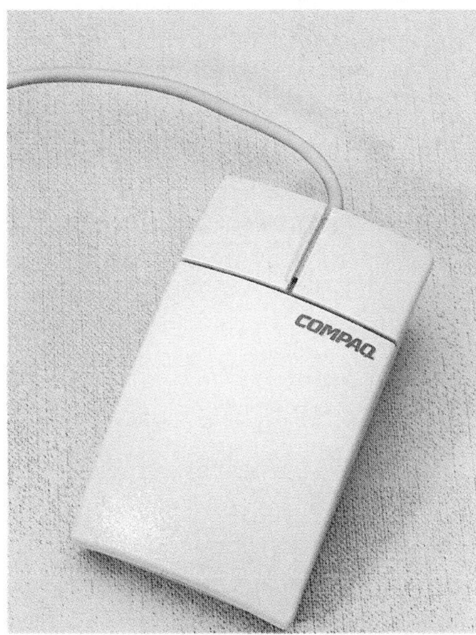

b

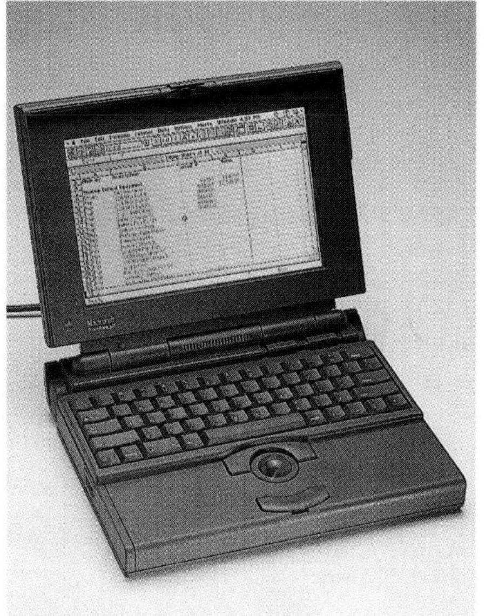

figure 3

(a) The mouse is frequently used to complement the keyboard and as a pointing device to select an option.

(b) Instead of moving a mouse around a desk, the user simply moves the trackball in the desired direction.

Graphics Tablet

A **graphics tablet** is a flat drawing surface, connected to the computer, on which the user can draw graphic figures (figure 4). A graphics tablet lets the user make new drawings, sketch freehand, or trace existing drawings. The drawing or tracing is input into the computer for viewing, alteration, or storage. Most graphics tablets are small enough to fit on a desktop, while some are as large as a drafting table.

figure 4

Graphics tablets are often used for engineering, architectural, and other professional applications.

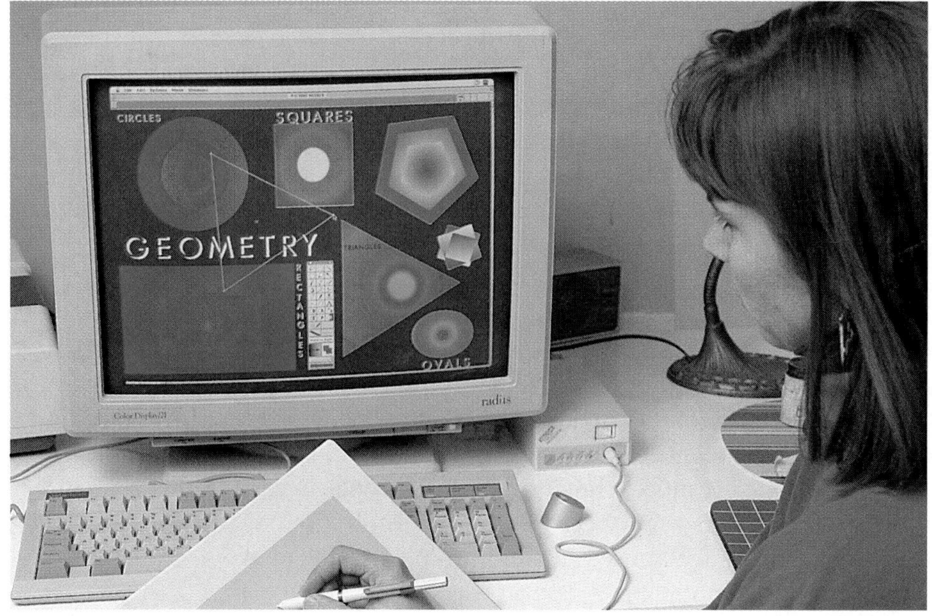

Touch Display Screen

The **touch display screen** is a display screen that allows users to use the most natural pointing devices of all—fingers (figure 5). It is perhaps the simplest and easiest to operate of all input devices. When the screen is touched, it converts the area of the screen touched into an *x,y* coordinate and sends this data to the computer's memory. Once the *x,y* location is in memory, a software program can determine what action or task is to be performed.

figure 5

Touch display screens are most often used for providing information, placing orders in self-service discount stores, business and industrial training, educational applications, and flight simulation.

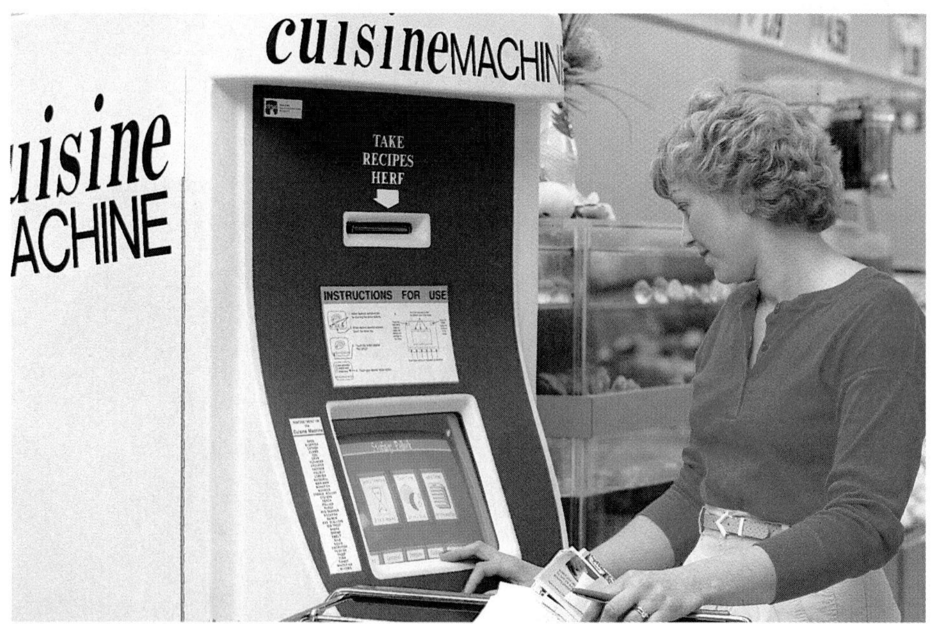

Speech Recognition Device

For many applications, the ability to instruct a computer by voice command is valuable. This can be done through the use of a **speech recognition device** (figure 6).

A computer technician may speak over the phone to a computer in the warehouse to determine the availability of a part. Spoken words may also be used to command a computer to perform common operational tasks, com-

figure 6

Speech recognition devices can be used by handicapped persons to command wheelchairs or robot arms.

mand a voice-controlled telephone to make a call, or program your voice-controlled VCR to record a television program while you are out.

As valuable as these applications are, the ideal speech recognition device would be one that could recognize freeform speech and every word in the dictionary, that is, ordinary conversational speech. Present systems have vocabularies of 20,000 words. Some systems must be "trained" to recognize different voices. Other systems compare the inflection, pitch, and so on of a spoken word to those the computer is capable of recognizing.

Scanners

Scanners are devices that can read special codes, printed characters, symbols, and graphic images for input to the computer. A summary of each scanner discussed here is provided in figure 7.

Type	Characteristics	Common Application
Bar-code Scanner	Reads Universal Product Code	Grocery stores at checkout counter
Optical character reader	Reads stock number or bar code from a price ticket	Department stores
Optical mark reader	Senses presence or absence of marks	Test scoring, data collection, inventory control, and other applications where the number of responses and volume of data are limited
Digitizer scanner	Reads photographs or graphic illustrations	Desktop publishing and newspaper applications
Magnetic scanner	Reads magnetic tape on a plastic card	Credit cards and bank teller machine cards

figure 7

Summary of scanners.

Bar-code scanner A **bar-code scanner** can read bars (lines) printed on a product. These bars, which represent data, are generally printed in a code known as the **Universal Product Code** (**UPC**). The code is printed on the product by the manufacturer and is a series of vertical bars with varying widths that reflect a laser beam from the scanner.

Retail stores (especially grocery stores) use bar-code scanners to automate the check-out process. Bar-code scanners transmit the product-identification characters directly to a computer. The computer then locates the correct price and description from data it has previously stored. The customer gets a sales slip listing the names of the items purchased, and the items are automatically deducted from the store's inventory.

Optical character reader An **optical character reader** (**OCR**) is an input device that operates on a principle similar to the reading method that humans use. For humans, when light is placed on a printed form, the reader scans the form. Images of the letters, numbers, or marks are reflected to the eye, and the images are transformed into nerve impulses and sent to the brain. The brain has been programmed through learning and experience to recognize these images. In a similar fashion, a character reader can read numbers, letters of the alphabet, and symbols directly from a typed, printed, or handwritten page.

Electronic elements placed in a matrix (row and column arrangement) inside the device react to light reflected from the page. The pattern of a letter, number, symbol, or bar code falls on the matrix (as it would on a human retina) and generates electronic impulses. The impulses being received are mathematically compared with stored records of what the impulses from various characters should look like. When a character is identified, its code is transmitted to the processor. Usually, the scanner reads a stock number or bar code rather than the price; the computer to which the scanner is attached then looks up the stock number in a price table to determine the amount to charge for the item (figure 8).

figure 8

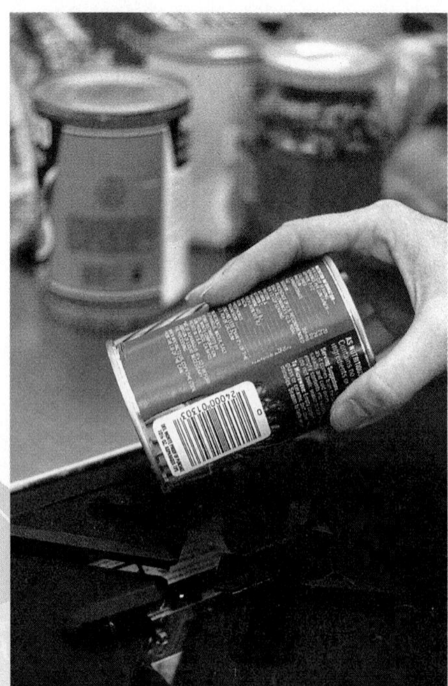

Optical character reading equipment is frequently used in grocery stores to read the price ticket on an item. This ensures that customers receive the sale prices on items that are specially priced. This type of system also makes it easy to change prices when necessary.

Optical mark reader The **optical mark reader** is a scanner that senses the presence or absence of marks made by regular pencil or pen on specially designed forms. This is the simplest form of optical reader, because it does not require the "intelligence" of a character reader.

A form is predefined into a matrix of marking positions. All that the mark reader needs to do is determine whether there is a mark (usually a rectangle or circle) at each of the positions. It is up to a computer program to determine what the presence or absence of a mark at a particular location means.

Digitizer scanner A **digitizer scanner** is another type of optical scanner used to convert shapes, pictures, graphic images, and so on into numbers for storage by computers (figure 9). For example, you can scan a photograph (some devices can scan 35-mm slides and filmstrips) or a graphic illustration and transfer it directly into the computer. Once in the computer, further work may be done to enhance the image or store it for later recall. These scanners are commonly used in desktop publishing and newspaper applications.

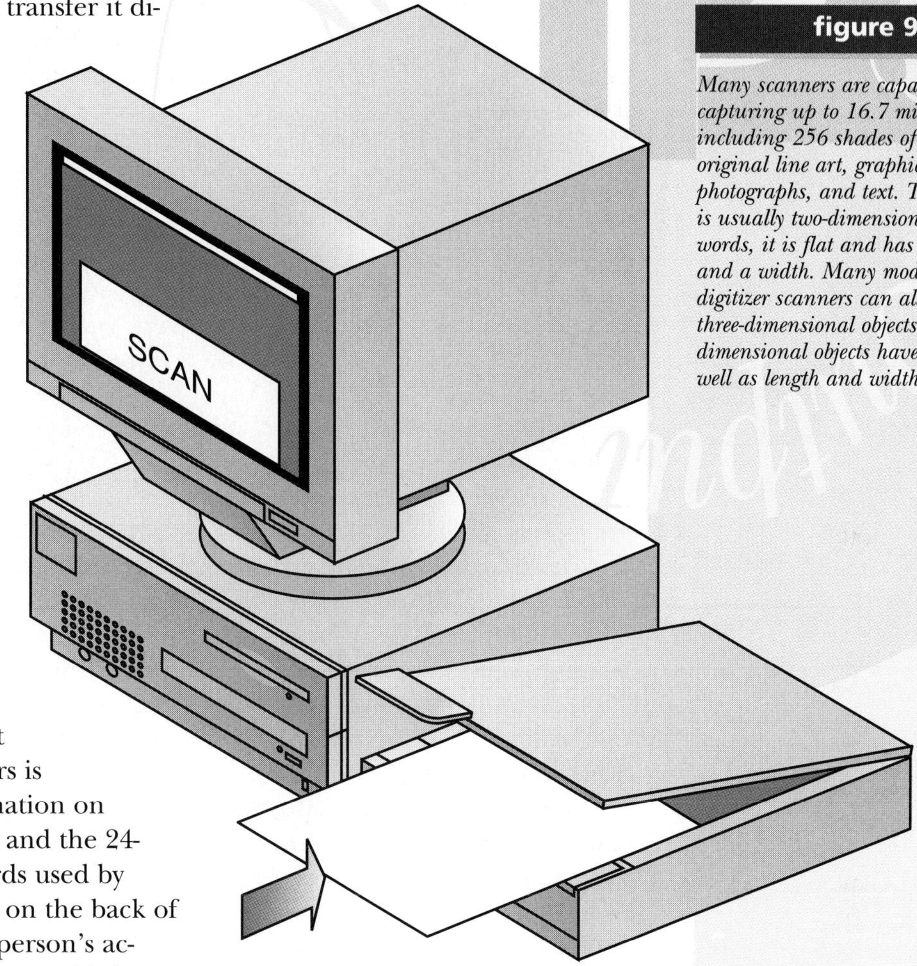

Magnetic scanner A **magnetic scanner** operates on the same principle as a videotape player. The tape that it reads, however, is usually only a few inches long. The largest use of magnetic scanners is to read encoded information on the back of credit cards and the 24-hour teller machine cards used by banks. A magnetic strip on the back of each card contains the person's account number. When the card is inserted, the magnetic scanner reads the tape on the back of the card and transmits the account number to the computer for processing.

figure 9

Many scanners are capable of capturing up to 16.7 million colors, including 256 shades of gray for original line art, graphics, photographs, and text. The picture is usually two-dimensional; in other words, it is flat and has a length and a width. Many modern digitizer scanners can also handle three-dimensional objects. Three-dimensional objects have depth as well as length and width.

Magnetic ink character recognition reader Banks in the United States use **magnetic ink character recognition** (**MICR**) input devices to help them keep accurate records of checks, deposits, and withdrawals (figure 10). Without MICR, it would be extremely difficult for banks to accurately process the many millions of transactions created daily.

Numbers and special symbols are printed in a special magnetic ink at the bottom of the check or deposit/withdrawal slip that identify the customer, bank, and so on. (There are no alphabet letters.) These unusual-looking numbers and special symbols are magnetized, creating differing electronic impulses when the documents go through the reader.

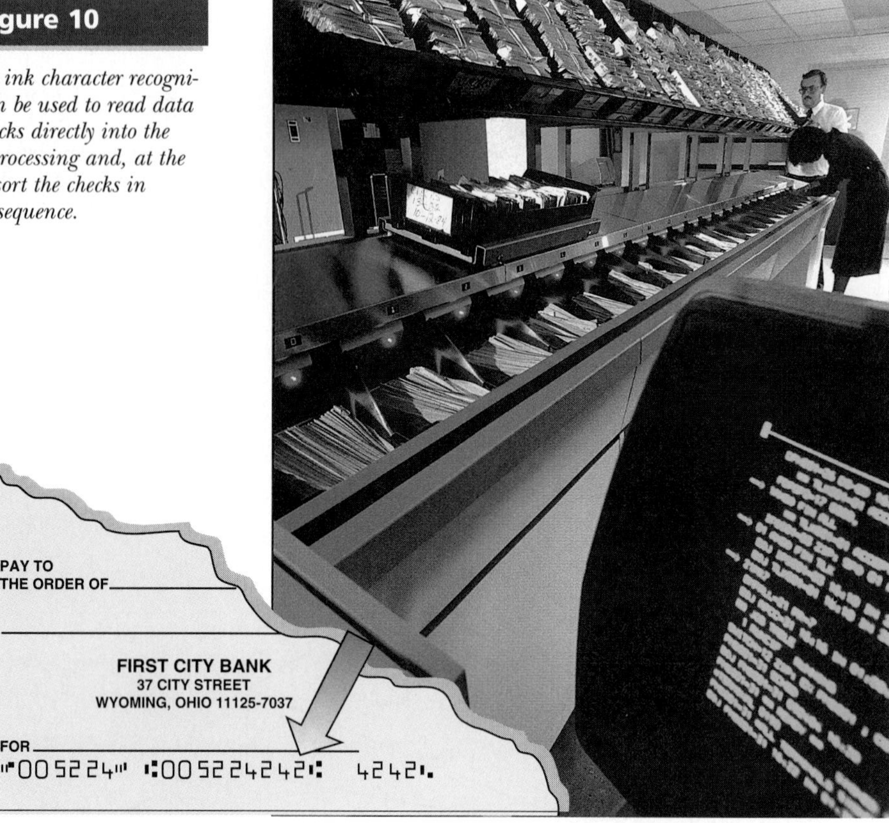

figure 10

This magnetic ink character recognition reader can be used to read data printed on checks directly into the computer for processing and, at the same time, to sort the checks in check-number sequence.

Real-Time Sensor

Real-time sensors are one of the most innovative and intriguing developments in computer input. *Real time* means "while it is happening." Therefore, a real-time sensor is like a sentry. It constantly monitors a process or event, and it transmits its findings to the processor without human assistance. Sensors constantly transmit data to the computer. As data is received, the computer processes the information and controls the output to achieve a desired level of efficiency.

Sound Boards

Devices called **sound boards** (also called **sound cards**) can be installed into the computer and used to mimic many different sounds, like musical instruments and human voices. The capabilities of the sound board depend on its sophistication and accompanying software programs. For example, one system may mimic only one type of instrument, while others enable the user to record different instruments on different tracks of tape and then combine the tracks (figure 11). The entire tape can be played back and

figure 11

This musician is using a sound board to record each of the different instruments shown and then will use the computer to combine them into a musical score.

Do It!

1 Prepare a list of the different input devices connected to the computer(s) at your school. If any input devices on your list were not discussed in the previous material, briefly describe the application(s) for which they are used and their physical characteristics (speed, size, and so on).

2 A mouse and a trackball are both used for the same purpose. Which of these two devices do you prefer? Justify your answer.

3 Have you ever used a scanner, or has a scanner ever been used to process data for you (at the grocery store, test scoring, and so on)? Prepare a chart similar to figure 7, listing the type of scanner, characteristics, and way in which it was used.

4 Visit a local business, fast-food restaurant, bank, or other establishment that uses terminals. Prepare a brief report, or give an oral report to the class on how these terminals are used. Explain how they interact with the main computer system and whether they are local or remote and smart or dumb terminals.

modified, and additional instruments can be added at the same time. New sound-board systems have been developed that store the actual, digitized sound of instruments in a wave table within the computer's memory. The computer searches the wave table and supplies an actual, digitized sound of the desired instrument when called for by the musician.

Terminals A **terminal** is any device that inputs or outputs data to or from a computer system. Each input and output device discussed in this module may be referred to as a terminal. However, terminals are commonly thought of as equipment that consists of a display screen, a keyboard, and a communication channel (a cable or telephone line) connecting it to the computer.

Terminals are often described as being dumb or smart. **Dumb terminals** do not have memory and therefore are totally dependent on the stored program in the computer to which they are connected. **Smart terminals**, however, do have memory and can be programmed to perform tasks ranging from simple text editing to sophisticated data processing. Smart terminals are often used to check input data being keyed for accuracy before the data is sent to the computer for further processing.

All terminals are considered to be either local or remote. A **local terminal** is a device (usually a display screen and keyboard) located near the computer (usually within 1000 feet) and directly cabled into the computer's processor. Local terminals can be used to input to a mainframe computer for processing the data that a company needs for maintaining records and conducting day-to-day activities.

A **remote terminal** is a device (usually a display screen and keyboard) located at a remote geographic site and connected to the computer by a telephone line. For example, a salesperson can use a remote terminal and

Profile

K. Philip Hwang

K. Philip Hwang developed the first "smart" computer terminal, which has revolutionized an entire industry. Quite an accomplishment, especially considering the setbacks Hwang overcame along the way.

At age 14, Hwang escaped from North Korea to the South Korean capital of Seoul to avoid possible execution after the Korean War. He lived with two friends behind a stationery store while he completed high school and 2 years of college. He took exams to qualify for over-seas study and received a scholarship to Utah State University that included tuition and a room in a dormitory. In 1973, Hwang purchased a 7-Eleven franchise in San Jose, CA as his source of income while completing college.

On graduating from Utah State with an electrical engineering degree, Hwang started his career in Detroit, where he worked for Ford and Burroughs—and earned his master's degree at Wayne State University. He then moved on to NCR in Dayton. He eventually made it back to San Jose, where he took a job with a video-game company that folded after a few months. Once again, his convenience store became his source of income.

In 1975, Hwang tried to start his own video-game business with $9000 he had earned from selling the 7-Eleven. Times were tough, but Hwang persevered. While assembling his video games, Hwang realized that by adding a $10 microchip, the "dumb" terminal—which dominated the market at the time—could be given processing capabilities and memory.

Optimistic about the market for his product, Hwang ordered enough parts to assemble 50,000 terminals, complete with fancy molded-plastic cases. Hwang's hard work and confidence paid off. Demand for the smart terminal was incredible, but Hwang was able to meet demand and maintain prices by keeping costs down.

In 1983, Hwang offered stock in his company (TeleVideo) to the public. At the close of trading on that first day, Hwang's 69% share of TeleVideo was worth $610 million. That same year, TeleVideo's sales were $169 million, up from $2 million just 4 years earlier. The company's success continued through the 1980s.

telephone to transmit an order to the central computer over a telephone line. When the order is received by the central computer, an invoice will be prepared and the merchandise shipped to the customer.

Computer Processing

The **central processing unit** (**CPU**) can be defined as the hardware device that stores data and programs, executes program instructions, and performs arithmetic and logic operations. The instructions the computer follows are stored in locations known as **memory**. Memory may also be referred to as **main storage** or **primary storage**. From memory, each instruction is executed (carried out) by the processor. Likewise, the data to be processed is loaded into memory and moved from there into the processor when necessary for processing. The processed data is then returned to memory for further use or output.

The memory of a computer is made of electronic circuits that, like the processor, are contained in tiny chips called **integrated circuits**. Memory can accept, hold, and release data as well as instructions for processing the data. Data and instructions are stored as electronic impulses at specified locations in the memory known as **numeric addresses**. You can imagine memory as being like a large number of mailboxes (memory locations), with each box being labeled with an identifying number (numeric address). Any desired "mail" (data and instructions) may be placed in any mailbox (memory location). Generally, the first storage location in memory is given an address of 0 and the second an address of 1. This process continues up to the number of memory locations that are available. The amount of data that can be stored in one memory location varies; however, with most computers, each location is generally capable of holding one **byte**. For now, think of a byte as the amount of space required to store one character or one value. For example, as figure 12 shows, the word "computer" requires eight locations, one for each letter (stored in bytes 101 through 108), while the value 25 can be stored in one memory location (byte 951).

Numeric Addresses

0	1	101	102	103	104	105	106	107	108	950	951
		C	O	M	P	U	T	E	R		25

figure 12

Data in a computer system is stored in memory locations, with each location containing one byte of data. Therefore, one memory location is equivalent to one byte. Bytes are numbered in terms of "K," which is short for "kilo" and means "1000." The numbering system inside of a computer is different, however, and one kilobyte (1KB) of memory is actually 1024 bytes (memory locations). Modern microprocessors address many "mega" (million) bytes; one million bytes (1MB) is actually 1,024,000 bytes, or 1024 KB.

There are many kinds of memory chips, and new ones are constantly being developed. Memory chips can generally be classified as RAM or ROM. Most computers contain both RAM and ROM memory (figure 13). **RAM** (**random-access memory**) is memory that loses the data or instructions that it stores when the power is turned off. It is called random access because the processor can jump directly from one location to another in random order as data is stored and retrieved. This is where data is stored while being processed.

ROM (**read-only memory**) is memory that does not lose its data or instructions when the power is turned off. It is frequently used to store the instructions necessary for getting the computer started when it is powered up (turned on). A computer can only read data from a ROM chip; it cannot write or store data on the chip. Most special-purpose computers have ROM chips containing the instructions that permit the computer to perform the specific tasks for which it was designed. For example, a ROM chip in a special-purpose computer may enable the computer to control a traffic light, do word processing, play an arcade game, or monitor instrumentation.

The Processor

All computers conduct processing by following the detailed instructions of a software program. The chip that receives and carries out these instructions, which is located in the CPU, is called the **processor**. Regardless of their size or make, all computer systems have processors. The processor is involved in all four of the computer's basic functions:

1. It interacts with program instructions and data stored in memory.
2. It controls and initiates the actions of the entire computer system by its ability to follow program instructions, such as reading data from an input device (keyboard) and transferring data to an output device (display screen).
3. It performs arithmetic computations.
4. It makes logical comparisons, such as determining if two numbers are equal.

Separate memory modules, containing 2 MB to 16 MB each, sit within the box that houses the processor. These modules are used to store programs and data and to help speed up specialized tasks, such as communications, video, graphics, disk access, and mouse and keyboard control. Several expansion slots are provided so that additional devices, such as a CD-ROM disk drive, can be added to the system (figure 13).

figure 13

The main circuit board (also called the motherboard) of a personal computer contains the processor, RAM, and ROM memory as well as other circuitry used to control the computer system.

Control Because the processor can follow the instructions of a stored program, it can also direct and control all other computer components (mouse, keyboard, display screen, disk drive, printer). Therefore, in addition to processing activities, the processor controls all of the input, output, and storage devices that are connected to the computer. It directs the transfer of data to and from these devices, and it maintains control over all activities of the entire computer system.

Arithmetic The vast majority of computer applications require arithmetic calculations (figure 14). Once read and stored in the computer's memory, numeric data often require such arithmetic operations as addition, subtraction, multiplication, and division. Most computers can accurately perform thousands, and even millions, of these calculations in 1 second. A math processor chip (called a math coprocessor) may be installed to greatly increase the speed of numeric calculations in computers used for math intensive applications.

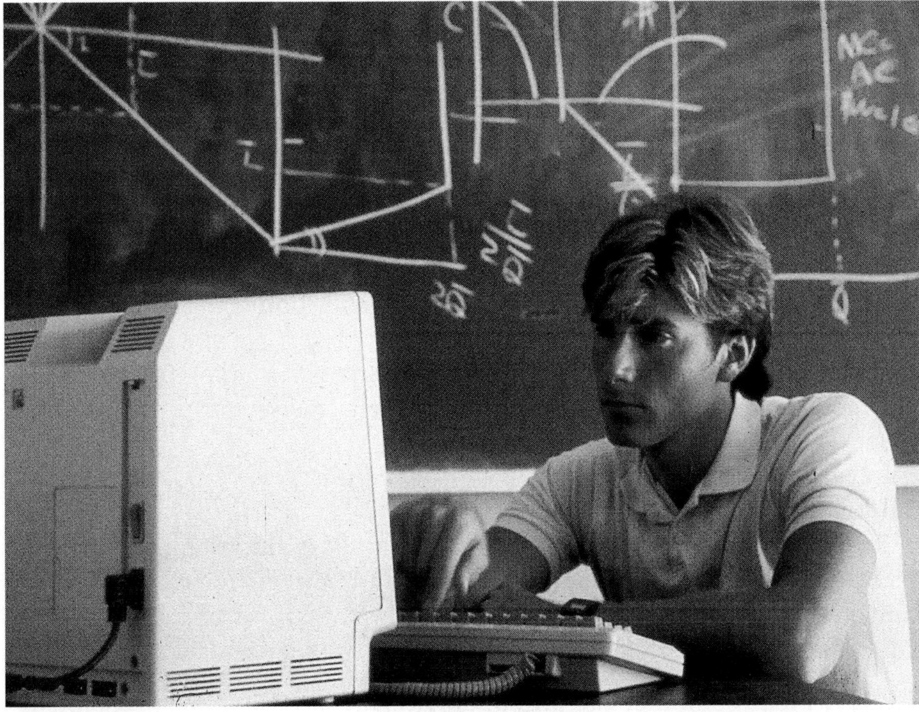

figure 14

This computer system is being used to learn math.

Logical comparisons Like arithmetic operations, logical comparisons are performed on data located in memory. The computer's processor is given instructions from a program stored in its memory to compare the data stored in one memory location with data stored in another memory location. Depending on the result of this comparison, the processor will be directed to follow appropriate instructions.

The Processing Cycle

Four steps make up the computer's processing cycle:

1. Retrieve instruction or datum.
2. Decode the instruction or datum.
3. Execute the instruction or datum.
4. Store the result.

Figure 15 illustrates the four steps of the processing cycle. Note that instructions or data are retrieved from primary memory. To increase processing speed, some computers use a small amount of very high-speed RAM called **cache memory**. Because cache memory is much faster than primary memory, instructions and data stored there can be retrieved much more

figure 15

The processing cycle consists of retrieving an instruction or datum, decoding the instruction or datum, executing the instructions or datum, and storing the result.

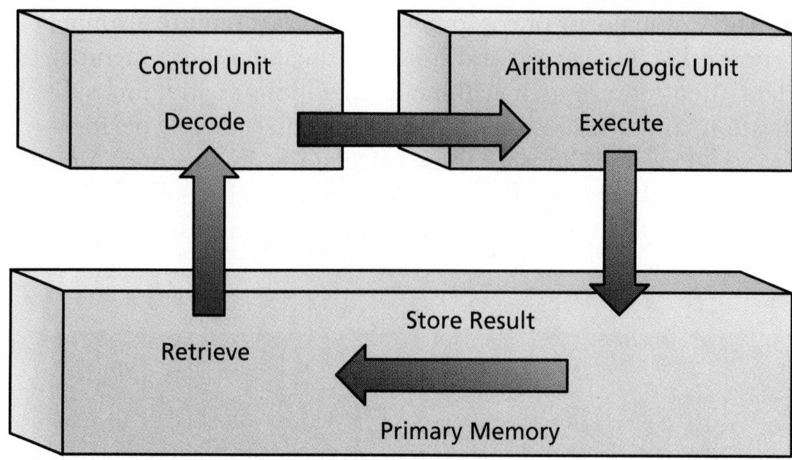

quickly, thereby increasing the speed of the processing cycle. Also note that decoding is done in the control unit, execution takes place in the arithmetic/logic unit, and results are placed in memory. One processing cycle is completed after all four steps are finished and the computer is ready to retrieve the next instruction or datum.

Although the processing cycle seems like a time-consuming process, recall that most modern personal computers operate at speeds measured over 66 MHz (66 million cycles per second).

Processing Functions

Recall that the processor can control all actions of the computer, move data from one memory location to another, and perform logical and arithmetic operations. Because of these capabilities, the processor can perform three specific tasks: classify data, sort data, and summarize data.

Classify data The computer can group similar data according to a predefined criterion. For example, in a student transcript system, each student may be classified by grade level: freshman, sophomore, junior, or senior. Or, as each student's transcript is processed, the computer can calculate the student's average grade for all completed courses. All students with an "A" average can then be classified as belonging to the "A Honor Roll," and all students with a "B" average can be classified as belonging to the "B Honor Roll."

Sort data Data stored in the computer's memory can be rearranged into any predefined order. For example, all students who have been classified as "A" students can be arranged in alphabetic order by name within their appropriate grade level.

Summarize data Lengthy, detailed data can be summarized by the computer to produce more meaningful and useful information for the user. For example, the principal of a school might want to know the number of "A" and "B" students by each grade level. As the computer processes each transcript, it can logically compare the calculated grade average with an "A" or "B." If equal, it would add a 1 to the "A" or "B" accumulator for the appropriate grade level. After repeating this processing cycle for each student, the desired, summarized information would be available for output.

Output Devices

Output devices have been designed for computer systems to help facilitate communication of the information they produce. This information may be communicated by devices that create such output mediums as printed reports, spoken words, music, pictures, graphics, charts, and microfilm, to name a few.

In many instances, the kind of information that must be communicated to a human determines which output device is best. In other instances, output equipment has been specifically designed and developed to facilitate communication and the reporting of processed information.

Display Screens

Video display screens are the most commonly used output devices. They are called **video display screens** because the images they produce can be seen. These images consist of virtually all output that the computer is capable of producing. Display screens are especially well suited for interactive applications requiring both input and output.

Display screens may be either monochromatic or color. A **monochromatic**, or monochrome, screen is a one-color (green, amber, or white) display. Full-color displays are the most commonly used screens. Graphic illustrations, charts, drawings, and pictures often depict information that is easier to understand in color.

Cathode-ray tubes Most computer display screens use the **cathode-ray tube** (**CRT**) technology in a device called a **monitor** to display information processed by the computer. Monitors are similar in appearance to television sets, with screen sizes that range from 11 to 15 inches (larger units are also available). The CRT technology consists of an electron gun, which is a device that shoots a narrow electron beam containing the data received from the computer into a yoke (a device located at the base of the tube), and a display screen coated with a phosphorescent material (a material that emits light). Wherever electrons hit the phosphorescent material on the screen, a small dot or light is lit. These tiny lights are called **pixels** (PIC-ture ELements). Each pixel can be lit (on) or not lit (off) to create images on the screen. The greater the number of pixels a given screen can display, the higher the resolution and sharper the picture.

Do It!

1 Find out how much primary memory is in a computer that you have access to. Express the amount of memory in MB. Calculate the actual number of numeric addresses (or bytes).

2 The CPU of a computer system is often compared with how a human brain functions. Provide an analogy (by using an example) that compares the four steps that make up the computer's processing cycle with how a human brain functions.

Careers

Careers in the Software Industry

In many ways, career opportunities in the software industry parallel those in the hardware industry. There are professionals who conduct basic research, those who apply the research to the development of specific software such as database or word-processing programs, and those who market the software.

As the hardware market has progressed, the software market has developed to keep up with improvements. For example, computer input, output, processor, and storage devices are useless without appropriate software to make them function.

In many ways, the development of software can be more difficult than designing hardware. Software development calls for the application of algorithms (problem-solving steps) that must be developed from scratch. Developers of software systems tend to have computer-science degrees. Some developers of applications software have a computer background, while others have a background in the area for which the program is being written. For example, people with accounting experience are needed to develop accounting software. Most major component parts of software are developed by teams, but significant programs may still be developed by only one or two individuals.

As with hardware, new software must be documented and user manuals prepared by technical writers. While the duplication of software is a very simple job compared with hardware manufacture, software must still be sold and marketed, opening up a host of career opportunities.

Once the software is in the hands of the user, problems or questions can arise. For most software manufacturers, software support means a staff of telephone support specialists to respond to every user's call for help. For simple software, the support specialist may be able to talk to the user about the symptoms of the problem. For more complex software, the user's computer may be equipped with a communications link that allows the software support specialist to query the computer directly to isolate the problem and solve it.

Monitors have many more pixels than television sets. For example, the resolution of a typical television set is 256 x 192 pixels (256 pixels horizontally by 192 pixels vertically), or a total of 49,152 pixels. By contrast, a popular high-resolution graphics monitor has a resolution of 640 x 480 (307,200) pixels and is capable of displaying over 200,000 different colors.

High-resolution monitors require a great deal of primary memory dedicated to holding information for the display; therefore, modern computers contain a **video graphics controller**. A video graphics controller is a separate hardware board inside the CPU that contains its own memory and greatly increases the computer's graphic and color capabilities. Several standard video graphics controllers have been established. The video graphics controller capable of the 640 x 480 resolution described above is called a VGA (Video Graphics Adapter) controller. Two controllers are the Super VGA (capable of an 800 x 600 resolution), and the 1024 (capable of 1024 x 768 resolution).

Liquid crystal displays and passive-matrix color screens Two flat-panel display screens that are commonly used with portable computers (notebooks, powerbooks, and so on) are the liquid crystal display and the passive-matrix color display screens. A **liquid crystal display** (**LCD**) screen is composed of an electrokinetic fluid (a fluid that changes color because of the effects of electricity in motion) positioned between two layers of glass. Each area of the display screen contains electrodes that when activated with electrical charges cause various light patterns (images) to appear on the screen. Until recently, most LCDs were monochrome (one-color) screens. Color LCD screens are now available to satisfy the needs of portable computer users.

Passive-matrix color display screens are flat-panel color display screens that are used with modern, portable computers (figure 16). Passive-matrix color display units, like the LCD color screens, are notorious for shadows that extend beyond the limits of the image displayed and for slow-speed screen redraws. For example, when scrolling through a word-processing document, a lingering shadow or blurry transition often occurs while an old screen image fades away and a new one appears.

Recently, a somewhat more costly but improved technology called active-matrix LCD has been making strong inroads into the portable computer

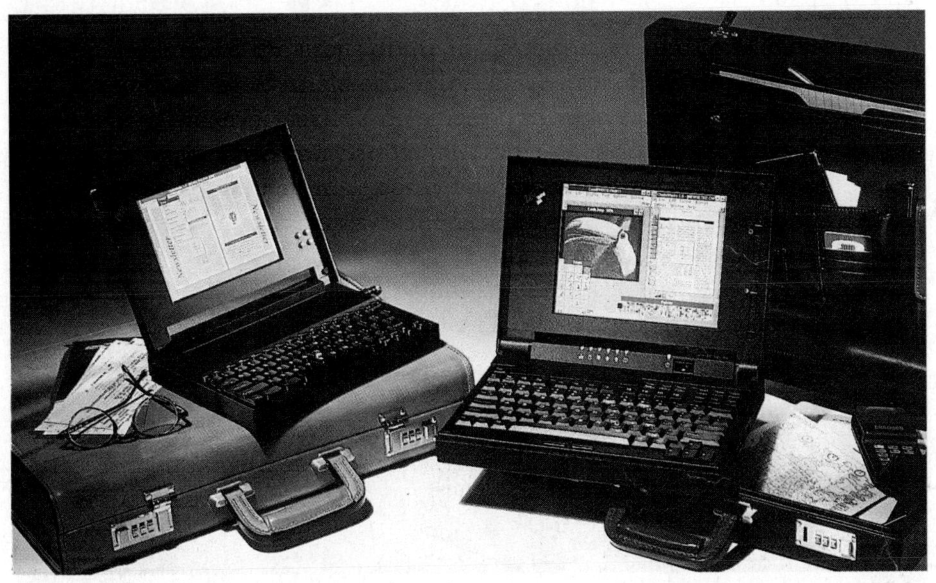

figure 16

Passive-matrix color displays are used in many modern laptop computers.

market. Another promising flat-panel display technology is called Field Emission Display (FED).

Printers

Printers are commonly used devices that place output on paper. Placing output on paper is generally called making a **hard copy** of the information. Printers are among the most common output devices, and nearly every computer application uses a printer in some way. There are tremendous differences in speed, print quality, price, and special features among the types and models of printers available. Some printers can produce only alphanumeric characters; others can print detailed graphics. Some printers print black-and-white characters and images, while others can print in several colors.

Printers use several different methods to place characters on a sheet of paper. With some, the paper is physically struck to form the images; these printers are known as **impact printers**. Impact printers are best used when multiple copies of the same document are required. **Nonimpact printers**, however, form the characters without actually striking the paper. Regardless of the method of printing, a character code(s) representing the character (or image) to be printed is sent to the printer from the processor. The printer then converts the code(s) and produces the proper mechanical or electronic action to print the character or image.

Dot-matrix printers The dot-matrix printer was once the most popular and widely used of all impact printers (figure 17). It creates an arrangement of dots, called a dot matrix (row and column arrangement of dots), to produce

figure 17

Dot-matrix printers are impact printers that are often used to print on multipart paper. Tiny pins in the printhead tap the paper through a ribbon to form an image, which is made up of dots.

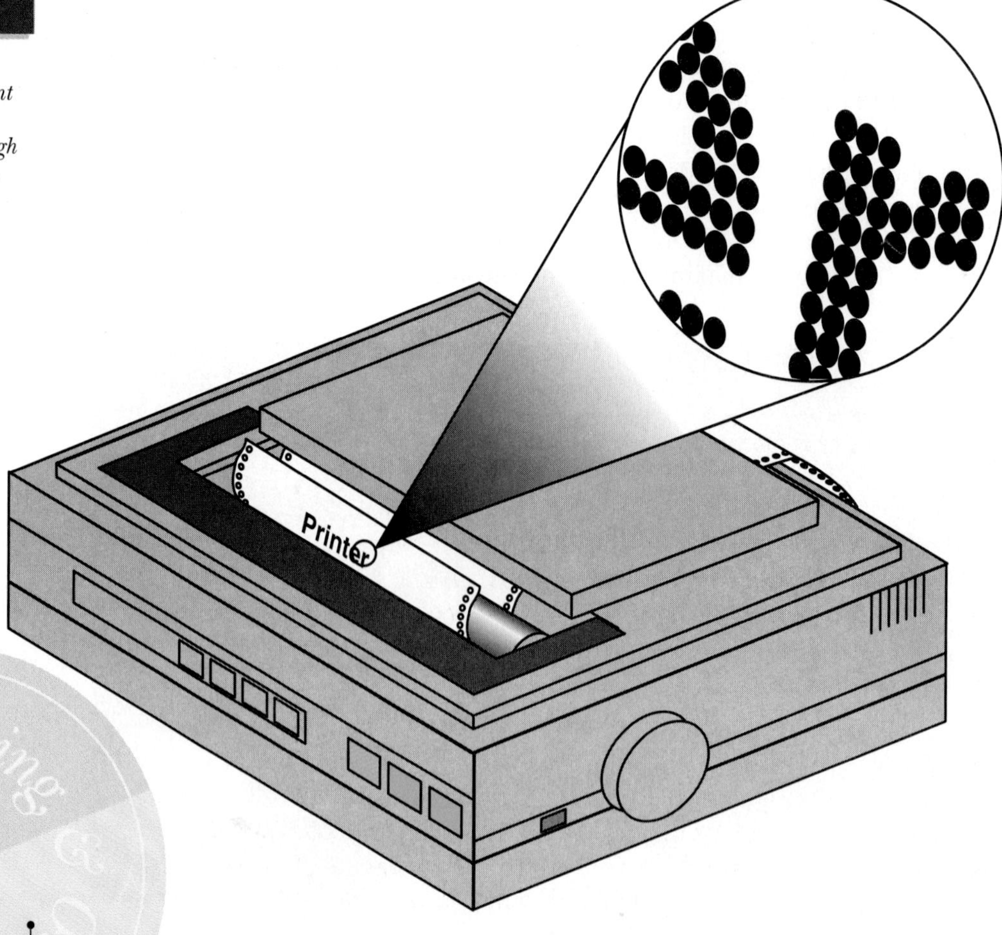

images. A **dot-matrix printer** can be defined as an impact printer that produces a character by forming images from rows and columns of dots. The mechanism of the printer that actually does the printing is known as the **printhead.** As it moves across the paper, tiny pins or wires in the printhead fire out to tap the paper through a ribbon and form the desired image, which is made up of dots. There is a wide variation in the number and arrangement of the pins or wires used to produce the printed images.

The print quality of dot-matrix printers varies depending on the number of dots (pins or wires) that form a character. Printers with printheads containing more pins can produce better-looking characters than those with printheads containing fewer pins.

Compared with other types of printers, no other printer can print on as many kinds of stock paper, including multipart forms. Most dot-matrix printers are fairly inexpensive, with low-end printers priced under $200. Dot-matrix printers are low-maintenance devices, and their per-page costs are about 0.3 to 2.5 cents, compared with about 6 cents for ink-jet printers and 3 cents for laser printers. Several modern dot-matrix printers also provide rudimentary color capabilities. The print speed of dot-matrix printers typically ranges from around 40 to several hundred characters per second (cps), which is quite adequate for most small computer systems.

Band and chain printers Band and chain printers are impact printers that operate on the same general principle. A **band printer** uses a moving band or belt that contains all printable characters; a **chain printer** uses a rotating chain that contains several sets of all printable characters. Both printers contain hammers that fire out to strike the appropriate characters after they are properly positioned against the paper. A ribbon between the characters and paper produces the images. Different fonts (shapes of print characters) can be used on either printer simply by replacing the band or chain.

Band and chain printers have been used for many years on mainframe computers. Both produce high-quality, solid character images. Both are also very reliable and can print at speeds ranging from 150 to 3000 lines per minute on continuous form paper.

Thermal printers A **thermal printer** is a nonimpact printer that produces images on special, heat-sensitive paper. It produces output via a matrix arrangement of heated rods. As individual rods representing the desired image are selected, they press against the heat-sensitive paper and burn the desired image onto it. The speed at which the rods move across the paper enables the printer to print at speeds between 30 and 150 cps. Thermal printers are some of the most inexpensive printers available and therefore are sometimes used with home computers and fax (facsimile) machines. Although the printer itself is relatively inexpensive, the heat-sensitive paper is often very expensive. Also, the quality of the output that is produced by most thermal printers is less than that of a standard typewriter.

Ink-jet printers The **ink-jet printer** is a nonimpact printer that has grown in popularity. Most ink-jet printers contain a mechanism, much like a miniature nozzle attached to a garden hose, that sprays liquid ink onto the paper (figure 18a). The spray pattern creates the desired characters. Ink-jet printers produce high-quality print, and many of them can produce different sizes

figure 18a

Ink-jet printers spray ink on paper to produce printed characters.

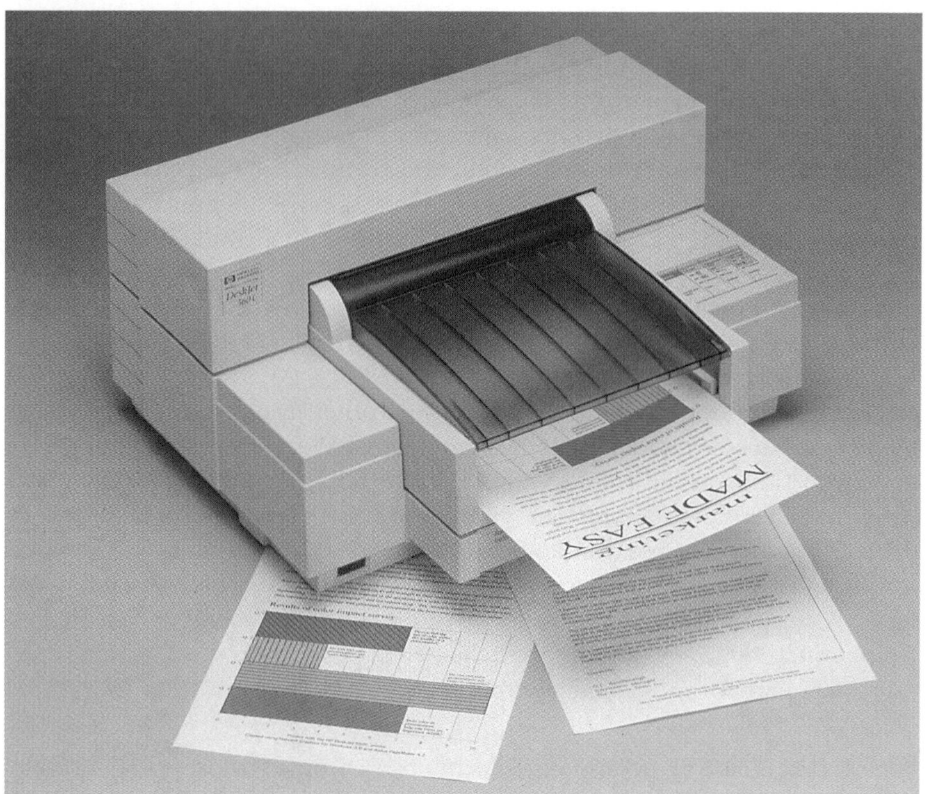

and styles of characters on the same line. Some can print in several colors by overspraying various colored inks to produce different color combinations. A typical ink-jet printer is capable of printing 150 cps.

Laser printers A **laser printer** is a nonimpact printer that works somewhat like a copying machine (figure 18b) and is also gaining widespread use. Laser printers use an electrophotographic process (in which a beam of light creates an electrically charged figure on a metal drum receptive to photographic

figure 18b

Laser printers can produce very high-quality text and graphic images.

images) to create its images. Tiny ink particles (called toner) stick to the image, which the drum rolls onto the paper. This technology permits high-resolution text and graphics to appear on the same page. In addition, different type sizes, styles, and fonts can be produced that exceed those of most other printing devices and approach typeset quality. Laser printers can produce output much faster than impact and ink-jet printers. Connected to mainframes, the most expensive and fastest ones can print over 20,000 lines (300 pages) per minute. Smaller, less expensive laser printers (which can be connected to personal computers) commonly print over 500 lines (8 pages) per minute. Today's laser printers are also capable of producing color output.

Choosing the best printer is not an easy task. The best guideline is to first determine what the printing needs are, then shop around to find the printer that meets those needs best. Many shoppers will be shocked to discover that the price of a good printer may exceed the price of the computer to which it will be connected.

Plotters

A **plotter** is most frequently used to print graphic output. It can draw maps, produce artwork, or draw any type of line (figure 19). A plotter draws output using one or more pens that are controlled by instructions from the processor. Because the pens can contain various colors of ink, multicolored output can be produced. Depending on the design of the plotter, the images created by the plotters are produced by either moving the pens over the surface of a fixed sheet of paper (flat-bed plotter) or by moving the paper under the pens (drum plotter). Therefore, most flat-bed plotters are limited to printing on standard-size sheets of paper, while drum plotters can work on continuous form paper of almost unlimited size.

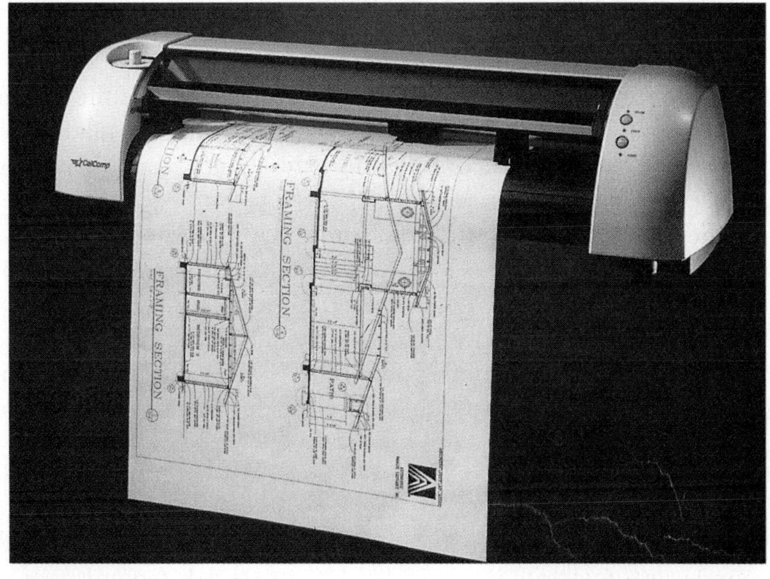

figure 19

Mapping, weather forecasting, drafting, architecture, and engineering are just some of the areas in which plotters are commonly used.

Computer Output Microfilm

Computer output microfilm, commonly referred to as **COM**, is used when large amounts of data must be printed and stored for future use. COM uses a photographic process similar to that of a camera. Computer output is reduced in size and recorded directly onto photographic film. As the unit reduces the size of the computer-generated text or graphics, it exposes the film in a manner similar to that in photography. Because the image of each character is greatly reduced in size, very dense storage (many characters in a small space) is possible. As a result, text and graphics can be recorded on microfilm much faster than they can be printed on high-speed printers and also at a considerable savings. The microfilm produced may be in long rolls or small, rectangular sheets called **microfiche**. To view either type, a person must use a special reader that magnifies the stored images to a size that can be read by the human eye. Many readers can produce a hard copy of any required information as well. Most machines also have automated search mechanisms to help locate desired data.

Sound Synthesizers

One of the most fascinating areas of development in computer science is use of the computer to generate sound. The devices that are connected to the computer to make this possible are called synthesizers. A **sound synthesizer** is a device that combines parts or elements of different sounds into a complex whole. Sound synthesizers can be categorized into two different areas: speech, and music.

Speech synthesizers Speech synthesizers are devices that project an imitation of the human voice. The process involves analysis by a computer program of words that are stored in the computer's memory. As each word is analyzed, phonemes (basic units of speech that provide the small changes in sound that differentiate between word meanings) representing various letter combinations are generated. The phonemes are combined into recognizable sounds by applying rules of voice inflection (accent) and emphasis, then projected over a speaker connected to the computer.

Another method of voice-generated output involves the storage of prerecorded spoken words and phrases. When an inquiry is made, the computer finds the appropriate recording and plays it back similar to the way in which a cassette player works.

The use of speech synthesizers and voice recordings is becoming more commonplace in modern society. Talking machines give phone numbers to persons who dial directory assistance. They perform electronic banking by using the phone as a terminal. Talking typewriters, calculators, and reading machines are also a tremendous aid for blind people. In addition, computer-assisted learning in areas such as foreign languages can be much more effective when the computer can speak.

Music synthesizers Music (or sound) synthesizers are devices that can blend sound waves to create music or brand-new sounds (sounds that are not commonly heard). With this technology, music (or other sounds) can be recorded on tape or disk. With a computer connected to the tape or disk and a synthesizer, the recording can be edited (figure 20). For example, the tempo can be changed, several other recordings merged together, pitch altered, and voices as well as other instruments added. The music and recording industry extensively uses specially designed computers connected to sound synthesizers to produce quality sound.

Real-Time Controllers

A real-time controller is an output device that converts computer output to some kind of action that controls a process. Often, the action consists of turning a valve on or off. In an automobile, the computer gives commands to controllers on the ignition and fuel systems. In an aircraft, computers constantly monitor and control cockpit instrumentation as well as engine operation.

figure 20

Musicians use music synthesizers to create music or modify prerecorded music.

Robots

Robots can serve as output devices. Under control of a computer, the robot produces output in the form of motion, which in turn performs work. If the instructions given to the computer are changed, the robot's motions can change, and it can do a different kind of work. Computer-controlled robots are commonly used in industrial environments (figure 21).

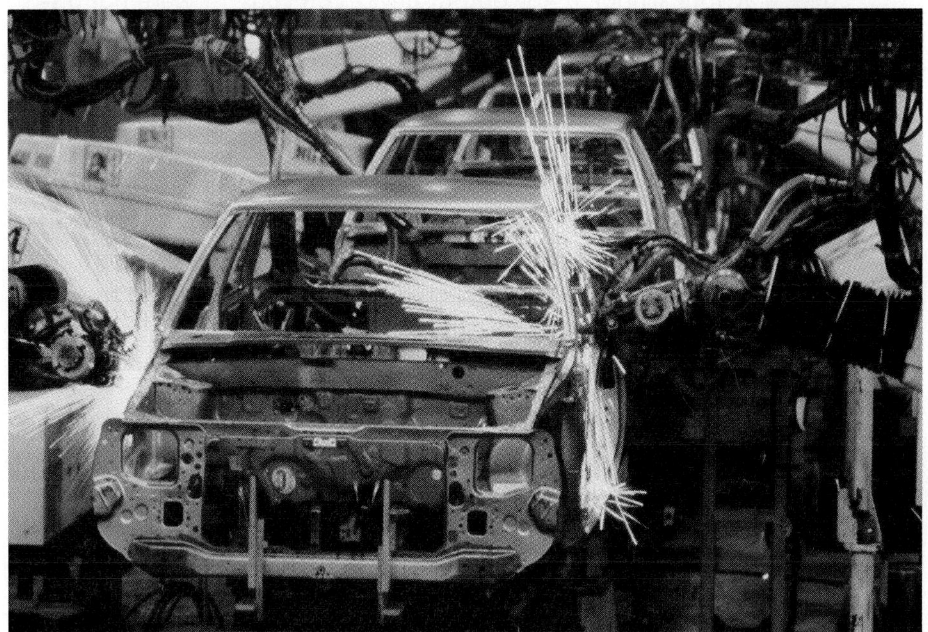

figure 21

This computer-controlled robot is being used to assemble automobile components.

Tasks that require repetition, situations that require very precise and finite work humans could not perform on a consistent basis, and jobs that require handling materials that are dangerous or harmful to humans all lend themselves to this type of technology.

Auxiliary Storage Devices

Many computer users have hundreds of software programs and huge volumes of data that cannot fit in the computer's primary memory at one time. Instead, they must be stored on an auxiliary storage device until they are needed. When required, the appropriate program can be loaded into the primary memory and, in turn, access the data it needs.

All auxiliary storage devices are either sequential-access or random-access devices. **Sequential access** is a term used to describe a device that records and reads back data only in a one-after-the-other sequence (similar to the tape of a movie rented from a local video store). **Random access** is a term used to describe a device that can go directly to the location of specific data without having to read through all of the data preceding it (similar to a CD player).

The purpose of all auxiliary storage devices is to record data for future access. Individual items or pieces of data stored on auxiliary storage device media are called **data fields** or **data elements** (employee name, street address, city, state, ZIP code). A collection of related data fields is known as a **record**; for example, all data fields pertaining to an individual employee make up one record. A collection of related records is known as a **file**. For example, all of a company's employee records that contain the same type of information (employee name, street address, city, state, and ZIP code) for each employee make up a file. This file could be called the Personnel File,

Do It!

1 Prepare a list of the different output devices connected to the computer(s) at your school. If any output devices on your list were not discussed in the previous material, briefly describe the application(s) for which they are used and their physical characteristics (speed, size, and so on).

2 Some people believe that use of computers and the various output devices that do not store data have reduced the amount of paper consumed. Others believe that high-speed printers contribute to a greater consumption of paper and waste of a precious national resource (trees). Do you think that use of computers has increased or decreased the consumption of paper? Justify your answer.

3 Visit a computer store or consult a computer magazine or other source to obtain information about printers that are used with personal computers. Obtain the price of three different types of printers (laser printer, dot-matrix, and ink-jet). Which is the least expensive, and which is the most expensive? Justify the difference in price.

because it contains a record for each employee (figure 22). Later, you will learn that a file may also be referred to as a database, but for now, think of a **database** as an organized collection of related data.

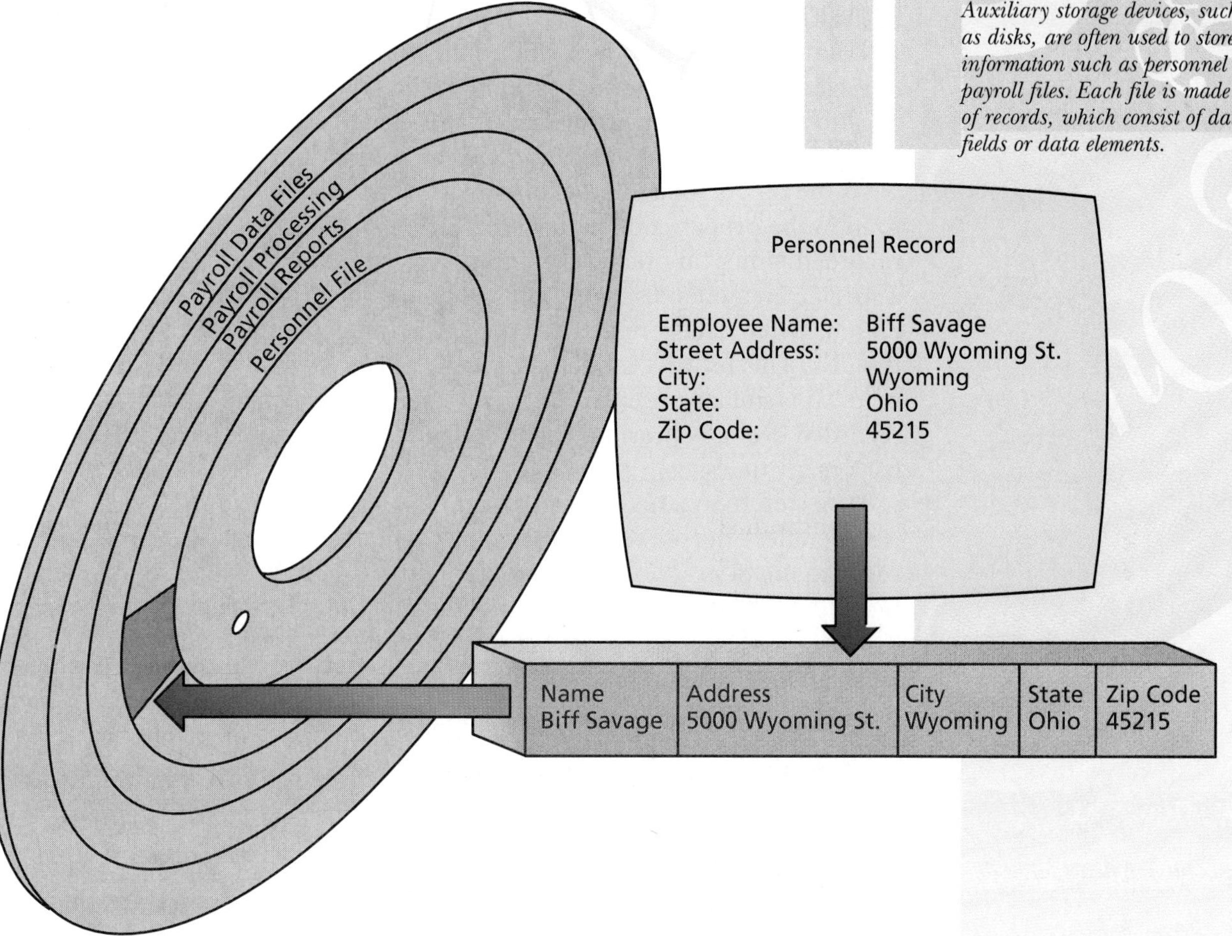

figure 22

Auxiliary storage devices, such as disks, are often used to store information such as personnel and payroll files. Each file is made up of records, which consist of data fields or data elements.

When a software program needs data, it references the appropriate file and then accesses and loads a record from that file into memory. Once in memory, the individual data fields can be processed to produce the desired output. The time it takes the computer to actually load the desired record from the auxiliary storage device into its memory is called the **access time**. Factors that affect the access time include:

1. The amount of time it takes to position the access mechanism over the desired data (called the **seek time** or **search time**).
2. The time it takes the record containing the desired data to pass under the reading mechanism while it is being read (called **latency**).
3. The time required to transfer the data from the device into primary memory (called the **data transfer rate**).

Access times vary greatly among auxiliary storage devices. For example, sequential-access devices may take several seconds, or even minutes, to access a given record of data. Random-access devices can access a given record of data within milliseconds (thousandths of a second). Transfer of data stored in primary memory–like devices to another area of primary memory can range from microseconds (millionths of a second) in microcomputers to nanoseconds (billionths of a second) in supercomputers (mainframes).

Magnetic Disks

Data to be processed by a computer is often recorded on a magnetic disk. A **magnetic disk** is an input, output, and storage medium similar in appearance to a CD with a smooth surface. It is coated on both sides with microscopic bars using a substance that can be magnetized.

As the disk is rotated beneath a read/write head, the tiny bars are magnetized in the proper code pattern for each character. Data on a disk may be recorded either on one or both of its surfaces. When new data is recorded to a specific area on a disk, any data previously recorded in that same area is erased. When data is read, however, there is no change; the data remains on the disk. This process is referred to as "destructive write/nondestructive read." It is similar to recording on a cassette; the new sounds will be recorded over any previous recording and, once recorded, can be played back many times.

Data stored on a magnetic disk can be accessed randomly. Random access is sometimes referred to as **direct access**. The read/write head can move directly to the desired location containing the data rather than sequentially moving through all of the unwanted data before it. If necessary, however, a disk drive can also access data sequentially.

Magnetic disks can be divided into two categories: flexible disks, and hard disks (figure 23). Flexible disks and their drives (devices that house the disk and contain the mechanisms for reading and writing) cost much less than hard disks and their drives. Flexible disks hold less data, however, and are much slower.

figure 23

Hard disks (a) and flexible disks (b).

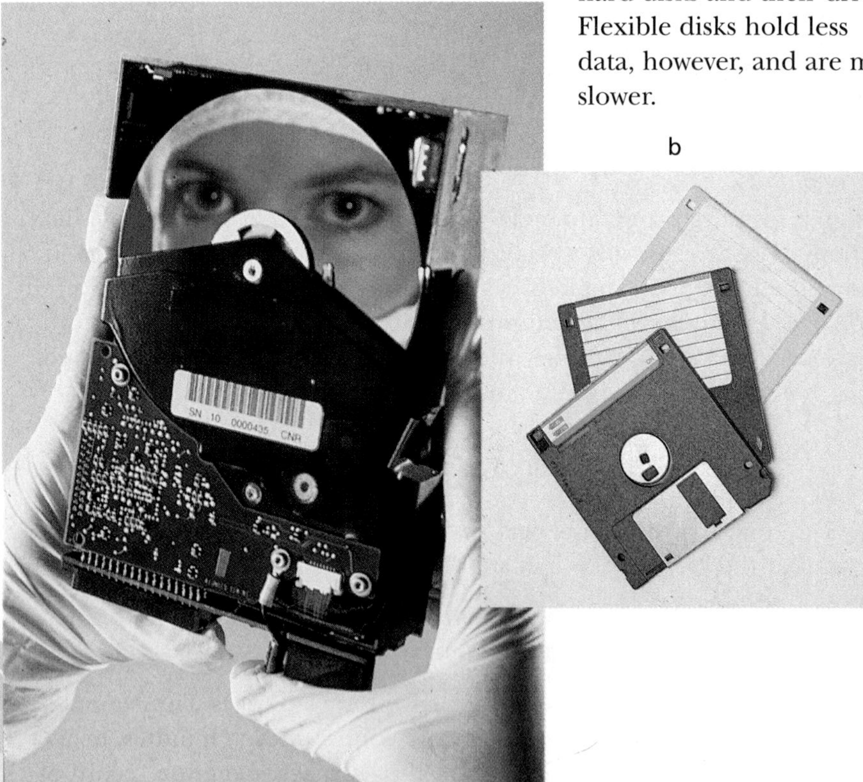

Flexible disks A **flexible disk**, frequently referred to as a **diskette** or **floppy disk**, is a small, pliable magnetic disk. Disks of $5\frac{1}{4}$ and $3\frac{1}{2}$ inches in diameter are commonly used as the main medium for microcomputer auxiliary storage. The amount of data that can be stored on one disk varies depending on the capabilities of the disk drive and the quality of the disk. Capacities from about 720 KB to 2 MB are common.

Hard disks A **hard disk** is a magnetic disk that gets its name from the fact that it is made of rigid material; it does not bend like a floppy disk. While the read/write head on a floppy disk actually makes contact with the disk surface, the head of a hard disk floats on a cushion of air a tiny distance above the disk surface (often less than 1 millionth of an inch). Because there is no physical contact, there is no wear of the disk surface. The biggest danger of losing data on a hard disk occurs if the read/write head loses its cushion of air and touches the disk. This is called a "head crash" and often causes physical damage to the disk surface. Rotating at about 3600 revolutions per minute, hard disks can transfer data to and from the computer at a much faster rate than floppy disks.

Hard disks are commonly used by personal computers as well as mainframe computers and generally are 5, 8, or 14 inches in diameter, although other sizes are available. Personal computers commonly use the $3\frac{1}{2}$-inch size, while mainframe computers use the larger sizes.

In a hard-disk drive, there may be one disk or several disks stacked atop one another on a common vertical shaft called a **spindle**. When there are several disks, the group of disks is referred to as a **disk pack**. There is just enough space between the disk surfaces to allow movement of the read/write heads.

A hard disk may be either fixed or removable. A removable hard disk (called a **disk cartridge**) may be taken out of the disk drive for storage and replaced by a different disk (figure 24). This permits the same disk drive to be used by additional hard disks for more storage. A fixed disk cannot be removed from the disk drive; it is permanently mounted. Because the fixed disk cannot be removed, its capacity is limited to what the disk itself can

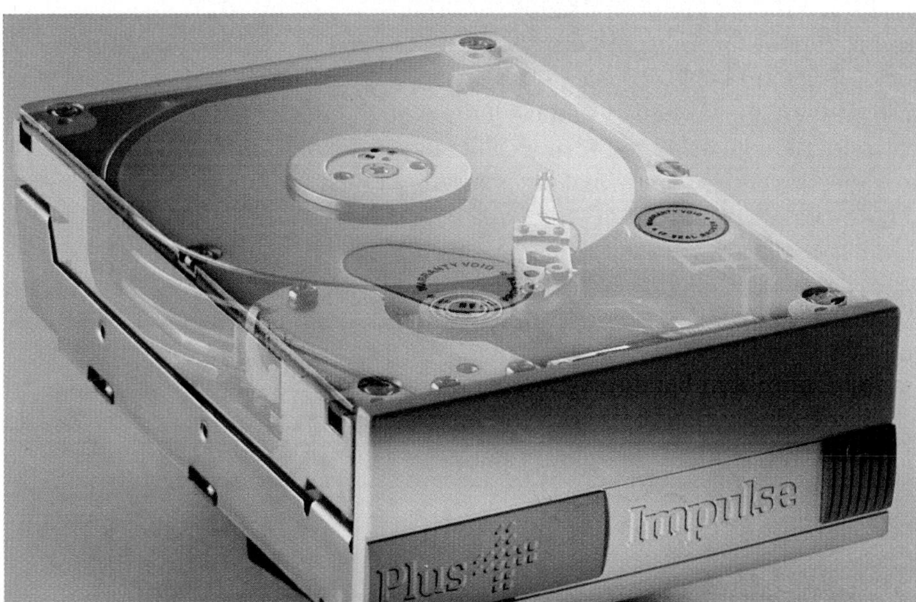

figure 24

A removable hard disk (disk cartridge) allows for greater storage than a fixed hard disk.

hold. When a fixed disk is filled to capacity, data files can be copied to other media for safekeeping, or data that has become obsolete can be erased to free additional space. Most mainframe computers use removable disks, while most personal computers use the fixed disk to meet their individual storage requirements.

Because a hard disk does not bend, data can be denser (packed much closer together) than it can be on a floppy disk. Typical hard disks used with today's personal computers have capacities in gigabytes (billions of bytes). Because many disk drives can be attached to the same computer system, the total amount of storage that can be online at any one time is almost unlimited.

Magnetic Tape

A tape is a long strip of flexible plastic wound on a reel, like the tape used in an ordinary cassette tape recorder. Most tape is called **magnetic tape** because it is coated with microscopic bars of a material that can be magnetized, similar to a magnetic disk. Magnetic tape may be on reels or contained in one of several types of cartridges.

Tape drives are devices that record data on the tape as magnetized spots in the proper pattern for each character. When the tape is read, the spots produce electronic impulses as they are moved past the read/write head of the tape drive. The heads either read the data already on the tape and transfer it to the computer for processing, or they write the processed data coming from the computer onto the tape.

Writing on tape erases any data previously recorded on it, just as with a disk. Recording new data erases the old; however, reading data on a tape does not erase it.

A tape drive is a sequential-access device. For a certain item of data to be found on a tape, the computer must read all of the items, one after the other, until it locates the desired one. The contents of the record can then be displayed on a monitor, printed, or otherwise processed. Tape is not practical for applications in which data must be stored or retrieved in random order. For some jobs, however, it is very appropriate. For example, suppose a historical log must be recorded each time an ambulance or police car is dispatched. All data relating to each call could be written onto a tape.

Tapes are also good for making a **backup** of data stored on a disk, which is simply a copy of all the data. The copy is made so that the data will still exist if the medium on which that data was originally stored is damaged or destroyed. Many companies regard the data stored on disk to be so valuable that they store the tape backups off-site (often in another building). That way, in case of a fire or similar disaster in which the entire computer system is destroyed, the backups (including the programs) can be copied to a similar computer, and the business can continue to operate. Two of the most common tape media are the tape cartridge and tape reels.

Tape cartridges

A **tape cartridge** is a device that is used primarily on personal computers to provide backup for hard disks (figure 25). The tape cartridge is similar in appearance to a cassette tape used in the home or automobile. It differs, however, in that it is longer (ranging from 450 to 600 feet), may be of different size, and is of much higher quality, thereby enabling more

figure 25

A tape cartridge is usually used to back up or transport large amounts of data.

storage of data in much higher densities. Because of modern tape cartridge speeds and storage capacities, they are quickly replacing tape-reel devices used for so long on minicomputers and mainframes.

Tape reels **Tape reels** contain $\frac{1}{2}$ inch-wide magnetic tape and are used primarily by minicomputers and mainframe computers for processing sequential applications or backup of data stored on disk. Tape reels are mounted on tape drives. Data is recorded to or read from the tape as it passes under a read/write head and is rewound onto a take-up reel. The area immediately below the tape reels contains two vacuum columns. The tape passes through the vacuum column on the left before it passes under the read/write head and through the vacuum column on the right before being rewound onto the take-up reel. These vacuum columns enable the tape to start and stop very quickly without breaking.

Optical Storage Devices

Many computer experts believe that optical storage technology is the alternative to standard magnetic disk and tape storage. This technology uses finely focused laser beams to cram at least 50 times more data onto a given number of square inches. The high densities of optical storage devices have encouraged development of a technology that includes CD-ROM and WORM disk devices.

CD-ROMs A **CD-ROM** (Compact Disk/Read-Only Medium) is one of the most exciting storage technologies developed during the past two decades. The present, 5-inch, silvery platter CD-ROM is a descendant of the 12-inch videodisks and, more recently, the audio compact disks of the 1980s. In general, the storage capacity of a CD-ROM is approximately 650 MB.

CD-ROMs are random-access devices. Both this and their large storage capabilities make CD-ROMs very valuable for applications where huge quantities of data must be stored and later randomly accessed. For example, companies that must store large volumes of historical data, like the contents of an entire set of encyclopedias, could make good use of CD-ROMs.

CD-ROMs are produced in factories using the same processes as audio CDs. Data is recorded by the presence or absence of holes burned onto the disk surface by a laser beam. These microscopic holes are read back as digital data by a mechanism of lenses and mirrors and fed directly into the computer, where they can be handled just like any other data.

WORM disks **WORM** (Write Once/Read Many times) optical disk storage devices use laser beams and precision optical technology. Information is depicted by patterns of reflected light compressed onto a single disk. This is equivalent to storing the contents of several hundred books or thousands of graphic images into a unit no larger than a floppy disk drive. WORMs have been designed to serve as high-volume backup devices used to create a permanent archive of information that must be kept.

All WORM disks store data as tiny holes made by a laser beam in the recording surface, similar to how a factory records data onto the surface of a CD-ROM. These depressions create physical changes on the disk's surface that cannot be changed or erased.

Trends

Wet-Head Technology: An Idea That's NOT All Wet

Hard disks will continue to become physically smaller, while their capacities continue to grow. One way to make these smaller, harder-working hard disks more dependable is "wet-head" technology.

This is an idea that is anything but all wet. Wet-head technology uses a liquid rather than air to float the read/write head(s) over the disk platter(s), increasing the aerial density of the disk platter. Compare wet-head to dry-head disks. In a conventional (dry-head) disk, the read/write head flies five thousandths of an inch above the platter in a vacuum within a sealed container. In a wet-head hard disk, however, a thin, slippery liquid is placed between the platter and the read/write head, allowing the head to ski to one thousandth of an inch above the platter. Because the head is closer to the platter, it can record data far more accurately, and that allows the manufacturer to pack data in higher densities on the disk.

Wet-head technology offer additional benefits as well. The lubricating film will make the drive quieter, and it may provide cushioning to protect the disk when used in portable computers.

Do It!

1 Visit a computer store or consult a computer magazine or other source to obtain information about disk drives used with personal computers. Obtain the price and storage capacity of three different auxiliary storage devices (floppy disk, magnetic hard disk, tape, CD-ROM). Calculate the cost per megabyte of storage by dividing the megabyte capacity by the price. Which of the three devices will store the most data for the least amount of money?

2 If you were responsible for the security of all data stored on a large company's computer disks, what would you do to protect that data?

Video Games: Gone Hollywood

Plop any kid in front of a video-game machine, and the child is immediately drawn into a world of action impossible to interrupt. Adults, on the other hand, just do not seem to understand the fascination with this technology. Perhaps that is why Hollywood—and the rest of the U.S. entertainment industry—has stayed out of the video-game business, dismissing it as a passing fad. After all, they have watched Pong, Pac-Man, and Atari video systems come and go.

Suddenly, American entertainment companies want a piece of the action. And there is plenty of action in the video-game market, with $5.3 billion a year in U.S. sales and $10 billion worldwide. Here is what really caught the attention of Hollywood: video games generate approximately $400 billion more each year than the U.S. population spends going to the movies.

Issues In Technology

In addition, advancements in technology are bringing the entertainment and video-game industries together. New computers with high-speed graphics chips that can create millions of colors and paint them on the screen in a split second, high-density storage, fiber-optic cable for fast transmission of data, and software that can produce three-dimensional images are revolutionizing the look of video games. Entertainment-industry professionals, working with video-game technicians, are transforming the cartoon-like characters of earlier games into more compelling entertainment with lifelike characters and plots.

The result of this Hollywood/video-game creative partnership? Dazzling new special effects, interactive movies with synthetic actors designed to allow players to take full control of the character's actions and with the proper equipment, enter a virtual reality in which the player becomes a character.

Meanwhile, Hollywood executives are exploring ways to distribute this new form of entertainment via cable television, computer networks, the telephone system, cartridges, or compact disks. Telemedia giants such as AT&T, Time Warner and TeleCommunications, Inc., are spending billions to turn television broadcasts into two-way, interactive media that can deliver movies, television shows, and yes, video games.

Summary

Input devices are used to enter programs and data into a computer's memory or storage devices. The computer's central processing unit (CPU) executes programs and performs arithmetic and logic operations. Output devices deliver the computer's information in a useable form.

- The CPU (central processing unit) can be defined as the hardware device that stores data and programs, executes program instructions, and performs arithmetic and logic operations. It is often referred to as the brain of the computer system.

- The computer keyboard is the most popular and common way of inputting data into the computer. A typical computer keyboard can be divided into four sections: function keys, typewriter keyboard, numeric pad, and directional keys.

- A joystick, mouse, and trackball are input devices that send *x* and *y* coordinates to the computer, which then determines movement and a specific location on the display screen.

- A graphics tablet is a flat drawing surface connected to the computer on which the user can draw or trace graphic figures.

- The touch screen is a display screen that lets the user point with a finger. It is perhaps the simplest and easiest to operate of all input devices.

- A speech recognition input device provides the ability to instruct a computer by voice command.

- Scanners are devices that can read special codes, printed characters, symbols, and graphic images for input to the computer. The most commonly used scanners are the bar-code scanner, optical character reader, optical mark reader, digitizer scanner, and magnetic scanner.

Summary

- Four steps make up the computer's processing cycle: retrieve an instruction or datum, decode the instruction or datum, execute the instruction or datum, and store the result. To increase processing speed, some computers use a small amount of very high-speed RAM memory, called cache memory, to retrieve instructions and data more quickly.
- Processing functions are made up of three specific tasks: classifying data, sorting data, and summarizing data.
- Most display screens use the cathode-ray tube (CRT) technology. Images are created on the CRT by patterns of tiny lit pixels. The greater the number of pixels, the higher the resolution and sharper the picture. Monitor is a term given to video display screens that are used for displaying information processed by the computer. Monitors are similar to television sets; however, monitors have many more pixels. Other types of monitors are liquid crystal display screens and the passive-matrix displays.
- Impact printers, such as the dot-matrix, band, and chain printers, use mechanisms that physically strike the paper to form images.
- Nonimpact printers, such as the thermal, ink-jet, and laser printers, form images without actually striking the paper.
- A plotter is most frequently used to print graphic output (draw maps, produce artwork, and so on).
- Computer output microfilm (COM) is used when large amounts of data must be printed and stored for future use. It uses a photographic process similar to that of a camera.
- Speech synthesizers are devices that project an imitation of the human voice.
- Real-time controllers are specifically designed devices that produce an action that controls a process or event.
- Under the control of a computer, robots produce output in the form of motion, which in turn performs work.
- Sequential access is a term used to describe a device (tape) that records and reads back data only in a one-after-the-other sequence.
- Random access is a term used to describe a device (disk) that can go directly to the location of particular data without having to read through all of the data before it.

Summary

- Individual items or pieces of data stored on auxiliary storage device media are called data fields or data elements. A collection of related data fields or data elements is known as a record. A collection of related records is known as a file. A file may also be referred to as a database.

- Access time is the time that it takes the computer to actually load a desired record from the auxiliary storage device into its memory. Factors that affect access time include seek time, latency, and data transfer rate.

- A magnetic disk is an input, output, and storage medium in which data is magnetically recorded on the surface of a rotating disk. The most popular magnetic disks are the diskette or floppy disk and the hard disk.

- A tape is a long strip of flexible plastic wound on a reel. Most tape is called magnetic tape because it is coated with microscopic bars of material that can be magnetized. Most tape devices are used to make backup copies of data stored on disk.

- A CD-ROM (Compact Disk/Read-Only Medium) is a technology with huge storage capacities. Data is recorded on CD-ROM disks by holes burned onto the disk surface by a laser beam. WORM (Write Once/Read Many times) optical disk-storage devices have been designed to serve as high-volume backup devices. A WORM disk can only be written to once, but it can be read as many times as desired.

The following key terms were defined in this module. For each of the following terms, write on a separate piece of paper the number of the definition followed by the letter of the appropriate term.

Terms

A. bar-code scanner
B. digitizer scanner
C. graphics tablet
D. joystick
E. keyboard
F. magnetic ink character recognition
G. magnetic scanner
H. mouse/trackball
I. optical character reader
J. optical mark reader
K. speech recognition device
L. touch display screen
M. band/chain printer
N. cache memory
O. dot-matrix printer
P. ink-jet printer
Q. laser printer
R. liquid crystal display
S. monitor
T. sound synthesizer
U. plotter
V. thermal printer
W. CD-ROM
X. magnetic disk
Y. magnetic tape
Z. WORM

Definitions

1 the most popular and common way of inputting data into the computer

2 a scanner designed to read data printed in magnetic ink with specially designed numbers and symbols

3 a pointing device that uses the movement of a ball to correspond to the movement of the cursor on the display screen

4 a flat drawing surface, connected to the computer, on which the user can draw graphic figures, sketch freehand, or trace existing drawings

5 an input device that can read numbers, letters, and symbols directly from a typed, printed, or handwritten page

6 an output device used to draw maps, produce artwork, or draw any type of line using pens that are controlled by instructions from the processor

7 a display screen that allows users to use their fingers as a pointing device

8 an input device that enables the computer to recognize and respond to voice commands

9 a scanner that senses the presence or absence of marks made by regular pencil or pen on specially designed forms

Matching

10 a scanner that converts shapes, pictures, and so on into numbers for storage by computers

11 a scanner designed to read encoded information on the back of credit cards and 24-hour teller machine cards

12 a type of impact printer that produces images from an arrangement of dots

13 an input device that uses a movable rod to input an x (horizontal) direction and a y (vertical) direction into the computer

14 a form of high-speed memory used to retrieve instructions and data during the processing cycle

15 a write-only device that can store huge amounts of data onto a single disk

16 impact printers used for many years on mainframe computers that can print at speeds ranging from 150 to 3000 lines per minute on continuous form paper

17 devices that are connected to the computer and enable it to generate speech and music

18 a type of nonimpact printer that produces images on special heat-sensitive paper

19 a scanner that reads Universal Product Code (UPC) bars printed on a product

20 a type of nonimpact printer that uses a miniature nozzle to spray liquid ink into patterns of desired characters on paper

21 a type of nonimpact printer that permits near typeset-quality text (in different type sizes, styles, and fonts) and high-resolution graphics to appear on the same page

22 a read-only random access device capable of storing huge amounts of data

23 a cathode-ray tube (CRT) screen that displays information processed by the computer

24 a random-access input, output, and storage medium in which recording is done magnetically by a method similar to that used by a cassette tape recorder

25 a sequential-access input, output, and storage medium in which recording is done magnetically by a method similar to that used by a cassette tape recorder

26 a type of display screen that uses an electrokinetic fluid (a fluid that changes color because of the effects of electricity in motion) and is used primarily with portable computers

Review

1. What are the four sections of a typical computer keyboard? (Obj. 1)
2. Where are membrane keyboards primarily used? (Obj. 1)
3. What is a real-time sensor input device? (Obj. 1)
4. Define terminal. What is the difference between a dumb terminal and a smart terminal? (Obj. 1)
5. What is the difference between local and remote terminals? (Obj. 1)
6. Identify the four basic functions a computer can perform. (Obj. 2)
7. What is a byte? (Obj. 2)
8. Describe the differences between RAM and ROM. (Obj. 2)
9. What is a processor chip? (Obj. 2)
10. Describe how the processor, located in the CPU, controls the computer's actions. (Obj. 2)
11. Describe how the processor performs arithmetic calculations. (Obj. 2)
12. Describe how the processor performs logical comparisons. (Obj. 2)
13. How many clock cycles per second are performed by a computer system running at 66 MHz? (Obj. 2)
14. What are the three specific tasks associated with the processing process? (Obj. 2)
15. What is a pixel? (Obj. 3)
16. What is a hard copy? (Obj. 3)
17. What is the difference between an impact printer and a nonimpact printer? (Obj. 3)
18. Name and describe two real-time controller devices or applications.(Obj. 3)
19. What is the purpose of an auxiliary storage device? (Obj. 4)
20. Identify three factors affecting access time. (Obj. 4)
21. Briefly describe a flexible disk (also called a diskette or floppy disk) and a hard disk. (Obj. 4)
22. What is a backup? Why are backups so important? (Obj. 4)
23. What is the primary use of tape cartridge and tape reel auxiliary storage devices? (Obj. 4)

Activities

1 *Speaking* Visit a local business or industry (grocery store, retail clothing store, library, and so on) that uses a scanner connected to a computer system. Ask the person using the scanner how it is used and what he or she believes are its advantages and disadvantages. Report your findings.

2 *Teamwork* With other classmates, organize into four or five teams. As a team, assume you have been asked to configure the computer system that your school will purchase to automate its grade-reporting system. All of the grades for each student must be stored and used to prepare each student's transcript each quarter or semester. Thereafter, all grades must be kept for 5 years after graduation. As a team, select the input, output, and auxiliary storage device(s) as well as processor capabilities that will best do the job. Justify why you selected each device, and explain how it will be used to do the job. Be sure to consider the number of students that must be handled, what other application(s) your computer could perform (if anything), and the ability of your system to expand in the future if needed. As a team, prepare a short (5 minute) presentation to share your chosen computer configuration with the other teams.

3 *Writing* Prepare a written report describing an application in which personal computers are using the large storage capacities of CD-ROM technology. Consult personal computer magazines and advertising literature, visit computer stores, check with your library, and so on for the information you will need to complete this report.

4 *Ethics* Susan works for a local business that uses personal computers. Her brother, who is taking a computer course, asks Susan if she would use one of the personal computers to complete an assignment for him. Her brother assures her that his homework will not take more than 15 minutes of computer time and suggests that she do this work after normal working hours. What do you think Susan should do? Justify your answer.

5 *Global Activity* Computers have been accused of being hazardous to the environment and to human health. For example, they have been accused of using too much electricity; wasteful consumption of printer ribbons, batteries, and paper that add to landfill problems; and personal injuries involving eye strain, back problems, and various trauma disorders. During the past few years, computer manufacturers have addressed many of these issues (use of less electricity, longer battery life, more efficient keyboard design, monitor screens). Consult a computer magazine, computer store, school library, or other sources, and identify one or more ways in which these environmental and health issues have been addressed.

6 *Math* Math coprocessors are added to the computer processing unit's motherboard to speed processing of numeric calculations. Consult a computer magazine or visit a computer store to find out the cost and advantages of a math coprocessor.

(Continued on next page.)

Activities

7 *Science* A commonly asked question in education over the past 15 years has been "Can computers be used to replace teachers?" The answer to that question has proven to be "No." However, computers have become invaluable tools that can help teachers. One area in which computers have been used in the classroom is in science. Computers are being used to simulate experiments and to predict the results of experiments in an effort to save money (cost of materials to conduct experiments) and for safety. Check your local computer store or educational publisher's catalog, and describe an application in which computers can be used as a teaching tool in science.

8 *Internet* If you have access to the Internet, use your Web software to find information about a new printer currently on the market. Obtain advertising literature, sales brochures, and technical notes that describe the characteristics of the printer. Use terms such as BUBBLE JET, INK JET, LASER, PRINTER and so on to help narrow your search. Report your findings.

Operating Systems

Overview

A philosopher once said that a computer without software might as well be a boat anchor. This is very true, because without software, the computer system will not work. Operating system software consists of the programs or instructions that enable the various components of the computer system to communicate and function. Without the operating system, the computer would be unable to accept strokes from the keyboard, to show anything on its display, to store and retrieve data from its disk drive, and to print anything.

All general-purpose computers have an operating system. This is true whether the machine is a state-of-the-art personal digital assistant, a desktop computer, the main computer on a network, or an archaic mainframe. Whatever operating system you are using, you must use application software that is written for that system. For example, you cannot buy software written for the Macintosh operating system and expect it to run on a PC.

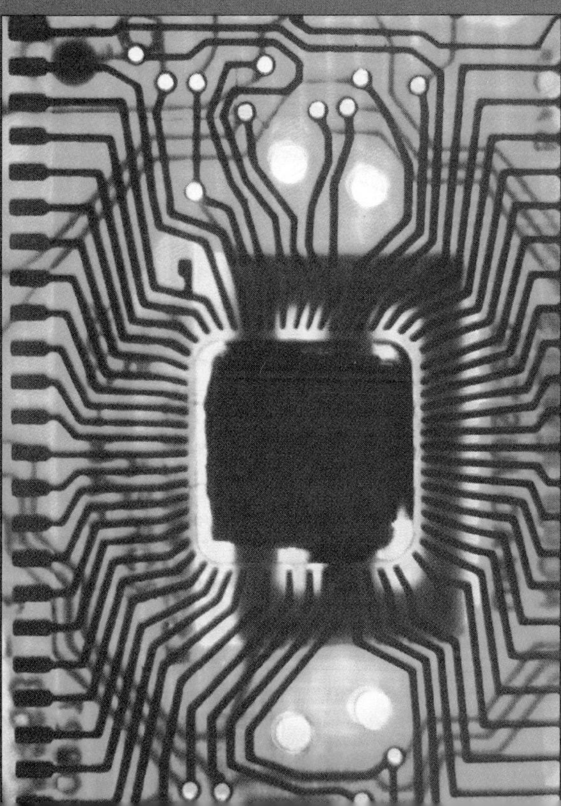

Objectives

1. Explain the purpose of an operating system.
2. Explain the functions of an operating system.
3. Compare and contrast the capabilities of single-user and multitasking environments.
4. Characterize common microcomputer operating systems.
5. Describe the functions of some commonly used utility programs.
6. Describe some issues of operating system compatibility.
7. Use the operating system of a computer to carry out typical functions.

The Purpose of Operating Systems

The software that controls operation of the computer and enables communication between components is called the **operating system.** It controls the operation of the processor, the auxiliary storage devices, and the input/output devices. The function of this software is in contrast to the function of applications software, which instructs the computer to perform a particular job, such as accounting or controlling factory equipment.

When the computer is started up (booted), the operating system software is loaded from disk into a designated portion of memory and control of the computer turned over to the operating system programs. There are at least enough instructions permanently stored in read-only memory (ROM) in the computer to start loading the operating system from disk into memory. Some computers store a large part (or even all) of their operating system permanently in ROM. The whole process is shown in figure 1.

Once the operating system software is loaded, the computer is under its control. The operating system starts programs that are to execute and deter-

figure 1

The processing work of the computer is done by the processor (1). On start up, the processor gets enough instructions from read-only memory (2) to begin copying the operating system instructions from the hard drive (3) into random-access memory (4). From that point, the processor carries out work as instructed by the operating system and the application programs to which the operating system may have given control. The operating system controls the operation of peripherals such as the diskette drive (5), keyboard (6), display (7), scanner (8), and printer (9). (Note that this diagram of the inside of a computer is not representative of any particular brand and model.)

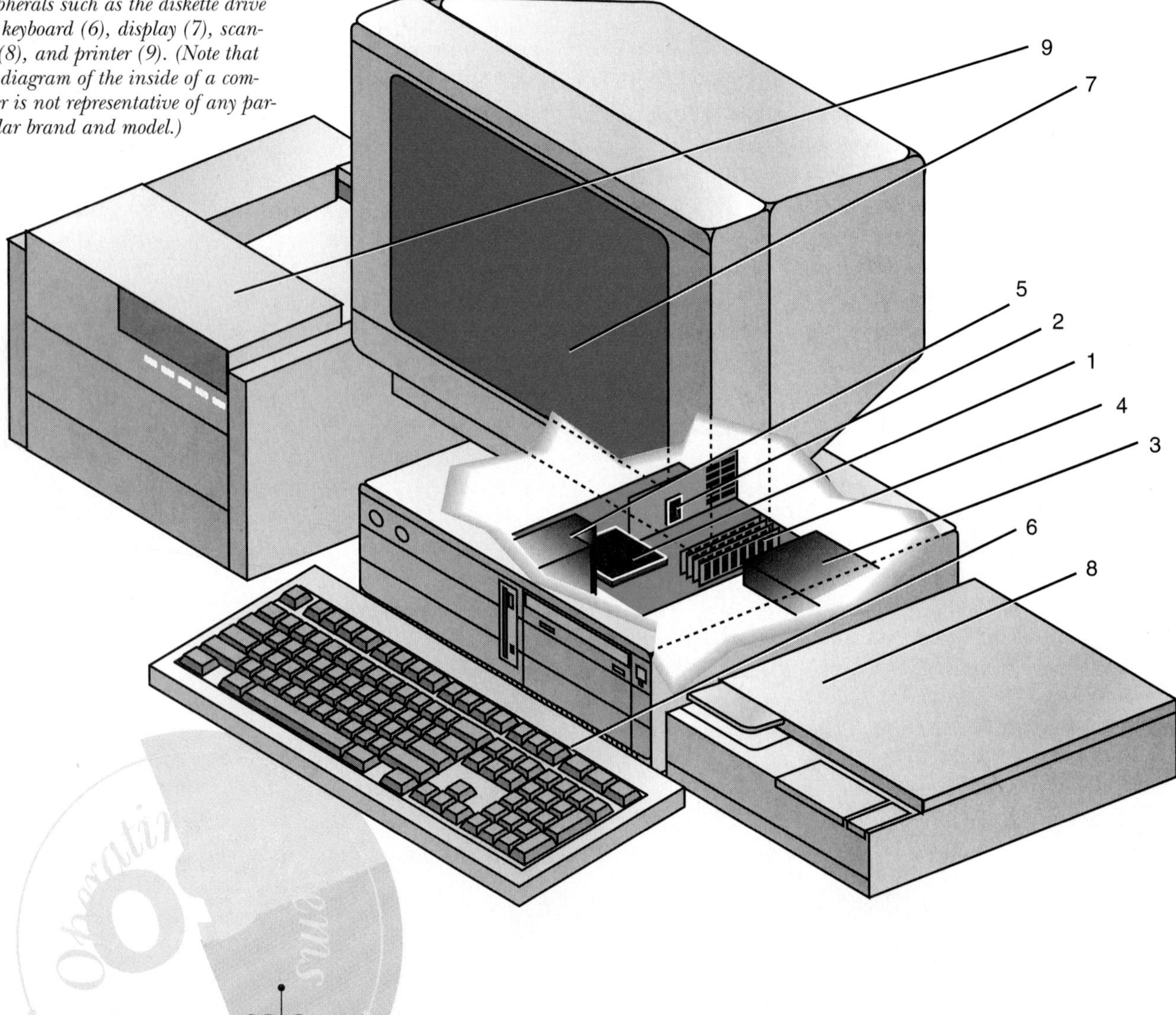

mines how much processor time they receive. Depending on how the computer is set up, the operating system may wait after boot-up for a command from the user or may immediately load and begin execution of specified application programs.

For each application program that is executing, the operating system provides the services of the computer's resources. These resources are the computer's processor(s), memory, auxiliary storage (usually one or more disk drives), and input/output devices such as keyboards, microphones, displays, and printers. The operating system controls the working of all these resources and makes them available when requested by an application program. Any application program that wants data stored on a disk, for example, informs the operating system, which actually handles the process of recording the data. The operating system is also in charge of communicating with and handling data from various input devices, such as a keyboard or scanner. Transmission of data in the proper format, to output devices such as a printer or a sound system is also under control of the operating system.

Do It!

1 Do you think that any one function of an operating system is more important than the others? Get with one or more fellow students and try to come up with some arguments, both pro and con. Write down your arguments for presentation to the class.

Types of Operating Systems

There are many brands and versions of operating system software. Each operating system is designed to work with one or more particular processor(s). All of them, however, can be classified into one of two categories: operating systems that provide for single-program execution, and those that provide for multiple-program execution or multitasking environments.

Single-Program Execution

Operating systems that only provide for **single-program execution** can execute just one application program at a time. These operating systems load the application program into memory and start execution of the application program's instructions. Meanwhile, the operating system continues to make its resource-management services available to the application program. Under such an arrangement, the main memory of the computer can be illustrated as shown in figure 2. This type of operating system, which is typified by DOS on stand-alone PC-type computers and Pro-DOS on the old Apple II family of computers, is becoming less frequently used.

When a different application program is run, the new program takes the place of the first one in memory. The amount of memory space into which the application program is loaded varies depending on the size of the pro-

Ethics

How Computers Keep Secrets

Have you ever written someone a secret message that you did not want anyone else to understand? You probably used a code that only you and your friend knew. Computers can do just that, putting normal words into a code and then unlocking the code for the person intended to get the message.

One of the tasks that can be performed by some operating systems is the coding and decoding of data. The coding of data is known as encryption; the reverse procedure—decoding—is known as decryption. In the encryption phase, readable data is turned into unreadable code; "Welcome" might become "*L#KsfS." In the decryption phase, unreadable code is turned back into readable data.

In the coding and decoding of data, an element known as a *key* is used. The key is an alphabetic or numeric value that is used by a mathematic formula that does all the work. Obviously, the key value is not transported or stored in the encrypted data. (Note that "readable data" means that it is readable to the computer, not necessarily to a human.)

What is the need for all these codes? Coded data has played a major role in military combat over the years. The outcome of wars has been determined by success of breaking codes, and military advantage has been maintained by keeping secret codes secret. In fact, much of the research that has contributed to today's sophisticated encryption techniques has come from the military.

Coding is not limited to these cloak-and-dagger type applications. Encryption is a technique used frequently by businesses. Much data, especially that in transit electronically from one location to another, is subject to piracy by electronic interception. By preventing unauthorized eyes from seeing this information, companies can maintain a competitive edge.

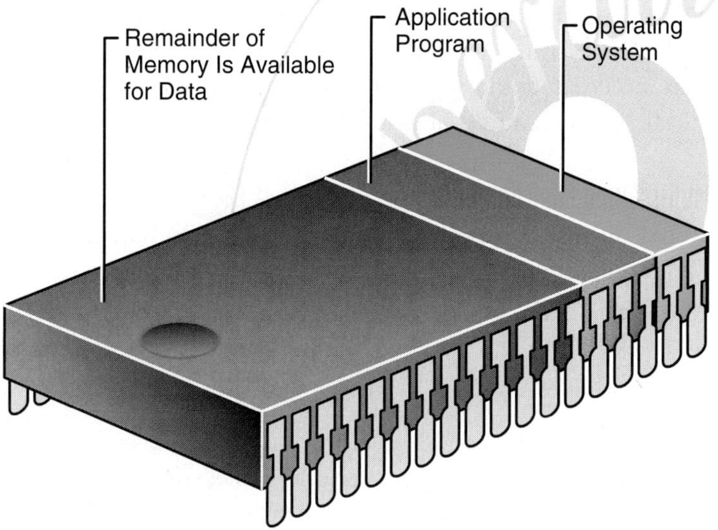

figure 2

With an operating system capable of running only one program at a time, memory (as represented by this chip) is shared by the operating system, the application program itself, and the data used by the program.

gram. If an application program takes up a large amount of space for its instructions, less memory space will be available for data storage; if an application program takes up little space for its instructions, more memory will be available for data storage.

While single-application operating systems can handle only one application program at a time, it is possible to load several programs into memory, where they stay resident until needed. These programs may be loaded by a special user-interface program that retains control of the computer and calls the loaded programs when they are needed. Alternatively, an additional program, called a **terminate-and-stay-resident (TSR) program,** is frequently used for such desktop accessory purposes as appointment calendars, phone directory/dialers, calculators, and so on. When a TSR program is used, it is loaded before any other application program. It puts itself into memory and sets up a watch over the flow of data coming (typically) from the keyboard. It then allows the user to load into remaining memory and execute any other application program desired. Because it is keeping watch over all keystrokes, however, it can recognize whenever a particular "hot key" combination is pressed. When the user strikes that combination, the TSR program takes back control; when it is finished, it returns control to the other application program.

As an example of how a TSR program works, assume that you load one that maintains a phone directory and dials the phone, then you load and begin using a spreadsheet program. While using the spreadsheet program, you decide to make a phone call. You hit the hot key combination, and the phone directory program's menu appears on the screen. You select the number, the program dials it, and you carry on the phone conversation. After you exit from the phone-dialer program, the spreadsheet program begins operating again.

Note that even though there may be two or more application programs simultaneously residing in the memory, only one is actually executing at a time. This is because a single-application operating system can handle execution of no more than one program at a time.

Under a single-program operating system, the application program that is executing generally has the freedom to use any portion of memory it desires.

This means that if you have a TSR program and another program in memory, and you are switching among them, one program may overwrite critical data that was created and will be needed later by the other. At best, such problems can be an annoyance; at worst, they can destroy a good deal of work.

Multitasking Environments

In contrast to an operating system that can handle only one application program, a **multitasking** operating system can juggle more than one action at a time (figure 3). In a small business, for example, the user may want to do word processing at the same time the computer is printing out monthly statements for customers (figure 4). A multitasking operating system could handle the task. All state-of-the-art operating systems are multitasking.

While the ability to handle more than one task at a time is valuable in many circumstances, it does require more complex instructions in the software as well as more computer memory. For example, while aging PC-DOS can get along in less than 640 K of memory, modern operating systems like OS/2, Windows, or Apple System 7 need from 4 to 16 megabytes (MB).

The additional complexities of a multitasking operating system can make it more difficult to use, but this is not necessarily the case if a good user interface is available. Although multiple tasks appear to the user to be happening at once, this is never the case in a computer with just one processor. In reality, the operating system is dividing the processor's time among the tasks by a technique known as **time slicing,** which gives each program a small slice of time in turn. When two or more programs are running simultaneously, one is frequently known as the **foreground task** and the others as **background tasks.** In the example of the small business, the word-processing application would be the foreground task; therefore, the computer would devote most of its time to that purpose. Some operating systems just give the foreground task most of the processor's time (perhaps 80%), while the background task gets less (perhaps 20%). You can frequently detect a slower response time when a computer divides its time between tasks in this manner. Figure 5 shows the dialog box for making changes in the amount of time Windows devotes to foreground versus background tasks.

figure 3

With multitasking, more than one program can be loaded into memory, and all can be executing simultaneously with processor time divided among them.

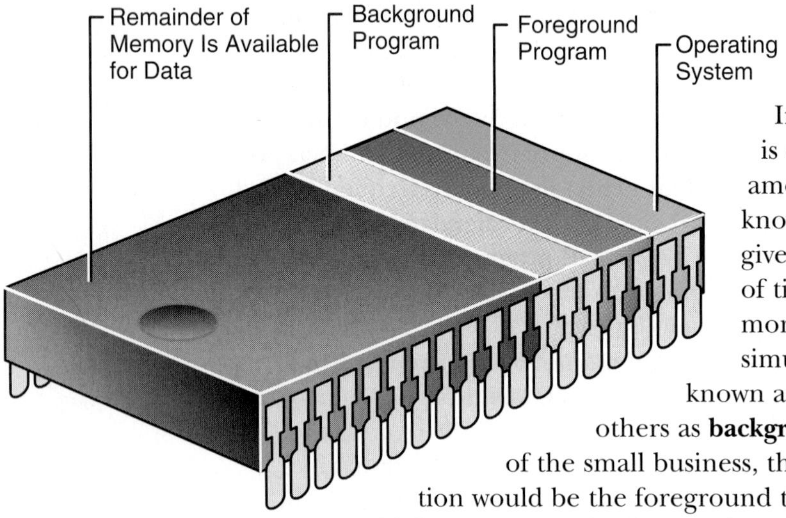

More advanced systems can vary the amount of time given to the tasks, depending on how much time the task needs. In the previous example, during pauses (even very short ones) in word-processing activity, all processor time can be devoted to printing the statements, which would be the background task. Any keystroke or mouse action from the word processor, however, immediately suspends the background task and activates the foreground task. With such a pre-emptive (meaning that a "more important" task can take over the processor from a "less important" task) multitasking

figure 4

With a multitasking operating system, a user can continue to interact with the computer while it processes another job, such as printing, in the background.

system, you are not likely to notice any slowing in the foreground task's response.

While multitasking operating systems are not mandatory on stand-alone computers, they are mandatory on computers that serve more than one user. These computers serving multiple users may be the file servers on networks or the minicomputers or mainframes to which a number of computers or terminals are attached.

Virtual Memory

Another feature of more advanced operating systems is the ability to use virtual memory. **Virtual memory** refers to the use of disk space to simulate memory. Any computer system has a limit to the amount of physical memory

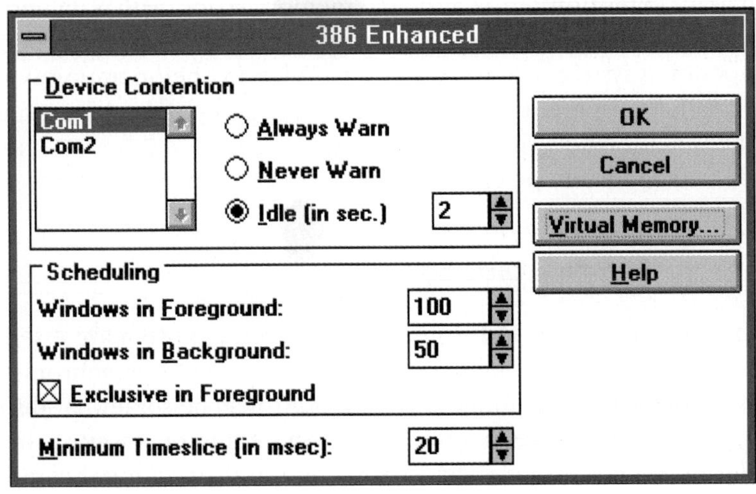

figure 5

With Windows 3.x, you control how much time is devoted to the foreground task and how much to the background task. You can also select from this dialog box to make changes in virtual memory settings.

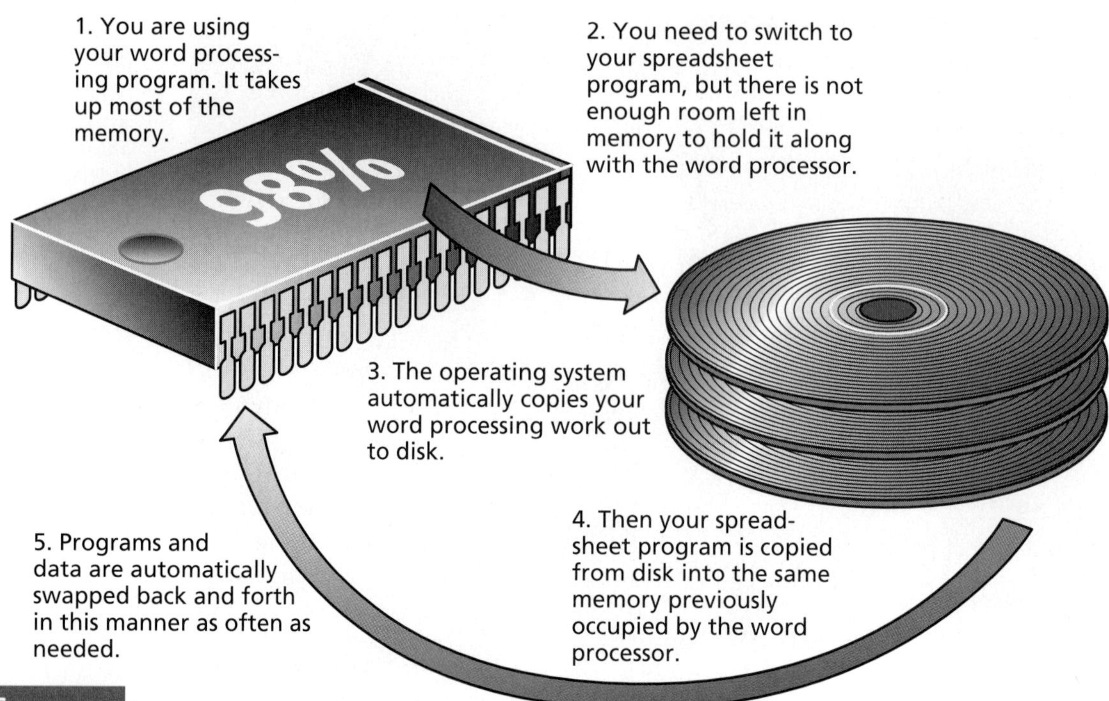

1. You are using your word processing program. It takes up most of the memory.
98%
2. You need to switch to your spreadsheet program, but there is not enough room left in memory to hold it along with the word processor.
3. The operating system automatically copies your word processing work out to disk.
4. Then your spreadsheet program is copied from disk into the same memory previously occupied by the word processor.
5. Programs and data are automatically swapped back and forth in this manner as often as needed.

figure 6

Virtual memory allows computers to access more memory than they actually have.

installed. When multiple programs are loaded into memory, it is easy to quickly exhaust that memory. When memory is full, it would be necessary to abandon some programs if it were not for virtual memory. Virtual memory is a method under which some of the data or program code from main memory is temporarily stored on disk while its application is not executing.

To illustrate this concept, suppose that six different programs are being executed at the same time and there is not enough memory to hold all of the programs and the necessary data at once. Remember, time slicing divides processing time between applications, and some tasks are designated as background and some as foreground tasks. Under virtual memory, as many of the six programs or their data as needed is temporarily stored on disk while they are not being processed, and they are reloaded into memory when it is their turn to be processed (figure 6). In other words, a disk drive is acting as an extension of the available memory space, with data and programs being swapped between the memory and the disk as needed. In a virtual operating system, these swaps are handled by the operating system and are totally transparent to the user of the programs. Swapping programs or data between memory and disk is very time consuming, however, and should be avoided when possible by having fewer active applications or adding memory.

Microcomputer Operating Systems

The primary functions performed by an operating system are essentially the same whether it is working on a microcomputer or an anachronistic mainframe computer. The number of functions may be somewhat different, however. Because in all likelihood you are using a microcomputer, the remainder of this discussion is devoted to commonly used microcomputer operating systems.

Where Is the Operating System?

Different parts of the operating system are stored in different places on most microcomputers. Part of it is in ROM. Part of it is also usually on a hard disk, though you can start a computer from a diskette as well.

The start up routine for a typical microcomputer is that the instructions in ROM first do some testing of the computer, including memory tests. If the computer tests out okay, the instructions in ROM then tell it to read the remainder of the necessary operating system instructions from the disk.

Commonly Used Microcomputer Operating Systems

There are several popular operating systems for microcomputers. As with all popular operating systems, these are constantly undergoing refinement and revision. If you are using a computer commonly referred to as a PC, you most likely will be using either DOS alone, a combination of DOS and a version of Windows, or a version of Windows alone. OS/2 is another operating system that is popular for PCs. If you are using a Macintosh, you will likely be using the Macintosh operating system, whose current version is known as System 7.

DOS DOS (short for Disk Operating System), written by Microsoft, has been the most commonly used operating system on IBM PCs and clones since IBM first introduced it in 1981. With each new version of the operating system, Microsoft has added new features and improved its functionality, but by itself, DOS is still a single-program execution system. At the time this text was written, the current version was 6.22. All of the versions of DOS operate on computers using Intel processor chips—the 8088, 8086, 80286, 386, 486, and the Pentium, as well as their clones from several other manufacturers.

DOS itself was written to be a character-based operating system. The user interacted with it by keying in commands. For example, to list all of the files on a disk, you would key in the word DIR and press the Enter key. When using DOS alone, you see what is known as the DOS prompt; at that point, you key in the command.

While these commands certainly get the work done, trying to remember (or having to look up) the correct way to key them could be quite a chore. To make the task of using DOS easier, various companies provided different "shells." These **shells,** which are just user-interface programs, placed a menu system around DOS so that the user picked items rather than having to remember the cryptic commands themselves.

Windows 3.1 and Windows for Workgroups 3.11 These versions of Windows work with DOS to add new extensions and functionality to the operating system as well as a graphic shell for easy operation. Because these two versions of Windows require DOS to operate, they are by themselves not complete operating systems. Among other things, they add multitasking ability, though it is not preemptive multitasking.

With the graphic shell provided by Windows, you have a graphic user interface, normally referred to as a GUI. To select functions performed by the operating system, you click their icon with a mouse. With Windows, the different applications installed on your computer appear as icons (small pictures) on the screen. The original installation of Windows sets up several groups of icons, including groups known as Main and Accessories. You can set up as many other groups as you want. Double-clicking on the icon for a

Do It!

1 Different types of operating systems are preferable under different circumstances. In a small discussion group with other students, consider which type would work best for an individual with a stand-alone computer who never does anything but simple word processing. For an author who prints out pages containing many graphics that take a long time to print but who would like to continue working while the pages are printing? For a business with a number of users who need to access the same accounting data at the same time? As a group, prepare a one-page report of your judgments for your teacher.

2 Determine whether a computer that is available to you uses virtual memory as described in the chart below. If it does, what is the amount of disk space devoted to virtual memory? What is the size of the hard disk on the computer? Note any other parameters that may be shown by the computer and compare the findings for your computer with those for others. Does there seem to be any relationship between the size of the hard disk and the amount of space reserved for virtual memory? If so, what is the relationship? If not, what do you think the relationship should be?

Windows	Select the control panel group, then double-click on the Enhanced icon. (If you have less than a 386 processor in your computer, you will not have this icon and will not have virtual memory.) In the dialog box that appears click on the Virtual Memory button. This will show you the virtual memory dialog box and tell you the current settings. From the dialog box, you can also make changes to the settings. Setting the virtual memory size too small can diminish its usefulness, while setting it too large consumes lots of disk space. Never set the size larger than that recommended in the dialog box. Click the Help button for more information.
Windows 95	Select the Start button, Settings, Control Panel, then double-click the System icon. Select the Performance tab, and click the Virtual Memory button in the lower right-hand corner. It is recommended that you let Windows 95 control your virtual memory.
Macintosh	From the Apple menu, choose Control Panels, then double-click on the Memory icon. This will bring up the dialog box that will give you the information. You can also make changes in the dialog box. As with Windows, setting the size too small or too large is less advantageous.

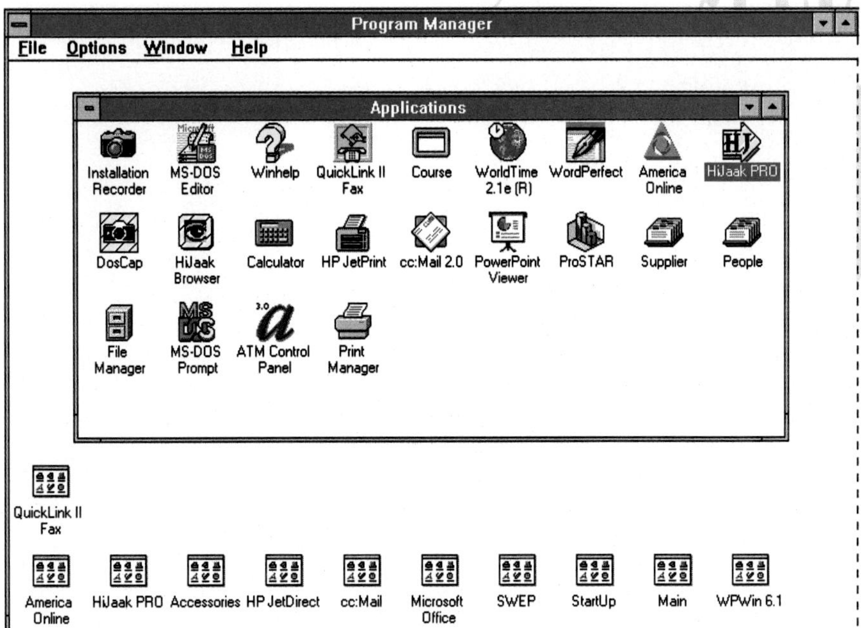

figure 7

The Windows Program Manager provides a graphic user interface for running programs. A double-click on any icon will bring up the icon for the programs in that group. The Applications window in the foreground of this illustration contains icons to start programs in that group.

group shows you a box in which you see icons for all applications in that group; just double-click on the desired application to start it up.

A Windows application known as the **Program Manager** takes care of creating the program groups and allows you to select the program you want to use. A typical Program Manager screen is shown in figure 7. A separate application that you run from the main program group, the **File Manager,** is used to look at disk directories and to copy, move, and erase files. If you double-click on the name of a data file or document while using the File Manager, the program that created the file will be started and the file loaded.

Several vendors sell alternate shells that work similarly to the Program Manager or File Manager but also have what the vendors consider to be improvements. Two of these alternate methods are the Norton Desktop and Dashboard. Windows-equipped computers can run software written for DOS as well as for Windows.

Windows 95 and Windows NT As opposed to Windows and Windows for Workgroups, Windows 95 and Windows NT are complete multitasking operating systems that provide a graphic user interface. Also different from the DOS/Windows duo, versions of NT run on several different computer processors in addition to those from Intel, including the Digital Alpha chip, the PowerPC chip from Motorola, and RISC chips from MIPS.

Windows NT is available in versions to work on individual computers and in a version to work as the file-server operating system when multiple computers are hooked together in a local area network. The look and feel of Windows NT is very similar to that of Windows for DOS and Windows for Workgroups. Windows 95 removes the separate program manager and file manager, and it replaces them with a more unified interface. A typical Windows 95 screen is shown in figure 8.

Software written specifically for Windows NT or Windows 95 runs faster under those operating systems than do applications written for other ver-

figure 8

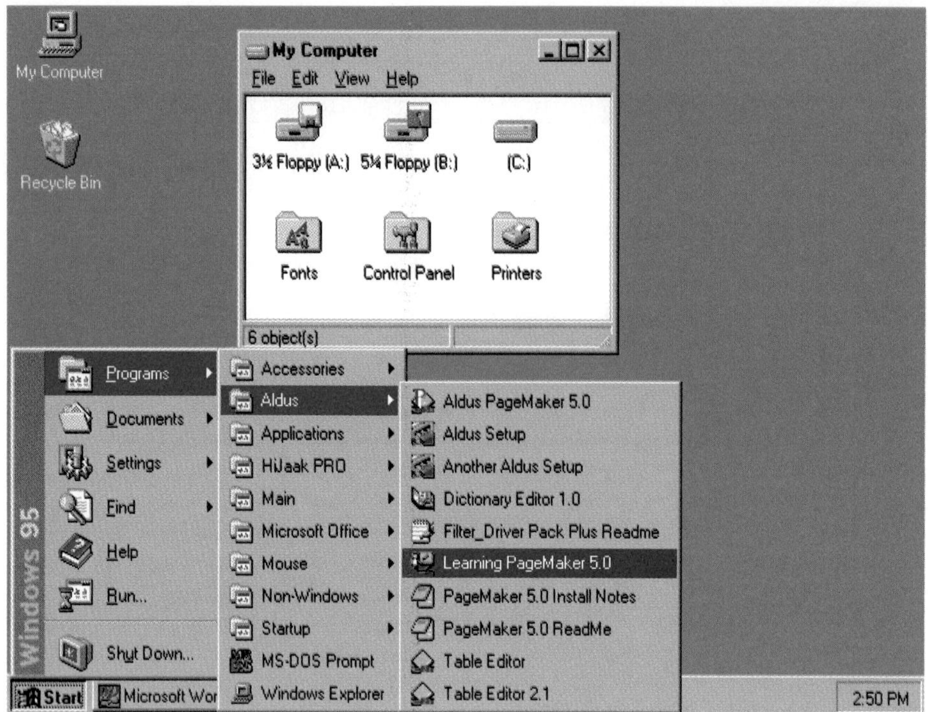

Access programs through Windows 95 by using the Task Bar (bottom of screen), or you can start a program or open a file by double-clicking the drive icon in My Computer and then selecting the file or program.

sions of Windows. These newer versions of Windows, however, can run programs written for the other versions.

OS/2 **OS/2** stands for Operating System 2. It originally started life as a joint venture of Microsoft and IBM. A parting of the ways, however, left IBM with OS/2 while Microsoft went on its way with Windows NT. OS/2 provides a graphic user interface that is quite similar to that of Windows—some would say it is even superior. OS/2 runs on chips in the Intel 386, 486, and the Pentium family as well as their clones. The most recent version, known as OS/2 Warp, is also available in a version to run on the PowerPC chip.

OS/2 can run the Windows interface and programs if the user desires. It does so more slowly than with programs written directly for OS/2, however.

Macintosh System 7 **System 7** is the multitasking, current version of Apple's operating system for the Macintosh. With the original version of its operating system, Macintosh first popularized the graphic user interface; however, Apple did not invent the interface. The idea of a graphic user interface was developed at Xerox's Palo Alto Research Center (PARC) and first brought to the marketplace in pre-Macintosh days in a product known as the Xerox Star.

The Macintosh uses a shell or application known as the **Finder** to launch programs, show the contents of disks, and move, copy, or delete files. The Finder shows the contents of a disk as folders. Double-clicking on a folder shows the contents of the folder, which can be other folders, applications, or data files. Double-clicking on an application's icon in a folder starts the application. Double-clicking on a data file or document starts the application that created the file and loads that file. A typical Finder screen is shown in figure 9.

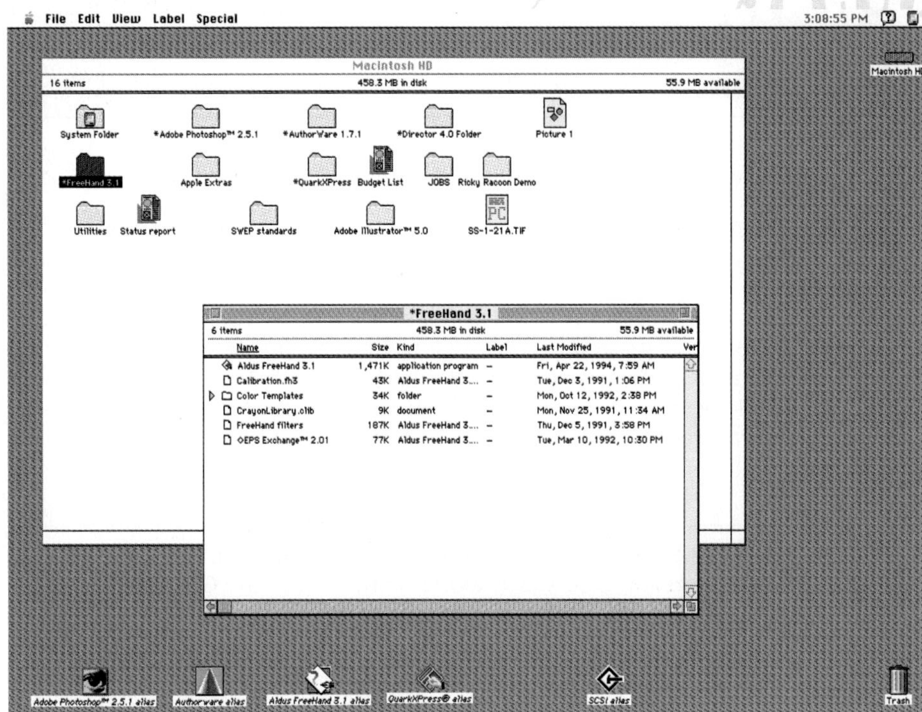

figure 9

Macintosh programs and data are accessed by double-clicking the folder that contains them, then double-clicking the program or data file. You can choose to see a list (inset) rather than icons if you wish.

Other companies can provide software than allows the Macintosh to run DOS/Windows programs under emulation (running a program that converts DOS/Windows instructions to Macintosh instructions), though at a much slower speed than on a PC. In 1993, Apple also introduced a Macintosh with an Intel processor chip as well as its standard Motorola chip so that it could run software written for either the Macintosh or the PC. Macintoshes with the PowerPC chip, introduced in 1994, can also run DOS/Windows programs under emulation.

Unix Unix is a multiprocessing operating system that was originally written years ago by Bell Labs to control telephone switching computers. It then became popular in the university and business communities as an operating system for minicomputers. Unix developed a reputation for having a difficult user interface (users keyed complex commands on what was called the command line), but it performed admirably. Recently, Unix has become available for a number of microprocessor chips, including ones from Intel, Motorola, and IBM. Various shells have been marketed to help insulate the user from the command line, which has made the system much easier to get along with. While Novell is now the owner of "official" Unix, variants of the language are available from several other vendors, including IBM (under the name AIX) and Apple (under the name A/UX).

Functions of Microcomputer Operating Systems

Many functions or commands of operating systems are built-in (internal or resident). In other words, the instructions to make them function are included in the operating system software that is stored in the computer's ROM or is loaded into memory on boot-up, staying there during operation.

Do It!

1 Is the computer you most commonly use a PC or a Macintosh?

2 Determine and write down the name and version of the operating system on the computer. Here's how:

DOS/Windows	Go to a DOS prompt and key VER to find out the version of DOS. If you have Windows on the DOS machine, find out what version Windows is by selecting Help . . . About Program Manager from the Program Manager's menus.
Windows 95	Select the START button, Settings, Control Panel. Double-click the System icon and read the version number under the General tab.
Macintosh	Select About This Macintosh from the Apple menu.

Other functions or commands are external (transients); the instructions to carry them out reside on disk. When needed, they are loaded into memory as a program and executed, then removed from memory.

The instructions required for resource management and control functions of the operating system are among those that typically remain in memory while the computer is running. Less commonly used instructions (or ones that require lots of memory) are loaded from disk when needed.

Many operating system functions are implemented through what are called **extensions** or **drivers.** (They tend to be known as drivers in the PC world and extensions in the Macintosh world.) These extensions, which you might think of as options because they are not part of the basic operating system, are additions to the operating system's basic functionality. Examples of extensions include software to enable the computer to communicate over a network, to add better sound capability, to add the capability to play "movies" on the screen, or to add the ability to recognize speech and convert it to menu choices or data input.

All of the extensions that have been designated in the configuration of your computer are loaded into memory one after another when the computer starts up. Some extensions require that they be loaded either before or after other extensions for them to operate correctly, so if your computer is acting strangely, one of the things to check is the order in which the extensions are loading. Figure 10 shows some typical control panel icons for setting various drivers; figure 11 shows some of the typical Macintosh extensions' controls.

Functions of microcomputer operating systems can generally be divided into the following areas:

- System control.
- System input and output.
- File handling.
- Memory management.
- Multitasking.

figure 10

Many of these Windows control panel icons allow you to configure device drivers.

To give you a "flavor" for the kinds of things that operating systems do, these five categories are discussed here. Keep in mind as you look at these functions, however, that they represent only a small sampling of the capabilities that are available.

System control At the heart of the operating system is the portion that serves as the nerve or control center for all other functions. Frequently referred to as the **executive,** this portion acts as the manager of all other operating system functions. It provides the interface between the demands of the user and the capabilities of the other parts of the operating system. In other words, the executive takes the commands entered by the user and determines which of the operating system's components needs to be used to carry out the command.

System input and output Another portion of the operating system takes care of transferring data from input devices to the computer or from the computer to output devices. Because many of these devices use different codes to indi-

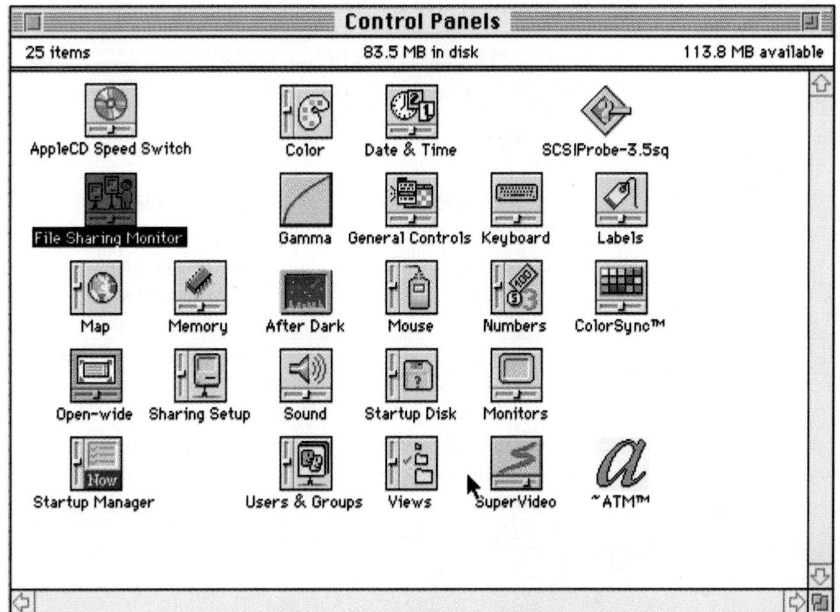

figure 11

Some of these Macintosh control panels are for extensions.

cate what they are transmitting or react differently to different codes when receiving them, the operating system needs to be able to tailor its responses or outputs to match the particular device. This is frequently accomplished by making a distinction between logical devices and physical devices. The physical device is the actual brand and model of printer, mouse, and so on, while the logical device is generic in nature. For example, an application program may just print to a device generically known as the "printer." The connection between the logical device of printer and the physical device (a particular brand and model, perhaps with unique commands to make it operate) is made by means of a device driver. The **device driver,** like any other driver or extension, is a piece of software that tailors the operating system to a specific task. In this case, the specific task is to provide the translation into the exact control codes required by the printer being used.

File input and output The file input and output portion of the operating system performs functions related to the use of files. These include creating files, opening files, reading a record from a file, writing a record to a file, and maintaining the record of where individual files are located on disk.

In maintaining the record of where individual files are located, most operating systems use something referred to as a **hierarchical directory structure.** Under this structure, the storage space on a disk appears to the user to be divided into directories, which are further divided into subdirectories (see figure 12). The scheme is similar to a file cabinet, which may have several drawers; each drawer may then have several folders with individual documents placed in the folders. This type of directory structure is also known as a **tree structure directory.** Instead of using the terminology of directories and subdirectories, the Windows 95 and Macintosh operating systems refer simply to folders. Because folders may be placed inside other folders, however, the idea is the same. For practical purposes, the terms *folder* and *subdirectory* are interchangeable.

figure 12

In this Windows 95 example, the frame on the left shows the hierarchical structure of the items stored on disk. The frame on the right shows the individual files in the directory.

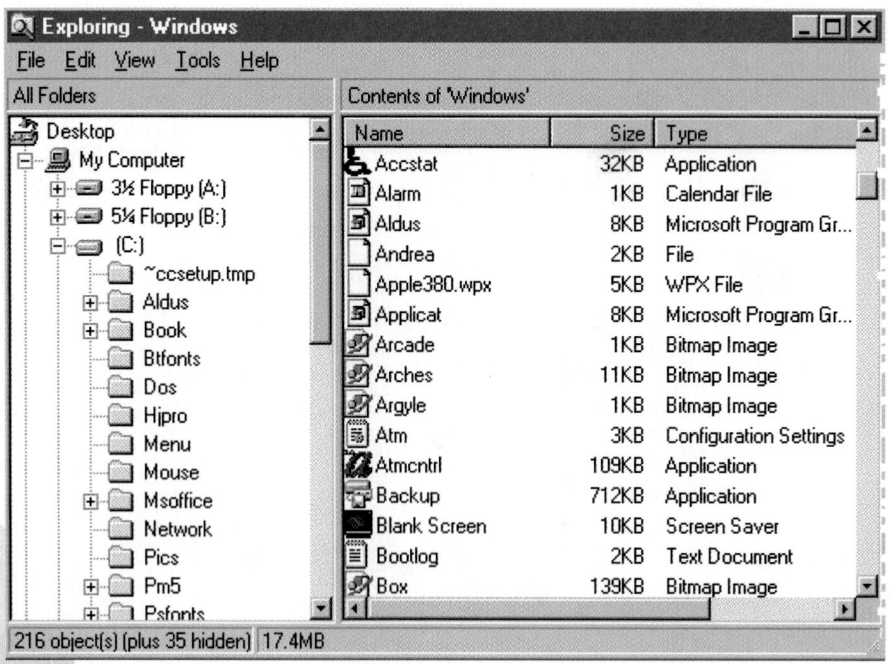

A hierarchical disk structure will contain a root directory, and the root directory may then contain several directories arranged according to the needs of the business or individual. For example, one business might want to arrange the disk with one subdirectory for accounting program files, one for spreadsheet files, and another for word-processor files. A more enlightened approach might call for dividing the disk into subdirectories based on business functions rather than categories of software (figure 12).

Memory management The memory-management portion of the operating system controls assignment of memory to various uses. For example, the memory needed for loading an application program or storing data is allocated by the memory manager. In a protected-mode, multitasking operating system, the memory manager "puts each application in a box" and makes sure it does not use memory outside of that area. In addition to its memory-assignment function, the memory manager also takes care of the actual movement of data into memory.

When an application is not executing, an advanced operating system can temporarily store its code and data in virtual memory by putting it on disk. You can control the operation of virtual memory in Windows and on a Macintosh using the dialog boxes shown in figures 13 and 14.

The amount of memory that can be addressed by the computer depends on the operating system as well as the processor in the computer. This is an area where the wildest imagination of some system designers in the past proved to be very inadequate. For example, the processor chip used in the original IBM PC could refer up to 1 MB of memory. That is, it could distinguish among 1,024,000 different memory locations. Because the most memory you could buy in the original PC was 64 K (64 x 1,024 memory locations), designers multiplied that by 10 and decided that 640 K was the most memory any application would ever need to deal with. Then, they designed DOS so that the memory addresses between 640 K and the 1 MB limit that could be addressed by the processor would be used for various device drivers—never by an application program. This boxed in the applications, creating a problem even through

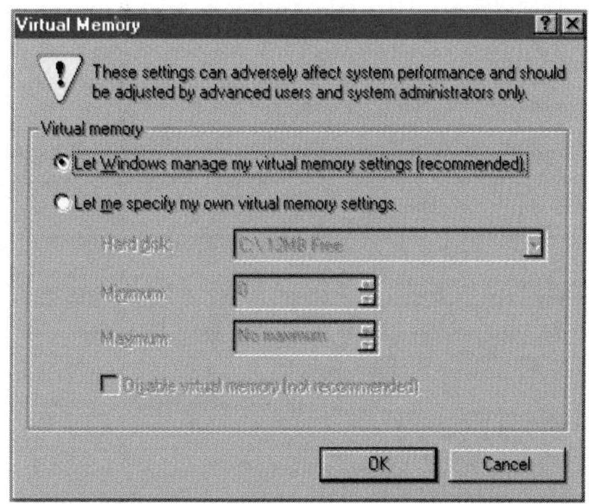

figure 13

Under Windows (this screen is from Windows 95), you can specify how you want virtual memory to be configured.

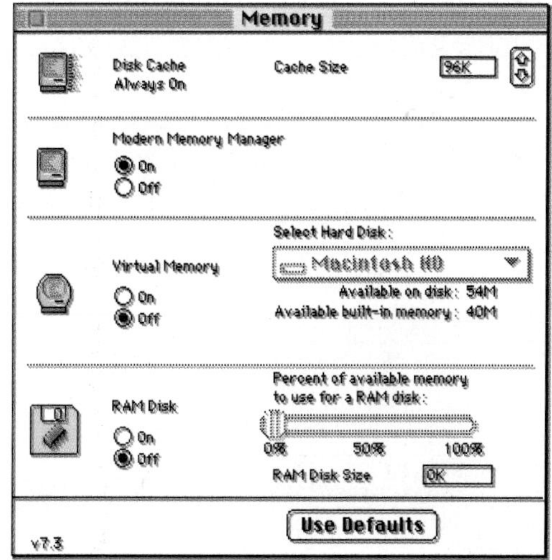

figure 14

As with Windows, you have control over the size of the swap file for the Macintosh.

Trends

The Evolution in Operating Systems

Trying to accurately predict which operating systems will gain immediate, widespread acceptance right from introduction and maintain that edge over time—and which will fall by the wayside—is like trying to guess which new investment opportunity will be the next McDonald's or Wal-Mart. Here is one potential predictor of success: the introduction of a new processor chip often leads to the development of a new operating system. If the chip is a success in the marketplace, the operating system grows in popularity with it. For example, when IBM introduced its personal computer in 1981, it also introduced PC-DOS by Microsoft, which led the IBM PC family and its 80xx processors into the forefront.

As more powerful processors have been introduced by Intel, software makers realized that a better operating system was necessary. To take advantage of the newer chips, Microsoft and IBM formed a partnership to develop the operating system called OS/2. The marriage did not last long, however, and the partners went their separate ways. IBM continued to develop and push OS/2, with its own unique graphic interface. Meanwhile, Microsoft focused efforts on its Windows NT. Software writers were caught in the middle as to the operating system on which to base their programs.

Watching these IBM/Microsoft developments was Apple Computer Company. Because Apple controlled both the hardware and operating system software for its Macintosh computers, no such fight over an operating system would develop, or could it? In a seemingly most unlikely alliance, Apple and IBM decided to jointly develop a new operating system for use on a new chip—the Power PC—to be manufactured by Motorola. Not to miss out on this opportunity, Microsoft announced Windows NT would run on the Power PC chip as well as several others on which the DOS/Windows combination could not function.

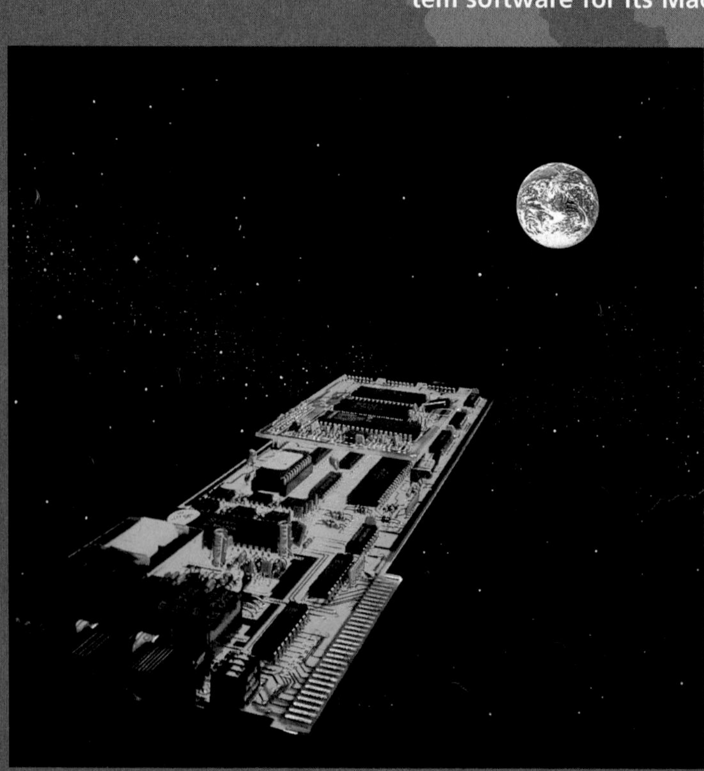

What does the future hold? One can safely predict that future operating systems will be able to address more memory and larger disks than current ones, offer much more stability (so your computer is less likely to crash), and be better able to handle multiple programs. And they will be better able to fully use the power of computers that have more than one processor chip.

DOS version 6. Various workarounds let newer Intel-type processors and applications deal with much more than 640 K of memory, but the process is not a neat, clean one.

As another example, the Macintosh operating system, through version 6, could address 8 MB of memory as the maximum. With the advent of Macintosh System 7 software, 8 MB became just about the minimum usable configuration. Fortunately, Apple dramatically increased the amount of memory that can be addressed by System 7 by going to a 32-bit number to represent each address.

The maximum amount of memory that can be directly addressed depends on the length of the binary numbers that are used to hold each address. This has nothing to do with the physical amount of memory installed in a computer, but rather with how high the computer can count in numbering the memory locations. The maximum locations for several lengths are:

16 bits (16 ones in binary) = 65,536 (64 K)

24 bits (24 ones in binary) = 16,777,216 (16 MB)

32 bits (32 ones in binary) = 4,294,967,296 (4 gigabytes)

Multitasking In a multitasking operating system, the processor's time must be divided among different applications that are executing, and memory must also be divided among the applications. In addition to these functions, the multitasking portion of the operating system ensures that a program's data and current status are remembered when its time slice is over, allowing execution to continue from the correct point when the program has processing time again.

Utility Programs

The instructions that are loaded from disk when needed to carry out DOS functions are usually referred to as **utility programs.** Depending on the operating system, these functions are accessible either by keying the appropriate command on a command line or by selecting a menu choice or icon.

Formatting Before a disk (or tape) can be used for data storage, it must be formatted. **Formatting** prepares the disk surface for storing data. You may purchase diskettes already formatted or format them yourself. Most formatting utilities perform two primary functions: checking the disk surface for defects and locking out of use any sectors that are defective, and setting up directory space and file allocation tables. The directory space that is set up is used to record the name and status of each file stored on the disk. As files are stored, the file allocation tables record exactly where on the disk the data is recorded.

The format of a disk generally varies from one operating system to another. Because of this, a disk formatted under one operating system is normally not usable by another.

Configuring Utility programs are frequently used to configure the computer system. **Configuring** refers to the process of making the desired match between logical and physical computer devices. Remember that each of the actual peripherals attached to a computer is a **physical device,** while operating sys-

Do It!

1 Make a list of the input and output devices attached directly to your computer or available to it through wiring. For each, write brief specifications (you can probably find these in the manual for the device, if it has one).

2 Determine how much disk space is available on your computer.

DOS	Get to a DOS prompt and type CHKDSK.
Windows	Double-click the File Manager icon if the File Manager is not already running. Click the name of the drive (C:, A:, and so on) for which you want to see data, and read the data off the status bar at the bottom of the screen.
Windows 95	Select the START button, Programs Windows Explorer; then click the icon for the drive you would like to scan. Finally, select Properties from the File menu. Alternately, you can click on a drive icon in My Computer and read the available space at the bottom of the window.
Macintosh	Double-click on the icon for your disk to open it, then read the data from the title bar of the drive's window.

3 Find out how much memory your computer has. Here's how:

DOS	Get to a DOS prompt and key MEM.
Windows	From the File Manager's Help menu, select About File Manager. Note that the memory figure you see here includes virtual memory available on the disk drive and is not, therefore, an accurate statement of the number of megabytes of memory your computer actually has in the form of memory chips.
Windows 95	Select the START button, Settings, Control Panel; then double-click the System icon.
Macintosh	Select About This Macintosh from the Apple menu.

4 Draw a diagram showing the structure of the directories or folders on your computer's hard disk or diskette. Use a format similar to that shown in figure 12.

tems frequently are designed to use **logical devices.** An operating system, for example, might direct output designed for a printer to a logical device. In configuring the system, the user could direct all output designated for the printer to a particular brand and model of printer attached to the system. Other examples of configuring include the speed with which you must click the mouse, the number of colors to display on the screen, and the way to set up a modem for communicating over a phone line.

When using a **graphic user interface,** such as that provided with Windows or the Macintosh, configuration utilities are accessed through control panels. With Windows, double-click the mouse on the Control Panel icon, which will be in the Main program group unless it has been moved elsewhere; then double-click on the icon for the configuration you want to do. With the Macintosh, pick Control Panels from the Apple menu; then double-click on the icon for the configuration you want to do. Figures 10 and 11 show how the control panels look very similar under Windows and Macintosh.

Backing up and restoring All data of any value stored on a computer system should be backed up on a regular basis. **Backing up** is the process of copying the data to another medium so that a duplicate is available for use should the original copy be destroyed or become unusable. **Restoring** refers to the process of copying data from the backup media to a hard disk after a failure has been rectified. When dealing with floppy disk microcomputers, backups are generally done on another floppy disk so that the user has two or more disks containing the same data. For larger computers, including microcomputers with hard disks, it is common to use tape as the backup medium.

Generally, there are two utility programs (or one program with two functions) associated with backups. The first makes a backup copy of all designated, or all, data on a disk. The other restores data to the disk by copying it from the backup medium.

The programs for backing up and restoring may come with the operating system, or they may be obtained from other vendors. The better backup programs can compress the files before sending them to the backup tape or diskette so that more files are stored in less space. Good backup programs can also do various levels of backups, such as backing up the entire disk, just files that have changed since the last backup, or just data files.

Providing accessories The common operating systems support small applications known as desk **accessories** or applets ("application-ettes"). Among those common both to Windows and the Macintosh operating system are a clock, a calculator, and one or more games to occupy idle time (or cut into work time). The creation of new desk accessories is fertile ground for some programmers. Figures 15 and 16 show the similarities of the typical Windows and Macintosh accessories. Your computer, however, may have different ones.

Issues
In Technology

An Olympic Challenge

When you watch athletes schuss or skate at the Winter Olympics, or swim or sprint at the Summer Games, computers probably do not come to mind. Computer systems deserve their Olympic moment of glory, however, for they make timing and scoring much more accurate and provide results to eager athletes and fans almost instantly. Computers also provide communication services for people connected with the games and information systems for broadcast commentators.

Computer systems have come a long way since they entered the Olympics in 1960. Now, the Games are something of an electronic show-place. For example, at the 1996 Summer Games in Atlanta, Seiko timers provided data almost instantaneously to IBM computers, which recorded the data, computed standings, and displayed results in less than 1 second. IBM promises even faster operation and more sophisticated processing for the 1998 Winter Games in Nagano, Japan, and the Summer Games in Sydney, Australia, in 2000.

In the acronym-driven world of computers, it is no surprise that designers of Olympic systems could not resist clever names for their efforts. For example at the 1994 Winter Games in Lillehammer the timing system was named LOLITA, or Lillehammer On-Line Interactive Timing Acquisition. The system used in Atlanta in 1996 was built on the Lillehammer system foundation.

Designing such a computer system is truly an Olympic effort that requires teamwork from scores of computer professionals. With venues spread over a fairly large geographic area, coupled with the need for split-second communications among them, the computer teams need professionals with computer-communication expertise. The system must handle data from a wide variety of sports, so experts in each athletic event must be consulted. Experts in data management must also have a place on the team.

Another Olympic challenge: computer systems and software must be up and running before the Games begin. There is no room for "vapor ware"—software that is announced but not shipped as scheduled. That puts the computer team under the gun for a marathon of work. For example, IBM's timing system at Lillehammer—the foundation for all Olympic systems through 2000—required more than 307,000 person-hours to create. That is equal to one person working approximately 150 years.

Comparison of Microcomputer Operating Systems

Figure 17 compares features and requirements of common microcomputer operating systems. Figure 18 shows how to accomplish common tasks using several such operating systems.

Do It!

1 Find out the names of operating system extensions or drivers that are loaded into memory when the computer starts up. While not all of these are technically utilities, many of them are. Here's how:

DOS	From the DOS prompt, key TYPE CONFIG.SYS, then hit the Enter/Return key. This shows you the contents of the file named CONFIG.SYS, which controls the loading of some of the extensions and drivers. Record the names, which typically will be in the form of name.SYS or name.EXE, then key TYPE AUTOEXEC.BAT and record the names of any additional files. Names in AUTOEXEC.BAT may not have the period followed by three letters. If you have version 5.x or 6.x of DOS, use the Help facility to see what each of the extensions or drivers does. At the DOS prompt, key HELP, and press Enter/Return. You can then find the names of the extensions and drivers in the contents and look up what they do. If you have an older version of DOS, look up the extensions in the manual. Regardless of whether you use the Help facility or the manual, record what each of the extensions/drivers does.
Windows	Double-click on the Control Panel icon in the Main program group; this will show you icons for a number of options. Record the names of the different controls you find here. Double-click on the icon for each option in turn, and record what choices are available to you. Then, double-click on the icon for Accessories, and record the names of the accessories you find there. Select each of the accessories in turn, and record its function.
Windows 95	Select the Start button, Settings, Control Panel. Record the names of the different controls you find here. Double-click on the icon for each option in turn and record what choices are available to you. Then select Accessories from the Program menu and record the names of the accessories you find there. Select each of the accessories in turn and record its function.
Macintosh	Double-click on the icon for the SYSTEM folder. If you have version 7 of the operating system, you will then see another folder named Extensions, which you should double-click to open. If you have a version older than 7, look in the SYSTEM folder itself. Record the names of any extensions you find there. (If you are using a version older than 7, you will likely need to look through a wild hodge-podge of all kinds of files.) If you have version 7, turn on balloon help, and point at each file with the mouse to find out what it does; if your version is older, refer to documentation to find out what each extension does. Record your findings. One by one, select the accessories from the Apple menu, and record the name and function of each accessory.

Profile

Bill Gates

No one can question the genius of Bill Gates as he has taken Microsoft to the leadership position in the microcomputer software industry—and kept it there. Nor can anyone doubt that Gates is among the richest people in the United States—*the* richest, according to one magazine that ranks the net worth of wealthy individuals. According to a widely circulated story, however, if Gary Kildall (president of Digital Research) had not gone on a vacation, you might be asking, "Who is Bill Gates? What is Microsoft?"

As IBM was developing its first PC, it decided to buy the CP/M operating system from Digital Research, purchase a BASIC language interpreter from Microsoft, and obtain a spreadsheet program from Visicorp. IBM's mainframe programmers were reluctant to do the programming for the new PC.

Because Digital Research's CP/M was the operating system used by 80% of the non-Apple computers at the time, it looked like a good choice for IBM. But when Big Blue showed up at Digital Research to make the deal, its president (Kildall) was away on holiday. No one else at the company had the authority to negotiate.

Miffed, IBM's folks went to their next scheduled stop, Microsoft, to negotiate purchase of the BASIC language. Though a fledgling company, Microsoft was a logical source for that program, because it had supplied the BASIC used on the Apple II computer. During their conversations, IBM mentioned the "snub" they perceived from Digital Research. Gates replied that he had an operating system he would provide to IBM on a royalty basis.

Actually, Gates really did not have an operating system, but he knew someone who did have a home-grown version. So, he went to the acquaintance who had the software and purchased the rights to it—some say for just $50,000. That investment paid off handsomely for Gates and Microsoft. Providing that software to IBM—and ultimately to hundreds of clone manufacturers—led Gates and his company on the road to riches.

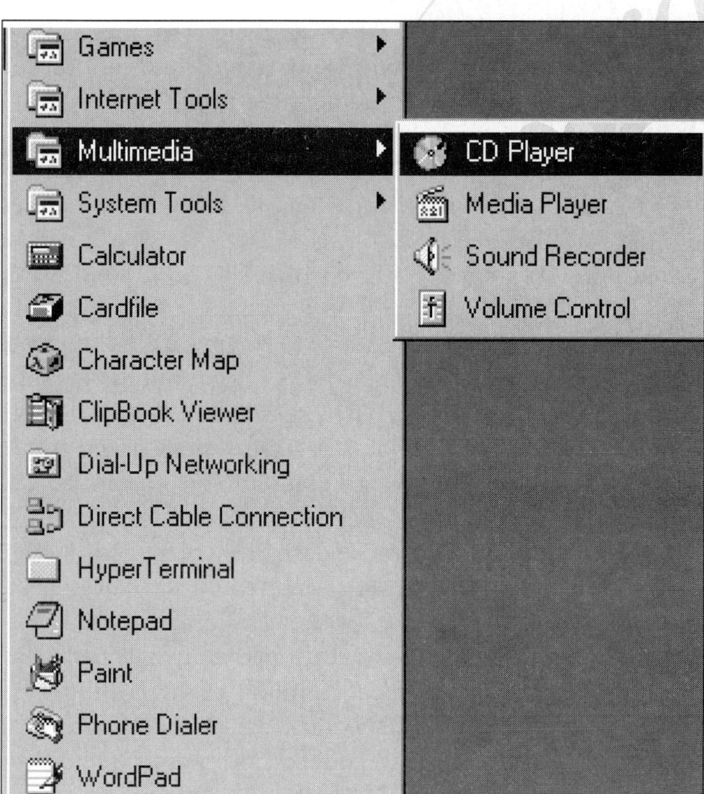

figure 15

These are typical accessories that are available under the Windows 95 operating system environment.

Compatibility Among Operating Systems

As you have learned, the data on disk drives is stored in the format that is required by the particular operating system, and this format varies from one system to another. Not only do different operating systems typically use different physical layouts for storing data on disk, the methods used for han-

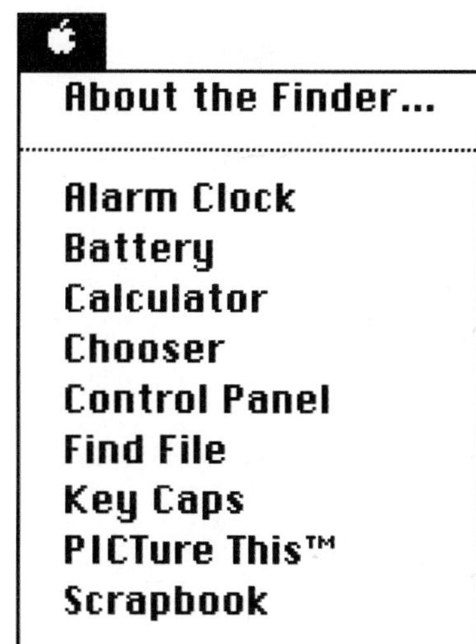

figure 16

The Macintosh accessories are available under the Apple menu.

dling directories and file allocation tables also vary. This means that one operating system cannot automatically use data recorded by another, even if both systems are designed for use with the same processor.

Generally, utility programs are available for converting data back and forth between the formats used by various operating systems, especially systems belonging to the same family. For example, it is quite easy to convert files between the formats used by Apple's old DOS 3.3 operating system and its almost-as-old ProDOS system, both of which run on the old Apple II machines.

It is also common for operating systems to be upwardly compatible within the same family. For example, IBM's PC-DOS started out as version 1.0. Later, versions 2.x, 3.x, 4.x, 5.x, and 6.x were released. Upward compatibility means that files created under version 1.0, for example, could still be used under versions 2.x and 3.x. This upward compatibility continued when OS/2 was introduced. Even though PC-DOS is a single-program operating system and OS/2 is multitasking, OS/2 can use data files created by PC-DOS. The reverse, however, is not usually true. Files created under newer releases of operating systems typically cannot be used by earlier versions.

Utility programs make it possible to convert file formats between DOS/Windows and the Macintosh. The most common of these utilities is the Macintosh File Exchange program, which comes with that computer's operating system. Macintosh File Exchange can convert both ways: DOS disks to Macintosh format, or Macintosh files to DOS format.

Features and Requirements of Common Microcomputer Operating Systems					
	Vendor	**Multitasking**	**Processors Supported**	**Recommended Memory**	**Built-in Networking**
DOS	Microsoft	No	Intel 8088, 8086, 80286, 386, 486, Pentium (and clones)	1 MB	No
DOS/Windows	Microsoft	Yes	Intel 386, 486, Pentium (and clones)	4 MB or more	No
DOS/Windows for Workgroups	Microsoft	Yes	Intel 386, 486, Pentium (and clones)	4 MB or more	Yes
Windows NT	Microsoft	Yes	Intel 386, 486, Pentium (and clones); DEC Alpha, MIPS	16 MB	Yes
Windows 95	Microsoft	Yes	Intel 386, 486, Pentium (and clones)	8 MB	Yes
OS/2	IBM	Yes	Intel 386, 486, Pentium (and clones)	8 MB	Yes
System 7	Apple	Yes	Motorola 680x0 family	4 MB or more	Yes

figure 17

Comparison of common microcomputer operating systems.

How do I do that?

	DOS (all as commands)	Windows
See what is stored on disk	Key DIR to see what is in the current directory. Follow DIR with a path name to see what is in a different directory. You can use wild cards to narrow the listing. For example, DIR *.DOC will show just those files whose names have an extension of DOC.	Activate the File Manager by double-clicking on its icon, then click on a drive letter button to display the contents of that drive. As you click on directory names in the left pane of the window, the file names appear in the right pane. You can use menu choices to set various parameters about the display.
Format (initialize) a diskette	Type FORMAT *x*:, where *x* is the name of the drive in which you have inserted the blank diskette. You can add /S to the end of the command to make a disk that can start the computer (known as a system disk or boot disk).	From the File Manager, select Disk . . . Format Disk, and respond to the dialog box prompts.
Configure the system	Make changes in the CONFIG.SYS and AUTOEXEC.BAT files in the root directory of the hard drive or boot disk. Making incorrect changes to these files can incapacitate your computer.	Windows with DOS uses the DOS CONFIG.SYS and AUTOEXEC.BAT files. Most changes you will want to make, however, are made by double-clicking the control panel icon and then double-clicking the icon for the item you want to change.
Copy a file	Key COPY *filex filey* where filex is the name of the file to be copied and filey the name to be given to the copy. If you are not working totally with the default (current) directory, you can include path names along with the file names.	In the File Manager, open windows for both the source and the destination. Drag the source name to the destination directory.
Delete a file	At the *DOS* prompt, key ERASE *filename* and press return. You may use wild card characters of * to mean anything on that side of the period in the filename and ? to stand for any character in its position.	In the File Manager, highlight the files you want to delete. Then, either hit the Delete key or select Delete from the File menu.

figure 18

How to accomplish common tasks with several microcomputer operating systems.

Windows 95	System 7
Double-click on My Computer; then double-click on the drive icon for the drive that you would like to scan. You can control how the information is displayed using the View menu. Alternately, you can click on Start, select Programs, then choose Windows Explorer and view the contents of any disk on your system.	Double-click on a folder to see what is in it. You can control whether you see icons or lists by making your choice from the View menu.
Double-click on My Computer; then click on the drive icon which contains the disk you would like to format. From the File menu, select Format.	Push an uninitialized disk into the drive. You will be presented with dialog boxes for initializing the disk.
Select the Start button, Settings, Control Panel; then double-click on the icon for the item you want to configure.	From the Apple menu, select Control Panels, then double-click on the icon for the item you want to configure.
Double-click on My Computer to open the My Computer window, then open windows for both the source and destination. Select the source file, and drag it to the destination directory. Alternately, click the file to select it, then click Edit from the window menu bar and select Copy. Next, open the destination folder, and click Edit, then Paste. Keyboard shortcuts Control+C and Control+V can also be used in place of menu selections, and the copy and paste icons can be made available through View, then Toolbar on the menu bar. In addition, you can copy files using Windows Explorer.	In the Finder, single click on the icon of the file you want to copy. Select Duplicate from the File menu, and an icon for the copied file will appear. Key a new name for the copy if you wish, and drag it to the folder in which you want it to reside.
Double-click on My Computer; then double-click on the drive icon which contains the file you would like to delete. Click on the file; then select Delete from the File menu or press the Delete key. Also, you may delete a file by dragging it to the Recycle Bin and selecting Empty Recycle Bin from the File menu.	Drag the icon for each file you want to delete into the trash can. Remember that the file is not really gone until you select Special . . . Empty Trash from the Finder menu.

Summary

The operating system is the software that controls the operation of the computer and the communication between its components.

- On booting up the computer, the first record of the operating system, called the boot record, is loaded from disk into memory. It then initiates the loading and running of the remainder of the operating system software.
- The resources of the computer are its processor, memory, auxiliary storage, and input/output devices. All of these are under control of the operating system.
- The operating system can monitor the use of system resources as well as track problems in the system.
- Operating systems can be categorized as either single-program operating systems or multitasking operating systems.
- While a single-program operating system can execute only one application program at a time, it is possible for more than one program to be in memory simultaneously.
- By using time slicing techniques, multitasking operating systems make the computer appear to do more than one task at a time.
- A foreground task is one that receives processor time priority. It is usually the one with which the user is interacting.
- A background task is one on which the computer works when the foreground task is not active.
- Virtual memory is used to enable multiple programs to run at once when there is not sufficient memory to handle all of their needs. It swaps data between memory and disk to give the appearance to the application programs that all of the memory needed is available.
- Some operating systems provide protected-mode operation, under which each application program is restricted to the use of an assigned portion of memory and prevented from destroying other programs or data.
- User interface with an operating system may be either by command line or graphic user interface.

Summary

- The heart of an operating system is the portion that controls the other functions of the system. This part is frequently known as the executive.
- Other parts of the operating system control system input and output, file handling, and memory management.
- Common microcomputer operating systems include DOS/Windows, Windows 95, and OS/2 on the PC and System 7 on the Macintosh.
- Device drivers are used to provide the connection between logical devices and physical devices.
- In a hierarchical directory structure, which is used by most operating systems, the directory is arranged as an inverted tree with multiple branches.
- Microcomputer operating systems generally perform the same functions as do the operating systems of larger computers.
- Utility programs are loaded from disk whenever needed to perform the housekeeping functions of the operating system, such as formatting disks, configuring the system, verifying file contents, or backing up data.
- Different operating systems are designed for use with particular processors and use different disk formats. Therefore, there is generally no true compatibility between operating systems. There is usually upward compatibility between different releases in the same family, however. Also, utilities are available to convert data from the format of one operating system to that of another.

The following key terms were defined in this module. For each of the following terms, write on a separate piece of paper the number of the definition followed by the letter of the appropriate term.

Terms

A. accessory
B. background task
C. backing up
D. command line entry
E. configuring
F. decryption
G. DOS
H. drivers
I. encryption
J. executive
K. extensions
L. external commands or transients
M. File Manager
N. Finder
O. foreground task
P. formatting
Q. hierarchical directory structure
R. internal command
S. logical device
T. multitasking
U. operating system
V. physical device
W. Program Manager
X. restoring
Y. single-program execution
Z. System 7
AA. terminate-and-stay-resident (TSR) program
AB. time slicing
AC. tree structure directory
AD. virtual memory
AE. Windows
AF. Windows for Workgroups
AG. Windows NT and OS/2

Definitions

1 an operating system command that remains in memory ready for use

2 takes care of creating the Windows program groups and allowing you to select the program you want to use

3 a type of program frequently used for desktop accessory purposes with a single-program operating system

4 software that controls the operation of the computer and enables communication between components to take place

5 the task that receives processor time priority, usually the one with which the user is interacting

6 complete multitasking PC operating systems that provide a graphic user interface

7 operating systems that can execute just one application program at a time

8 portion of the operating system that acts as the manager of all other operating system functions and provides the interface between user demands and the capabilities of the other parts of the operating system

9 is used in Windows to look at directories and to copy, move, and erase files

10 the instructions to carry out functions or commands and that reside on a disk and are loaded into memory as a program and executed

Matching

11 the coding of data

12 the term usually used in the PC world to refer to extensions to the operating system

13 the task that the computer works on when the foreground task is not active

14 devices that operating systems are frequently designed to use on a generic basis

15 a shell or application used by the Macintosh to launch programs, show the contents of disks, and move, copy, or delete files

16 a structure that is used by most operating systems in which the directory is arranged as an inverted tree with multiple branches

17 an operating system that can juggle more than one action at a time

18 a type of directory structure similar to the scheme of a file cabinet

19 refers to the use of disk space to simulate memory

20 a small "application-ette"

21 an addition to the Macintosh operating system to provide additional functionality

22 a method in which commands are entered by typing them on a keyboard

23 the operating system originally used on IBM PCs

24 a version of Windows that runs with DOS and provides built-in networking

25 the multitasking, current version of Apple's operating system for the Macintosh

26 the process of copying data from the backup media to a hard disk after a failure has been rectified

27 each of the actual peripherals attached to a computer

28 prepares the disk surface for storing data

29 the decoding of data

30 the process of copying data to another medium so that a duplicate is available for use should the original copy be destroyed or become unusable

31 refers to the process of making the desired match between logical and physical computer devices

32 an extension to DOS that provides a graphic user interface

33 the process of devoting a portion of processor time to each of several tasks

Review

1. What is the purpose of an operating system? (Obj. 1)
2. What is the difference between the function of operating-system software and application software? (Obj. 2)
3. What is the first function performed by an operating system when a computer is turned on? (Obj. 2)
4. Name the resources of a typical computer system. (Obj. 2)
5. Differentiate single-program and multitasking operating systems. (Obj. 3)
6. Support the fact that a single-program operating system can execute only one application program at a time, although it is possible for several programs to be in memory at once. (Obj. 3)
7. How does a terminate-and-stay-resident (TSR) program function? (Obj. 3)
8. What is the difference between a foreground task and a background task? (Obj. 3)
9. How does an operating system seem to perform several tasks at once? (Obj. 3)
10. When is virtual memory useful? How is it implemented? (Obj. 3)
11. Describe the two methods of user interface with operating system commands. (Obj. 4)
12. What are logical devices and physical devices? What is the relationship between them? (Obj. 4)
13. Name and describe three typical PC operating systems. (Obj. 4)
14. Name and describe the operating system typically used for the Macintosh. (Obj. 4)
15. Describe the structure of a hierarchical directory. (Obj. 4)
16. What is the purpose of utility programs? (Obj. 5)
17. Describe the process of formatting a disk. (Obj. 5)
18. What is the purpose of backup and restore utilities? (Obj. 5)
19. How compatible are different operating systems? Substantiate your views. (Obj. 6)

Activities

The following activities call for hands-on use of some of the facilities of the operating system. As you do these activities, remember that help is available on the computer if you are using newer versions of the operating systems. From a DOS prompt, key HELP followed by the name of what you want help about (such as HELP FORMAT); if you do not know what the desired function is called, just key HELP by itself and then select from the listings provided. From within Windows, press the F1 key at any time to get a help screen, or click on Help on the right end of the menu bar. For System 7 on the Macintosh, turn on balloon help by using the "Question Mark" menu item, then a brief help message will appear whenever you point the mouse at things on the screen.

1 Format a diskette for storing data. Label the diskette with your initials plus the number 1, for example, JMC1 or RLM1.

2 Select any two files that you created and stored on the computer's hard disk or any diskette you use with the computer. Copy the two files to the newly formatted diskette; the diskette then serves as your backup.

3 *Writing* Write a short essay on why it is okay to copy files such as ones you create, but it is not acceptable to copy many other files—such as program files or reference works such as an encyclopedia.

4 Your computer can be told to automatically run one or more programs on start up. Do the following to determine the status of your computer:

DOS	Use an editor program to examine the file named AUTOEXEC.BAT. At the end of this file may be the names of one or more programs, such as a menu program, word processor, or some other application. If your computer starts Windows automatically, you will see the file name WIN. Modifying the AUTOEXEC.BAT program without really knowing what you are doing can be disastrous to the operation of your computer, especially if it is on a network.
Windows	Look at the program group called Startup. Any programs whose icons are in this group will start up automatically when Windows starts. You can place the icons for several programs in this group, and all of those programs will start up. You can then switch among them. As an experiment, drag a program icon from another program group into the Startup group. Then, exit and restart Windows, and note that the application starts up.

(Continued on next page.)

Activities

Windows 95	Select the Start button, Settings, Start Menu; then double-click the Programs folder. Drag the program that you would like to start automatically into the Start Menu window.
Macintosh	Any program whose icon is in the Startup folder will start up when the Macintosh starts. Look in the Startup folder, and see what applications are there. As an experiment, drag an application's icon from another folder into the Startup folder. Then, restart your Macintosh, and watch the application begin.

5 *Writing* If you are using a PC with DOS or DOS and Windows, finding enough memory to run DOS applications can be a challenge. Remember that the original design of the PC provided the first 640 K of memory for the use of programs and data and reserved the memory from there through 1 MB for the use of various hardware devices such as video display cards.

If your computer had 1 MB of RAM, the part above 640 K was not used because those memory addresses were allocated to other devices. Not all of that reserved space is actually used by devices, however. With versions of DOS since 5.0, some parts of the operating system device drivers can be loaded into high memory addresses that are not being used. MEMMAKER is a program that comes with DOS 5 and 6 to find available space and automatically modify your computer's configuration to use the memory. Programs available from other vendors can also do the same thing.

Research the use of MEMMAKER by studying manuals or HELP screens. Also find magazine articles about memory configuration in a PC. With your instructor's permission, try out MEMMAKER or a similar program. Note the amount of memory available before and after you use the program. Using a word-processing program, write a short (2 to 3 pages) summary of your findings.

6 *Speaking* The compression of data on disk drives has become a hot topic with the proliferation of large files on today's computer systems. Graphics files and program files in particular consume huge amounts of space. Using periodicals or online services to which you have access, research the several kinds of file compression. Cover static compression (in which a file is compressed under user command for storage and then decompressed under command for later use) versus active compression (where every file is automatically compressed when saved and decompressed when needed by an application). Also cover no-loss versus lossy compression. Which kinds of compression can save the most space? Which types of applications and files are most appropriate for compression with the various kinds of compression? If your instructor directs so, different portions of the research may be done by different students and integrated back into a group report to be presented to the class.

7 *Math* One of the extensions available for both Windows and Macintosh is for playing full-motion digital "movies" on the computer screen. Windows calls it Video for Windows or Multimedia, and Macintosh calls it QuickTime. One of the biggest problems with development of these movies has been the enormous amount of data that must be moved to create the screen displays. As you go through the following activities, record your results and answers for each step:

- For a screen photo to look good requires that it use 256 colors. How many binary digits (bits) are necessary to store each dot of color (pixel) if you have a range of 256 possible colors? How many bytes per pixel is that? (Remember that the binary system is based on powers of 2 and that a byte contains eight binary digits.)
- How many bytes of data are required to store one frame of a 300 x 200 pixel picture using 256 colors?
- You are accustomed to seeing video at 30 frames per second, that is, thirty different images appear and disappear each second. Your eyes are thus fooled into thinking the image is moving. How many bytes of data are necessary to represent 30 frames of the 300 x 200, 256-color movie?
- Assume that you now move to a 640 x 480 size movie. How many times more bytes of data are necessary for 1 second of a 30-frame movie?

(Continued on next page.)

Activities

- Last but not least, assume that you need a true color movie—one with a range of 16.7 million colors rather than 256. How many bytes per pixel are necessary to represent that many colors? How many bytes of data are necessary to store 30 frames of 640 x 480 at 16.7 million colors? Is the hard disk on your computer large enough to hold the data size you derived?
- Applying what you have learned about compression, does it make more sense to use lossy or non-lossy compression for video? Why?

8 Both Windows and the Macintosh may be configured to be compatible with the conventions of various countries. On whichever machine you have available, determine how to change the setting for the country in which you are operating. If necessary, use the help facility of each computer, or consult the user's manual. Change the country, then use an application program. Note the differences you see, and then change the country setting back to the one you are really in.

9 Divide the class into teams, one team each for Windows, OS/2, and the Macintosh. Each team researches its operating system and makes a case before the class as to why they consider it to be the best operating system.

10 *Internet* If you have access to the Internet, use your Web software to look for helpful hints about the operating system you are using. You can often find helpful hints on the Internet for how to make better use of software. Software publishers often have Web pages, but other sites also may offer help or comments. Use your word processor to make notes of at least five of these hints (try to find ones that seem useful to you), and develop a report of your findings.

Networks NT

Overview

Before microcomputers, computing power resided in large machines called mainframes or in mid-sized machines called minicomputers. Users worked on terminals (keyboards and displays) connected to the computer. Applications on the large computer were typically limited to accounting or manufacturing applications. Software such as word processors and spreadsheet programs did not—and still usually does not—exist on the larger computers.

When microcomputers first came into existence, each person's computer was a stand-alone device. If you wanted to produce a letter, draw a picture, or do a spreadsheet, your computer would load from its disk drive(s) the software for each of the applications you would use. If you wrote a document with your word processor and wanted to give it to someone else to edit with their word processor, you would have used what was affectionately known as the "sneaker net." That is, you put the document on a diskette, and the sneakers on your feet walked over to the other person and delivered the diskette.

It was not long, however, until people began imagining what they could do if their computers were hooked together in some way to enhance the applications being done on microcomputers. Instead of putting a document on diskette and taking it to another person, that other person could simply ask his word-processing program to open the document, and it would be retrieved. Networks make such sharing possible.

Objectives

1. Define a computer network, and distinguish between the different kinds of networks.
2. Identify and characterize common network topologies, standards, and transmission carriers.
3. Name and describe the roles of common operating systems used on networked computers and file servers.
4. Describe the directory and security structures typically implemented on networks.
5. Describe some applications that are enabled by use of a network.
6. Carry out common operations on a network that is available to you.

What Is a Network?

By definition, a network refers to things that are hooked together. For example, your personal network consists of people who are connected to you through their friendship. A network of television stations consists of stations that are connected by virtue of getting much of their programming from the same source, such as ABC, CBS, NBC, or Fox. By the same line of reasoning, a group of computers that are connected together is known as a **network** (figure 1).

The definition of a computer network may be further refined by referring to the geographic territory covered by the group of machines. If all of them are close together, such as in the same school or building, the network is referred to as a **local area network**, or **LAN**. Figure 2 shows the general idea behind a local area network. In such a setting, the users of the various computers can access the same data, which might include documents, calendars, lists of phone numbers, and accounting records.

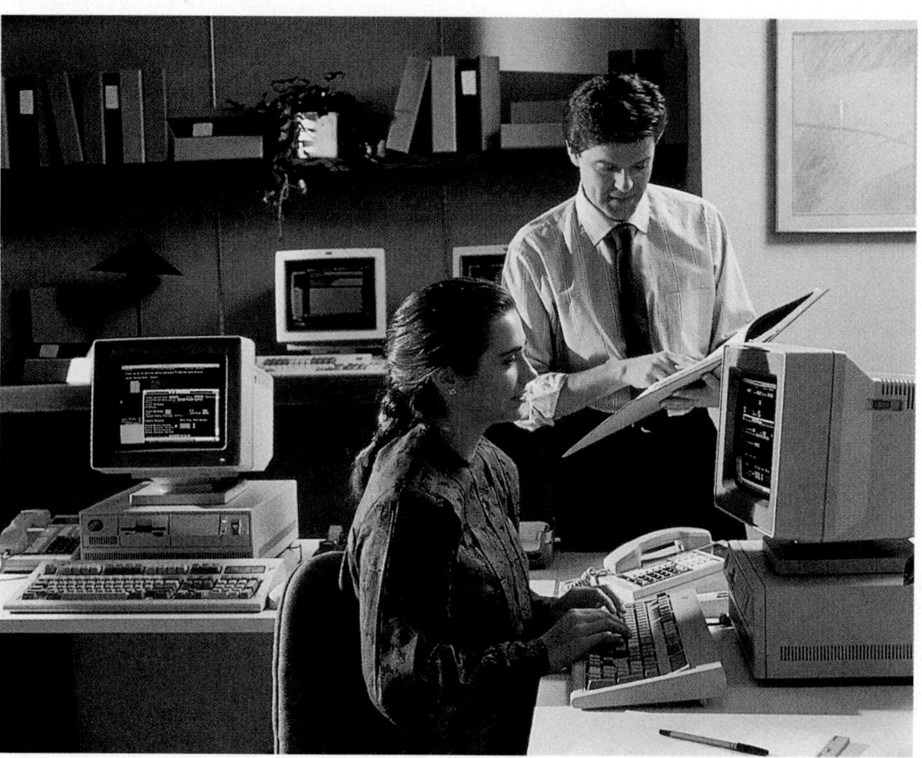

figure 1

A network enables employees to access resources throughout a company.

If the attached computers are spread apart geographically—such as across a state, the country, or the world—the network is known as a **wide area network**, or **WAN**. Within a WAN, you may have a number of local area networks. For example, each school in a school district may have a local area network, and those may be connected across the county or city to make a wide area network. Figure 3 shows the concept of a wide area network, in this case local area networks in different areas of the country that are connected through communications lines.

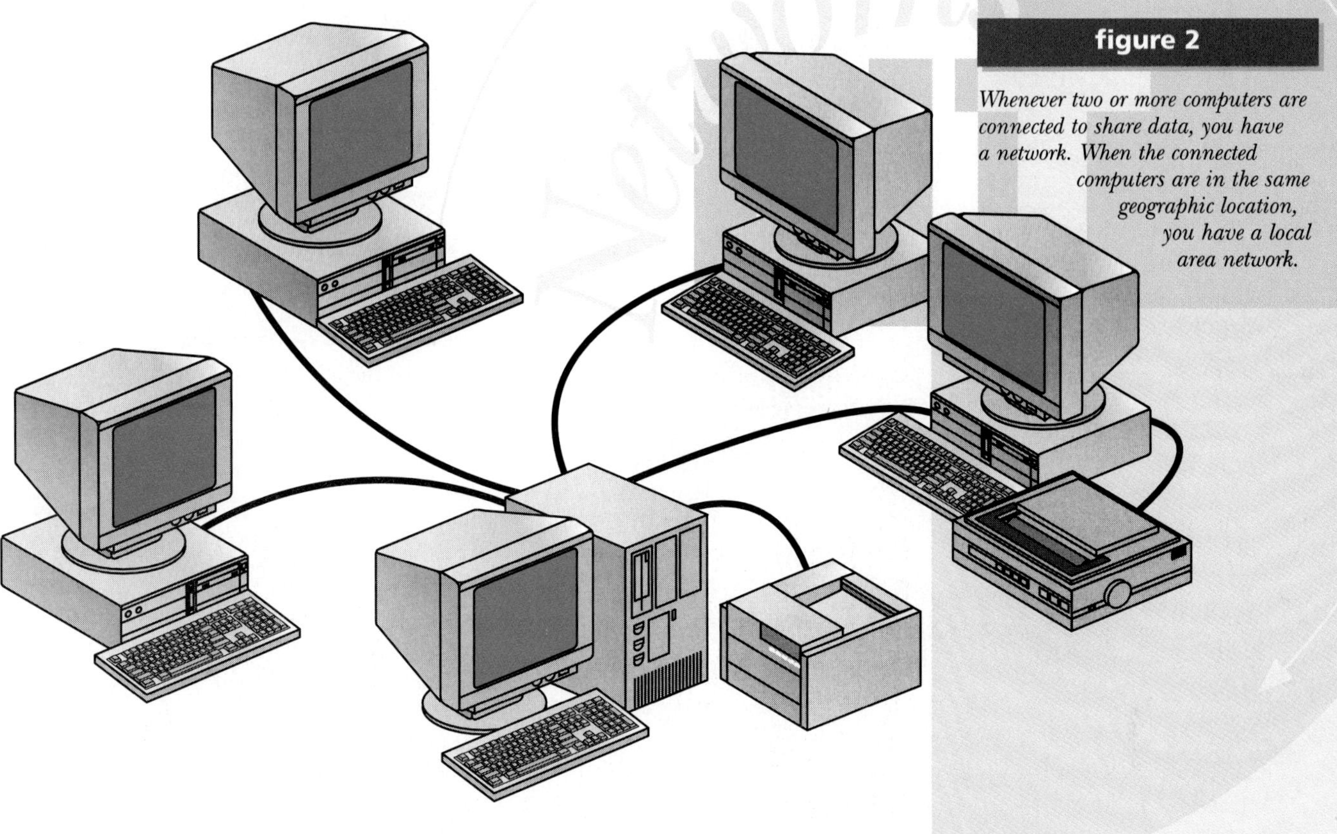

figure 2

Whenever two or more computers are connected to share data, you have a network. When the connected computers are in the same geographic location, you have a local area network.

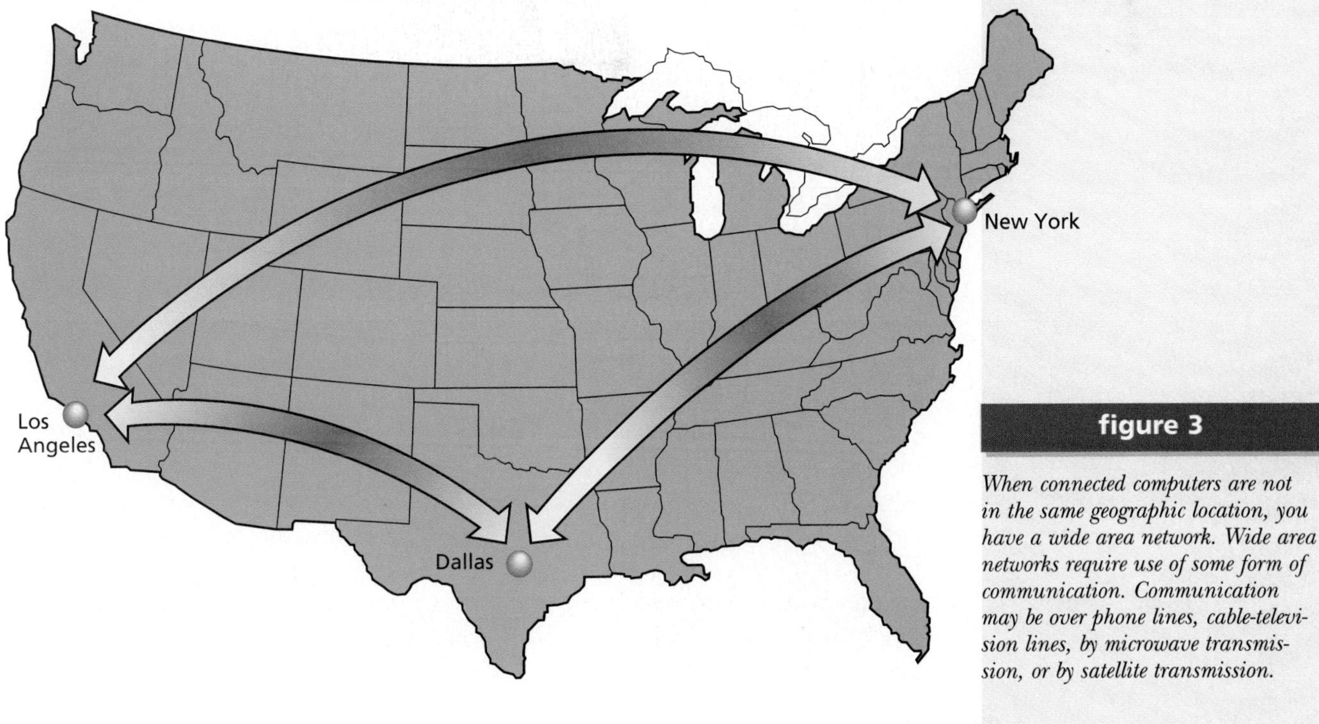

figure 3

When connected computers are not in the same geographic location, you have a wide area network. Wide area networks require use of some form of communication. Communication may be over phone lines, cable-television lines, by microwave transmission, or by satellite transmission.

E-mail, Ego, and Ethics

Think about the various ways that one person communicates with another. The method that conveys the most information is talking face to face. You have spoken words conveying meaning, of course, but you also convey meaning through voice inflection, posture, gestures, eye contact, and general demeanor. And all those elements can say as much—if not more—than words.

When you pick up the telephone, you still have the words and voice inflection. However, you have lost the meaning conveyed through the other methods.

Communicate in written form, and all meaning is gone except for the words themselves. That applies to electronic mail (e-mail) on the computer. It offers some advantages over letters and memos in that it is easy to compose and the message is delivered almost instantaneously to its recipients. Those advantages, however, can lead to problems if e-mail is misused.

With e-mail, it is just as easy to send a message to a huge group of people as to one. This capability leads some to use e-mail for non-business purposes, thus wasting hundreds of hours of other employees' time as they screen these "garbage" messages before deleting them.

A potentially more costly problem could be called "quick to anger." If a network user gets mad at someone, it is tempting to immediately compose a nasty e-mail message and share it with everyone. Before e-mail, when thoughts had to be put on paper for delivery, at least there was an automatic "cooling-off period" enforced by the process itself. There is particular danger when supervisors transmit messages that have accusations that violate legal standards and open up potential employee lawsuits. Likewise, angry messages from employees can contain comments that lead to firing.

Some words of advice for e-mail users. First, remember that e-mail is *not* private. Network administrators have access to all data stored on the network; supervisors may also be able to look at e-mail of employees. Second, follow your company's policies regarding e-mail use. In addition, keep these thoughts in mind: never send an e-mail message that you would not want everyone to see, and do unto others with e-mail as you would like them to do unto you.

This module concentrates on local area networks. As you study these networks, keep in mind the primary difference between local and wide area networks. Local area networks' computers are connected directly on-premises—usually through wiring but occasionally with infrared signals (similar to your TV remote control) or low-power radio signals. A wide area network, however, uses external communication facilities such as phone lines, cable-television lines, or satellite transmission to carry data over longer distances. Wide area networks are discussed in the Telecommunications module.

Characteristics of Local Area Networks

The popularity of local area networks is growing rapidly. As more and more small computers are used for more and more applications, users are finding these networks to be a convenient way to share hardware, software, and data as well as to reduce cost. Businesses are finding that they can often be more productive and spend less money by converting their computer applications from mainframes and minicomputer systems to networked microcomputer systems.

With a local area network, you may use either of two methodologies in deciding where to put files for common access. These are peer-to-peer networking and server-based networking.

Peer-to-Peer Networking

Under **peer-to-peer networking** (figure 4), all computers on the network belong to users and are equal as far as the network is concerned. That is, your computer and my computer are peers (equals). If I want to make a document on my computer available to you, your computer can open it just as if it were on your own computer. If I want to see something on your computer, my computer can open a file from your hard drive (assuming you have given me permission to do so).

Peer-to-peer networking is accomplished by connecting cables between computers and installing software that will let the various computers share data. If our computers are DOS machines, each computer's hard drive will appear to the other computers as a drive letter beyond C: (remember that drive C: refers to the built-in hard drive). Therefore, my hard drive might show up as drive D: on your computer, and your hard drive might show up as drive D: on my computer. If our computers are Macintoshes, my hard drive may show up on your desktop as Jim's Computer, while your computer might show up on my desktop as Sue's Computer or Sam's Computer (or whatever your name is).

If the computers you want to connect in a peer-to-peer network all use the same operating system, you may need to add only the physical connection to create a network. This is true for Macintosh System 7, Windows for Workgroups, Windows 95, Windows NT, OS/2, or Novell DOS version 7. If you have computers with built-in networking hardware, such as the Macintosh and a growing number of PC models, just connect cable from computer to computer.

For PCs without built-in networking hardware (or to speed up communication for Macintosh models with LocalTalk rather than Ethernet), you need to install a network interface card (NIC). These cards can be purchased for

figure 4

A peer-to-peer network allows each user to access what is stored on the hard drives of the other computers on that network.

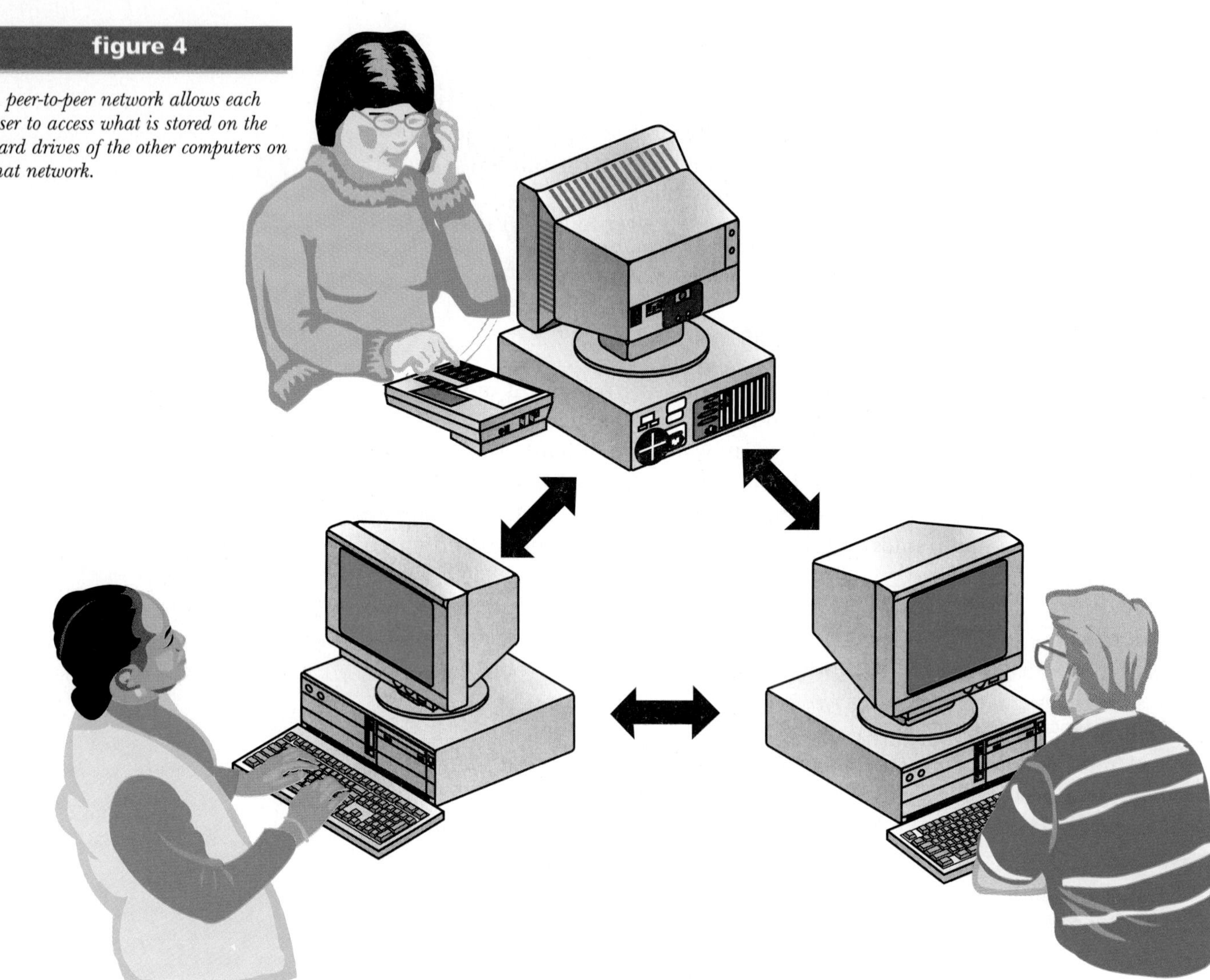

under $100 per computer, and the cable to run between a pair of computers is only a few dollars. (It is possible to do simple peer-to-peer networking using the parallel or serial ports of PCs and appropriate software such as INTERLNK and INTERSVR that comes with DOS 6. This form of communication, however, is very slow and most often used for functions such as copying files from a desktop computer to a notebook computer and vice versa.)

File-Server Based Networking

As opposed to computers having access to other users' computers, a network may be set up so that a main computer "serves" files to the users who need to access them. The main computer in such a network is called a **file server** (named for its main function).

Under some circumstances, a file-server computer may also be used by a worker, but it is typically restricted to its file-server duties because it works much faster when there is no user on it. Any files that are to be shared by more than one user are stored on a hard disk on the file server rather than

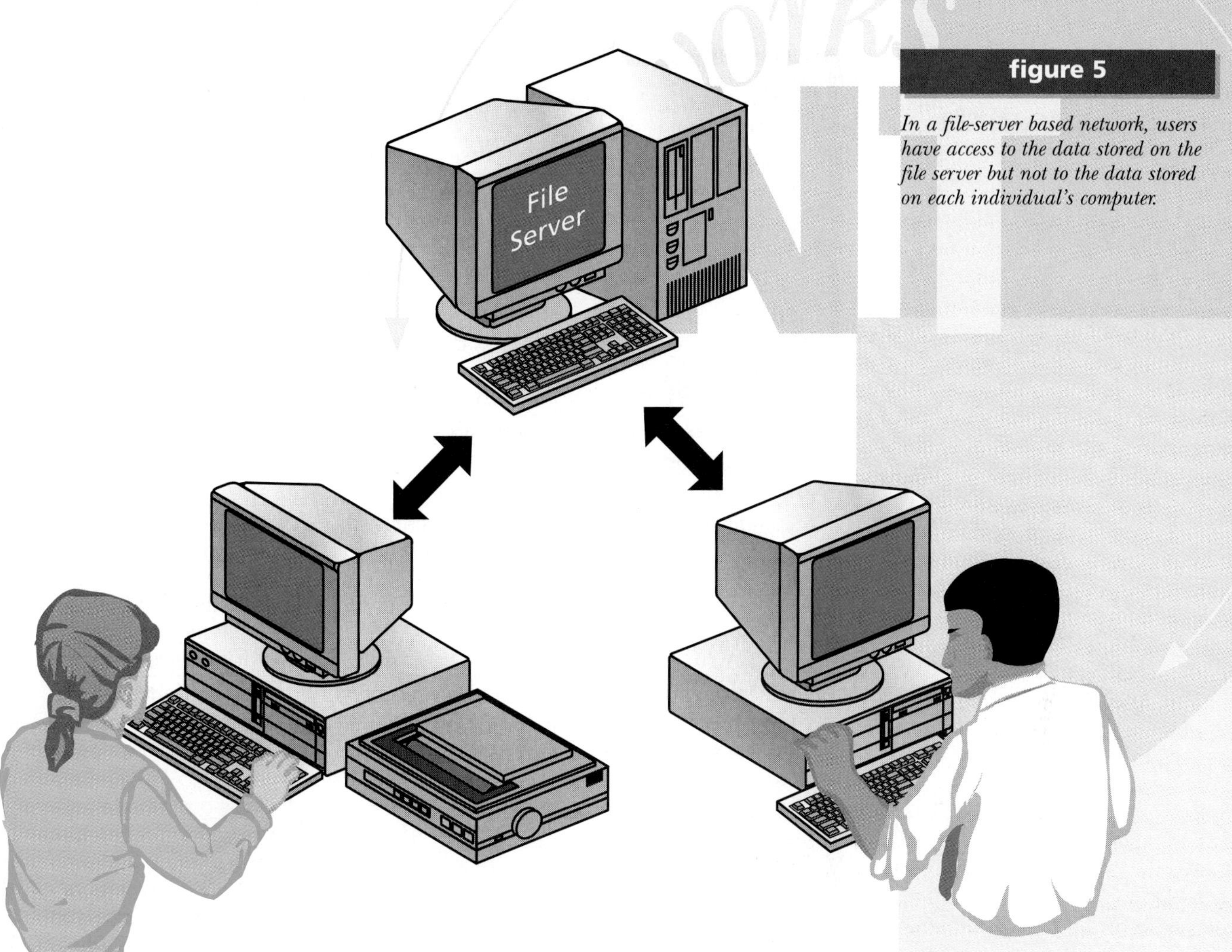

figure 5

In a file-server based network, users have access to the data stored on the file server but not to the data stored on each individual's computer.

the hard disk on an individual user's computer. Files stored on the file server typically include application (program files) as well as documents and data. Individual users can still store files on their local hard drives; however, files on local hard drives are typically not available to other users on the network (figure 5).

The physical connections for a file-server network are the same at each computer as for a peer-to-peer network. Each computer must have hardware for networking (either built-in or add-on NICs). Network cable (and occasionally infrared or radio signals) connects to the NIC. For a small network, the cable may just be strung from computer to computer. Usually, however, a more sophisticated wiring scheme is used where the cable from each computer goes to a central point for connection.

Peer-to-Peer Versus File Server

There are advantages and disadvantages to both ways of setting up a network. Figure 6 compares the two.

figure 6

A comparison of peer-to-peer and server-based networks.

Feature	Peer-to-Peer	Server-Based
Cost	$	$$
Complexity	Fairly simple	Can be very complex
Computers required	Only the users' computers	File server in addition to the users' computers
Effect on network if one user's computer goes down	Other users cannot access data stored on the computer that is down	None
Effect on network if the file server goes down	Not applicable	No users have access to data stored on the server
Complexity of wiring	Can be as simple as a cable strung between two computers	Can be simple cable strung between computers or can be as complex as a building-wide structured wiring system
Maximum number of computers in network	Preferably no more than a handful; keeping up with what's stored where becomes just about impossible after that	Can be hundreds or even thousands
Ease of control or administration	There is no central point of control, so administration can get sloppy in anything more than a minimal-sized network	The file server provides a central point of control, making it much easier to administer a larger network
Size of business or workgroup for which appropriate	Small	Any size
Ease of keeping up with where data is stored	Can be iffy because data can be stored on any computer	All shared data is on the file server, so there is no question where it is
Ease of backup	Can be complex because data can be stored on several different computers	Easy because all critical data should be on the file server

Do It!

1 Find out what kind of network, if any, is used in your school. Is it a file server based or a peer-to-peer network? Talk with the network administrator about the advantages and disadvantages of the network being set up the way that it is; your instructor may want this interview to be a class activity.

2 Find a business in your community that uses a local area network. Discuss with that business how they use the network and what advantages it gives them in operating the business. Prepare a report of your findings.

What Are Networks Made from?

You have learned that networked computers are connected through means of a network interface, which can be either built-in or on a plug-in card. Each interface must be attached to a conductor such as wire, fiber-optic cable, or even infrared or radio transmissions.

A network must also use a "communication language" that all of the individual computers can speak. This is like having a German and a Spaniard in a room together trying to communicate. If one speaks only German and the other speaks only Spanish, not a whole lot of meaning will be conveyed. If they both know English in addition to their native language, however, they will be able to carry on a conversation.

Topologies and Standards

The way that signal flow is logically arranged is known as the **topology**, while the way in which data is transmitted or "spoken" is known as the **transmission standard**. Standards are necessary to control the flow of traffic on the network. If every computer on the network were allowed to transmit data whenever it wanted to with no regard to other nodes, the resulting rush of data on the network cabling would result in garbled codes, and the network would fail to operate. Therefore, these standards are something like the "rules of the road" to keep signals flowing smoothly.

Each computer in a local area network is referred to as a **node**. Each connection or communication channel over which the computer "talks" is referred to as a **link**. Nodes and links can be arranged in a variety of different arrangements (called network topologies). Two of the most commonly used topologies are the ring topology and the bus topology.

Ring topology In a **ring topology**, one or more computers may act as host systems or file servers. As figure 7 illustrates, all of the computers and other terminal devices are attached to each other through a ring configuration. This means that data transmitted from any computer or terminal device on the network may be received by any other device. Data simply travels around the ring until

Profile

Ray Noorda

Novell shares several things with Wal-Mart. Among them are leadership positions within their respective industries, and that their corporate leaders defined themselves by their easygoing manner—and pickup trucks. One could say that Novell's Ray Noorda is the Sam Walton of the computer networking industry.

In fact, it is hard to picture Novell *before* Ray Noorda became president. Having received a degree in electrical engineering in 1949, Noorda worked for GE until 1970. He then worked with several start-up companies before joining Novell in 1983. In that year, Novell's sales were $3.8 million. Projected sales for 1994 were $1.2 billion, or 316 times as much. Noorda is credited for being the driving force behind this phenomenal growth.

Novell's first networking product was a disk server for handling multiple CP/M computers. When IBM introduced the PC, Novell built an interface card to attach the MS-DOS computer and CP/M computer on the same network. Then, a file server was designed that would allow the different operating systems to exist on the same network. After the IBM XT was introduced in 1983, Novell decided that their network software should be independent of the hardware and software of the computer user station. By keeping their NetWare product on the leading edge over the years, Novell was the software of choice for over two thirds of all computer networks in 1993.

Novell's primary competition is Microsoft, who seeks to dominate network software in much the same way they have desktop operating systems. To maintain its leadership position, Novell has made several key software acquisitions. Among them have been Digital Research, a company that developed a DOS-compatible operating system. Novell also purchased the UNIX operating system from AT&T, and the QuattroPro spreadsheet software from Borland. Their biggest acquisition was the purchase of WordPerfect Corporation in 1994 for $1.4 billion in stock and options. This purchase gave Novell ownership of the dominant word-processing program.

Under Noorda's leadership, Novell specialized in what he calls "coopetition." That is, he cooperated with competitors whenever that was good for networking and, thus, for Novell.

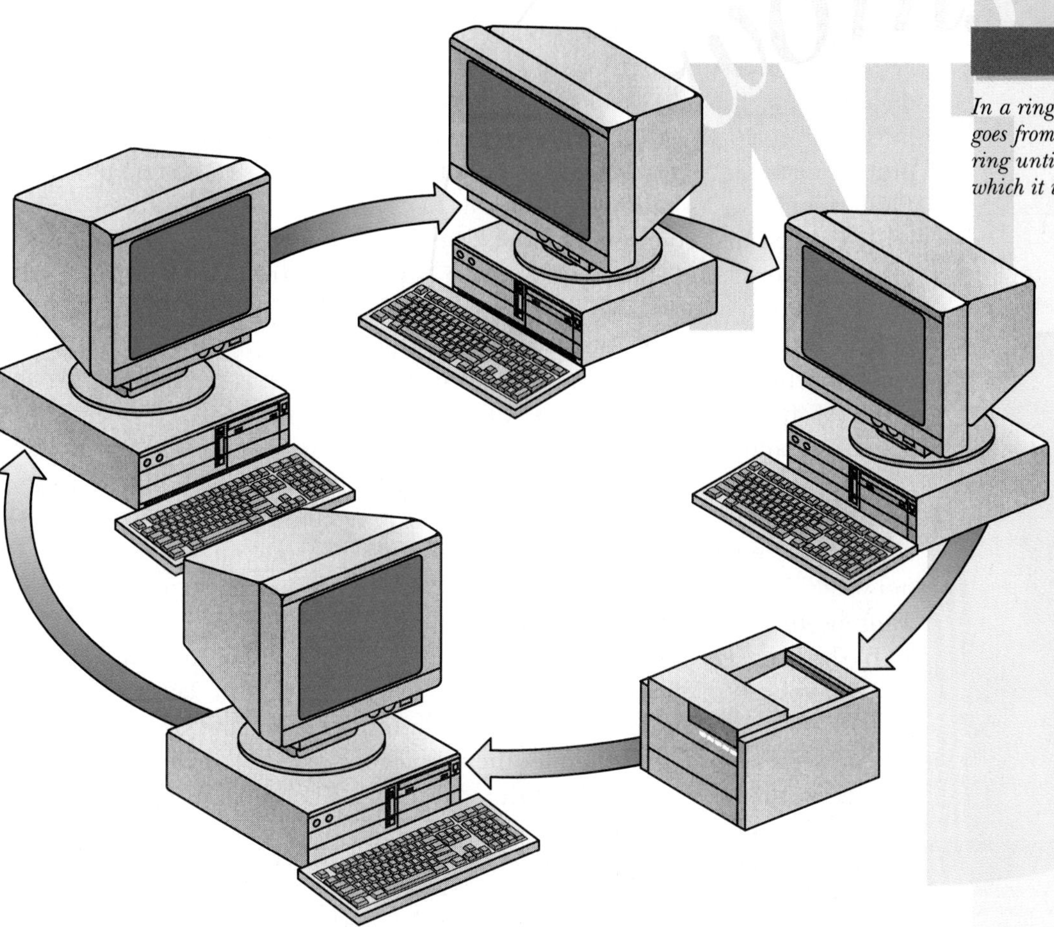

figure 7

In a ring topology, communication goes from one computer around the ring until it reaches the computer for which it is intended.

it comes to the communicating device for which it is intended (addressed). A device on the ring network can easily be bypassed without disrupting the rest of the network. IBM has been the biggest proponent of ring topology.

Networks using a ring topology generally use a transmission standard called token passing. **Token passing** may be thought of as being similar to a train. Assume that you have a circular track and a train with one freight car circles the track continuously. At various points around the track are businesses that want to ship things by train to other businesses along the track. When the train comes by a business, the business looks to see if the freight car is empty. If it is empty, the business stops the train, loads it, and tells it the name of the business that is to get the load. If the freight car has freight on it when it comes by a business, the business looks to determine if the load is addressed to it. If it is, it unloads the freight; if the load is intended for someone else, the train just keeps moving. With only one train on the track, there is never a possibility of a train collision, and freight keeps moving smoothly. The greater the number of businesses wanting to ship freight, however, the longer it will likely take for all of them to get served, because it will be a longer wait for an empty train.

If you make the railroad track be your network wiring and each of the businesses along the way a computer that shares information on the network, you have an analogy to a token-passing network. In a token-passing system, a packet of data, called the token, controls access to the network. Only the computer that gets possession of the token may transmit on the network. For example, assume that Node 1 has the token and wants to send some data to Node 4. Node 1 will put Node 4's address into the packet of token information along with the data and its own address as sender. Once it has put the necessary information in the token, Node 1 passes the token onto the network.

The token first comes to Node 2, where the card attaching the computer to the network takes a quick look at the "ship to" address on the token. Not finding its own address, Node 2 simply passes the token along to the next node. The same thing happens again at Node 3.

When the token gets to Node 4, Node 4 finds that it is the intended receiver of the token. Therefore, it takes the data, puts a "received" message in the token, and releases the token back onto the ring. The token continues to travel around the ring until it comes back to Node 1, which intercepts it and examines the return message from Node 4. Finding that its network access was successful, Node 1 puts a new "available to anyone" token on the network. This token then repeatedly circles the ring until the next node wanting to use the network takes control of it.

In short, token passing controls network traffic by requiring that a node have possession of the token (its address is in the packet of data) before it can use the network. The time that is required for a node to examine the token for its address and then let the token continue its journey may typically be in the range of 1/30,000th of a second. Therefore, as long as the network has a reasonable number of nodes and the work performed by the network computers is not extremely time critical, token passing operates at a good speed.

The most commonly used token-passing standard is known as **token ring** and has been heavily promoted by IBM. It is typically available in two transmission speeds (the slow freight and the fast express, if you will). The hardware for connecting computers to token-ring networks is frequently adjustable between the two speeds. Slow speed is typically 4 megabits per second, while fast speed is 16 megabits per second. That is, with 16-megabit speed, roughly 16 million ones or zeroes of binary numbers with which computers communicate travel over the wire in 1 second. Note that the speed is expressed in terms of megabits per second (Mbps), with each bit being a one or zero, as opposed to being expressed in characters per second.

With a token-ring network, the size of the information packet being transmitted (the size of the "train car") can be set to several different values, the largest being 4096 bytes of data for the 4-Mbps speed and 16,384 bytes of data for the 16-Mbps speed. Whenever the packet size can accommodate all of the needed data for a transmission in one "load," the network can be more efficient.

In a token-ring network, the cable from each computer goes to a connection point known as a multistation access unit, or MAU. As shown in figure 8, the data flow is still in a ring shape.

Bus topology In a **bus topology**, each computer or terminal device is linked to a single communication channel by a "drop" line (figure 9). The drop line may be as short as the half-inch of metal on a T-shaped connector attached to the back of a computer, or it may be as long as several feet (such as if it drops down from a cable in the ceiling). Data that is transmitted by any device on the bus network travels down the entire length of cable. Similar to a ring net-

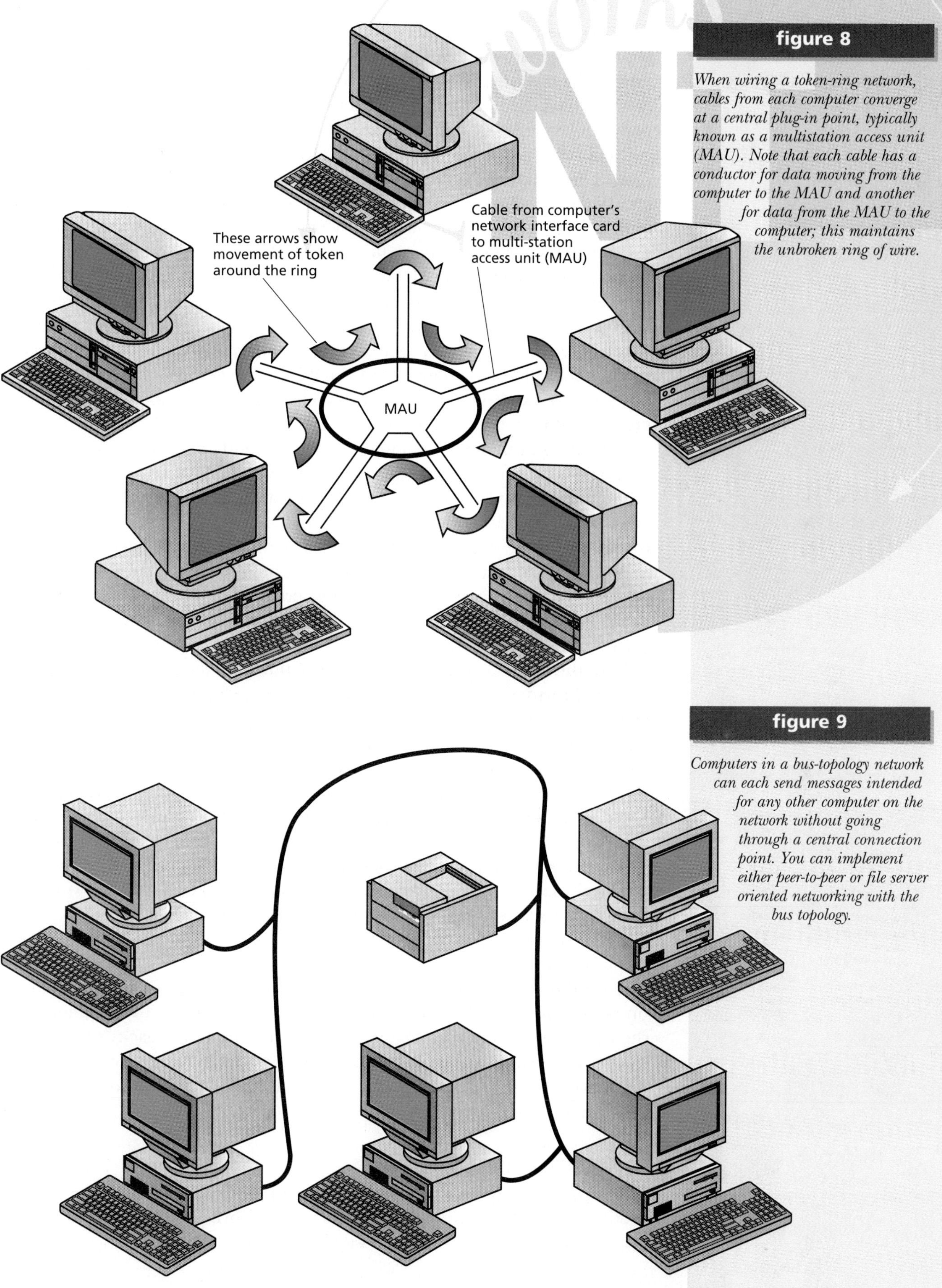

figure 8

When wiring a token-ring network, cables from each computer converge at a central plug-in point, typically known as a multistation access unit (MAU). Note that each cable has a conductor for data moving from the computer to the MAU and another for data from the MAU to the computer; this maintains the unbroken ring of wire.

figure 9

Computers in a bus-topology network can each send messages intended for any other computer on the network without going through a central connection point. You can implement either peer-to-peer or file server oriented networking with the bus topology.

work, a computer or other terminal device that becomes inoperative may be bypassed or unattached without affecting the other devices on the network as long as the main trunk of the cable remains undisturbed. The bus topology is almost always used with small, inexpensive networks, and it is also the major player in larger local area networks.

Networks using a bus topology typically operate with a **contention standard**. This is like having a one-lane road connecting all of the businesses in a city. When a business wants to ship something, it looks at the nearby street and, seeing no traffic, puts its delivery truck onto the street. Unseen in the distance, another business may have put its truck in the street at the same time. In this circumstance, the two trucks will inevitably collide at some place on the one-lane street. If two trucks do collide and the merchandise is not delivered, the businesses just wait a short time, put new merchandise on a new truck, and try again. As long as there is not much traffic on the one-lane road, there will not be many collisions. With increased traffic (more computer users), however, the number of collisions goes way up, and the overall speed deteriorates markedly.

For networks that operate on a contention standard, also known as carrier-sensing multiple access with collision detection (CSMA/CD), any node wishing to use the network first "listens" to see if it can hear a signal on the network indicating that another node is using it. If the first node does not hear the signal, known as a carrier signal, it transmits a packet of data onto the network. It then listens for the echo signal from the "transmitter" to see if its data remains uninterrupted by any other node's data. If it senses a disruption to the data, it sends a "blocking" signal that cues all of the nodes to disregard the transmissions that are being mixed. When the transmission is interrupted, the node must wait for a period of time and then try again. The length of the delay before retry is different for each node so that the same two will not try again at exactly the same time.

As long as the quantity of data being transmitted on the network is reasonable, the contention standard operates nicely. As the volume of data increases, however, the number of collisions increases, and the operating speed slows down. Therefore, the contention standard is most appropriately used where the volume of transmissions does not become extremely heavy. The most common contention standard is known as Ethernet. Growing in popularity are the Fiber Distributed Data Interface (FDDI) for use with fiber-optic cabling and the similar Copper Distributed Data Interface (CDDI) for use with copper wire. Another common contention standard is Apple's LocalTalk.

With Ethernet, the maximum amount of data that can be contained in one transmission is 1518 bytes. With FDDI, it is 4096 bytes. Depending on the typical amount of data that needs to be transmitted in each "transaction," these smaller sizes can be a performance disadvantage compared with a token ring.

Transmission Carriers

Transmission carriers refers to the kind of cable or other medium that is used to connect the various computers in a network. This section discusses the most commonly used transmission carriers for local area networks.

These include twisted-pair wire, coaxial cable, and fiber-optic cable. (Transmission carriers for wide area networks are discussed in the Telecommunications module.)

Unshielded twisted-pair wire **Unshielded twisted-pair wire** is similar to common telephone wire, but each of the pairs of wire is twisted with a different number of turns per inch to cancel out electrical noise between the pairs. Figure 10 illustrates one of these pairs. Usually, four pairs are packaged together in one outer sheath. The "unshielded" part of the name refers to the fact that there is no wrapping of metallic braid or metallic foil surrounding the wires inside the outer sheath. (For token-ring networks, you can also use shielded twisted pair, which contains two pairs of wires covered with a metallic shield, but this wire is expensive and bulky and thus not that widely used.)

figure 10

Pairs of twisted wires may be used for network communication. A typical cable installed in a building contains four of these pairs.

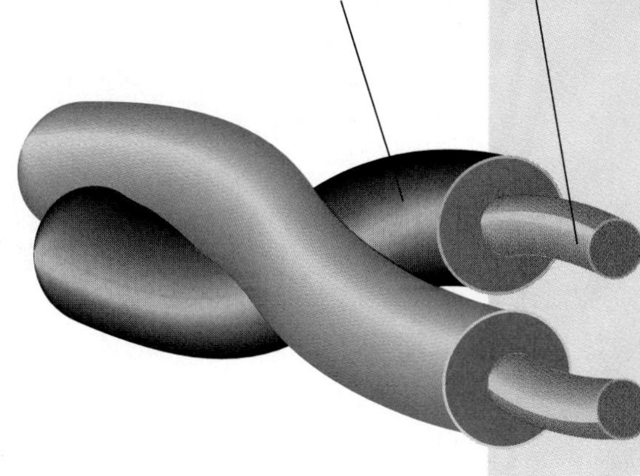

Unshielded twisted-pair wires are inexpensive carriers that can easily connect one device to another. Probably the most frequently installed carrier, twisted-pair wire is used to link local-area-network devices within short distances of each other. These copper wires are vulnerable to outside interference; for example, wires that are too close to high-voltage electrical lines, air conditioner fans, photocopiers, and so on can cause the data bits being transmitted to become distorted or lost. The longer the distance, the more chance of outside interference. Therefore, users of this type of carrier try to keep the length of twisted-pair wires under 250 feet.

There are several quality levels for twisted-pair wiring. The higher the quality, the faster and more reliable the communication that can be conducted. For example, a lower grade of wire may be able to handle only a 4-Mbps speed, while higher grades can handle 10-Mbps, 16-Mbps, and even 100-Mbps speeds.

Coaxial cable **Coaxial cable** (figure 11) is a high-quality communication channel. There are several grades or levels of coaxial cable.

Coaxial cables are more expensive than twisted-pair wires. Because of their heavy shielding (a metallic wrapping inside the outer covering of the wire), however, they are much less vulnerable to outside interference. They are also able to carry data over longer distances (usually up to 1000 feet) before the strength of the signal denoting data bits diminishes.

Fiber-optic cable **Fiber-optic cable** is made from glass fibers as thin as human hair (figure 12). It transmits laser light instead of electricity and can carry more data faster and over longer distances than any of the other transmission mediums. It is also more expensive. It is common practice in putting networks together to use fiber optics for portions of the network that have heavy traffic and longer distances and to use a less expensive transmission medium for the portions without as much traffic.

Figure 13 compares network cabling. Figure 14 shows the relative merits of the most common network standards.

figure 11

Coaxial cable can generally carry more data at faster speeds than twisted-pair wiring can. The shielding makes it more resistant to outside interference, so it can be used for longer distances.

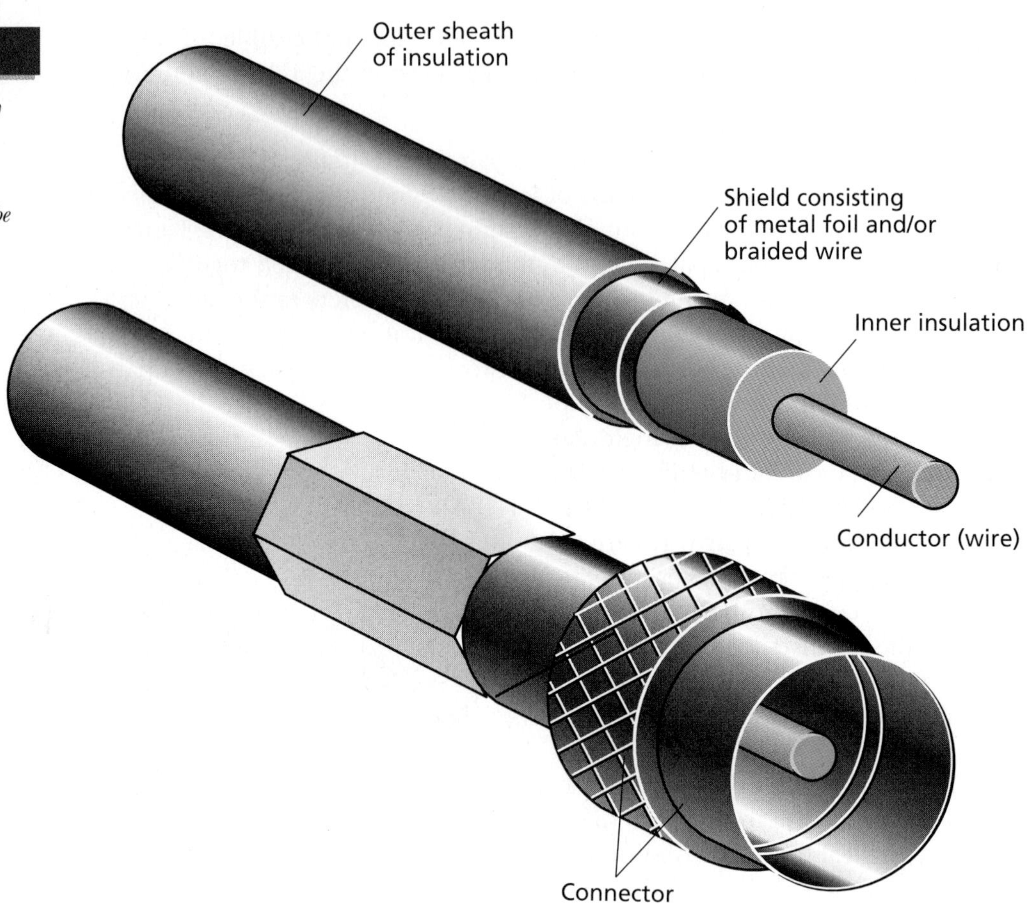

figure 12

Fiber-optic cable provides the fastest speed and the greatest capacity for data transmission.

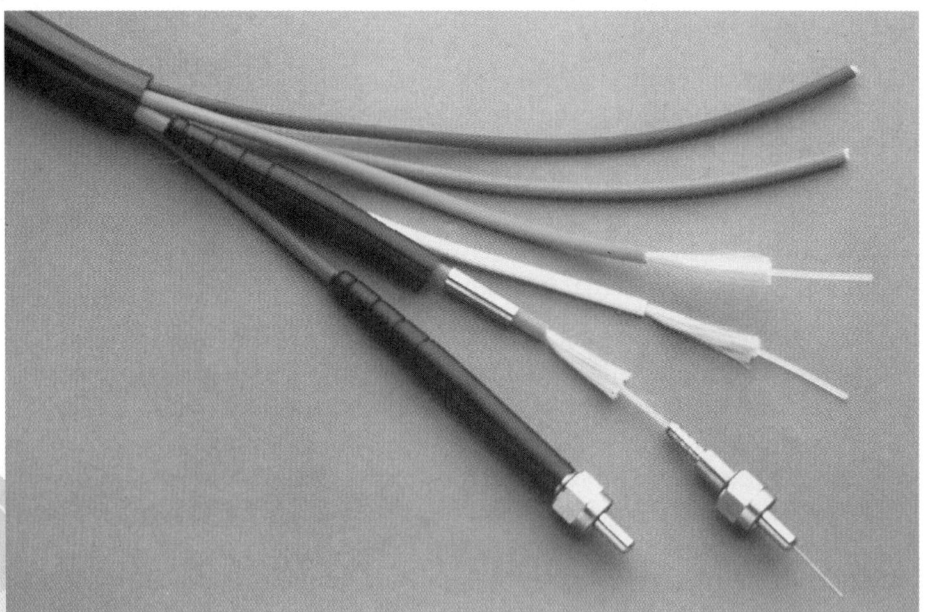

Type	Cost	Speed	Distance
Unshielded twisted pair	$	Slow to fast depending on number of pairs used and configuration	Short
Coaxial cable	$$	Fast	Medium
Fiber optic	$$$	Fastest there is	Longest there is

figure 13

A comparison of network cabling.

Protocol	Cabling That Can Be Used	Stated Speed	Rate of Slowdown With Increased Traffic (Flat or Increasing)	Cost	How Much of the Network May Go Down When Cable Is Cut?
LocalTalk	Twisted pair	280 KB	Increasing	$	Entire network
Standard Ethernet	Coaxial cable	10 MB	Increasing	$	Entire network
10BaseT Ethernet	Twisted pair	10 MB	Increasing	$$	Only computer(s) on the cut segment
Fast Ethernet	Twisted pair	100 MB	Increasing	$$$	Only computer(s) on the cut segment
Token ring	Twisted pair	4 or 16 MB	Flat	$$	Only computer(s) on the cut segment

figure 14

A comparison of the most commonly used network transmission standards.

Network Interface Cards

The network interface of your computer, whether it is built-in or in the form of an add-in card, must match the standard of the network to which you are going to attach the computer. If you are going to attach your computer to a token-ring network, it must be equipped with a token-ring interface. If you are going to attach to an Ethernet network, it must be equipped with an Ethernet network interface.

Manufacturers are more frequently including network attachment hardware (most typically Ethernet) as a standard part of their computers. All Macintosh computers have built-in network attachment capability, either LocalTalk or Ethernet, depending on the model.

Trends

ATM: Bringing Together Network Communications

An emerging standard in network communications that can provide computer data, video, and audio all on the same link goes by the acronym *ATM*. No, it is not to be confused with automated teller machines, or Adobe Type Manager. This ATM is asynchronous transfer mode, and it can move data at the maximum rate of 155 megabits per second.

The biggest difference between ATM and other network technologies, however, is that it "guarantees" a particular quality of service or transmission speed. When a device needs to send video or voice, the network can guarantee the high, sustained speed that is necessary to accomplish that task. When the need for constant speed is not there, the network can set up the connection at a variable speed rate or an available speed rate (acceptable for normal data transfer). Whatever the circumstance, the sending device tells the network what sustained and peak speeds it needs. In return for the network's agreement to provide those speeds, the sender agrees not to overwhelm the network by sending more than it indicated. Thus, the network "turns on" the capability needed at a particular time by a network user. It is this guarantee of sustained transmission availability that makes ATM a viable option for delivering voice and video on the same network that is delivering data.

While large-scale experimental implementations of ATM were underway at this writing, the standards for the system were still evolving. The system can be implemented, however, on a local area network or wide area network. The promise of technology is that devices spread across the country can share data, including voice and video, with as much speed as those situated locally. That speed comes at a very steep dollar cost, however; like most technology breakthroughs, the cost should decline very significantly with large-scale implementation.

The Concept of Structured Wiring

It is often advantageous to install a structured wiring system in a building. This is certainly the case when a new building is being constructed or major renovations are taking place in an old building.

A structured wiring system is simply a set of wires installed throughout a building, with the idea that the wires will serve the communication needs of the building for a long time—even though computer networking technology will certainly change. The basic idea is very simple. At each work location throughout the building is an outlet into which computers may be connected. A cable runs from each of these outlets back to a cross-connect panel in a central location, which is usually referred to as the **wiring closet** (figure 15). Typically, there is one wiring closet for each floor of a building, but there can certainly be variations from this norm depending on the building's construction and the communication needs of its occupants. The panels in the different wiring closets of a building are then connected to each other.

The cabling that runs from individual computers back to the wiring closet is typically of the twisted-pair variety. The beauty of this type of wiring is that you can install the networks of your choice on the cabling. For example, you can connect all of the computers to token ring, all of them to Ethernet, or

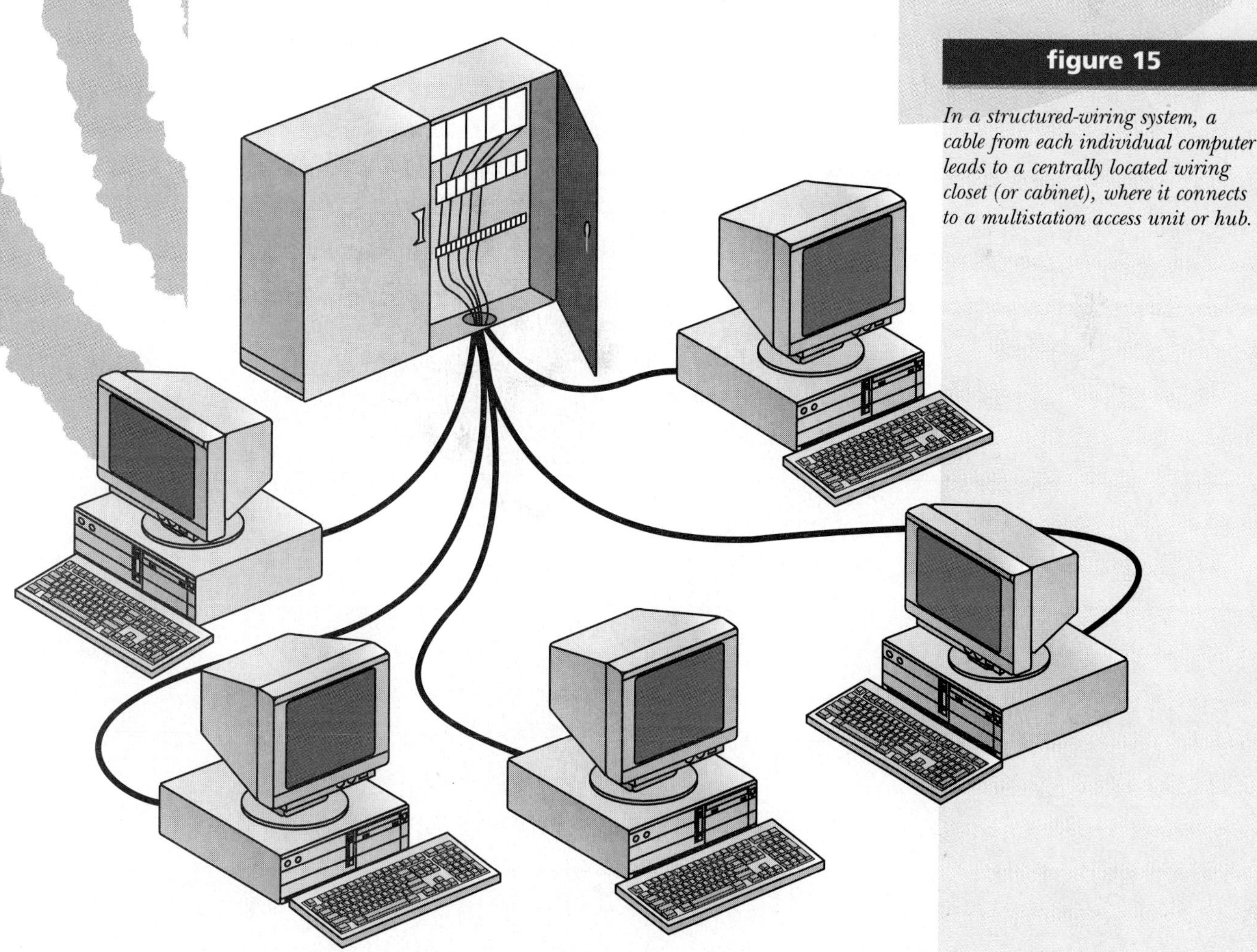

figure 15

In a structured-wiring system, a cable from each individual computer leads to a centrally located wiring closet (or cabinet), where it connects to a multistation access unit or hub.

Careers

Network Administrators in Demand

The shift toward a growing reliance on computer networks directly affects career opportunities, and that can be good or bad, depending on your computer background. For instance, if you have a background in microcomputers and networking, you can apply those skills to administer or manage computer networks—careers that are in high demand. That is not so great news, however, for those who made a career in the care and feeding of mainframe computers. The skills needed for keeping networks going are quite different than those acquired in the world of mainframes.

The importance of keeping networks up and running can be seen in the fact that almost all jobs now rely on computers in some way. This is true whether the business in question is a law office, auto-repair shop, retail store, or manufacturing company. In many of these businesses, employee productivity will hit rock bottom if the network is down, or if particular employees cannot access the computer applications or data they need. In cases where everything comes to a standstill for whatever reason, the network specialist is the doctor who holds the health of the business in his or her hands.

Networks do suffer from occasional hardware breakdowns. Most network problems, however, can be traced to the software. Among the typical responsibilities of a person supporting or administering a network are troubleshooting and resolution of network problems; installation of software on the network; addition of new users to the network; control of access privileges; training users; fine-tuning network parameters for the best performance; controlling the user interface to the network; addition and control of printers and other peripherals; administration of electronic mail; backing up data on a rigorous basis; and helping users understand the idea of disk conservation and to remove data that is no longer needed.

While network management can be routine, there can be emergencies that really make network managers earn their pay. And according to a 1993 survey by *LAN Magazine*, they are well rewarded: the average salary for network professionals was $49,450 in 1993.

some to a token ring and some to Ethernet. The choice is made by how you connect jumper (connector) cables in the wiring closet. If you want a token ring, you install token-ring multistation access units (MAUs) in the wiring closet and connect the wires coming from individual computers to the MAUs. If you want Ethernet, you install 10-BaseT hubs in the wiring closet and connect the wires from the individual computers to the hubs.

When you use a structured wiring system, you are still using the topologies discussed earlier. Even though it probably does not look like it to a casual observer, the connections still take the shape of a ring or a bus.

Connecting Local Area Networks to Each Other

Many times, a building will contain more than one local area network. Each network typically serves a logical workgroup, such as one department of a business. Most of the time, users in the workgroup access data on their own network. At times, however, they may need to access one of the other networks. To take care of that need, the multiple networks are connected.

There are two common methods used for connecting networks: bridges, and routers. **Bridges** are used for connecting similar networks; for example, two different token rings might be connected by using a microcomputer that is set up to function as the bridge between the two. The connection can be as simple as the server computer having two token ring cards, one for each ring. Data travels across the bridge only when that data originates on one of the networks and has a destination on the other network. Messages whose origination and destination are on the same network remain on that network.

For connecting a network to a dissimilar network, such as a local area network to a mainframe, a processor functioning as a **router** is used. Frequently, the connection is made over a long-distance carrier as part of a wide area network, and a router is used at each end of the connection. The router does more work than a bridge, however, because it must translate signals from one protocol or "language" to another.

Network Operating Systems

In addition to the hardware connections that are required to hook up a network, your computer must have an operating system that—either natively or by using extensions—knows how to send and receive data across the network. The operating system is the software that controls the operation of all parts of the computer system, such as the storage and input/output devices. In addition, if the network is file-server oriented, the file server computer must have an operating system that is designed for providing services to other computers.

Operating Systems for User Computers

Any of the operating systems typically used on microcomputers can access a local area network. Whether they can do it natively or require extensions in the form of additional programs obtained from the network software vendor depends on the operating system of the user computer and that of the file server (if applicable). Typical operating systems that are used with microcomputers accessing a network are DOS (driver required), DOS with Windows (driver required), Windows for Workgroups (networking built-in), Windows

NT (networking built-in), Windows 95 (networking built-in) OS/2 (networking built-in), Novell DOS (networking built-in with version 7), and Apple System 7 (networking built-in). When networking is built-in, it uses a particular protocol; other protocols can be added by adding drivers or extensions.

When a networked computer needs to access a disk drive or other device, the operating system or an extension of it determines whether the request for service should go to the local computer or the network. If your computer is using DOS and the network Novell NetWare, for example, a shell program (NETx or the Requester, depending on the version of NetWare you are using) intercepts commands for operating system services and determines whether they should go to the local computer or the network file server. All of this takes place transparently to the user.

Operating Systems for File Servers

Windows NT and OS/2 can both be used on file servers. By far, however, the most commonly used file-server operating system is Novell NetWare. The protocols used by different operating systems may be different, but that is not a concern unless you are interconnecting them.

With NetWare, you can have a local area network consisting of dissimilar user computers as well as using a wide variety of wiring options. Therefore, if some users have PCs and others Macintoshes, they can all use the same network and store data on the same file server. Likewise, you can have both Ethernet and token-ring segments attached to the same file server. Networks are complex, however, and combining different types of machines makes life that much more difficult for network support personnel.

Even though PCs and Macintoshes can use the same file server, this does not mean that PCs can run Macintosh application programs and vice versa; this can only happen if the user computer has been specially adapted to do so. A growing number of application programs, however, are available for both the PC and Macintosh, and many of these use the exact same file formats on both platforms. In this case, users of both machines can freely access documents created with the other type of computer.

Data Storage on the Server

With a server-based network, data that must be accessible to multiple users is stored on the file server. This section discusses how this data is stored, accessed, and protected. Because the great majority of server-based networks are implemented with Novell NetWare, all examples will refer to that product.

Volumes and Directories

Hard drives on file-server computers are typically a good bit larger than the hard drives on user computers. In fact, disk capacities of several gigabytes (billions of characters) are common. The disk space on the server may be divided into several **volumes**, each of which can be thought of as equivalent to a file cabinet (but with much more capacity).

Every Novell NetWare server has a main volume that is named SYS; it may also have additional volumes with other names. Each volume has **directories** that can be thought of like drawers in a file cabinet. In turn, each directory can have subdirectories, which you can visualize as equivalent to hanging folders inside the file cabinet. Going still further, you can have more levels of subdirectories, which you can visualize as manila folders inside the hanging folders.

Data and programs reside in files that can be visualized as paper documents. Each of these files can be placed either in a directory or subdirectory. This kind of filing system is very similar to the way that files are stored on the local hard drive of your PC or Macintosh.

Directories and subdirectories may be created by the network administrator or users (assuming that the administrator has given the user permission). Directory names should make sense for the particular business that is using the network. For example, a high-school office might have a directory structure similar to that shown in figure 16; note that the structure matches fairly closely what goes on in a school.

figure 16

The best way to set up a directory structure is so that it fits the kind of business being conducted.

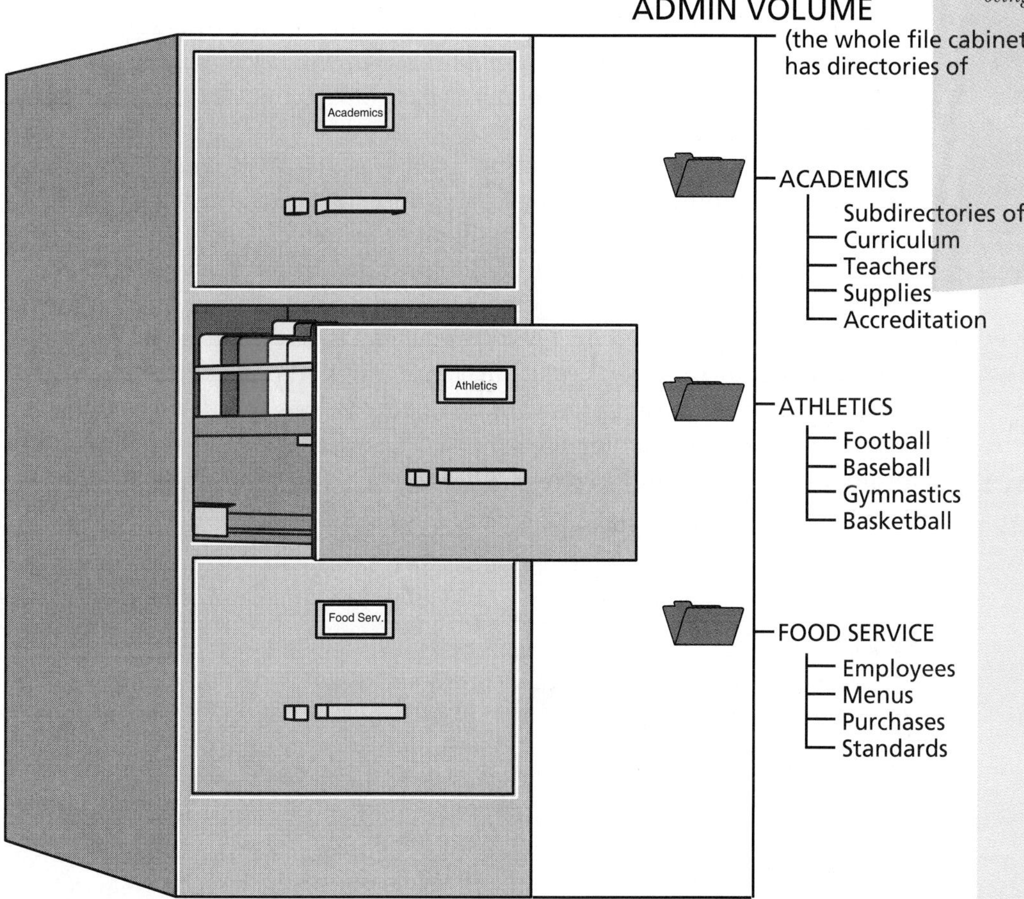

Mapping

To the user of a Novell network, the data stored on the file server looks just like another hard disk. It is possible, therefore, that a user could see the entire SYS volume on the file server as one large hard drive. For networks with a fairly small directory structure, that would probably work okay.

For many networks, however, there are literally thousands of directories and subdirectories on the file server. With this many possibilities, wading through them all would be difficult for the user, so Novell made life simpler with something called mapping. **Mapping** simply means that any directory or subdirectory on a server volume can be made to look like a separate disk drive.

Consider again the example of the school-administration network. If one employee in the office deals with nothing but curriculum, she could have the subdirectory named CURRIC mapped to appear as a drive. If she uses a PC, the drive might appear as D:. Therefore, she can easily save documents simply to drive D: and needs to know nothing else about where the data goes. In the absence of mapping ability, she would have to select the SYS volume, the ACADEMIC directory, and then the CURRIC subdirectory.

Drive mappings are not permanent settings. They are simply "pointers" that are set up for the current computer session; the pointer for drive D: can "point to" the subdirectory named CURRIC. If you are at a prompt and enter the command to change the directory of drive D: to ACCRED, you have changed the mapping, and D: now points to the ACCRED subdirectory of the SYS volume, and not the originally mapped CURRIC subdirectory.

The network administrator will most likely have set up for each user particular drive mappings that are created automatically on start up. Most users will not need to change these start-up mappings. In fact, changing them can result in erratic software behavior when programs try to access a particular directory to which a drive letter was supposed to refer.

At this point, you are aware of two kinds of disk drives that a Novell user may access. The first is the local drive or drives on the user's own computer. The second is the mapped network drive. There is also a third kind, which is called a search drive. If you are familiar with a DOS PATH command, you know that it tells the computer all of the places to look for an executable file if it is not in the current directory. A search drive is essentially the same thing for programs stored on the network. It simple tells NetWare, "If a program I try to run is not in the directory I am currently using, go look in the place(s) specified by the search drive mappings."

Network Security

To help ensure that unauthorized persons do not access data or programs, the makers of network software build in rather elaborate safety precautions. These precautions act as locks to keep out everybody other than authorized persons. Just as the door to your home can be left unlocked, however, so can all of the security built into your network. This security only works if you as a user take the necessary precautions to make sure that "all the locks stay locked." With that big caveat (figure 17) behind us, how security is implemented on a typical computer network is now examined.

User names and passwords The first level of security is implemented through use of user names and passwords. For each person who can legitimately use the network, the person designated as the network administrator issues a **user name**. The network administrator makes up these names, and they are frequently some version of the user's actual name, such as the first initial and last name combined. A password is also assigned to each user. There is a

figure 17

Leaving your network data unsecured invites mischief and worse, just like leaving a file cabinet open to anyone who may want to explore what it contains.

good chance that you will also be assigned to a group of users. For example, users in the principal's office might be assigned to one group, while users in the counseling office are assigned to a different group.

Before being allowed to use the network, the user must do what is known as logging on. Logging on simply means entering your user name and password. A person who does not know a valid user name and password combination is not allowed on the network. Good practice mandates that you change your password at regular intervals. In fact, there is a very good chance that your network administrator has set the network software to require you to do this after a given time, for example, once a month.

Access privileges Assuming that you have a valid user name and password, you still have access only to the directories or files for which the network administrator has given you privileges. The network administrator may limit access in either or both of two ways:

- He or she may impose blanket limitations on the use of certain directories or files. For example, the files that contain the network operating-system software itself would always be locked to all users so that they cannot change or erase them.
- She or he may give varying levels of access to particular users.

In granting access privileges, the network administrator may grant them to all users, to members of a certain group of users, or to individual users. There are several different levels of access that can be made available, including the following:

- Read-only: You can look at files but cannot change or delete them.
- Create: You can add new files to a directory.
- Modify: You can change the contents of files stored in the directory.
- Delete: You can delete files stored in the directory.

The rights to directories can be hierarchical in nature. If you have the right to create documents in the root of the volume, you have rights to create documents in any of the directories and subdirectories. In other words, you have the rights to the directory for which the rights were given, plus all of the directories below that one. In the school-office example, you could be given the right to create documents in the Academics directory, which would then allow you to create documents in the subdirectories under it (namely, Curriculum, Teachers, Supplies, and Accreditation).

The network administrator has total rights to everything on the network. Other users will have lesser rights, as given by the administrator. For example, the administrator in one network may reserve for herself the right to add users. In another situation, the administrator might delegate the authority of adding and removing users to the managers of individual departments. In all cases, the combination of user name and password represents the key that provides access.

Using a Network

This section considers some of the more basic things to know about using a Novell NetWare network. Many of the concepts can also apply to other networks.

A Novell NetWare network can be command driven. In other words, you can type in commands at a DOS prompt or simulation of a DOS prompt. NetWare then carries out these commands. It is becoming the norm, however, that the commands are carried out behind the scenes for you by one of a number of front-end programs or shells that may use either a character or graphic user interface. For example, you may choose to connect to a printer somewhere else on the network by making a menu choice or clicking on an icon. In the following paragraphs, study the effect of some of the more common NetWare commands, then look at how they are implemented in Windows for Workgroups, which provides a graphic front end for accessing a Novell network.

Logging In and Out

The command to log in or log on (these terms mean the same thing) is, logically enough, LOGIN. If you are using a command line interface, simply key the word, followed by your user name, and press the Enter key. For example, key LOGIN JSMITH. Windows for Workgroups, along with most other front-end programs, will ask you for your user name and password when it starts up.

When you are through using the network for a period of time, you should log out. From the command line, simply key LOGOUT and press Enter. From the Windows File Manager, just select Disconnect Network Drive from the menu or click its icon on the toolbar. In this case, you will be shown a list of all network drives to which you are connected, and you click on the one(s) to disconnect. Also, most front-end programs will ask if you want to disconnect from the network when you exit the programs.

Controlling the Drives That You Are Using

Remember that NetWare maps directories from the file-server disk volumes to Drive names. From the command line, you may key MAP and press enter to see a list of all drive letters to which you are connected, along with the path showing where the files are physically located. This command will show you the local drives, network drives, and search drives. With Windows, the network drives appear in the File Manager directory listings along with your local drives.

The initial drive mappings will have been set up for you automatically when you logged on the network. To add or change the drive mappings, you can use the MAP command from the DOS prompt. The command is:

```
MAP M:=[SERVE1/SYS:/BUDGETS]
```

If you are familiar with BASIC programming, you will recognize this syntax as being similar to a BASIC assignment statement. That is, what is on the right side of the equals sign is assigned to what is on the left side of the equals sign. Note the logical sequence of what goes on the right—the server name, followed by the volume name, followed by the directory name. Note that you could have additional levels of subdirectories at the end of the statement if need be. Any drives that you map from the command line will not show up as mapped the next time you come back on the network; they are temporary connections only available during the network session in which you map them.

With Windows for Workgroups, you use the File Manager to map drives. Select Attach Network Drive from the menu, or click its icon on the tool bar. You are then shown the dialog box in figure 18, which displays the names of the available network drives for you to pick from. Note that a drive letter is proposed for the new connection; in other words, the drive letter will be mapped to the directory you choose. Note that you can tell Windows whether to re-establish these mappings when it is started up the next time. With the Macintosh, you select a network drive by using the Chooser from the Apple menu.

If you cannot see or find the directory to which you want to map a drive, it is probably because you do not have sufficient access rights to that drive or directory. In this case, see your network administrator.

One other thing to note about drive mapping is that using the DOS Change Directory command can also change your mappings. For example, suppose you map M: to be SERVE1/SYS:/BUDGETS. If you then use the

figure 18

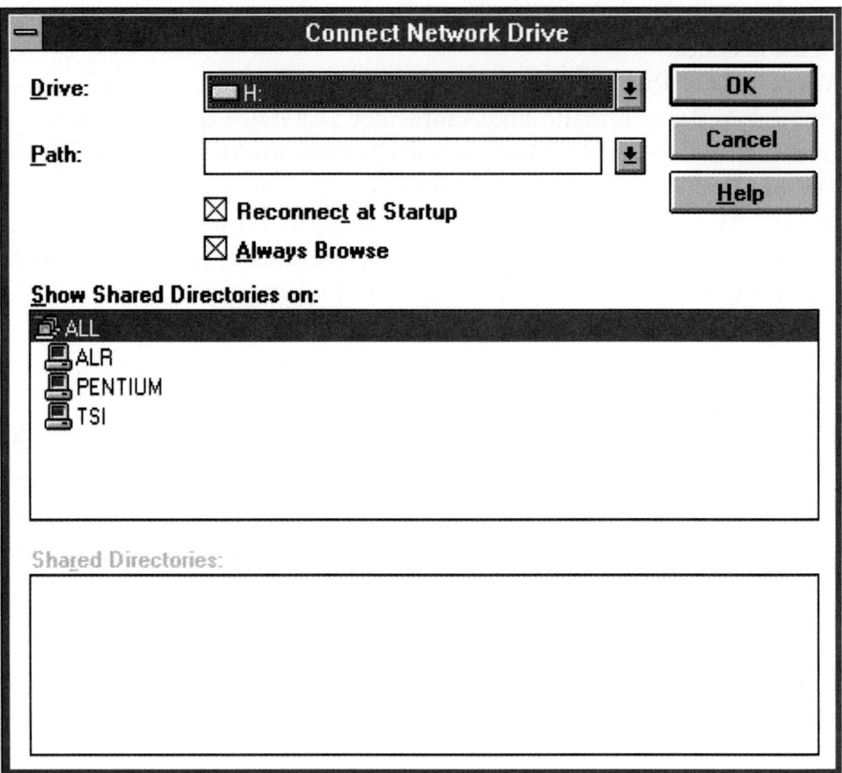

With Windows for Workgroups as well as a number of other "front-end" programs, you connect to network disk drives by choosing them in a simple dialog box. The screen for Windows 95 is very similar.

Change Directory command to backup one level in the directory structure (CD . .), M: will no longer refer to the BUDGETS directory but to the root of the SYS: volume.

Printing with a Network

When you are attached to a network, you can print documents to a printer somewhere else on the network as well as to a printer that may be attached to your local computer. You simply choose to print from your application program as usual (File… Print for most applications). Whether the printing goes to a local or a network printer depends on whether NetWare has "captured" the print. If it has been captured, it goes to the network printer.

Your network may automatically set itself up to **capture** printing; on the other hand, you may have to tell it when you want the printing to go to another printer on the network. An example of the command for sending successive printing to a network printer is:

CAPTURE Q=QMS860

The Q= portion of the command tells the network which print queue (which printer waiting line) the print jobs should be placed in. In this example, QMS860 is the name of one of the printers and the name that has been assigned to the print queue by the system administrator. Once you issue the command, all printing goes to that printer until you enter the command ENDCAP, which will bring printing back to the local printer.

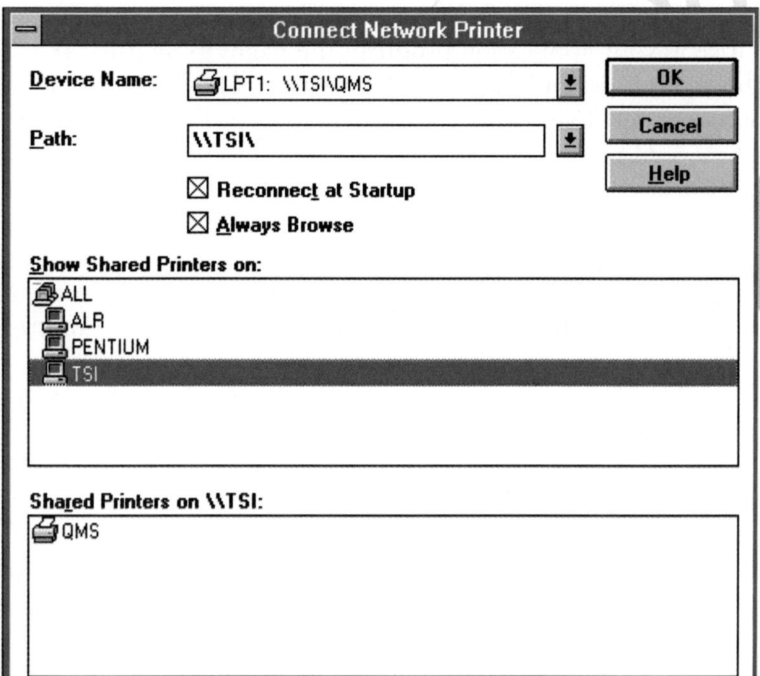

figure 19

With Windows for Workgroups, use this dialog box to connect to a network printer. The screen for Windows 95 is similar.

With Windows, you go into the Print Manager and select Connect Network Printer or Disconnect Network Printer to accomplish the capture steps. (Use the menu choices or the toolbar icons.) Figure 19 shows the dialog box for connecting to a network printer. Simply choose the desired print queue from the list that you will be shown. With the Macintosh, select a printer from the Chooser dialog box under the Apple menu (figure 20).

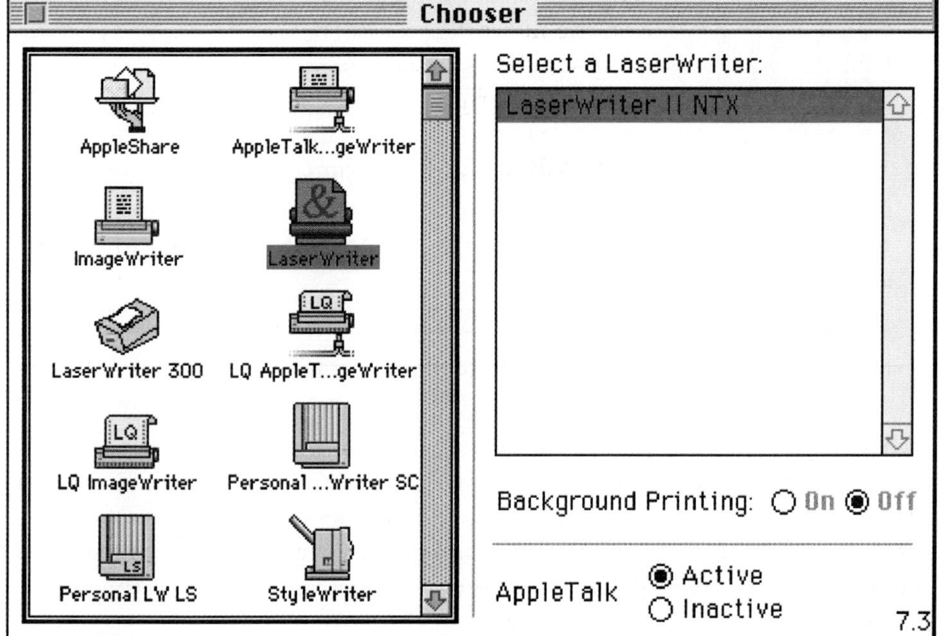

figure 20

On the Macintosh, use the Chooser to select network printers.

Whenever you are printing to a network printer, the print job is stored on a disk drive as your application produces the pages to be printed. Once your application has finished its print work, the print job is fed from the file on disk to the printer. The reason for this way of operating is quite logical. Suppose that several people on a network are trying to print something and no print queues are on disk—all three are connected straight to the printer. The printer will receive a little of the first user's job, a little of the second user's job, and then perhaps a little more of the first user's job. By putting data on disk as an application works on printing, the entire, finished job can be delivered to the printer as one whole job that the printer can process in an unbroken fashion.

There will be times when you want to see what print jobs are in the queue. From the command line, you may key PCONSOLE (short for printer console), select the name of the file server where the print queue is located, select Print Queue Information from the Available Options menu, and then select Current Print Job Entries. If you are using Windows, you can simply look at the print queues as they are shown in the Print Manager's window.

If you have sent a job to the printer and then decide that you do not want to print (perhaps because of an error you just discovered), you may cancel the job while it is still in the print queue. To do this from the command line, first follow the steps from the previous paragraph for displaying the list of print jobs. Then, when the list is displayed, move the cursor to highlight the name of the job you to want delete and press the Delete key. Note that unless you have been given power by the network administrator to delete other jobs, you can only delete print jobs that you sent to the queue. From Windows, you may delete a print job by clicking on its name in the Print Manager's window, then hitting the Delete key or selecting Document . . . Delete Document from the menu.

Do It!

1 Find out what operating system is on the network to which you have access. Does your network use a shell that allows the user to control it from menu choices rather than by keying in commands? If so, what is the shell called?

2 Is your network wired as a token-passing network or as a contention network? What is the name of the standard it uses?

Depending on how your network is set up, the network printers to which you can print may be attached to the file server or to the computers of other users. In some cases, printers may have the intelligence built in to them to be their own stations on the network rather than being attached to any computer at all. Regardless of the setup, the printing process remains the same to the user.

Application Software That Takes Special Advantage of Networks

Just about any application software can be stored on a file server and loaded from that point onto individual computers for use. There are, however, several categories of software that cannot operate in the absence of a network. Often, these applications—the three most common are electronic mail, group calendars, and client-server databases—may be the justification for installing a network.

Electronic Mail

With an **electronic mail** application, which comes with some network-ready operating systems and is also separately available from other vendors, any computer user on the network can send messages and files to any other user on the network. A given message may be sent to any number of people, from one up to everybody on the network. Electronic mail (usually just called e-mail) provides almost instantaneous communication and can also save a good many trees if people will just read the messages on their displays, save them to a disk if they are important, and not print them.

Group Calendars

One of the hardest things to do in most organizations is scheduling a meeting at a time when all of the desired participants can attend. With group-calendaring programs, each individual keeps his or her appointment and meeting calendar on the network. While individual schedules can be kept confidential with most software, a search mode allows the software to look at the calendars of all persons who should attend a particular meeting and suggest to the scheduler times when everyone is available. After choice of a date and time by the scheduler, the system transmits information on the newly posted meeting.

Client-Server Databases

A database is a collection of data—about customers, students, products, and so on. In the case of a database about students, among the kinds of information included would be the name, address, parent data, grades earned, and courses currently being taken.

If all of the data about students is on a file server, as is most likely the case, any authorized user on the network can access the data. This is true whether the file server is a microcomputer, minicomputer, or mainframe. Counselors might use the data while talking with students about what courses to take. Assistant principals might use it while working with students to resolve discipline problems. The football coach might use it to determine who is academically eligible to play ball.

In any of these cases, there are two possible ways in which data can be handled. Taking the case of the football coach, look at the differences in the two methods (figure 21):

- The coach's computer says to the file server, "Send me all of the academic data for all the students." As the academic record for each student

figure 21

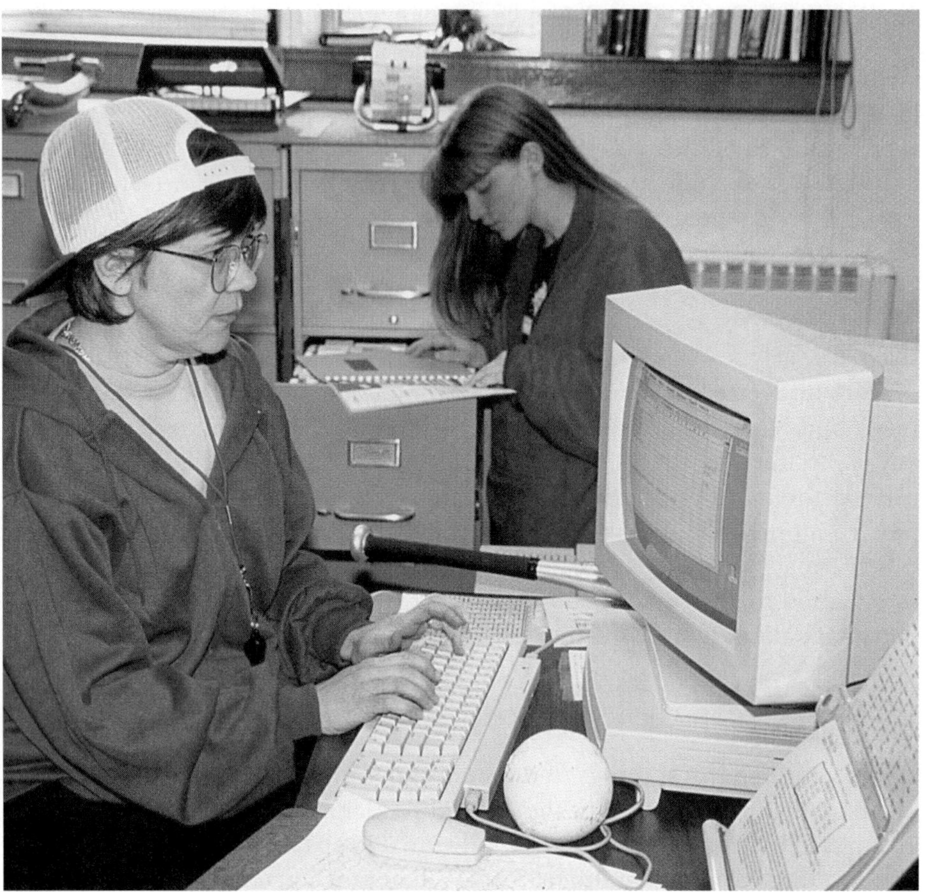

Only authorized users can access database information stored on a network file server.

travels over the network and arrives at the coach's computer, that computer examines the data to see if the student has a C average and can therefore play. The software in the coach's computer places the name of each eligible student on a list and discards all of the other data.

- The coach's computer says to the file server, "Send me the names of all students with a C average or better." The file server looks at the records, which are stored on its own disk drive, and transmits over the network only the names of eligible students.

The big difference in these two methods is in the amount of network traffic. In the second case, only the names of eligible students travel the wire, while in the first case, the names of all of the students as well as their entire academic records make the journey. For the file server, it is more work to pick out the desired records before transmitting than it is to blindly transmit everything, but by keeping the amount of traffic on the network down, network performance is improved for everyone using it. This reduced traffic may often be enough to allow use of slower, less expensive network hardware while still maintaining good performance. Limiting the amount of data traveling the network is especially critical in wide area networks, where the communication costs can be astronomic.

This advantageous second scenario is known as **client-server** computing. In other words, the coach's computer is a client, and the server "serves" it with just the information it needs. Client-server computing is growing in popularity as the quality of software has improved and more applications are being converted.

Note that client-server computing is done on a standard network. It is not the network that is different, but rather the application software that is used to maintain the database.

Summary

A network is a group of computers that are connected together for sharing files and peripherals, such as printers.

- A local area network (LAN) is a network whose computers are located in the same place, such as the same building or campus.

- A wide area network (WAN) consists of computers or local area networks that are dispersed geographically but are connected through communication lines to share data.

- A network may be set up either on a peer-to-peer basis or with a file server acting as the central repository for programs and data.

- Each computer that is attached to a network is known as a node, and the communications method by which it is attached is known as a link.

- The two most common network topologies are the ring and the bus. In a ring topology, signals carrying data travel around the unbroken wiring loop from computer to computer. In a bus topology, signals travel down a terminated cable and bounce back.

- Network signals may travel over various kinds of media, including twisted-pair wire, coaxial cable, fiber-optic cable, or wireless transmission.

- The two most common network standards are token passing and contention. In token passing (token ring), a packet of electronic signals is loaded with data for transport to another location on the network; because there is only one packet at a time on the wire, there should be almost no garbled data needing retransmission. Under a contention standard (Ethernet, AppleTalk), a computer is free to transmit a message whenever it does not "hear" another computer already on the wire. Because at times more than one computer will broadcast at once, collisions of data are inevitable, requiring rebroadcast after a random time out.

- Buildings are frequently wired so that the cable from each computer goes to a central wiring closet. There, the cables may be interconnected as needed to form the computer network.

- Similar networks (such as two Ethernets) may be connected by a simple bridge. Dissimilar networks may be connected by a device known as a router, which is able to translate between different protocols.

Summary

- The most commonly used network operating system is Novell NetWare. Other well-known systems include Windows NT, OS/2, and AppleTalk.
- Volumes on a Novell file server are analogous to file cabinets; directories are equivalent to file drawers. Any directory may be mapped so that a particular drive letter refers straight to the directory.
- Network security is enforced through the use of user names and passwords. The degree of access that is available to each user is determined by settings made by the administrator.
- Each directory on the network may be set for read/write, read only, or no access. Additionally, each user's access to particular directories may also be set to read only, read/write, or no access.
- The network operating system may capture printing from a user's application and send it to a printer attached elsewhere on the network.
- Some applications that take great advantage of networks are electronic mail, group calendars, and client-server databases.

The following key terms were defined in this module. For each of the following terms, write on a separate piece of paper the number of the definition followed by the letter of the appropriate term.

Terms

A. bridge
B. bus topology
C. capture
D. client-server
E. coaxial cable
F. contention standard
G. directories
H. electronic mail
I. fiber-optic cable
J. file server
K. link
L. local area network (LAN)
M. mapping
N. network
O. node
P. peer-to-peer networking
Q. ring topology
R. router
S. token ring
T. transmission carriers
U. transmission standards
V. unshielded twisted-pair wire
W. user name
X. volumes
Y. wide area network (WAN)
Z. wireless
AA. wiring closet

Definitions

1 refers to the kind of cable or other medium used to connect the various computers in a network

2 each connection or communication channel over which a computer "talks"

3 uses radio transmissions or microwaves

4 a computer on the network whose job is to store and make available programs and data for other computers

5 used for connecting a network to a dissimilar network

6 a centrally located cabinet where wires from individual computers are connected to a multistation access unit or hub

7 cable that is similar to standard telephone wire

8 what the network does to your printing to send it to a network printer

9 a network of computers in the same building or campus

10 the identification by which a user is known on the network

11 a configuration in which computers are attached to a single communication channel by a "drop" line that has a beginning and an end

12 a high-quality communication cable like that used for cable television

13 a configuration in which one or more computers may act as host systems or file servers and are attached to each other through an endless looping ring

Matching

14 the network equivalent of a file cabinet

15 a network whose computers are spread apart geographically

16 the kind of cable that can carry more data farther than any other

17 a protocol under which one packet containing data passes around a ring

18 used for connecting similar networks

19 each computer in a local area network

20 a protocol that is like having a one-lane road connecting all of the businesses in a city

21 a group of computers that are connected together

22 networking in which each computer can be accessed by others and are equal as far as the network is concerned

23 the network equivalent of a file drawer

24 the process of making any network directory look like a disk drive to the user's computer

25 a database program where the server selects data before sending it to the user's computer

26 an application for sending messages among computer users on a network

27 standards that define how electronic messages are handled on the transmission medium

Review

1. What is a computer network? (Obj. 1)
2. What distinguishes a local area network from a wide area network? (Obj. 1)
3. What are the similarities of and differences between a peer-to-peer network and a server-based network? (Obj. 1)
4. Compare the advantages and disadvantages of a peer-to-peer network versus a server-based network. (Obj. 1)
5. What are the two most commonly used network topologies? (Obj. 2)
6. Describe the typical physical layout of each of the two most common network topologies. (Obj. 2)
7. What is the difference between a link and a node? (Obj. 1)
8. What are network standards? (Obj. 2)
9. Describe how a token-passing network operates. (Obj. 2)
10. Describe how a contention network works. (Obj. 2)
11. What are the names of the most commonly used token-passing and contention network standards? (Obj. 2)
12. Compare the strengths and weaknesses of a token-passing standard versus a contention standard. (Obj. 2)
13. Name and describe four transmission carriers that can be used with a network. (Obj. 2)
14. Which of the transmission carriers that you named in question 13 has historically been the slowest and can carry signals for the shortest distance? (Obj. 2)
15. Which transmission carrier offers the fastest speeds and longest distances? (Obj. 2)
16. What is meant by the concept of structured wiring? What are its advantages? (Obj. 2)
17. Compare and contrast the roles of bridges and routers. (Obj. 2)
18. What is the most popular operating system used on network file servers? What are some others that are also used? (Obj. 3)
19. What are some common operating systems used on computers attached to networks? (Obj. 3)
20. Can computers of different types be attached to the same network? If so, what are some of the limitations and advantages? (Obj. 2)
21. Describe the typical arrangement of storage on a file server. (Obj. 4)
22. What is the difference between a volume and a directory on a file server? (Obj. 4)
23. Describe the concept of mapping as implemented on Novell file servers. (Obj. 4)
24. Why is network security important? (Obj. 4)

25 Describe the role of user names and passwords in implementing network security. (Obj. 4)

26 List and describe the various kinds of access that can be made available on a network. (Obj. 4)

27 How would you decide what kind of access to give a particular network user? (Obj. 4)

28 With a Novell network, what do you do to start using the network? What do you do to stop using the network? (Obj. 6)

29 Describe the Novell command used to map a drive. (Obj. 4)

30 Describe the Novell command used to print to another printer on the network. (Obj. 6)

31 Discuss the advantages of client-server databases. (Obj. 5)

32 How can electronic mail and group-calendar programs be used to complement each other? (Obj. 5)

Activities

To perform the following activities, refer to the documentation provided by your instructor. For some of the activities, the network administrator must give you the necessary access rights. Be guided by your instructor as to whether there are any activities that you cannot carry out on your network.

1 *Writing* Keep a log of the following steps:

- If you have access to electronic mail on the network, send a message to a friend or co-worker. Ask him or her to respond to your message indicating that it was received and read.
- Print a copy of the electronic mail you sent and the response you received, and give them to your instructor.
- Where did the electronic mail print out? Was the printer attached directly to your computer or to the network?
- Look at network screens to see what other printers are available for your use.
- Determine which network tools are available for your use. These may include such things as utilities to control printing, show the names of network users, help you change your password, change access privileges, or get help. List the tools and what they do.

2 *Speaking* Work in a group with several other people who are interested in the same kind of business that you are. For example, you may be interested in an automobile dealership, medical practice, publishing company, international distributorship, or farming business. Prepare a presentation for the class showing the benefits that your particular kind of business could get from using a computer network. If you have multimedia capabilities on a computer in your classroom, make this a multimedia presentation; otherwise, you may want to prepare some overhead transparencies on the computer. Be sure to cover some of the ways that the network could keep costs down, increase productivity, and increase customer service.

3 *Ethics* Using magazine and newspaper indexes that are available, find an example of a company or school that had problems because the security of their computer system was violated. Write a report on the case that you find. Include a precaution that you think the company or school could have taken that would have prevented this problem.

4 *Math* One challenge of installing a network is providing enough disk space to handle all of the data that must be stored. Suppose you already know that a file server needs a hard drive of at least 300 MB to handle the operating system and application software to be placed on it. The main application that will be placed on the server is a client information system to keep up with the records of all clients in your company. Working in a group with several other people, consider the kinds of data that must be stored about each client, and estimate how much additional disk space would be needed to hold that data for the number of clients in your company. After all groups have made their estimates, hold a discussion comparing the findings.

5 Keep and turn in to your instructor a log of the following activities:

- Log on to the network to which you have access. It will be necessary for your teacher to have arranged to have you added as a network user before you do this.
- Change your password on the network.
- Under your private subdirectory on the network, create three new directories. Name them with your initials plus a digit (1, 2, or 3). Set up directory xxx1 so that no user other than you (or the network administrator) can read or write anything to it. Set up directory xxx2 so that all network users can read from it. Set up directory xxx3 so that all network users can write to as well as read from it.
- If you are using Novell NetWare, map a drive letter to each of the three directories you created.
- Using a word processor, store a file in each of the three directories you created. The file should contain a sentence identifying the directory in which you place it.
- Add a new user to the network. The identification should be your initials plus the letters NEW. Give this user access to the three directories you created.
- Ask a classmate to log on to the network using the new user name you created. Have him or her use a word processor and try to access the files you stored in the three new directories you created. Have the classmate use the word processor to write down the results.

(Continued on next page.)

Activities

- Ask your classmate to try saving his or her report in each of the three new directories you created. He or she should add to this document to indicate the results. The report should also include suggestions on what could be done on the network to enable saving the file to all three of the directories. Your classmate should print out a copy of the report for the instructor as well.

6 *Internet* If you have access to the Internet, use your Web software to locate specifications and prices for the parts you might use to put together a local area network for your classroom. Find at least two sources/brands of each of the following components: file server computer, network operating system, and network interface card. Select the components you think provide the best balance between price and performance. Use your word processor to write a 2- to 3-page report describing and explaining your selections.

Telecommunications

Overview

Some computer systems are stand-alone systems—that is, one computer serves one user and is connected to no other computers. The computer may be performing word processing, accounting, or any number of different applications. Other computers are connected. A group of computers is often connected within the same building; this arrangement is called a *local area network*, or LAN. Often, however, computers need to communicate with remote systems—that is, they need to talk with other computers that may be in another city, state, or nation. When such remote communication is needed, telecommunications are used to make the connection, and the resulting group of connected computers is known as a *wide area network*, or WAN.

Telecommunication is the process of transmitting and receiving information from one location to another. (*Tele* means far, and *communication* means talking.) In this chapter, you will learn how communication hardware and software enable computers to communicate with each other. In addition, you will learn how several of the common transmission carriers (i.e., telephone lines, satellites) facilitate this communication and review several common environments in which data communication is used.

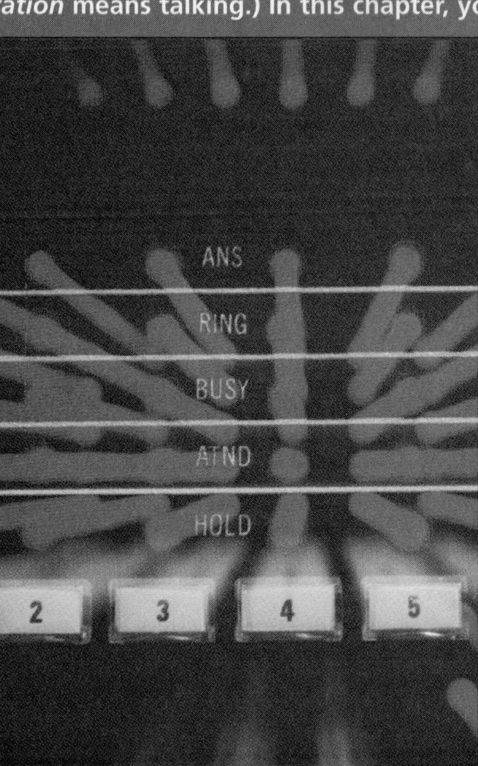

Objectives

1. Define and give examples of telecommunications.
2. Describe how a simple telecommunications connection works.
3. Identify the characteristics of data communication setups (hardware and software).
4. Compare the relative speeds and costs of various communication media.
5. Identify and use the services provided by bulletin board systems.
6. Identify and use the services provided by an information service.
7. Identify and use the services available over the Internet.

Examples of Telecommunications

Telecommunications can be beneficial to anyone from the home user of a computer to the largest corporations. Here are some examples.

The home user, with the least expensive of telecommunications hookups, can access a multitude of information. From reading the daily news and sports scores, looking at weather maps, making airline and hotel reservations, paying bills, doing in-depth research on a topic, to just "chatting" with other computer users, the individual has access to services that could only be dreamed about a few years ago.

figure 1

This store uses telecommunications to receive pricing information from headquarters and to send sales and inventory data to headquarters.

Think about any business, and you can see a multitude of areas in which telecommunications are crucial. Electronically transmitted orders for merchandise zip instantaneously from continent to continent. The package you ship by an express service is continuously tracked from pickup to delivery by an electronic data stream. Large retailers know every night how many dollars of sales each one of thousands of stores made during the day, and reorders for merchandise are calculated and transmitted to manufacturers and wholesalers through the telecommunications network.

A Simple Telecommunications Connection

The simplest kind of telecommunications connection is when two computers are connected together over a phone line to share data. The data may be a "chat" between two users of the computers, a document going from one computer to the other, or data related to a business. Regardless of the type of data being shared, the connections of the computers could be the same.

Assume that you need for your computer to be able to talk with my computer and we are located in different places. All that needs to take place is for you to plug your computer into the phone line and for me to plug my computer into the phone line. This seeming simplicity, however, masks several complicated things that, fortunately, happen pretty much invisibly to the users of the computers. First, there has to be a way of making the electronic connection between the computer and the phone line. Second, both computers must be using communications software that "speaks the same language" over the phone line. These two important issues are discussed in the following sections.

The Phone Connection

Remember that phone lines were originally constructed to transmit sound. Therefore, the phone system was put together so that the sound waves produced by a person speaking into the phone modulated or changed an electric current passing through the phone line. Because the electric current changed in response to sound, the phone system was known as an analog device. (Remember that an analogy is a way that things are similar; in other words, the "shape" of the current flowing on the wire mimics the "shape" of the sound that was spoken.) Computers, however, are digital devices. They work with numbers—specifically, ones and zeroes. Everything in the computer is represented by a combination of these two digits. Therefore, the basic operating methodology of phone lines and computers was different.

Modems To make the connection between the phone system and a computer, a device called a **modem** was invented. The word modem is taken from the terms *modulator/demodulator* and describes what the device does. As shown in figure 2, it modulates the digital signals from the computer into analog signals for the phone system. At the receiving computer, it demodulates the analog signals from the phone system back into the digital signals required by the computer.

To establish communication, software on the initiating computer causes the modem to dial the phone number of the remote computer.

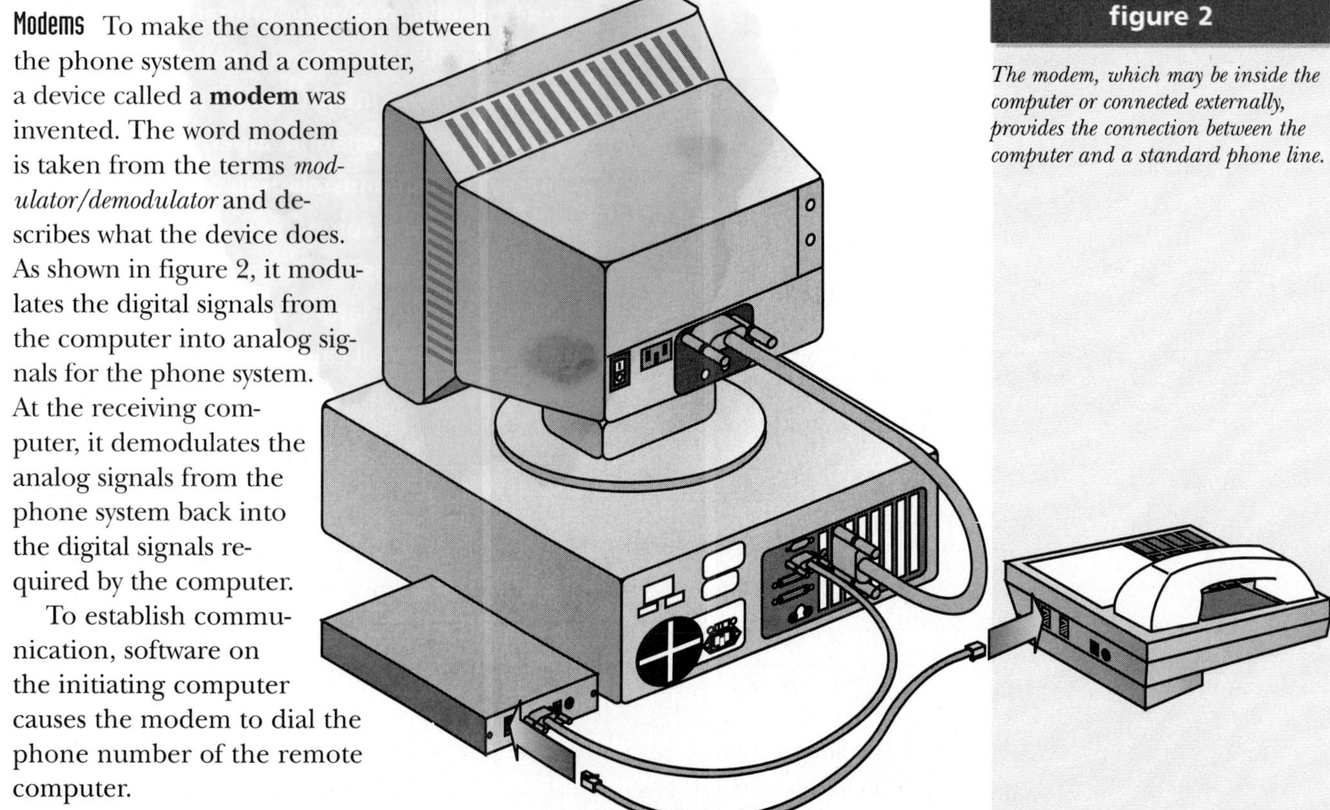

figure 2

The modem, which may be inside the computer or connected externally, provides the connection between the computer and a standard phone line.

Trends

Phone Companies and Cable TV Race Toward the Information Superhighway

Even if you are not into computers, you have probably heard the terms *convergence* and *information superhighway*. These buzzwords describe trends that are taking place right now in the telecommunications industry.

Convergence means "coming together." In telecommunications, this refers to the fact that cable-television companies and telephone companies, which in the past were totally separate industries, are beginning to provide the same services. Cable-television companies are rushing to provide two-way communications through their cable, while telephone companies are working to get government permission to provide television channels through phone lines. In many cases, this convergence actually opens up direct competition between phone companies and cable-television providers. In some parts of the country, however, various phone and cable companies have formed alliances.

One product of this convergence is what is called the information superhighway—a concept that is still being defined. The basic idea is that each home and business in the country will have ready access to high-speed data communications possibilities. One vision is that each potential user could choose from at least two different companies who would provide telephone service, interactive television service, and data communications service.

Much of the infrastructure necessary to provide an information superhighway is in place. The rapid installation of fiber-optic cable by phone companies in recent years has made it possible for phone companies to carry a much larger volume of data than possible when all cabling was made of copper wire. Similar developments in the cable-television industry now make it possible for a cable to carry a growing number of signals at once, thus opening the door for two-way communications.

One more player in the development of the information superhighway is the government. Because government regulates communications companies, it will have a say in granting additional services, whether they are provided by telephone companies or cable-television providers. An even bigger question: what role should government play in planning and implementing the infrastructure of the information superhighway?

Software on the remote computer causes its modem to answer the phone, and communication is set up.

Interestingly, phone systems are rapidly converting to digital transmission for sound. Your conversation is converted to digital signals (i.e., the same ones and zeroes that computers use) before it is transmitted over the phone lines and then is converted back to analog form to operate the speaker or headset you use to listen to the sound. This digital phone technology is called **ISDN**, for **integrated services digital network**.

Transmission speed Data can be transmitted over phone lines at various speeds. The speed at which data can be transmitted is stated either as the **baud rate** or the number of **bits** (ones and zeroes) **per second** (bps). A baud rate can be defined as the number of signal events per second. Because data is transmitted a bit at a time and each bit represents a signal, the terms baud rate and bits per second are commonly used interchangeably. However, there is a technical difference between them.

The transmission speed is determined by the capability of the particular modems being used. However, there is also a speed limitation imposed by the quality of the phone lines over which the transmission is taking place.

Not very many years ago, the most common transmission speed was 300 baud, or roughly 30 characters per second. Anything higher resulted in too many errors coming over the line. As a result of improved technology (both hardware and software) and a generally higher quality of phone lines, that rate is now considered to be woefully archaic. The commonly used speed has continued to rise, until the most commonly sold modem now features a speed of 28,800 bps. With advanced data compression, quality phone lines, and compatible modems at both ends of the line (modems by their nature are compatible except for the newest technology, which must exist on both ends for maximum speed), substantially higher rates are possible.

Thus, transmission speed over common phone lines is typically 96 times as fast as it was a few years ago. Compared to the transmission speed between computers that are connected within the same building or campus to a local area network, however, modem speeds are still incredulously slow. If you compare 28,800 bps to a very common (but fairly slow) local area network (LAN) running at 10 megabits per second, the network is 347 times faster than the modem.

Two new technologies can speed up non-LAN communication: satellite transmissions can be used for the download side, and cable TV lines can totally replace the telephone connection. At the time of this writing, however, these two technologies were not widely available.

Physically, modems are available in three forms. First, they may be manufactured as an integral part of the computer's main circuit board (motherboard). Second, they may be in the form of a circuit card that plugs into the computer's motherboard; this type of modem is called an internal modem. Finally, they may be in an external enclosure that plugs into a port on the computer such as the PCMCIA port of a laptop computer.

Figure 3 shows two variations of modems: an internal modem designed to fit into a slot on the computer's motherboard, and an external modem designed to plug into a computer's serial port. Regardless of their physical format, they do the same work.

figure 3

These internal and external modems are typical of those used with desktop computers.

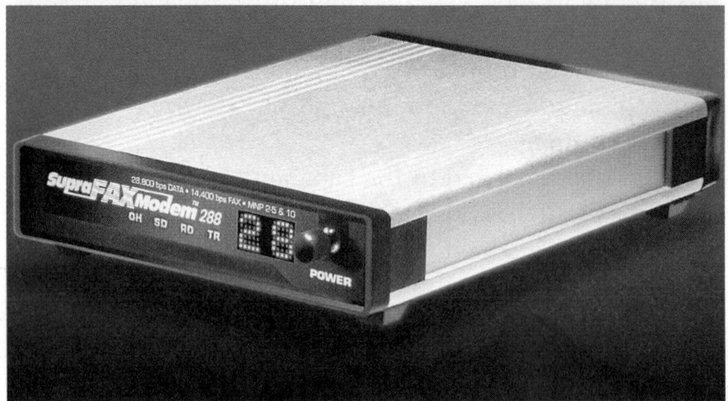

Both the host computer and the computer that it communicates with must set their modems the same regardless of the type of modem used (built-in, internal, or external). For example, the transmission speeds of both the sending and receiving modems must be the same, and the protocol (the "language") used by both must be the same. Specifications regarding speed and protocols are typically adjustable under software control. The user simply runs the software and makes menu choices to control the setup parameters for the modem. Once this information is known by the communications software, it can interact with the communications hardware to allow communication to take place. Most modems can automatically change speeds so a match is made at both ends of the line without operator intervention.

If you have direct access to digital phone lines, the services provided by a standard modem (modulation and demodulation) are not needed to make a phone connection that will share data. There must still be a physical connection, however, and it may still be referred to as a modem.

Installing your external modem Modems communicate with your computer through a **serial port** on the computer. A serial port is a connection through which the ones and zeroes of computer language march in single file. The speed at which the port and the modem are operating designates how many of these ones and zeroes (binary digits or bits) go through the connection each second.

If you are using a Macintosh computer, the modem plugs into a serial port that is known as the **modem port**. If you are using a PC, the modem will usually use a port known as COM1 or COM2 (figure 4). COM is short for communications. COM3 and COM4 may also be available, but these ports generally are not used because their implementation is not standard on some computers. Depending on the modem, you may have to set a jumper or a switch on it to indicate which port you are going to use.

When installing a modem, you need to try not to use the same port name for more than one device. On a PC, other devices that may use a serial port include the mouse, printer, and others. If you have a serial mouse and a modem, for example, be sure that one uses COM1 and the other uses COM2. The software you will use may have a configuration option where you need to tell it which COM port the modem is using. If you are using what is known in the PC industry as a "Plug and Play" computer and modem, you should not need to be concerned about such things as which port the modem is using. Neither should you be concerned with this if you are using a Macintosh.

Setting up software Without appropriate software, the modem in your computer is useless. When you install a modem, you also install the software that operates it. In addition (or in place of) the software that comes with a modem, you may use a special communications software package for particular purposes. For example, services such as Prodigy, CompuServe, and America Online have their own communications software that uses your modem to access their services. The installation process for the software may show you a list of modems and ask you to select the brand and model you are using; if not, you usually make such a selection from a menu the first time you run the program.

Typically, specialty software comes already configured to match the requirements of the service with which it is to be used. For general-purpose communications software, however, a number of parameters need to be set. Such general-purpose software comes with the modem or as a part of an operating environment such as Windows, or it can be purchased separately. It is typically used to access computer bulletin boards and networks. Figure 5 shows the Terminal software that comes with

figure 4

Modem ports of a typical Macintosh (top) and PC (bottom).

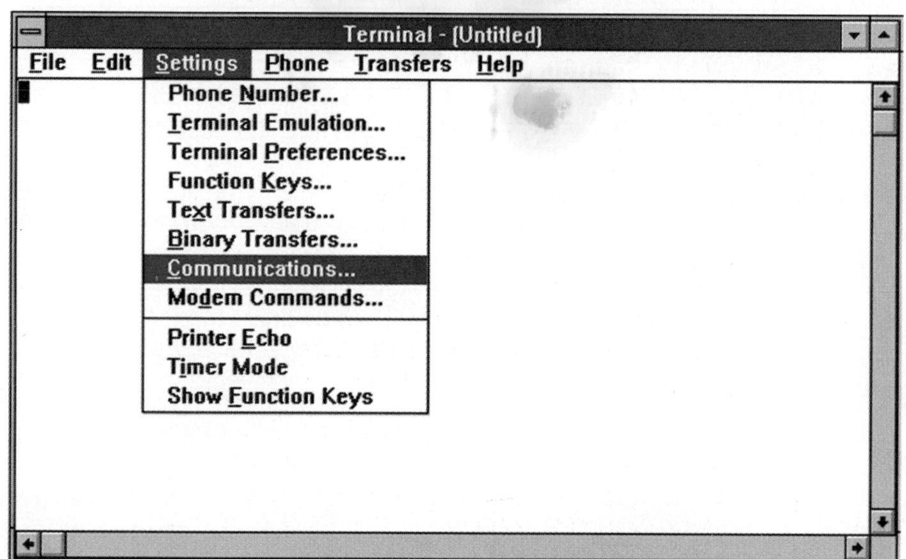

figure 5

Communication settings can be changed through menus and dialog boxes, such as these in the Windows Terminal software.

Issues In Technology

Voice Mail: Caller's Friend... Or Foe?

One product of the convergence of computer and telephone technology is voice mail—the automated phone service that many businesses use to direct incoming phone calls and take messages. You already know voice mail if you have called a company and heard a recorded voice telling you how to reach a particular person or department. ("If you know the extension, please enter that number now...") Even the smallest businesses can have voice mail. All it takes is placing a card that costs only a few hundred dollars into a computer and plugging it into a phone line.

Properly designed, voice mail can help cure many of the problems that businesses have in trying to make telephone contact. After all, the computerized voice that answers the phone is able to determine whether a person is answering his or her phone, can play a message stating where the person is and whether he or she will be available, and can record a message for delivery to the person. The caller's message can be any reasonable length and immediately channeled to a particular individual if it is a confidential message, or it can be routed to a company bulletin board for broadcast to all—all with just one phone call. Another attractive feature to callers: The ability to store messages at any time is particularly useful for callers from different time zones or who cannot call during normal business hours.

There is a downside to voice mail, however. Callers can become frustrated when they cannot reach a human being. Often, the problem is not with the technology itself but with how it is implemented. The first rule of thumb: a person in an office should always answer the phone if he or she is there. Frustration builds if the caller has reason to believe someone is refusing to pick up the phone. Another implementation problem involves how many hoops a caller must jump through to reach a particular person. Some businesses' voice mail is so complex, the caller must listen to as many as three or four menus of choices before proceeding. This can lead to a feeling of "getting lost inside the voice mail," seemingly unable to reach a human being. Even if the phone is eventually answered by the intended receiver, the "hassle factor" for the caller has immediately erased any feelings of goodwill for that business.

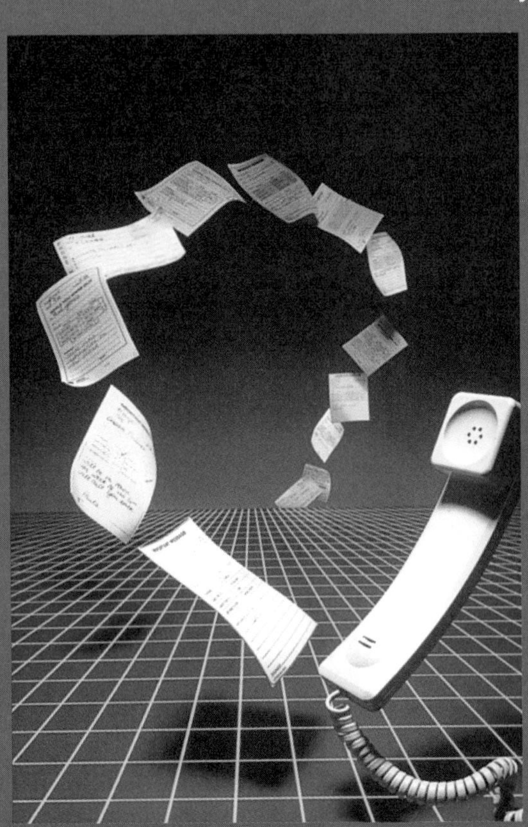

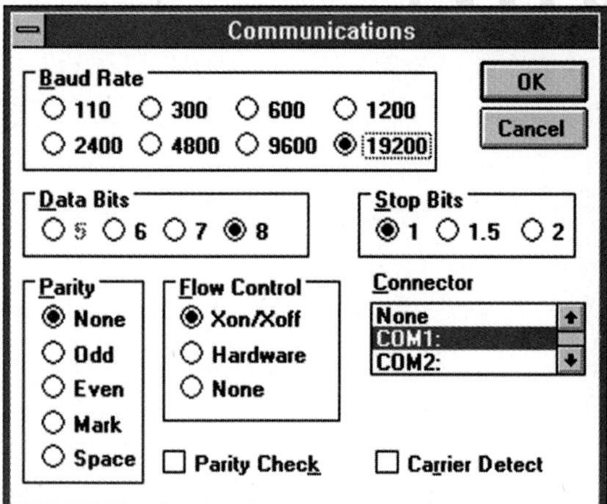

figure 6

This screen from the Windows Terminal software shows some of the commonly used settings for modem communications.

Windows. Note that the menu pulled down is the one used to set the many user parameters. Then, the communications settings have been chosen. In the following sections, you will find out more about some of what you may need to set by selecting these menu items; figure 6 shows the common settings as entered with the Windows Terminal software.

Speed Modems are capable of operating at lower speeds as well as at their maximum speed. In any case, you will need to tell the software the speed at which to operate. The software will then send the proper commands to the modem to set that speed.

Remember that modems at each end of a connection must be running at the same speed. Typically, however, a modem that receives a call has the ability to sense the speed at which the initiating modem is transmitting and adjust its own speed accordingly. This is not always the case, however.

Number of data and stop bits The dialog box you just looked at in figure 6 also allows you to set the number of data and stop bits. The number of data and stop bits refers to the number of ones and zeroes used to represent each character. Data transmission with microcomputers uses a coding system known as the **American Standard Code for Information Interchange**, or ASCII pronounced "as-kie"). As first set up, this code used seven bits (ones and zeroes) to represent each character. Because 128 is the largest decimal number (or number of different combinations) that you can represent using seven binary digits, the code was capable of handling all letters of the alphabet, digits, punctuation marks, and a few other special characters. Each of the 128 possible codes represents a character.

Along the way, makers of microcomputers added an eighth binary digit to the code, so that a total of 256 different characters could be represented. These extra characters tend not to be standard, and they are used for different characters by different software vendors.

This possibility of using either seven or eight bits to represent each character led to modem software settings for either seven or eight data bits. Most computers with which you will wish to communicate will likely be set up for eight data bits.

Stop bits are bits that come after the digits representing the character itself. They designate the end of the character. When you are using eight data bits, you will usually use one stop bit.

Profile

Dennis Hayes

Modems have been around since the 1960s. Those early boxes, however, had no software. Even the phone number to call was stored inside the hardware itself. Want to dial a different number? Open up the box, and rearrange some wires.

Dennis Hayes knew these first modems very well; he installed them for rural electric cooperatives in Georgia. From this hands-on experience, Hayes designed a modem that allowed the user to control its functions through software rather than the hardware. In 1977, Hayes started Hayes Microcomputer Products by hand-assembling modems at a kitchen table with a partner. From these humble beginnings, the company quickly grew, until it commanded over half the modem market. Hayes modems and software commands quickly became the industry standard. Competitors soon entered the modem market, but their products had to be Hayes compatible to have any hope of selling.

While Hayes has been challenged by low-cost competitors, the company has continued to focus on quality. With that focus, Hayes Microcomputer Products has grown into a major enterprise, with estimated sales of $120 million in 1989 according to Dataquest. Actual sales figures are not available because the company is privately held, which is a rarity in the computer and communications industries. Because the company remains privately held, it retains Dennis Hayes' leadership and unique vision.

What happens to Hayes' company when digital phone lines (ISDN) make modems totally obsolete? Hayes' newest product is a board that plugs into the computer and attaches it to a digital phone line, providing communication for voice, data, and video. Hayes sees the definition of the modem to be evolving into any device that connects a computer to a phone line, as opposed to the original meaning of the word: modulator/demodulator.

Terminal emulation **Terminal emulation** is a leftover from the days when mainframe computers ruled the computer world and used something called "dumb terminals" to connect with users. The computer sent various codes to the terminals to do such things as clearing the screen and positioning the cursor. When people started attaching microcomputers to mainframes, the mainframes knew nothing about microcomputers and continued sending the same terminal codes they had always sent—so the microcomputer software had to pretend to be one of the dumb terminals.

Many computers with which you communicate may still be using the mainframe codes, so you have to set up your software to match this. Your software will probably allow you to make a choice between pretending that your computer is a TTY (teletype machine, the dumbest of all terminals), a DEC VT-100 (a terminal that met something called ANSI standards [the American National Standards Institute]), or other models. As with all other settings discussed here, there needs to be a match on both ends of the line. Bulletin board systems and other remote systems to which you attach can typically send signals appropriate for a number of different settings as long as you tell them (by answering online configuration questions) which setting you are using.

Local settings Communications software packages allow you to set many things about how your computer will behave while it is talking with another computer. As examples, you may be able to set the length of line it will display or what action the function keys on the keyboard will control.

File transfers One thing users typically do with modem-connected computers is copy files. To ensure that the files are received just as they were sent—that is, that no data got garbled along the way because of noise on the phone line or other reasons—several different data-verification schemes are available by which the software checks the received data for accuracy and requests a retransmission if anything is wrong. You will frequently have a choice between these different transmission protocols. Again, the rule is that both ends of the connection must be using the same one.

Modem commands **Modem commands** refer to the signals the software sends to the modem to make it do various things. For example, to cause the modem to initiate dialing a phone number, the software might send it the characters ATDT. Hayes (see profile in this chapter) is the manufacturer that really popularized microcomputer modems, and most other manufacturers emulated its commands to sell their units. Some communications software gives you access to the modem commands so that you can change them, and some modems come with long lists of all the possible commands. However, modems generally operate properly without your doing anything to these settings (in fact, some software totally hides them from you). The rule to operate under is to leave the default commands alone unless you are having trouble and are instructed by a technical support person to change them.

When Is Using a Standard Phone Line Appropriate?

Using a standard phone line for communication between computers is appropriate only when the volume of data to be moved is small. With computer bulletin boards and online services, this criterion is usually met.

For example, a modem operating at 28,800 bps transmits about 2880 characters per second. Thus, it would take about 6 minutes to move 1 megabyte of data, figured as follows:

2880 characters per second x 60 seconds per minute
= 172,800 characters per minute

1,024,000 characters (1 megabyte)/172,800 characters per minute
= 5.93 minutes.

Figure 7 shows the approximate amount of time it takes to move 1 megabyte of data using different bits per second. Your computer may have several files that are as large as or even larger than 1 megabyte. From the time required, you can see that dialup connections with regular phone lines are not very appropriate for the routine movement of large volumes of data.

figure 7

Moving large quantities of data over a regular phone line is a time-consuming process.

Approximate Time to Move 1 Megabyte of Data

Speed (bps)	Time
2400	1 hour, 11 minutes
9600	18 minutes
14,400	12 minutes
28,800	6 minutes

Techniques for compressing data for transmission are becoming better and more widespread. Compressing data lessens the transmission time required. The data is mathematically "scrunched" by the communications software so that it is accurately represented in fewer bytes than the original. If you have an ISDN phone line rather than a regular analog phone line, you can get a basic transmission speed of 144,000 bps, compared with the 28,800 bps of a typical modem.

Do It!

1 Determine whether there is a modem attached to a computer you have access to. If so, is it external, internal, or built-in? (A built-in modem will not be on a separate plug-in card in the computer but will be part of the main circuit board.) What is its maximum speed?

2 What is the name of the communications software that is available on a computer you use? If you have both general-purpose and specialized software, list both categories.

3 Call up the configuration menu for the communications software you have, and examine the options that are available.

Typical Dial-Up Services

It was estimated that in the early 1990s, 10% of all microcomputers were connected to some type of communication network, either a local area network or telecommunications services. By 1993, however, it was the norm for PCs being sold to come equipped with a modem. In short, the number of communicating computers has exploded.

This growth has been driven in large measure by the increasing availability and quality of services providing dial-up connections. Here are some examples of the more popular services.

Bulletin Board Systems

The term **bulletin board system** (BBS) refers to any computer that may be called by other computers for exchanging messages, uploading files (remote computer to the BBS), or downloading files (from the BBS to the remote computer). Just about any computer can serve as a BBS simply by installing a modem and bulletin board software. Most of these systems are equipped to handle multiple incoming phone lines instead of just one. You access a BBS using general-purpose communications software that came with your modem or operating system or that you purchased separately.

Literally thousands of these systems are available. Many serve the needs of users of a particular product or those with a particular interest. For example, many manufacturers of computer hardware and software operate a BBS to provide information and technical support to their customers.

A BBS typically provides three different services: electronic mail, general messages and announcements, and a file library that can be downloaded to the user's computer. The communications software that drives a BBS can range from a simple program permitting one computer to communicate with another to sophisticated networking software servicing thousands of users over a vast geographic area. Typically, the more sophisticated the software, the greater the number of different devices that can access the service and the greater the number of applications that are available to its users.

With **electronic mail** (e-mail), users with valid passwords can log on (establish connection by dialing the telephone number and keying the valid password) to a BBS and then post and read messages to and from each other. All valid users have their own "mailbox" on the disk of the host computer. Messages can be directed to another user's mailbox. When that user accesses his or her mailbox, the messages that it contains are sent to the proper terminal for display or printout.

The **public message service** performs a function similar to the bulletin board in your school. Messages and announcements are placed in a special mailbox for all valid users. The user can then access this special mailbox to receive all of the messages and announcements it contains. Depending on the sophistication of the software providing the BBS services, messages may be categorized by subject or date to make accessing them easier.

The files contained on a BBS may cover a wide range of topics, depending on the purpose of the BBS. They may include such things as updates to software and various graphic images that can be downloaded for inclusion in documents created by the user.

Information Services

CompuServe, Prodigy, America Online, Delphi, and other similar offerings are known as information services or online services, and they provide services far beyond those provided by a BBS. Typically, information services consist of sophisticated software running on large mainframe host computers with large databases capable of providing a wide variety of services to thousands of users across the country. These systems provide services related

figure 8

Online services provide information relating to many interests, including travel and tourism.

to local and national news, weather, sporting events, travel, recipes, shopping, tax advice, computer games, theater listings, and home record-keeping, to name a few (figure 8). Commercial users (businesses and industries) as well as individuals subscribe to the service. A subscriber is given a valid password and telephone number that permits access to the information service's host computer's databases. The user may contract for all or any of the services available and, once logged on, can access any of the contracted services. The subscriber is usually billed for the amount of connect time (time spent communicating with the host computer over a communication channel). Additionally, some services may carry a premium charge. Billing is usually done to a credit-card account.

The popularity of these networks has led to an increased number of users and, in turn, an increase in the revenue generated. This increased income has been reinvested in additional hardware, software, and databases capable of serving even more users. This has created a "snowball-rolling-down-the-hill" effect. That is, as the use of these systems grows, the revenue they generate increases, and this enables the money to be reinvested to expand the services in an effort to interest even more users in using the network.

Some of the most popular information services include CompuServe, Prodigy, and America Online. All of these major services can provide communications software tailored specifically to the service, making it easier to access than if you were using generic software. While you can access some of the services with generic communications software, the specialized software is required for some and is certainly preferred for all of them. Figure 9 shows a CompuServe menu screen; note the different categories of service that are available as indicated by the different icons and menu choices. Figure 10 shows an e-mail screen from America Online.

The range of services provided by these systems is extremely broad and is growing every day. While there are variations from one service to another, the following sections will give you a good flavor for what is available.

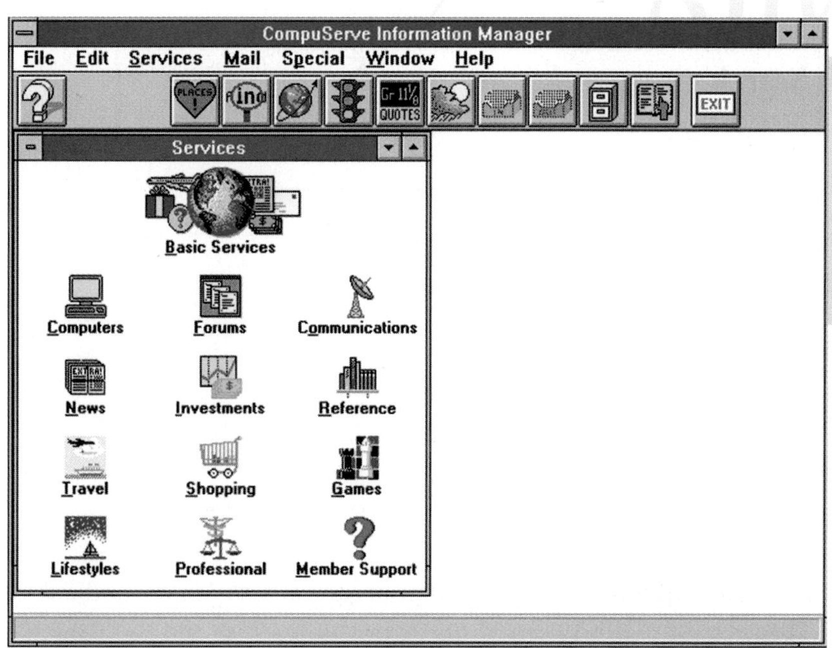

figure 9

Typical of specialized software used to connect with an information service, CompuServe's Information Manager makes it easy to select services using a graphic user interface.

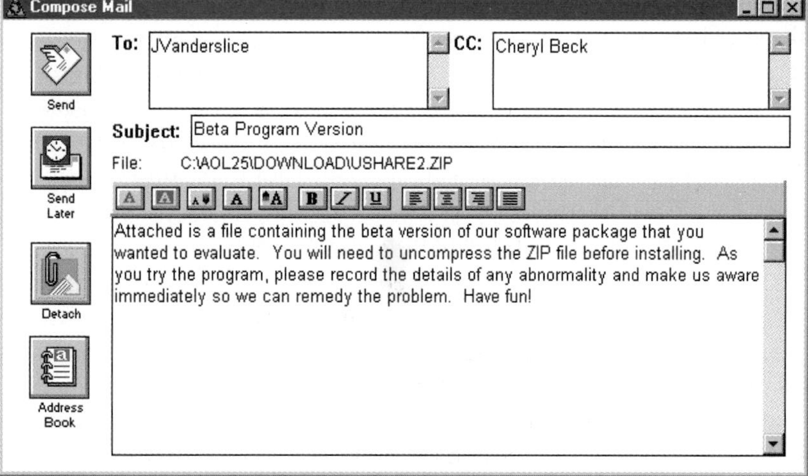

figure 10

This electronic-mail dialog box from America Online is typical of that provided by many information services.

Research Services

Research services provide retrieval of data from a wide variety of sources, such as newspapers, magazines, reference volumes, and various scholarly works. It is often much easier to obtain this information through the computer than from a school or local library. The data that is available through the computer often is not available in a local library.

Sophisticated software running on the host computer accesses large databases to provide this service. You may search for information in several different ways. You may look for items by their author's name, by the name of an article, by the subject area, or by a keyword search. A keyword search is the most powerful, because it looks at the actual text of all available articles to see if it contains the terms you are looking for. For example, if you were looking for articles about Lincoln automobiles, you might do a keyword search for all magazine articles containing the word *Lincoln.* If you did this search, however, you might be surprised to get a lot of references about President Lincoln and Lincoln pennies, and no telling what else related to various Lincolns. To get more of the result you want, you might narrow the

figure 11

Searches can be done using a number of different criteria. This screen from America Online is typical of those provided by many information services.

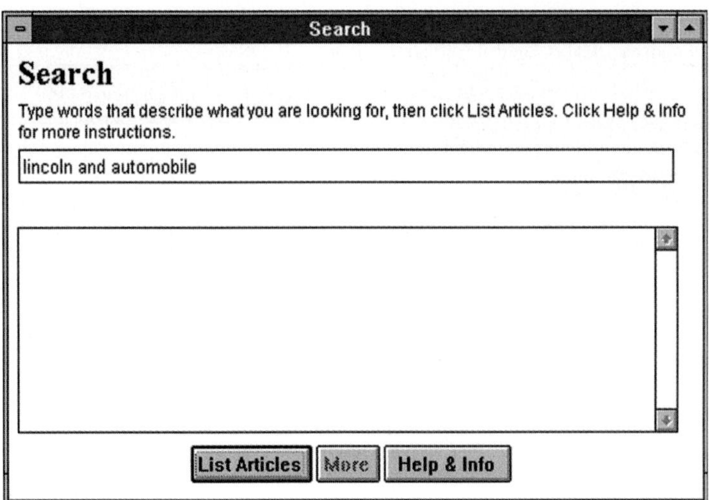

search by requesting articles containing the words *Lincoln* and *automobile*. Figure 11 shows an America Online screen used for doing such a search.

Many information services are able to connect you with databases that are not on their computers but are on other computers located in different places. This connection is made for you when you choose from a list the database you want to use. The connection is handled transparently for you by the information service; at most, you may see nothing more than a small message informing you that a connection is being made to the database.

Some of the databases you can access through an information service require user IDs and passwords of their own. These are in addition to those you use to log on to the information service itself.

News Services

Information services generally make available access to a wide variety of current news. Whether your interest is world politics, sports, computers, weather, or whatever, you can call up the latest stories as soon as they are written. The sources available vary with different information services but can include items gathered by various news organizations as well as the entire text of various newspapers and magazines. Some services allow you to construct your own "newspaper dummy" in which you specify the kinds of news you want to appear on each page of your "newspaper." When you access the service, the computer then scans all of the news items to select those related to your chosen topics and displays them in the positions you have chosen. For example, if you owned a lot of stock in a particular corporation and wanted any news about it to be placed in a "front page" position, the service would put it there. If you want the news related to your local professional team to appear as the "front page story," the service will put it there. Figure 12 shows a typical America Online screen.

Travel Services

You can have do-it-yourself access to airline, hotel, and rental-car reservations systems (figure 13). You can browse schedules and fares, or you can have the computer select the flights with the lowest fares. You can ask for help from the computer in selecting a hotel that meets your preferences for

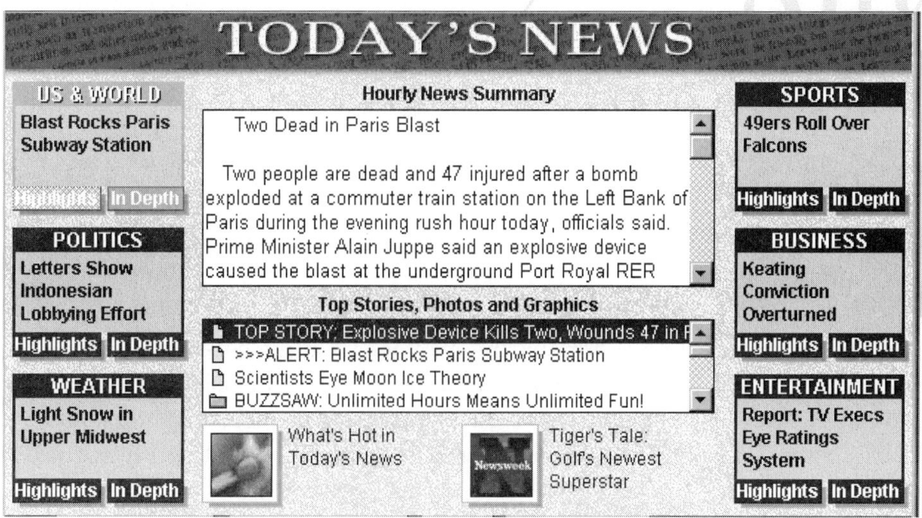

figure 12

By using an online service, you can get news stories or classified ads before they are printed in a newspaper.

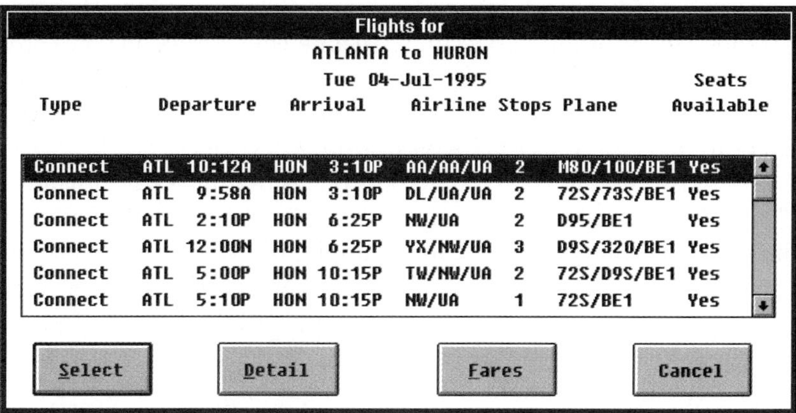

figure 13

By using travel services, you can access the same reservations system used by travel agents.

location, price range, and amenities. After making selections on the computer, you can have tickets sent to you or can pick them up at a local ticket office.

Stock Exchange Services

One of the popular available resources is the data on financial markets provided by various vendors on the information services. Among the services that can be provided are:

- Comprehensive company profiles for interested investors, including earnings forecasts, price/volume charts, and financial history.
- Up-to-date stock prices and quotes.
- Market news and analysts' opinions minutes after they are written.
- The ability to buy and sell directly over the computer.
- Individual customer portfolio management.
- Alerting the customer to critical situations and times, including when stock prices reach a certain limit established by the customer, stock options are about to expire, and bonds are about to mature.

- Individual reporting capabilities, including all investment activities, gains/losses, and year-to-date summaries.
- Tracking of individual securities or selected stocks.

Depending on the information service you are using and the degree of sophistication of the financial markets service you are accessing, there may be a premium charged for the service.

Forums

Forums provide a place for sharing messages. Unlike e-mail, which can be somewhat private, forums serve the same purpose as old-fashioned town meetings. They are a place to pose questions, hear proposed answers, and debate issues. A typical information service provides many different forums, each of them related to a particular subject.

There obviously are forums related to computer issues, typically with a separate forum for each popular hardware and software product. In these forums, users of the product who have questions can effectively post their question where others can read it. Anyone who has an answer can then post the answer. Forums provide a valuable service in support of computer products, and sometimes an angry flood of complaints will force a product's producer to make significant changes.

There is no limit to the range of subjects that may have forums available. If someone wants to fund the operation of a forum for those interested in the culture of the honey bee, for example, there is no reason such a forum could not exist.

File Library

The **file library** service enables users of an information service to download various computer files as well as (in some instances) to upload programs to share with other users. A list and brief description of each file stored in the library may be accessed. From the list, a file can be selected and downloaded to a user's computer for subsequent use.

Typically, files that are available for download are categorized as being in different libraries, where each library contains files related to a common subject. For example, one library might contain files related to a particular word-processing program, while another might contain various graphic images for use with drawing programs.

File libraries are often associated with forums. In this way, they are conveniently at hand when the user is accessing the forum.

Chat Modes

By going into chat mode, you may type messages that are seen on the screens of whichever other users happen to be in chat mode at the same time. Many have taken advantage of this method to meet new people, but you definitely are not getting the full dimension of the other person when your only contact is the words they type on a keyboard.

Depending on the service, you may have control over which users are in chat mode with you. For example, you might want to include only those who have a mutual interest in the same forum as you.

Do It!

1 Sign on to a BBS to which you have access. Examine the different menu choices that are available to you.

2 Sign on to an information service that is available to you. Explore the different services that are available to you.

While chatting over a computer network certainly lacks some of the personal contact of face-to-face communication, there is at least one documented case of a couple who met in chat mode and became engaged to be married before they ever spoke or saw each other. They did hold the wedding ceremony in person, however.

Wide Area Networks

As you are probably aware, a group of connected computers is known as a network. When all of the computers are in the same general location, the network is known as a local area network. Many businesses, however, have several different locations, with computers at each and the need for computers at one location to communicate with those at others. When these computers that are geographically separated from each other are connected, you have what is known as a wide area network. See figure 14 to learn about some typical applications of wide area networks.

How Are Wide Area Networks Connected?

Wide area networks can be connected by either or both of two broad categories of telecommunications connections. One is an **on-demand connection**, which basically means a phone line that has a dial tone and can be accessed as needed. The other involves a **dedicated communication connection**, which is connected at all times. In most cases, implementing a wide area network involves buying time on communication lines from a company that specializes in providing these services, such as phone companies and satellite communication companies.

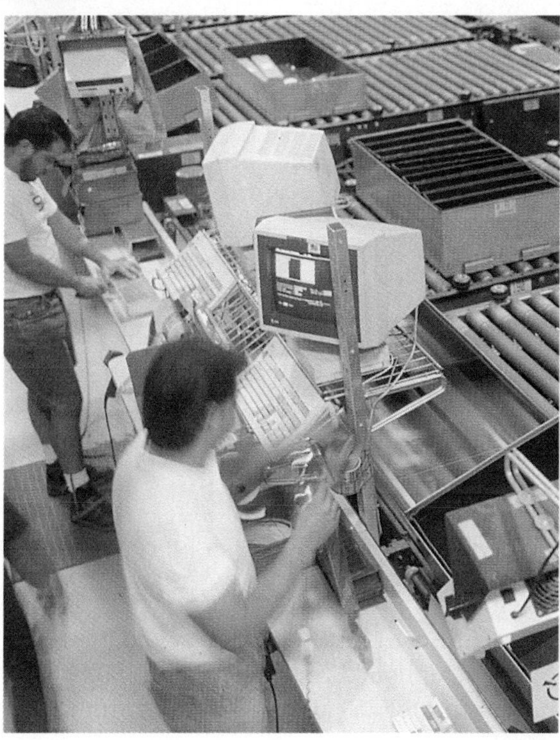

figure 14

Electronic data interchange is used to process purchase orders and invoices. When an automobile manufacturer's computerized system determines that a particular quantity of parts is needed, it electronically sends a purchase order to the supplier of the parts. The parts supplier then electronically sends an invoice to the auto manufacturer; whose system then electronically has the proper funds transferred. The transfer of paper forms is eliminated. Without EDI, the "just in time" delivery of parts and the resulting efficiencies would be impossible.

When the volume of data is such that high speed is needed, either a T1 or T3 line can be used. T1 lines are those that typically provide a transmission speed of 1.544 mbps, while T3 lines typically provide a 45 mbps speed. Keep in mind that these kinds of lines are extremely expensive compared with regular phone lines.

If the need for communication from one location to another is constant, a dedicated line probably is preferable. On the other hand, if the need is sporadic, a dial-up line is preferable. For some businesses that have a constant communication load plus a need for additional "spike handling" capability, a combination of the two methods may be appropriate, with dial-up lines supplementing the dedicated lines as needed.

Whether you use dial-up service or leased lines, the process of communicating with computers in other geographic areas is similar. For low volumes of data transmission, the entire connection may be made with regular telephone lines. For higher volume, phone lines may connect your computers to a higher-speed link, such as fiber-optic cable. A **fiber-optic** cable consists of one or more hair-thin strands of material capable of conducting light images. These light images can transmit more data over more channels at higher speeds than wire cables.

figure 15

Microwave towers provide the links for long distance, wireless communication.

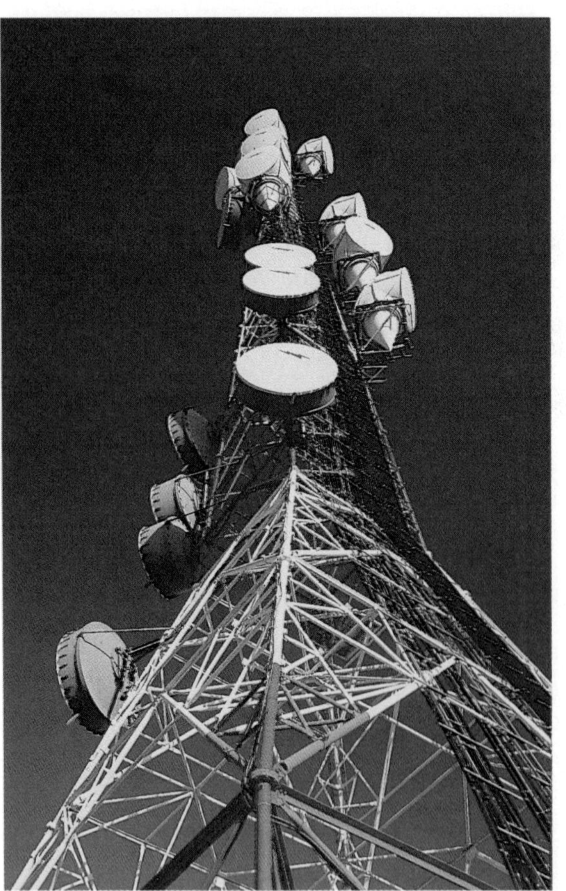

When long-distance communication is required, the communication links carrying the transmission may connect to and use a microwave carrier (figure 15). **Microwave carriers** transmit data on a straight path from one microwave station to another. Each station must be in a direct line with another station to pass the transmission along. Microwave stations vary in their distances from each other depending on the location, height, and obstructions between the dishes. Microwave dishes are frequently mounted on water towers or other types of high antenna towers to maximize the distance between stations. After a transmission enters a microwave carrier, it is directed from one microwave station to another. When it reaches the area closest to its destination, it once again enters a telephone line to complete its journey to the receiving communicating device.

The telephone line or fiber-optic cable carrying data may also connect to and use a satellite carrier when long-distance communication is required. A communication satellite maintains a stationary position by orbiting above the earth at a distance and speed that correlates to the earth's rotation. Figure 16 shows a typical earth station that sends and receives data from a satellite. Frequently, a combination of communication channels will be used; figure 17 shows one possible scenario. Fortunately, the computer user does not have to be concerned about how the data travels.

Bandwidth Versus Budget

figure 16

Many strategically located earth stations similar to this one direct their antennas toward satellites to send and receive data.

Bandwidth refers to the volume or speed at which a communication channel operates. Moving a little bit of data over a communication line costs little money—like placing a phone call; moving a lot of data over a communication line costs more—a lot more. In fact, most of the costs for implementing a wide area network go into paying rent on the communication lines even including ones under the sea (figure 18). Suppose you have computers in four different cities and each uses one regular phone line for 8 hours a day for communication, which is the equivalent of 32 hours of long distance calls per day. If you lease a line, the typical cost starts at thousands of dollars a month and varies depending on the data-carrying capacity and distance.

The catch for developing a wide area network is that even the faster communication links operate rather slowly compared with the local area network speeds to which users have become accustomed. While there are communication links in place that can operate at billions of bytes per second between their main points of presence, communication from any one user's local area network to the departure point for data that is perhaps going across country is likely to be much slower. Refer to figure 19 to see a speed comparison for some of the commonly used communication links (common local area network speeds are shown as comparisons). Most of the local area network speeds considerably surpass most of the telecommunications speeds. To get really fast speeds, you need to go to fiber-optic cabling, whose speed advantage is shown graphically in figure 20. To obtain the same volume and speed of data transfer over a wide area network that is typical on a local area network costs a very significant sum of money. The sum is so significant that persons designing wide area networks are wise to put a big chunk of their

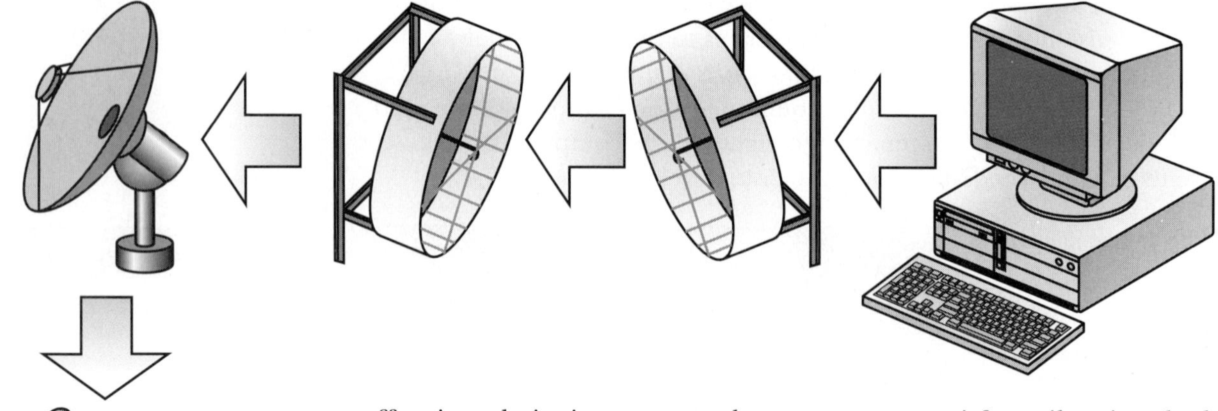

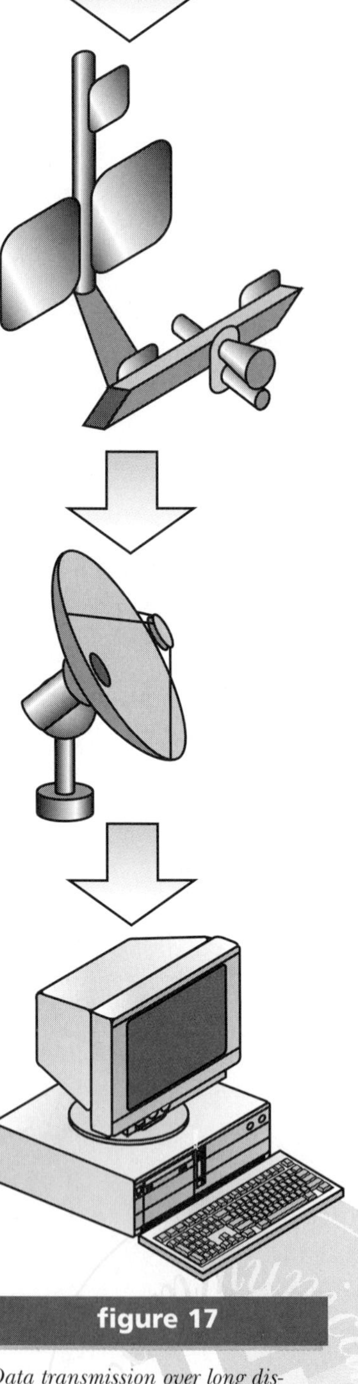

figure 17

Data transmission over long distances may use varying combinations of transmission carriers.

effort into designing a system that can operate satisfactorily using the least expensive communication link that will get the job done in a satisfactory manner.

Internet

The Internet is a worldwide interconnection scheme for accessing various computer networks from other computer networks. That is, it is the world's largest wide area network. For example, a student at one university can access data stored on the computer network at a university in another country, or a person who uses an information service such as CompuServe can send electronic mail to a person who uses the Pentagon's computer network.

The Internet was originated by the U. S. Department of Defense and for years operated in relative obscurity. It was not particularly user-friendly and was limited mostly to the government and university communities; commercial use was excluded on the government-funded network. Over the years, it grew into a collection of thousands of different networks. Then, commercially funded communication channels were added as alternatives to the government-funded ones, and the world discovered the Internet. During one brief period in 1993, more than 250,000 new computers were connected to the Internet. Even more indicative of the spectacular growth that occurred was that in one month of late 1993, the traffic carried by the Internet was more than double the volume carried the year before. Figure 21 gives an indication of its size.

Where the Internet once was the domain of computer mavens and users with direct connections to it, the Internet is now routinely used as well for such things as routing e-mail from parents on an information service to their college kids, whose in-room computers are connected to their university's computer network.

How Do I Get on the Internet?

The networks of many colleges, universities, governments, and businesses are attached directly to the Internet. If you want to use the Internet and are not part of an attached network, you can gain access through a service provider. If you are going to use a provider, you will need to sign up to become a subscriber. Just about any ordinary communications software can be used on the Internet; however, specialized programs can make connection and navigation easier. You can even attach to the Internet directly from some word-processing programs.

figure 18

In an age of satellites you might think all transoceanic phone calls travelled that way. But this special cable-laying ship belonging to AT&T is installing fiber-optic cable along the ocean floor. Each of the strands of glass can carry 20,000 simultaneous phone calls, and just 16 strands of the many in a cable can handle all transAtlantic phone traffic.

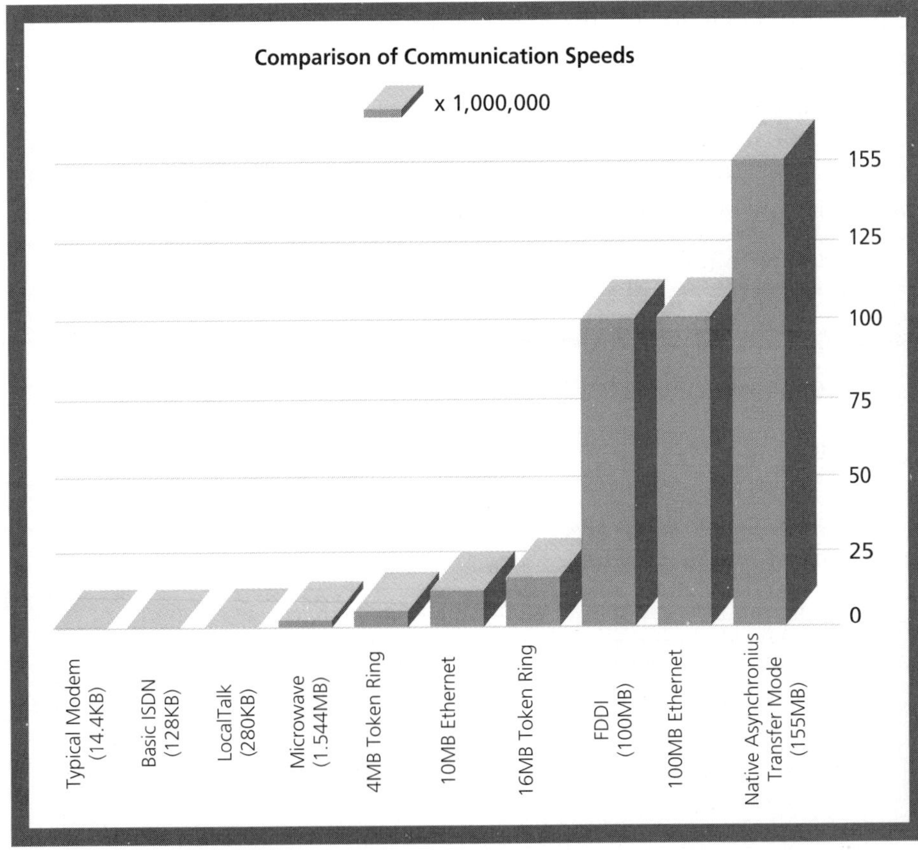

figure 19

The more economical telecommunications options are very slow compared with typical local area network speeds

figure 20

Fiber-optic cable can carry much more data than copper cable.

Once you have a way to attach to the Internet, you will need an address by which you are known on the network. These addresses take the form of words and numbers separated by punctuation. They begin with some form of your name, include the name of the network from which you are accessing the Internet, and end with a domain—*domain* meaning a sphere of activity (figure 22). Basically, the domain names indicate what the accessing organization does. Here are some examples:

jclark@delphi.com

In this example, *jclark* is the name of the user, *delphi* is the service provider network, and *com* is the domain.

38987, 2343@compuserve.com

The *numbers* at the beginning of this address will be familiar to CompuServe users as the identification of a user. *CompuServe* is the name of the provider network, and *com* is the domain.

president@whitehouse.gov

figure 21

The number of Internet users has exploded. While estimates of usage vary, these "guestimates" indicate the vastness of the Net.

A Glimpse at the Internet	
Number of countries with Internet access in 1996	170+
Number of host computers (servers) in 1996	10 million
Number of users in 1996	38 million
Projected number of users in 2000	200 million+
Number of bytes of data transfered on the World Wide Web in 1996	50 trillion/month

Internet domains	
com	Commercial
edu	Education
gov	Government
mil	Military
net	Network support
org	Other organizations

figure 22

Each network attached to the Internet is placed in one of these six categories.

This one should be obvious. Yes, you can send e-mail to the President of the United States over the Internet.

If what you are doing on the Internet involves a file server and not an individual user, just leave the user name off the address.

What Can I Do on the Internet?

There are four main activities you can do on the Internet:

- Send and receive e-mail.
- Transfer files from one computer to another. This capability is limited by the security in place on the member networks. There are many files that you can look at and copy, but there are vastly more that you are blocked from simply because they are nobody's business but their owner's.
- Take part in forums or discussion groups. A feature that is available on the Internet that may be a bit different from what you have experienced with forums on a BBS is the idea of subscribing to mailing lists. On the Internet, you can add your name to any of numerous computer mailing lists related to your interests. Whenever anybody sends a message to that mailing list, you will receive the message. Usenet is the Internet feature that allows you to access various subject-area topics or messages; it can be thought of as a BBS. The main difference in the mailing lists and Usenet is that you automatically receive everything that is sent to a mailing list while you must use viewing software to select and see messages in Usenet.
- Look for information.

As you have probably figured out, these are the same things you can do on a BBS or an information service. This is logical because the Internet provides the connection between different computer networks. For example, if you are a user of America Online and I am a user of CompuServe, we can send e-mail because the two services are connected through the Internet.

How Is the Internet Different from an Information Service?

Because the services available on the Internet look so similar to those provided by services such as CompuServe, Prodigy, and America Online among others, you may be wondering what the differences are. Indeed, much data can be obtained through either route.

Here are two characterizations that will help you see the differences:

- Information services or online services present you with an organized, coherent view of available data and services. You deal with one point of contact and access services by selecting items from menus or clicking on icons. Even when these services are accessing data on a computer many miles from their own computer, the action is transparent to you as the user. You are, however, limited to the services that have been chosen by the provider.
- The Internet has no central point of contact. The Internet in and of itself does not store and provide data and services to users—its only purpose is to *inter*connect different *net*works. The Internet is a wide area network that allows you to connect with any attached network for which you have access privileges. In comparison with the organized presentation on information services, the resources available through the Internet can appear chaotic. There are, however, many networks attached to the Internet that are not available to you through an information service.

Whew! How Do I Find My Way?

It is understandable that many new users of the Internet are somewhat overwhelmed by the enormous quantity of data that is available to them. Just thinking about the difficulty of finding a "lost" file on their own computer is enough to make them think that finding things on the Internet's vast resources must be next to impossible—and it would be without a little help from your friends on the system. A **Web browser** is software installed on the user's computer. It uses the computer's modem to connect to the Internet service provider. The provider may be an on-line service such as CompuServe or America Online, a phone company, or a company specializing in Internet services. Figure 23 shows an example of a dial-up screen for a Web browser. Once the connection is made, the browser software receives, across the Internet, data that is stored on remote computers that run Web server software. The network formed of the Web server software and Web browser software talking across the Internet is known as the World Wide Web. Files received from the World Wide Web by the browser software contain pages to be displayed on your computer; each page contains codes that the browser interprets to determine how it should look. These pages can contain virtually any kind of information imaginable—sports scores, financial reports, world news, weather radar, movie schedules, medical research, or even a "live" picture of the mountains on Maui. The creator of a Web page may have made provision for you to send a response or download a file. You may pull up a page for viewing by keying in its universal resource locator (URL), which is its location name, or you can move among the various Web pages through hypertext links, which are icons or underlined text on a Web page. Clicking on a link brings up the Web site that the link refers to. (See figure 25 for an example of using a Web browser.)

To help find material you are looking for, you may use a **search engine.** The home pages of many Internet service providers show the different

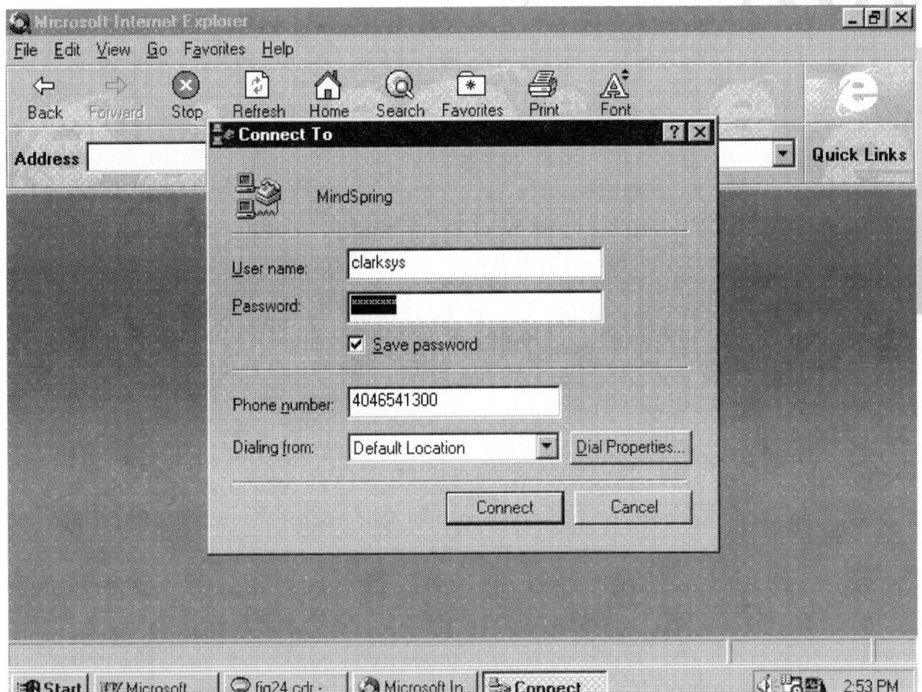

figure 23

Each Internet session starts with a login to the service provider with which you have made arrangements.

search engines that are available. You can link to a desired engine or type in its URL. Basically, to use a search engine, you type in "key words" that are related to the topic for which you want information. The engine then usually provides a descriptive list of links to Web pages or sites that contain the words you entered. The capabilities of different search engines vary. Some try to categorize Web sites, similarly to cataloging a library, while others do a free-form search of all pages they know about.

While the World Wide Web is the most common way of accessing things on the Internet, it is not the only one. Many Internet sites still provide at least part of their data without using the graphic method of the Web. For those sites, several utilities that are located on the remote computers can make life easier.

How Does a Browser Get that Stuff on my Display?

When you use a Web browser to view text, some characters are larger than others, some are bold, and some are underlined. Also, there may be specialized layouts such as bulleted lists or tables. Your browser formats these items according to the rules of a markup language.

To understand a markup language, consider a report that you prepare for a school course. The report probably has a main heading, your name as the author, perhaps some subheadings throughout, and (of course) some normal text in paragraphs. In preparing the report, you decide how large the main heading should be and what font it should use. You also decide the font and size to use for the author's name, subheadings, and paragraph text.

Text on Web pages is sent from the Web server computer to your browser computer with each of its parts (headings and so on) marked as to what it is. Your browser then reads the markings and displays the text using various fonts and sizes. You can change your browser's definition of how headings, paragraphs, and other items are supposed to look. Therefore, the same Web page, viewed on different computers, may look different. The following is a very simple example (using just a few of the many available codes) of how a page may be marked up. Note that many page-creation programs hide the codes so that you never actually see them. If you enter the example with a text editor or word processor, however, and save it under a name such as index.htm, you then can open it with a Web browser and see how it looks. Find the codes in figure 24 as you learn about them here:

- *<HTML>* This stands for **H**yper**T**ext **M**arkup **L**anguage and appears at the top of the page to let your browser know what set of codes has been used to create the page. HTML is a set of markup codes that was created or defined using what is known as SGML, or **S**tandard **G**eneralized **M**arkup **L**anguage. SGML is known as a metalanguage and can be used to create any number of different markup schemes. While some web browsers are capable of handling codes other than those in HTML, HTML is the standard that all browsers know how to interpret. If you look at the end of the example, you will see the code </HTML>. The only difference in this code and the opening <HTML> is the addition of the slash mark. The <HTML> means the start of HTML code, while the </HTML> means the end of HTML code. This is standard syntax, where the slash mark is used to indicate the end of a particular type of item.
- *<Head>* This code indicates the name or heading of the page that you are defining. If you find the </Head>, which indicates the end of the heading, you will see that the words "FJ Software Home Page" are the heading of the page.
- *<Title>* This code indicates that the page heading is to be displayed according to the rules your browser has been set to for a title.

figure 24

This example shows a portion of the markup codes that are available.

```
<HTML>
<Head>
<Title>FJ Software Home Page</Title>
</Head>
<H1>Welcome to FJ Software</H1>
Welcome to the FJ Software home page. Here you can find answers to frequently asked technical support questions. If you cannot find what you need here, please call us at 800-555-1212.<P>
Last Updated 5/17/96
<P>
<I>Click a product name to see tips for optimizing product use as well as answers to frequently asked questions.</I><P>
<A HREF="amax.html">AMax</A> software for home crafters<Br>
<A HREF="crex.html">CRex</A> software for church recreation leagues<Br>
<A HREF="sfan.html">SFan</A> software for steam train aficionados
<p>
</HTML>
```

- <*H1*> The following text, in this case "Welcome to FJ Software," will be displayed as a level 1 heading, which is usually the largest and boldest heading your browser is set up to display. Remember that the </H1> shows the end of the level 1 heading.
- *Normal text* After the level 1 heading, there is text with no code or tag. This means that it is displayed as normal text. Generally, your browser will show such text at a small size and without bold or italics.
- <*P*> This is the paragraph mark. Usually your browser will be set to put some extra space between paragraphs.
- <*I*> This is the code to begin italics. The </I> code shows where the italics stop.
- <*A HREF="amax.htm"*>*Amax*<*/A*> This code sets up a link to another web page. In this case, the name of the file containing the web page is amax.htm. The word "Amax" just before the </A> closing code will be displayed on the screen and underlined as the item on which the user clicks the mouse.
- <*Br*> This is a break code, which tells the browser to go to a new line but without inserting the extra blank space that is typically placed between paragraphs.
- **Gopher** is probably the most used of these utilities. (You might think the name comes from the fact that it "goes for" information, but in reality, it is named for the mascot of the University of Minnesota, where the first such utility was developed.) There are different gophers on different servers, and each gopher aims to provide a menu-driven interface to certain data that is available on the server. For example, the gopher on a university server might allow you to access the library's catalog, daily news, or on-line registration.
- **Telnet** provides the capability to log on to another computer network and use it just as if you were at its location. For example, you can log on to a university computer in another city and use it just as if you were sitting in a computer lab on that campus. Telnet is often invoked for you by a gopher.

Do It!

1 On the Web itself are numerous pages devoted to explanations of HTML and to various software packages that help you create Web pages without having to know the codes. Locate at least one site that shows and defines codes, and make yourself a list giving the codes you think would be most useful. Then, investigate several of the Web page creation programs, many of which can be downloaded from the Internet. Download one of your choice, and create a Web page with it. Then, open the Web page with your browser and look at it.

figure 25

Use the arrows to move backward and forward through pages you have already looked at.

Click Refresh to cause the contents of the page to download again.

Move from wherever you are back to the home page that you have selected.

See a list of your favorite pages so you can immediately go to one of them.

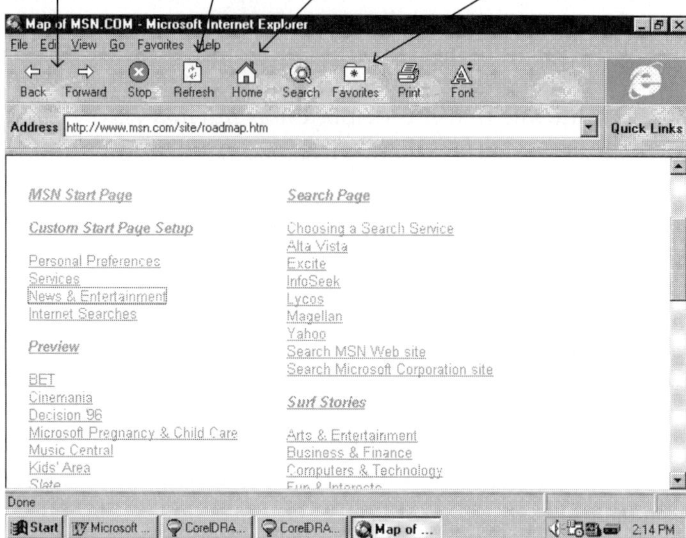

When you log in to your Internet service provider, your browser software will display a start page. While this can be any web page you specify, it initially will default to the start page of your service provider. Other choices, which are indicated as underlined links or icons, may be visible on the screen, or you may have to scroll down to see them. In this example, you are looking at the MSN start page, which among other things shows you the names of different search engines you may select. Because the different search engines perform differently, you will probably want to read the description of each of them and, perhaps, try them all.

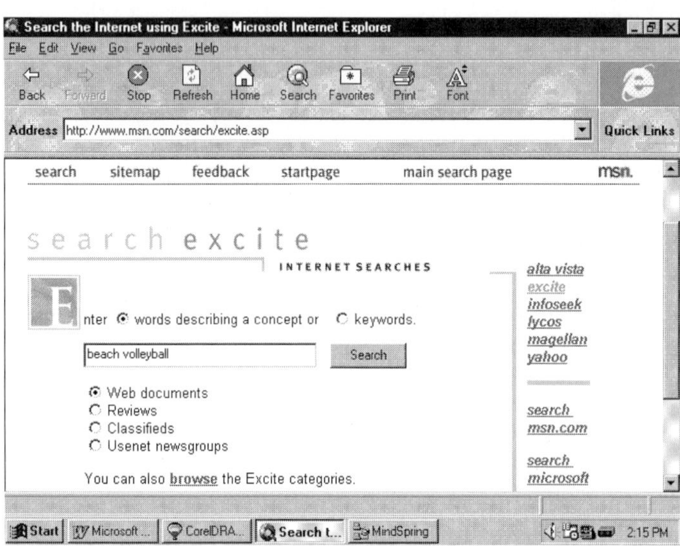

To get to this screen, we clicked on the name of one of the search engines. Note that we have keyed in the term "beach volleyball," which is the subject about which we want to locate information. With most of the search engines, you don't type "and" or "or." In this case, "and" is assumed so the search engine will look for pages that include both the words "beach" and "volleyball." After keying the words to search for, click the button to begin the search.

The search engine presents us with the list of pages it has found. Note that this particular engine has assigned a "goodness" percentage to each find. That is, the items with the highest percentage figures are the ones the search engine software thinks are closer matches to the criteria we keyed in. Now all you have to do is click on the individual item you want to see.

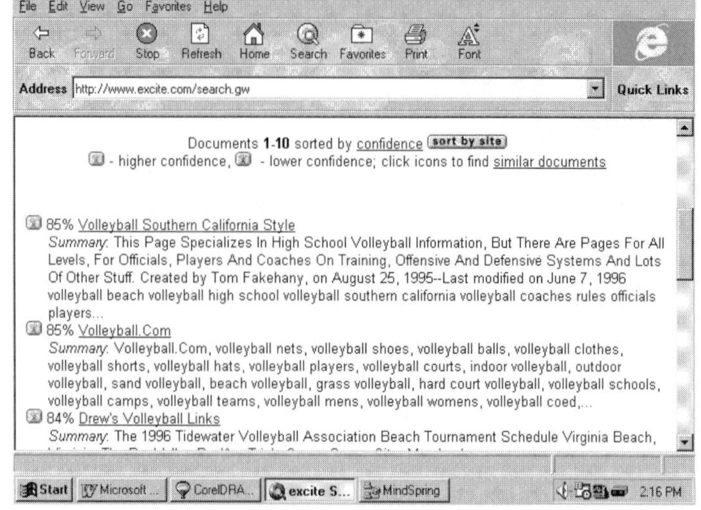

Several utilities available on the Internet make it easier to find items in the vastness of the network. Among them are the following:

- **Archie** helps you to find files you may want to copy from some other site on the Internet. Archie will search the hundreds and hundreds of sites with files available for transfer and find what you are looking for.
- The **Wide Area Information System**, or **WAIS**, enables you to look through the entire text of hundreds of sources of information and find particular words. This utility is also where you find the names of all mailing lists and Usenet topics on the system.
- **Veronica** might be called a smarter version of Archie and Gopher combined. It lets you use Boolean searching (AND and OR) and can look at all of the different gopher menus to find what you are looking for.

Intranet

Most large companies have turned to Internet technology to implement data communication networks that serve only their company and customers. These networks, called "intranets," because they are internal to the company, have several advantages. Compared to using the Internet, the limited access to an Intranet provides a much higher level of security. All the communications connections can be privately arranged, so intranets are not subject to capacity overloads as the Internet is. Because the format of the data that travels between the Web server software and the browser software is independent of the operating system, problems of getting different brands of hardware and software to work together are minimized as well. The uses to which an intranet can be put are myriad, including sales and purchasing, transmission of accounting data, documentation of company products, and the dissemination of company policies and procedures.

Do It!

1 Determine whether you have access to the Internet. If you do, what steps must you carry out to log on?

2 Pick a subject you would like to research. Using your Internet browser, use different search engines to look up the subject and explore some of the Web sites located for you. Analyze the differences in what you found. Then, based on your trials, decide which search engine(s) you like the best.

3 Is there a gopher on the server to which you connect to access the Internet? What services are provided by that gopher?

Summary

In the computer industry, communication of data from one location to another is known as data communication. Data communication is accomplished by using communications hardware, software, and transmission carriers. Computers connected within the same building or campus are known as a local area network.

- Data communication is used by all manner of people, from the home user to the largest corporation.
- The simplest data communication setup is simply two computers equipped with modems "talking" with each other over a regular phone line.
- A modem is the device that translates the digital signals of your computer into the analog signals required by most phone lines and vice versa.
- Transmission speed, expressed as the baud rate or bits per second, is typically 28,800 bits per second with most current modems.
- Modems may be built into the computer's circuitry, added as a plug-in card inside the computer, or attached externally to the computer's serial or modem port.
- In addition to the modem, which provides the hardware connection to attach your computer to the phone line, communications software is needed to send and receive the proper data over the line.
- Data is transmitted to and from microcomputers in a code known as the American Standard Code for Information Interchange. The basic code uses seven bits per character but has been extended by many manufacturers to eight bits; modem software can be set to handle either.
- To use some communications software, your microcomputer must emulate (pretend to be) one of several terminals that were used with mainframes.
- Using a standard phone line for communication is appropriate when the volume of data to be moved is fairly small.
- Typical dial-up services include bulletin board systems providing electronic mail, public messaging services, and file upload and download services.
- Commercial information services such as CompuServe, Prodigy, and America Online provide a wide range of data services, including research, news, travel information and reservations, stock exchange services, interest forums, and file libraries.

Summary

- When the need exists to connect local area networks to one another (or to connect microcomputers to distant mainframes), a wide area network is constructed. Wide area networks can use on-demand lines (dial-up) or dedicated communication links.

- The price of communication links for wide area networks grows in proportion to the bandwidth (speed and quantity of data) that the line can carry. The bulk of the cost for operating most wide area networks is to pay for the communication links.

- Wide area networks are commonly used for, among other things, electronic banking, funds transfer, and electronic communication of purchase orders and invoices.

- The Internet is a worldwide interconnection scheme for computer networks. It allows a user on one network to access the resources of a distant network.

- Internet resources are commonly accessed through the World Wide Web (WWW), which contains pages of information downloaded from Web servers. Use of the WWW is made possible through Web browser software and an Internet service provider.

The following key terms were defined in this module. For each of the following terms, write on a separate piece of paper the number of the definition followed by the letter of the appropriate term.

Terms

A. American Standard Code for Information Interchange (ASCII)
B. Archie
C. bandwidth
D. baud rate
E. bits per second (bps)
F. bulletin board system (BBS)
G. data communication
H. dedicated communication connection
I. electronic data interchange
J. electronic mail (e-mail)
K. fiber optics
L. file library
M. gopher
N. forums
O. the Internet
P. local area network (LAN)
Q. microwave carriers
R. modem
S. modem commands
T. modem port
U. on-demand connection
V. public message service
W. research services
X. serial port
Y. stop bits
Z. telecommunication
AA. Telnet
AB. terminal emulation
AC. Veronica
AD. wide area network (WAN)

Definitions

1 is the name for a serial port on a Macintosh computer

2 a place for the sharing of messages

3 communication of data from one location to another

4 refers to the number of signal events per second

5 a device used to make the connection between the phone system and a computer

6 refers to the signals the software sends to the modem to make it do various things

7 refers to any computer that may be called by other computers for purposes of exchanging messages, uploading files, or downloading files

8 a type of connection on wide area networks that basically means a phone line that has a dial tone and can be accessed as needed

9 provide retrieval of data from a wide variety of sources, such as newspapers, magazines, reference volumes, and various scholarly works

10 a service that enables users of an information service to download various computer files as well as (in some instances) to upload programs to share with other users

11 bits that come after the digits representing the character itself and that designate the end of the character

Matching

12 a way that your terminal uses some communications software, in which your microcomputer must "pretend to be" one of several dumb terminals that were used with mainframes

13 a coding system used for data transmission

14 the resulting group of connected computers when remote communication is needed

15 an arrangement in which computers within the same building are connected

16 the process of transmitting and receiving information from one source (or location) to another

17 an Internet utility used to search for files

18 a connection through which the ones and zeroes of computer language march in single file

19 allows you to post and read messages to and from each other on a bulletin board system

20 refers to the volume or speed at which a communication channel operates

21 a service that performs a function similar to the bulletin board in your school, in which messages and announcements are placed in a special mailbox for all valid users

22 transmit data on a straight path from one microwave station to another

23 a manner of connecting wide area networks that is connected at all times

24 a cable that consists of one or more hair-thin strands of material capable of conducting light images

25 a system for electronically transmitting purchase orders, shipping orders, and invoices

26 the speed of a modem expressed as the number of binary digits that go across the line

27 the largest wide area network

28 the basic navigation tool for Internet users

29 an Internet utility used for connecting with other servers

30 an Internet utility that lets you do Boolean searching

Review

1. What is telecommunications? (Obj. 1)
2. Describe some typical uses of telecommunications using computers. (Obj. 1)
3. What device is used to connect a computer to a typical phone line? What does this device do? (Obj. 2)
4. Will modems be necessary as time goes by? Why or why not? (Obj. 2)
5. What has been the trend in the speed of data communication using modems? (Obj. 3)
6. What kind of port do modems use to communicate with your computer? What are the characteristics of this port? (Obj. 3)
7. List the modem settings that must be the same at both ends of a communication link for communication to take place. (Obj. 3)
8. What is the ASCII code? What are its characteristics? (Obj. 3)
9. How many different characters can be represented during data communication if your modem software is set for seven data bits? For eight data bits? (Obj. 3)
10. Discuss the factors to consider in deciding whether a regular dial-up phone line is adequate for data communication. (Obj. 4)
11. What is the difference between a computer bulletin board system and an information service? (Obj. 5, 6)
12. List and describe some of the services provided by typical computer bulletin board systems. (Obj. 5)
13. List some of the information services available to computer users. (Obj. 6)
14. List and discuss some of the typical application areas provided by information services. (Obj. 6)
15. What is the relationship between communication speed and cost of the communication line? (Obj. 4)
16. Compare the relative speeds of typical local area networks with that of typical communication connections for wide area networks. (Obj. 4)
17. Describe some typical applications of wide area networks. (Obj. 4)
18. What is the Internet? What benefit does it provide for the computer user? (Obj. 7)
19. Describe some of the utilities that are typically available on an Internet server. (Obj. 7)

Activities

1 *Writing* Does a computer that is available to you have a modem? If so, write a profile about the modem, giving its brand and model, what its possible transmission speeds are, and whether it is built-in, internal, or external. Also, include information on the communications software that is available for use with the modem.

2 *Writing* Working as a group member, consult a personal computer magazine, your local newspaper, a computer store, or other sources for information to prepare a brief report about the modems currently available for popular microcomputers. As a group, decide which brand/model provides the best combination of price and value and which source seems to provide the most value. Prepare a handout supporting your conclusions for other groups in the class to study.

3 *Global Perspectives* Working with your instructor, decide on a computer bulletin board system that you will access. Each class member or group (depending on your teacher's instructions) should pick a different system. Dial into the bulletin board, and explore the services available on it. Prepare a report describing those services, and share the report with the class. As a class, discuss the relative value of the different services that were discovered. With your instructor's permission, one or more groups may want to access a bulletin board system in a different country.

4 *Ethics* As an individual or group (depending on your teacher's instructions), select a particular service area provided by an information service to which you have access. Connect to the service, explore the area, and report to the class on your findings. Among the areas to choose from would typically be making travel reservations; accessing news, weather, and sports; shopping; doing research in a database; playing games; "chatting" with other users; retrieving financial information; and sending electronic mail. After exploring the area, write a brief paper dealing with the ethics of using the service.

5 *Writing and Speaking* If you have access through the Internet or some other connection, attach to the media-center catalog of a library at a major university. Retrieve a listing of all resources the library has available about a subject in which you are interested, and compare this listing with the resources that are available in your local school's media center. Share your results in a written report and an oral report to the class.

6 *Math, Speaking, and Writing* Assume that you are in charge of the computers for a library system that has one location in each of three adjoining counties in your state. Because you want the users at any one location to be able to research the holdings of all the locations, you have decided to use one file server in a central location to store the catalogs of all three locations. Access to the catalog for library users will be through a wide area network. The question to be answered now is whether to use a client/server database system, which would be about $6000 more expensive to install than a non-client/server system. You have wisely decided to look at communication costs before making your decision.

Activities

The three libraries together have about 100,000 books. Many of the library patrons like to do keyword searches because they identify many more books than just an author, subject, or title search. This means the catalog program must search all of the notes that have been entered in the catalog as well as searching the title, author, or subject. To help speed things up, you can set up the system to index the words in the notes, but that index consists of about 40,000 entries with an average length of 20 characters per entry.

If you do not use a client/server database, all of the data in the index must travel across the communication line each time someone does a keyword search. If you use a client/server database, the server sends back to the local computer only the records for the books that contain the desired keyword(s).

Working with a partner, determine how long it will take for a patron to do a single keyword search without client/server technology if the computers are attached by a standard phone line. Is this length of time acceptable? If not, decide what speed would be necessary for acceptable performance, and investigate the cost of a communication link working at that speed.

Prepare a written report making a recommendation to your instructor on whether to go with a client/server database. Be sure to include all of the supporting data and reasons that you have developed. If you have access to the software to do so, include graphs to support your recommendation.

7 *Writing* If you have access to the Internet, compare what is available to you on it as opposed to what is available on an information system such as CompuServe or Prodigy. Because of the enormous quantities of data available on both sources, this comparison will, of necessity, be somewhat superficial. Prepare a one- or two-page comparison of your findings, and include a conclusion about which service you prefer to meet your own needs. Be sure that you explain why you picked the one you did.

8 *Math and Science* Work in a group with several other students. Pretend that you have $10,000 to invest in stocks. Use the resources of an information service or the Internet to do research on companies in which you might like to invest. Prepare two portfolios, one of various stocks of your own choosing and the other of biotechnology stocks. Make a decision on which stocks you would buy.

Enter the data on your stock purchase in the two portfolios into a spreadsheet program, being sure to include the number of shares, price per share, and value. Once a week for the number of weeks specified by your instructor, use the computer to look up the current prices of the stock and add that data to your spreadsheet. Use the spreadsheet to maintain a line graph showing the changes in individual stock prices as well as the total value of your portfolios. Compare the performance of your mixed portfolio and your biotechnology portfolio.

9 *Internet* The available options for computer communication are constantly changing. Modem speeds are increasing, ISDN service is becoming more common, and cable modem service is becoming more widespread. Using your Web browser, search the Internet for data on the communication options that are available in your area, along with their costs. Prepare a spreadsheet listing the different options, their maximum speeds, and the typical monthly cost.

Word Processing

WP

Overview

Word-processing software is software that is designed to assist individuals or businesses in preparing documents. Modern word-processing software is often referred to as being full-featured software, which means that the software has the capabilities to perform a wide array of tasks. For example, full-featured word processors allow the user to enter text, revise text, incorporate graphics, check spelling, reference a thesaurus, check grammar, print, and store documents electronically. The software will also allow you to add, move, and delete individual characters, sentences, pages, and large blocks of text. In addition, you may specify margins, page length, and a variety of character fonts and print styles. It makes no difference whether the text is in the form of a memo, letter, report, newspaper, or legal document; word processing can make its preparation faster and more accurate. While businesses operated successfully for years with only handwriting and typewriters, the advent of word-processing software has made working with text much more efficient.

Objectives

1. Describe the need for word-processing software.
2. List advantages of using word-processing software.
3. Enter, edit, process, output, and store documents.
4. Explain and demonstrate how word-processing software is used for document construction.
5. Use spell checking, thesaurus, grammar checking, mail merge, and mailing label features to improve the quality and accuracy of a document.
6. Understand how word-processing software is used by writers.
7. Understand how word-processing software is used for desktop publishing.
8. Determine hardware needs in relation to the word-processing capabilities being anticipated.

Careers

Word Processing Software : A Writer's Best Friend

Word-processing software has made life easier for writers—and for editors and publishers.

In the not so-distant past, writers laboriously typed manuscript for books or articles, frequently retyping pages to correct misspellings or enhance the wording. Large volumes of paper manuscript were exchanged between writers and editors, and scissors and paste were often used to rearrange the sequence of the material. Marked-up, pasted-together material then went to a typesetter, who had to decipher the markings and key the material into a machine that produced clean, typeset copy. Sections of material were pasted onto boards, along with pictures, to develop the desired layout. After much proofreading and further copy corrections, the laid-out material was photographed, and plates were made from which the material was printed.

Word-processing software has changed all this by allowing writers and editors to make many kinds of changes much more easily. In addition, files can be sent by modem between the computers of a writer and editor, and finished manuscripts can be printed by a laser printer or sent to a typesetting machine for final production.

Following are nine advantages of word-processing software for writers, and for businesses in general:

1. Keying errors that are made when creating a document are easily corrected by backspacing and rekeying.
2. After initial keying of the document, errors can easily be corrected by moving the insertion point to the error and rekeying.
3. Revisions to the entered document can be made at any time. Blocks of text (phrases, sentences, paragraphs) can be copied or moved to new locations. In addition, font styles and sizes can be changed without rekeying text.
4. A spelling checker, thesaurus, and/or grammar checker can be used to improve accuracy and readability.
5. Mail merge eliminates the need to rekey a document for each entry on a mailing list.
6. Documents (or parts of documents) can be stored for later reuse.
7. Documents are more accurate because revisions do not require a retyping of the entire document, and text portions that are used repeatedly can be stored on disk and re-used. This reduces the likelihood of introducing errors into a document after proofreading.
8. Documents can be stored and retrieved electronically, eliminating the need for distribution of paper copies.
9. Documents can be transmitted electronically from one location to another, or put on floppy disks and passed from one office to another or even mailed to another location.

How a Word-Processing System Functions

After you enter the command to load the word-processing application into memory, the opening screen appears. Figure 1 shows an opening screen for a full-featured word-processing program.

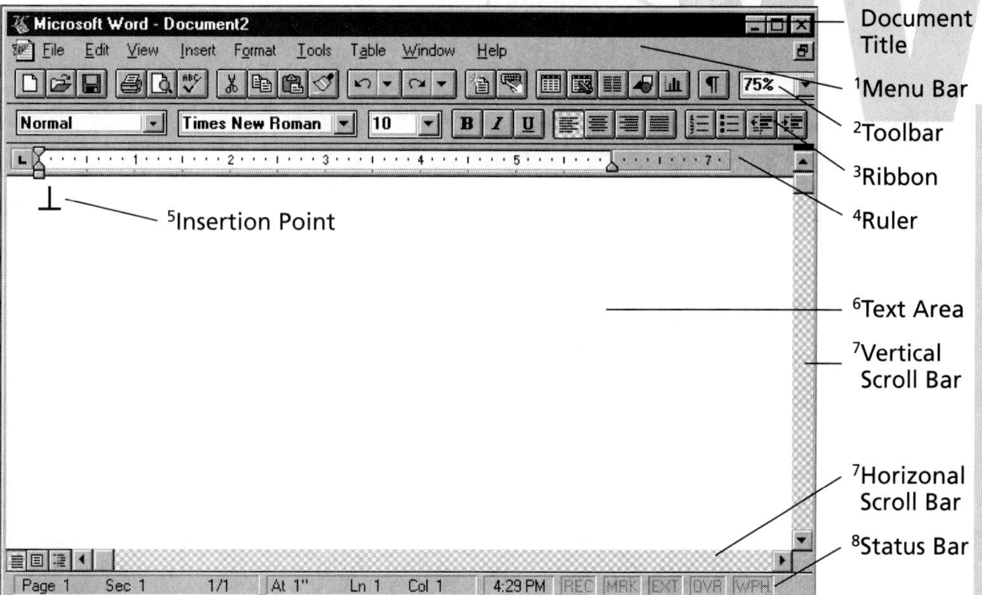

figure 1

Example of a full-featured word-processor Screen Display (Microsoft Word).

A **menu** is used to display and select the commands to operate the word-processor software. For example, commands that retrieve, store, print, and format data in the document are chosen from menus. The **toolbar** contains icons (often referred to as buttons) from which the most frequently used commands may be quickly chosen. For example, when the icon depicting a printer is chosen, a hard copy of the word-processed document will be printed on an attached printer. The **ribbon** is used to change the appearance of selected text. For example, selected text may be changed to a different font and point size or displayed and printed in bold, italics, or underlined characters. The **ruler** is used to change paragraph indentation and margin settings, and the **insertion point** appears as a blinking vertical bar that indicates where text will be inserted when typed. The **text area** is the large, empty portion of the screen display that displays text as it is keyed or graphics that are incorporated into the document; in figure 1, this area is blank because no text has been keyed in. The **vertical** and **horizontal scroll bars**, which are located along the right side and bottom of the display screen, respectively, are used to move a document through the text area for viewing. The **status bar** displays information such as the current page number, total number of pages in the document, current line and column of the insertion point, and the status of several keys such as CAPS and NUM, which indicate that the Caps Lock and Num Lock keys are engaged.

Menus

A menu-driven operating environment is easy to use. Drop-down menus, icons, toolbars, and other user-friendly features make operating the software an intuitive process rather than a completely learned one. Training is quick and the learning curve short. Extensive "Help" systems also mean that even a beginner can be productive immediately.

Another advantage of menu-driven software is that because all programs operate the same and use similar commands, users can soon be up and running other applications that use a similar menu-driven design (called a standard user interface). For example, notice the similarities in the File menus of the popular full-featured word processors shown in figure 2. They each contain commands to create a new document, open (load) an existing document file, save a document, print a document, and exit the software.

figure 2

Examples of file drop-down menus.

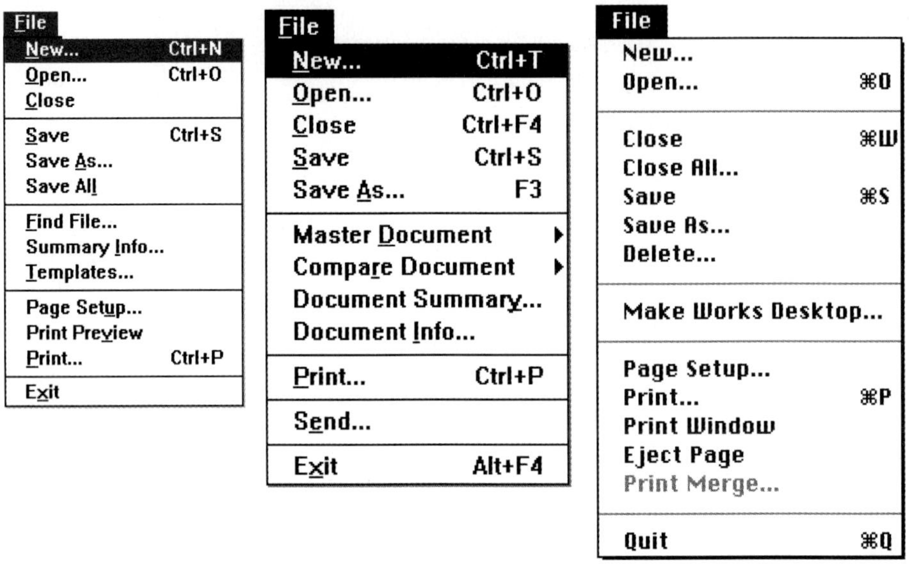

File
New... Ctrl+N
Open... Ctrl+O
Close
Save Ctrl+S
Save As...
Save All
Find File...
Summary Info...
Templates...
Page Setup...
Print Preview
Print... Ctrl+P
Exit

File
New... Ctrl+T
Open... Ctrl+O
Close Ctrl+F4
Save Ctrl+S
Save As... F3
Master Document
Compare Document
Document Summary...
Document Info...
Print... Ctrl+P
Send...
Exit Alt+F4

File
New...
Open... ⌘O
Close ⌘W
Close All...
Save ⌘S
Save As...
Delete...
Make Works Desktop...
Page Setup...
Print... ⌘P
Print Window
Eject Page
Print Merge...
Quit ⌘Q

Entering Documents

Entering a document refers to the task of inputting text and graphics into the computer. Typically, text is entered through use of the keyboard and graphics are inserted from art (called clipart) stored on disk, even though scanners are increasingly used for entering previously keyed text and graphic images from other sources. For example, a company logo may be read by a scanner and stored on disk. Later, the logo image can be read from disk by the word processor and inserted into a document as part of the business' letterhead without having to redo artwork for use by the computer.

Text appears on the screen as it is entered by the operator. If desired, formatting that includes specific character fonts, point sizes, line spacing, margin settings, left/center/right justification, boldface, underline, or italics may be included when the text is initially entered or specified later.

When word-processing software is capable of showing the document on the screen the same way that it will look when printed, it is said to have **WYSIWYG** capability. WYSIWYG stands for "What You See Is What You Get." Obviously, it is preferable that what you see on the screen resembles as closely as possible what is going to come out on paper when a document is printed.

The degree to which WYSIWYG is implemented with word-processing software depends not only on the software itself but on the hardware as well. Most of today's computers, printers, and word-processing software are capable of showing not just simple enhancements, such as boldface print, but also graphics, various type fonts and sizes, and proportionally spaced print.

Editing and Processing Documents

Processing by word-processing software can occur either during the text-entry process or the editing and revision process. When editing and revising text, the user is changing the text. Changes may be made either to correct errors or improve the technical quality of the writing. Even after an entire document has been entered, the insertion point can be moved back to an error and the correction keyed in. The insertion point can be moved either by the directional keyboard control keys or a mouse. Use of a mouse has become increasingly popular with word-processing software, and a mouse is especially appropriate for making menu choices, moving the insertion point to a distant location in the document, and selecting portions of text.

Inserting Text

You can easily insert characters, words, phrases, sentences, and even pages of text while you are editing a document. Use the following steps to insert the word "former," which was omitted from the sample letter, as illustrated in figures 3 and 4:

1. Position the insertion point at the desired location.
2. Make sure the insert function is turned on. (Press the key labeled Insert or Ins to toggle the insert function on or off.)
3. Key in the desired text.

As each character is keyed, the following text will move one space to the right to allow for the insertion. Also, notice in figures 3 and 4 that the word "for" at the end of the line containing the insertion automatically moved down and to the beginning of the next line to make space for the inserted word.

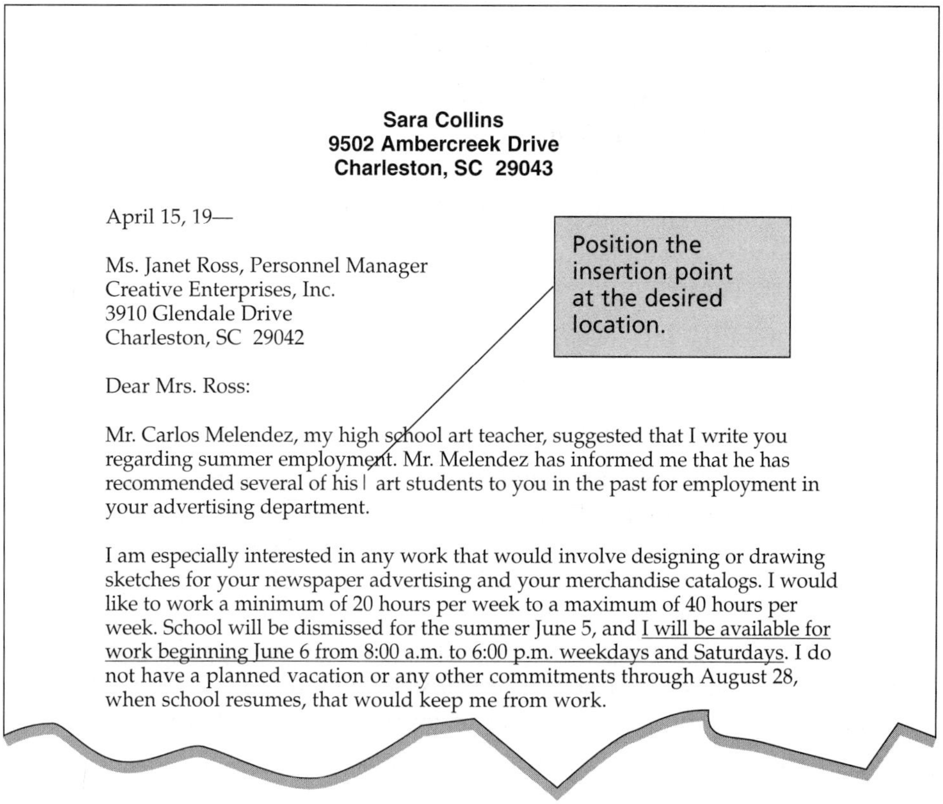

Sara Collins
9502 Ambercreek Drive
Charleston, SC 29043

April 15, 19—

Ms. Janet Ross, Personnel Manager
Creative Enterprises, Inc.
3910 Glendale Drive
Charleston, SC 29042

Dear Mrs. Ross:

Mr. Carlos Melendez, my high school art teacher, suggested that I write you regarding summer employment. Mr. Melendez has informed me that he has recommended several of his | art students to you in the past for employment in your advertising department.

I am especially interested in any work that would involve designing or drawing sketches for your newspaper advertising and your merchandise catalogs. I would like to work a minimum of 20 hours per week to a maximum of 40 hours per week. School will be dismissed for the summer June 5, and I will be available for work beginning June 6 from 8:00 a.m. to 6:00 p.m. weekdays and Saturdays. I do not have a planned vacation or any other commitments through August 28, when school resumes, that would keep me from work.

Position the insertion point at the desired location.

figure 3

Position the insertion point at the location where a correction or insertion is desired.

figure 4

Key the correction or added text (in this case, "former").

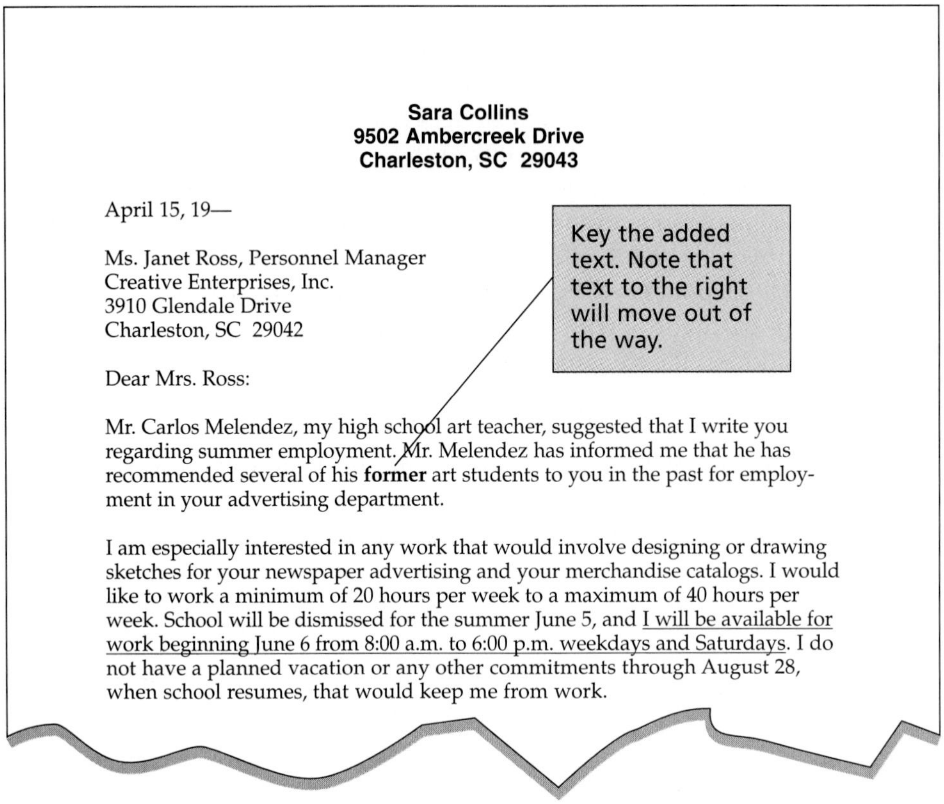

Sara Collins
9502 Ambercreek Drive
Charleston, SC 29043

April 15, 19—

Ms. Janet Ross, Personnel Manager
Creative Enterprises, Inc.
3910 Glendale Drive
Charleston, SC 29042

Dear Mrs. Ross:

Mr. Carlos Melendez, my high school art teacher, suggested that I write you regarding summer employment. Mr. Melendez has informed me that he has recommended several of his **former** art students to you in the past for employment in your advertising department.

I am especially interested in any work that would involve designing or drawing sketches for your newspaper advertising and your merchandise catalogs. I would like to work a minimum of 20 hours per week to a maximum of 40 hours per week. School will be dismissed for the summer June 5, and I will be available for work beginning June 6 from 8:00 a.m. to 6:00 p.m. weekdays and Saturdays. I do not have a planned vacation or any other commitments through August 28, when school resumes, that would keep me from work.

Key the added text. Note that text to the right will move out of the way.

Moving Text

Moving a block of text is another revision that you can make. Moving or rearranging a block of text is called **cutting-and-pasting**. The block of text that you move may include only one character, or it may include several pages. Use the following steps to switch the second and third paragraphs of the sample letter, as illustrated in figures 5 and 6:

1. Select the text to be moved. If you are using a mouse, simply move the mouse to the beginning of the block of text, then click-and-drag the mouse to the end of the block that you wish to move.
2. Cut the text from the current location. (Cut text is temporarily stored in memory in a place called the clipboard.) The Cut command is usually located in the Edit menu.
3. Position the insertion point where you want the text to be moved.
4. Paste the text in its new location. The Paste command is usually located in the Edit menu.

Copying may be done in a similar fashion. When copying, the selected text remains in its original location and is duplicated in the new position (the original copy is then cut from the document). Many full-featured word processors permit the selected text to be dragged with a mouse to its new location, where it is automatically inserted.

The amount of editing or revision that can be done on a document is unlimited. Likewise, the number of sessions at which this work can be done is unlimited. For example, a document may be entered and saved to disk.

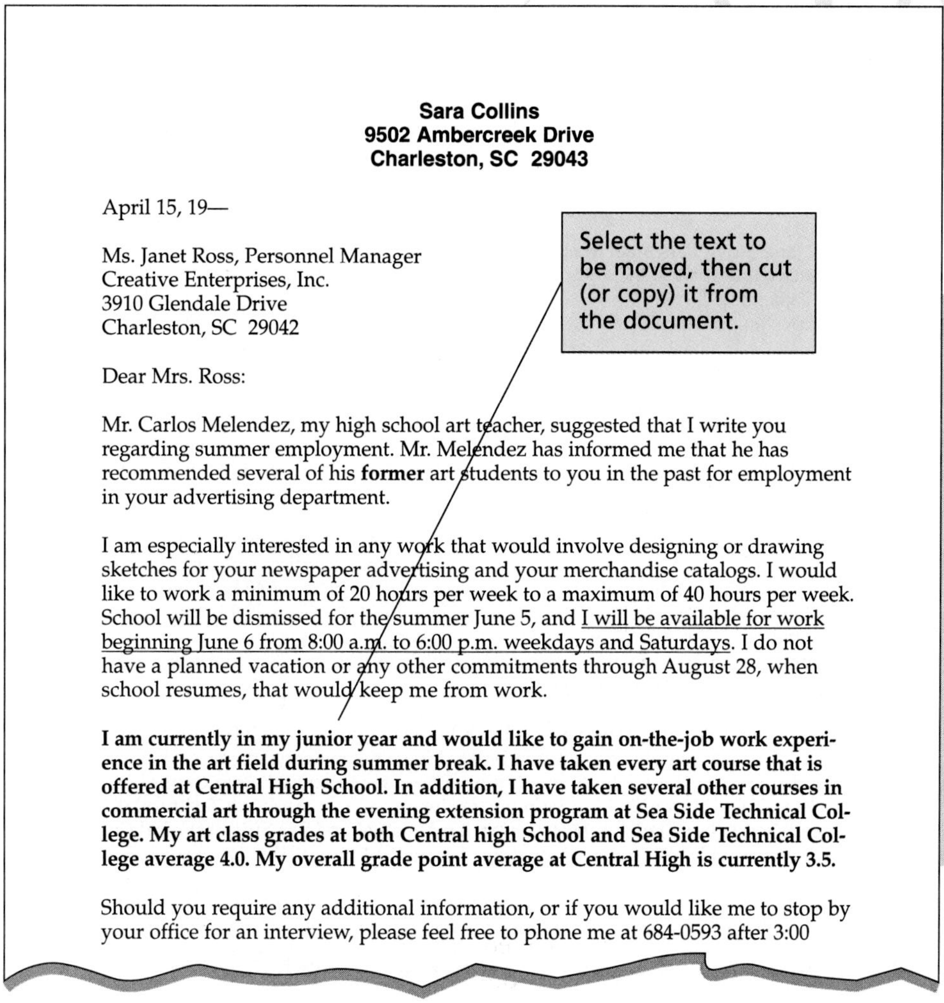

Sara Collins
9502 Ambercreek Drive
Charleston, SC 29043

April 15, 19—

Ms. Janet Ross, Personnel Manager
Creative Enterprises, Inc.
3910 Glendale Drive
Charleston, SC 29042

Dear Mrs. Ross:

Mr. Carlos Melendez, my high school art teacher, suggested that I write you regarding summer employment. Mr. Meléndez has informed me that he has recommended several of his **former** art students to you in the past for employment in your advertising department.

I am especially interested in any work that would involve designing or drawing sketches for your newspaper advertising and your merchandise catalogs. I would like to work a minimum of 20 hours per week to a maximum of 40 hours per week. School will be dismissed for the summer June 5, and I will be available for work beginning June 6 from 8:00 a.m. to 6:00 p.m. weekdays and Saturdays. I do not have a planned vacation or any other commitments through August 28, when school resumes, that would keep me from work.

I am currently in my junior year and would like to gain on-the-job work experience in the art field during summer break. I have taken every art course that is offered at Central High School. In addition, I have taken several other courses in commercial art through the evening extension program at Sea Side Technical College. My art class grades at both Central high School and Sea Side Technical College average 4.0. My overall grade point average at Central High is currently 3.5.

Should you require any additional information, or if you would like me to stop by your office for an interview, please feel free to phone me at 684-0593 after 3:00

Select the text to be moved, then cut (or copy) it from the document.

figure 5

To rearrange text, the text to be moved must first be selected.

Later, the user may come back, load the document from disk into memory, make as many revisions as desired, and again save the text to disk.

Formatting a Document

One of the advantages of word processing is that you can control exactly how you want your document to look when it is printed. Controlling those characteristics that affect the appearance of a document when printed is called **text formatting**.

Word processors have been designed with several features that facilitate text formatting to give documents a more professional appearance. For example, you may use a variety of different character fonts, sizes, styles, and colors to draw attention to selected text in a document. Figure 7 shows an example of how to specify several character format options; most word processors permit setting these options via buttons in the toolbar or drop-down menus.

You may also format a document by changing the text indentations, alignment, spacing, margins, and by creating tables, borders, and frames. Figure 8 shows an example of how to specify several paragraph format options; most word processors permit setting these options via buttons in the toolbar, drop-down menus, or icons in the ruler.

figure 6

Words, phrases, sentences, paragraphs, and entire pages may be moved anywhere within a document by positioning the insertion point to the new location and using the appropriate command to move or "paste" the text into that location.

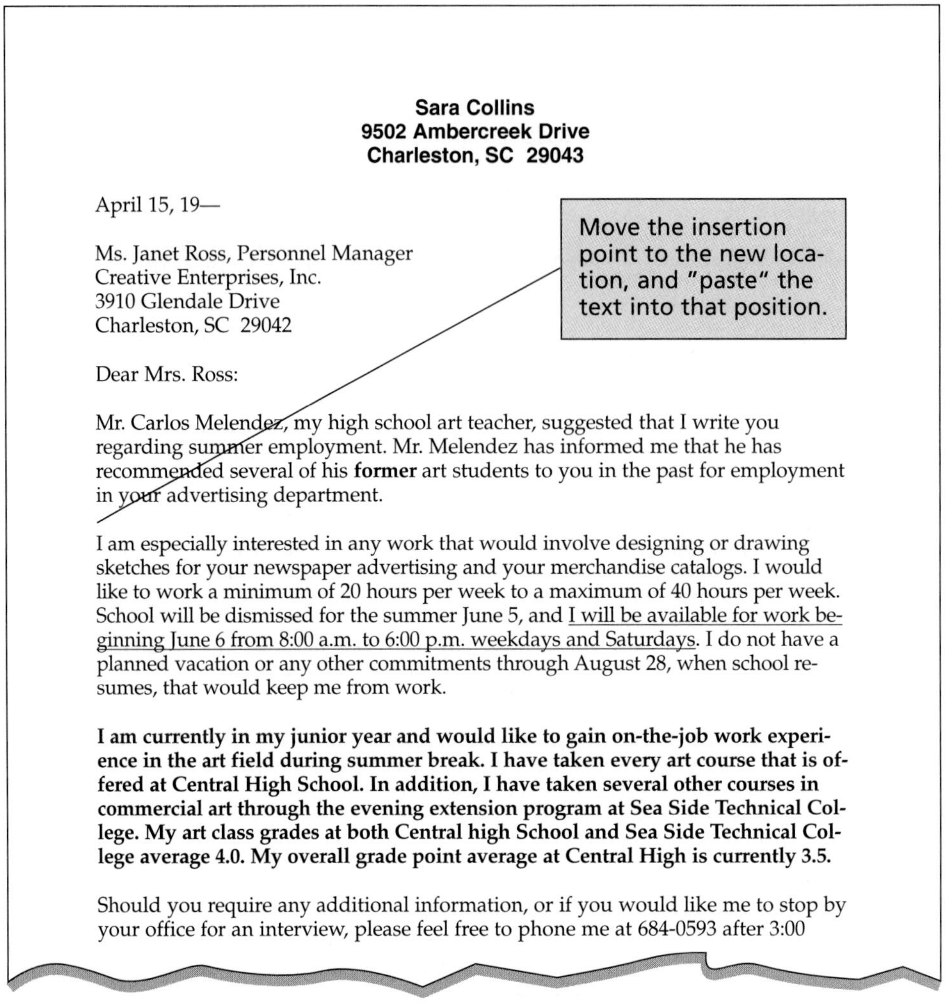

Sara Collins
9502 Ambercreek Drive
Charleston, SC 29043

April 15, 19—

Ms. Janet Ross, Personnel Manager
Creative Enterprises, Inc.
3910 Glendale Drive
Charleston, SC 29042

Dear Mrs. Ross:

Mr. Carlos Melendez, my high school art teacher, suggested that I write you regarding summer employment. Mr. Melendez has informed me that he has recommended several of his **former** art students to you in the past for employment in your advertising department.

I am especially interested in any work that would involve designing or drawing sketches for your newspaper advertising and your merchandise catalogs. I would like to work a minimum of 20 hours per week to a maximum of 40 hours per week. School will be dismissed for the summer June 5, and I will be available for work beginning June 6 from 8:00 a.m. to 6:00 p.m. weekdays and Saturdays. I do not have a planned vacation or any other commitments through August 28, when school resumes, that would keep me from work.

I am currently in my junior year and would like to gain on-the-job work experience in the art field during summer break. I have taken every art course that is offered at Central High School. In addition, I have taken several other courses in commercial art through the evening extension program at Sea Side Technical College. My art class grades at both Central high School and Sea Side Technical College average 4.0. My overall grade point average at Central High is currently 3.5.

Should you require any additional information, or if you would like me to stop by your office for an interview, please feel free to phone me at 684-0593 after 3:00

Move the insertion point to the new location, and "paste" the text into that position.

Outputting a Document

Once a document is entered and in the form desired, it may be printed or transmitted to another location. While most documents are printed in hard-copy form, the number of electronically transmitted documents is growing. If a computer is equipped with a laser printer, the quality of printouts can be higher than those from other types of printers.

Printing output is accomplished by giving the appropriate command or making the appropriate menu choice (choosing the Print command from one of the File menus shown in figure 2). When the Print command is chosen, a Print window similar to that shown in figure 9 will appear; using this, you may specify the number of copies, a specific page or range of pages, as well as other options. If the word processor being used to produce the document has full WYSIWYG capability, the screen display will show the different fonts just as the printer does.

Storing a Document

As indicated earlier, any text that is entered into the computer with word-processing software can be stored for later use. Some word-processing software require that a document be stored before it can be printed; others allow it to be printed before it is stored. It is a good idea, however, to store the document first. Then, if the printer has problems and hangs up the computer, the document will not be lost.

figure 7

Examples of font, size, and style options.

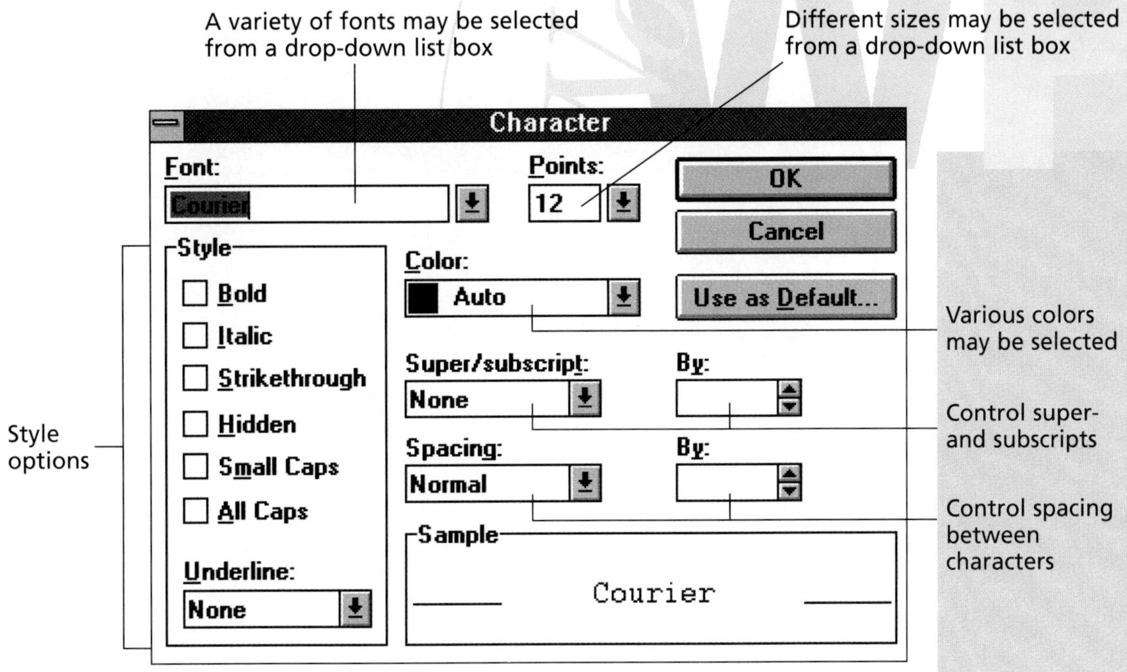

A variety of fonts may be selected from a drop-down list box

Different sizes may be selected from a drop-down list box

Character

Font: Courier

Points: 12

OK

Cancel

Style

Bold

Italic

Strikethrough

Hidden

Small Caps

All Caps

Underline: None

Color: Auto

Use as Default...

Super/subscript: None

By:

Spacing: Normal

By:

Sample

Courier

Style options

Various colors may be selected

Control super- and subscripts

Control spacing between characters

figure 8

Examples of alignment, indentation, and spacing options.

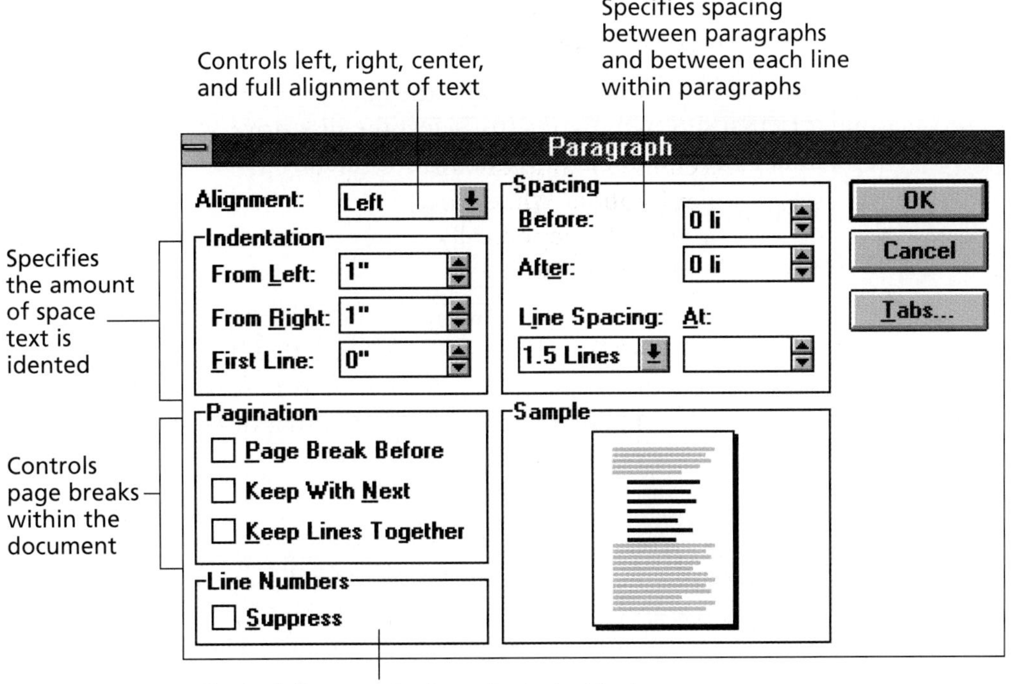

figure 9

Example of a Print window.

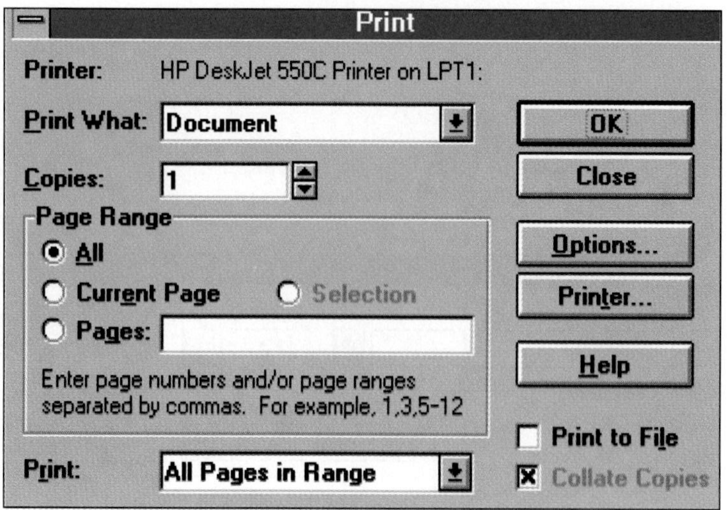

Storing a document is done by giving the appropriate command or making the appropriate menu choice. Most word processors use the Save and Save As... commands to store a word-processing document to disk. The Save command enables you to save your work to disk under the current file name (the first time data is saved, you will be asked to supply a file name). The Save As... command is identical to the Save command, but it permits you to save a document to disk with a different file name each time it is chosen. This command is very useful for making a backup, which is simply a copy of an existing file. Use the following steps to save the sample letter to disk with a file name of SWCLETTR:

1. Choose the Save As... command from the File menu.
2. When the Save As... window appears (the Save As... window may be similar to that shown in figure 10), select the disk drive and the directory/folder where you wish to save the document.
3. Key the desired file name (SWCLETTR).
4. Press the OK button.

Once a document is stored, it may be recalled whenever desired for further revision or printing. Some word processors require that the user know the name of the document to recall it. Others allow users to search for documents by using keywords contained in them or by browsing through a directory of file names.

Word-Processing Features

In addition to the basic functions of word processors discussed previously, there are many other features, or enhancements, available. The quantity and quality of these features depends on the particular software. This section covers the most common features included in full-featured word-processing software, including spelling checkers, thesaurus software, grammar and style software, mail merge, and mailing label generation. Figure 20 identifies additional featues of most full-featured word processors. These include capabilities to do the following: perform basic mathematical functions, sequence a

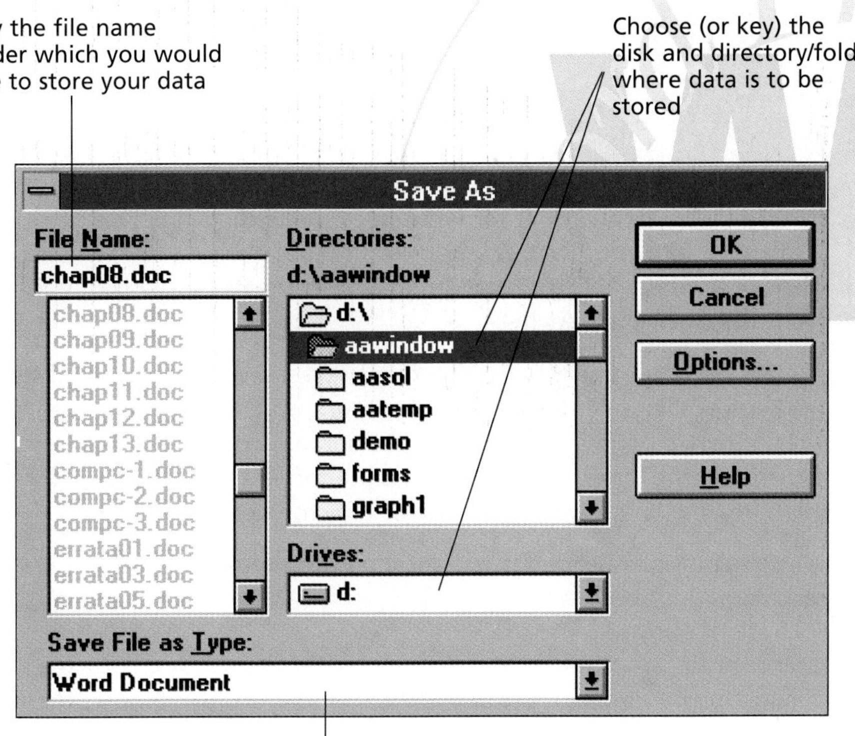

figure 10

Save As... window.

list of numbers or alphabetic data, permit multiple documents to be active at the same time, split the viewing window to permit working with two or more documents, and perform automatic backup at various time intervals.

Spelling Checkers

Spell-checking capability is built into most full-featured word-processing software, while it is optional as a separate program for use with others. When the capability is built-in, a simple command or menu choice invokes execution of the spelling checker.

Essentially, a **spelling checker** looks up words of text in its dictionaries and calls attention to the not-found words. Usually, there is a general dictionary consisting of many thousands of words stored on disk. In addition to the general dictionary, there may be special dictionaries for particular disciplines, such as law or medicine, plus individual dictionaries made up of words added by the user over a period of time. Typically, spelling checkers can be asked to check varying amounts of text, anywhere from one word to the entire document.

Most spelling checkers operate while in edit mode and stop at each word that is not found in the dictionary to allow for correction. More capable spelling checkers stop at each suspect word, but they also display suggested words that may have been intended and allow the chosen replacement word to be entered into the document by a simple keystroke or mouse click.

Figure 11 shows a screen during a typical spell-checking operation. Note that the spelling checker has found a word that it did not find in its dictionaries, and it is suggesting dictionary words that are phonetically close to the misspelled word. Also, note that the user can choose a word from the list by

Do It!

1 Using any word processor at your disposal, enter the text provided by your instructor (without formatting) of the letter. After the text is entered, save it to your data disk or directory/folder with a file name of XXXWP-A (where *XXX* are your initials, *WP* is the module code, and *A* identifies this Do It! activity).

2 Format the letter you just entered. Use a similar font, size, and style. Also, use similar indentations, margin settings, and spacing between the lines of text. If your word processor has border capabilities, place a border around the letter. When you complete formatting, print your document, then save it to your data disk or directory/folder.

3 Prepare your own letter to a local business regarding summer employment.

using keyboard control keys or the mouse and then indicate the action to take by striking one key or clicking the mouse on the choice. If the choice is made to correct the highlighted word, the erroneous spelling is immediately replaced by the correct one. Many spell checkers are also capable of checking the spelling for different languages.

Thesaurus Software

A thesaurus is a list of synonyms and is useful in finding alternative words to express ideas. **Thesaurus software** functions very similar to spelling-checker software, except that the user selects the word for which a synonym is desired. The program then looks up the word in a thesaurus stored on disk and suggests alternative words (and in many cases, their definitions). For example, if the person entering the document wished to use a word

figure 11

A spelling checker can look up words in its dictionary and call attention to those misspelled.

Words not in the dictionary are identified
The ease with which spelling erros can be corrected, and the minimal amount of time it takes to run the spelling checker software, justifies its use with every word processed document. In the long run, it will save time and enhance the quality and accuracy of the document.
To use the spelling checker, simply choose the spelling checker icon button in the toolbar after keying the document. Please note that formal names, addresses, technical terms, etc., are not available in the word processor's di
ellings,
check them cl
Spelling: English (US)
Not in Dictionary: erros
Change To: errors
Suggestions: Eros errs errors error arose eras
Ignore
Ignore All
Change
Change All
Add
Undo Last
Suggest
Cancel
Add Words To: CUSTOM.DIC
Options...
The user may choose a word from the list of suggestions that appears

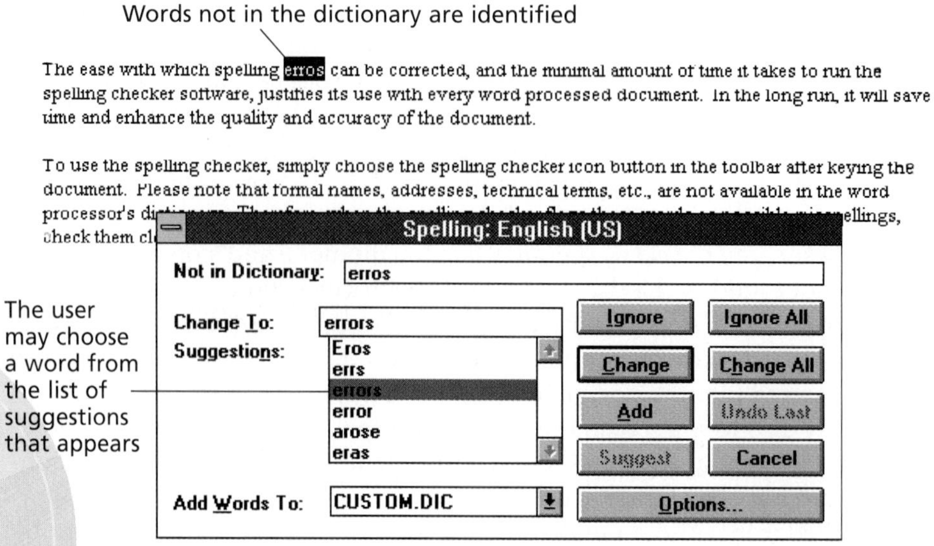

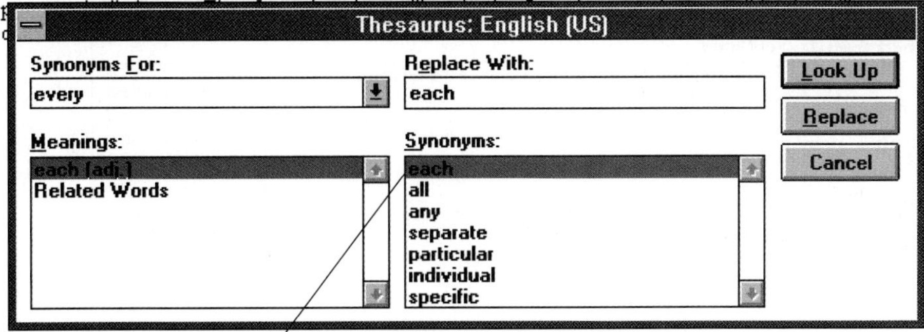
A word is selected in the text
The ease with which spelling errors can be corrected, and the minimal amount of time it takes to run the spelling checker software, justifies its use with every word processed document. In the long run, it will save time and enhance the quality and accuracy of the document.
To use the spelling checker, simply choose the spelling checker icon button in the toolbar after keying the document. Please note that formal names, addresses, technical terms, etc., are not available in the word
Thesaurus: English (US)
Synonyms For:
every
Replace With:
each
Look Up
Replace
Cancel
Meanings:
each (adj.)
Related Words
Synonyms:
each
all
any
separate
particular
individual
specific
A replacement word may be chosen from a list of available synonyms

figure 12

A thesaurus program allows the user to choose a replacement word from a list of alternatives.

other than "every," as entered in the second line, the screen might look like that in figure 12. At this point, the word "every" has been selected, and the thesaurus software has been invoked. The user would then use keyboard control keys or a mouse to choose a replacement word ("each" in this illustration). As soon as a replacement word is chosen, the new word will automatically take the place of the original one in the document. Note that many full-featured word processors have thesaurus software that is also capable of providing the same capabilities for many different languages.

Grammar and Style Software

Grammar and **style software** can do various types of grammatical error checking once a document has been entered into the computer. Grammar and style software may be either built into the word-processing software or provided as a separate program that is capable of reading the word processor's document files. While the capabilities vary depending on the software, some of the commonly made checks are shown in figure 13.

Depending on the software, corrective action may be suggested. For example, the sentence shown in figure 14 has been identified by a grammar checker. The checker has suggested that the sentence be revised because it may contain a long sequence of noun modifiers.

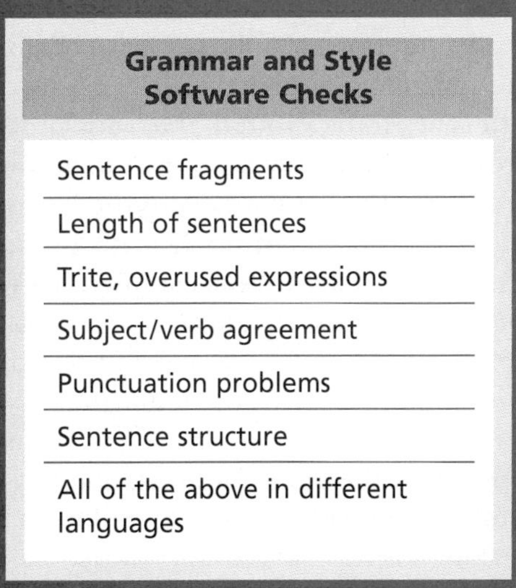

Grammar and Style Software Checks
Sentence fragments
Length of sentences
Trite, overused expressions
Subject/verb agreement
Punctuation problems
Sentence structure
All of the above in different languages

figure 13

Grammar and style software checks.

figure 14

A grammar checker can identify sentences containing possible error(s) and make suggestions.

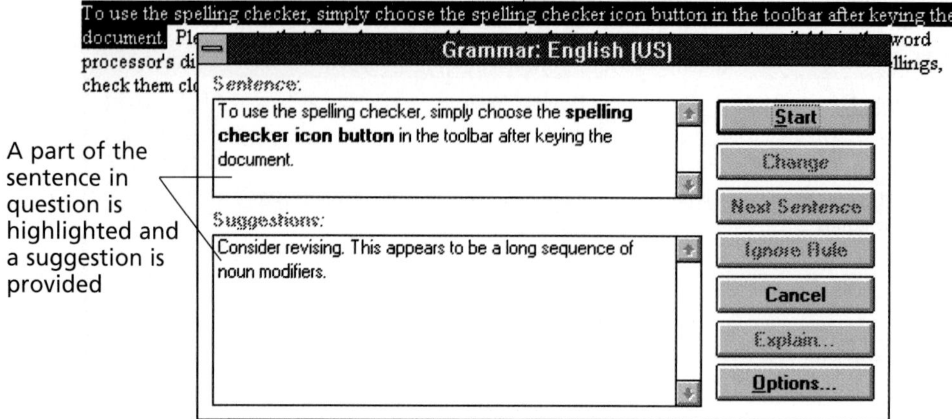

A sentence in the text containing possible grammar error(s) is selected
The ease with which spelling errors can be corrected, and the minimal amount of time it takes to run the spelling checker software, justifies its use with each word processed document. In the long run, it will save time and enhance the quality and accuracy of the document.
To use the spelling checker, simply choose the spelling checker icon button in the toolbar after keying the document.
Grammar: English (US)
Sentence:
To use the spelling checker, simply choose the spelling checker icon button in the toolbar after keying the document.
Suggestions:
Consider revising. This appears to be a long sequence of noun modifiers.
Start
Change
Next Sentence
Ignore Rule
Cancel
Explain...
Options...
A part of the sentence in question is highlighted and a suggestion is provided

Mail Merge

Mail merge functions are found in almost all commercial word-processing programs. Adding tremendous power to the basic word-processing functions, mail merge allows the software to insert varying values into documents as they are being printed. The basic characteristics of the mail merge feature are:

1. The same letter can be sent to different persons, with the name and address customized for each letter.
2. Varying values can be placed in documents to customize them as required. A lease, for example, could have the street address of the property and the amount of monthly rent entered as appropriate at the time of printing.
3. Address labels can be printed for the mailing of various materials.

Mail merge typically uses data obtained from a separate file. For example, the separate file might contain names and addresses for a letter. When the letters are to be printed, the word processor will read the names and addresses from the file and print them on the letters. Figure 15 illustrates this process; note that markers in the letter body indicate where the name and address should be printed.

Most word processors can use data from a separate file to perform mail merge functions. In addition, many of them can ask for data from the keyboard at print time. When using one of these programs, the user would tell the program to print the letter that is stored in a particular file. Based on prompts stored in that file, the word-processor program would ask the operator to key the name, address, and any other variable data. The letter—containing the variable data entered from the keyboard—would then be printed. Note that the variable data, whether from a file or the keyboard at print time, are not limited to names and addresses; they may consist of any data located at any point in the document.

Mailing Labels

After mail merged letters have been printed, **mailing labels** must be created for the envelopes of the mail merged letters. The same data file used to prepare the mail merge letter is also commonly used to create mailing labels. As illustrated in figure 16, name and address information from the data file is used to print mailing labels in the same way that mail merge documents are created. A mailing label can be created for each individual record in the data file.

Uses of Word Processors

The capabilities of word-processing software were discussed previously. Now, some of the common applications for which the software may be used are explored.

Correspondence

In many companies, virtually all correspondence is performed with word-processing software. This means internal memoranda as well as letters going to customers, vendors, and other contacts outside the company. Mail merge and mailing label capability are extremely important in using word processors for correspondence, because the time that is required for keying documents and addressing envelopes can be drastically reduced when the same or similar letters are used for several persons.

Many full-featured word-processor programs contain several **document templates** that automatically allow the use of common formats. Common document templates include memoranda, various personal and formal letter styles, mailing labels, facsimile sheets, overhead presentations, proposals, and term-paper formats. The desired format may be selected when starting a new document. For example, if a Memorandum format were chosen, the word "Memorandum" along with the headings To, From, Date, and Subject would appear in the proper memorandum format. The computer automatically inserts the current date and can recall previously stored information to supply the To and From data, or it can permit the user to key this information. Figure 17 shows an example of how a Memorandum and Facsimile document template might appear on the screen before the text is entered.

Document Construction

The term **document construction** refers to the act of combining various pre-saved paragraphs or sentences and graphic images to produce a finished document. One area where such capability is frequently used is the legal profession. Attorneys frequently prepare leases for their clients, and for this

figure 15

The computer merges a data file (containing names and addresses) with a document to produce a personally addressed letter for each person in the data file.

Courtesy_Title	First_Name	Last_Name	College_Name
Mr.	Edward	Hatcher	Normandale College
Ms.	Shirley	Myers	Springfield College
Mrs.	Leslie	Sasser	Wade University
Mr.	Ralph	Topazio	Embassy University
Mrs.	Linda	Webel	Boyers College

Phyllis Waxler
1201 Snyder Rd.
Atlanta, GA 30314-6210

March 4, 19—

<<Courtesy_Title>> <<First_Name>> <<Last_Name>>, Admissions
<<College_Name>>
<<Street_Address>>
<<City>>, <<State>> <<Zip>>

Dear <<Courtesy_Title>> <<Last_Name>>:

As the end of my junior year nears, the time has come to start gathering information from the colleges and universities that I am interested in attending. Please send me admissions material, financial aid and scholarship information, a course/subject catalog, and any brochures that you may have describing your campus environment. Also, please send me any specific information you may have about your degree programs in engineering

figure 16

Name and address information from a data file is used to produce a mailing label for each person in the data file.

Courtesy_Title	First_Name	Last_Name	College_Name
Mr.	Edward	Hatcher	Normandale College
Ms.	Shirley	Myers	Springfield College
Mrs.	Leslie	Sasser	Wade University
Mr.	Ralph	Topazio	Embassy University
Mrs.	Linda	Webel	Boyers College

<<Courtesy_Title>> <<First_Name>> <<Last_Name>>
<<Company_Name>>
<<Street_Address>>
<<City>>, <<State>> <<Zip>>

Street_Address	City	State	Zip
4611 Circle Dr.	Atlanta	GA	30342-4591
824 State St.	Memphis	TN	38101-6539
16 Arbor Rd.	Newport	KY	41071-9085
930 Cook Ave.	Vinton	VA	24179-3527
1475 Lindale	Girard	PA	16417-5530

Phyllis Waxler

At

March 4, 19—

Mr. Edward Hatcher, Admission
Normandale College
4611 Circle Dr.
Atlanta, GA 30342-4591

Dear Mr. Hatcher:

As the end of my junior year nea
tion from the colleges and unive
send me admissions material, fi
course/subject catalog, and any
campus environment. Also, plea
have about your degree program
of this letter.

Phyllis V
1201 Snyde
Atlanta, GA 3

March 4, 19—

Ms. Shirley Meyers, Admissions
Springfield College
824 State St.
Memphis, TN 38101-6539

Dear Ms. Meyers:

As the end of my junior year nears, the
tion from the colleges and universities
send me admissions material, financial
course/subject catalog, and any broch
campus environment. Also, please send
have about your degree programs in en
of this letter.

Street_Address	City	State	Zip
4611 Circle Dr.	Atlanta	GA	30342-4591
824 State St.	Memphis	TN	38101-6539
16 Arbor Rd.	Newport	KY	41071-9085
930 Cook Ave.	Vinton	VA	24179-3527
1475 Lindale	Girard	PA	16417-5530

Mr. Edward Hatcher
Normandale College
4611 Circle Dr.
Atlanta, GA 30342-4591

Ms. Shirley Myers
Springfield College
824 State St.
Memphis, TN 38101-6539

Mrs. Leslie Sasser
Wade University
16 Arbor Rd.
Newport, KY 41071-9085

figure 17

Examples of a Memorandum and Facsimile document template.

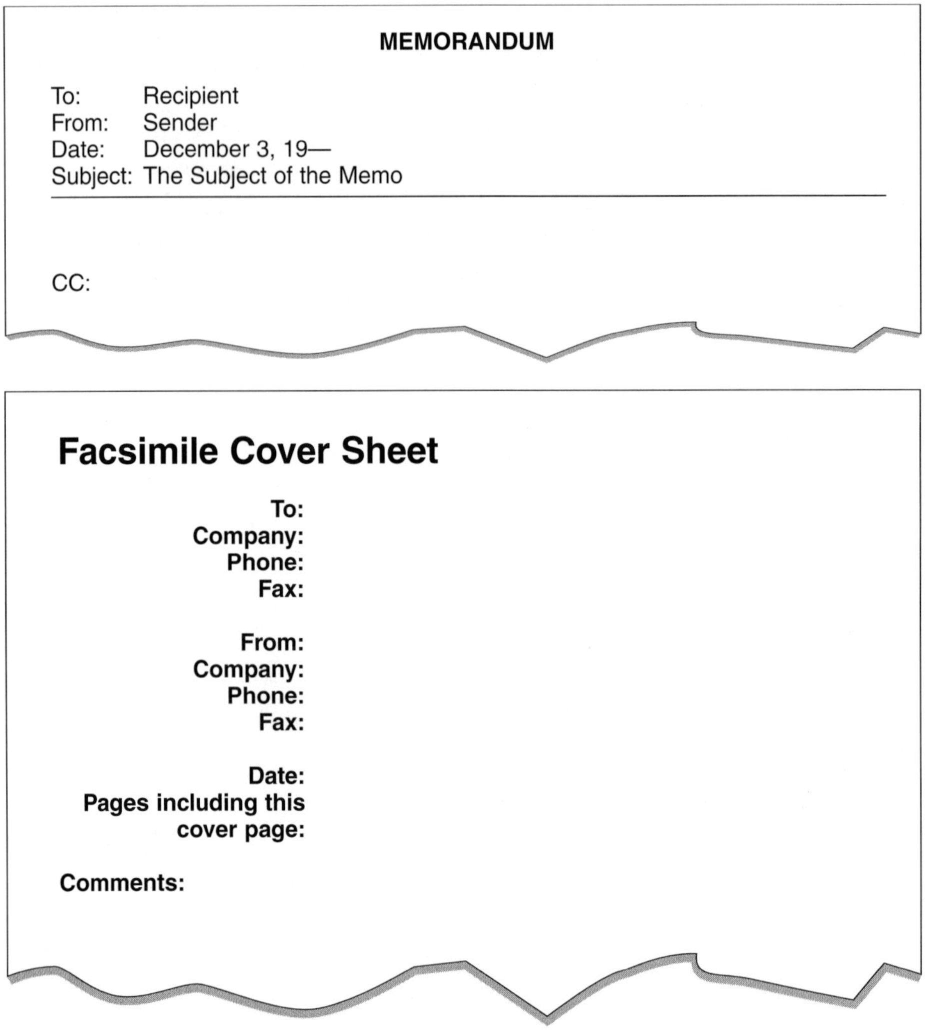

MEMORANDUM

To: Recipient
From: Sender
Date: December 3, 19—
Subject: The Subject of the Memo

CC:

Facsimile Cover Sheet

To:
Company:
Phone:
Fax:

From:
Company:
Phone:
Fax:

Date:
Pages including this cover page:

Comments:

purpose, standard paragraphs have existed for years, each for a particular application. For example, if a person who rents property is prohibited from renting it in turn to another individual, paragraphs will be needed in the lease to indicate this. If it is acceptable for the renter to rent to someone else, different paragraphs will be needed.

These various standard paragraphs, which may number into the thousands on some word-processing applications, are known as **boilerplate text**. They are pre-stored on an auxiliary storage device and combined with custom text as needed to produce the desired document. Figure 18 illustrates this concept.

Note that the assembly of pre-saved paragraphs into new documents is typically done in memory as text entry and revision and not at print time. Once the paragraphs are assembled and any desired changes made in the pre-saved wording, the document may be saved and printed just like any other document that has been created.

Preparation of Manuscripts

Word-processing software can provide many valuable functions to writers when producing manuscripts. In addition to the normal text entry and revi-

figure 18

Boilerplate text is stored on the computer and can be combined with other text to produce a new document.

sion functions previously detailed, many word processors can also automatically produce tables of contents and indexes for manuscripts, format and place footnotes, and prepare bibliographies.

Desktop Publishing

One of the most exciting developments related to word processing is desktop publishing. **Desktop publishing** refers to the process of using the computer to produce an original layout for material that is to be printed. The software that does desktop publishing can produce a wide variety of print fonts on a laser printer (dot matrix can be used, but the quality is much lower), combine graphics with text, and print text in multiple columns. Graphics can be prepared with a drawing program or by scanning them in with a scanner. Additionally, many "clipart" graphics are available from various publishers that are ready to be included to enhance documents such as newsletters.

In the early days of desktop publishing, it was necessary to enter the text using a word-processing program, then a separate publishing program would combine the text with any desired graphics and put them in the format for printing. While the use of two programs (word processing and publishing) is still common, the two are now merging. It is increasingly common to find desktop-publishing capabilities in word-processing programs and to find full word-processing features in desktop-publishing programs. Figure 19 illustrates an example of a document produced through use of the desktop publishing capabilities of a full-featured word processor. (Everything shown in the example was printed by a laser printer; nothing was pasted together after printout.)

Comprehensive List of Features and Capabilities

A comprehensive list of word-processing features and capabilities is provided by figure 20. As new software is developed and existing software updated, many of these features will become standard built-in capabilities of all word-processing software.

Trends

Sony: Bringing Computer Users Face-to-Face With Technology

Sony's Computer Science Laboratory (CSL) in Tokyo is developing advanced software that could dramatically change the way that humans interact with a computer. Sony's future computers will recognize and respond to its users with voice and image.

The graphic user interface you already know from computers may be replaced by a life-like digital face (of your choosing) that would carry out your spoken commands. The face that would appear on the screen is a speaking face, with expression, personality, and communication skills. (Working with this Sony system could give new meaning to the word *interface*.)

To construct this three-dimensional interface, CSL researchers built a face-modeling system by wrapping a polygon mesh over a series of still photographs of the desired face. Then, using mathematics, they were able to move the surface of the model to simulate the actions of facial muscles, jaw rotation, and eye movement. Additional control editing software is used to match emotional states, including generating wrinkles. The head-animation system is coupled with a speech-dialogue system that listens to the user's command, decodes the meaning, and chooses an appropriate audible and visual response. Sony hopes to have computer products based on its face-to-face communications interface model on the market in the next 5 to 10 years.

figure 19

Example of a document produced by a full-featured word-processing program using desktop-publishing features.

cfm international

NEWS

N e w s l e t t e r V o l . 1 1 9 9 4

Engines Achieve Impressive Milestone

Twelve years after entering revenue service, CFM International's fleet of CFM56-2, -3, and -5 engines has logged 50 million flight hours while establishing the industry standard for both commercial and military aircraft engine reliability. Total flight hours are expected to double to 100 million by 1998.

The CFM56 fleet currently logs nearly a million flight hours per month and averages 10,000 takeoffs per day, or one takeoff every 9 seconds.

The CFM56 fleet leader is the CFM56-3 powerplant for the Boeing 737-300/-400/-500 series of short-to-medium range aircraft. Since entering service with Southwest Airlines and USAir in late 1984, the -3-powered 737 has logged more than 33 million flight hours. The CFM56-powered 737 has become the fastest-selling aircraft in history, with more than 1,400 currently in service. Its engine is the industry leader in terms of reliability, with an in-flight shutdown (IFSD) rate of only .003, which translates to one IFSD per 300,000 flight hours, and a dispatch reliability rate of 99.96 percent, or fewer than one engine-caused delay or cancellation in 2,500 departures.

The CFM56-5A, which powers more than 300 Airbus Industrie A320 aircraft, has logged more than 4 million flight hours since April 1988. The engine maintains an impressive 99.94 percent dispatch reliability rate.

The CFM56-5C is the newest engine to enter service and powers the long-range, wide-bodied, four-engine Airbus Industrie A340. In its first year of service, the A340 has logged 200,000 flight hours.

The CFM56-2 was originally selected to re-engine the DC-8 Super 70 commercial and the KC-135 military tanker aircraft and was the first CFM56 to enter service. Since April 1982 these engines have logged nearly 12 million flight hours.

Cumulative CFM56 Flight Hours

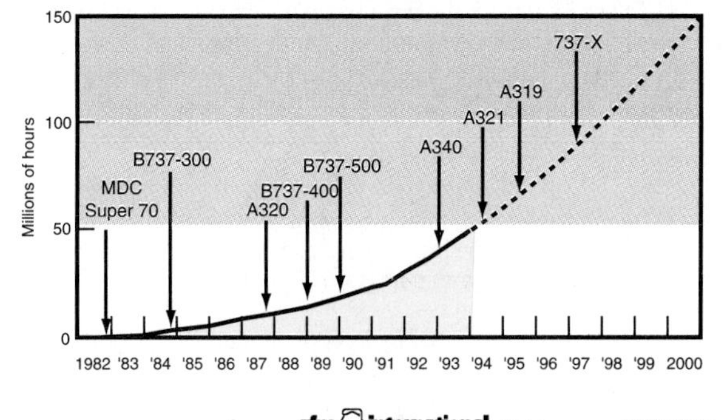

cfm international A joint company of SNECMA, France and GE U.S.A.

Hardware Requirements

The kind of hardware that is required for word processing depends on the sophistication of the software. With some programs, word processing can be done on the most minimal microcomputer systems. Although word-processing software is available for virtually all computers, there are several points to keep in mind when selecting software and hardware:

figure 20

Features and capabilities of full-feature word processors.

Feature/Capability	Description
Memory and Disk Usage	
Networkable	Will execute on most of the common network systems.
Expanded memory	Automatically uses additional expanded memory if available.
Files opened	Will permit several files (document) to be opened at once.
Commands	
Mouse	Supports a mouse.
Internal codes	Formatting uses codes inserted in the document.
Menus	Uses a menu-driven interface.
Quick/hot key	Uses key combinations to choose commands.
Command line	Display area that shows commands available.
Screen Display	
Ruler	Ruler can be used to set margins/tabs and can be suppressed from view.
Ribbon	Ribbon containing icon buttons available for choosing font and text attributes.
Page breaks	Page breaks are shown while user is typing.
Paragraph markers	Special symbols identifying paragraphs may be displayed or hidden.
Graphics preview	Graphics can be previewed before they are inserted in a document.
Print preview	Document pages previewed in condensed format as they will appear when printed.
Editable WYSIWYG	When document is displayed in WYSIWYG format, it may be edited.
Adjustable zoom	Document, or parts of a document, may be enlarged or reduced in size.
Text and Page Layout	
Document templates	Commonly used formatted styles sheets.
Non-printing text	Comments and specially selected text may be hidden.
Centering	Text can be automatically centered on the page.
Orphan control	Single words (called orphans) are controlled so that they are not left on a line or page by themselves.
Paragraph indentation	Indent entire paragraphs without changing margin settings.
Conditional page breaks	User can force a page break.
Snaking (columns)	Pages can be formatted and printed in Newspaper column style.
Expandable box	Text may be enclosed by an expandable box.
Text and Editing Entry	
Search-and-replace	Searches document using wild card, case-sensitive, whole-word, format, text attributes, and font search arguments and replaces desired text.
Non-standard character sets	Supports characters (math symbols, drawing symbols, and other special symbols) not in the standard character set.
Keyboard shortcut key	Keys can be designated to include non-keyboard characters in the document.
Hyphenation and Grammar	
Spell checker	Checks words to standard or special dictionaries. Checking may be done as words are typed, single selected words, or the entire document.
Hyphenation	Hyphenates words in the document using algorithms and dictionaries.
Thesaurus	Displays the meaning(s) of a selected word and a list of synonyms from which a replacement word may be chosen.
Grammar checker	Checks the document for grammatical errors.
Tables and Numbers	
Table editor	Automatically creates tables with multiple rows and columns that can be edited (rows and columns can be inserted or deleted).
Graphics in table	Capable of inserting a graphic within a table cell.
Math within document	Basic mathematics may be performed by inserting a mathematic operation (+, -, and so on) between numeric values.
Graphics	
Line drawing	Lines can be drawn using keyboard or mouse.
Line insertion	Lines may be inserted from menu options.
Graphic import formats	Commonly used graphic formats may be accessed.
Resize graphics	Graphics (illustrations, pictures, clipart, and so on) imported into the document can be resized and moved.

Feature/Capability	Description
Text wrap around graphic	Text will automatically wrap around a graphic moved into the text area.
Drawing tools	Drawing/paint tools are included or accessed in such a way as to be integrated into the word-processing software.
Graphics in text	Graphic images can be inserted directly into text within a document.
Complex Document Features	
Outline	Outline format and numbering.
Tables of contents	Can automatically generate multiple-level tables of contents.
Indexing	Can automatically generate multiple-level indexing.
Footnotes/endnotes	Automatic numbering of footnotes and endnotes.
Headers and footers	Includes user header and footers with current date, page numbers, and so on.
Cross-referencing	Automatically creates a cross-reference of selected key words.
Spreadsheet links	Can connect to a spreadsheet to send and receive data via cut-and-paste or via dynamic data-exchange linkage.
Database links	Can connect to a database to send and receive data via cut-and-paste or via dynamic data-exchange linkage.
Text-file links	Can connect to other application software via cut-and-paste or dynamic data-exchange links.
Printing	
Background printing	Can print as a low or high priority while the user performs other tasks.
Print queue	Documents that are to be printed and are temporarily stored in a print queue may be modified by priority.
Prints block	Can print only a user defined (selected) block of the document.
Prints discontinuous pages	Can print discontinuous ranges of pages within a document.
Prints current page	Can print only the current page.
Envelope creation	Automatically formats and prints envelope mailing information.
Landscape/portrait	Documents may be printed to paper in portrait (vertical) orientation or in landscape (horizontal) orientation.
Collates	Different print jobs may be collated together into one document.
File Management	
Timed backup	A backup copy of a document is automatically made based on a fixed time period.
File manager	Can manage files (delete and rename document files) and print files from a list of filenames.
Document descriptions	Can accept and store user supplied (name, title, and so on) and computer generated information (version number, current date) about each document.
Search files	Can search disk for files and text within files.
View files	Can view the contents of files before opening them.
Senses import files	Can sense files that are being imported (files not created by the word-processing software).
Import/export formats	Can read from and write to disk in several of the most common word-processor formats.
Macros	
Record keystrokes	Can record keystrokes for later replay.
Programmable macros	Can enter instructions to program macros.
Remappable keyboard	Keyboard keys may be changed and remapped to simplify macro usage.
Glossary	Frequently used text (macros, keystrokes, instructions, and so on) that have been stored and can be inserted without typing or creating again.
Professional	
Mail merge	Can merge a data file with a document to produce personally addressed letters.
Data imports	Can import data for mail merge from common database programs.
Select field names	Data fields to be included in a mail merge operation can be selected from a menu (need not be typed).
Sorting function	Can arrange selected text or fields alphabetically or numerically.
Mailing labels	Name and address data from a data file are used to create mailing labels to address envelopes.
Revision marking	Used to track changes made to a document.
Comparison	Compares one document to another and notes any differences.
Password protection	Uses a password to protect a document from being modified.
Encryption	Can encrypt a document stored on disk so that others who access it cannot read what is stored.
Direct e-mail link	Can be integrated directly into an electronic-mail service.
Help and Documentation	
Online tutorial	Software that provides tutorial help and examples of how to use commands and features.
Context-sensitive help	Online help information that may be displayed relative to the current command or task being performed.
Keyboard templates	Cardboard or plastic-coated templates that can be laid over the keyboard to identify functions performed by certain keys.

Issues In Technology

Internet Links Adoptees

Many adults who were adopted as children have joined an Internet computer "mailing list" for adoptees looking for their biologic parents or who are dealing with legal, emotional, or other issues. Currently, about 200 people nationwide who are concerned with birth-parent searches and other adoption issues are plugged into this electronic information exchange. Word processing plays an important part in this electronic information-sharing process.

Adoptees are among the 20 million people worldwide (over 13 million in the United States) who are using word-processing capabilities to compose letters of information that are communicated through electronic mail (e-mail) on the Internet. Anyone who has a computer with a modem can subscribe to services that offer electronic bulletin boards and mailing lists, which work like automated newsletters. When a subscriber submits an article or writes a letter to the service, the mail is duplicated and sent to the other subscribers. Information is shared and exchanged electronically.

Adoptees have found e-mail services to be invaluable for conducting research to find their birth parents. There have already been several success stories of adoptees making contact with one or both birth parents.

Adoptees using the birth-parent focus network have received help from other adoptees and other subscribers who are willing to help in a particular search. For example, adoptees using the e-mail system have received responses that include suggestions for places to contact, questions to ask, what to say when a parent is found, what to tell the adoptive parents, emotional considerations, and a wide range of other issues relating to the past history of the birth parents.

1 Today's more sophisticated, full-featured word-processing programs require a hard disk for satisfactory performance. If a hard disk is not available, you can still obtain a very workable but less powerful word processor.

2 The more sophisticated a word-processing program is, the more memory it will require. It is common for full-featured word-processing programs to require 6 MB or more of memory.

3 Word-processing software with true WYSIWYG capability (showing on screen the different fonts and sizes as they will actually appear) requires a high-resolution display monitor as well as a fast processor for satisfactory operation.

Do It!

1 Using your school's word processor, prepare a letter to your favorite college or university asking for information about admissions, specific degree programs, and so on. (Use the letter shown in figure 15 as a guide.) When you are finished, save the letter to your disk and directory/folder with a file name of XXXWP-B (where *XXX* are your initials).

2 If your word processor has spelling and grammar features, use them to check the letter you just prepared. Use the thesaurus feature to improve the quality of your letter. When finished using these features, save the letter back to your disk and directory/folder.

3 Does the word processor you are using have document templates? If yes, open and print the memo and fax templates; if not, use your word processor to make your own memo and fax templates. Save them to your disk and directory/folder with file names XXXWP-C and XXXWP-D. Use the format of the memo and fax templates shown in figure 17.

Summary

Word-processing software assists in the preparation of documents for businesses and individuals.

- Word-processing software allows easy correction of keying errors, either at the time they are made or later, and easy revision of documents.
- Preparing similar documents for various recipients is easy with word processing's ability to modify standard text, either in memory or during the mail merge function.
- Documents prepared with word processing can be stored for reuse.
- Word-processed documents can be more accurate because of the lessened amount of rekeying.
- Documents can be stored, retrieved, and transmitted electronically rather than on paper.
- Input to a word-processing program is usually through use of a keyboard, even though scanners are used to convert existing documents and graphics for computer storage and revision.
- A menu is used to display and select the commands to operate the word-processor software.
- A toolbar contains icon buttons that enable the user to quickly select frequently used commands.
- The ribbon portion of a word-processor screen contains icons and features that are used to change the appearance of selected text.
- The ruler is used to change paragraph indentation and margin settings.
- The text area is the large portion of the screen display that displays text as it is keyed or graphics that are incorporated into the document.
- Vertical and horizontal scroll bars are used to move a document through the text area for viewing.
- A status bar displays information such as the current page number, total number of pages in the document, current line and column of the insertion point, and the status of several keyboard keys.
- Many full-featured word processors contain document templates that automatically allow use of common formats, such as memoranda, various personal and formal letter styles, mailing labels, facsimile sheets, overhead presentations, proposals, and term-paper formats.
- WYSIWYG means "What You See Is What You Get" and refers to the ability of a word processor to display material on the screen as it will appear on the printed page.
- During processing of a document, errors may be corrected and text moved or copied through a process known as cut-and-paste.

Summary

- Output may be directed to almost any printer; alternately, the document may be transmitted electronically to another computer(s).
- Storage of documents is done on disk, with the storage taking place either before or after printing depending on the brand of software or user preference; however, storage before printing is a good safeguard in case of printer problems.
- Word-processing enhancements include spelling checkers, thesaurus software, grammar and style software, mail merge, and mailing label functions.
- Spell checkers locate document words that do not appear in their dictionaries and call attention to them, frequently giving the operator a list of potentially correct words to choose from.
- Thesaurus programs present synonyms for desired words on the screen for operator choice.
- Grammar and style checkers can help the operator produce more technically correct compositions.
- Mail merge functions make it easy to produce the same or similar documents that are customized for various recipients.
- Mailing labels may be created from a data file containing name and address information to reduce the amount of time it takes to address envelopes.
- Word processors are frequently used for correspondence, document construction, for the preparation of manuscripts, and for desktop publishing.
- While word processing programs are available for even the most minimal microcomputer, sophisticated, full-featured programs used in business require computers with more speed and memory, as well as hard disks.

The following key terms were defined in this module. For each of the following terms, write on a separate piece of paper the number of the definition followed by the letter of the appropriate term.

Terms

A. WYSIWYG
B. boilerplate text
C. ruler
D. scroll bars
E. document construction
F. document templates
G. menu
H. word-processing software
I. cut-and-paste
J. text area
K. grammar and style software
L. spelling checker
M. status bar
N. thesaurus software
O. mail merge
P. toolbar
Q. desktop publishing
R. mailing labels
S. ribbon
T. insertion point
U. text formatting

Definitions

1 pre-stored, standard paragraphs that may be assembled in desired order to help create a customized document

2 the process of removing text from one location and putting it in another; moving text

3 the process of using word-processor software to produce an original layout (newspaper layout) for material to be printed

4 the process of combining various pre-saved paragraphs or sentences to produce a finished document

5 a display used to select the commands to operate the word-processor software

6 used to change paragraph indentation and margin settings

7 commonly used formats such as memoranda, facsimile sheets, proposals, and term papers that are contained in many full-featured word processors

8 software used to check a document for sentence fragments, overused expressions, subject/verb agreement, punctuation, and sentence structure

9 icons (often referred to as buttons) from which the most frequently used commands may be quickly chosen

10 the process whereby the word-processing software merges a data file (containing names and addresses) with a document to produce a personally addressed letter for each person in the data file

Matching

11 displays information such as the current page number, total number of pages in the document, current line and column of the insertion point, and the status of several keyboard keys

12 used to change the appearance of selected text such as fonts, point sizes, bold, italics, and/or underlined characters

13 the process whereby name and address information from a data file are printed in a format used to address envelopes

14 software that checks the words in a document to a dictionary and calls attention to not-found words

15 a blinking vertical bar that indicates where text will be inserted when keyed

16 software that presents a list of synonyms from which the user can choose to replace a selected word in the document

17 the large portion of the screen display that shows text as it is keyed or graphics that are incorporated into the document

18 controlling those characteristics that affect the appearance of a document when printed

19 software specially designed to assist in the preparation of documents for individuals or businesses

20 used to move a document through the text area for viewing

21 what you see is what you get

Review

1. What does word-processing software do that makes it a necessary part of today's business world? (Obj. 1)
2. List nine advantages of using word-processing software. (Obj. 2)
3. What devices are commonly used to input data into a word processor? (Obj. 3)
4. What kinds of processing are typically performed with word- processing software? (Obj. 3)
5. What kinds of output are possible with word-processing software? (Obj. 3)
6. What kind of storage is usually used with word-processing software? (Obj. 3)
7. Why do you think that document templates have been provided in many of the modern full-featured word processors? (Obj. 4)
8. What is the advantage of WYSIWYG? (Obj. 3)
9. What is meant by "cut-and-paste"? (Obj. 3)
10. Describe the operation of a typical spelling checker. (Obj. 5)
11. Describe the operation of a typical thesaurus program. (Obj. 5)
12. Describe the operation of a typical grammar and style checker. (Obj. 5)
13. What is the purpose of the mail merge function? (Obj. 5)
14. What is the purpose of mailing labels? (Obj. 5)
15. Describe four applications of word processing. (Obj. 4, 6, 7)
16. What is the relationship between word-processing software capability and hardware requirements? (Obj. 8)

Activities

1 *Writing* A friend has asked you to help purchase a word-processing program. Write a memo to your friend advising him or her about the features that should be included in the purchase decision. Refer to the list of features and capabilities in figure 20, and itemize those in your memo you think are the most important. Use a memo document template if available, the memo template you created earlier in the Do It! activity, or create your document using the memo format shown in this module.

2 *Writing* Use your word processor to create the cover sheet of a school newspaper (using a format similar to that in figure 19) or a small brochure describing your school. Check your software's technical manual or help feature to find out how to display and print your newspaper or brochure in multiple columns. Add graphics (if available) to enhance the appearance of your output.

3 *Math* Because mathematics plays such an important and direct part in our lives, the developers of many modern full-featured word-processing software have included the capability to enter mathematic symbols into word-processed documents. Check your software's technical manual or help feature to find out how to access these symbols.

Your math instructor has asked you to share important information about an assignment with a classmate who has been home sick. Because you have a fax machine at your home and you know that the sick student also has a fax machine at home, you decide to prepare the information in a facsimile format and send it via a fax machine. Complete the following facsimile:

Facsimile Cover Sheet

To: Classmate Name
Fax: Area Code and Phone Number

From: Your Name
School: Your High School
Fax: Area Code and Phone Number

Date: mm/dd/yy
Pages including this cover page: 1

Comments:

The following hint, given in class today, will help you complete yesterday's assignment:

The bar of the radical sign should be treated like parentheses. That is, you must work under the bar before doing anything else. For example, to simplify

$$\sqrt{36 + 49}$$

you must add 36 and 49 first, then take the square root.

$$\sqrt{36 + 49} = \sqrt{85} = 9.2195$$

I hope you are feeling better and will be back in school soon.

Activities

4 *Science* Science instructors and students often use word-processing software to report their findings or research. Often, the table-generation capabilities of a word processor are used to illustrate data within their reports. Use the table feature of your word-processing software to create and print the following Electron table. (Check the software's technical manual or help feature to find out how to use this feature if necessary.)

GP	AN	AS	K	L	M	V
1	1	H	1	–	–	±
18	2	He	2	–	–	0
1	3	Li	2	1	–	+1
2	4	Be	2	2	–	+2
13	5	B	2	3	–	+3
14	6	C	2	4	–	±4
15	7	N	2	5	–	–3 +5
16	8	O	2	6	–	–2
17	9	F	2	7	–	–1
18	10	Ne	2	8	–	0
1	11	Na	2	8	1	+1
2	12	Mg	2	8	2	+2
13	13	Al	2	8	3	+3
14	14	Si	2	8	4	±4
15	15	P	2	8	5	–3 +5
16	16	S	2	8	6	–2
17	17	Cl	2	8	7	–1
18	18	Ar	2	8	8	0

5 *Global Activity* You have learned that some word processors with spelling, grammar, and the thesaurus features have the capability of working with different languages or special disciplines. Often, this is accomplished by instructing the software to reference different dictionaries and different language rules. Does your word-processing software have any of these features? If yes, what languages are supported with each feature? If your word processor does not have any of these features, find one that does by checking a computer magazine or a local computer or software store.

6 *Teamwork* Divide into four teams. Using a word processor with mail merge and mailing label generation capabilities, perform the following tasks. Note that teams 2, 3, and 4 must obtain information (field names) from team 1.

Team 1: Creates a data file containing the addresses of at least five companies that members of the team would like to ask to advertise in the school newspaper. If you know a contact person, use that person's name; if not, address the letter appropriately to the owner, president, manager, and so on.

Team 2: Creates a short form letter explaining two or three options detailing the costs and sizes of ads. Be sure to include an inside address and courtesy title line.

Team 3: Uses the mail merge feature to create a personalized letter to the contact person, president, and so on for each company in the data file.

Team 4: Uses the mailing label feature to create a mailing label for each company in the data file.

7 *Speaking* Choose an application for which you would use word-processing software (math reports, science reports, business correspondence, school work, and so on). What hardware and software factors might you consider in deciding what word processing would be best for your chosen application? Why would you consider these factors? Give a short presentation to your class identifying the factors you think are important and justifying your choices. Prepare a handout itemizing the important factors.

(Continued on next page.)

Activities

8 *Ethics* Software called shareware software has been around for many years. Authors of shareware make their programs available to the public to copy but retain the copyright to their work. They hope that the user will like their program well enough to make a donation. Users of shareware are encouraged to make copies and give these to others as a means of distributing the product. The basic philosophy behind shareware is that users will pay for a program that has value, and authors will be encouraged to produce quality products based on the fees they receive. What do you think would happen if the users of shareware did not send a donation to the authors even though they liked and used the software?

9 *Internet* Access the Internet, and use your search engine to find specific information about word processing, such as word processing used in a language other than English or for type-setting. Also gather usage tips and information on standards, training, or template files that are available. Report your findings.

Spreadsheets

SP

Overview

While this module addresses the spreadsheet as it is implemented by computer software, a manual form of the spreadsheet (also commonly called a worksheet) has been used for many years. A *spreadsheet* is simply a row-and-column arrangement of data—a grid of labels, values, and numbers computed through the use of formulas. Individuals and businesses have used manually prepared spreadsheets for years by writing in the figures and performing the computations. Computations were originally done by hand and then by mechanical adding machines, mechanical calculators, and electronic calculators. Recently, computerization of the spreadsheet has created an electronic version that has made its use much easier and enabled much more complex computations to be completed.

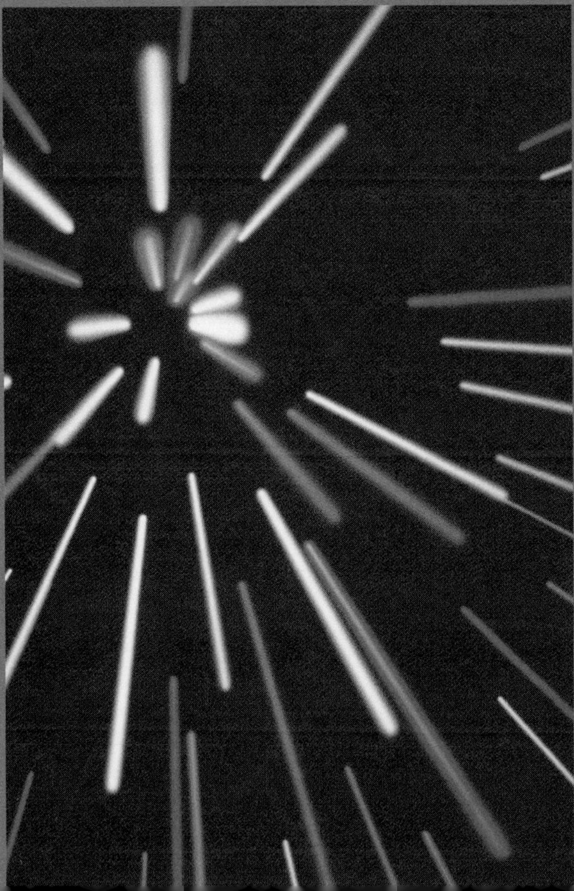

Objectives

1 Explain the purpose of spreadsheet software.

2 Describe how a spreadsheet is organized.

3 Enter labels, values, formulas, and functions into a spreadsheet.

4 Generate charts and graphs.

5 Print a spreadsheet document, and save data to disk.

6 Insert and delete rows and columns, format a spreadsheet, protect spreadsheet data and files, hide spreadsheet cells, lock titles, and use macros and template files.

7 Use a spreadsheet program for planning, modeling, linking with other spreadsheets, and integrating with other software.

8 Describe the hardware requirements for spreadsheet software.

The Purpose of Spreadsheet Software

The spreadsheet illustrated in figure 1 was prepared by Nathan, a high-school student, to keep track of the expenses he incurred to operate his car for the months of January, February, and March. He then computed the results.

In examining the spreadsheet in figure 1, note that each row shows the results for each expense. The columns labeled January, February, and March contain the amount of each expense incurred during the month. The Total column contains the sum of each expense for all three months. The Cost/Mile (cost per mile) column is calculated by dividing the total amount of each expense by the total miles traveled; for example, the cost of insurance of $0.06 per mile would be calculated as :

Total insurance expense ÷ Miles Traveled = $222.00 ÷ 3495 = $0.06

Finally, the last row contains a total of each of the spreadsheet columns. Notice that during the months of January, February, and March, it cost Nathan $0.21 to operate his car. If Nathan continues to use his spreadsheet for succeeding months, he will be able to use the cost-per-mile calculation results to alert him when it is time to purchase a new vehicle. That is, when the cost per mile to operate his car becomes excessive, it may be cost justifiable to buy a new or different vehicle.

Note that in the example of Nathan's spreadsheet, the data represents a report of existing conditions. In other words, the results of car operating expenses are presented. Examples of other existing conditions for which spreadsheets may be prepared are accounting records of a business, sports statistics, and grades from a teacher's grade book.

Spreadsheets may also be used to make projections or predictions of data. For example, a user might compute the predicted population of various

figure 1

Spreadsheets are often manually prepared by both individuals and businesses.

Nathan's Car Operating Expenses					
Miles Traveled: 3495					
	January	February	March	Total	Cost/Mile
Insurance	$74.00	$74.00	$74.00	$222.00	$0.06
Gas	$42.00	$36.00	$45.00	$123.00	$0.04
Oil and Filter	$21.50	$0.00	$19.95	$41.45	$0.01
Repairs	$35.00	$0.00	$57.00	$92.00	$0.03
License	$0.00	$58.00	$0.00	$58.00	$0.02
Tires	$38.00	$0.00	$0.00	$38.00	$0.01
Depreciation	$47.50	$47.50	$47.50	$142.50	$0.04
Totals	$258.00	$215.50	$243.45	$716.95	$0.21

cities assuming that their growth continues at the present rate. Or, if over the next 5 years you want to save $25,000 for a down payment on a house, you can compute how much you will need to invest each month at an assumed rate of return to obtain the desired amount.

While any of these spreadsheet applications can be done by hand, computer software makes the job easier and more accurate. The job is easier because the spreadsheet software already knows how to make many kinds of computations by use of built-in formulas. The job is more accurate because the computer will not make computational errors as a person might. It is good to keep in mind, however, that the computer software does what its user tells it to do. Therefore, if the user instructs the software to use the wrong formula or data, for example, the results will be inaccurate.

The Organization of a Spreadsheet

A spreadsheet is a row-and-column arrangement of data, as shown in figure 1. Different names or descriptions are applied to various parts of a spreadsheet. Any single horizontal area extending across a spreadsheet is called a **row**, and this is illustrated by the highlighted area in figure 2. Note that the row number (at the beginning of each row) is supplied automatically by the spreadsheet software and is used to identify the row.

A single vertical area running through a spreadsheet is known as a **column**. The spreadsheet in figures 2 and 3 use columns A through F. Note also that the spreadsheet software supplies column labels or numbers, again for referring to designated locations. The first column in the example is A, the

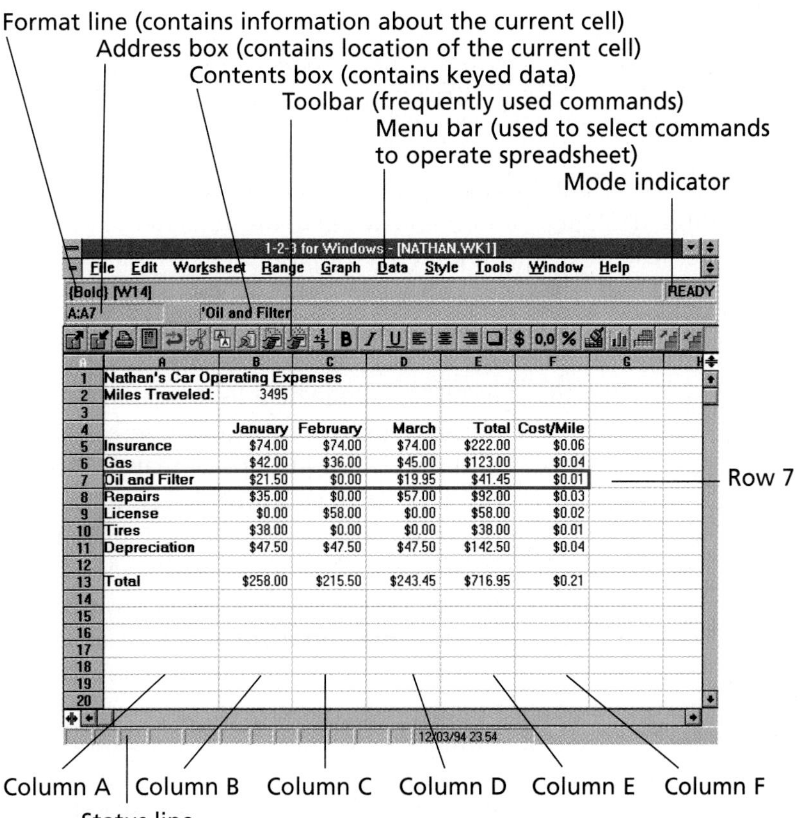

figure 2

Example of a full-featured spreadsheet display.

figure 3

Elements of a spreadsheet.

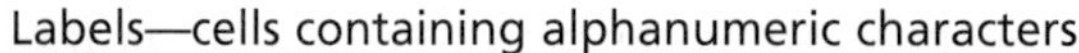

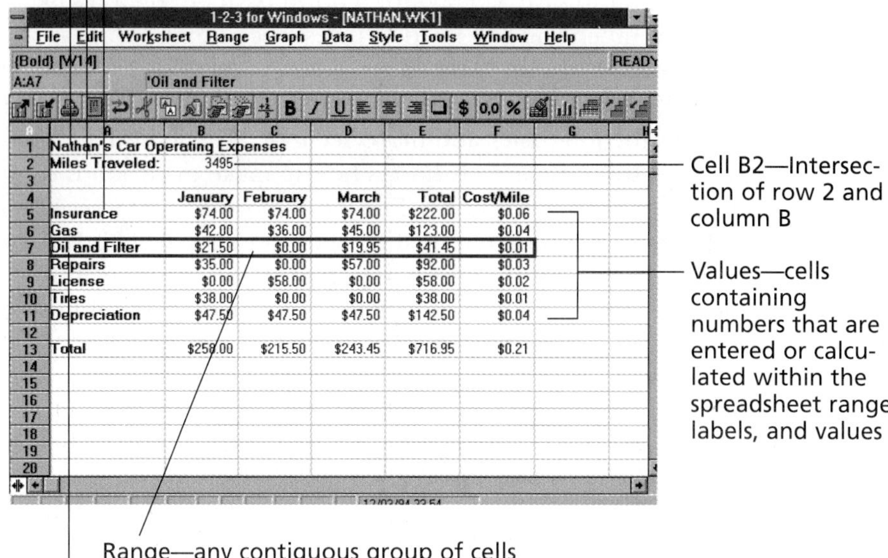

	A	B	C	D	E	F
1	Nathan's Car Operating Expenses					
2	Miles Traveled:	3495				
3						
4		January	February	March	Total	Cost/Mile
5	Insurance	$74.00	$74.00	$74.00	$222.00	$0.06
6	Gas	$42.00	$36.00	$45.00	$123.00	$0.04
7	Oil and Filter	$21.50	$0.00	$19.95	$41.45	$0.01
8	Repairs	$35.00	$0.00	$57.00	$92.00	$0.03
9	License	$0.00	$58.00	$0.00	$58.00	$0.02
10	Tires	$38.00	$0.00	$0.00	$38.00	$0.01
11	Depreciation	$47.50	$47.50	$47.50	$142.50	$0.04
12						
13	Total	$258.00	$215.50	$243.45	$716.95	$0.21

second column is B, and so on. When the alphabet is exhausted with column Z, labeling starts with AA, BB, and so on. While there are variations in row and column numbering from one brand of software to another, they all serve the same purpose.

While rows and columns refer to more than one value on a spreadsheet, the term **cell** is used to refer to the space on the spreadsheet used to store one value, number, character label, or formula. Note that in figure 3 cell B2 (the intersection of row 2 and column B) contains the value 3495. Also, note that cell A7 (along with the other cells in row 7) has been selected (highlighted or outlined). One or more selected cells are referred to as the **current cell(s)**, because it is the current cell(s) that will receive data that is entered or be affected by the computer's next processing action.

While row and column refer strictly to the arrangement of cells, the term **range** refers to any contiguous group of cells. In other words, any group of cells next to each other may be called a range of cells. The range that is highlighted (called the current range) in figures 2 and 3 consists of the cells in columns A, B, C, D, E, and F in row 7. It is just one of many possible ranges in the spreadsheet, however. A range may include several columns and rows of numbers, alphabetic items, special symbols, formulas, and other data. Ranges are useful for specifying cells that are to be deleted, moved, copied, or otherwise manipulated. Many spreadsheet programs allow you to select and work with more than one range simultaneously.

In addition to categorizing parts of a spreadsheet by its physical arrangement, as has been done to this point, each cell may also be classified by whether its contents are alphanumeric (any character) or numeric. Alphabetic (or alphanumeric) characters that are entered into cells are called **labels**, while cells containing numbers that are entered or calculated within the spreadsheet are referred to as **values**.

Entering Data into the Spreadsheet

You may enter characters, numbers, and formulas into a spreadsheet. Usually, you enter data into a spreadsheet by keying it; however, you may also cut-and-paste data from another program (such as a word-processing or database program) into a spreadsheet.

Entering Character Data

Character (alphanumeric) data is not used for computation. This type of data is most frequently used to identify the numeric values that appear in the rows and columns. For example, the row and column labels shown in figure 3 (Insurance, Gas, January, February, March, and so on) identify the numeric values that appear within the spreadsheet.

To enter character data, first move the **cell pointer** to the desired cell. If necessary, select the desired cell by clicking with the mouse button. Then, enter the data.

With some software, the characters appear directly in the current cell, while with other software, the characters appear in a **contents box** before they are moved into the current cell. Figure 4 shows two partially completed spreadsheets. Cell A8 (column A, row 8) is the current cell. In figure 4*A*, the label "Repairs" appears in the contents box as you key the letters. When you press Enter/Return, the label will move to the current cell. In figure 4*B*, the label appears in the contents box and directly in the current cell when you key it.

In certain instances, you must enter a special symbol (some spreadsheets use a single quote mark ['], others use a double quote mark ["]) preceding numbers that should be treated as characters. For example, key a single or double quote mark preceding a street address that begins with a house number, your student identification number, class number, or social security number.

Changing Column Width

Often, the width of one or more columns is too small to accommodate large labels or numeric values. Both spreadsheets in figure 4 have had the width of column A expanded to 14 (other columns have a width of 9) to accommodate the labels identifying the expenses. To change the column width, use the following steps:

1. Make any cell in the column to be changed the current cell.
2. Choose the column width from the appropriate menu.
3. Enter the desired size of the column, and respond to any additional information that may be required.
4. Choose the appropriate command (press the OK button) to execute the format command. As a shortcut, you can change the column width of most full-featured spreadsheet programs by positioning the pointer between the column labels (the pointer will turn into a crosshair symbol), then clicking and dragging left or right to the desired width.

figure 4

To enter alphanumeric data, the cell pointer must be used to select the desired cell (which becomes the current cell) that is to receive the data.

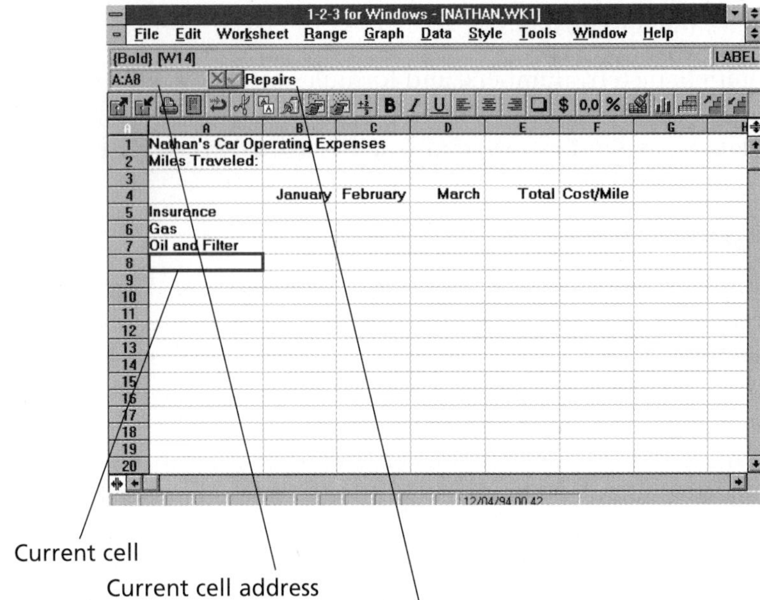

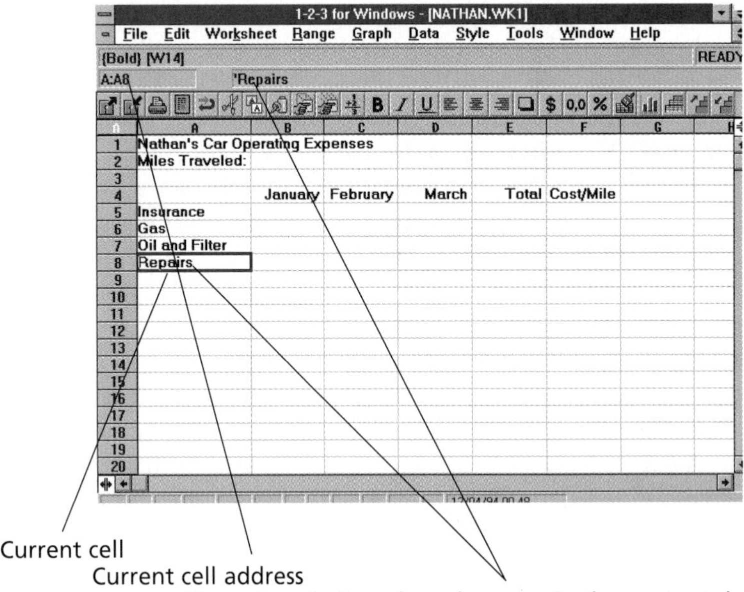

The height of cells may also be changed to accommodate large font sizes or leave more spaces between each row of data. The procedure to change the height of the cells in a selected row(s) is very similar to that used to change column width.

Entering Numeric Data

Numeric data is entered into a spreadsheet using the same procedure as character data. Simply move the cell pointer to the desired cell, and key in the desired data. Figure 5 illustrates this procedure.

Character and numeric data in a spreadsheet may be entered in any order desired. After data entry, the sample spreadsheet appears as shown in

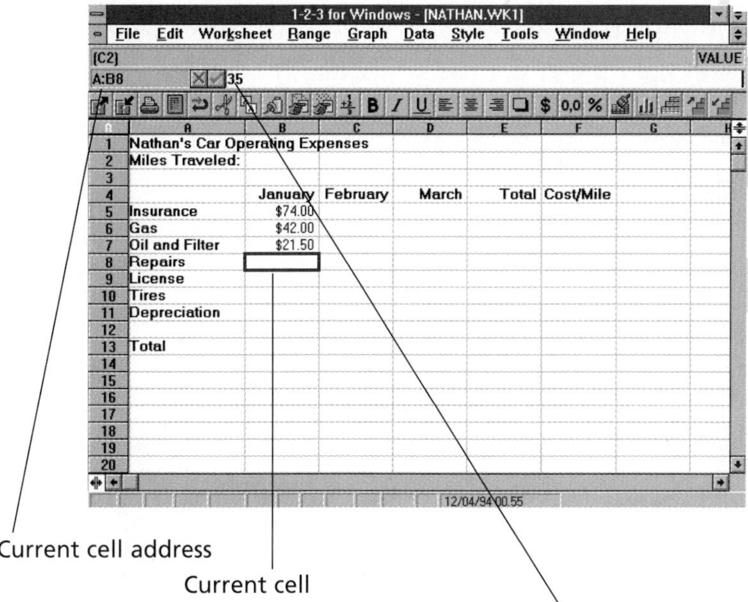
Current cell address
Current cell
Values that are keyed appear in the contents box.
When Enter/Return or a directional key is pressed,
the value is moved to the current cell.

figure 5

To enter numeric values, the cell pointer must be used to select the desired cell (current cell) that is to receive the value from the contents box.

figure 6. While studying this figure, note that no computed values yet appear (the Totals in row 13 and the Cost/Mile in column F), but formulas could have been entered during the process of entering character (labels) and numeric (values) data.

1-2-3 for Windows - [SSCHAP7.WK1]

File Edit Worksheet Range Graph Data Style Tools Window Help

(C2) READY

A:B13

	A	B	C	D	E	F
1	Nathan's Car Operating Expenses					
2	Miles Traveled:	3495				
3						
4		January	February	March	Total	Cost/Mile
5	Insurance	$74.00	$74.00	$74.00	$222.00	
6	Gas	$42.00	$36.00	$45.00	$123.00	
7	Oil and Filter	$21.50	$0.00	$19.95	$41.45	
8	Repairs	$35.00	$0.00	$57.00	$92.00	
9	License	$0.00	$58.00	$0.00	$58.00	
10	Tires	$38.00	$0.00	$0.00	$38.00	
11	Depreciation	$47.50	$47.50	$47.50	$142.50	
12						
13	Total					

figure 6

Nathan's spreadsheet after alphanumeric and numeric data are entered.

Entering and Copying Formulas

The computed values in a spreadsheet are calculated by means of **formulas**. A formula is a mathematic equation that is used to compute spreadsheet values. In our example, the total amount of expenses for the month of January is computed by adding, or summing, the seven values of $74.00, $42.00, $21.50, $35.00, $0.00, $38.00, and $47.50. These values are in Cells B5, B6, B7, B8, B9, B10, and B11. To perform this computation, you must select cell B13 as the current cell (the point at which the total should appear) and enter the formula. Figure 7 shows how this is done with an example of a formula and a function appearing in the contents box.

Profile

Mitch Kapor

Take a look at the resume of Mitch Kapor, the father of Lotus 1-2-3 software, and you will find some pretty interesting jobs. Before becoming the multimillionaire head of Lotus Development Corporation, Kapor was a Transcendental Meditation instructor, hospital counselor, and even a rock-radio disk jockey.

After earning his bachelor's degree in psychology from Yale in 1973, Kapor wandered in and out of various jobs. In 1978, while waiting to get into a doctoral program in psychology, Kapor became interested in microcomputers. He started helping people set up computer programs for their own personal use. Kapor thought that the program he had written for a graduate student at MIT could be marketed to others. With the help of MIT's Dr. Eric Rosenfield, Mitch made a few changes and sold the program as *Tiny Troll*, which did line charts, statistics, regressions, and editing.

Kapor's software career was taking off. At an Apple user group meeting, he met Bob Frankston, who along with Dan Bricklin created VisiCalc, the first electronic spreadsheet. Through Frankston's connections, Kapor developed two new programs based on *Tiny Troll*: *VisiPlot*, and *VisiTrend*. Both were introduced in 1981, and these two programs brought him royalties of half a million dollars in just 6 months. In 1982, Kapor sold the rights to these programs for $1.5 million.

Next, Kapor created the Lotus Development Corporation. Teaming up with expert programmer Jonathan Sachs, Kapor's newest product was Lotus 1-2-3, a powerful, integrated electronic spreadsheet with data-processing and graphics functions. To launch Lotus 1-2-3, Kapor needed money—and lots of it. Kapor approached Ben Rosen, a high-tech venture capitalist who had purchased the *Tiny Troll* program years earlier. Rosen and his partner L. J. Sevin agreed to give Kapor $5 million. Lotus was introduced to the public at the Fall 1982 COMDEX convention and by an unprecedented, nationwide advertising blitz.

By the following April, Lotus 1-2-3 had hit the top of the bestselling software charts. In October 1983, just 18 months after its founding, Lotus Development Company went public. Mitch Kapor received $5.4 million in cash, plus shares worth over $50 million. Rosen and Sevin's $5 million investment exploded to more than $100 million.

When you enter the formula +B5+B6+B7+B8+B9+B10+B11 (as shown in the figure 7 contents box) and strike the Enter/Return or directional key, the computed sum is placed in the current cell (B13). This formula works fine; however, it is somewhat inconvenient, especially when the number of cell references is large. Therefore, a shorter, easier method may be used. To do this, a **function** is used. A function is simply an entry representing a procedure or calculation that the spreadsheet software knows how to do, such as sum. Most spreadsheets require that a special symbol, such as the @ symbol, precede the function. For example, to sum column B in the spreadsheet shown in figure 7, key @SUM followed by the range of cells (separated by two periods) to be summed inside parentheses: @SUM(B5..B11). (With some spreadsheets, the range is entered by moving the cell pointer over the cells to be added rather than by keying the cell numbers.) Another popular spreadsheet uses a slightly different SUM function format: =SUM(B5:B11). While the exact syntax may vary depending on the software, the result will be the same. Some spreadsheet software also lets you take a short cut in selecting an entire row or column as a range by positioning the cell pointer on the number of the row or column and clicking the mouse or striking a key combination. Note that while the answer or solution is what appears in the cell, the formula is still considered to be the actual contents of the cell.

Functions to perform various actions are built into spreadsheet software. Commonly used functions include those that average numbers, round numbers, count data, and perform logarithmic functions.

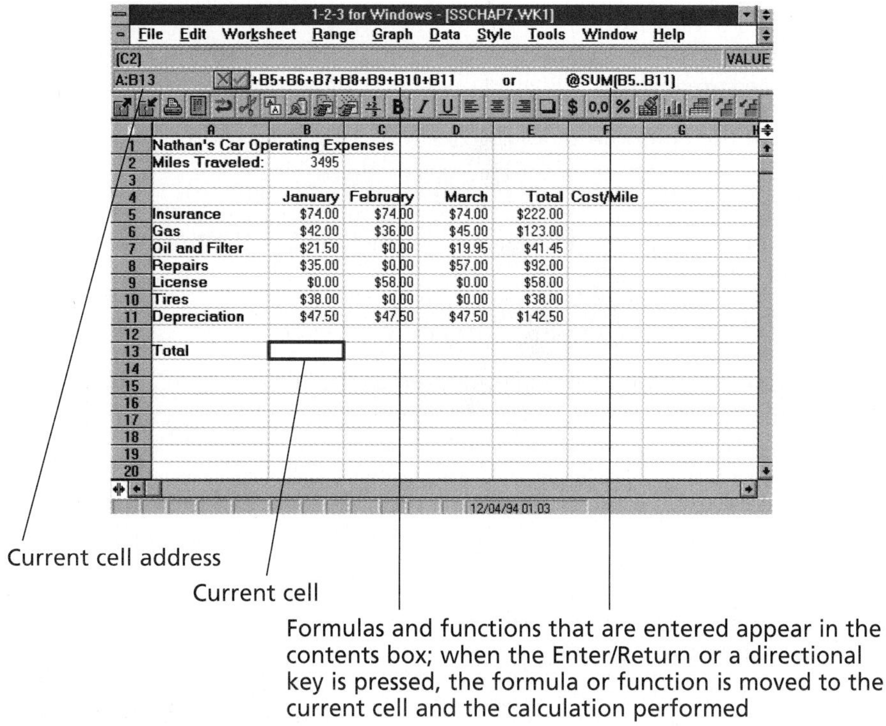

1-2-3 for Windows - [SSCHAP7.WK1]

File Edit Worksheet Range Graph Data Style Tools Window Help

[C2] VALUE

A:B13 +B5+B6+B7+B8+B9+B10+B11 or @SUM(B5..B11)

	A	B	C	D	E	F
1	Nathan's Car Operating Expenses					
2	Miles Traveled:	3495				
3						
4		January	February	March	Total	Cost/Mile
5	Insurance	$74.00	$74.00	$74.00	$222.00	
6	Gas	$42.00	$36.00	$45.00	$123.00	
7	Oil and Filter	$21.50	$0.00	$19.95	$41.45	
8	Repairs	$35.00	$0.00	$57.00	$92.00	
9	License	$0.00	$58.00	$0.00	$58.00	
10	Tires	$38.00	$0.00	$0.00	$38.00	
11	Depreciation	$47.50	$47.50	$47.50	$142.50	
12						
13	Total					

12/04/94 01.03

Current cell address

Current cell

Formulas and functions that are entered appear in the contents box; when the Enter/Return or a directional key is pressed, the formula or function is moved to the current cell and the calculation performed

figure 7

To enter formulas or functions, the cell pointer must be used to select the cell that is to receive the calculated value.

Use the following procedure to **copy-and-paste** the formula or function in cell B13 to the remaining total cells:

1. Select cell B13 as the current cell (if it is not already the current cell).
2. Choose the Copy command from the Edit menu to copy the formula or function to the clipboard (the clipboard is a temporary storage location in memory).
3. Select the range of cells C13 through E13 by positioning the pointer on cell C13, clicking and dragging (click the left mouse button and move the mouse to the right) to and including cell E13, then release the mouse button.
4. With cells C13 through E13 selected, choose the Paste command from the Edit menu to paste the formula or function with relative cell references into the selected cells.

This type of cell referencing is called **relative cell referencing**, because the cell addresses are automatically changed, or updated, by the program when the formula or function is copied to another cell.

Now that you know how to sum a column of data and copy the formulas, look at the procedure used to compute the cost per mile in Nathan's Car Operating Expenses spreadsheet. To compute the Cost per Mile, simply divide the total expense by the miles traveled. To accomplish this calculation, move the cell pointer to the desired location for the answer, then enter the formula or function. Match the following steps with those shown in figure 8; numbers in parentheses indicate where each of the following steps take place on the spreadsheet:

1. Move the cell pointer to the desired answer location.
2. Begin keying the formula by entering a plus sign (+).
3. Enter the first cell reference to be included in the formula. In this case, the cell is +E5.
4. Enter the division sign (/) from the keyboard.
5. Enter the cell reference to be used as the divisor, B2. (This reference must be absolute, because each of the following calculations must reference the data in this same cell.)
6. Strike Enter/Return, or press a directional key to indicate completion of the formula. The answer of $0.06 will appear in the current cell.
7. Copy-and-paste the relative cell addresses in the formula or function to cells E6 through E11.

Note that cell reference B2 is called an **absolute cell reference**. Absolute cell references remain the same no matter where the formula is copied. Dollar signs ($) are used so that the spreadsheet software can tell the difference between them and relative references.

After the formulas to compute the Cost/Mile have been entered and copied for each expense, the total Cost/Mile must be calculated to complete the spreadsheet. Either the formula +F5+F6+F7+F8+F9+F10+F11 may be entered, or the Sum function @SUM(F5..F11) may be entered in cell F13 to total the cost per mile column.

1-2-3 for Windows - [SSCHAP7.WK1]

File Edit Worksheet Range Graph Data Style Tools Window Help

(C2) VALUE

A:F5 +E5/B2

	A	B	C	D	E	F	G
1	Nathan's Car Operating Expenses						
2	Miles Traveled:	3495					
3							
4		January	February	March	Total	Cost/Mile	
5	Insurance	$74.00	$74.00	$74.00	$222.00		
6	Gas	$42.00	$36.00	$45.00	$123.00		
7	Oil and Filter	$21.50	$0.00	$19.95	$41.45		
8	Repairs	$35.00	$0.00	$57.00	$92.00		
9	License	$0.00	$58.00	$0.00	$58.00		
10	Tires	$38.00	$0.00	$0.00	$38.00		
11	Depreciation	$47.50	$47.50	$47.50	$142.50		
12							
13	Total	$258.00	$215.50	$243.45	$716.95		
14							
15							
16							
17							
18							
19							
20							

12/04/94 01.10

(1) (2) (3) (4) (5)

figure 8

Steps to enter the formula to calculate cost per mile.

When using a spreadsheet, all of the labels, values, formulas, and functions are entered in a manner similar to that described here. If you later change any value that is used in a formula or function, remember that the formula will automatically recalculate using the new value and place the updated result in the formula's cell.

Do It!

1 Using any spreadsheet program at your disposal, enter the spreadsheet shown in figure 8. Enter the expense data for January, February, and March, and then input the miles traveled, the formulas or functions to total the rows and columns, and finally, the formula to calculate the cost per mile. *Don't worry about formatting (using bold labels and values that appear as dollar and cents) your spreadsheet at this time.* When the spreadsheet is completed, save it to your data disk or directory/folder with a file name of XXXSP-A (where *XXX* are your initials, *SP* is the module code, and A identifies this activity).

2 Modify the miles traveled and expense amounts in the spreadsheet you just entered for your own (or a family member or friend's) car expenses. Enter the expense amounts for any 3-month period you wish. When you complete your spreadsheet, print it, and then save it to your data disk or directory/folder with a file name of XXXSP-B (where *XXX* are your initials).

3 Research your spreadsheet's online help system, and describe the mouse or keystroke procedure to copy an individual cell or range of cells.

Trends

Imagine: Office Equipment "Talking" to Each Other

Imagine a telephone that walks you through the steps of making a conference call, or lets you view a summary of phone messages rather than listen to all of them in detail. Or how about a digital fax machine that lets you insert a disk containing a word-processing or spreadsheet document that can be broadcast to a whole group of people simply by touching a display screen.

No, you have not seen this office-of-the-future on *The Jetsons*, nor is it far-out fantasy. Right now, Microsoft is working to develop a new operating system architecture that it calls "At Work" to link various pieces of office equipment together: fax machines, printers, telephones, copiers, and computers.

In this new, integrated work environment, you can use your personal computer to communicate with other freestanding machines in the office, giving you command of their functions. For example, copy machines will notify you when their toner is low, and printers can let you know when they are out of paper or it is time for maintenance. In addition, this "At Work" technology will include security features for handling data encryption, signature authorization, rendering technology for screen drawing, and document viewing. Companies that are working with Microsoft to incorporate this technology into their products include Delrina, Hewlett-Packard, McCaw Cellular, U.S. West, and Yamaha.

Printing Reports

As you have seen, spreadsheet data and the calculated results are displayed on the computer's display screen as the user works with the spreadsheet program. In addition, the worksheet portion of the spreadsheet display is frequently printed to obtain a hard copy or displayed or printed in a variety of graph formats.

Any of the data stored in a spreadsheet may be printed to produce reports. The user is free to define the items to be printed. Frequently, the entire spreadsheet will be printed for reference and filing; however, selected portions or ranges of information often produce more meaningful reports.

Other Spreadsheet Features

There are several additional features that increase the effectiveness and efficiency of spreadsheet use. These features include the generation of graphs and charts, insertion and deletion of rows and columns, formatting, protecting spreadsheet data and files, hiding spreadsheet cells, locking titles, and the use of macros and templates. Also, more than one spreadsheet (also referred to as a worksheet) can be loaded and active simultaneously. Additional features are identified in the comprehensive list provided by figure 14.

Graphic Output

Many spreadsheet programs are capable of producing graphs from the data both in screen display and printed form. Computer graphic images are often used to enhance information and thus improve communication. Most spreadsheet programs can use the data that appears in the worksheet to create many different types of graphs: line, bar, stacked bar, XY, pie, and mixed graphs. Most spreadsheets use the following procedure to create a chart or graph:

1. Select the range of cells to be graphed. Note that the range of cells to be graphed in the Car Operating Expenses spreadsheet are E5 through E11.
2. Choose the New Graph command from the appropriate menu. At this time, you may be asked to key the name you want to identify your graph or chart.
3. Select the type of graph desired.
4. Choose the Data Labels command (or similar command) from the appropriate menu, then provide the additional cell reference data that enables the spreadsheet program to display descriptive information such as *x* and *y* axis labels, keys, and so on with the graph or chart.
5. Copy the graph to the clipboard, exit the graph generator, define a range of cells where you would like to place the graph, and then paste the graph from the clipboard into the spreadsheet.

The three-dimensional pie chart and bar graph shown in figures 9 and 10 illustrate Nathan's total car operating expenses for the months of January, February, and March.

figures 9 & 10

Graphs and charts produced by the spreadsheet can be displayed and printed in black and white, shades of gray, or full color. Graphs and charts may appear in a separate worksheet or on the same worksheet with the data from which they were derived. If any of the labels, values, formulas, or functions are changed, the graphs or charts will be automatically redrawn to reflect the changes.

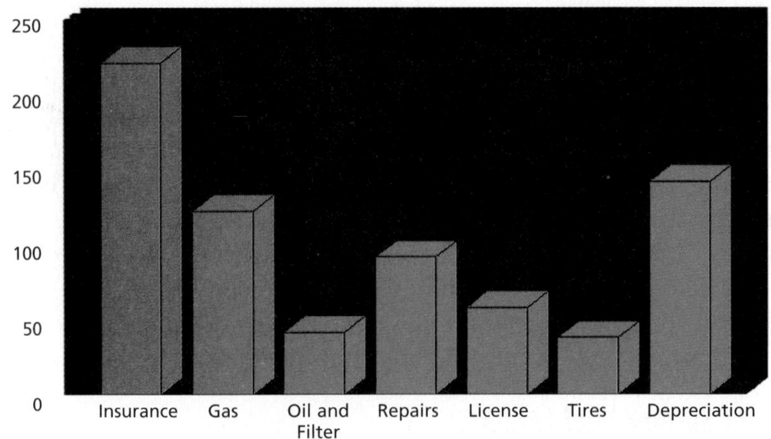

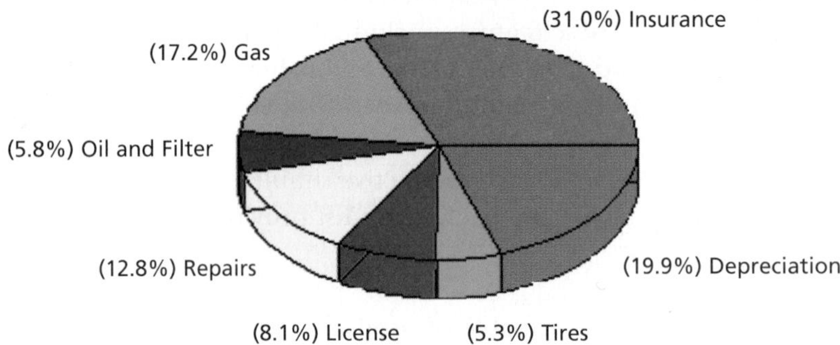

Insertion and Deletion

During the development or modification of a spreadsheet, you may discover that you need to add an explanatory note or title or insert additional data or results (figure 11). Spreadsheet programs provide an Insert command, which is used to insert new rows and columns. When a new row is added, all cells that are adjacent to it are moved up or down (depending on your choice) to accommodate it; similar adjustments are made when new columns are added. To insert one or more blank rows or columns, use the following procedure:

1. Select any cell as the current cell in the row or column adjacent to the one you want to insert.
2. Choose the Insert command, and then specify whether you want to insert a row or column and if the new insertion should appear before or after the row or column containing the current cell.
3. Choose the appropriate command (OK button) to execute the insertion.

It may also be necessary to remove rows or columns that are no longer needed. The procedure for deleting rows and columns is almost the same as for inserting. Once the command is given and the deleted row or column specified, the vacated row or column is filled with the contents from the adjacent cells. It is with the use of insertion and deletion that the advantage of relative cell addressing in formulas becomes obvious. For example, assume that you have entered a formula in cell B13 to add the values in cells B5 through B11. Later, if you need to insert another row whose value you would like to have added into the total, your formula will not include it. The only solution is to change the formula. If you use relative cell addressing, however, and sum the cells in column B, any new row that is added within that range will automatically be included in the formula, because the range of cells will automatically be expanded by the software. Therefore, changing formulas is unnecessary when insertions are made. The same is true for deletions, because the software will contract the range of the formula when a row or column is deleted.

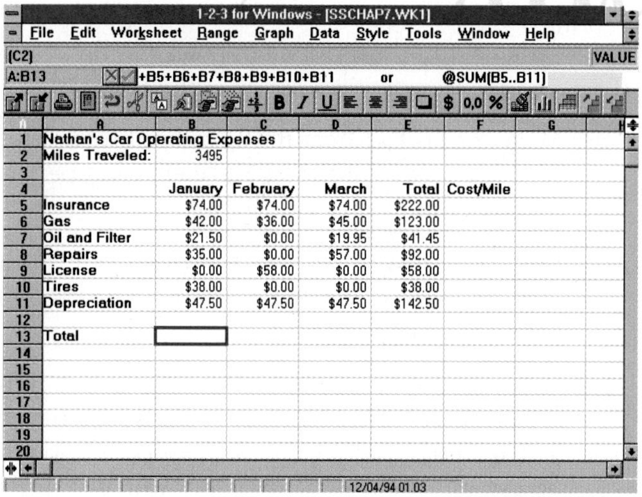

1-2-3 for Windows - [SSCHAP7.WK1]

File Edit Worksheet Range Graph Data Style Tools Window Help

(C2) VALUE

A:B13 +B5+B6+B7+B8+B9+B10+B11 or @SUM(B5..B11)

	A	B	C	D	E	F
1	Nathan's Car Operating Expenses					
2	Miles Traveled:	3495				
3						
4		January	February	March	Total	Cost/Mile
5	Insurance	$74.00	$74.00	$74.00	$222.00	
6	Gas	$42.00	$36.00	$45.00	$123.00	
7	Oil and Filter	$21.50	$0.00	$19.95	$41.45	
8	Repairs	$35.00	$0.00	$57.00	$92.00	
9	License	$0.00	$58.00	$0.00	$58.00	
10	Tires	$38.00	$0.00	$0.00	$38.00	
11	Depreciation	$47.50	$47.50	$47.50	$142.50	
12						
13	Total					

12/04/94 01.03

figure 11

Spreadsheet programs allow you to edit an existing spreadsheet to change figures, add comments, and insert or delete columns and rows.

Formatting

Most spreadsheet programs have been designed and developed with several commands that facilitate formatting. These formatting commands enable you to control the appearance of your spreadsheet document when it is printed.

Figure 12 illustrates the result of using several formatting commands with Nathan's Car Operating Expenses spreadsheet. Note that all the grid lines have been removed; the title has been centered and appears in bold, Arial MT 24 point size font; the column headings are bold and underlined; a total line has been added under the column data; the total Cost/Mile value is shaded and enclosed within a border; and a double total line has been added under the totals.

To use the formatting features, use the following procedure:

1. Select the cell or cells to be formatted.
2. Choose the desired formatting command (font, bold, print size, border, shading, alignment, and so on).
3. Respond to any additional information that may be required regarding the chosen formatting command.
4. Choose the appropriate command (press the OK button) to execute the format command.

Protecting Spreadsheet Data and Files

Most spreadsheet programs can be instructed to protect the data contained within a spreadsheet or spreadsheet file. Initially, all cells and files are considered to be unprotected; however, they may become protected in a variety of ways. For example, you can do any of the following:

1. Assign a password to a file when it is saved. Once a file is password protected, anyone who wishes to open and load the file must first know the password. If you use passwords, be sure to remember your

password as well as the exact capitalization and characters. Password-protected files cannot be opened without the password, and there are no provisions to find out what the password is if you forget it.

2. Make the spreadsheet file a read-only file. When a file is a read-only file, other users of the spreadsheet can open and load the file into memory but cannot change the data.

3. Protect individual cells, cell ranges, or the entire spreadsheet from change. Once protected, the specified cell contents cannot be changed except by you.

4. Prevent other users from changing and updating a spreadsheet file that is accessed by many individuals on a network. When your file is protected on a network, other users can open the file with read-only access, but you are the only user who can save changes to the file.

figure 12

Example of a formatted spreadsheet.

All labels appear in Arial font

Column headings are bold and underlined

Title is centered and appears in bold, Arial MT 14 point size font

Nathan's Car Operating Expenses

Miles Traveled: 3495

	January	**February**	**March**	**Total**	**Cost/Mile**
Insurance	$74.00	$74.00	$74.00	$222.00	$0.06
Gas	$42.00	$36.00	$45.00	$123.00	$0.04
Oil and filter	$21.50	$0.00	$19.95	$41.45	$0.01
Repairs	$35.00	$0.00	$57.00	$92.00	$0.03
License	$0.00	$58.00	$0.00	$58.00	$0.02
Tires	$38.00	$0.00	$0.00	$38.00	$0.01
Depreciation	$47.50	$47.50	$47.50	$142.50	$0.04
Totals	$258.00	$215.50	$243.45	$716.95	$0.21

Single total line

Double total line

Total Cost/Mile is shaded and enclosed within a border

Hiding Spreadsheet Cells

Spreadsheet programs can be instructed to hide various parts of a spreadsheet from displaying and/or printing. Commands may be used to hide comments, labels, numeric values, graphs, and other items that you do not want to display or print. Specifically, most full-featured spreadsheets permit the hiding of:

1. Individual cells.
2. Range(s) of cells.
3. All data in a spreadsheet.

4 Rows and columns.

5 Graphs, charts, and the data in them.

6 Colors denoting information in graphs and charts.

7 Text and data ranges in a graph.

8 Slices of a pie chart.

9 Percentage labels of a pie chart.

Locking Titles

When working with large spreadsheets, it is often necessary to scroll right or down to columns and rows that do not initially appear on the screen. When the spreadsheet is scrolled, the leftmost or topmost columns that often contain identifying label information no longer appear on the screen. Most spreadsheet programs have a lock column and row feature that fixes specified columns or rows on the screen. For example, if column A and rows 1 through 2 were locked, they would remain on the display screen regardless of what columns or rows are scrolled.

Using Macros

As used with computer software, the term **macro** refers to a series of keystrokes or program instructions remembered by the software so that the sequence may be executed quickly whenever desired. For example, all of the keystrokes necessary to copy a formula from one cell to the cell below it might be recorded by the program. Then, when the user wants to copy a formula, only one or two keystrokes are needed to cause the series of stored commands to be carried out. Some macros may already be stored when spreadsheet software is purchased; others may be recorded at the option of the user.

Do It!

1 Format the spreadsheet you entered and saved as XXXSP-A in the previous Do It! activity to match figure 12. (If you did not complete this activity, enter the spreadsheet shown in figure 12.) When you finish formatting the spreadsheet, print and then save it to your data disk or directory/folder (with a file name of XXXSP-C (where *XXX* are your initials).

2 If your spreadsheet has graphic capabilities, create a pie chart and a bar graph depicting your (a family member's or friend's) total car operating expenses from the spreadsheet named XXXSP-B (where *XXX* are your initials) that are prepared in the previous Do It! activity. If you did not complete this activity, use the spreadsheet in number 1 above.

3 Using the spreadsheet from number 1 above, insert "Car Washing" as a new expense category between the "Gas" and "Oil and Filter" categories. Enter an expense amount of $10.00 per month, then enter the formulas to compute the sum and cost per mile. Delete the "Depreciation" expense category and all of its associated data. Print the completed spreadsheet.

Using Templates

A **template** is a "skeleton" spreadsheet that includes labels, formulas, and perhaps macros but has incomplete or no data. The data is then entered by the user, and the computations are made. Templates are often included in spreadsheet programs, sold by software vendors, or created by individual users.

As an example of how a template is used, assume that a person who invests in stocks wants to use a spreadsheet to keep transaction records. The investor also wants to predict what the value of the stock investments might be under various market conditions, along with the tax consequences of various investment decisions. As an alternative to entering all of the data and formulas from scratch, the investor might purchase a stock-investment template. This template would already include all of the formulas and labels indicating where to key in the price paid for a stock, tax rate, and so on. Additionally, it might include data related to tax laws and the buying and selling of stock. On keying in data, all of the pre-defined computations take place with no further effort by the user.

The mortgage and loan analysis report shown in figure 13 was created from a template in a popular spreadsheet program. The template was loaded into the spreadsheet, and then the principle, annual interest rate, length of loan, number of payments per year, and date of the loan entered. The rest of the data was calculated by the formulas contained in the template. Note that the monthly payment for a $15,000.00 car loan at 8.5% over 3 years is $473.51 per month. Also, note that the total amount of interest is $2,046.47, and the total cost of the loan is $17,046.47. The body of the report shows the detailed data for each of the 36 monthly payments.

Comprehensive List of Features and Capabilities

A comprehensive list of spreadsheet features and capabilities is illustrated in figure 14. As new software is developed and existing software updated, many of these features will become standard, built-in capabilities of all spreadsheet software.

Using a Spreadsheet

As you learned earlier, spreadsheets can be used to record data that already exists or predicts what might happen in the future. In this section, you learn more details about using spreadsheets.

Using the Spreadsheet for Planning

One of the most common uses of spreadsheets is as a planning tool. A plan is a way of deciding what you want to do. As an example, suppose that Anna, a high-school student, wants to use a spreadsheet to help budget her spending and savings each month during the year. She wants to be able to enter the money she earns from her part-time job and deduct her expenses to compute how much she will have left to put in a savings account for college. She would also like to be able to ask "what if" questions (what if I get a raise in pay, what

MORTGAGE AND LOAN ANALYSIS

figure 13

Completed mortgage and loan analysis template for a car loan.

ANALYSIS

Principle	15,000.00
Annual interest rate (eg: 8.25)	8.500
Length of loan (in years)	3
Payment periods per year	12
Start date of loan	6/96

Monthly payments	473.51
Number of payments	36

To calculate final Total interest and Total loan cost, extend the table to row: **53**

Principle	15,000.00
Total interest	2,046.47
Total loan cost	17,046.47

PAYMENT NUMBER	PAYMENT DATE	BEGINNING BALANCE	INTEREST	PRINCIPLE	BALANCE	ACCUMULATIVE INTEREST
1	6/96	15,000.00	106.25	367.26	14,632.74	106.25
2	7/96	14,632.74	103.65	369.86	14,262.87	209.90
3	8/96	14,262.87	101.03	372.48	13,890.39	310.93
4	9/96	13,890.39	98.39	375.12	13,515.27	409.32
5	10/96	13,515.27	95.73	377.78	13,137.49	505.05
6	11/96	13,137.49	93.06	380.46	12,757.03	598.11
7	12/96	12,757.03	90.36	383.15	12,373.88	688.47
8	1/97	12,373.88	87.65	385.86	11,988.01	776.12
9	2/97	11,988.01	84.92	388.60	11,599.42	861.03
10	3/97	11,599.42	82.16	391.35	11,208.07	943.20
11	4/97	11,208.07	79.39	394.12	10,813.94	1,022.59
12	5/97	10,813.94	76.60	396.91	10,417.03	1,099.19
13	6/97	10,417.03	73.79	399.73	10,017.30	1,172.97
14	7/97	10,017.30	70.96	402.56	9,614.75	1,243.93
15	8/97	9,614.75	68.10	405.41	9,209.34	1,312.03
16	9/97	9,209.34	65.23	408.28	8,801.06	1,377.27
17	10/97	8,801.06	62.34	411.17	8,389.88	1,439.61
18	11/97	8,389.88	59.43	414.08	7,975.80	1,499.03
19	12/97	7,975.80	56.50	417.02	7,558.78	1,555.53
20	1/98	7,558.78	53.54	419.97	7,138.81	1,609.07
21	2/98	7,138.81	50.57	422.95	6,715.86	1,659.64
22	3/98	6,715.86	47.57	425.94	6,289.92	1,707.21
23	4/98	6,289.92	44.55	428.96	5,860.96	1,751.76
24	5/98	5,860.96	41.52	432.00	5,428.96	1,793.28
25	6/98	5,428.96	38.46	435.06	4,993.91	1,831.73
26	7/98	4,993.91	35.37	438.14	4,555.77	1,867.11
27	8/98	4,555.77	32.27	441.24	4,114.52	1,899.38
28	9/98	4,114.52	29.14	444.37	3,670.15	1,928.52
29	10/98	3,670.15	26.00	447.52	3,222.64	1,954.52
30	11/98	3,222.64	22.83	450.69	2,771.95	1,977.34
31	12/98	2,771.95	19.63	453.88	2,318.07	1,996.98
32	1/99	2,318.07	16.42	457.09	1,860.98	2,013.40
33	2/99	1,860.98	13.18	460.33	1,400.65	2,026.58
34	3/99	1,400.65	9.92	463.59	937.06	2,036.50
35	4/99	937.06	6.64	466.88	470.18	2,043.14
36	5/99	470.18	3.33	470.18	0.00	2,046.47

figure 14

Features and capabilities of full-featured spreadsheet programs.

Feature Capability	Description
Memory and Disk Usage	
Networkable	Will execute on most of the common network systems.
Expanded memory	Automatically uses additional expanded memory if available.
Files opened	Will permit several files (worksheets) to be open at once.
Commands	
Mouse	Supports a mouse.
Internal codes	Formatting uses codes inserted in the worksheet.
Menus	Uses a menu-driven interface.
Quick/hot key	Uses key combinations to choose commands.
Content line	Display area that shows data entered.
Screen Display	
Cell adjustment	Width and length if cells can be adjusted.
Ribbon	Ribbon containing icon buttons for choosing frequently used functions.
Style	Font, style, shading, and color attributes can be changed.
Page breaks	Page breaks are shown and can be inserted.
Hide cells	Hides columns in a worksheet, or entire worksheets, to prevent display and printing data.
Cell protection	Cells may be protected from updates.
Print preview	Spreadsheet pages previewed in condensed format as they will appear when printed.
Adjustable zoom	Worksheet, or parts of a worksheet, may be enlarged or reduced to size.
Pivot table	Allows user to view data from different perspectives (each product line by quarter sales, or quarter sales for each product line).
Lock columns and rows	Locks (or freezes) columns along the top of the current worksheet, rows along the left edge of the worksheet, or both. These columns and rows (which usually contain labels) remain in view as the worksheet is scrolled.

figure 14

Features and capabilities of full-featured spreadsheet programs (continued).

Feature Capability	Description
Cell Entry and Editing	
Cell editing	Permits editing within the current cell.
Keyboard shortcut keys	Keys can be designated to include non-keyboard characters in the worksheet.
Tips/suggestions	Monitors users work and suggests quicker and more efficient alternative to performing tasks.
Find/replace	Finds or replaces specified characters in labels, formulas, or both in a range.
Move	Transfers a range of data, including cell formats, protection status, and formatting, to another range in the same spreadsheet.
Copy	Copies a range of data, including cell formats, protection status, and formatting, to another location in the same spreadsheet.
Multiple layers	Can support many different worksheets within the same spreadsheet (Worksheet A, B, C, and so on).
Transpose	Changes the data from a horizontal arrangement to a vertical arrangement or vice versa.
Go to	Moves the cell pointer to a specified cell or range.
Format	Can change the cell format to currency, percentage, scientific notation, and so on.
Graphics	
Graphs	Can generate several different types of graphs and charts (area, bar, HLCO, line, mixed, pie, and XY) in any of the following options: 3-D effect, stacked or unstacked data ranges, vertical or horizontal orientation, and table of values.
Graphics inserted in worksheet	Graphic charts can be inserted within the worksheet.
Drag-and-plot	Selected range(s) of numeric values can be dragged to a chart and the chart will automatically be redrawn with new figures.
Auto update	Graph is automatically updated with the data used to create it is changed in the worksheet.
Complex Spreadsheet Features	
Spreadsheet links	Can connect to another spreadsheet to send and receive data via cut-and-paste or dynamic data-exchange linkage.

figure 14

Features and capabilities of full-featured spreadsheet programs (continued).

Feature Capability	Description
Database links	Can connect to a database to send and receive data via cut-and-paste or dynamic data-exchange linkage.
Word-processor links	Can connect to a word processor to send and receive data via cut-and-paste or dynamic data-exchange linkage.
Text-file links	Can connect to other application software via cut-and-paste or dynamic data-exchange linkage.
Printing	
Background printing	Can print as a low or high priority while user performs other tasks.
Print queue	Worksheets that are to be printed and are temporary stored in a print queue may be modified by priority.
Prints range	Can print a user defined (selected) range of cells within the worksheet.
Landscape/portrait	Documents may be printed to paper in portrait (vertical) orientation or in landscape (horizontal) orientation.
File Management	
Timed backup	A backup copy of a worksheet is automatically made based on a fixed time period.
File manager	Can manage files (delete and rename spreadsheet files).
Spreadsheet descriptions	Can accept and store user supplied (name, title, and so on) and computer generated information (version number, current date) about each spreadsheet.
Senses import files	Can sense files that are being imported (files not created by the spreadsheet software).
Import/export formats	Can read from disk and write to disk in several of the most common spreadsheet formats.
Macros	
Record keystrokes	Can record keystrokes for later replay.
Programmable macros	Can enter instructions to program macros.
Remappable keyboard	Keyboard keys may be changed and remapped to simplify macro usage.
Functions	
User-defined functions	User may define functions, store them, and recall them for later use.
Built-in functions	Full compliment of over 100 pre-recorded functions.
Tutorial functions	Prerecorded functions that provide step-by-step procedures for use.

Feature Capability	Description
Automatic usage	Software remembers functions that are used most often.
Auto-functions	Commonly used functions (sum, count, average, and so on) can be selected from the toolbar to perform appropriate tasks for a selected range of cells.
Professional	
Sorting	Can arrange selected cells alphabetically or numerically.
Password protection	Uses a password to protect a spreadsheet from being modified.
Encryption	Can encrypt a spreadsheet stored on disk so that others who access it cannot read what is stored.
Help and Documentation	
On-line tutorial	Software that provides tutorial help and example of how to use commands and features.
Context-sensitive help	Online help information that may be displayed relative to the current command or task being performed.
Keyboard templates	Cardboard or plastic coated templates that can be laid over the keyboard that identify functions performed by certain keys.

figure 14

Features and capabilities of full-featured spreadsheet programs (continued).

if I spend more or less each month) that could help her plan for college. Figure 15 shows how such a spreadsheet might be arranged and how data and computed values appear for the first half of the year. Once the budget data and earnings are entered, the amount that can be saved for college can be calculated. If the amount of savings is low (or negative), Anna must then decide where to cut her spending.

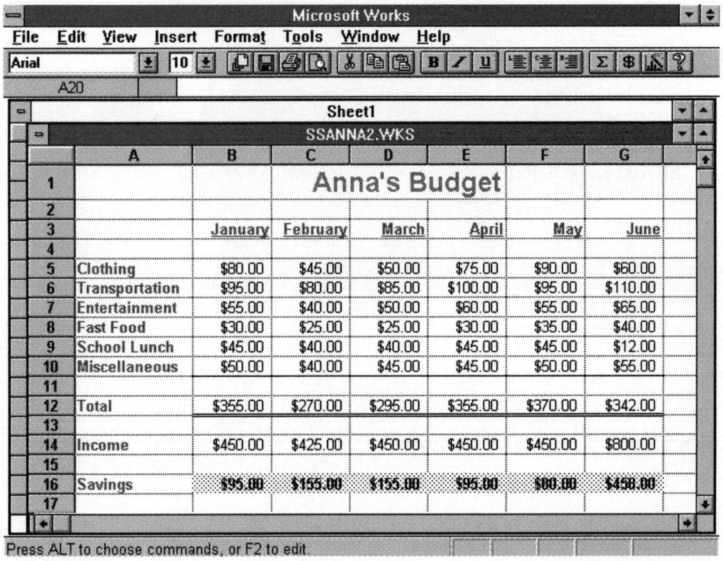

Microsoft Works

File Edit View Insert Format Tools Window Help

Arial 10

A20

Sheet1

SSANNA2.WKS

	A	B	C	D	E	F	G
1			Anna's Budget				
2							
3		January	February	March	April	May	June
4							
5	Clothing	$80.00	$45.00	$50.00	$75.00	$90.00	$60.00
6	Transportation	$95.00	$80.00	$85.00	$100.00	$95.00	$110.00
7	Entertainment	$55.00	$40.00	$50.00	$60.00	$55.00	$65.00
8	Fast Food	$30.00	$25.00	$25.00	$30.00	$35.00	$40.00
9	School Lunch	$45.00	$40.00	$40.00	$45.00	$45.00	$12.00
10	Miscellaneous	$50.00	$40.00	$45.00	$45.00	$50.00	$55.00
11							
12	Total	$355.00	$270.00	$295.00	$355.00	$370.00	$342.00
13							
14	Income	$450.00	$425.00	$450.00	$450.00	$450.00	$800.00
15							
16	Savings	$95.00	$155.00	$155.00	$95.00	$80.00	$458.00
17							

Press ALT to choose commands, or F2 to edit.

figure 15

A spreadsheet can be used as a planning tool to answer "what if" questions.

Careers

Management Opportunities

Not surprisingly, the top computer jobs in any business are management positions. Top job titles include Vice-President for Management Information Systems and Director of Management Information Systems, to name two. Career opportunities for information management personnel working under the President (or Chief Executive Officer) depend on the size and organization of that particular company. The duties of the information management executive include working with other executives to develop strategic plans for the management information function of the company, making detailed plans for carrying out that strategy, and overseeing the daily operations of the company's computers.

More and more businesses are recognizing the importance of information management, and they are now making the information management executive an integral part of the company's top management team. Most individuals who hold these top management jobs have extensive college backgrounds and work experience in information systems. Many also bring to their jobs valuable expertise in other business areas, such as finance or marketing, from which they acquire the necessary information processing skills.

Using the Spreadsheet for Modeling

Modeling is a term used to describe the process of mathematically simulating something that happens in the world. If the mathematic simulation is good enough, the model can be used to predict future action with at least some degree of confidence in the prediction. For example, economists use models to try to track the performance of the economy and predict when depressions, recessions, and good times will happen. Similar modeling is done by others to try to predict when the stock market will go up or down and by approximately how much. Most models such as these involve many variables and complex formulas; however, spreadsheet software can provide the means to record the variables and compute the desired prediction outcomes.

Linking Spreadsheets

Some spreadsheet programs have the ability to link several spreadsheets together to provide consolidated reporting. Assume, for example, that you operate three restaurants. The manager of each restaurant fills in financial data using a spreadsheet template that you provide. You then retrieve those spreadsheets from the managers and link them together to form one spreadsheet that automatically sums all of the data from the three underlying spreadsheets. In this way, you can examine the financial position of your entire restaurant group and use the consolidated data as a company-wide decision-making tool.

Integrating the Spreadsheet with Other Programs

While much spreadsheet use involves nothing beyond the spreadsheet software, the number of applications that use spreadsheet information is growing. As a result, several methods have been developed to permit spreadsheet data-sharing. For example, most full-featured spreadsheet programs can be linked with database, word processors, and a host of other software programs through processes known as **linking** and **dynamic data exchange**. When two or more of these programs are linked together, data from one may be passed to the other for display and further manipulation; likewise, if data is changed in any one of the linked software programs, all of the others will automatically be updated. This process is often referred to as dynamic data exchange because changes to data dynamically affects all of the other programs that are linked to it.

Another method that can be used to share spreadsheet data with other software programs is the **cut-and-paste** method. Data in the spreadsheet that is to be shared with another program, such as a word processor, is selected, cut (or copied) from the document (where it is stored in memory in a place called the clipboard), and then pasted to its new location in the receiving program.

Other spreadsheet programs can store their output to disk in a format (called an export file) that can be read by other programs. For example, spreadsheet data stored on disk can be merged (imported) into a word-processing document, where it can be further formatted and included with other information.

Online Catalog Marketing

Mention the word catalog and what comes to mind? A glossy, colorful book filled with page after page of merchandise. Now, catalogs do not have to be printed on paper; they can be placed on computer disks or CD-ROMs and viewed at your personal computer.

Perhaps you have already seen one of these online catalogs. Companies such as AT&T, Buick, Ford, Goodyear, CTE, MCI, and Chrysler are using them to expand their marketing strategies. These companies are using software developers to create interactive disks containing product information that they can distribute to dealers or prospective customers. Just pop one of these disks or CD-ROMs into a personal computer and you have an online catalog, complete with colorful graphics and sound that make for a very compelling marketing presentation. Disks can incorporate all of the information necessary for a customer to make an informed decision, including product specifications, product options, and pricing. Some even have interactive activities such as games to involve the prospect—and make the product offerings even more interesting.

Issues In Technology

Catalogs on disk offer companies an entire catalog of benefits. They save companies money because they can be easily updated (without tossing out an investment in printed catalogs) and cost less to mail to a large audience than bulky, book-like catalogs. Because they are a reusable medium designed to replace paper catalogs (which are eventually discarded), computer disks do a better job protecting the environment.

Software is now available that lets companies produce their own interactive catalogs on disk. The software puts together a database of text and graphics in a catalog layout, complete with search-and-print capabilities. This technology makes it possible for individuals to learn about new products from their personal computers.

Hardware Requirements

The same hardware guidelines that apply to most other application software apply to spreadsheet software as well. Some type of spreadsheet software is available for almost all computers. Each new program that is introduced, however, seems to have greater capability and requires more memory and disk space than the program it replaces or competes with. In general, the greater the capability of a spreadsheet program, the greater the memory and disk space that are required. As the size of a spreadsheet grows, the execution speed of the hardware becomes more important. In a small spreadsheet, all of the formulas can be recalculated almost instantaneously; newer spreadsheet programs recompute only formulas whose underlying cells have changed. Even with that computational advantage, however, the increased speed of a faster computer is desirable for very large, complex spreadsheets.

Do It!

1 Using any spreadsheet program at your disposal, enter the spreadsheet shown in figure 15. Be sure to use the format commands at your disposal to make the spreadsheet appear similar. After the spreadsheet is completed, save it to your data disk or directory/folder with a file name of XXXSP-D (where *XXX* are your initials).

2 Modify the spreadsheet you just entered for your own budget. Use the Insert and Delete commands to add and remove budget categories as necessary. Use as many of the formatting features that you have available to make your spreadsheet attractive and easy to read. When your spreadsheet is completed, save it to your data disk or directory/folder with a file name of XXXSP-E (where *XXX* are your initials).

3 Does the spreadsheet program you are using have template files? If yes, open and print at least one of them. If not, use your spreadsheet program to make a template that you can use to record the grades you earn from homework, test, quizzes, projects, and so on for *each* of your classes. Be sure to have your template file compute an average grade. (Remember that the template should contain all of the labels and formulas but no values.) Save your completed template to your disk and directory/folder with a file name of XXXSP-F (where *XXX* are your initials).

Summary

A spreadsheet (also called a worksheet) is a row and column arrangement of data—a grid containing labels, values, and numbers computed through the use of formulas.

- A single horizontal area extending across a spreadsheet is known as a row, and a single vertical area running a spreadsheet is known as a column.
- Rows and columns are designated with letters or numbers, for example, columns A, B, C, and so on, and rows 1, 2, 3, and so on.
- The space that exists between the intersection of a row and a column is known as a cell, and it may be referenced by its column and row numbers, such as C3. A cell is used to store one value, character, label, or formula.
- A cell that has been selected (highlighted or outlined) to receive data is referred to as the current cell.
- Any contiguous group of cells is known as a range.
- Cells containing alphanumeric characters are referred to as labels, while cells containing numbers that are entered or calculated are referred to as values.
- A cell pointer (also called the cursor) is used to select cells and indicate where data is to be entered.
- When data is entered, they appear in a contents box before being moved into the current cell.
- Formulas entered into cells designate what operations are to be performed and the values to be used in performing the operations.
- The use of pre-defined mathematic functions and procedures simplifies the entry of formulas.
- Relative cell references refer to a cell by relating its position to other cells. Thus, if the spreadsheet is expanded or contracted, cell references change accordingly. Conversely, absolute cell references refer to a particular row and column intersection on the spreadsheet and do not change when the spreadsheet is changed.
- Printed reports can be portrait or landscape orientation and may include all or a selected part of a spreadsheet.
- A variety of charts and graphs may be generated from data contained in a spreadsheet.
- New rows and columns may be inserted into an existing spreadsheet, and unwanted rows and columns of data may be deleted.

Summary

- Formatting refers to the use of commands that enable the user to control the appearance of the spreadsheet.
- Data within a spreadsheet or stored in a file on disk may be protected from unauthorized changes by other users.
- Various parts of a spreadsheet may be hidden from displaying or printing.
- Specified columns or rows may be fixed on the display screen so that the data within them will not scroll out of view.
- Macros are "recordings" of sequences of keystrokes for later "replay" during spreadsheet use; they simplify spreadsheet use by making it possible to take complex actions with only one or two keystrokes.
- Templates consist of spreadsheets that already have labels and formulas in them but no or incomplete data. They are available for many common applications, and on entry of the values by the user, they provide computed results.
- Spreadsheets are commonly used as a planning tool, for modeling, to link several spreadsheets together, and to integrate data with other software applications.
- Generally, the greater the capability of a spreadsheet program, the greater the hardware requirements.

The following key terms were defined in this module. For each of the following terms, write on a separate piece of paper the number of the definition followed by the letter of the appropriate term.

Terms

A. absolute reference

B. cell

C. cell pointer

D. column

E. formula

F. function

G. label

H. macro

I. range

J. relative reference

K. row

L. spreadsheet

M. template

N. value

O. current cell

P. contents box

Definitions

1 cell addresses within a formula that remain the same no matter where the formula is copied

2 cell addresses that are automatically changed or updated when the formula is copied to another cell

3 a built-in procedure or calculation

4 a mathematic equation used to compute spreadsheet values

5 an image that appears on the screen and is used to select cells

6 the place where entered data appears before being moved to the current cell

7 cells containing alphanumeric characters

8 cells containing numbers

9 any contiguous group of cells

10 the cell that will receive entered data, or the cell(s) that will be affected by the computer's next processing action

Matching

11 the space in a spreadsheet used to store one value, label, formula, or function

12 a single horizontal area extending across a spreadsheet

13 a single vertical area extending downward through a spreadsheet

14 a row and column arrangement of data—a grid of labels and values computed through the use of formulas

15 a series of keystrokes or program instructions that is remembered by the software so that the sequence may be executed quickly whenever desired

16 a skeleton spreadsheet that includes labels, formulas, and perhaps macros but has incomplete data

Review

1. Explain how cell address C5 is derived? (Obj. 2)
2. What is the difference between a label and a value? (Obj. 3)
3. How is entering a formula into a cell different from entering a label or a value? (Obj. 3)
4. What is the purpose of functions? (Obj. 3)
5. What part do ranges play in entering formulas? (Obj. 3)
6. Briefly describe the procedure to copy-and-paste a formula from cell B15 to cells C15 through F15. (Obj. 3)
7. What is an absolute cell reference? What is a relative cell reference? (Obj. 3)
8. What is the advantage of relative cell references? (Obj. 3)
9. Describe the procedure to create a chart or a graph. (Obj. 4)
10. What is the difference between portrait and landscape orientation? (Obj. 5)
11. When a printed report is desired, what portion of a spreadsheet is printed? (Obj. 5)
12. What happens to formulas when a row or column is inserted or deleted? Is this always the case? Explain. (Obj. 6)
13. Do you think it is important to use formatting commands to enhance the appearance of a spreadsheet? Support your answer. (Obj. 6)
14. Why would anyone want to protect individual cells or spreadsheet files from being changed? (Obj 6.)
15. Why would anyone would want to hide data that is in a spreadsheet? (Obj. 6)
16. Why would it be convenient to lock columns or rows from scrolling out of view? (Obj. 6)
17. Define a macro. What is its purpose? (Obj. 6)
18. What is the purpose of a template? (Obj. 6)
19. Define planning and modeling. What is the difference between the two? (Obj. 7)
20. What is the purpose of linking together several spreadsheets? (Obj. 7)
21. What is the purpose of dynamic data exchange or linking spreadsheets with other software application programs? (Obj. 7)
22. What can be said of the relationship between spreadsheet capability and computer hardware requirements? (Obj. 8)

Activities

1 *Writing* A friend who has never used a spreadsheet program before has asked you to provide her with your opinions regarding the most important features to look for when purchasing a spreadsheet program. Open and load one of the spreadsheets that you prepared in one of the Do It! activities, or enter one of the spreadsheets illustrated in this module. Use formatting and graphing to prepare an example that illustrates several of the features your friend should consider. Print your example spreadsheet document, and use a pen or pencil to identify these features on the hard copy. Save your spreadsheet to your data disk or directory/folder with a file name of XXXSP-G (where *XXX* are your initials).

2 *Math* In this activity, you create a spreadsheet in the format shown below to compute compound interest. Compound interest is computed on both the principal and accumulated interest. For example, if you borrowed $1000.00 for two years at 7% compound interest, you would pay a total of $144.90 in interest. The amount of interest would be $70 (7% of $1000.00) at the end of the first year and $74.90 (7% of $1070.00) at the end of the second year. The formulas have been provided below. You are to create the spreadsheet, enter the following loan amounts and rates, and then determine the total amount that must be paid at the end of 10 years for each loan:

	Amount	Interest Rate
Loan 1	15,000.00	.07
Loan 2	15,000.00	.08
Loan 3	20,000.00	.06

Save your spreadsheet to your data disk or directory/folder with a file name of XXXSP-H (where *XXX* are your initials).

Compound Interest

Your Name:
Class:
Date:
Amount of Loan: $0.00
Interest Rate: 0.00%

Year	Amount	Interest	Amt + Int
1	+B6	+C10*B7	+C10+D10
+B10+1	+E10	+C11*B7	+C11+D11
+B11+1	+E11	+C12*B7	+C12+D12
+B12+1	+E12	+C13*B7	+C13+D13
+B13+1	+E13	+C14*B7	+C14+D14
+B14+1	+E14	+C15*B7	+C15+D15
+B15+1	+E15	+C16*B7	+C16+D16
+B16+1	+E16	+C17*B7	+C17+D17
+B17+1	+E17	+C18*B7	+C18+D18
+B18+1	+E18	+C19*B7	+C19+D19

Activities

3 *Science* Use a spreadsheet to record the freezing point of the following solutions, then generate a bar graph depicting this information, which is:

Solution	Freezing Point
Salt	–2
Sugar	0
Distilled water	2
Calcium	–6

Save your spreadsheet to your data disk or directory/folder with a file name of XXXSP-I (where *XXX* are your initials).

4 *Global Perspectives* The purpose of this activity is to track and analyze foreign currency exchange rates. Divide into teams of four students each. Each team should choose a country with a different exchange rate from that of the United States. Your task is to convert $100.00 U.S. dollars per day to your designated foreign currency. Each team member should be responsible for a part of the project. One possible division of the responsibilities is:

Student 1: Research the daily foreign currency rate for the team's chosen currency, and report this rate to your team for each of the 5 days.

Student 2: Create the spreadsheet in the format shown below. Enter the data and formulas, and then print the results. Save your spreadsheet to your data disk or directory/folder with a file name of XXXSP-J (where *XXX* are your initials).

Student 3: Use the spreadsheet graphing capabilities to prepare a graph or chart showing the change in your chosen currency from day 1 to day 2, from day 2 to day 3, and so on for each of the 5 days. Label the graph or chart, and print it so that you can show it to your class.

Student 4: Present your team's results to the class.

Team:
Name of Currency:
Class:
Date:

U.S. Dollars:

Days	Exchange Rate	Amount In Other Currency
Monday	Amount	Formula
Tuesday	Amount	Formula
Wednesday	Amount	Formula
Thursday	Amount	Formula
Friday	Amount	Formula

5 *Teamwork Project* In this activity, you participate in a team competition dealing with stock investments. The purpose of this activity is to simulate stock investment and tracking. Divide into teams of four students each. For this simulation, each team should assume they have $5000.00 to invest in stocks. Each team should refer to their daily newspaper and purchase whatever stock(s) that they believe will yield the greatest return (all of the $5000.00 must be invested). After each team has purchased its stock, members of the team must track each stock, report changes, and update their spreadsheet so that their investment(s) can be recalculated. The team with the most profit at the end of 4 consecutive days is the winner. Each team member should be responsible for a part of the project. One possible division of the responsibilities is:

Student 1: Obtain the daily changes for the team's chosen stock(s), and report this information to your team for each of 4 days.

Student 2: Create a spreadsheet in the format shown below. Enter the data and formulas into the template provided (SPFILE-C) on the template disk, and then print the results.

Student 3: Use the spreadsheet graphing capabilities to prepare a graph or chart showing the total change in your investments from day 1 to day 2, from day 2 to day 3, and so on for each of the 4 consecutive days. Label the graph or chart, and print it so that you can show it to your class. Save your spreadsheet to your data disk or directory/folder with a file name of XXXSP-K (where *XXX* are your initials).

Student 4: Present your team's results to the class.

Stock Investments

Team:
Class:
Date:

Stock	Shares Purch.	Cost/ Share	Initial Cost	Day 1	Day 2	Day 3	Day 4
Totals							

Activities

Activities

6 *Speaking* Prepare a spreadsheet that will record and calculate the results of a survey that you conduct in your school. For example, you could ask several juniors and seniors which of the current Top-10 recordings are their favorites. Be sure to calculate the percentages of each group's responses. Give a 2- to 4-minute presentation to your class regarding the results of your survey. Have a printout of the results available to pass around the class. Save your spreadsheet to your data disk or directory/folder with a file name of XXXSP-L (where *XXX* are your initials).

7 *Ethics* Using a computer to access another computer user's data can actually be a criminal activity. This activity is commonly referred to as "hacking." The term hacking is often used by computer enthusiasts to describe the challenge of breaking codes or other protection schemes that prohibit unauthorized access. Hackers that break codes to access other users' confidential information, records, computer time, and so on are committing a crime. Do you think that most hackers realize they are committing a criminal act? What can be done to deter hacking?

8 *Internet* Access the Internet, and use your search engine to find information about spreadsheet template files that can be used for spreadsheet applications. Identify the template file(s) found, and describe how it/they can be used with a spreadsheet program. Use terms such as SPREADSHEET, TEMPLATE, FILES, and so on to help narrow your search.

Publishing PB

Overview

The publishing industry has been revolutionized by the use of computers. Virtually everything that was done manually just a few years ago is now fully computerized (figure 1).

For those just getting into publishing, the first big hurdle is likely to be the vocabulary. Just as with most crafts (be it medicine, plumbing, or whatever), publishing has its own jargon. This module helps you to "speak the tongue."

Along with speaking the language, you learn about the different typefaces, fonts, and formatting styles that are available. These words all refer to how the print looks—its artistic design, if you will.

Many of the functions that were previously available only with professional desktop publishing software are now available in most word-processing programs. Some advanced functions, however, are still available only in high-end publishing applications. This is especially true when working with long, complexly formatted documents. Distinctions between the program types are made clear in this module, and you will able to determine which application to use for a given purpose.

A significant portion of this module is devoted to how documents are actually created with a computer application program, whether it be a word processor or a high-end publishing program. This discussion carries you from the original entry of text and graphics through the page-layout process to the final output. It includes a thorough discussion of color as well as black-and-white output.

Objectives

1. Define publishing.
2. Understand and use the measurement system of the publishing industry.
3. Distinguish among typefaces, fonts, and styles. Describe the three categories of typefaces, and give examples of each.
4. Understand the concept of compound or object-oriented documents.
5. Understand and use the tools that publishing software typically provides.
6. Describe the parts that typically make up long documents.
7. Understand the tradeoffs involved in scanning images and in printing images.
8. Evaluate different products for their suitability to short, design-intensive documents and long documents.
9. Describe the concepts of color models and color separations.
10. Successfully produce a publication.

figure 1

The production area of this publisher shows how pervasive computers have become in the publishing industry.

What Is Publishing?

Historically, publishing has been the process of getting composed writings (manuscripts) into printed form. For a typical book or magazine produced in the 1970s or 1980s, the process involved steps such as:

- The writer wrote the material, probably using a typewriter.
- A person known as a typesetter (using a special machine or manual methods) converted the words to "typeset" form; that is, he or she put the words into a proportional typeface as opposed to the monospaced typing in which they were originally entered. The typeset words appeared in a single, long column of text called galleys.
- A paste-up person cut the typeset columns into segments and pasted them down onto a piece of pasteboard in the desired arrangement. If photos and illustrations were desired, space was left for them when the pasteup was done.
- A printing plate was made to place on an offset press (a printing press in which ink is attracted to the image on the plate and then "offset" from the printing plate onto paper). The pasted-up text was photographed with a camera to produce a negative, and the negative was then used to produce the positive-reading paper or metal plate to put on the press to produce the copies. Any photos that appeared on a page were manually screened; that is, a fine-meshed screen was laid on top of the picture to break it into a fine pattern of dots; it was photographed to make the negative.
- If the page was to be printed using color photos, a manual process involving differently colored filters (similar to colored glass) was used to trick the plate-making camera into seeing only the areas that were to appear in a particular color. Thus, different plates were made for each of four colors, from which other colors may be made.

With the use of computers for publishing, these steps may be condensed. Indeed, it is possible to do all of them directly with your computer system. Figure 2 shows some of the results that can be attained when using the computer for publishing. Using one or more application programs (depending on their capability), you do the following steps directly:

figure 2

Publications as varied as these can all be produced on a desktop or a notebook computer.

- Key in text (or enter it through scanning, handwriting, or voice recognition), and it appears on the screen already in a proportional typeface. Different typefaces may be applied to different text either during entry or later.
- Scan photographs into the computer using one of several different types of scanners. Once stored in the computer, the photos may be enhanced or artistically modified. Details on many of these effects will be found in the Graphics Presentation module.
- Create drawings and illustrations directly on the computer.
- Layout pages on the screen, arranging text, photos, and illustrations according to a predetermined design.
- Send finished pages directly to a laser printer (quality) or an imagesetter (higher quality) to produce a negative or positive image on film from which the printer can make a plate for the offset press. Some laser printers can produce an offset plate directly, with no intervening steps on the part of the printer. For small quantities, output directly from a laser printer is satisfactory; this completely removes an offset press from the process.

Use of computers in publishing has certainly fostered profound changes in the industry. While you can still find some companies and printers doing things the old way, the overwhelming majority of publishing today is done with computers.

Speaking the Language of Publishing

As you work with publishing software on your computer, you will find many instances of references to terms that are part of the jargon. By studying the following sections, you will be familiar with these terms.

Basic Units of Measure

While you have spent your life using measurements based on inches and feet (and perhaps some familiarity with the metric system), publishing has its own traditional measurement system. This system is based on **points** and **picas**. As shown in figure 3, 12 points make up a pica, and 6 picas make up an inch. Common usage in the printing industry would refer to a 30-pica line—not a 5-inch line.

Some publishing software allows you to choose which measuring system to use. For example, you may be able to set the software to show all sizes as points, picas and points, inches, or millimeters. Regardless of your software's capability, it is wise to learn the lingo of the industry.

figure 3

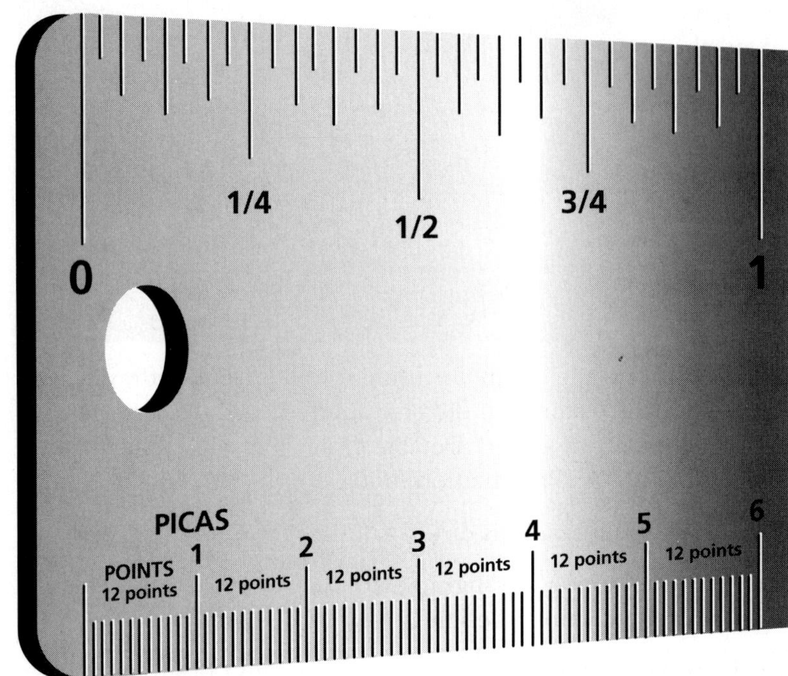

In publishing, measurements are usually in picas (1/6 inch) and points (1/12 pica or 1/72 inch).

Size and Spacing of Type

Letters printed on a page are measured by their approximate height, not their width, and the size is always specified in points. While any size may be used, common sizes for the body text of publications such as books and newspapers are 8 through 12 points. For headlines and text that require special emphasis, such as in advertisements, very large type may be used. For example, 1 inch–tall letters are 72-point type. The **type size** is measured from the top of the capital letter to the base of the text. Figure 4 shows how type is measured as well as some new vocabulary about type.

Once you have picked a size for the characters that make up the words of

figure 4

The letters of type rest on the baseline. Ascenders and descenders extend above and below the main part of the letters, which is known as the x-height.

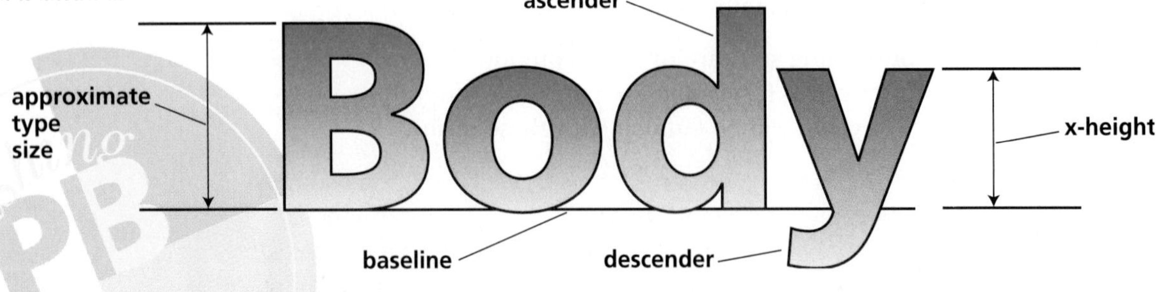

your publication, you can also pick what is called the **leading** (rhymes with sledding). Back in the olden days, when type was made from metal, typesetters would put thin strips of lead between the lines of type, thus the derivation of the term. Essentially, leading means the distance from the top of one line to the top of the following line.

When you talk about type sizes and leading, you generally say that you have set the *type size* on *leading*. For example, if you are using 10-point type and the leading is 12 points, you are setting 10 on 12; in shorthand notation, you can write that as 10/12. As a general guideline, text is easier to read if the leading is at least 120% of the typesize. For example, 120% of 10-point type gives 12-point leading. Figure 5 shows examples of how leading affects readability.

This paragraph is set 10 on 10. It is close, making it difficult to read

This paragraph is set 10 on 15, making it a bit easier to read.

This paragraph is set very open at 15 on 30. It gives a very stylistic effect and would look right at home in some advertisements.

figure 5

The amount of leading makes a big difference in appearance.

A Tapestry of Typefaces

A **typeface** is a set of letters, digits, and symbols that share a particular design or artistic look. You can categorize typefaces in three different groups (figure 6). These are:

- **Serif typefaces**, which consist of characters that have small horizontal lines (called **serifs**) attached at the ends of strokes. Serifs are designed to help guide the eye horizontally along a line, making these typefaces easier to read (other things being equal). Serif typefaces are commonly used in the body text (regular paragraphs) of a publication.
- **Sans serif typefaces**, which do not have the small horizontal lines known as serifs (*sans* means *without*). Sans serif typefaces are frequently used in headlines or when a clean look is desired in body text.
- **Decorative** or **display typefaces**, which are those that have very noticeable design features. In other words, they are not what you would consider to be "plain, everyday type." Decorative faces may or may not have serifs. Some decorative faces are very difficult to read, while others are quite easy to read. They are used primarily to grab a reader's attention, such as in main headings.

Figure 6 gives you a very small sample of the thousands of typefaces that are available. It is very common to find hundreds of different ones installed on a particular computer. If you do not like any of the typefaces to which you have access, you can even design your own (if you have appropriate software). Different typefaces can give very different "feels" to publications. Whether the intent of a publication is to convey fun and frivolity or staidness and security, the selection of an appropriate typeface helps set the mood.

A given typeface may be available in different styles. Typical **type styles** are bold, italics, and underscore. These styles can also be combined. In addition,

Issues
In Technology

A Whale of a Tale: The First Coffee-Table Book Typeset with a Desktop Computer

In 1986, both the Macintosh computer and laser printers were in their infancy. That year, however, they made history by being used for the first time to produce a full-color, glossy-photo, coffee table book on Hawaiian whaling.

All of the text was entered, edited, and typeset on a Macintosh Plus computer, then the output was printed on an original Apple LaserWriter. These pages were then photographed to make printing plates for the offset press.

Titled *Whale Song,* the book was written by MacKinnon Simpson, with photography, design, and editing by Robert Goodman, who did his work on the Macintosh. Commissioned by the Lahaina Whaling Museum in Maui, Hawaii, the book showcases many of the museum's artifacts as well as the beauty of the whale in its natural oceanic environment. The book truly is a treasure, for it chronicles a portion of Hawaiian history previously not covered by any other text.

Robert Goodman went to Hawaii as a photojournalist and later joined the National Geographic Society as a photographer, working with Jacques Cousteau in the Red Sea. Later, he formed his own publishing company, producing several award-winning books the old-fashioned way before doing *Whale Song* electronically.

By today's standards of what is considered to be the bare minimum for desktop publishing, the equipment used to produce *Whale Song* was more like a minnow than a whale. The Macintosh used had only a 20 MB hard drive.

Decorative

Shelley Script
changing a font not only changes the style of the text,
But it also changes the width of spacing in the text.

STENCIL
CHANGING A FONT NOT ONLY CHANGES THE STYLE OF THE TEXT,
BUT IT ALSO CHANGES THE WIDTH OF SPACING IN THE TEXT.

CASTELLAR
CHANGING A FONT NOT ONLY CHANGES THE STYLE OF THE TEXT,
BUT IT ALSO CHANGES THE WIDTH OF SPACING IN THE TEXT.

Serif

Palatino
Changing a font not only changes the style of the text,
but it also changes the width of spacing in the text.

Times Roman
Changing a font not only changes the style of the text,
but it also changes the width of spacing in the text.

Sans Serif

Frutiger Roman
Changing a font not only changes the style of the text,
but it also changes the width of spacing in the text.

Tekton
Changing a font not only changes the style of the text,
but it also changes the width of spacing in the text.

figure 6

Typefaces can be categorized as decorative, serif, or sans serif, as illustrated by these examples.

some typefaces may come in several different weights, such as light, normal, medium bold, bold, and extra bold. Some may also come in expanded or condensed versions, referring to the width consumed by the characters. Any combination of a typeface, style, and weight is known as a **font**; for example, a typeface known as Hero in normal weight and normal style is one font, while the same typeface in bold weight and italics is another font.

You are probably accustomed to referring to "spaces" and "dashes." Quality typefaces typically include at least two widths for each of these: an en width, and an em width. **En spaces** and **dashes** are generally the width of the letter *N*; **em spaces** and **dashes** are the generally width of the letter *M*.

Almost all typefaces are proportionally spaced, that is, wide letters take up more space than narrow letters. The Courier typeface is a notable exception, in that it is monospaced (all letters consume the same width). The proportional spacing makes the print look very nice, because each letter consumes only the amount of space that it needs. Even with proportional spacing, however, some particular combinations of letters look as if they are spaced too far apart. This problem is especially apparent when the combinations are printed in large sizes, and to make the appearance better, the letters are **kerned**. That is, they are placed closer together than their width would call for. Examples of kerning are shown in figure 7. All high-end publishing programs are capable of automatically kerning letter pairs, even though you can manually change the letter spacing if you wish.

AVAIL
AVAIL

DELTA
DELTA

figure 7

When letter pairs with "nestling" shapes occur, they can make words look like they have "holes" in them, especially in large type sizes. Kerning pulls the pairs closer together to improve the appearance, as in the AV, VA, LT, and TA combinations shown here.

Do It!

1 Working with a partner, study the typefaces in several magazines. Find the easiest-to-read and the most-difficult-to-read typeface. Discuss why you selected the particular ones. Did each magazine tend to use a lot of the same typeface to help give it a particular image? Make a report of your findings to the class, showing examples of the typefaces you chose.

2 Enter the text from figure 6, and format it using three different decorative typefaces, three different serif typefaces, and three different sans serif typefaces. Print out the result. If your computer does not have that many typefaces available, use as many as you have.

How Does a Publishing Program Differ from a Word-Processing Program?

In the early days of desktop computing, there was a very distinct difference between word-processing programs and publishing programs. In fact, the publishing programs were more accurately referred to as page-layout programs. These differences were:

- Word-processing programs were used to enter and edit text. After you keyed in text, the programs allowed you to correct it, rearrange it, and perhaps look for spelling errors. As far as layout, however, the programs were basically limited to setting margins on the page and controlling the number of blank lines between each pair of text lines.
- Page-layout programs were not designed to enter text; rather, they specialized in importing text that was originally entered with a word processor. They could also import graphics that had been created with a graphics program. Their strength was applying complex elements of layout to each page. For example, they could arrange text in multiple columns, make shaded backgrounds for items on the page, and make various-sized headlines.

As time went by, it seemed that each revision of a word-processing program added not just more text-handling features, but also more of the page-layout features that were previously the exclusive domain of publishing programs. And each revision of publishing programs added not just additional layout features, but also more of the text-handling capabilities that previously belonged only to word processors.

Now, word-processing programs can combine text and graphics on the page in a wide variety of layouts. This makes them suitable for producing many of the documents that otherwise would have required a publishing program (figure 8). Publishing programs have also continued to add word-processing features such as find and replace, spelling checkers, and thesauruses, until they can now serve as the vehicle for doing all of the text entry as well as the page layout.

With the changes in both products, it would seem they would converge into one program. This is precisely the case for many users. By choosing the

figure 8

Word-processing programs can be used to create professional-looking documents.

right word processor or the right publishing program, you can eliminate the need for the other. While an exact comparison of features must be between particular brands of products, there are a few generalities that can be made. For the most part, publishing programs are more powerful than word-processing programs in three main areas:

- Documents where precise control over the placement of items on the page is necessary. For example, publishing programs allow you to set any amount of space that you desire between lines, while many word-processing programs restrict you to a choice of a half-line, a whole line, or no line of space.
- Long documents with a lot of structure, such as reference manuals and price lists.
- Production of color separations for printing presses.

The Objects from Which a Publication Is Constructed

For this discussion, a publication can be anything from one page to an entire book. Any publication is made from some combination of text and graphics. Each piece of data in a publication, whether it be a chunk of text or a graphic, is known as an object. Where do these objects come from?

Text

Text for a publication can be entered directly using the program that will lay out the pages (either a word-processing or a publishing program). It can also be imported after having been created with a different program.

Different word-processing programs store their text using different file formats. Most word-processing and all publishing programs, however, include filters (small, built-in computer instructions) that can read the formats of all major word-processing programs.

Graphics

Most likely, the graphics included in a publication will have been generated with a program other than the one doing the page layout. While the built-in graphics abilities of word-processing and publishing programs have improved tremendously, they are still no match for the capabilities of programs that are dedicated to graphics. Graphics fall into two groups: pixel based, and line or vector based. This module does not cover graphics programs, but the type of graphics that you use can have a great impact on the quality of your finished publication as well as on its storage-space requirements and print times. Therefore, it is helpful to know the differences at this point.

Pixel-based graphics A computer display is made from dots. Each dot that makes up an image is known as a pixel (picture element). If you are working in black and white, each dot is either black or white. If you are working in color, each dot can be one of numerous colors. **Pixel-based graphics** are stored in the computer as the pattern of these dots; for example, if you have a graphic that is 600 dots wide and 600 dots high, the image is made of 360,000 dots (600 x 600). The amount of space that is required to store this image in the computer depends on how many colors you are using (figure 9).

Going to a larger-size graphic consumes much more storage space. You can see that to store many images you need a very large hard drive. Of course, files can be compressed so that they require less space. The lesson, however, is that graphics take disk space—the bigger the picture and the more colors there are, the more space is required. Bigger pictures and more colors also slow down the operation speed of the publishing program and increase print times very significantly.

If you are using photos in your publication, you will use pixel-based graphics, because that is the only way to get photographic quality (figure 10). You get photos into the computer by using a scanner, and you may then touch them up or make major modifications in them using any of various "photoshop"- type programs. You may also create pixel-based images with painting programs.

When deciding on the resolution of pixel-based graphics, whether they are scanned-in photos or created with a paint program, keep in mind the resolution of your intended output device. It is simply a waste of storage space and time to use a higher resolution than will have any impact on the quality of your output.

Other than their required storage space, the biggest drawback to pixel-based graphics is that resizing them results in a loss of quality. While reducing their size may not result in any noticeable degradation, enlarging them can result in the "jaggies" or "fuzzies," depending on how your software enlarges the image.

Line-based graphics **Line-based (vector) graphics** are usually created with a drawing or a CAD (computer-aided design) program. In a line-based program, each shape that you create is represented by a mathematic formula. This is true whether the shape is a line, alphabet letter, circle, rectangle, or free-form shape. To make an object larger or smaller, the size values in the formulas are changed by the application program. This means that the storage space required for a line-based drawing does not escalate simply because

figure 9

The greater the color depth used when scanning and/or saving images, the higher the quality. The trade-off is that higher quality requires much more storage space.

True Color Image

16.7 million colors

Requires 3 bytes (24 bits) per pixel

Actual file size of this image 5,357 kilobytes

Relative file size:

Beautiful true-color images such as this one require three bytes of storage for each pixel. Remember that one byte (8 bits) can represent the values 0-255, for a total of 256 values. Thus, one byte represents 256 different levels of red light, another 256 different levels of green light, and the third 256 different levels of blue light. Also remember that combining the full intensities of red, green, and blue light produces white. The total absence of all three of these light colors produces black. By varying the amount of each color in the mix, 16.7 million different colors can be represented.

256-Color Image

256 colors chosen in a palette by software

Requires 1 byte (8 bits) per pixel

Actual file size of this image 2,206 kilobytes

Relative file size:

This image is the same as the one above, with the number of colors reduced to just 256 possibilities. This reduces the amount of storage required from three bytes per pixel to one byte per pixel but reduces the quality of the image.

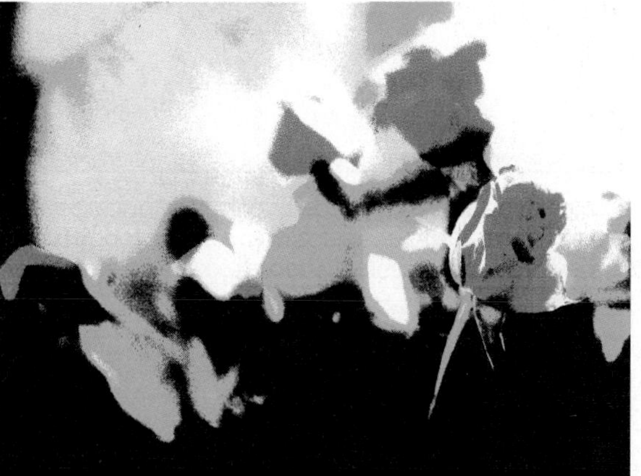

16-Color Image

16 colors

Requires 1/2 byte (4 bits) per pixel

Actual file size of this image 1,419 kilobytes

Relative file size:

Reducing the color depth still further, in this case down to a maximum of 16 colors, degrades the image severely. But it doesn't take much storage space — just half a byte per pixel, since 16 different colors can be represented with four binary digits.

Trends

Whatever Happened to the Paperless Office?

For years, futurists have predicted the demise of paper in offices. With the widespread use of networked computers, everybody was supposed to just read everything from the computer screen rather than printing documents on paper. Surprise! As the number of computers has increased, so has paper usage.

Whatever happened to the idea of the paperless office? Perhaps part of the increased use of paper results from the ease of correcting mistakes with computers. Before computers, a minor mistake may have been taken care of with a handwritten correction; now an office worker is likely to make the correction on the computer and reprint the entire page—or the entire document.

Fax machines are also doing their part to create more paperwork. Even with the ability to send documents via electronic mail, it is still common for an office worker to compose a document, print it, and then send it by fax to the intended receiver; now there are two paper copies of the document instead of one. To add to the puzzlement of the situation, the received fax is often scanned into the receiver's computer for further processing or storage.

Still another reason for the continued use of paper has to do with appearances—the "look" of the document. Until recently, the professional appearance of the document created on one computer would get lost on the receiving computer; the receiver would see an ugly page with nothing but lines of unformatted text. If both computers happened to have the same application programs, a document file sent over a network or phone line could be opened, but if the machines had different fonts, the look of the document would still be different. This problem of appearances is now being solved with the advent of software that can preserve the look—including the different fonts—of documents when they are shared between unlike computer systems. There are several competing systems available; the market will decide which will survive and serve as a standard. This new software may at last make the futurists' predictions come true—and the resulting decline in the use of paper would preserve a lot of forests.

figure 10

To store photographs, a pixel-based format is used. An editing program can help you to improve the image or transfigure the picture in numerous ways. As you see from the revision here, the edited photo can be much more appealing than the original.

you choose to reproduce the drawing at a larger size. Neither, however, does the required storage space shrink if you decide to reproduce the drawing at a smaller size. For an extremely complex drawing, file sizes can become very large.

Except for photographic-type images, line-based drawings are preferred. This is because of their scalability—the ability to reproduce them at both smaller and larger sizes than the original with no loss of quality (figure 11).

The Construction of a Page

The program you are using for page layout, whether it be a word-processor or a publishing program, enables you to place the various objects that make up a page in any position you want them to appear. For example, a typical newsletter page might include the name of the publication (the nameplate), the date of publication, some headlines, some photos, and some text. Figure 12 takes such a newsletter page and illustrates its various pieces so that you may see the parts from which it was assembled. Today, most programs fortunately provide plenty of online help that shows you how to perform various actions. Therefore, competence in using a program becomes the knowledge of what can be done, with the more exotic things being looked up in help when needed.

figure 11

Line-based drawings like this horse can be reproduced at wildly different sizes with no loss of quality.

During the early days of page-layout programs, the programs made copies of the files containing the underlying text and graphics and placed them in the one file containing the entire document. Many programs now do a much better job in that they simply keep up with the externally created file and use it directly rather than making a copy of it. This means that if you use a particular illustration and later modify it using the program that created it, the changes will appear in your document.

The most current of today's programs go a step further. The publication that you create can be thought of as a container for holding objects created by other applications. Because of the container/object orientation, you can do in-place editing of text or graphics that were created by the other

figure 12

A typical, highly designed page is made from a number of parts. Each part may have been created by the layout or other programs.

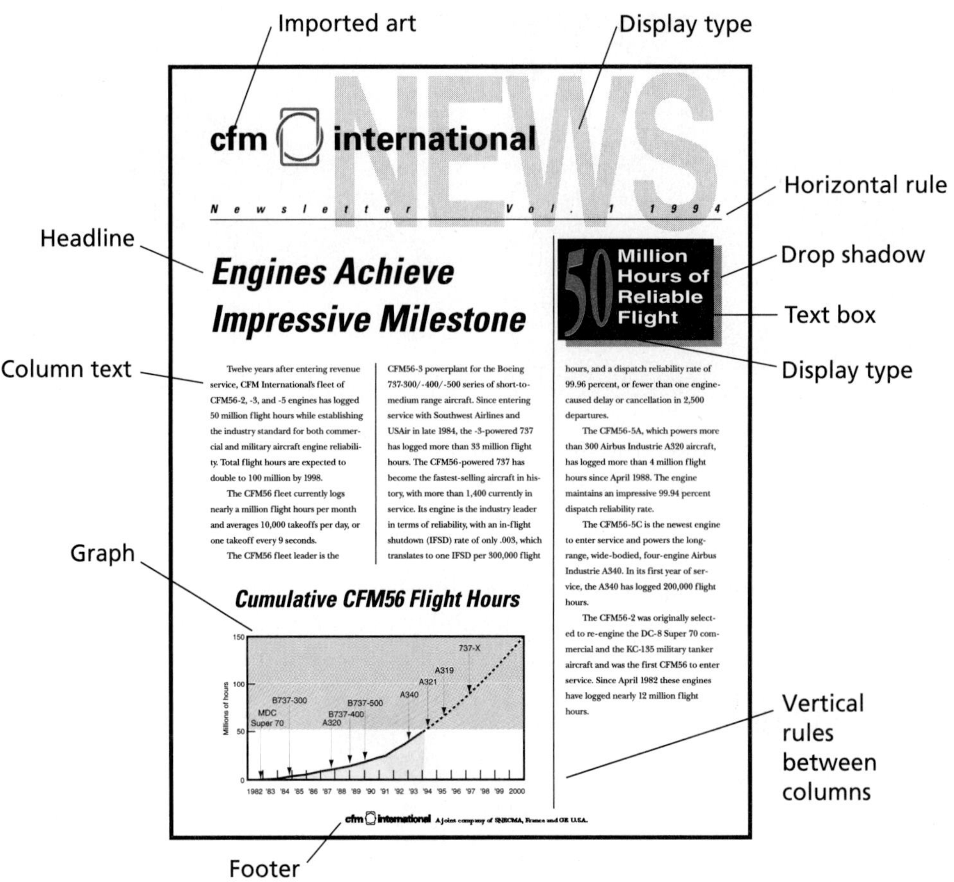

cfm international NEWS

Newsletter Vol. 1 1994

Engines Achieve Impressive Milestone

50 Million Hours of Reliable Flight

Twelve years after entering revenue service, CFM International's fleet of CFM56-2, -3, and -5 engines has logged 50 million flight hours while establishing the industry standard for both commercial and military aircraft engine reliability. Total flight hours are expected to double to 100 million by 1998.

The CFM56 fleet currently logs nearly a million flight hours per month and averages 10,000 takeoffs per day, or one takeoff every 9 seconds.

The CFM56 fleet leader is the CFM56-3 powerplant for the Boeing 737-300/-400/-500 series of short-to-medium range aircraft. Since entering service with Southwest Airlines and USAir in late 1984, the -3-powered 737 has logged more than 33 million flight hours. The CFM56-powered 737 has become the fastest-selling aircraft in history, with more than 1,400 currently in service. Its engine is the industry leader in terms of reliability, with an in-flight shutdown (IFSD) rate of only .003, which translates to one IFSD per 300,000 flight hours, and a dispatch reliability rate of 99.96 percent, or fewer than one engine-caused delay or cancellation in 2,500 departures.

The CFM56-5A, which powers more than 300 Airbus Industrie A320 aircraft, has logged more than 4 million flight hours since April 1988. The engine maintains an impressive 99.94 percent dispatch reliability rate.

The CFM56-5C is the newest engine to enter service and powers the long-range, wide-bodied, four-engine Airbus Industrie A340. In its first year of service, the A340 has logged 200,000 flight hours.

The CFM56-2 was originally selected to re-engine the DC-8 Super 70 commercial and the KC-135 military tanker aircraft and was the first CFM56 to enter service. Since April 1982 these engines have logged nearly 12 million flight hours.

Cumulative CFM56 Flight Hours

cfm international A joint company of SNECMA, France and GE U.S.A.

programs. For example, suppose you make an illustration with a drawing program and place that illustration on a complex page of text and graphics. By double-clicking the mouse on the illustration, the menus of the program that created it will appear on the screen and allow you to make changes. This is a simple concept, but it is one that took a tremendous amount of planning and programming by both the companies that produced the operating system of your computer and your application programs.

The menu choices and dialog boxes used to create a document vary widely depending on the software that you use. Typically, however, you make settings that control the appearance of text on the base page of your publication. Various other items that you place on the page can interact in various ways with the base page, and each typically has its own settings to control its appearance. Figure 13 shows the base-page settings that were selected through menu choices at one stage during the development of this book. Note that all of these settings were entered into the program by making menu choices or completing dialog boxes. Some programs can print out a specifications sheet, such as shown here, for checking purposes.

Predefined Styles

Most publishing programs enable you to use **predefined styles** to control the arrangement of items on a page. Some of these styles may come with the publishing software, and others can be created by the user. Depending on the program, these may be called by names such as tags, styles, or templates. You control the appearance of each piece from which the publication is made.

C:\DC14CA\C8\SAMPLE.STY

Base Page Settings

Page Size & Layout

Orientation: Portrait
Paper Type & Dimension: Letter, 8.5 x 11 in.
Sides: Double
Start On: Right Side

Margins & Columns

# of Columns: 1
Settings For Left Page
Top: 06,00 picas & points
Bottom: 06,00 picas & points
Left: 12,00 picas & points
Right: 06,00 picas & points
Widths/Gutters—1:33,00 picas & points
Settings For Right Page
Top: 06,00 picas & points
Bottom: 06,00 picas & points
Left: 06,00 picas & points
Right: 12,00 picas & points
Widths/Gutters—1:33,00 picas & points

figure 13

Simply selecting a menu choice caused the publishing program to print out these base page settings, which can be reviewed to confirm that the specifications are as desired.

For example, a document such as a long report or a book is likely to be made (at a minimum) from the following parts. Except for the main title, you will have at least several occurences each of the following kinds of parts:

- The main title.
- Major headings (known as level 1 headings).
- Intermediate headings (known as level 2 headings).
- Minor headings (known as level 3 headings).
- The text of paragraphs.

When you use **tags** or **styles**, all of the text typically defaults to a particular style, such as "body text." Then, by using the mouse and selection lists (or alternately, function keys with some programs), you mark each of the other parts as a particular style. In other words, you "tag" each heading to indicate to the program whether it is level 1, level 2, or level 3. All level 1 headings take on the appearance that is defined for level 1, all level 2 headings take on the appearance that is defined for level 2, and so on. There are several advantages to this system, including:

- You can use the same style for various different documents without having to redefine it.
- If you decide to change the appearance of one component (level 2 headings, for example), you just redefine the style and every occurence of that component changes its appearance automatically.
- The appearance given to each part of the publication is selected through dialog boxes. Figure 14 shows several of these dialog boxes

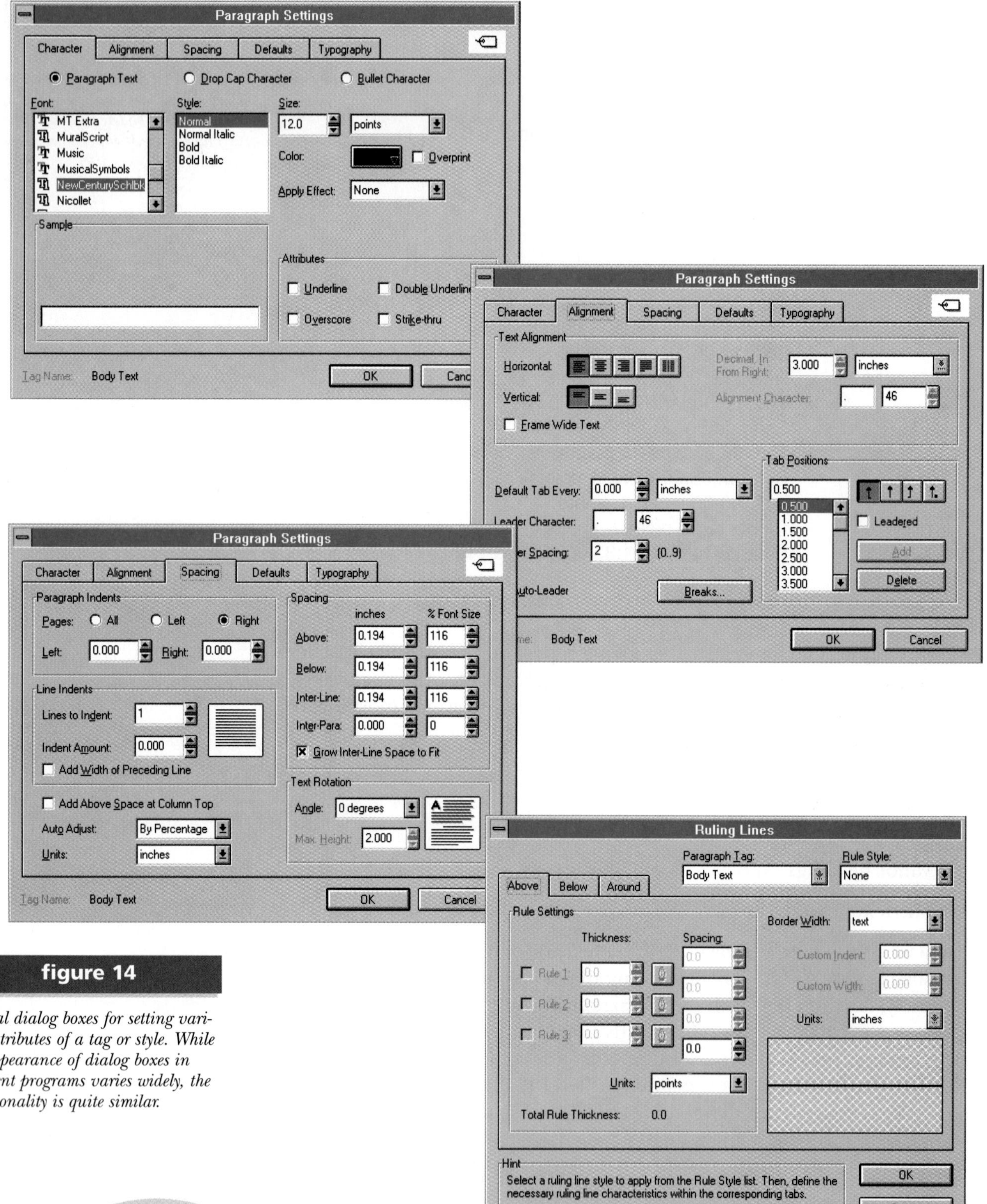

figure 14

Typical dialog boxes for setting various attributes of a tag or style. While the appearance of dialog boxes in different programs varies widely, the functionality is quite similar.

from one popular publishing program. If your program is capable of doing so, you can print out the specifications that you have assigned for each tag or style. An example of the description of body text (the default tag) at one point while working on this book is shown in figure 15.

C:\DC14CA\DC14CA.STY

Body Text

Font
Face: NewCenturySchlb
Size: 12 points
Style: Light
Color: Black
Overscore: Off
Strike-Thru: Off
Underline: Off
Double Underline: Off

Alignment
Horz. Alignment: Left
Vert. Alignment: Top
Text Rotation: None
Hyphenation: US DICT
Successive Hyphens: 2
Overall Width: Column-Wide
First Line: Indent
Relative Indent: Off
In/Outdent Width: 00.00 inches
In/Outdent Height: 1
In From Right to Decimal: 03.00 inches

Spacing
Above: 15.00 points
Below: 15.00 points
Inter-Line: 15.00 points
Inter-Paragraph: 00.00 points
Add in Above: When Not at Column Top
In From Left (Left Page): 00.00 points
In From Right (Left Page): 00.00 points
In From Left (Right Page): 00.00 points
In From Right (Right Page): 00.00 points

Breaks
Page Break: No
Column Break: No
Line Break: After
Next Y Position: Normal
Allow Within: Yes
Keep With Next: No

Tab Settings
Leader Char: 46
Leader Spacing: 2
Auto-Leader Off

Special Effects
Special Effects: None

Attribute Overrides
Line Width: Text-Wide
Overscore Height: 0.010/0.173 inches
Strike-Thru Height: 0.010/0.054 inches
Underline 1 Height: 0.010/0.010 inches
Underline 2 Height: 0.010/0.030 inches
Superscript Size: 10 points/0.078 inches
Subscrript Size: 10 points/0.018 inches
Small Cap Size: 10 points

Paragraph Typography
Automatic Pair Kerning: Off
Grow Inter-Line To Fit: On
Letter Spacing: 0.100 Ems
Tracking: 0.000 Ems Looser
Minimum Space Width: 0.600
Normal Space Width: 1.000
Maximum Space Width: 2.000
Vert. Just. At Top of Para: 0.208 inches
At Bottom of Para: 0.208 inches
Between Lines of Para: 0.000 inches

Ruling Line Above
Width: None

Ruling Line Below
Width: None

Ruling Box Around
Width: None

figure 15

This printout shows all of the settings for one tag or style of text. Note that each section shows the choices that have been made in a particular dialog box. A complex project may have dozens of different tags or styles, each with different settings in the combination of these or similar dialog boxes.

Do It!

1 In figure 13, many measurements are given in picas and points. Translate those picas and points into inches.

2 Measure the margins of a typical page of this text, and report your results in picas and points. Measure the size of various levels of headings (main headings and subheadings), and report your results in points.

Steps in Creating a Publication

The steps that you use to create a publication will differ depending on the program you are using. Several typical steps, however, can be examined for creating the simple, sample publication shown in figure 16. These steps are:

- Using the publishing program, start a new document and make page settings.
- Place the text file on the page, and make settings to control the appearance.

figure 16

This advertisement is an example of a document made from imported text and an imported graphic. The text is in plain format in the text file, and the typefaces, sizes, and styles are applied in the publishing program. The graphic can be moved by dragging it, and its size can be changed by clicking on it and then dragging a resizing handle.

- Place the graphic on the page, and make settings to control the appearance.
- Make any desired changes in the appearance of the text and graphic on the page.

Start a New Document

With most programs, you start a new document by selecting File . . . New from the pull-down menus (figure 17 is typical). You will probably not name the document until you select File . . . Save from the menu the first time. After the blank document is open, you will be able to select other menu choices to set, among other possibilities, the size of the page, whether it is a portrait or landscape orientation, and what the margins should be. Figure 18 shows a typical menu choice to select this.

figure 17

A typical menu from which to create a new document.

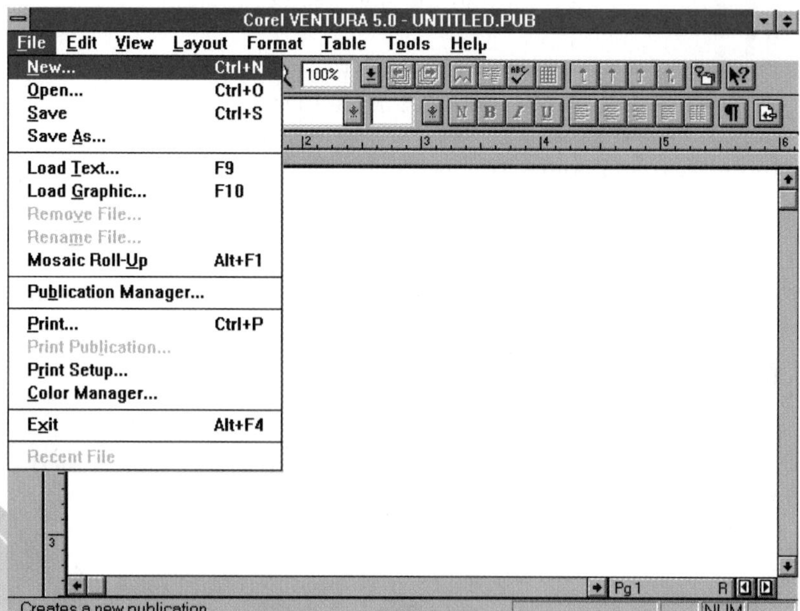

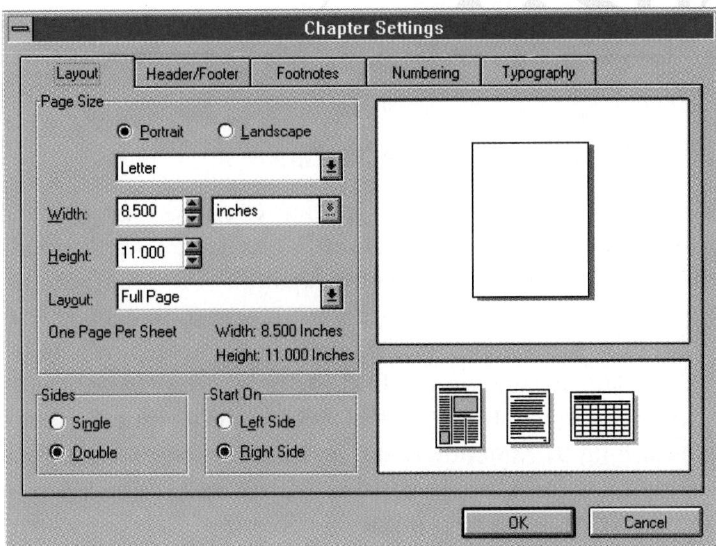

figure 18

A typical menu for setting the page size and layout.

Place the Text File on the Page

Depending on your program, you may place text directly on the page or may need to draw a frame on the page first into which the text will be placed. If you need to draw a frame, there will be a button or menu choice that allows you to do so. Once that is taken care of (or if you do not need a frame), use a menu choice or button to put the text on the page. While the name of the menu item will vary depending on which program you are using, it will typically be similar to one of these: File . . . Insert, File . . . Import, File . . . Load, Edit . . . Insert, or Object . . . Insert. (In figure 17, you would use the Load Text choice.) If your software is older, it may copy the original text file and place it on the page; more current software will directly use the original file to place the text. If you have the most capable software, you will be able to maintain a "live" link between the original file and your laid-out page. If this is the case, any change that you make back in the original document (using the program that created it) will show up immediately on your page layout.

After the text is on the page, tag it with a particular style to control its appearance, or select it with the mouse and make menu choices to set the appearance. What exactly you do will depend on the capability of your program.

Place the Photograph

The photograph will be placed on the page in almost identical fashion to the text.

Arrange the Photograph and Text

Once the photograph and text are on the page, you can manipulate them. When you click the mouse on one of them, most programs will show a set of resizing handles around the object. Just drag the handles to resize or reshape the objects. With the photo, you will be able to crop it or change its size. A menu choice will allow you to choose your desired action.

If the photo is in the center of the text, you will need to make a menu choice to tell the program to make the text flow around the picture rather than printing on top of it. You may also be able to tell the program how much blank space to leave between the edges of the picture and the text.

At this point, you can highlight and modify the appearance of particular words as well. For example, you can make the headline larger and a different typeface.

The Construction of Long Documents

Many programs, including just about all word processors, can be used for making short documents. Naturally, the more complex and stylized you want the document to be, the greater capability the program must have. It is in the preparation of long documents, however, that specialized publishing programs "show their stuff." Long documents typically have a standard look all the way through, and publishing programs can consistently apply that look pretty much automatically. Books and technical manuals are two examples of long documents. While magazines also consist of many pages, they frequently do not use a consistent layout and thus are less amenable to the automated features of publishing programs. In other words, more manual work will be necessary when the layout is not consistent.

While the terminology used by different programs varies, look now at what makes up a typical long document, such as a book.

Publications

An entire long work may be known as a **publication**. A publication is a collection of individual chapters or sections.

Chapters

Some publishing programs use the name **chapter** to designate a particular document. This is true whether the document is one page or many. Other programs refer to such a collection of pages simply as a document or a file.

Table of Contents

A **table of contents** generally appears at the beginning of a long publication, such as a book, and it gives the page numbers on which the various chapters and sections begin. Competent publishing programs can automatically create the table of contents by using the different levels of headings as entries.

Frames

Many programs use the concept of **frames** to contain objects on the page. Each chunk of text will be in a frame, each photo will be in a frame, and each graph will be in a frame. Typically, each frame can have margins, a multicolumn breakdown if it is holding text, and padding to separate it from the text on the page. You can usually also control the color of the frame's background, as well as the design and color of a border (if you want one) around the frame. Figure 19 shows a representative menu.

Anchors and Captions

One of the things that sets major-league publishing programs apart is their ability to attach figures (photos, graphics, and so on) to points (**anchors**) in the text and "drag them along" if the text in front of the figure should grow or shrink. Suppose, for example, that you have a long document with an illustration on page 16 that deals with the content that is on

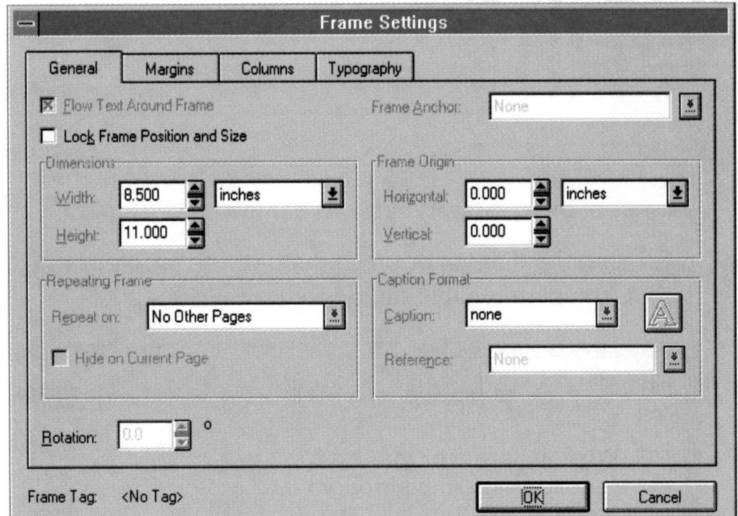

figure 19

A typical menu for making frame settings.

page 16. Now, during the revision process, eight new pages are added before page 16. By using the anchor capability of high-end programs, the illustration would automatically move to the new page 24, where it would still be with its descriptive text.

Captions are "labels" that apply to figures and illustrations. They are usually attached to the figures (you can control above, below, left, or right) so that they move along automatically.

Cross-references

Cross-references are those insertions in text that refer the reader to some other point in the publication, such as "See review on page 139." The automated function of some publishing programs eliminates the need to manually keep up with whether the review is still on page 139 as revisions are made. Instead of entering a particular page number on which the review appears, you enter a cross reference (using menus) that refers to an invisible marker you place on the actual review. Then, as revisions are made in the document, the program looks to see what page the marker is on now and refers to that page.

Indexes

Without an **index**, many books would be much less valuable. This is especially true with technical and reference books. Some publishing programs allow you to indicate in your publication the items that you want to appear in the index. The program then takes care of arranging the items alphabetically and applying the correct page numbers to them. This makes a previously labor-intensive task a bit more palatable.

Final Output

The final output of your publication may be done on just about any printer. Of course, the higher the resolution of the printer, the better the output will look. This section describes some of the characteristics to consider in choosing the best output device and settings to use for a particular application.

Do It!

1 Determine which program available for your use is the most capable with publishing tasks. What is its name and version?

2 Using the manual or online help of the program you identified in step 1, complete a table similar to the following:

Question	Answer
1. What are some of the text file formats that can be brought into a document?	
2. What are some of the graphic file formats that can be brought into a document?	
3. Describe the steps for starting a new document and making page settings.	
4. Describe the steps for bringing a text file into the document.	
5. Describe the steps for bringing a graphic into a document.	
6. Does the program use tags or styles to control the appearance of text or graphics?	
7. Describe how to apply a tag or style to a paragraph of text.	
8. Describe how to change the specifications for a particular tag or style.	

Resolutions

The maximum **resolution** with which an output device can print makes a big difference in print quality. All printers use dots to form images. With an inexpensive dot-matrix printer, the dots are formed by wires hitting the paper through a ribbon. With an inkjet printer, the dots are formed by small droplets of ink hitting the paper. With laser printers, the dots are formed from toner particles. With color printers, the dots may be formed from ink droplets, melted "wax," or vaporized colorants.

Most laser printers now on the market use a resolution of 600 dots per inch (dpi). This means that for each square inch on the paper, there can be a maximum of 600 dots across and 600 dots down, for a total of 360,000 dots. This is four times as many dots as with a resolution of 300 dpi. The most capable laser printers use 1200 dpi, while imagesetters (the highest quality output devices, which can print to either paper or photographic film) can do thousands of dots per inch (figure 20).

While you can set many printers to use less than their maximum resolution, the best resolution is a function of the hardware itself. This cannot be changed.

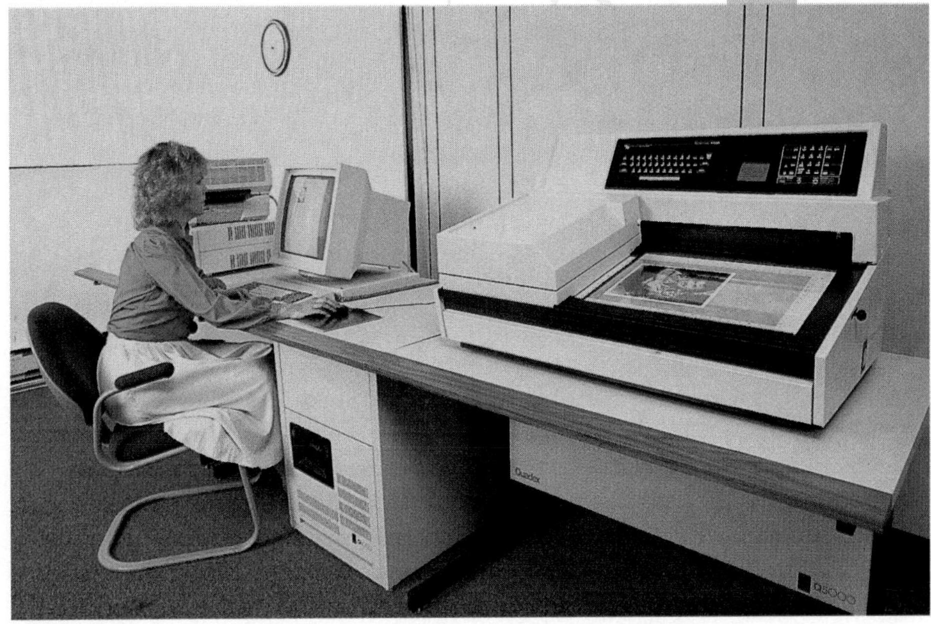

figure 20

Among the output devices that you can use for publishing are an inexpensive printer, laser printer, plain-paper typesetter, imagesetter (shown here), color inkjet printer, color thermal transfer printer, color dye sublimation printer (photographic quality), slidemaker, and banner maker.

Line Screens

For printing solid black areas or characters, the output of just about all laser and inkjet printers looks fine. The differences come into focus, however, with gray-toned text, illustrations, and photographs. A non-color printer has only one color with which to work—usually black. So, to make a gray color, it has to lay down a pattern of black dots with white space between them, fooling your eyes into thinking the area is gray.

To give the appearance of gray, programs use what is known as a **screen**. This is a term left over from precomputer days, when printers would actually lay a screen over a photo and make a picture of it for the printing plate. The wires in the screen broke the photo into "dots" as the plate was made. Note that screens are applied only to objects on the page that are not a solid ink color; they are less-than-complete coverage of the color. Screens can apply to colored ink as well as black ink.

The way that screens are made with the computer is analogous. Each square inch of printing area is divided into smaller areas. For example, with a 600-dpi printer, you might use a 60-line screen. This means that the 600 vertical dots per inch are divided into 60 ten-dot segments, while the horizontal dots are divided the same way. This means that each square inch of print surface is now made up of 3600 ten-dot x ten-dot "cells." Each of these cells has a total of 100 dots (10x10), and each of these dots can be either black or white. Therefore, by using different patterns of black and white dots, the eyes can be fooled into seeing (theoretically) a maximum of 100 different levels of gray.

The number of lines that you specify for a screen works with the maximum resolution of the printer to determine how many different levels or

Careers

Desktop Publishing: Designing New Career Opportunities

The advent of powerful desktop publishing software led to a massive career shift in the publishing industry. Previously, typesetting could be done only by very complex, expensive machines, so it was reserved for such items as books, magazines, catalogs, and advertising literature. The vast majority of routine written material was produced by the typewriter.

Now just about anything that is written can have the appearance of typeset material, and businesses of any size (even one-person enterprises) can produce sophisticated layouts. Projects that were previously sent to outside typesetters can now be handled in-house by a person skilled in the use of desktop publishing equipment and applications software. In many cases, the only need for an outside service provider is to produce the final output using higher-resolution equipment not readily available to all.

What are the skills necessary to be successful in desktop publishing? For starters, the person must know how to obtain the data (words and graphics) that are to be used; this requires knowledge of where to get this data, and how to use the computer. Obviously, the desktop publisher must also have the skill to lay out pages. This involves not only the technical skill in operating a particular publishing program but also an artistic eye to help ensure a pleasing arrangement that communicates information effectively. The last part of the process involves choosing the most appropriate output methodology. This can be anything from a laser printer to a slide recorder to an imagesetter in a full four-color process. For persons who possess these skills, there is the potential for freelance or home-based work as well as employment within a company.

shades of gray or a color you can imitate. For example, if you specify a 60-line screen, you will be able to imitate more gray shades than if you specify a 106-line screen. The flip side is that as you decrease the number of lines in the screen to get more shades, you cut the amount of detail that can be represented. Thus, you are always dealing with a compromise between shades of gray or color and the level of detail (figure 21).

figure 21

Coarse line screens lose detail; fine screens cut the number of available shades.

45-Line Screen

85-Line Screen

133-Line Screen

When you scan an image into the computer, you can save a lot of storage space as well as speed up processing by scanning at a dpi setting that is appropriate for the final output. For example, if you are going to print using a 60-line screen at the actual size of the scanned photo, it makes no sense to scan at 400 dpi, because most of the information in the image will just be disregarded during printing. If you are going to print larger than the original scan, the extra pixels in a higher-dpi scan can help keep the quality high as the size increases. One formula for determining the ideal dots per inch for a scan is the following:

Scan dpi = Line screen to be used x 1.2 x Enlargement factor.

Using this formula, here are some settings that you might compute and use:

Screen	Enlargement	Computed Scan	"Next Higher" Scanner Setting
60 line	1.0x (original size)	72 dpi	75 dpi
80 line	2.0x (double size)	192 dpi	200 dpi
106 line	1.5x	191 dpi	200 dpi
225 line	1.0x	270 dpi	300 or 400 dpi

Color Separations

If you are working on a color publication and are only going to print it on a color printer (perhaps with copies made by a color copier), consider your life to be easy. Just make your publication and print it. If, however, you are going to reproduce your output on offset presses (which is the only economic method for large quantities), you must delve into the world of **color separations**. In other words, your computer program must produce a different printout for each color of ink that will be used on the press.

There are two methods of doing color with printing presses. One is spot color, and the other is process color.

Spot color With spot color, you define various parts of your publication to appear in certain colors of ink. For example, you might print big headlines in bright red and the remainder of the publication in black. This would involve two printing plates: one for red, and one for black (figure 22). When using spot color, areas that are to be solid ink come out of the printer as black; areas that are to be lighter shades of the same color of ink come out as screens (areas of black dots interspersed with white space).

Process color With **process color**, there are always four colors of ink and four printing plates. The paper passes under four print rollers, one for each color. The four inks are yellow, cyan, magenta, and black. Theoretically, all colors can be created by combining portions of these four inks.

When doing process color, your computer program will produce a different printout for each of the four ink colors. Each printout contains only what is to be printed in its designated color. Areas that are to be printed

WRAP UP THE ANNIVERSARY SAVINGS NOW

DINETTES FROM $99
SOFAS FROM $129
OCCASIONAL CHAIRS FROM $39
COLOR TELEVISIONS FROM $99

555-1234

figure 22

When printing spot color on a press, a separation is made for each of the different colors of ink to be used.

solid in one of the primary colors (cyan, magenta, yellow, or black) will come out on only one printout page. Areas that are to be a mixed color will come out as screened areas on two, three, or all four printouts, depending on the color. For example, a color made by combining yellow and magenta will appear on the printouts for both of those colors (figure 23). The actual printouts are done in black and white, with screens for less than full coverage. If the technical process to be used by a commercial printer requires it, you can tell the computer to produce a negative image, which reverses all the colors—white backgrounds are black and black text is white, for example.

A different printing plate is made from each of the process color separations, and the four different colors of ink are printed onto the paper one after another. Depending on the press, this may be done by running the paper through a one-color press four times, through a two-color (two sets of rollers) press twice, or through a four-color (four sets of rollers) press once.

figure 23

When printing process color on a press, you produce a separation for each of the colors of cyan, magenta, yellow, and black. When all four colors are printed on the page, you get a full-color picture, such as the dog shown here.

Color models There is one vexing problem that many publishers endure: the color on your computer screen is not necessarily what you get when you print on a color printer or an offset press. Today's most sophisticated hardware and software do a much better job of making things look the same than earlier equipment did, but even the best hardware and software are not perfect.

These problems arise because color is produced differently on the screen than in printing; in other words, they use different **color models**. The computer screen makes colors by producing light. The printer or press makes colors by absorbing light into a surface such as toner or ink. If you see green on a computer screen, this is because green light is being produced. If you see green on a printed page, light of all colors is hitting the page and only green light is bouncing back; the ink is absorbing all other colors.

figure 24

It is a challenge for computers and printers to reproduce all colors of the spectrum.

On the typical computer monitor, three electron guns light up pixels on the screen in the three colors of red, blue, and green. If all three colors of light are produced equally, you see white; if no colors are produced, you see black. This is known as additive color. What you see on paper, however, is known as subtractive color; as you put more coloring or ink on a page, more light is absorbed and less reflected. Whatever is left to be reflected is the color you see (figure 24).

Various color standards exist to help ensure that you get the printed results that you expect, not necessarily what you see on the screen. One of the more commonly used is known as the Pantone Matching System, or PMS colors. Most printers and serious users of publishing software will have a set of Pantone colors (or a similar brand) on hand for reference. These colors are actual samples of the ink colors. Many computer programs allow you to specify colors by their Pantone name.

Trapping and spreading Printing presses are not absolutely accurate in feeding paper. The paper may not hit the cyan ink roller exactly the same way as it hits the magenta roller. That is, the registration may be just a hair off. This can lead to some interesting defects, such as a white shadow where two colors of ink are supposed to meet. To help make registration problems less noticeable, publishing software may automatically do what is known as **trapping** or **spreading**. Trapping is making a "hole" in a color slightly smaller so that it "traps" the color that shows through the hole. Spreading is making the color that shows through the "hole" slightly larger so that it spreads larger than the hole. Done improperly, trapping and spreading can make output look worse. Fortunately, most programs have default settings that do a pretty good job.

Tips for Attractive Layouts

When you look at a printed page, you automatically know whether you like or dislike its appearance. While we could give you a long list of "dos" and "don'ts" for design and tell you to obey them, that would only stifle your creativity. Some of the most attractive pages you will ever see violate the "rules" of layout; on the other hand, some that follow the "rules" are absolutely awful. Of course, what you think is awful, someone else might think is wonderful. The bottom line is, good design in page layout is totally subjective, and what is "in" changes over time.

There are some things to think about, however, that can help you keep your designs looking good. These might be called "guidelines to think about" rather than "rules." Here are some things to consider:

- For the beginner, using only two typefaces helps ensure a cohesive look. Use one serif face for body text and one sans serif face for headings.
- Use plenty of white space so that pages do not look overly crowded.
- Use good contrast between the background and the text that appears on it. Do not put black text on a dark gray background, for example. Instead, use a light gray background.
- Reserve decorative type for decoration. Use easy-to-read type for the body of your publication.
- Use varied margins or placements on the page as appropriate for your project. Figure 25 shows the difference in feel provided by different placements.

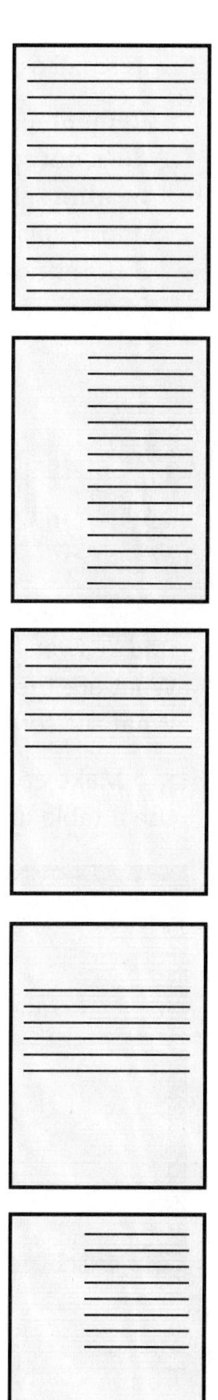

figure 25

Changing the margins on a page can have a dramatic effect on the overall appearance.

Publishing to the World Wide Web

If you wish, many publishing programs can produce final output in the form of a World Wide Web file. Typically, you can select a menu choice such as File . . . Publish or save the file as a Web document, and the program will automatically insert the necessary formatting codes for the file to display correctly as a Web page. Sometimes, a converter program is used to "map" the formats from the text document to a Web document.

If you plan to publish a document as a Web page rather than print it, you should keep in mind some guidelines specific to Web publishing:

- While graphics are beautiful on the computer screen, they take a long time to download if a user has a slow modem or the network is heavily loaded. Therefore, be judicious in your use of graphics, keeping them as small as will still look good on the page.
- Remember that under current Web browser software, your Web page does not specify the exact typeface or size. It specifies different levels of headings, for example, and the browser software on the user's computer displays them according to its settings. Therefore, a page will look different on different computers; it may not look the way you intended in your design.

Do It!

1 If a scanner is available for your use, try it out. As you work with it, find answers for the following questions: Is it monochrome or color? What are the different resolutions you can set through its software? What file formats can its software save in?

2 Make an inventory of the printers that are available for your use. Use a table in format similar to the following:

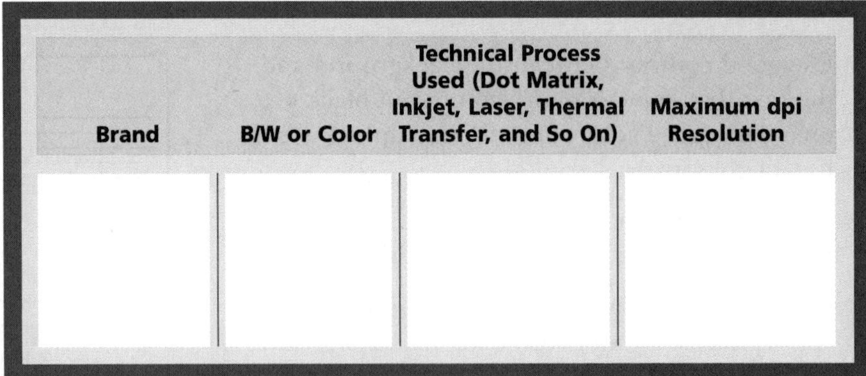

Brand	B/W or Color	Technical Process Used (Dot Matrix, Inkjet, Laser, Thermal Transfer, and So On)	Maximum dpi Resolution

Summary

The use of computers has revolutionized the publishing process, eliminating many of the manual steps that were previously necessary.

- Publishing measurements are traditionally expressed in terms of picas and points. There are 12 points in a pica and 6 picas in an inch. Therefore, there are 72 points in an inch.
- Leading is the measurement of line spacing used in the publishing industry. It is the distance from the top of one line to the top of the next line, and it is expressed in points.
- Typeface refers to the design of the letters. Typefaces may be categorized as decorative, serif, or sans serif.
- Type styles refer to such things as regular, bold, italics, and bold italics.
- Kerning is the process of varying the space between different pairs of letters to make each pair look its best.
- While word-processing and publishing software are on a converging path, publishing programs still tend to be superior for doing long, highly structured documents.
- Publications are made from a combination of text and graphics.
- The greater the resolution and the number of colors, the more storage space an image requires.
- Line (vector)-based graphics retain their detail as their size is changed. Pixel-based graphics lose detail as their size changes but are required for photographic images.
- Tags or styles can be used to "automatically" control the appearance of paragraphs in a document or publication.
- The basic steps in making a new publication are to open a new file, import or type text, import or create graphics, and make the desired stylistic adjustments to the pages.
- Among the capabilities of some advanced publishing programs are the creation of anchored frames, automatic captions, cross-references, indexes, and tables of contents.
- On final output, screens are used for objects that contain shades of colors or gray. Finer screens provide more detail but fewer color variations.
- Color may be spot or process. Spot color is typically used when a publication uses fewer than four colors. Process color, which uses four colors of ink, is used when there are more colors in the output and to produce photographic-quality images. While a color printer does the whole job, output going to an offset press requires the creation of a different printout for each of the ink colors to be used. Color printers are fine for small quantities, but offset printing is much more economic for larger quantities of the finished product.

The following key terms were defined in this module. For each of the following terms, write on a separate piece of paper the number of the definition followed by the letter of the appropriate term.

Terms

A. anchor
B. ascender
C. baseline
D. font
E. color model
F. cross reference
G. display typeface
H. descender
I. em space
J. en space
K. frame
L. index
M. kerning
N. leading
O. line (vector)-based graphics
P. pica
Q. pixel-based graphics
R. point
S. process color
T. publication
U. resolution
V. sans serif typeface
W. screen
X. color separations
Y. serif typeface
Z. spot color
AA. styles or tags
AB. table of contents
AC. trapping and spreading
AD. type size
AE. type style
AF. typeface
AG. x-height

Definitions

1 an entry that refers to another part of a publication

2 a space the width of the letter *n*

3 a typeface without horizontal lines on the letters

4 the imaginary line on which the letters of a typeface rest

5 graphics in which each shape is represented by a mathematic formula

6 a detailed list of items referred to in a publication, along with the pages on which they appear

7 the method used by a display or printer to produce color

8 characteristics or appearances of particular type, such as bold or italic

9 a point in text to which a graphic is attached for automatic moving as text is lengthened or shortened

10 printouts done for each of the different colors of ink to be used on a press

11 a typeface that uses small extensions to the letters to help guide the eye from left to right or as decorations

12 the part of a letter that extends above the height of most of the letters

13 a list of the major contents of a publication along with their page numbers

Matching

14 a container on the page into which text or graphics can be placed

15 color that is printed on the page by using a different ink for each color

16 a graphic printed with tiny dots of toner or ink to give the impression of different shades

17 a typeface that is distinguished by a stylish or unique appearance

18 bringing a pair of letters closer together for better appearance

19 the part of a letter that hangs below the baseline

20 a measurement equal to 12 points or one sixth of an inch

21 a space the width of the letter *m*

22 a measurement equal to one seventy-second of an inch

23 the distance between lines of type

24 any combination of typeface, style, and weight

25 a document that is created with a publishing program

26 defined appearances that can be attached to particular paragraphs of a publication

27 graphics in which the image is represented by data that stores the color of each dot in the picture

28 the process of making portions of a publication slightly over- or under-sized to prevent unsightly gaps in color when the printing press alignment is not perfect (handled automatically by many publishing programs)

29 the number of dots per inch that can be scanned or printed

30 the height of a typeface, measured from the bottom of the lowest letter to the top of the highest letter

31 color created by combining the four colors of cyan, magenta, yellow, and black

32 a set of characters with the same artistic design features

33 the height of the main body of the letters of a given typeface

Review

1. What is publishing? (Obj. 1)
2. What are the differences in publishing and word processing? (Obj. 1)
3. List and define the different units of measurement used in publishing. (Obj. 2)
4. The terms *typeface, font,* and *style* are frequently, and erroneously, used interchangeably. What are the correct definitions of these terms? (Obj. 3)
5. Some publishing programs use the concept of object orientation, while some do not. How can you determine whether a particular program is object oriented? (Obj. 4)
6. List and describe the functions typically performed by publishing software. (Obj. 5)
7. How does the current relationship between word-processing and publishing programs differ from the same relationship several years ago? (Obj. 5)
8. Explain the concept of a publication made from chapters. (Obj. 6)
9. What are anchors, and what are their advantages? (Obj. 6)
10. How do a table of contents and an index differ? (Obj. 6)
11. What is the relationship between the coarseness or fineness of a line screen and the quality of the printout? (Obj. 7)
12. Describe how to determine the resolution at which graphics or photos should be scanned to provide the highest quality image while at the same time saving storage space and optimizing processing time. (Obj. 7)
13. Name and describe two color models. What devices use each of the two models? (Obj. 9)
14. Why do colors on the screen usually not match those that come from a color printer? (Obj. 9)

Activities

1 *Writing* Prepare a one-page publication that resembles figure 16. Enter your own text, and select a graphic that is available to you. Place the items on the page, and select the margins, typefaces, sizes, and styles that you think look best. Remember that everything must fit onto one page. Try a number of different variations until you find the one that you like the best.

2 *Writing/Teamwork* Working with one other student, prepare a multipage publication. As with the first activity, select graphic files that are available to you, and enter your own text. Make choices on how many columns to use for the text (it does not have to be the same on all pages), how large to make the pictures, and what typefaces, sizes, and styles to use. Try to place each picture on the same page with the text that refers to it. Place captions with each of the pictures. Present your finished work to the class, and be sure to explain why you made your particular layout choices.

3 *Writing/Teamwork/Ethics* One of the great advantages of electronic publishing is that many different people can create the underlying files from which the entire publication is constructed. For this activity, a great deal of organizational work must be done under the instructor's direction. The entire class should take on the role of a newspaper or book publisher. The publication can be about whatever area the instructor or class decides—for example, a school newspaper, a sports newspaper reviewing sports figures and happenings, or a magazine of anecdotes and stories obtained through interviews with the elder individuals of the community. Different stories, art, or photographs of the covered news should be assigned to various students for completion and storage in electronic form. Each student should be sure that plagiarism and copyright violations are avoided. If you are using networked computers, store the stories and pictures on the network. Other students should be responsible for the design or "look" of the newspaper. Once all of the items are ready, they should be assembled in the newspaper document and arranged according to the already-adopted design. Make sure the writers, artists, and photographers receive credit for their work in the publication. The finished product should be printed and copies distributed to all interested parties, such as the publication's creators, fellow students, parents, or community members.

4 *Writing* Working from advertisements, periodicals, displays in stores, and other sources, make a table comparing several different publishing and word-processing programs. In the left-hand column, make a list of features, and in a column for each brand of software, indicate whether or how that feature is implemented. Decide which product you think is best for short, design-intensive documents and which is best for long, highly structured documents. Record the reasons for your decisions. If your instructor desires, each student can be responsible for researching one brand, with the results combined.

5 *Speaking* Tour a local publishing company or commercial printer, and observe the activities that go on there. Make an oral report to the class.

Activities

6 *Science* Inks and other chemicals used in the printing industry can be a pollution concern. Research the kinds of chemicals that are used and the impact they may have on the environment. Find out what manufacturers and printers are doing to lessen any potential damage. Write your findings.

7 *Science/Global* Extensive use of paper has led to concerns about the loss of forest. Research the impact of deforestation in different areas of the world and what positive effects recycling may be having. Present your report in oral or written form.

8 *History* The art of printing was developed in China in the sixth century. It was not until the fifteenth century, however, when Johann Gutenberg invented movable type in Germany, that publishing consisted of more than manually writing a copy of a handwritten document. While some ultraexpensive computer aids to publishing were introduced in the 1970s, it was not until the introduction of the Macintosh computer (1984) and the Hewlett-Packard LaserJet printer (1985) that desktop publishing became a reality.

9 *Internet* If you have a publishing program that can prepare HTML pages for Internet access, use it to design a "welcome" or "index" page for a Web site for your school. Use a Web search engine to locate a downloadable graphic to use on the page; it may represent your school mascot or some other image to lend personality to the page. Remember that use of small but effective graphics will result in much faster performance when the page is accessed by a browser. If you have access to do so, place the page on the Web and then access it with your browser to see how well it works. Make a screen print of the page to hand in to your instructor.

Graphics & Presentations

Overview

In this module, you will learn about application software that enables you to produce graphics. *Computer graphics* refers to any pictorial representation that can be produced by the computer, either on the display, printer, plotter, or other output device. In many cases, graphics make communication much clearer than the use of words alone. Graphics take many forms—from logos to product illustrations to graphs, to name a few.

Graphics software is a term generally applied to any program that produces "pictures" or "art." *Paint programs* are graphics programs that enable you to do "art" by changing the colors of pixels on the display. Photo touch-up and modification is a specialized area for painting programs. *Drawing programs* enable you to draw images that are stored as mathematically defined objects. Drawing programs are especially useful for technical illustration. *Computer-aided design* (CAD) programs are a specialized type of drawing program. *Graphing programs* produce graphs or charts from data. Therefore, paint programs, drawing programs, and graphing programs are three kinds of graphics software.

Presentation software takes graphic images (created by the presentation software itself or another source) and organizes them as a slide show. Many popular word-processing, spreadsheet, and database programs also include powerful graphic capabilities.

Objectives

1. Define and give examples of the use of computer graphics.
2. Describe and experience the use of paint programs.
3. Describe and experience the use of drawing programs.
4. Describe and experience the use of graphing programs.
5. Describe and experience the use of presentation programs.

Uses of Graphics Software

Graphics software is used for many purposes. Among them are computer art, computer-aided instruction, CAD and drafting, scientific study, television and movies, and presentation graphics. While all of these areas have common roots in computer graphics, each is unique in its purpose and implementation.

Computer Art

The computer has replaced the palette and brush for a growing number of artists. The wide range of available colors, ability to easily repeat patterns, and ease of performing special effects, when added to the much higher resolution now available with many computers, have led to the growth of computer art. Figure 1 exemplifies what may now be accomplished.

figure 1

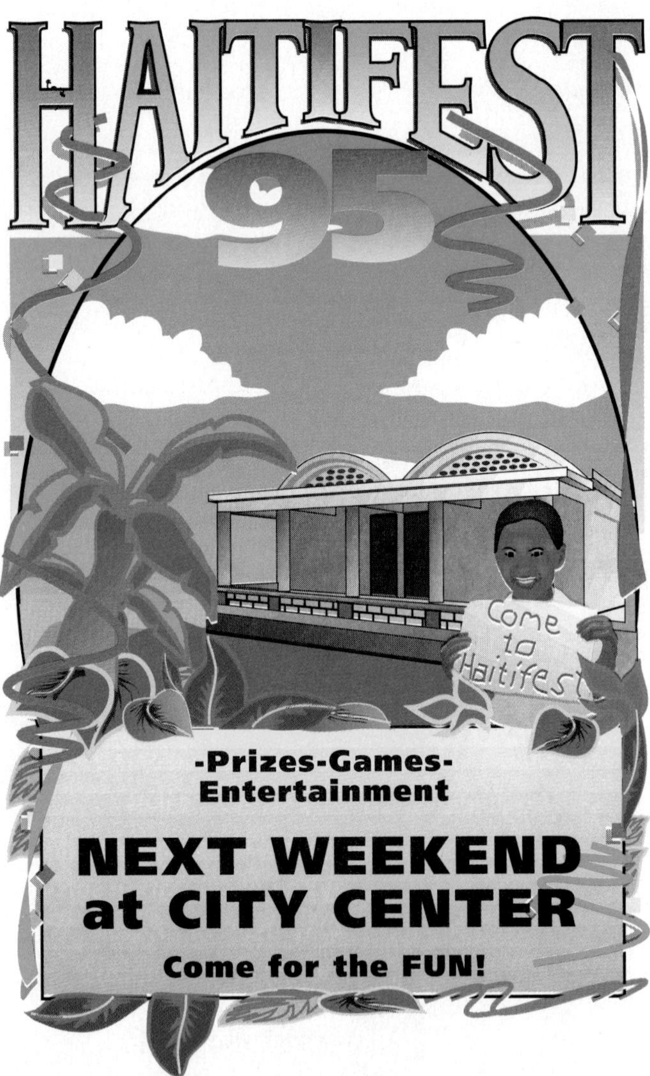

A complex, color computer graphic illustration.

Computer-Aided Design

Virtually all technical illustrations and blueprints (designs) are now done with the computer. Whether they are plans for mansions or motorcycles, increased accuracy and efficiency are made possible by CAD software. This software provides many automatic functions, such as dimensioning (providing measurements for the object being drawn). More advanced programs include additional functions, such as calculating material strength requirements and simulating behavior of the actual object being designed. Objects now being designed by use of the computer range from automobiles to houses to bottle caps to spacecraft. A tremendous advantage to using the computer is the ability to produce three-dimensional drawings: an object can be drawn and then viewed (even in motion) from any angle with the computational and display abilities of the computer software. Figure 2 shows how the computer can provide a "walk-through" of the three-dimensional space you have drawn.

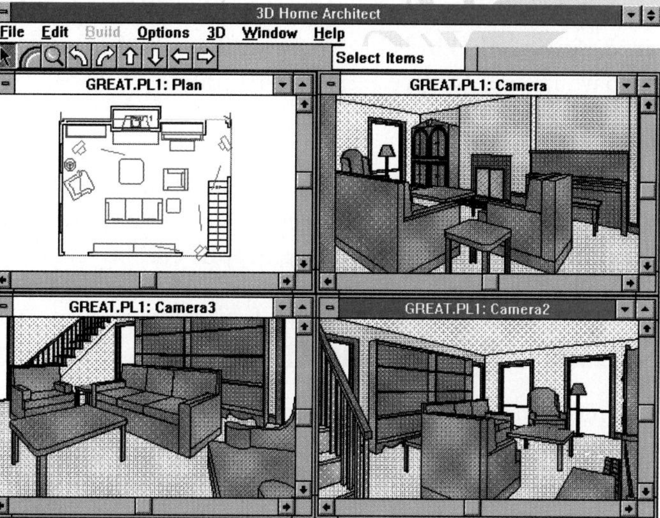

figure 2

Using a three-dimensional design program, you can do computerized "walk-throughs" of what you have created. This allows you to see the aesthetic effects of your design, especially when designing buildings.

Scientific Study

In many areas of scientific study, graphics are used extensively. From fields as diverse as medical imaging to modeling the behavior of weather, the computer is proving to be an invaluable tool.

Photo Editing

Many application programs are available whose specialty is the clean-up and modification of photographs. Once an image is scanned into the computer, special routines in these programs can do things such as enhancing sharpness, giving a soft appearance, emphasizing detail, cleaning up background clutter, and giving artistic effects.

Television and Movies

Virtually every television show and movie now produced uses computer graphics in some way. Whether just for titles and special effects or for the total production, as in the case of computer-generated cartoons, computers help to make the production more interesting and economic.

One of the most interesting phenomena made possible by computer software is "morphing." In morphing, the computer provides all of the intermediate images to make a movie of one original image changing into the second original image.

Presentation Graphics

Presentation graphics are produced by the computer for use as visual aids. Images included in these presentations may be created by the user or imported from any of numerous image libraries that are available. These visual aids may be used for everything from business presentations (figure 3) to classroom instruction to special effects at concerts. Computers are assisting tremendously in the production of visual presentations such as slide shows; images can be created on the computer and quickly converted to slides by exposing film with a specially

figure 3

Presentation graphics are designed to help convey ideas, usually in a group meeting of some kind.

fitted camera. As an alternative to making slides, a series of images may be produced with computer software, stored on disk, and "played back" with special software on the computer display or a large projector whenever desired. Any of the kinds of programs described in this module can be used to prepare images for presentation graphics.

Graphing Software

Graphing software, which may be part of another package, typically takes numbers that have been entered in the form of a spreadsheet and turns them into graphs. The resulting graphs can be used in other graphics or in presentations (figure 4).

Microcomputer Graphic Software

This section discusses painting software, drawing software, and graphing software. These are three of the most commonly used types of programs. While they are discussed separately in this module, keep in mind that with a growing number of programs, you may create "container" documents. The container document (which is often a word-processor or page-layout program document) can contain components or objects created with various kinds of programs. Thus, part of an image could be created with a paint program, part with a drawing program, and part with a word processor, for example.

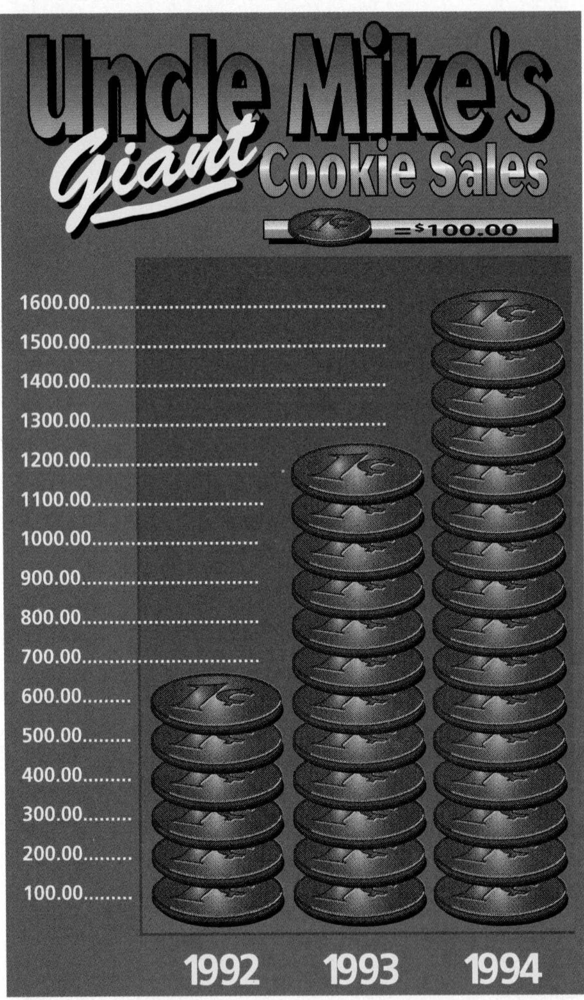

figure 4

There is no need for graphs to be boring.

If you have access to appropriate software, you will want to try many of the things you learn. This section obviously addresses the software in generic terms because many different programs are available, each of which has its own user interface. You may find it advantageous, therefore, to refer to the user's manual for the software you have available as you study these sections. The help screens of most programs are quite good and provide an excellent resource for you.

Using Paint Software

Paint programs work with pixel-based images (figure 5). That is, they work by changing the colors of the individual dots that make up the image on the computer display. These programs enable a designer to create art, logos, or just about any kind of graphic desired. Paint programs use the computer screen as a canvas and allow the "painter" to paint with computerized tools that give the same general effect as brushes, paint rollers, paint sprayers, and other tools. However, many other effects are possible. These include mirror images of part of the screen, flipping part of the screen, or smearing the image across the screen, to name a few.

figure 5

Left, Pixel-based images become "blobby" or lose detail as their size is changed. Right, Drawing-program images are vector based, so they retain detail at all sizes.

The number of colors that you can see on the screen depends on the display hardware with which your computer is equipped. Some programs are able to save only the number of colors you can see, while others can save more than can be displayed. To display 256 colors requires one byte of memory per pixel, 65,536 colors requires two bytes per pixel, and 16.7 million colors (true color) requires three bytes per pixel. You can easily see that all other things being equal, the more colors you are displaying, the slower the display will refresh (update to show your changes) as you work because of the additional data to be moved. You will find that most persons who work with large, true-color images want accelerated display hardware to help handle the load.

The amount of disk space required to store a pixel-based image also depends on the size and color depth of the image. The following table shows how the required storage space goes up as you save more colors and as the size of the image becomes larger. You can see how you can quickly fill the computer's hard disk with graphic image files even if your computer can compress them.

Bytes of Memory Required to Store Pixel-Based Images, +, +, +

Image Size (Pixels)	Black & White (1 bit per pixel)	256 Color (8 bits or 1 byte per pixel)	16.7 Million Colors (24 bits or 3 bytes per pixel)
320 x 240	9600	76,800	230,400
640 x 480	38,400	307,200	921,600
800 x 600	60,000	480,000	1,440,000
1024 x 768	98,304	786,432`	2,359,296

Ethics

Before Using That Image. . .

The widespread use of CD-ROMs and online services such as CompuServe and America Online have made it very easy to obtain graphic images of almost any subject. Need a stellar shot taken from an orbiting spacecraft or a photo of a world leader? Today's technology can give you easy access to these images.

With this easy access comes the temptation to use any graphic, regardless of its source and the intended use, but fair play—as well as the law—demands more. Suppose you created a masterpiece image using a drawing or painting program. After toiling over it for untold hours, would you want someone else selling it—and profiting from *your* work?

To help protect their rights, many photographers and artists copyright their images. Copyrighting makes it illegal to use an image without permission from the copyright owner. In addition, the ways in which copyrighted images can be used are strictly limited according to the wishes of the owner. With this in mind, be sure to read the documentation for a given library to determine how the images can be legally used. For example, a publisher will give permission to use the copyrighted image in newsletters and flyers but place restrictions on selling the image in any form to others.

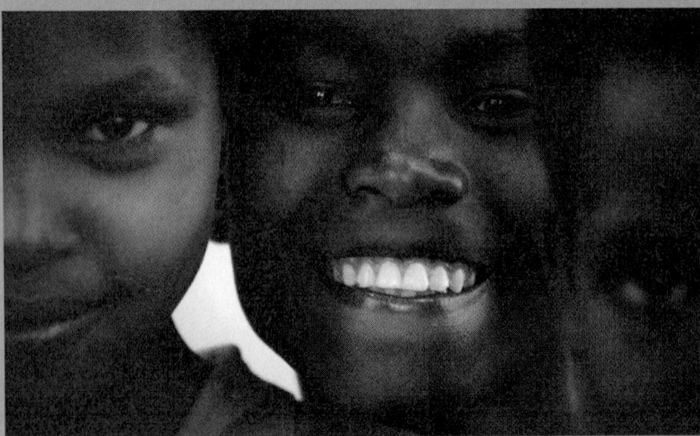

The Paint Working Environment

The initial screen of most paint programs will look something like that shown in figure 6, which is from the Paintbrush program that comes with Microsoft Windows. While this example screen is similar to that of many programs, remember that others may be different in both the arrangement and the exact items shown on the screen.

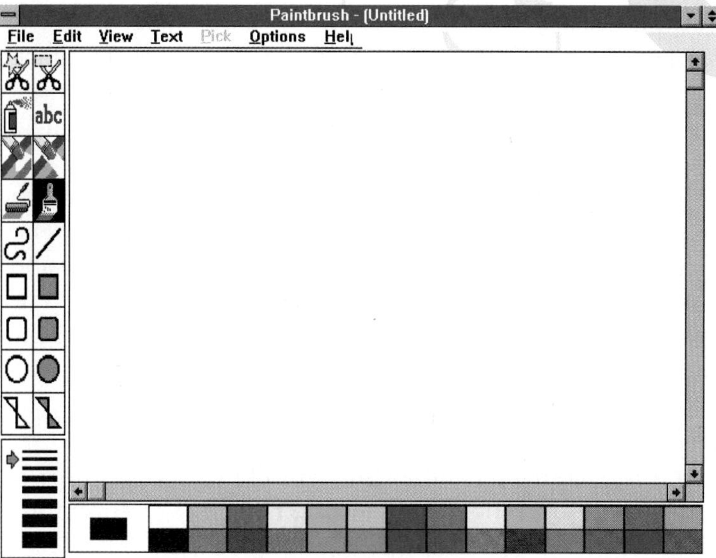

figure 6

The Windows Paint program is a simple application, but it illustrates the functions of paint programs in general.

Note that across the top of the example paint screen are menu choices: File, Edit, View, Text, Options, and Help. By selecting the Help menu, you can find out just about anything you need to know about using the program. Shown down the left side are the tools that may be used. Tools refer to the "computerized implements," such as pencils and erasers, that are used for drawings. The tools are selected by moving the mouse pointer to the desired one and clicking the mouse. From top to bottom, they represent the following:

1. Scissors: Used to "cut" portions of the screen, either to remove them, move them to another part of the screen, or make duplicates of them on another part of the screen.
2. Spraycan: Used to "spray" color onto the screen. The effect is quite similar to putting spray paint on a wall as you move the can at different speeds.
3. Text: Used for entering any alphabetic characters on the screen.
4. Erasers: Used to erase any part of the drawing from the screen. The color replacer changes one color to another; the regular eraser removes everything on the screen at the point of erasure.
5. Painting tools: Use these tools to fill in enclosed areas of the drawing with a chosen color.
6. Drawing tools: A variety of drawing tools are available, from the line-drawing tool to tools for both open and filled rectangles, rounded-corner rectangles, ovals, and freeform shapes.

At the bottom left of the screen is the width control; use it to change the width of the drawing or erasing line. Across the bottom of the screen are different patterns or colors of "paint" (known as a palette) that may be used with the drawing tools and the paint bucket. As with other items, these are chosen by pointing at them with the mouse pointer and clicking the mouse button.

Making a Freehand Painting

To make a painting, just select the color you want to use by clicking on it. Select the appropriate tool, and go to work. To find out how to use any of the tools in your software, just use the help menu if you have one; otherwise, refer to the user's manual.

The thing to remember about painting is that you usually have some ability to move shapes around on the screen when you first create them. For example, you might be able to move a line of text or a shape to position it just where you want it. Once you "release" the shape, however, it becomes indistinguishable from the rest of the screen, except for its color, and cannot again be independently selected for movement or modification.

Saving a Painting

Once a drawing has been completed, you will probably want to save it. In almost all programs, this is done by selecting File . . . Save from the drop-down menus.

Working from External Input

In the painting examples created in this module, a clean screen was used, on which a drawing was made. In many cases, however, the initial input can come from some other source, with touch-up work being done on the computer. For example, a scanner can be used to input any printed material. The surfaces in figure 7 were scanned from everyday materials and will work nicely as the background for a painting.

figure 7

Scans of everyday materials can make interesting backgrounds for paintings. Many paint programs include files of such images for easy importing by the user.

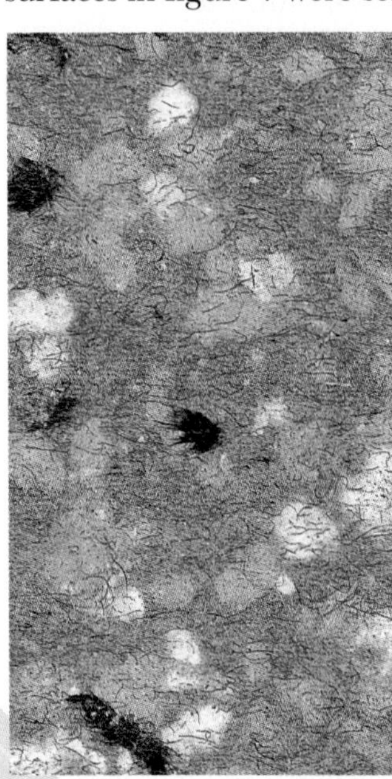

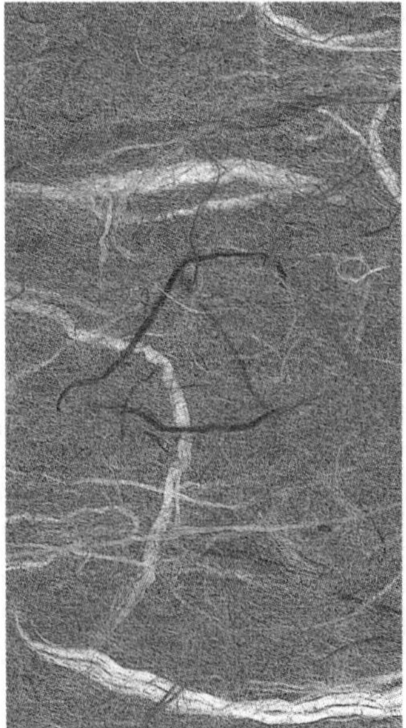

In using a scanner to input materials to the computer, remember that the original creator has a legal right to the work. Copyright law that protects the creator's rights should not be violated when selecting materials to scan.

Photographic Clean-up and Modification

Some paint programs are especially equipped for working with photographs. Once a photo is scanned in, these programs can do such things as:

- Improve the exposure range.
- Improve the contrast.
- Sharpen the image.
- Emphasize the detail.
- Diffuse the image.
- Clean up backgrounds.
- Duplicate portions of the image.
- Create artistic effects with the image.

Look at figure 8 to see an example of various things that can be done to a photograph.

Original Scanned Photograph

Background Cleaned up

Image Converted to Crystallize

figure 8

Here are just a few of the things that you can do with a paint program designed for photo touch-up.

Using Image Libraries

Image libraries are computer files that contain predrawn art for use with painting and drawing programs. Typically, these files are available in collections of related work, such as images for holidays, seasons, business promotions, and so on. Most graphics programs come with an image library, and many additional libraries are available from other vendors. The images can be loaded from the disk into the paint program and manipulated as desired, including merging them with other images and performing special effects. A very popular recent addition to image libraries has been the photo-CD, which is a CD-ROM packed with full-color photographs that can often be used royalty-free as long as it is for a noncommercial use. Be sure to check the licensing agreement of any materials you obtain, however.

Image libraries can make the work of a designer or artist much easier. Again, however, keep in mind that the images are copyrighted by their creator or publisher. The ways in which the images can be used are strictly limited; therefore, be sure to read the documentation that comes with a given library to determine how the images can be legally used. Many times, for example, the publisher will give permission to use the image in such items as newsletters and flyers but place restrictions on selling the image in any form to other persons.

Natural Media Simulation

Among the advanced features available in the best of today's paint programs is the ability to more closely simulate natural media. Each of the

Looking Good . . . Thanks to the Computer

Do you have trouble finding clothes that fit right and look great on you? Or do you feel frustrated when your hair stylist can't make you look exactly like one of those glamorous models in the photo books? Don't despair! Help is on the way via computer technology—and some interesting applications of software.

Let's start with clothes. Sure, you could go to the time and expense of having a tailor custom-make your clothes to your exact measurements and tastes, or you can take advantage of computer applications now in use in jeans stores that let you select the desired design at the store and be measured *by computer*. In addition to taking standard measurements, the computer can even take into account your posture. This information is used to size the pattern you select, then the jeans makers go to work. Your new garment is delivered back to the store in a few days—tailored to your physique.

Trends

What's next? Custom-designed fabric. With a new technique developed at the Georgia Institute of Technology, a fabric print is created on the computer using standard graphic design software. Then, the design is printed onto fabric using a color copying machine.

Computer technology can also be used to prevent bad-hair days caused by unflattering cuts. A growing number of salons now use a computer system that stores the images of a large number of hair styles, just like you'd find in a printed portfolio. The same style might even be shown in several variations to take into account differences in head shape. At the salon, your face is framed by a television camera that feeds its output directly into a computer for storage. Then, with the image of your face and all of the hair styles stored into the computer, the stylist can instantly call up your image with any hair style you might be considering. Want to see what you'd look like in a new hair color? The computer can show you that, too. All risk-free.

natural mediums of painting has its own "personality." You can tell by looking whether a particular work is watercolor, oils, or acrylic, for example, and you can tell whether something is painted on paper, canvas, or another surface. Advanced algorithms in some programs now allow them to simulate these types of surfaces and paints. Included among the surfaces are all kinds of papers, fabrics, and woods, for example, and the tools that can be simulated range from pencils to chalk to finger-paint to watercolors to oils. You can also control the "sharpness" of a pencil or the kind of brush that you are using.

Producing Output

Once a painting is finished, it can be printed by selecting the Print command. Generally, the size of the printout can be controlled at this point.

Do It!

1. What painting software is available for your use?
2. Try out each of the tools and effects included in the software that is available to you. Use the help feature of the program to find out how to use tools that are not familiar to you.

Using Drawing Software

Drawing software is mathematically based. You can use programs primarily intended for artistic-type creations, or you can use design software. CAD is a category of graphics software designed to assist in the preparation of plans (traditionally called blueprints) for a variety of projects to be constructed. These projects might range from a golf course to a house to an airplane to a highway (figure 9). In this module, we first look at software intended primarily for artistic purposes and then examine the unique characteristics of drafting software.

The Geometric Foundation of Drawing Programs

Drawing software can be contrasted to paint software in the way that its images are handled. As stated previously, paint software allows the computer display to be used as an artist's palette, with the user "painting" on it with various tools. Although drawing software allows total freedom of what is placed on the screen, it works with objects that are mathematically defined. A circle,

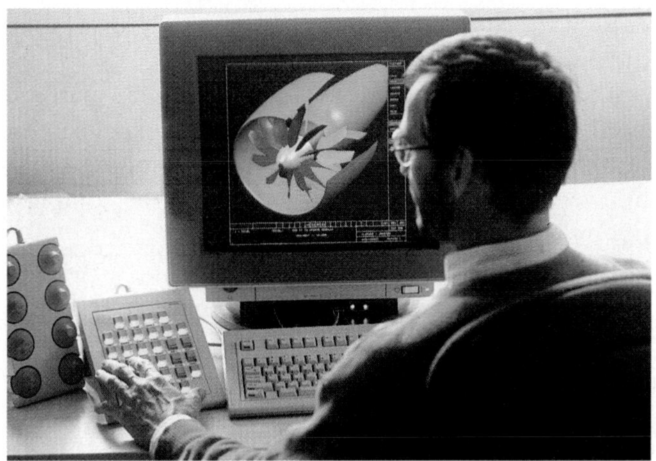

figure 9

Computer Aided Design (CAD) software uses the power of the computer to produce technically accurate designs.

for example, is mathematically defined for a drawing as having a defined reference point (which determines its placement in the drawing) and a defined radius (which determines its size).

Because of the mathematic definition of all shapes, there are some inherent capabilities of drawing software that cannot exist in painting software. Additionally, objects can be moved easily from one place to another, even when they overlap other objects on the screen or have objects drawn on top of them.

Everything in a drawing is made of geometric shapes of some kind, such as straight lines, circles, and so on.

A Drawing Program's User Interface

The user interface varies significantly from one drawing or CAD program to another. You may use either a mouse or a digitizer pad. Figure 10 shows the interface for one popular drawing program, CorelDraw.

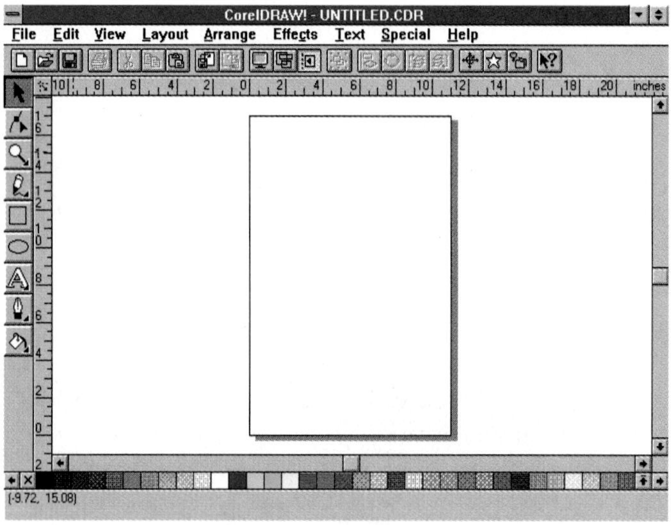

figure 10

The interface for a drawing program is quite similar to that for a paint program. Note the tools on the left for adding various shapes or text to your drawing. The highlighted tool is the selection arrow for picking an already drawn object that you want to change. The second tool from the top is the node-edit tool for working with an object's reference points.

Drawings are made on a blank screen using the geometric shapes that can be handled by the drawing program. To help keep the drawing accurate, points on objects can automatically snap to a grid of defined size. To understand the concept of "snapping" to a point, imagine a drawing on a piece of graph paper. Every line on the drawing must start and stop at an intersection on the grid. Using the computer, the grid is similar to drawing on computerized graph paper. As the designer draws, the drawing point "jumps" (or snaps) from one grid intersection to another—no point of a drawing can be defined as being anywhere other than on the intersection of a horizontal and vertical rule. For example, when a straight line is drawn, the ends of the line will automatically go to the nearest intersection on the grid.

Drawing programs are not appropriate for manipulating photo-like images. Many of them, however, can import pixel-based images and incorporate them as part of a finished work. The amount of storage space required by a vector-based image is dependent on the complexity of the image and not on its size or numbers of colors.

Using Objects

While just about anything can be drawn from scratch using geometric shapes, the use of predrawn objects can make the work much easier and faster. Objects may be drawn and named by the user of the drawing program. Programs include a number of objects, however, that can fulfill many of your needs. In fact, the most popular programs include tens of thousands of predrawn objects, which cover categories from animals to architectural features to people to parks.

Editing

Editing simply means making changes in something. In the case of a drawing program, it means making changes or modifications to objects that are in the process of being used in a drawing. Keeping in mind that each object drawn is represented in the computer as a mathematic formula—not as a pattern of pixels that are turned to particular colors—will make the concepts of editing easier to understand.

Moving reference points Each object drawn has **nodes** (usually shown as tiny squares or circles) that represent changes in the direction of the lines. Each object also has **reference points** (usually shown as heavier black squares) indicating the edges of an imaginary rectangle surrounding the object. For example, a straight line has a node on each end. A circle has a node on the circumference. An ellipse has four nodes: one on each end, and one on each side. Any of these nodes may be moved, and when that is done, the size, shape, or position of the object will change accordingly. For example, a straight line can be moved from a vertical position to a horizontal position by moving the reference point for one of the ends. Figure 11 shows how the nodes on an object can be moved to create different shapes.

Moving and copying objects Entire objects, or groups of objects, can be moved from one place on the screen to another. One object can be moved by pointing to one of its reference points and then pointing to a new location. One or more objects can be moved by putting a "window" around them and then moving the window. In similar fashion, objects already on the screen can be copied to other locations on the screen or even other drawings.

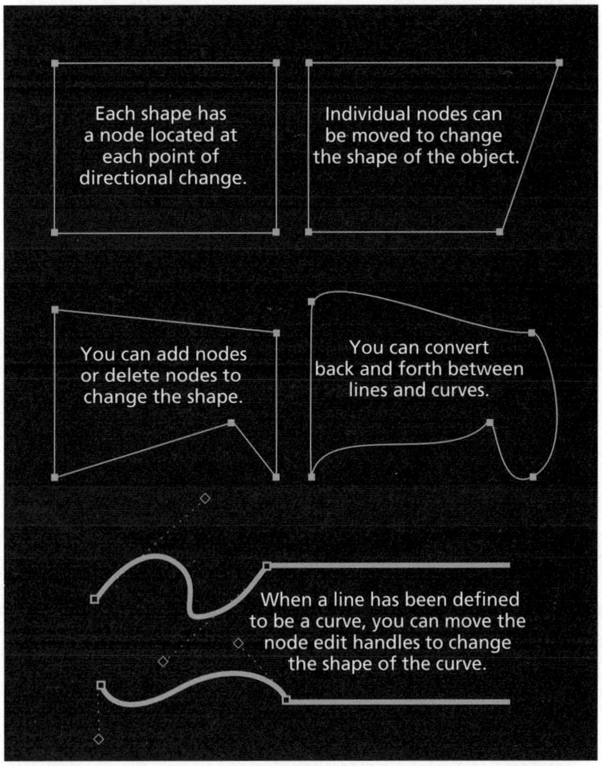

figure 11

One of the great powers of a drawing program is the ability to manipulate objects through their nodes or reference points.

Object effects Objects already on the screen can be changed by applying various effects. Some of the effects that can be done are shown in figure 12. Remember that the exact ones available to you will depend on the particular brand of software you are using. Also, the particular menu choice or tool used to accomplish the effect will vary considerably from one program to another.

Profile

Michael Cowpland

Dr. Michael Cowpland's Corel Corporation started as a computer systems integrator. As a sideline, Corel created a graphic product that added utility to Ventura, the original publishing program for PCs. That "sideline" utility program eventually became CorelDraw, which is now the focus of Corel Corporation.

And that's not the end of the Corel/Ventura relationship. In what might be characterized as a mouse swallowing an elephant, the Ottawa-based Corel purchased Ventura Publisher from Xerox in 1993. Cowpland's company now offers the entire Ventura program as part of the Corel fold—considered by many to be the leading family of graphic products for the PC.

Cowpland's venture has enjoyed explosive growth in a few short years. In 1990, the first year after introducing its market-leading CorelDraw package, the company had approximately $50 million in sales. In 1994, sales were estimated at over $200 million. Corel's tradition of releasing a major product upgrade at least once a year helps to boost sales.

While Corel's products are judged to be excellent by most independent evaluators, a large part of the company's high-flying success can be attributed to its incredibly aggressive marketing and advertising campaign. From a glitzy international design contest fueled by big prize money to advertisements in general-circulation media as well as computer publications, Corel never lets its products escape public attention. All of its marketing and advertising activities are handled by an in-house staff, allowing Corel to take quick advantage of opportunities.

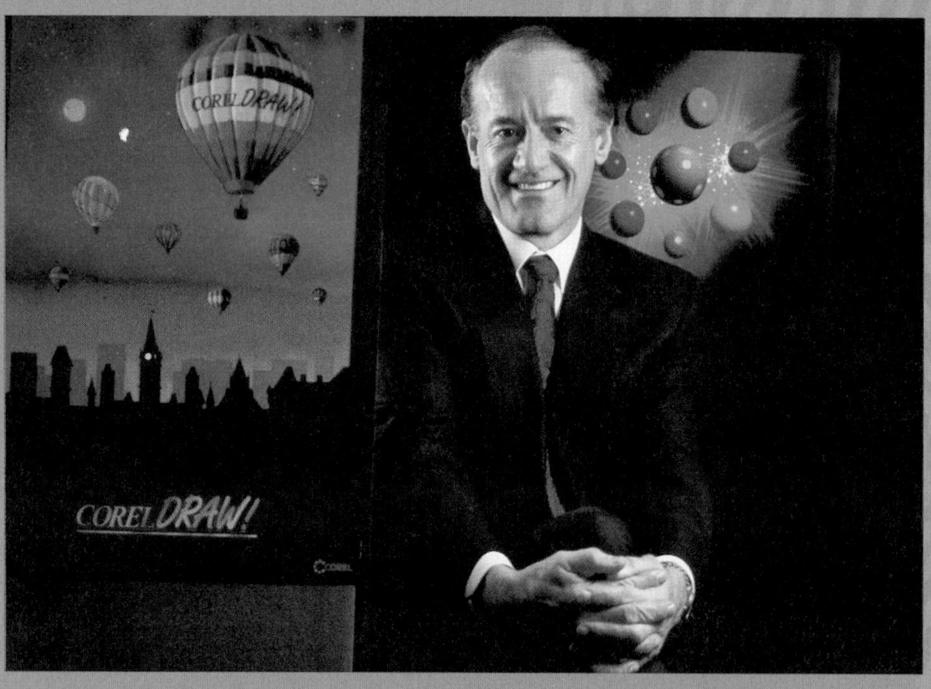

Corel's founder is a native of the United Kingdom. Cowpland, who is an engineer with a Ph.D., once headed up a company called Mitel. With Mitel, Cowpland earned a reputation as one who enjoyed the good life, spending lavishly on mansions and helicopters. Now, Cowpland leads a more down-to-earth lifestyle and lets his company soar.

One effect—mirroring—is particularly useful when symmetric objects are being drawn. In this case, half of the object can be drawn and then mirrored to create the other half automatically. Mirroring can be done vertically, horizontally, or at an angle. The mirrored object can be touching the original or placed any desired distance away. While mirroring is somewhat similar to flipping a defined area when using a paint program, it generally offers more powerful alternatives than the flip operation.

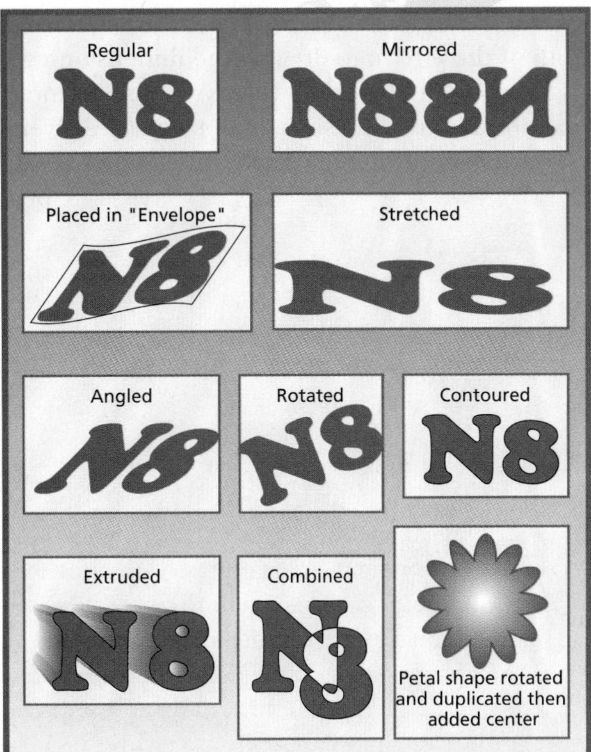

figure 12

A wide variety of effects is available in drawing programs. The exact effects will vary from one software package to another.

Adding Text

Text can be added in a drawing wherever desired by selecting the text tool, clicking on a location, and keying the text. Letters of text are essentially the same as predefined objects on the drawing. Each letter is made up of geometric shapes. For example, a capital "A" is made of three straight lines with defined beginning and ending points; a lower-case "e" is made of a defined arc and a defined straight line. Because letters are made of these mathematically defined components, they can be manipulated the same as any other object once they are in place—that is, they can be resized, moved, or rotated.

Using Layers

Drawing programs typically provide the ability to work in layers on a given drawing. This makes it possible to isolate different kinds of components to make working on them easier. In the design of a house, for example, one layer might contain the layout of the walls, another the fixtures, another the electrical plan, and another the heating and air-conditioning plan. By selecting options, the designer can have any number of layers visible at the same time, while drawing and editing are done on one selected layer. In other words, while the designer is working on the fixtures for a house on one layer, the walls on another layer are entirely unaffected by anything that is done, even though they are visible on the screen at the same time.

When plotting or printing finished drawings, selections can again be made by layers. For example, the designer could plot just the wall and electrical layers for the electrician or just the walls and the heating and air-conditioning layers for the contractor.

Special Features of Computer-Aided Design Software

The basic abilities of CAD software reflect very closely those of drawing software designed for artistic use or illustration. Several features not usually included with illustration software are standard, however, for CAD software. Both of these have to do with the dimensioning of objects in the drawing.

Virtually all blueprints (plans) contain dimensions. For example, in the plan for a house, the sizes of all rooms are given. While dimensions can be placed on a drawing manually, much labor is saved by the ability of CAD programs to automatically compute and print all of the desired dimensions on the drawing, as shown in figure 13. The operator simply indicates the points at which dimensions should be given, and the program does the rest. As a complement to automatic dimensioning of what has been drawn, CAD programs allow the user to enter the exact dimensions for the object, and the program sizes the object to those exact requirements.

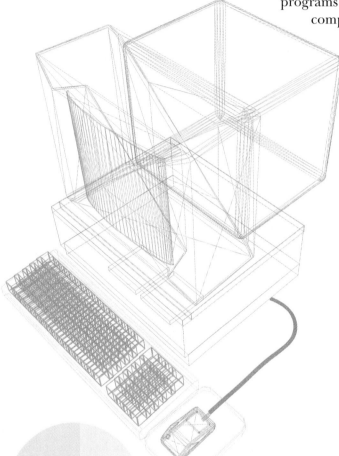

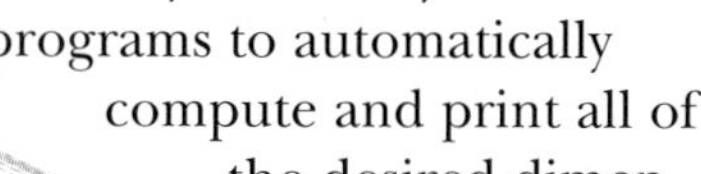

figure 13

CAD software can automatically calculate and print all dimensions in a drawing.

Do It!

1. What brand of drawing software is available for your use?
2. Try out each of the tools available in your drawing software.
3. Try out all of the special effects available in your drawing software, such as stretches, blends, extrusions, envelopes, and so on.

Using Graphing Software

In contrast to paint programs, which work from artistic input, and CAD programs, which create and place mathematically defined objects, graphing programs do their work from existing data. The data is converted by the software into graphic images that represent the data.

The user interface varies tremendously from one graphing program to another. Many popular word-processing, spreadsheet and database programs contain modules for making graphs of their data. Additionally, a number of stand-alone programs are still available.

Graphs are also frequently known as charts. Among the frequently used types of graphs are bar graphs, pie charts, line graphs, and area charts; these are discussed in this section. With each graph is an example of the data used to create it, with the data shown in the format in which it would appear on a spreadsheet.

Bar Graphs

Bar graphs represent data quantities by the lengths of the bars that are drawn, and these graphs are good for showing differences between items (figure 14). Each item is represented by one bar, whose length indicates the value of the item. The bars may be either vertical or horizontal. Some programs use the terms "bar chart" when referring to graphs with horizontal bars and "column chart" when referring to graphs with vertical bars.

figure 14

Bar graphs are ideal for comparing quantities.

Fruit Flavor Preferences
Westland Mall, July 18, 19--

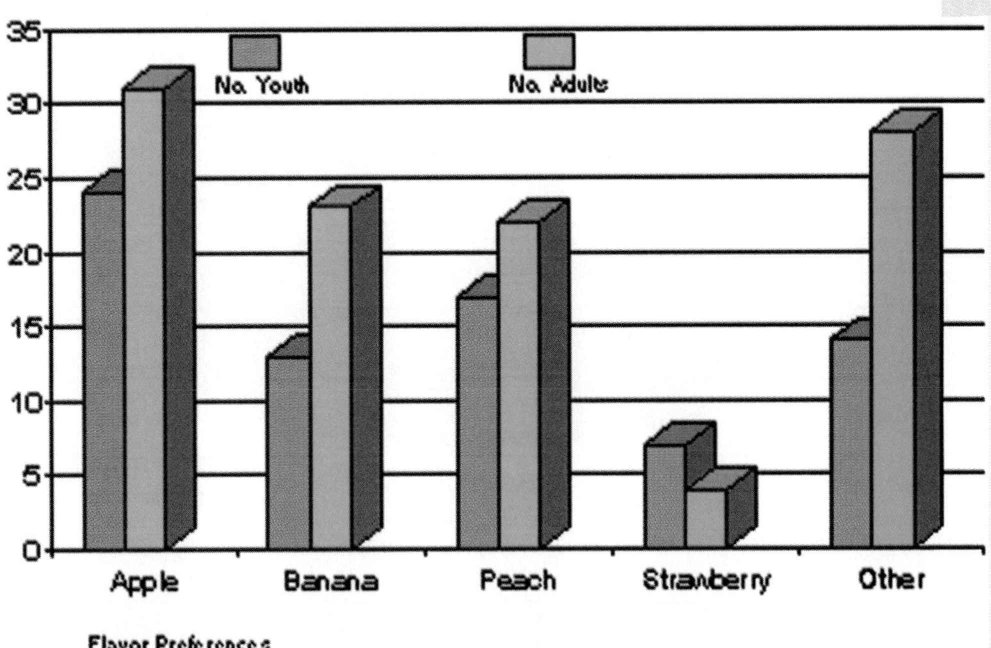

Flavor Preferences

Flavors	No. Youth	No. Adults
Apple	24	31
Banana	13	23
Peach	17	22
Strawberry	7	4
Other	14	28

In preparing bar graphs, the entire length of the bars should be shown. That is, the bars should begin at zero on the scale and extend as far as necessary. For example, if the smallest quantity being graphed is a test score of 80 and the largest a score of 100, the temptation might exist to cut off the portions of the bars representing scores from 0 to 70. This would result in a graph with bars starting at 70 and extending to 100. This would then have the effect of amplifying or exaggerating the differences. Under these circumstances, for example, the bar of a person who scored 90 would be twice as long as that of a person who scored 80, making it appear that the better score was twice as high. Obviously, that is not the case, as showing all of the bars would quickly indicate.

Pie Charts

A **pie chart**, as the name implies, divides a total entity into its component parts. In other words, it slices a pie into various-sized pieces to represent the different percentages of each component. To illustrate the concept, look at figure 15. It combines the flavor choices for youths and adults that were used in figure 14. Note in figure 15, however, that the spreadsheet has added a third column, which represents the total number of youths and adults. This new column is used to produce the graph. The graphing program automatically computes the percentages from the values in this column.

figure 15

Pie charts are ideal for showing the division of a whole into its component parts.

Fruit Flavor Preferences
Westland Mall, July 18, 19--

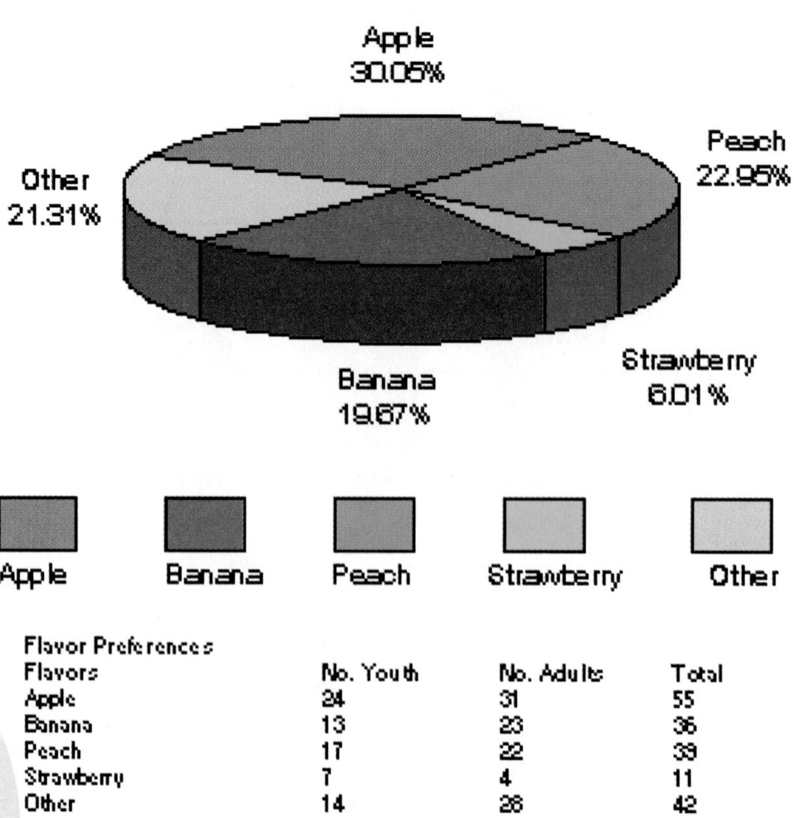

Flavor Preferences

Flavors	No. Youth	No. Adults	Total
Apple	24	31	55
Banana	13	23	36
Peach	17	22	39
Strawberry	7	4	11
Other	14	28	42

Line Graphs

While bar graphs are generally used to show comparisons and pie charts to represent a division of a whole into its parts, **line graphs** are used to show changes in the same data series over a period of time. For example, to chart the sales of a business over a period of months, a line graph would be appropriate. Assume Shirlann's Snack Shack, located in a local shopping mall, sells three lines of merchandise: frozen yogurt, hot dogs, and beverages. The sales for each of these lines of merchandise are plotted for each month, and the plotting points are connected. This results in a line for each item. The line moves up and down as the sales volume moves up and down from month to month (figure 16).

Shirlann's Snack Shack
19-- Sales Volume

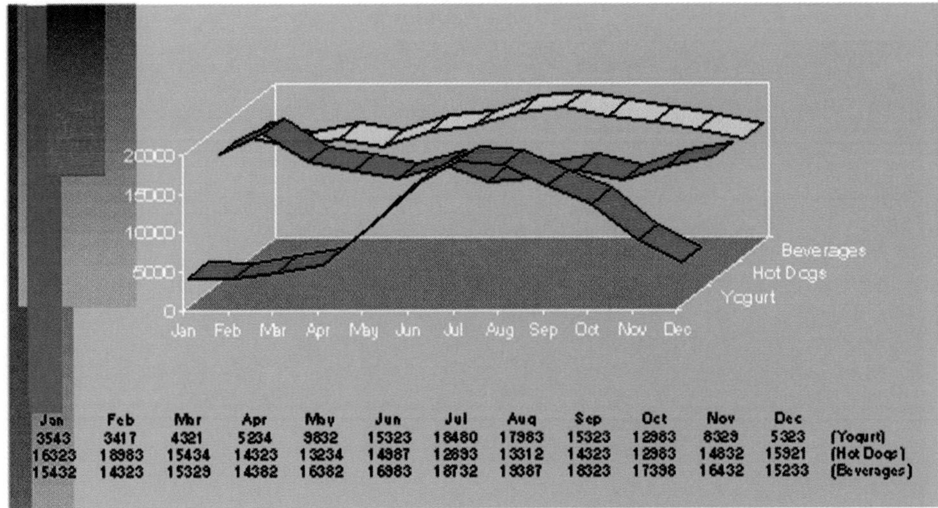

Jan	Feb	Mar	Apr	May	Jun	Jul	Aug	Sep	Oct	Nov	Dec	
3543	3417	4321	5234	9832	15323	18480	17983	15323	12983	8329	5323	(Yogurt)
16323	18983	15434	14323	13234	14987	12693	13312	14323	12983	14832	15921	(Hot Dogs)
15432	14323	15329	14382	16382	16983	18732	13387	18323	17398	16432	15233	(Beverages)

figure 16

Line graphs readily show changes that occur over time.

Area Charts

The line graphs in the previous section show change over time for each of the three items being sold. It would be advantageous to Shirlann, however, to see the total sales of the shop as well as the sales of the individual items. To do this, she may use an **area chart**. Such a chart adds the total sales figures for each month and shows the total as well as the size of the individual components. This is illustrated in figure 17, which shows two graphs. The first is based on a bar graph, while the second is based on a line graph. The data for these charts is the same as that in figure 16.

Here is an example of how to read the graphs. In January, Shirlann's sold $3543 of yogurt, $16,323 of hot dogs, and $15,432 of beverages. The total of these three figures ($35,298) is shown on the graphs. Note that the total for the month is divided into three parts on the graphs, one part for each of the three products sold.

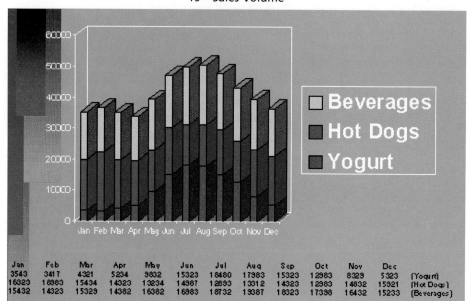

figure 17

An area chart readily shows the contribution of the parts to a whole.

Shirlann's Snack Shack
19-- Sales Volume

60000
50000
40000
30000
20000
10000
0
Jan Feb Mar Apr May Jun Jul Aug Sep Oct Nov Dec
Beverages
Hot Dogs
Yogurt

Jan	Feb	Mar	Apr	May	Jun	Jul	Aug	Sep	Oct	Nov	Dec	
3543	3417	4321	5234	9832	15323	18480	17983	15323	12983	8329	5323	(Yogurt)
16323	16983	15434	14323	13234	14987	12893	13312	14323	12983	14832	15921	(Hot Dogs)
15432	14323	15329	14382	16382	16983	18732	13387	18323	17398	16432	15233	(Beverages)

Shirlann's Snack Shack
19-- Sales Volume

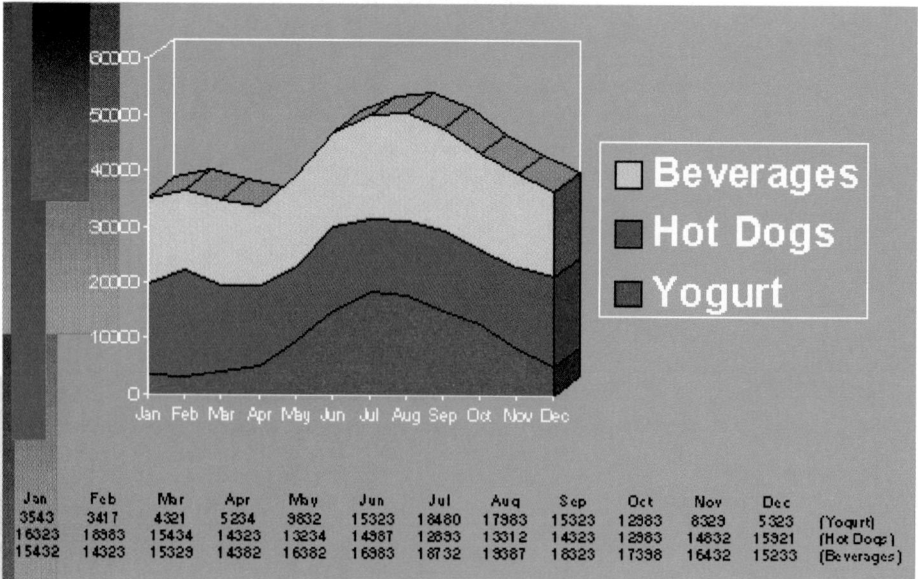

Jan	Feb	Mar	Apr	May	Jun	Jul	Aug	Sep	Oct	Nov	Dec	
3543	3417	4321	5234	9832	15323	18480	17983	15323	12983	8329	5323	(Yogurt)
16323	16983	15434	14323	13234	14987	12893	13312	14323	12983	14832	15921	(Hot Dogs)
15432	14323	15329	14382	16382	16983	18732	13387	18323	17398	16432	15233	(Beverages)

Do It!

1 What graphing software is available for your use? Do not overlook such things as the graphing ability of a spreadsheet program or other software package you may have.

2 Make a graph of your budget, showing what portion goes to each category such as savings, clothing, food, transportation, and entertainment.

Using Presentation Software

Presentation software shows one graphic image after another on the computer screen. That is, it makes a computerized slide show. Beyond this basic definition, there are many differences from one brand of presentation software to another. These include:

- Some programs take images that have been created by other programs and simply handle the job of getting them to the screen one after the other.
- Other programs create images from a script or outline entered by the user. In these cases, the words from the script appear over backgrounds selected by the user. With this type of program, the user typically selects a template that is supplied with the program. The template controls the graphic appearance of the screens on which the user's words appear.
- Some programs can handle motion and sound, tending to place them more in the category of multimedia software, which is discussed in a different module.

Creating a Presentation

The following steps are somewhat typical of many presentation programs. Keep in mind, however, that there is a wide range of capabilities, and the interface used to create presentations can vary considerably from one brand of software to another. Typical steps are:

1. Select a template on which to base the presentation. The template provides the background appearance. Often, it contains predone screens in standard formats such as titles and bullet lists, and you can simply edit the wording to reflect what you want to display.
2. Select the type of display for each screen or "slide." Typically, you have choices such as title, introduction, bullet, text, graph, and conclusion.
3. Enter or edit the text to appear. With many programs, this may be done directly on the screen image or in a script.
4. Set controls for how to move from screen to screen. Usually, you can set a timer to change screens automatically, or you can set the program to wait until the user clicks the mouse or presses a key before continuing.

Figure 18 shows a very simple presentation and the script that created it. Keep in mind that software can create much more complex presentations than this sample. Just about all programs, for example, can place images created by other programs.

figure 18

Many presentation software packages let you work from a script, such as this one.

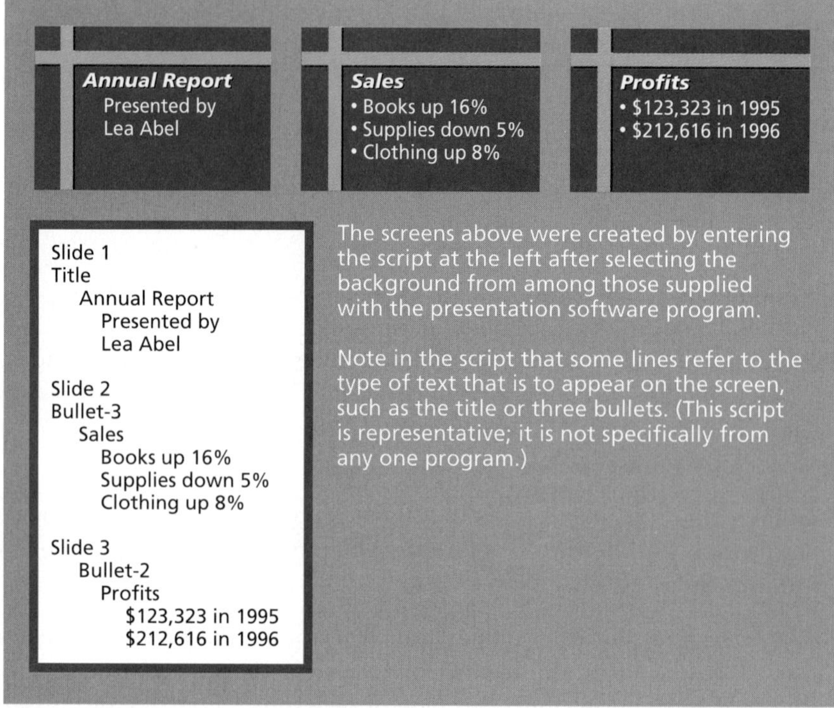

Editing a Presentation

Once a presentation is done, you will probably want to make changes to it. Changes in wording are simple; just use the mouse and keyboard to edit the text. Another thing you may frequently need to do, however, is to rearrange the order of the screens or "slides." Many programs provide a screen sorter for this purpose. As shown in figure 19, a sorter simply places and shows small images of all of the screens, and you can use the mouse to move them to different locations. Note in the figure that the kind of template used for each image appears beneath its picture.

figure 19

You can rearrange a presentation's sequence by using the mouse to move the slides on the screen sorter.

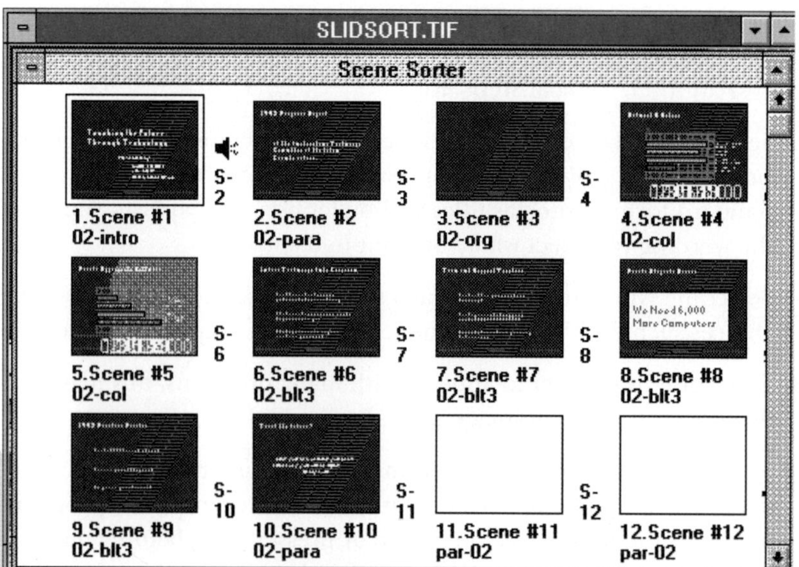

Publishing a Presentation on the World Wide Web

You can use a presentation program to prepare pages for publication on the Internet's World Wide Web. With programs equipped to do the job, a simple menu choice such as File . . . Publish is generally all that is required. The software can automatically convert graphic file formats to match the requirements of the Web, and it can automatically place the formatting codes to control how the content looks on the Web. Keep in mind, however, that the more graphics (and the larger the graphics) you include in a presentation, the longer a page will take to load into a viewer's Web browser. Once the presentation program has created the files, you will need to use services provided by your Web server site to upload those files for use.

Common file formats are listed in the following table:

Some Commonly Used File Formats for Graphics

These are just a few of the many different file formats in which different programs store graphic images. Fortunately, many programs can store and retrieve several different formats. There are also a number of conversion programs on the market that can convert from one format to another, including conversion of Macintosh files to PC formats and PC files to Macintosh formats.

Format Name	Pixel/Vector	Primarily Used With
PICT Picture	Vector	Macintosh
EPS (Encapsulated PostScript)	Vector	Macintosh & PC
TIF (Tagged Image Format)	Pixel	Macintosh & PC
PCD (Kodak Photo-CD)	Pixel	Macintosh & PC
PCX (PC Paintbrush)	Pixel	PC
CDR (CorelDraw)	Vector	PC
WMF (Windows Metafile)	Vector	PC
JPEG (Joint Photographics Experts Group)	Pixel	World Wide Web
GIF (Graphic Interchange Format)	Pixel	World Wide Web

Summary

Graphics refers to any pictorial representation that can be produced by the computer.

- Graphics software is any software that can produce "pictures" or "art."
- Paint programs allow a person to do "art" on the computer screen.
- CAD programs are used for computer-aided design and drafting.
- Graphics programs can produce graphs or charts from data.
- Among other things, computer graphics are used for art, computer-aided instruction, computer-aided design and drafting, scientific study, television and movies, and presentation graphics.
- Paint programs give the user access to computer versions of commonly used tools, such as pencils, brushes, paint rollers and paint sprayers, as well as to erasers and special effects tools.
- Freehand drawings may be made with paint programs.
- Text may be entered into the images made with paint programs.
- Paint-program images are made from individual picture elements (pixels) that are set to the appropriate color.
- Paint programs can use image libraries to assist in the development of pictures.
- Drawing programs base their images on objects made from mathematic formulas.
- Among the shapes that can be drawn with drawing programs are straight lines, rectangles, polygons, circles, arcs, ellipses, and complex curves.
- Any object drawn using the geometric shapes of a drawing program can be named and used as a component in the drawing.
- Component libraries are available for drawing programs.
- Because drawing-program objects are mathematic, they can easily be moved, reshaped, resized, copied, or mirrored.
- Text may be added as desired to drawing images; the text is also represented as mathematic formulas.
- Many drawing programs allow the use of different layers for different purposes in the drawing.
- Dimensions can be computed and placed automatically by computer-aided design (CAD) programs.

Summary

- Graphing programs produce their output from inputs of existing data.
- Bar graphs are good for comparing different data items, with the length of each bar representing the data value.
- A pie chart shows the divisions of a "whole" into its component "slices"; it is excellent for showing any situation where a total is made up of several lesser amounts.
- Line graphs show changes in one or more series of data over a period of time.
- Area charts show the sum of the parts, usually over a period of time.
- Presentation software enables you to prepare "slide shows" on the computer.
- Presentation software varies considerably in capability, ranging from simply showing one screen after another to handling motion and sound, which places it in the category of multimedia software.

The following key terms were defined in this module. For each of the following terms, write on a separate piece of paper the number of the definition followed by the letter of the appropriate term.

Terms

A. area chart

B. bar graph

C. computer-aided design (CAD) program

D. component or object

E. computer graphics

F. drawing program

G. graphics software

H. graphing program

I. image library

J. line graph

K. node

L. paint program

M. pie chart

N. pixel

O. presentation graphics

P. reference point

Q. tools

Definitions

1 a point on an object that can be used to resize the object

2 the points on an object that indicate a change in direction

3 a chart that shows the contribution of parts to the whole

4 a collection of stock images that may be used with a painting program

5 an individual dot in an image

6 a chart that divides a whole into its component parts

7 the different "instruments" provided by a drawing or painting program

8 a graph that shows comparisons between different quantities

9 a program designed for producing plans and blueprints

10 a predefined shape that may be used repeatedly in a drawing

Matching

11 the generic terms for any "art" or "pictures" done on the computer

12 a program that uses mathematically defined shapes to create images

13 the generic term for any software that makes "art" or "pictures"

14 "slide shows" made with the computer

15 a graph showing changes in data over time

16 a program that produces graphs from data entered in a spreadsheet

17 a program that enables the user to produce images by changing the color of individual pixels on the screen

Review

1. What is meant by computer graphics? (Obj. 1)
2. List the three common types of graphics software. (Obj. 1)
3. Name and describe six uses for computer graphics. (Obj. 1)
4. What characteristics define a paint program? (Obj. 2)
5. Describe the general method of using a paint program. (Obj. 2)
6. What is the purpose of image libraries? (Obj. 2)
7. What characteristics define a drawing program? (Obj. 3)
8. Describe the general method of using a drawing program. (Obj. 3)
9. What are objects, and what is their purpose? (Obj. 3)
10. What characteristics define graphing software? (Obj. 4)
11. Describe four common types of graphs, and tell the kinds of data they are best at graphing. (Obj. 4)
12. What characteristics represent the strong points of painting software? Under what circumstances do these characteristics become weak points? (Obj. 2)
13. What characteristics represent the strong points of drawing programs? Under what circumstances do these characteristics become weak points? (Obj. 3)
14. Internally, is graphing software more likely to be based on a painting or a drawing program? Why do you believe this to be true? (Obj. 4)
15. What characteristics distinguish CAD software from drawing software? (Obj. 3, 4)
16. List and describe the use of some of the commonly found paint-program tools. (Obj. 2)
17. List and describe some of the commonly found drawing-program tools. (Obj. 3)
18. List and describe some of the common effects in a drawing program. (Obj. 3)
19. If you did not have a graphing program available and needed to make a graph, could you make one with a painting or a drawing program? Which would be preferable? How would you go about making the graph? (Obj. 2, 3, 4)
20. What distinguishes presentation software from drawing, painting, and graphing software? (Obj. 5)

Activities

For the following activities, decide whether painting, drawing, or CAD software is the most appropriate to use. If you have the most appropriate type of software available, use it to complete the project. Most of the projects can be completed with the nonoptimum type of software if the ideal is not available.

1 *Speaking* Bring in examples of graphics or container documents, and explain what kind of program (draw, CAD, graphing, paint) was probably used to create their components. Describe the clues that helped to suggest the kind of program that was used. Also, point out any portions of the documents that were probably created using images from a library.

2 *Art* Create an image of your school mascot.

3 *Math* If you have the software available, learn how to use a CAD program. Draw the layout of your classroom or your home.

4 *Math* If you have the software available, learn how to use a graphing program to graph the record of one of your school's athletic teams over the past several years.

5 *Science* Visit an architectural or engineering firm and observe how CAD and drafting software are used there.

6 *Speaking* Visit a television station, and observe how graphics software is used there. Report what you learn to your class.

7 *Writing* Prepare a research report on how the movie and television industry uses graphics.

(Continued on next page.)

Activities

8 *International Business* Working with a small group of other students, decide on an international business that you would be interested in operating and on a name for the business. Use painting or drawing software (you which is most appropriate if both are available) to design a logo that you think reflects the ideals of the business. Do research to make sure there are no negative connotations to the name or logo in the countries where you would operate. (As an example of what you would not want to do: A number of years ago Chevrolet had a model they called the Nova, and sales in Spanish-speaking countries were incredibly poor. Chevrolet eventually found out that in Spanish, Nova means "no go.")

9 *Speaking* Using software that is available to you, create a presentation to sell a product or an idea. Make your presentation to the class.

10 *Internet* Use a graphics program that is available to you to prepare an image for publication on a World Wide Web page. Save the image in a format generally usable by Web browsers—that is, GIF or JPEG. Size the image appropriately for use (remember that a standard computer display is 640 x 480 pixels and the image should only consume a portion of the screen). Also, make sure you save the image in 256 colors. If you have access to do so, place the image on a Web page and look at it with your browser to see how it looks. If it needs improvement, modify it until you are satisfied. Make a screen print of the page to turn in to your instructor.

Multimedia & Hypermedia

Overview

The most technologically advanced way to do a presentation is with multimedia. The first use of multimedia that likely comes to mind is interactive games; however, more important uses include business presentations and training materials. Also, information kiosks at airports and other locations use multimedia software.

By definition, *multimedia* involves more than one kind of presentation element. Among the elements a developer may choose from are graphics, sound, animations, and movies (either captured or stored on computer media, retrieved from videodiscs, or retrieved from a CD-ROM).

A prevailing characteristic of multimedia (in addition to its use of multiple presentation mediums) is interactivity. That is, the course of the presentation can be changed by choices made by the user. For example, you touch the screen of an information kiosk to tell the computer what information you want to see, then you see only that information.

Objectives

1. Define multimedia and hypermedia.
2. Distinguish between graphics software and multimedia software.
3. Describe the various kinds of objects that can go into a multimedia presentation.
4. Describe the hardware characteristics that are necessary for successful multimedia production and presentation.
5. Describe the difference between multimedia and hypermedia.
6. Describe some typical applications of hypermedia.
7. Use multimedia programs on your computer.
8. Develop a multimedia production.

What Is Multimedia?

In one sense, *multimedia* is a generic word meaning "more than one medium." Therefore, if you stand in front of a group and show them how to tie a knot, you are using multimedia—the medium of your voice and the medium of your hands manipulating the rope. Likewise, if you are an artist and put on a show containing both watercolors and oils, you have done a multimedia show. When referring to computer multimedia, most people mean they are using software that accesses multiple kinds of sensory producers, usually including graphics, text, and sound (figure 1).

What Are the Characteristics of Multimedia?

There are three characteristics that generally set multimedia software apart from other software. The program:

figure 1

People of all ages use computer multimedia.

1. Uses some combination of text, graphics, animation, movies, and sound. Each of these is an object that is manipulated by the program, and it is this combination of media that distinguishes multimedia from graphics software. Images created with graphics software are used in multimedia productions, however.
2. Is usually based on timelines. Elements in each frame or slide of the presentation appear and disappear at designated times. Additionally, changing of the frames or slides may proceed under timed control.
3. Is interactive. While major portions of the presentation may be under timed control, the user can jump to different frames, slides, or even a different place in the timeline by touching the screen, clicking the mouse, or entering a selection from the keyboard.

Find out more about these characteristics in the following sections.

Types of Media

Multimedia programs can use images and sounds that have been created or captured from a wide range of sources. Some of the more common ones are listed on the next page. The program controls the entrance, duration, and exit of each object that makes up a portion of the presentation.

Types of Media Used in Multimedia Programs

Media Category	Common Types
Graphics	Pixel-based from paint programs Pixel-based images consist of dots of various colors arranged to form an image.
	Vector-based from drawing programs Vector-based drawings are stored as math formulas representing the different shapes in the image, and the computer constructs them from the formulas when they are needed for display. Because the images are stored as formulas, some programs can independently animate the various objects that make the vector-based image.
Sounds	Digitally recorded words and/or music Can be high quality or low, depending on the hardware, software, and the sampling rate (how much detail of the sound is recorded). Higher sampling rates require much more memory.
	CD audio When this option is used, sound is played directly from an audio CD through the computer's speakers.
	Synthesized sounds Require much less storage space, because they are instructions to synthesizer chips on what kind of sound to produce rather than recordings of the actual sound. Quality generally is not as good as digital recording unless you have expensive hardware.
Animations	Computer-generated animations These are usually in the Autodesk Animator or Macromedia movie format.
Computer-based Video	Apple QuickTime, Microsoft Video for Windows
External video	Multimedia programs can control external laserdisc players or VCRs to show video on separate screens (or on the computer's screen if the computer has the proper hardware to do so).

Timeline Orientation

Multimedia productions are usually divided into scenes. Movement to a given scene may be automatic on completion of a previous scene, or it may happen on the choice of the user. The clock controls when objects in each multimedia screen appear as well as how long they remain visible or continue to play.

Profile

Marc Canter

Macromedia, Inc., is a leading company in multimedia production software. Their software, which includes titles such as Director and Action, have provided the vehicle for creation of some truly astounding productions, from city information kiosks to instructional and training materials (and annual reports) for a pizza company.

Perhaps it is appropriate that a multimedia company was created by a person of multiple talents. Macromedia's founder, Marc Canter, is an accomplished opera singer who has also tried his hand at such things as video games, laser light shows, holography, kinetic sculpture, and computer programming. After earning his degree from Oberlin College, Canter and some like-minded artistic types founded MacroMind, Inc. The company lured away several Apple Computer executives, including John Sculley, who became MacroMind's chief executive. At first, the company's software ran only on Macintosh computers, which at the time had a large technologic edge for handling multimedia applications. Later, Windows versions were added to extend the product range to IBM-compatible machines. Through mergers, Canter's company became today's Macromedia, which rang up sales of $30 million in 1994.

Macromedia's software, which has always provided state-of-the-art capabilities, has now reached the level where there is binary file compatibility between the Macintosh and Windows versions. This means that a presentation created on one platform can be used on the other. The latest announced versions of the software will offer three to five times the performance of previous versions. This kind of leading-edge development has kept Macromedia at the forefront of the multimedia revolution.

Macromedia will have to go on without Marc Canter, however. Having left the company he helped to create, Canter is still the visionary. He has been working on technology to take advantage of interactive cable television as it becomes more commonplace. He visualizes a multimedia product with which the listener/viewer interacts with music videos in real time to control the sequence of events.

As an example of the concept, let's do a human presentation for the introduction of a school talent show. The presentation is equivalent to a scene, takes 30 seconds, and uses various "actors," who are equivalent here to computer objects. The basic flow of events is:

- Spotlights come on.
- Orchestra begins playing.
- Announcer announces, "Ladies and gentlemen…"
- Dancers come on stage and dance.
- The orchestra and dancers stop, and the spotlights go out.

If we put that sequence of events into a timeline to see how it looks, we get something like the following. Note that time goes across the page and that the start of a bar indicates the entrance, and the end of the bar the departure, of an actor.

0"	4"	7"	10"	13"	16"	19"	22"	25"	28"
Spotlights									
Orchestra									
	Announcer								
			Dancers						

By looking at this timeline, anyone can see exactly when each of the participants comes on and when they leave. Also, adjustments can be made to the timeline to indicate changes. For example, if you decide to have the spotlights go out slightly before the orchestra stops and the dancers leave, just drag the right end of the spotlights bar a little to the left. (If you are working on the computer instead of with this human example, moving the end of the bar would actually cause the lights to turn off at the end of the changed time.) Note that there is usually a separate timeline for each element of a production.

Interactivity

Most multimedia productions are **interactive**. That is, either a presenter or the program's user can select what should happen next. For example, suppose you approach the kiosk at the airport and are greeted by a screen displaying a picture that shows a hotel, a restaurant, a taxi, and a limousine. Wording on the screen requests that you touch the item you want to know more about. Suppose you touch the restaurant. The next screen that appears has a map with the city divided into areas, and the text asks you to touch the part of the city in which you would like to dine. This is followed by a screen that finds out what kind of food you want. Finally, a listing with photos of individual restaurants appears, and you can touch as many in turn as you like to find out more information. Lastly, when you have decided on a restaurant that requires reservations, you can touch the telephone icon beside it and be instantly connected to make your reservation. Another example of interactivity is the exhibit at the Indianapolis Children's Museum that is shown in figure 2.

Making a Multimedia Production

In this section, we discuss the process of actually creating a multimedia production. We will use Macromedia Action, a program that is available for both the PC and the Macintosh, in creating our example production. Very similar steps are used with other programs, although menus, dialog boxes, and mouse action may be somewhat different. Two other commonly used programs include Hypercard on the Macintosh and LinkWay on non-Windows IBM PCs.

Start the Program

When you click on the Action icon, you get a screen that looks very familiar. It has the usual menu across the top and a toolbox down the left side. You have a blank screen with which to work, and you are ready to begin. While you can do very complex things with Action, we are going to do one simple scene. We could add additional scenes later. Here are the steps.

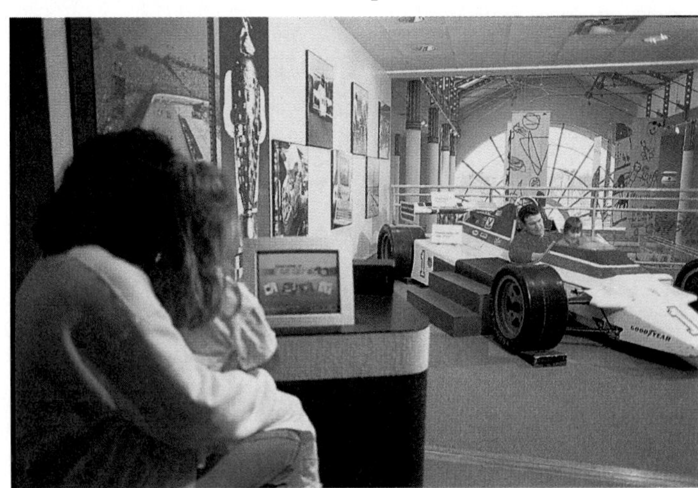

figure 2

This multimedia production at the Indianapolis Children's Museum helps visitors learn about the laws of physics as they relate to the Indianapolis 500 auto race.

Import a Background

Using the File . . . Import menu, bring in a background for the scene. We could bring an entire template categorized as to whether it is a title, ending, graph, bullet chart, or whatever. Instead, let's just bring in a simple bitmap image. We select it from the dialog box, and our screen looks as shown in figure 3, with the image covering the entire presentation area. Note that we went to the Window menu and turned on Timeline so that we can see the timeline that is maintained by the program. The background object has been automatically placed on the timeline by the program with a default length of 10 seconds.

Add Some Music

Music will help make the presentation much nicer. So, once again, go to the File . . . Import menu, change the selection drop-down box to WAV and

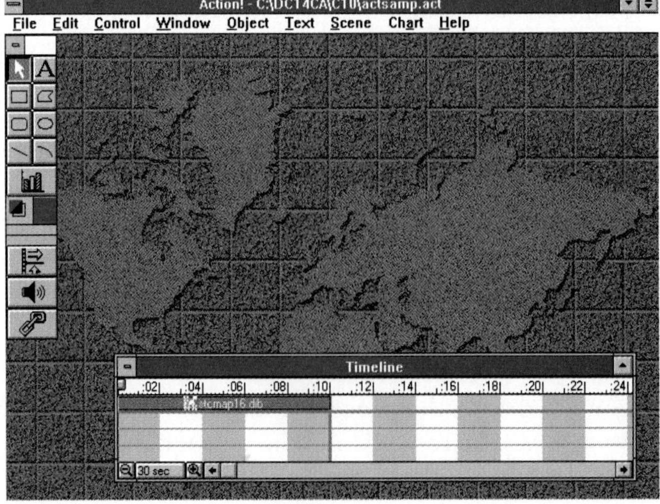

figure 3

Just about any image may be used as the background for a multimedia screen.

select a sound; this dialog box is shown in figure 4. Next time we show you the timeline, you will see that the music has been added. If you are actually working on a computer doing this, you can try your presentation by using the play controls at the top right of the screen.

If we wanted to add a video or animation, the process is the same as that for adding the music. We would just pick a file containing the desired video or animation.

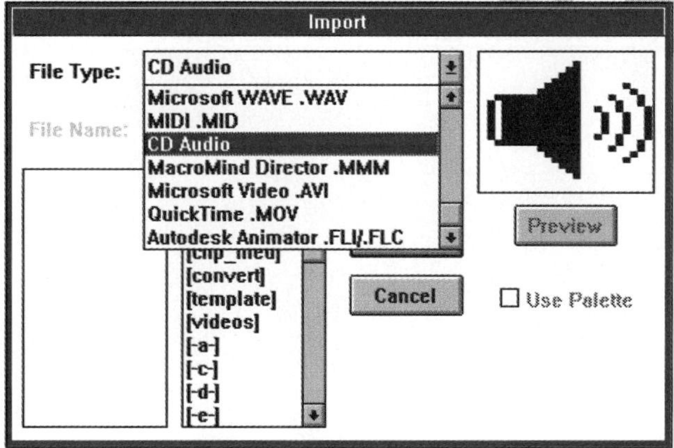

figure 4

The import dialog box shows the numerous kinds of files (for sound, video, and animations) that can be used in a multimedia presentation.

Add Some Text

The name of the company doing this production is Global Partners Ltd. Their name will move onto the screen from the right and then sparkle.

Under Action, each object has an entry phase, a duration or hold phase, and an exit phase. You can define the kind of action that is to happen with each object during each of these phases. A few of the possibilities include objects moving onto stage from any of several directions, materializing from out of the background, or being exposed as if by blinds.

Now, to add the text, use the text tool (A) from the toolbox to put text on the screen in its final position. Then, use the Text menu to select the font and size that you want. Use the color tool to set the color. Then, double-click on the text to bring up the dialog box to control its actions, as in figure 5; in this figure, you see the dialog box in two different states: one to control the entry stage, and another to control the hold phase. Note that the sparkle put on it during the hold phase is automatically applied and animated by the program.

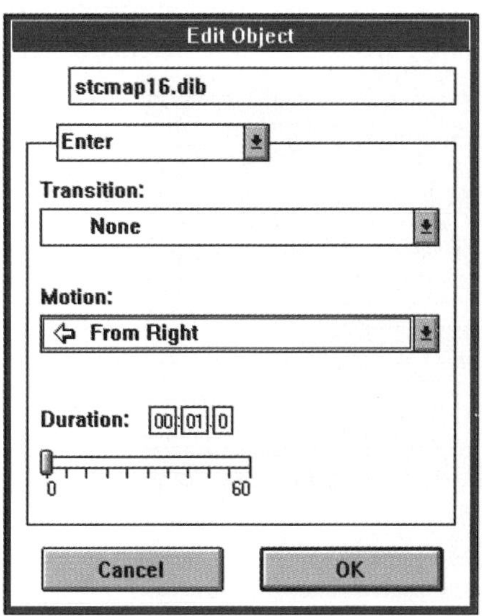

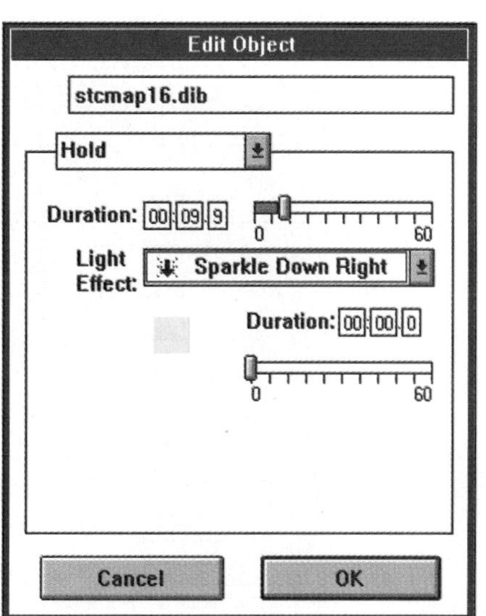

figure 5

This dialog box controls the movement, effects, behaviour, and appearance of objects.

Look at the result in figure 6. The timeline shows the addition of the new objects. If you look carefully, you will see that we have moved the left end of the text bar in the timeline to make the text begin its entry from the right of the screen about 1 second after the background and music. If you look still more carefully, you will see a faint, vertical line in the bar for the text. This marks the point where the entrance phase ends and the hold phase begins. The point can be moved with the mouse.

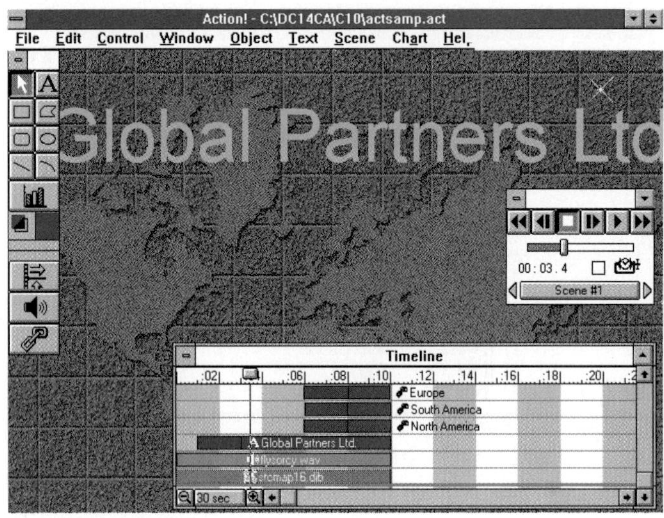

figure 6

As each object is added to a screen, it appears in the timeline. By moving an object on the timeline with the mouse, you control its entry time, duration time, and exit time.

Adding Buttons

To make a production interactive, you add buttons. Each **button** is then told where to take the presentation when the user clicks the mouse on it. To add a button to an Action presentation, select Object . . . Add New . . . Button from the menus. Double-clicking on the new button brings up a dialog box for giving it the desired name and for controlling its entry, hold, and exit phases, just as with any other object. Using the link tool from the toolbox then allows you to specify the action to be taken when a user chooses that button. If you want to make the button invisible (so that the user clicks on some portion of the map, for example), you can do that, too.

Look at figure 7 to see our example with buttons added to name different places where Global has operations. We told these buttons to move in from the edges of the screen to their resting points. To finish the presentation, we

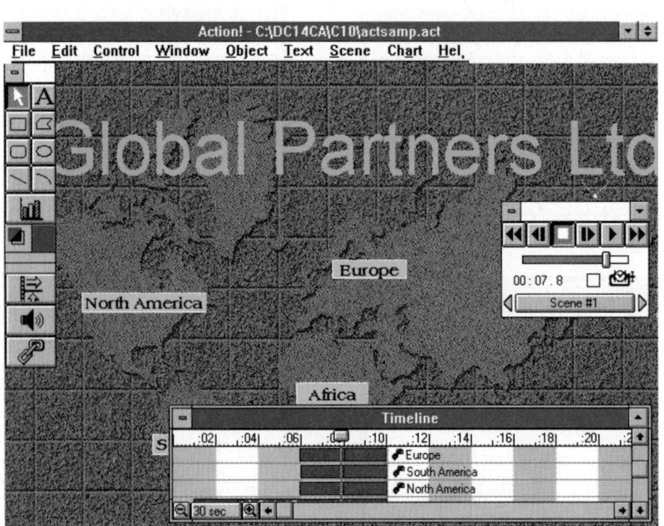

figure 7

The buttons with continent names are linked to other screens to which the program moves when a user clicks on the button. To make the screen more lively, the buttons were set up to glide onto the screen after the main heading has appeared. Note that all the buttons appear in the timeline and can be adjusted from that point.

would add additional scenes for operations on each of the continents, and we would link the buttons to go to those screens.

At any time during creation of the production, you can use the play and rewind buttons on the screen to see what you have done in action. Once you have finished, the program may allow you to use menu choices to create a stand-alone version. The stand-alone version is frequently referred to as a *run-time version.* It can be played back and interacted with by a person who does not have the program that you used in putting the production together.

Do It!

1 What multimedia productions do you have available for use? These may include various instructional programs and games. Make a list of their features—that is, what they are capable of doing. Try out the productions to see how the user interacts with them. Working in a group, evaluate the productions, and report to the class their good features and how the applications could be improved.

2 What programs are available to you for producing multimedia presentations? Try any sample productions that are available with those programs. Evaluate the samples, and write down what you consider to be their most and least appealing features.

3 Complete any tutorial that may be a part of a multimedia program that is available for your use.

Going Beyond Multimedia to Hypermedia

If you look in the dictionary for the meaning of the prefix *hyper-*, you find such words as *above, beyond,* and *super.* So, you may want to remember the definition of **hypermedia** as going "beyond" multimedia to get to the level of "super" media. Hypermedia distinguishes itself by obtaining data or information from a variety of sources. That is, it combines the user interface of multimedia with connections to one or more sources of data. By responding to user choices, the program can extract data and present it to the user in the form of the needed information.

Hypermedia for Research

One of the applications of hypermedia with which you are probably familiar is a CD-ROM encyclopedia. Such an encyclopedia uses multimedia, of course, because it has text, graphics, and sound. What makes it hypermedia is that under user selection, it can look up articles in the full text of an encyclopedia. It can also look up definitions in a dictionary. Figure 8 shows a dialog box from a typical encyclopedia; in this box, you specify the topic you want to research.

Another example of hypermedia is provided by online information services that use a graphic user interface and can, under user request, go out and search through a wide variety of different databases looking for information related to the requested topic. This information can then be presented on the screen as full text and graphics from the source.

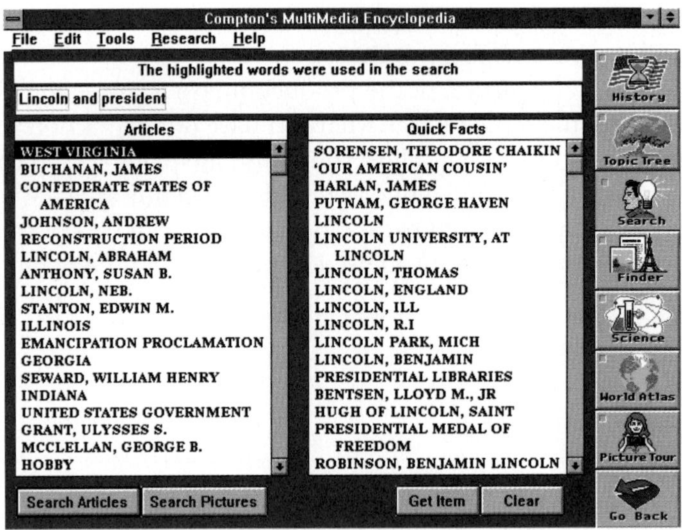

figure 8

By specifying a topic you want to research, a hypermedia application such as this encyclopedia can search out the desired data.

Hypermedia for Teaching

A growing number of products are available that use hypermedia for teaching purposes. Most of these products allow students to explore by creating their own paths through data. For example, a product used in biology classes allows the student to click on different parts of a human body on the screen. Depending on the user's choice, several actions are possible. He or she can see the body part's name and its definition from the program's medical dictionary. He or she can "dig deeper" or "cover up," depending on what layer (skin, underlying tissue, bones, and so on) they are on. He or she can also perform surgery on the body, seeing the results of each step graphically on the screen. Figure 9 shows a typical screen from one such program.

Some people see the use of hypermedia in the classroom as a great advance. Others are concerned that when a student is allowed to explore, there is not enough structure to the learning. While there have been some studies on the effectiveness of hypermedia-based learning, they have not yet provided definitive answers as to when it is most appropriate. One thing is for sure, however: you can do things with hypermedia (like performing surgery) that you could never do without it.

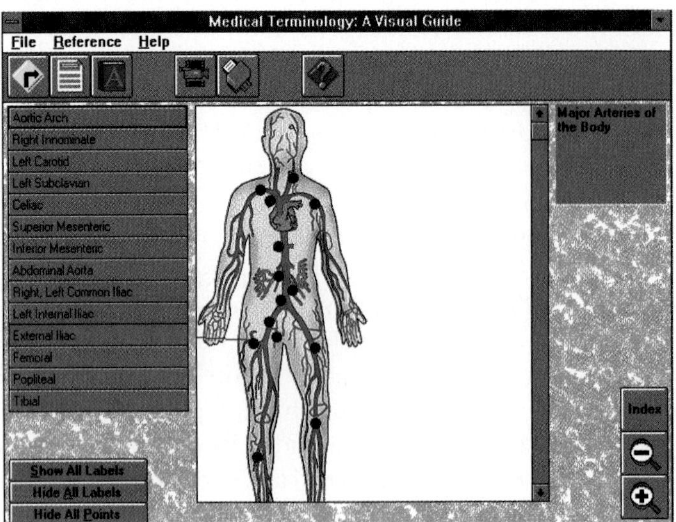

figure 9

This hypermedia product adds a new dimension to classroom learning by enabling students to explore inside the human body.

Hypermedia for Business Decision-making

A quickly developing area in which hypermedia plays a large role is in what are known as **executive information systems**. The persons who manage businesses must base their decisions on valid data if they are to succeed. Historically, managers could access two kinds of data: summarized data and detail data. However, they could only see it after other people had done the summarizing, and by then, it was frequently out of date. Another problem was that the summary might contain so little detail that it would be useless, or the detail would be so voluminous and unorganized that no information could be seen in the data.

Now that just about all of a company's data is on a computer system, the computer is capable of providing data at whatever level of summary or detail is needed—and of doing it close to instantaneously. The only catch is that managers have not yet been expert enough in using computers to get at the information.

Now, hypermedia-based executive information systems have ridden to the rescue. Using a graphic user interface, developers have been able to tie managers straight to the corporate database system. Instead of issuing arcane commands to retrieve the data, however, the manager uses the mouse to select the kind of data he or she wants to see and the manner in which he or she wants to see it.

Frequently, a number of predefined views of the data will be developed by the information-systems staff of a business. Then, whenever a manager desires, the computer will go look at the current data and present it to the manager in the predefined format. Easy-to-fill-in query screens can also make it easier for a manager to summarize data at a level and in a fashion that has not been previously defined. Figure 10 shows a screen that a manager might use to access an executive information system.

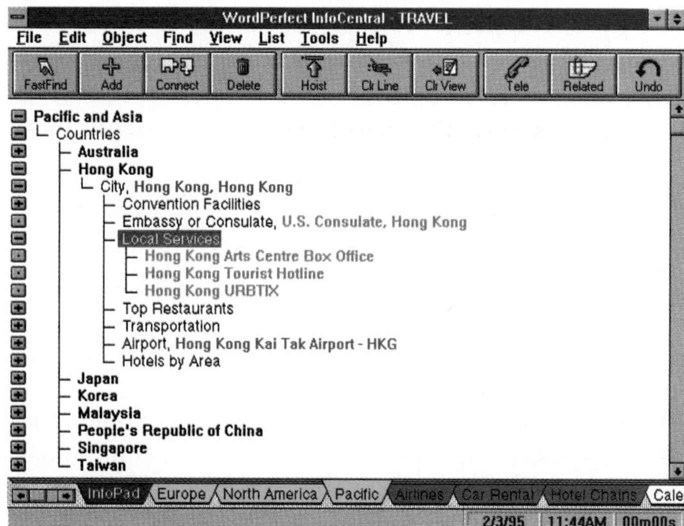

figure 10

Hypermedia-based executive information systems make it possible for managers to get to the data they need in order to make the best decisions.

Hardware Requirements for Multimedia

Most computers now sold are capable of handling at least simple multimedia applications. Many older computers still in use, however, do not have enough power to use multimedia software. The typical hardware needed for multimedia (figure 11) can be described as follows:

figure 11

The hardware necessary for multimedia may be included as a standard part of the computer or may be implemented by adding on additional equipment.

- A fast processor. For satisfactory performance with a PC, you need at least a 486SX processor, and for a Macintosh, at least a 68030 processor.
- Lots of memory. Typically, at least 8MB of RAM are required.
- Lots of storage capacity. Many commercial multimedia applications come on **CD-ROM**, and you must have a CD drive (figure 12) in your computer to use them. CD-ROMs are used because they have lots of storage space to hold the massive graphics and sound files that are used by the application. For productions you make yourself, you will need a very large hard disk drive, a magnetic optical disk, or an alternate storage device, such as a PC-CD or removable magnetic cartridge drive. PC-CDs combine the ability to read a standard CD-ROM with the abilities to both read from and write to an optical disk. You simply put the disk you want to use (CD-ROM or optical) into the drive. When you insert an optical disk, you can record (and rewrite numerous times) up to 650 megabytes of data per disk. To the user, the optical disk appears to work just like a hard drive. Since you can have as many disks as you wish, the storage capacity is unlimited. Magnetic disk drives with removable cartridges offer another form of unlimited storage. Some of these cartridges use "floppy" disks, while others use fixed or "hard" disks. Speed and capacity for these drives varies according to the brand and model.
- A 256-color or better display. To get realistic-looking photographs on screen requires at least 256 colors; 16 just will not do it. While a display offering up to 16.7 million colors looks nicer (if the images are stored at that depth), it requires much faster hardware to be satisfactory. Keep in mind that the number of colors you can see depends on the computer video output, not the monitor itself.
- Sound capability, which may be built-in or added with a separate sound card.

Do It!

1 Check with media specialists and teachers as appropriate to determine what multimedia and hypermedia instructional applications are used in your school. List the applications, decide whether each is multimedia or hypermedia, and list the courses in which they are used. If possible, try out at least one multimedia and one hypermedia application, and report to the class on your experience. Give your evaluation on how well the program uses its multimedia or hypermedia capabilities.

The Low-Down on Sound

There are two ways of producing sound: creating it with synthesized or digitally sampled sound, or playing back digitally recorded sound. Sound cards usually are capable of both.

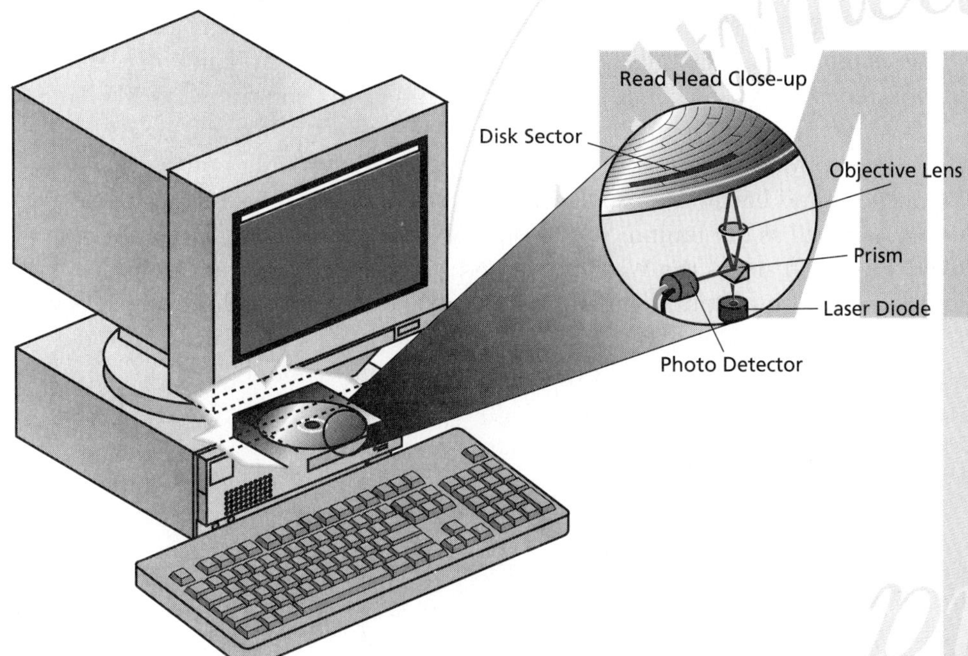

figure 12

CD-ROMs started in the audio world and were adapted to computers. Because of that background, the recorded data is arranged on one long spiral rather than discreet tracks. Each sector is the same size, and the speed of the disk changes as the read head moves from edge to edge of the disk so that there is always a constant number of bits per second passing by the laser beam that reads the data. A CD-ROM can store up to 600 megabytes and is read only, making it ideal for distributing multimedia productions.

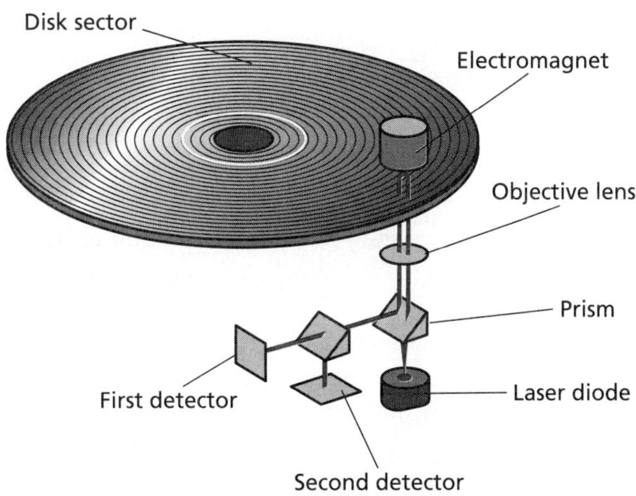

figure 13

For high-capacity read-write storage, a magneto-optical disk is useful. A 3.5" disk can hold up to 250 megabytes of data, while a 5.25" disk can handle up to 1.3 gigabytes (1,300 megabytes). In addition to storing much more data, a magneto-optical drive and disk is much less likely to fail than a standard magnetic disk. Thirty years of storage time is estimated for magneto-optical disks before failure of the medium (the drive mechanism probably won't last that long). The magneto-optical disks are removable media, somewhat like giant capacity floppy disks.

Synthesized and digitally sampled sound When you do **synthesized sound** or **digitally sampled sound**, the sound card or an attached MIDI musical instrument creates the sound requested by the computer. (MIDI stands for Musical Instrument Digital Interface and is a standard for making connections among "digitally aware" instruments and computer equipment.) No sound is stored anywhere on the computer; essentially, there is just a list of the required notes, along with the name of the "instrument" that is to play them, and durations. Storage space is not critical with synthesized or digitally sampled sound. In fact, you could store the instructions for producing about an hour of sound in about half a megabyte of disk space.

The difference between synthesis and digital sampling is fairly simple. In synthesis, the card or instrument creates sound from scratch using formulas that tell it how to produce the sound of a guitar versus a piano, for example. In digital sampling, the card or instrument constructs the different notes to be played by basing them on a brief digital recording of the instrument to be mimicked.

Digitally recorded sound **Digitally recorded sound** stores an "image" of the sound on computer media and "gobbles" disk space. For example, if you pick up your computer's microphone and speak into it, the computer takes a "snapshot" of the sound many times per second. Each snapshot may be recorded on the computer using either 8 bits or 16 bits, depending on the capability of the sound hardware installed in the computer. Most sound cards sold now, as well as the built-in sound on "AV" Macintoshes, use 16 bits.

Figure 14 shows the Windows Sound Recorder, which you can use to record your own sound and store it on disk. Even with an application as simple as this, you may apply various editing effects. The Macintosh Sound control panel is similar. More advanced software allows you to do even more with sound.

figure 14

The Windows Sound Recorder gives the ability to record and play back digital sound. You can edit the sound by cutting out portions of it, inserting sound from another file, or mixing with sound from another file (second frame). You can also speed up, slow down, or put echo effects on the sound (third frame). The Macintosh Sound control panel gives similar capabilities.

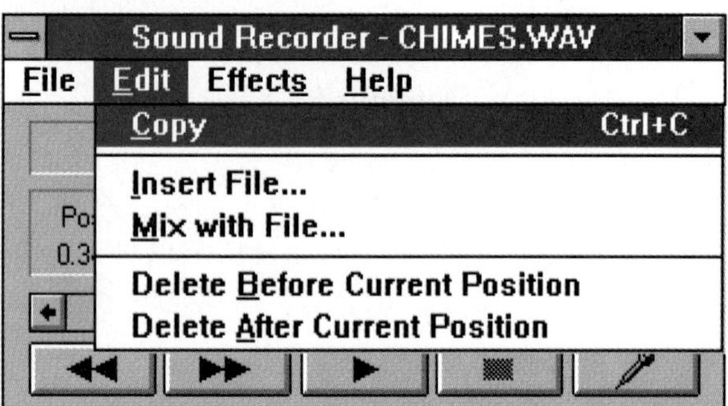

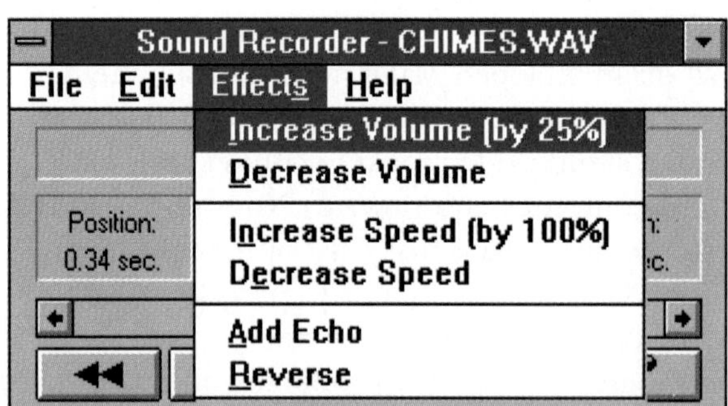

If you remember your binary numbers, you will recall that with 8 bits (two raised to the eighth power) you can have only 256 different values. With 16 bits (two raised to the sixteenth power) you can have 65,536 different values. Obviously, 8-bit sound is going to register on your ears as being rather pathetic compared with 16 bit.

Another factor in the quality of sound is the **sampling rate**, which is the number of times per second that the computer stores the sound. The multimedia PC standard (MPC) states that the minimum sampling rate the hardware is capable of should be 22.05 KHz, which is also the Macintosh standard sampling rate. KHz is short for kilohertz, which literally means "thousand times." Therefore, a frequency of 22.05 KHz means that the computer records slices of sound 22,050 times per second.

Most recording software is capable of handling the standard rate as well as variations such as half or double the standard rate. If you use half the standard rate, the quality will be much lower. Double the standard rate, or 44.1 KHz, is the sampling frequency used on audio CDs—and you know how spectacularly good that sound is. Hardware that is capable of handling the 44.1-KHz rate is becoming more common.

If you are recording nothing but the spoken voice, a lower sampling rate and 8-bit samples may be sufficient; music really pleads for 16-bit recording and at least the standard sampling rate. As you decide the sampling rate to use in recording sounds, remember that the higher the rate, the more storage space will be required.

Catching the Motion

Playing video images on the computer screen carries with it even more challenges than those brought on by the use of sound. This is because of the much greater storage requirements for video.

Storage requirements for video As you may be aware, the number of different colors that can be displayed depends on the amount of storage devoted to the dot. If one byte (8 bits) is used, you can store up to 256 different colors for each dot. This is the minimum number of colors for a barely acceptable photographic image. By increasing the storage to two bytes (16 bits), you get 65,536 different colors. (Note that these are the same number of combinations that you get for sounds with the equivalent storage.) For really superior-looking color, however, you need three bytes (24 bits) per pixel, giving 16.7 million color combinations.

If you want to fill a 640 × 480 pixel area (a "standard" 14-inch screen) with video, look at the work to be done. First, multiply 640 × 480 to get the number of dots on the screen, or 307,200. Using just 256 colors, this means that 307,200 bytes are needed to hold one screen of video. To get smooth motion requires 30 frames or screens per second. So, 307,200 × 30 gives 9,216,000 bytes (roughly 9 MB) of data for one second of full-motion video. At that rate, how many seconds of video can be stored on the hard drive of your computer?

Besides storage space requirements, another major difficulty with full-motion video has been the inability of computer hardware to make that many changes in the screen. In other words, the hardware has been too slow to display 30 different images each second.

Ethics

Once-Dead Stars "Live Again" Via Computers

Is it legal to trade on the fortunes of those who have been brought back from the dead? That is a new dilemma brought on us by the ever-increasing speed and capability of computers—and their decreasing price per unit of performance.

No, we are not saying that computers will actually resurrect people who are long gone, but computers can reconstruct their images and voices through simulations. This means that Clark Gable could come back to star in the sequel to *Gone With The Wind*, or Marilyn Monroe could extend her career by "appearing" in completely new films for a new generation of fans.

To this point, the expense of ultra-high-resolution computer animations—which are required to produce "human-quality" output—have prevented their use for anything other than brief scenarios. (Perhaps you remember the Diet Coke commercials of a few years ago in which contemporary stars such as Elton John "interacted" with departed actors such as Jimmy Cagney and Humphrey Bogart, or the more recent campaign for Chanel No. 5 perfume "starring" Marilyn Monroe.) With the cost of the hardware required continually going down, however, the possibility of making entire movies using "reconstructed" screen stars is becoming technologically feasible.

This raises interesting legal and ethical questions. Who owns the likeness of the departed? Is it the person's estate? Is it the movie studio to which the person was under contract? Who has the right to decide, years after a celebrity's death, whether he or she would have any interest in doing a particular movie? And could a simulated performance trash the reputation of a star long after his or her demise? Perhaps today's living legends and their agents should consider these questions now—or otherwise risk being haunted forever by the consequences of emerging computer technology.

Making video work with lesser equipment To make video feasible with less-than-the-fastest computers and smaller disk drives, three techniques are used:

1. The frame rate is reduced. Video may be shown at 15 frames per second, for example, rather than 30. While this makes the picture appear jumpy, it helps the hardware to keep up.

2. The video size is reduced. For example, a video image of 320 × 240 pixels requires manipulation of only one fourth as many pixels as a 640 × 480 image. Of course, the viewer sees an image that fills only one fourth of the screen. For many purposes, however, using video of much less-than-full screen size is very appropriate.

3. On-the-fly **compression** is used to reduce the size of files needed to store the images. Like that for sound, this compression uses patterns to enable file size reduction. There are, however, two categories of video compression: nonlossy compression, and lossy compression. Nonlossy compression retains all of the data from the video image, and playback upon **decompression** is just like the original. Lossy compression allows still greater reduction in file size but at the expense of some minute detail when the image is brought back.

Capturing video Before you can use video in a multimedia presentation, you must have a way of getting it into computer format. Fortunately, all this requires is a card known as a video capture card. You attach to this card a standard VCR or video camera with which you have captured the image you want to use. Then, run the capture software that comes with the card, and play the video into the computer. This setup (figure 15) typically compresses the images as it brings them in and stores them on disk. Most cards can also capture single frames of video when you need a still image. Once the image is stored in a file on the computer, it is placed into the multimedia presentation just as any other object.

When you are in the market for a video capture card, be sure to get one that works in real time. Less-expensive cards can capture only one frame at a time, which makes them suitable only for still images.

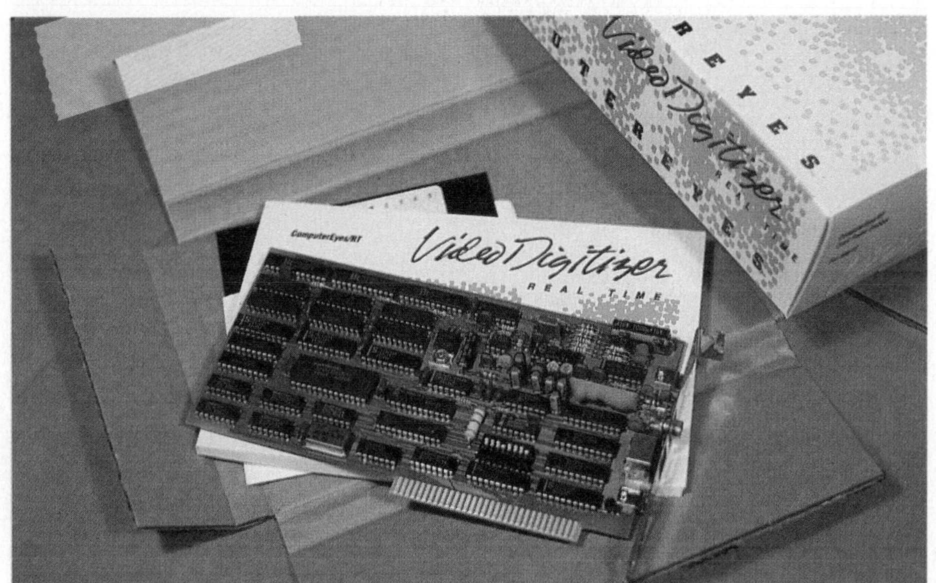

figure 15

With the proper equipment, transferring video from a camera or VCR into computer format is as simple as pressing the play button.

Virtual Reality: Multimedia's Next Step

Most people think of multimedia as a combination of pictures, sound, and text presented on the computer screen. The user has a limited degree of interactive capability in choosing which of several different program "branches" the presentation should take.

Aficionados of virtual reality look at multimedia and see even broader possibilities. Rather than merely viewing a screen and making choices with a mouse, the user become an integral part of the action. By donning various sensors such as gloves, the user's movements are transmitted to the computer. The computer then controls what is seen through special video goggles or on a large screen—and what is heard through the sound system.

Perhaps the oldest form of virtual reality is represented by cockpit simulators, used to train pilots. Today, virtual reality can enable a person to "walk through" a city or building, even if it only exists inside a computer. For example, a virtual reality presentation allowed members of the International Olympic Committee to walk through various venues being proposed by Atlanta for the 1996 Olympics long before a single structure was built.

Trends

Would-be Olympians and other athletes can get valuable, realistic sports training via virtual reality, whether it's perfecting their baseball throw or straightening out their golf swing. Even armchair athletes can participate in action adventures in which their virtual selves play an active role.

The Internet's World Wide Web: Ultimate Hypermedia?

Web browsers, which can now handle video and sound as well as static graphics, are capable of showing multimedia presentations downloaded from a Web server. Search engines on the Web can look for data in individual Web pages all over the world, and this puts the Web in the category of hypermedia. While the World Wide Web is capable of multimedia and hypermedia, the slow speed of downloading sound and images over a standard modem limits this use. As more users connect to the Web by using satellites or cable TV lines, however, this limitation will erode.

Do It!

Check the configuration of a multimedia computer that is available for your use.

1 Does it have a CD-ROM player? If so, what is the average access time, and what is the data transfer rate? Why would these two figures be important if you were to playback video from a CD-ROM?

2 Is sound built-in, or does it have an add-on sound card? If it has an add-on card, what is the brand and model?

3 Does your computer use 8-bit or 16-bit sampling for sound recording? What sampling rates is it capable of using?

4 Play the "standard" sounds that come with Windows or the Macintosh, as described here:

Windows Double-click on the Sound Recorder icon, which is normally in the Accessories group. Use the Sound Recorder's File menu to load a sound; the sounds that come with Windows are normally in the Windows directory. Click on the play button to hear the loaded sound. Note that your computer must have sound capability for this to work. To record a sound, click on the microphone button, and speak into the microphone. You can then use the File menu to save the sound.

Macintosh From the Apple menu, choose Control Panels, then double-click on the Sound icon. Click on a sound name to make it play. To record a sound, click on the Add button to bring up the record dialog box, then click on the record button and speak into the microphone. You can then click on the Save button to save the new sound.

Summary

Multimedia involves the use of different presentation elements.

- Among the presentation elements used with multimedia are graphics, text, sounds, animations, and full-motions videos.
- The scenes of multimedia presentations are usually based on timelines that control the appearance and action of objects in the scene.
- Multimedia presentations are interactive, allowing the user to choose what to see or hear next.
- Graphics may be either bit mapped or vector based.
- Sounds may be synthesized or digitally recorded and played back.
- External video players may be controlled by multimedia programs, or the programs can produce motion directly on the computer screen.
- Buttons are screen areas on which the user may click the mouse to answer questions or select what to do next.
- Hypermedia involves the attachment of external data sources to a multimedia production. The user interacts through the multimedia interface, and the underlying program extracts information from numerous data sources, all done behind-the-scenes to the user. Hypermedia is useful for research, teaching, business management, and so on.
- Executive information systems are designed to extract from huge databases the information that executives need to make sound decisions. These systems are much easier to use when they are set up as hypermedia.
- To use multimedia effectively, you need a fast computer with lots of memory and disk space.
- Multimedia productions are often distributed on CD-ROM because of the huge storage space available on each disk.
- For multimedia presentations that you develop, a magneto-optical disk can provide vast amounts of removable storage space.
- Synthesized sound is created at playback time by the computer using stored instructions on what kind of sounds, what notes, and what durations. Because actual sound bites are not recorded, the storage space required is minimal.

Summary

- Digitally recorded sound produces a faithful reproduction of original sounds, but it can require huge amounts of storage space depending on the quality and length of the sounds.
- Higher sampling rates and 16-bit sampling result in higher-quality digitally recorded sound, but these require the most storage space.
- On-the-fly compression and decompression of sound files can reduce the amount of storage space required.
- Full-motion video requires the movement of huge volumes of data to the display each second. There is a tradeoff between size and quality of the playback.
- Compression of data can make video more feasible. It can be either nonlossy (full retention of detail) or lossy (more compression but minor loss of detail).

The following key terms were defined in this module. For each of the following terms, write on a separate piece of paper the number of the definition followed by the letter of the appropriate term.

Terms

A. button

B. CD-ROM

C. compression

D. decompression

E. digitally recorded sound

F. executive information system

G. hypermedia

H. interactive

I. PC-CD drive

J. multimedia

K. sampling rate

L. synthesized sound

Definitions

1 restoring a recorded sound or video to its full character on reading it from a storage medium

2 sound made by a sound card following instructions from the computer

3 a screen area on which a user can click the mouse to answer a question or select an action

4 a read-only storage medium capable of storing huge quantities of data that is read back by a laser beam

5 the number of times per second the computer records an image of the sound being recorded

6 an application that connects a multimedia "front-end" to a number of data sources for information retrieval

7 the use of several different mediums, such as sound, graphics, text, animation, and video

8 the reduction in size of a sound or graphics file by recognizing repeating patterns in the data

9 combines the ability to read a CD-ROM disk with the abilities to read from and write to an optical disk

10 a method of storing sound under which thousands of "snapshots" or "slices" of the sound are recorded each second

11 the operation of a program under which the user has control of the progression of events

12 a system designed to allow business managers to easily retrieve needed information from large data systems

Matching

Review

1. What are the necessary components of a multimedia presentation? (Obj. 1)
2. What is added to multimedia to get to the level of hypermedia? (Obj. 1)
3. Is multimedia or hypermedia most appropriate when presenting data that change frequently? Why? (Obj. 1)
4. Because graphics software is capable of producing pictures and text, what distinguishes multimedia software from graphics software? (Obj. 2)
5. Describe the interaction between graphics software and multimedia software. (Obj. 2)
6. List and define the different kinds of objects that can go into multimedia presentations. (Obj. 3)
7. What are some things to consider in deciding whether to use synthesized or digitally recorded sound in a presentation? (Obj. 3)
8. For the kind of computer that you use (Macintosh or PC), describe the slowest processor, slowest speed, and smallest memory size required for satisfactory use of multimedia applications. (Obj. 4)
9. Why does multimedia require a fast computer? (Obj. 4)
10. Why does multimedia require lots of memory and disk space? (Obj. 4)
11. What distinguishes multimedia and hypermedia? (Obj. 5)
12. List and describe at least three applications of hypermedia for which multimedia would not be appropriate. (Obj. 6)
13. Describe the typical steps in putting together a multimedia scene. (Obj. 8)

Activities

1 Many standard applications can be considered multimedia when you attach another medium to them. For example, you can attach a spoken phrase or sentence to a cell in a spreadsheet. Or, you can put a spoken note on a written report to describe something about it or ask a question of someone else who is looking at it.

Determine whether your computer and software are capable of attaching spoken notes to documents. If so, open a document, attach a spoken note, and then have another student open your document and listen to the note.

2 Plan a multimedia or hypermedia project. Work in a group with two or three other students. First, enumerate what you want the project to accomplish; that is, what would the outcome be for its users if it were produced. Next, write an outline or script of what should happen as a user interacts with the product. Then, sketch what the various screens should look like, and specify the sources of the information that will appear on each.

Under your teacher's guidance, select one of the following or another idea as the subject of your project:

- A kiosk to place at the main entrance to your school for the benefit of visitors.
- A production to make new students aware of your school—its physical facilities, its traditions, and its instructional program.
- A production to teach someone to dance.
- A production to teach someone to play golf.
- A production to provide "story starters" for students who are embarking on the task of writing a composition for English class. The product might ask various questions of the student or present various visual images as an initiative to write about a particular subject. It would be appropriate to get suggestions from English teachers on what to include.

(Continued on next page.)

Activities

3 As a group, present the plans for your project to the class. If appropriate, use computer-generated images or a presentation program to get your ideas across. Get suggestions from the class on how the project could be improved. Consider the suggestions and decide which ones to incorporate in an update of your plans.

4 If you have appropriate software available, produce the project you designed in activities 2 and 3. Implement the project as appropriate.

5 *Internet* If your Internet Web browser is capable of doing so, you can listen to sounds and watch videos on Web pages. If your browser can do so, locate several sites on the Web that use sound and video and experience them, then use a search engine to locate information on how to implement sound and video on your own Web page. Use your word processor to make notes about how to include sound and video. If you have access to do so, construct a Web page that contains at least one sound and one brief video.

Databases

DB

Overview

In this module, you will learn about using computers to maintain the data of a business or individual. This is done by using software that is frequently referred to as a database management system (DBMS). The name is derived from the fact that the software manages (processes) a database (an organized collection of facts).

A database management system keeps up with records that otherwise would have to be recorded on paper. By having the data in the computer, the computer's power can be used to easily search for any desired information. The computer also makes routine processing such as sending bills to customers or ordering merchandise much easier. Thus, the maintenance of records is much more efficient when done with a database management system. There are kinds of processing that also can be done with the computer that simply cannot be done manually because of time and cost restraints.

While you can program your own database management system using a programming language, this is rarely done. Usually, you use a commercially available program and define the data you want to keep up with. The program then takes care of all the details of storing, retrieving, and reporting.

There are several general categories of database software available, ranging from simple to complex. The kind that you use depends on the complexity of data you will keep up with. In this module, you learn about the two most common database types and will be able to decide which is best for a given situation.

Objectives

1. Define and state the purposes of a database.
2. Describe the functions performed by database software.
3. List and describe the main features of flat file and relational databases.
4. Plan a database.
5. Use and share database files.
6. Describe the purpose and characteristics of physical and logical views.
7. Explain the functions of database administration.
8. Describe the relationship between database capability and hardware requirements.

Purposes of a Database

A **database** is a collection of organized data whose elements are in some way related to one another. Thus, all data maintained by a club about its members is a database. Also, the records of accounts and sales of a business make up a database. In any event, the purpose of a database is to maintain all relevant data in a form that is useful to its owner for record keeping and decision-making. For a club, the database can be used to prepare directories, mail form letters to members, or analyze the characteristics of the membership. For businesses, the database can also aid in making and recording sales and in analyzing data to provide information for management decision-making.

As an example of a database, look at figure 1 to see a card containing data about an individual. Other cards contain data about other individuals. Each kind of data about the person is known as a **field**, and all data about the individual is known as a **record**. If you desire, you can look at the data in the form of a table, such as in figure 2. In this case, each column represents a field, while each row represents a record.

figure 1

Each piece of information (last name, first name, and so on) about a person is known as a field. The whole group of data about one individual is known as a record. A group of records is known as a file or database.

Last Name: Abels
First Name: Marguerite
Street Address: 32 Simons Street
City: Brooks
State: GA
ZIP: 30216
Telephone Number: 404-555-3987

figure 2

When data is shown as a table, each row represents a record and each column a field.

Last Name	First Name	Street Address	City	State	ZIP
Abels	Marguerite	32 Simons Street	Brooks	GA	30205
Farquahar	Wilhelmina	8643 Central Lane	Brooks	GA	30205
Jackson	Lea	981 Posey Place	Fayetteville	GA	30214
Rodriguez	Jose	563 First Avenue	Tyrone	GA	30215
Smith	Lawrence	389 Roselawn Ave.	Fayetteville	GA	30214
Tunnicliff	Kenneth	974 April Court	Fayetteville	GA	30214

You can do many things using this data. Among them are:

1. Add new names and addresses to the list.
2. Change the data if a person changes his or her phone, address, or name.

3. Print mailing labels for sending a monthly newsletter or other announcements. Assuming that your list becomes long enough to make it worthwhile, you can print the labels in ZIP-code order to qualify for reduced postage rates.
4. Print directories showing names, addresses, and phone numbers. Directories will probably be printed in alphabetic order by member name.
5. Print a membership list by original membership date for honoring those with the longest service.
6. Print reminder letters to members who have not yet paid yearly membership dues.
7. Update data easily whenever an item changes.

With a list as short as that shown in figure 2, you can easily do all of these functions manually with pen and ink. However, the data can also be easily transferred into a computer database—a step that becomes almost a necessity as the number of records grows. Any one of numerous database software packages on the market can handle the job.

Functions of Database Software

By using commercial database software, the functions needed for entering data, manipulating data, and reporting information from the data are available without programming. One way of categorizing these functions is as follows:

- Creating the structure of the database.
- Adding data to the database.
- Editing data already in the database.
- Selecting and retrieving data.
- Designing reports.
- Modifying the structure of the database.

Note that once the database has been created, the functions can be performed in pretty much any sequence as needed.

With most database software, think of the data as being contained in a table in the computer. This makes it easy to make the transition from a paper form of the data to the computer form.

Creating a Database

The first step in moving from a paper form of a database to the computer form is to plan the data to be stored in the database. Along with deciding what fields are to be stored, you also need to determine how much space is needed for each field and what kind of data the field will contain. For a simple database, you can determine these factors while using the software to set up the database; for more complex systems, you will certainly want to do planning ahead of time.

When you are ready to create the database, run the database application software and select the proper menu choice or click on the proper icon to create a new database. You may be asked for a database name up front, or you may not be asked for one until the end of the process.

Assume that your database consists of data about students, and you plan to use this data as the basic demographic information about students in a dance school you operate. This data is to include the social security number, name, address, and birthdate. If you are using Microsoft Works, begin a new database by selecting it from the opening screen. When a blank form is shown to you on the display, take the following steps for each field:

1. Click the mouse at the point on the screen where you want the field to appear.
2. Key the name of the field, being sure to put a colon (:) at the end of the name.
3. A pop-up box will appear asking you how long the field should be. In deciding on the length, you do not need to reserve enough space to hold the absolutely longest data that may ever occur. Someone somewhere may have a last name of MacBurghermeister-Smithamptondale (33 characters). It is highly unlikely you will encounter a name of such length, however, and if you specify 33 characters for the last name, most database programs will use that much space on the disk for every last name in the database, whether it is needed or not. Try for field lengths that will hold the vast majority of data but not the rare exceptions. If you are using a database that uses only the number of characters actually entered for a field, such as Microsoft Access, go ahead and make the specified field lengths long enough to hold the lengthy exceptions.

Figure 3 shows what the works form looks like after you have entered field names into it. Once you place a data field on the screen using the above steps, you can move it to a different location by using the mouse. You can also change the field length by clicking on the field, then selecting Format . . . Field Size from the menus. By clicking a field and selecting Format . . . Show Field Name (a toggle), you can control whether the name of the field appears on the screen along with the data-entry area.

If you prefer, you can switch to a spreadsheet view by using the View menu or button-bar button and then enter data into the spreadsheet without

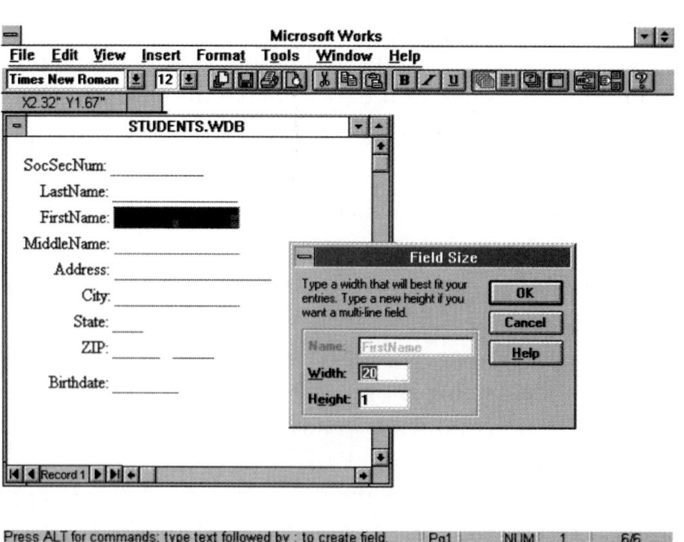

figure 3

After selecting the menu choice to create a new table, fill in the names and lengths of the fields for the table.

predefining field names. Works will place default names (Field1, Field2, Field3, and so on) at the tops of the columns. You can change the default field name to whatever you desire by first clicking the mouse on the name you want to change and then selecting Edit . . . Field Name from the menus.

You will note that in using Microsoft Works, you are not asked for the kind of data to be entered into a field. Many packages, however, do ask for that information. Among the most common types of data from which you can choose are:

- Text.
- Numbers (perhaps of different types, such as integers or currency).
- Date/time.
- Yes/no.
- Note.
- Picture.

A database that asks for the data type will simply include the choice as part of a dialog box that sets up the fields. Many database programs also allow (or require) you to specify a field to use as an index. Use of an index makes retrieval of data much faster, especially if there are many records in the database. The index of a computer database works just like the index of a printed catalog. Suppose you have a large general merchandise catalog and want to find an exercise machine. You can either flip through the pages until you happen on it, or you can look it up in the index to and go directly to the correct page.

Adding Data to the Database

Entering data into a table of a database is commonly known as **appending** data to the table, or **loading** the table. Depending on the software and the application, data is appended with a very simple default screen form or with a screen form specially designed by the developer of the application. In Microsoft Works, you define the screen form at the same time you define the fields to be included in the database.

Once the fields are defined for your Works database, use the same screen to enter the data. Simply click on the forward arrow at the bottom of the window to move forward to a blank form for the next record.

Editing Data Already in the Database

Data stored in the computer change from time to time, such as when someone moves, gets a new phone number, or pays dues. Also, an error that requires a correction may have occurred in entering the data. In all such cases, the already-entered data may be edited. This is done by selecting the appropriate menu choice or icon to display the existing data on the screen and then keying the corrections. Depending on the program and form you are using, you may scroll through records until you get to the desired one, or you may enter a small portion of the person's name and go directly to his or her data. Most database software allows editing to be done in either a row-by-row display, which looks like a table on the screen, or by using the screen form that is used for data entry. Figure 4

figure 4

In Microsoft Works, the same form used to define the database fields can be used to enter or edit data.

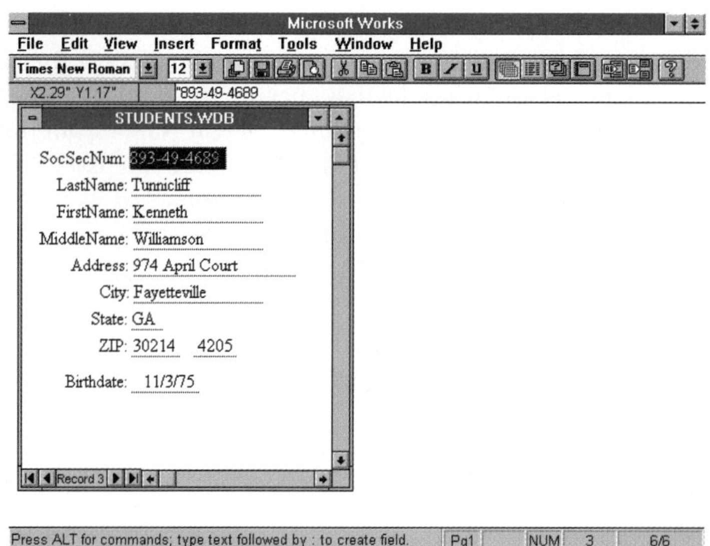

shows the Works form view, while figure 5 shows the table view. Switch between the two views by using the View menu or clicking on the appropriate view button.

Selecting and Retrieving Data

Data from a database may be displayed whenever desired by using either a menu or a command, depending on the software. For example, suppose you want to look up the address of Lawrence Smith. After you select the Edit . . . Find item from the Works menu, you are asked for the item to find. At that

Relational Databases: A Language All Its Own

You'd think that a relational database is so named because you define relationships between tables, but that's not the case. In fact, in the academic world of relational databases, you'll discover a whole new vocabulary—with a language you probably won't find in the user manuals of commonly available software packages.

Want to learn a new language? Here's your first lesson in relational database-speak:

- A table is known as a relation.
- A column or field is known as an attribute.
- A row is called a tuple.

Relational databases are modeled on two mathematic principles: the theory of arbitrary degree, and multivalued first-order predicate logic.

End of lesson!

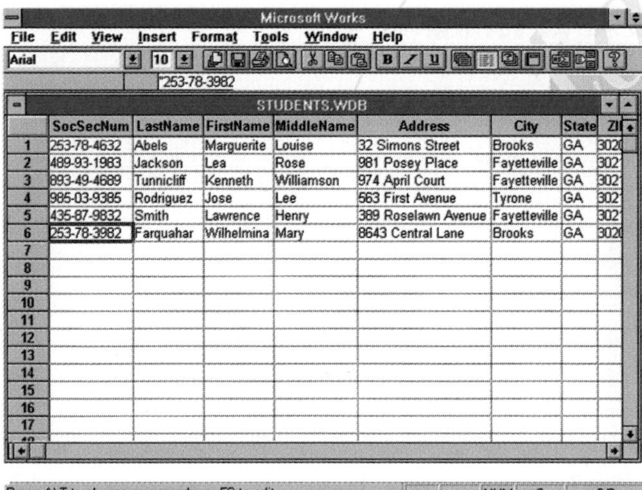

figure 5

As an alternate to using a data-entry form, you can work in the table view. To switch between the two screen layouts, select from the View menu or click on the appropriate view button in the button bar.

point, key in the name Smith. The first record containing Smith will appear on the screen; if it is not the right Smith, use the forward arrow to move to the next one.

Querying the Database

With most software, virtually any column or combination of columns can be searched to display various data items. For example, you may want to see just the dance students with an address in Fayetteville. You make this query through the use of menus and dialog boxes. With Works, you first select Query from the View menu. You will see a dialog box, which will show some named views that have been stored earlier. You can use one of them or define a new query by clicking on the OK button. To define a new query, you see a screen form (figure 6) that looks just like a regular data-entry

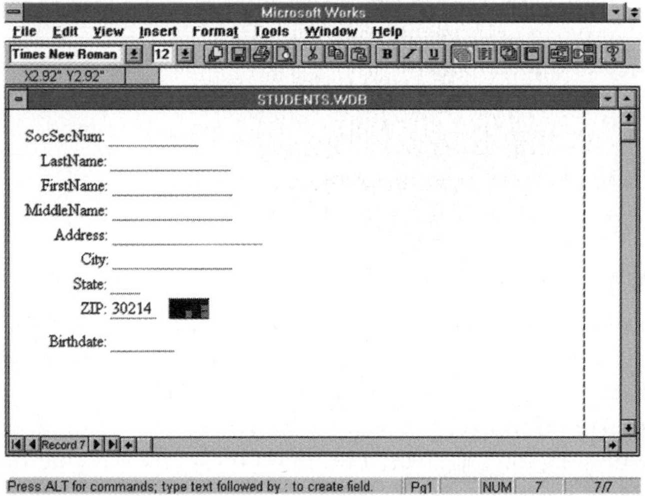

figure 6

By keying the desired matches on the query screen, you can limit or filter the records that you see.

query. This time, however, you key the selection criteria on the screen. For example, to limit the record display just to people who live in Fayetteville (ZIP 30214), you can key 30214 into the ZIP line on the form. The result of this is shown in figure 7, displaying just those residents (note that not all fields are visible on this screen).

The criteria that you can enter on the query definition screen follow the usual Boolean logic rules. **Boolean logic** is based on comparisons of data items. For example, one data item can be equal to another one, not equal

figure 7

After entering the parameters for a query, you will see only the records that match those criteria.

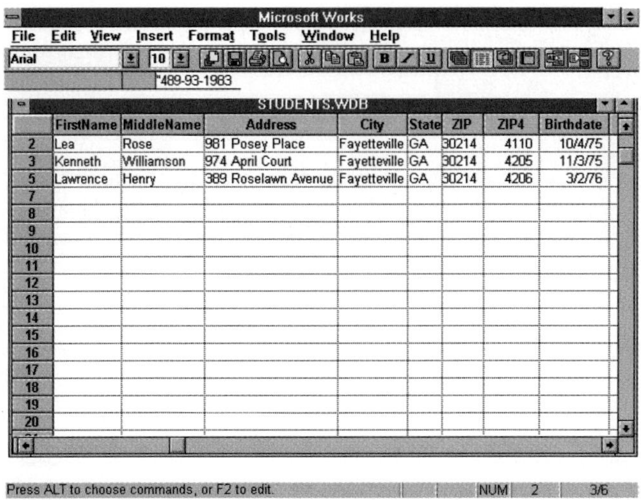

to another one, greater than another one, or less than another one; the conditions can also be combined, such as an item being greater than or equal to another one. For the field or fields into which you key selection criteria, the following choices are usually possible:

Operator	Meaning
= or blank	Equal to the entered data
>	Greater than
<	Less than
>=	Greater than or equal
<=	Less than or equal
<>	Not equal
Not Null	Not blank

Designing Reports

Reports can be designed from stored data by using the database software's function for creating reports. By an interactive process using a report writer portion of the software, the headings to be placed on the report and the data to be printed in each column of the report are defined. Data to be included may be sorted and selected in much the same way that data is sorted and selected with the query language. An example of a report created by means of a report writer is shown in figure 8. It lists the students by birthdate in chonological order. Note that the report is arranged differently from the order of data in the database in figure 5 and does not include all columns of data, even though it could. While this illustration is a screen preview of the report, a simple print choice can commit it to paper. Figures 9 and 10 show how the report was created in Works.

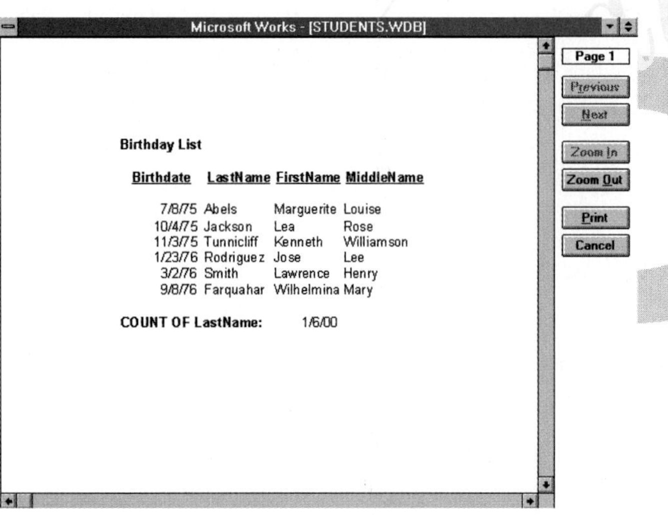

figure 8

The automated report generation feature of most database programs makes it easy to create reports such as this one.

Modifying the Structure of a Database

Even with the best of planning, a column (field) may be omitted from a database, or a column may be narrower than it needs to be. With most database programs, you can go back at any time, regardless of the amount of data in the database, and make modifications. Unless a column is made narrower or removed, data will not be lost when a database structure is modified. For example, if the NAME column is modified to make it wider than originally defined, no data is lost. The exact method of modifying the structure depends on the software. With Microsoft Works, you can change the width from either the list or form view. Whichever view you are in, select Format . . . Field Width from the menus.

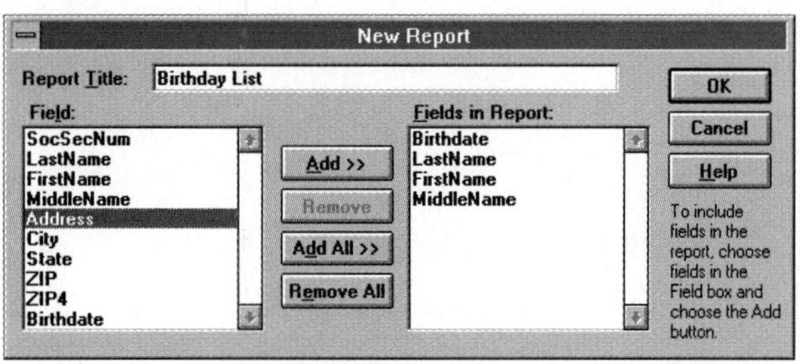

figure 9

On selecting Tools . . . Create New Report from the Works menu, you are shown this dialog box. Use the buttons to transfer the desired fields to the report.

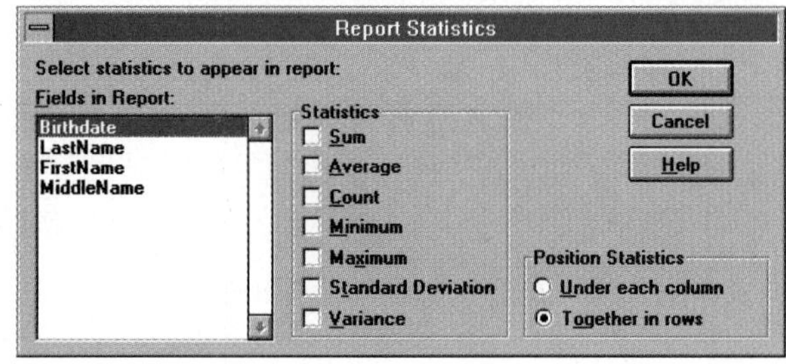

figure 10

After you tell Works which fields to include, you will see this dialog box, which allows you to specify which summary data are to be printed on the report.

Note that you can change the width of the display area by dragging with the mouse—at the end of the data entry area in form view or on the bar between field names in list view. Changing the view size in this manner has no effect on the maximum width in the underlying database.

Database Types

There are several types of databases. The more commonly used ones are discussed here.

Flat File Database

The kind of database you have studied to this point is known as a **flat file database**. A flat file database is limited to one table of data. Each row in the

Profile

Dr. Edgar F. Codd

Dr. Edgar F. Codd is known as the father of relational databases. Before the relational model, most database applications were based on the hierarchical model: data was designed to look like roots of a tree. For example, there might be an entity known as a student and like roots growing under the student, there would be first name, last name, birth date, and whatever other attributes were to be included. The only way to access specific data such as the birth date would be to first find the student and then look for the birth date.

According to Codd, one of the great strengths of relational databases is that it frees users from the programmers by making it possible for users to formulate their own queries of the databases. Codd came up with the relational database model while working for IBM on their Series 360 mainframe computer operating system in the late 1960s. He wrote the seminal papers on relational databases in 1969 and 1970. He had to struggle against IBM's bureaucracy to get the computer giant to accept the relational model, which was *not* what they had chosen to market at the time. IBM finally came around only when customers demanded the relational model. In 1979, IBM awarded Codd its Outstanding Innovation award; three years later, Big Blue introduced a relational database product. It was many years before this model was accepted as a mainstream idea.

A native of Great Britain, Codd came to the United States with degrees from Oxford in 1948. After earning his Ph.D. at the University of Michigan, Codd joined IBM to work on an early precomputer prototype. He left IBM after a dispute in 1953; by 1957, he returned to Big Blue at their invitation.

In 1984, Codd left IBM to form Cobb and Date, Inc. Two years later, he published his famous "12 Rules for Relational Databases." These rules set forth the criteria against which database vendors' products can be measured to see whether they are really relational databases. According to Codd, many products that claim to be relational meet only some of the requirements.

table is a record, while each column is a field. Flat file databases are fine for many applications, such as mailing lists, club membership lists, and inventories of collections.

Do It!

1 Arrange for a representative from your school office to discuss with the class the kind of database that is used to maintain student records.

2 If your school media center has a computerized database program (perhaps on CD-ROM), use the program to research a topic of your choice. The database programs typically found in media centers include magazine and periodical indexes, encyclopedias, and various other reference works. If you use one of the CD-ROM indexes, write down a description of the fields you think the database uses to locate the information you are looking for.

When using flat file database software, many different databases—of one table each—can be created. There is no connection between the various tables, however; each of them is a stand-alone collection of data. The programs supplied as part of the flat file database package are used to set up the structure of the data to be stored, provide for the addition and editing of data, and provide facilities for locating and retrieving the data. Frequently, the user is limited to the capabilities provided in the purchased package of software. If other processing functions are needed, they must be written in a programming language that creates its own data files separately from those of the database package.

For all practical purposes, the use of a flat file database is limited to simple applications. For more complex applications such as maintaining student records in a school or college, their use is much less than satisfactory. Look at some of the problems that would arise in a college system (figure 11):

- Everything your database knows about a student must be contained in one row in a table; therefore, to track courses taken and grades earned, you would need to add a new field for each course. If a student typically takes 36 courses before graduation, you would have to add 36 fields for the course name and 36 fields for the course grade. With that arrange-

figure 11

Flat file databases are not suited for large collections of data, like student records, with many related groups of information. Relational databases are better suited for this purpose.

ment, however, most software programs would not be able to do any kind of grade summary or reporting. Then, there is the problem of the students who take more than 36 courses—what do you do with the extra grades? In short, you could handle grades, but only very awkwardly.

- You must do a dean's list each quarter. To do this report, you must compute the average of all academic courses the student took during the quarter. How do you tell from your flat file database which of the courses were taken this quarter? And how do you get your software to do an average of some of the 36+ grade fields in the record?
- You want to record honors and awards received by each student, but some students receive no honors or awards, and others receive dozens. How many fields do you add to the record? How do you process it if you want to know the names of all students who received a particular honor?

The more that you decide to have your database do, the more difficulty you will encounter. To get a full-fledged student information system going, you would probably be using hundreds of fields per record, and you would have a totally unworkable operation.

To create a student record system without the drawbacks of a flat file database application, several other types of database organizations are available that provide more capability. The most commonly used on microcomputers is the relational database.

Relational Database

In the view of the user, a **relational database** also presents its data in the form of tables—multiple tables as opposed to one. The different tables created may be "connected" or "related" (each table is technically known as a relation). In the college's case, therefore, one Microsoft Access table might be created, as in figures 12 and 13, to contain data regarding students'

figure 12

In Microsoft Access, a desired action is chosen from the main control panel. For example, to create a new table, click on the Table button and then on the New button.

names and addresses (just as a table did in the flat file database). Once you enter data in the database, you can view it with a default form (if you have created one by clicking on Forms . . . New Form and telling Access which table to base it on) or in list view. Figure 14 shows a sample of both views. You may switch views by clicking on the desired view icon on the tool bar or by selecting it from the View menu.

While a database with one table is useful, the power of a relational database becomes obvious when you add a second table. Do this with Access by clicking on a New Table button and defining the fields—just as you created the original table. In the case of college recordkeeping, it makes sense to create a second table to store the records of courses taken by students. Look in figure 15 to see a handful of grade records recorded in such a separate table; note that the social security numbers in the grade table can be found in the student table to determine who the grade belongs to.

Table: Students

Field Name	Data Type	Description
SocSecNum	Text	
LastName	Text	
FirstName	Text	
MiddleName	Text	
Street	Text	
City	Text	
State	Text	
ZIP	Text	
ZIP4	Text	
BirthDate	Date/Time	

Field Properties

Field Size	11
Format	
Input Mask	
Caption	
Default Value	
Validation Rule	
Validation Text	
Required	No
Allow Zero Length	No
Indexed	Yes (No Duplicates)

The data type determines the kind of values that users can store in the field. Press F1 for help on data types.

figure 13

After defining the fields for your Access table, highlight the field that will be unique, then click the key icon on the toolbar. This defines the key field. Then, close the window by double-clicking the close button at the upper left corner; Access will ask you for a name for the table.

a.

Table: Students

SocSecNum	LastName	FirstName	MiddleName	Street	City	State	ZIP
253-78-3982	Farquahar	Wilhelmina	Mary	8643 Central Lane	Brooks	GA	30205
253-78-4632	Abels	Marguerite	Louise	32 Simons Street	Brooks	GA	30205
435-87-9832	Smith	Lawrence	Henry	389 Roselawn Ave	Fayetteville	GA	30214
489-93-1983	Jackson	Lea	Rose	981 Posey Place	Fayetteville	GA	30214
893-49-4689	Tunnicliff	Kenneth	Williamson	974 April Court	Fayetteville	GA	30214
985-03-9385	Rodriguez	Jose	Lee	563 First Avenue	Tyrone	GA	30215

Record: 1 of 6

figure 14

When working with a relational database table, you can usually choose between a list view (panel A) *and a form view* (panel B)*. This form was created using the Access Form Wizard.*

This common field (in this case, social security number) connects the data in the two tables. We can look at this relationship graphically in figure 16, which shows the two tables and a line connecting the common field in the two of them. Many databases, including Access in this example, can show you the structure of the database in such graphic fashion. With Access, you may create the relationship by using the Edit . . . Relationship menu or by dragging between fields in a query (explained on page 17).

b.

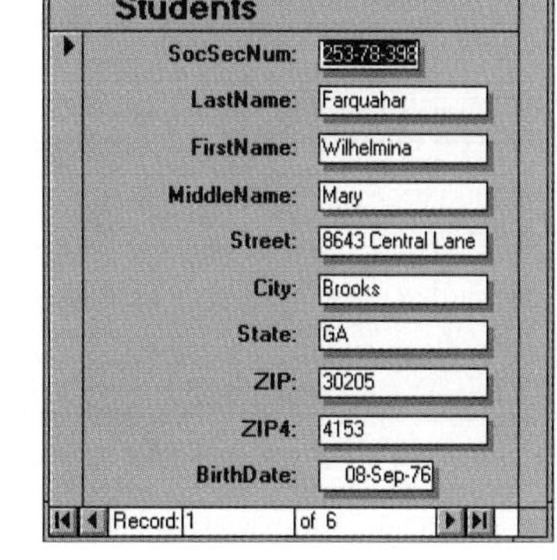

As good as it is, there are some problems with the design shown in figure 16, however. These include:

- The course name is stored in full in the table. This opens the possibility that the name may be recorded differently for different students. It also wastes a lot of storage space to spell out the full name for each student who ever takes the course.

Table: CoursesTaken

ID	SocSecNum	Year	Qtr	Course	Grade	Instructor
1	893-49-4689	95	1	Freshman English 101	A	Akin, Ronald
2	893-49-4689	95	1	Beginning Algebra 101	B	Deanna Creekmore
3	253-78-3982	94	3	U.S. History 501	C	S. Johnson
4	435-87-9832	95	2	Accounting 301	B	Harold Dowe
5	893-49-4689	95	1	Freshman English 101	A	Speck, Cheryl
6	253-78-3982	94	3	Beginning Algebra 101	C	Creekmore, D.
(Counter)						

Record: 6 of 6

figure 15

When using a separate table to record grades, you use one row for each course taken. There can be as few or as many rows for each student as needed, and the rows need not be contiguous as the database software can easily select only the rows that belong to a particular student.

figure 16

By defining a common field in two tables, the computer is able to look up data from one table in the other. If the relationship has not been defined earlier, drag the mouse from one of the connecting fields to the other (as shown in this screen).

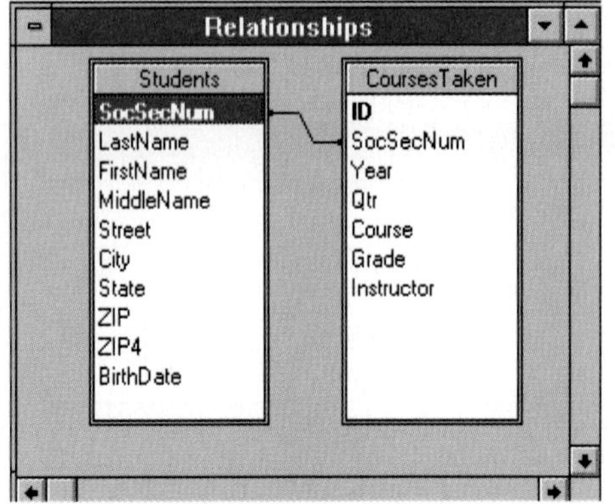

- The instructor's name has the same problem. By increasing the likelihood of different degrees of "fullness"—first initial, spelled out first name, first and second initial—the possibility of analyzing data by instructor is diminished. Likewise, much storage space can be wasted.

These problems can be alleviated and the data kept much more accurately by storing a coded form of the course name and the instructor's identification number (perhaps his or her social security number). When the structure of the database is improved in this manner, it appears as shown in figure 17. Note that each table is tied to another by a common field. The database can be set up so that in the CoursesTaken table, entries for the grade earned, course name, and instructor are restricted to the values appearing respectively in the GradingSystem, CourseCatalog, and Faculty tables. Restricting what may be entered in this manner keeps the data more accurate, because it is impossible to enter a grade, course, or instructor that does not exist.

figure 17

A well-designed relational database consists of a number of interrelated tables. Many of these tables contain the details behind a code that is entered into another table.

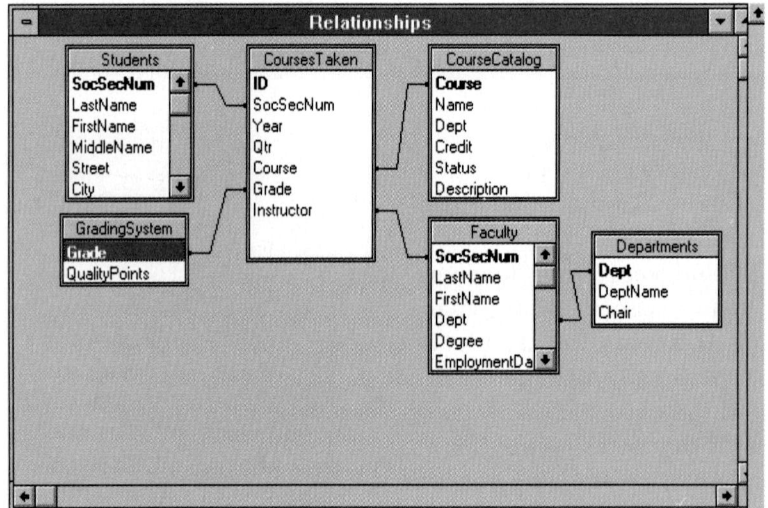

Making a query yourself By using several tables together, you, as a human, can extract various kinds of information. Among these are lists of just about anything desired, as well as counts, a report of high and low values, or items within a certain range. How can we determine the amount of credit earned to this point by a student, such as the total amount of credit earned by Kenneth Tunnicliff in figure 18? This screen was created in Access by opening tables and then resizing them so that they would all fit on the screen. Here are the steps to determine the credit earned:

1. Look up Kenneth's name in the Students table, and get his social security number, which is 893-49-4689.
2. Look in the CoursesTaken table for all entries for Kenneth's social security number. In the part of the table that is visible on the page, that number is found in rows 1, 2, and 5.

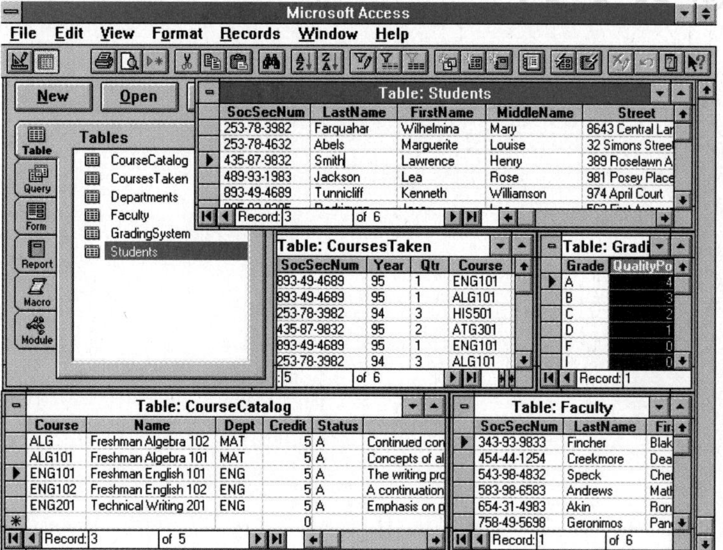

figure 18

With a relational database, there is no physical connection between the different tables, but the computer can look at different tables to extract data just as a human can.

3 For each course that Kenneth passed (grade of A–D), look in the CourseCatalog table under the course number and find how much credit the course is worth. In this case, each of the courses is worth five quarter-hours of credit, for a total of 15 hours for the three courses we can see in the table; of course, when the computer does this computation, it will look at all of the table, whether it is visible to human eyes or not.

Telling the computer to make a query Requesting that your database application run a query for you is a bit different from one brand of software to another. The method used by Access, however, is typical. To see how this is done, have the computer do the same query that we just had a human do; that is, determine the total amount of credit earned by a student. The procedure is:

1 In the main Access control panel, click first on Query, then on the New button. A window will pop up that you use to tell which tables are needed in the query. In figure 19, the screen looks as it does after we have selected three tables to be used in the query. Once this is done, click on the Close button to make the selection box go away.

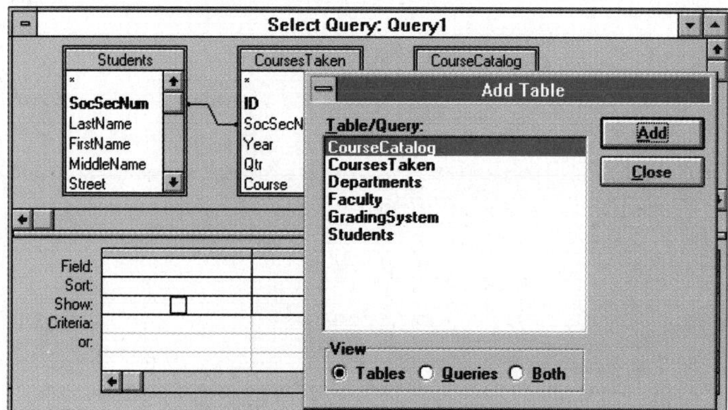

figure 19

The first step in creating a query with Access is to add the tables containing the data that is needed to derive the result.

2 By looking at the three tables as they have appeared at the top of the query in figure 19, you see that there are lines between them con-

Trends

ER Databases

Despite what you might think, ER databases have nothing do with hospital emergency rooms. In this case, ER stands for *entity-relationship* database, just one of many new approaches that combines the advantages of relational databases (which account for most database management software sold today) with the positive features of other database approaches.

The primary goal of these new database approaches—with ER considered to be the most promising—is to make it easier for developers to represent the operation of a school, business, or other organization in the database. When developing a database under ER, the user begins by defining the structure of the organization for which the data is to be maintained. As examples, consider the following statements for a high school:

- The school *has* students.
- Students *have* last names, first names, addresses, social security numbers, and so on.
- The school *employs* teachers.
- Teachers *have* last names, first names, social security numbers, areas of certification, and so on.
- Courses are *taught* in rooms.
- Rooms *have* numbers, types, and capacities.
- Students *take* courses.
- Courses *have* IDs, names, descriptions, credit amounts, and so on.
- Courses *are taught* by teachers.

While this is a very brief example, you can see that there are *entities* (students, teachers, rooms, courses) and *relationships* (has, have, employs, are taught, take). Looking at things in this manner helps the user to visualize how the data must fit together for a database system to function.

While no popular commercial database management program is directly based on this ER approach, there is software on the market that allows the developer to use ER methods to define the database. This software typically uses a graphic interface and helps the user set up the relationships by making simple menu and dialog choices—and in many cases, simply by dragging the mouse. Once the database has been described, the software automatically creates the proper relational database tables to implement the database.

necting the common fields. This means that someone has previously made the connection. If the lines were not there, you would just use the mouse to drag between the field names that should be connected.

3. Place field names in the columns of the query. Either double-click on the field names one at a time or drag them with the mouse. The screen will appear as shown in figure 20.

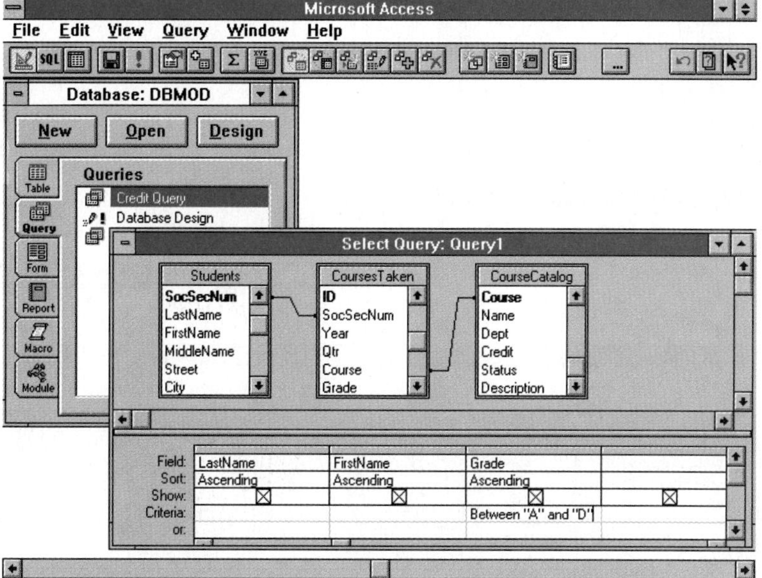

figure 20

Finish defining a query by placing field names, criteria, and operations in the columns.

4. Because we want this query to total the amount of credit for a student, click on the sum button on the button bar, or select Totals from the View menu. This adds a line for total computations to the query window, with a default entry of "Group By" in each column.

5. The default "Group By" entry on the total line is appropriate for all fields except Credit and Grade. We want a sum of the credit, so use the drop-down box to select Sum as the type of total operation for that column. If we leave Grade with a "Group By," we will get a total for the As, a total for the Bs, and so on. If that is what we want, leave it grouped. Otherwise, change the "Group By" to "Where" because we want a total where the grade is between A and D (the passing grades).

6. Click on the data view icon or the Do It! icon to get an answer to the query. The result shown in figure 21 will appear on the display.

Another query example Suppose that Prof. Creekmore has just received national recognition for her excellent teaching and research. You want to invite all of the students she has taught to a reception in her honor. You need their names and addresses. By defining a query, you can easily get this information. Figure 22 shows the query you will construct, while figure 23 shows a portion of the results. Note that if we wanted the results sorted in ZIP-code order, we could insert a Sort option (either ascending or descending) into the ZIP-code column when defining the query.

With some database software, a query is known as a view. Note that when you create a query or a view, you are not creating a new table, and the data in your database is not copied into a new structure. Rather, the term *view* is

figure 21

After you define the query and tell the database software to execute it, you receive the result—in this case, the hours of credit earned by Kenneth Tunnicliff.

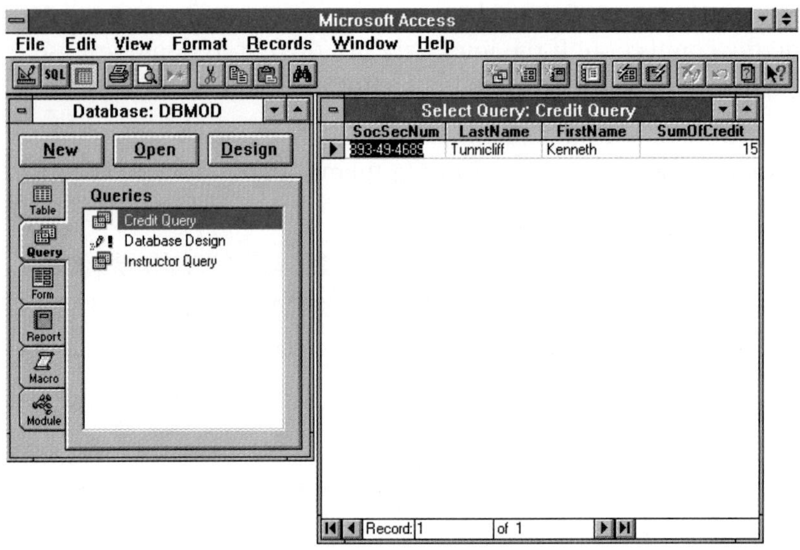

figure 22

Combine data from the CoursesTaken table and the Student table with an instructor number criterion to get a list of students who have had a particular teacher.

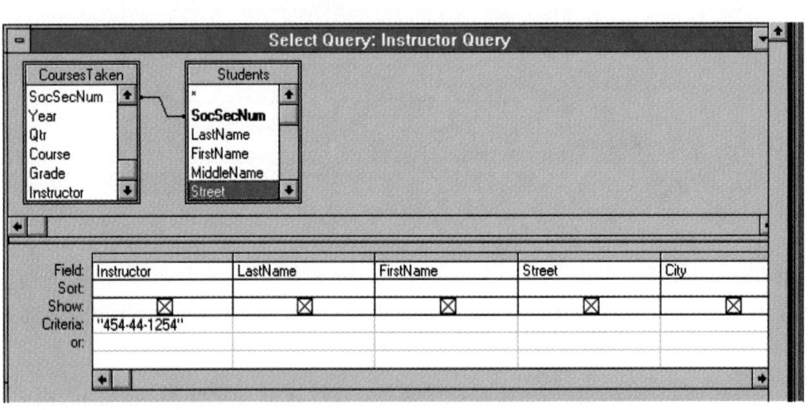

figure 23

Partial results from running the query in figure 22.

Select Query: Instructor Query

Instructor	LastName	FirstName	Street	City	State	ZIP	ZIP4
454-44-1254	Farquahar	Wilhelmina	8643 Central Lane	Brooks	GA	30205	4153
454-44-1254	Tunnicliff	Kenneth	974 April Court	Fayetteville	GA	30214	4205

Record: 1 of 2

probably more accurate here—you are looking at data that can be residing in several different tables, but you are looking at it in the arrangement that is most valuable to you at the moment.

After defining this query to pull out the data we need, we could go back to the main control panel, click on Report . . . New Report, and let Access print mailing labels based on the data we just retrieved. In the case of reports and forms, Access will ask you which table or query on which to base its work (as well as some "cosmetic" questions), then it will automatically do the work of creating the report or form. You can modify the automatically created form or report, or you can create a form or report from scratch. The way you do this is beyond the scope of this text, but the Access help screens can lead you through the process.

With a relational database, it is possible to easily add, delete, or change tables. Also, because relationships between data may be established whenever needed, previously unthought-of computations or queries are easily handled. Because of its ease of use and flexibility, the relational database is very desirable. This flexibility, however, yields a slower operating speed and requires much more complex software than some other types of database software. Much progress is being made in improving the speed, however, thus helping the relational database become a standard.

Planning a Relational Database

Planning an efficient database involves setting up the structure of the actual database as well as designing applications that will use it to the greatest advantage. Just because you have a relational database application does not mean that the computer will plan everything for you. You can create a bad application quite easily if you do not plan ahead. The following sections discuss how to plan for the tables needed and design appropriate applications.

Planning for Tables

Planning for tables should normally start at the desired end result and work backward. In other words, what reports should the database be able to produce? What analyses of data should it be able to do?

If you are planning to develop a database system to handle all aspects of your business, it helps to consider what goes on during it's normal operation. In the college example, it would help to consider statements such as:

- Students take courses and receive credit.
- Students have addresses.
- Instructors teach courses.
- Instructors have degrees and hire dates.
- Courses are offered by departments.
- Courses carry credit.

These kinds of statements can help you see the relationships between different kinds of data. In fact, you can purchase software packages that enable you to tell the computer what all of the relationships are; once you have finished, the software automatically creates a database with all required fields and relationships.

Once you know what the desired outcome is, you can start figuring which pieces of data must be maintained to produce the results. If you have described the entities within your business, that will give you a head start. Another way to identify the data is to have brainstorming sessions with the persons in your business who work with the data.

In any event, you will probably be identifying field names without necessarily placing the fields in a table when they are identified. One interesting methodology here is to write each field name on a self-adhesive note when you identify it. These notes can later be posted on pages representing the tables of the database. Because the notes can be easily removed and attached elsewhere, it is easy to make as many changes as needed as you go through the design process.

Deciding Which Fields Belong in Which Tables

The first thing to remember when deciding on the tables to be contained in your database is that each table should contain the data about one category of items. In the college example, this means separate tables for stu-

Careers

Database Administrators

With the widespread adoption of microcomputers in business, many more databases are being set up without the expertise of database professionals: however, there is still a need for database administrators, primarily in large organizations and for complex databases. These managers are responsible for developing and maintaining the integrity (correctness) of the database used by the organization.

Database administrators plan the design of the data elements (tables and fields) in the database, and they define their relationships to one another. After the initial planning, the database must be upgraded continually—that is, new data elements may be added, relationships between different data elements may be redefined, and some data elements may be dropped because they have outlived their usefulness. The database manager's duties are not performed in a vacuum but in close consultation with users of the database.

It is the database administrator's responsibility to coordinate the data needs of many different persons in the organization. Their needs must be met while at the same time avoiding undesirable replication of data from one application to another.

Most database administrators have a bachelor's degree in information systems along with extensive database experience gained from planning database systems and programming. As businesses move toward a unified database for their entire operation, the database administrator's job becomes even more critical to the success of the organization.

Database administrators typically report to the director of information systems, and they usually receive compensation second only to their immediate supervisor. Average salaries in the mid-1990s are in the $60,000 to $65,000 range.

dents, faculty, courses taken, and the course catalog, among others. Even with this general idea in place, however, you will encounter situations that require a little more analysis.

To help with the more difficult situations, numerous articles have been written by theoreticians concerning the best way to set up the tables in a relational database. What we provide for you here is the "meat" of how to do it without much of the jargon that fills the literature.

Making sure that the columns of your database are in the right tables is known as normalizing the database. In this chapter, we consider what can be called three "levels of acceptability" in developing the tables of your database. To be considered legitimate, a table must be in what is known as **first normal form.** This simply means that *a table must have no repeating fields (columns).* For example, a college could try to include the courses you have taken in your student record table. It could use columns named Course1, Course1Grade, Course2, Course2Grade, Course3, Course3Grade, and so on. Obviously, different students will take differing numbers of courses, so there may not be enough fields to record all courses taken by a given student. Additionally, analysis of the data becomes almost impossible because of the great number of differently named columns in which course records are stored. The right way to do it is to create a separate CoursesTaken table, as we did in our earlier example. The fact that none of our tables have repeating fields means that they are in first normal form.

A table must already be in first normal form before it can be carried to the higher level of **second normal form**. Second normal form means that *each field (column) must be dependent on the primary key.* The **primary key** is the field or combination of fields that makes each row or record unique. Access and most other database software force you to define a primary key. In our Students table, SocSecNum is the primary key; it is different for every student. LastName could not be a primary key, because you may have lots of people with the same last name. Even the combination of LastName and FirstName would not make a good primary key because of the likelihood of having more than one student with the same last and first names.

Using the social security number as the primary key does not mean that the database cannot find students by name, because it certainly can index on name fields as well. However, the primary key is what makes the record unique; it is the value that by definition is different for each record in the database.

Here is what is meant by the other fields all being dependent on the primary key. If you look up a record based on the social security number, there is only one LastName associated with that number. Likewise, there is only one FirstName, one MiddleName, one Street, one City, one State, one ZIP, one ZIP4, and one BirthDate. Because these fields are dependent on the primary key, you will never pull up two different birthdates for the same student, for example. This means that our Students table is in second normal form.

A table must meet the requirements for first normal and second normal form before aspiring to **third normal form.** Third normal form says that *fields (columns) must be dependent on only the primary key.* To illustrate what is meant by this one, assume we have added two fields to our student table: Advisor, and AdvisorOffice. The Advisor field is to contain the social security number of the professor who has been designated to serve as counselor to the student. The AdvisorOffice field is to contain the room number of the advisor's office. On analyzing these new fields, Advisor turns out to be good. It is not a repeating field, and it is dependent on the primary key (the student's social security number). The AdvisorOffice field, however, cannot be allowed in the table, because the adviser's office number is not dependent on the student's ID but on the advisor's ID. The advisor's ID is not the primary key for this table; therefore, the AdvisorOffice field would have to be moved—probably to the Faculty table.

With each step up the ladder of normalization, our database has passed harder and harder tests. Generally, once all of your tables are in third normal form, you are considered to have done a good job (figure 24). There are higher levels of normalization, but they are beyond the scope of this chapter.

While the names of first normal, second normal, and third normal perhaps suggest that these are three sequential steps to take in designing your tables, this is not necessarily true. Once you have designed a few databases, you will probably find that you intuitively create your tables in third normal form simply because you know what it takes to make them that way, so you just do it right the first time. Does that mean you will never make changes in tables as you work on a design? Of course not. Even the most experienced designers add fields, delete fields, add new tables, delete old tables, and re-establish previously deleted tables as the design of the overall database proceeds. The more experience you have, however, the less likely you are to need to take corrective actions.

Maintaining Integrity of the Database

The very thing that makes a relational database such a powerful tool can also be its downfall if it is not implemented properly. What makes it powerful is the ability of the system to pull data from a number of different tables as needed, but the data that connects the tables must remain intact if the database is to work. While most database software can enforce the rules of integrity for you, it is still important that you be aware of what they are.

The primary key must never be blank If the database is to work, every record entered into a table must have a primary key, and that key must not be blank or null. For example, when our database uses the social security number as the primary key, that field can never be left blank. Of course, that raises interesting questions about what to do if a given student cannot supply a social security number. We would probably have a policy that we make up a pseudo–social security number, perhaps one that begins with the college initials and then is followed by the year of entry and a sequential number, so that it would look like BCC-95-0001.

A record on which others depend cannot be deleted Assume that we have a student who has taken the course coded as ATG301. If that portion of the CourseCatalog table was reproduced in the text, you would find that this course is named Introduction to Cost Accounting and carries 7 hours of credit. If the record for the course was removed from the CourseCatalog, however, all references to it in the CoursesTaken table would be left as orphans; there would be no way to find more detail about the course known as ATG301.

For this reason, a record should be nonremovable if any record in another table makes reference to it. While most software can automatically enforce this provision, you typically must make sure that the option to do so has been activated with a menu choice.

figure 24

This illustration shows the steps from a poorly designed database to one that meets the requirements of third normal form. Experienced designers don't go through these steps, however. Their original design of tables tends to be good.

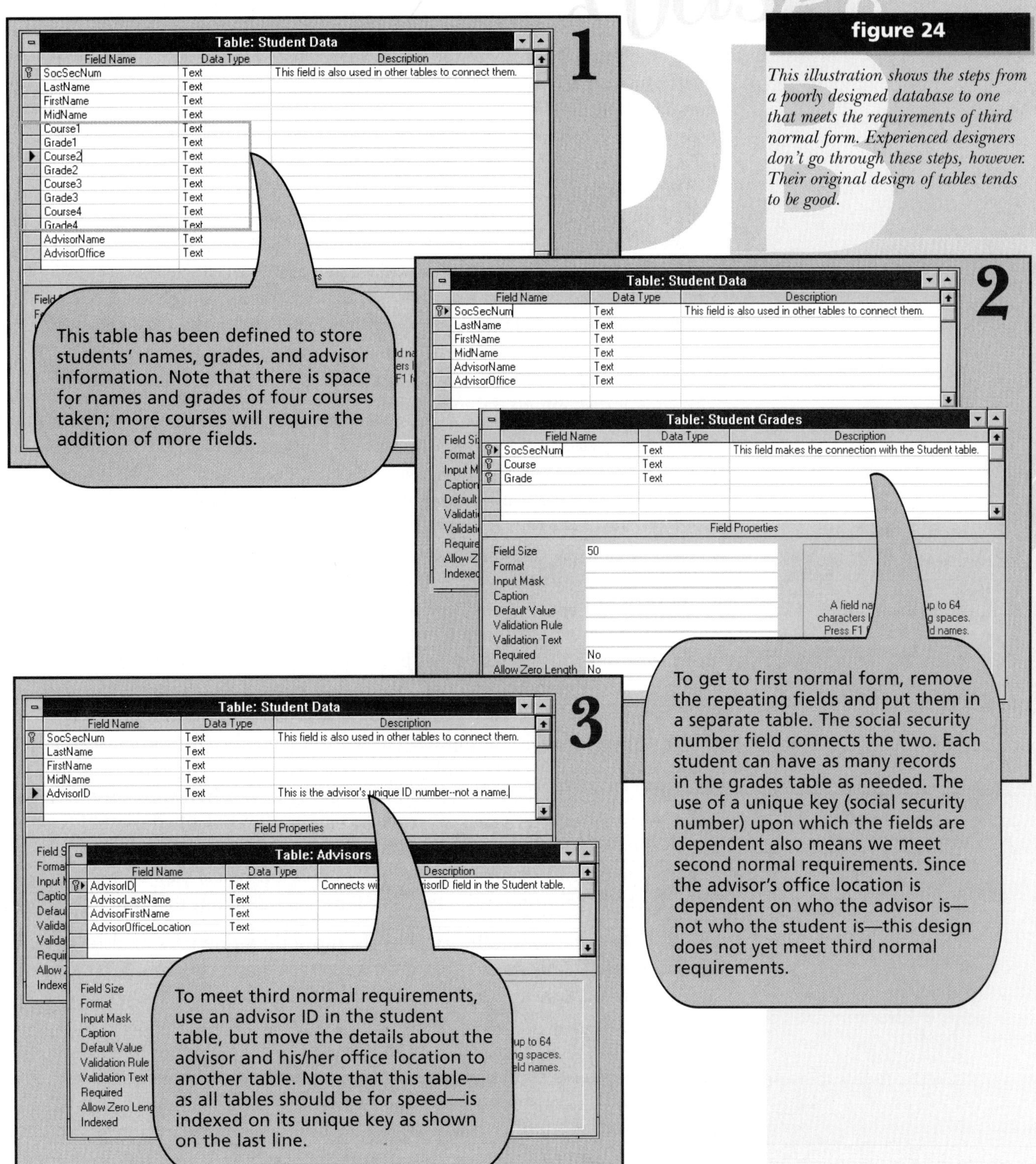

Sharing Database Fields

In the simplest implementation of a database, the data is on your computer and you are the only person who uses it. Most databases, however, contain data that must be accessible to more than one person. This is equally true whether you are using a computer attached to a local area network or a terminal attached to a mainframe computer.

Database data to be accessed by different persons has typically been stored on one central computer. Leading edge technology, however, now allows different tables of a relational database to be stored on different computers. With these computers networked together, all of the data is available to all authorized users on the network. In such a case, a user need not know which computer the data is stored on. If the desired data exists, access (regardless of physical location) is made automatically by the system. Such a database with data stored in different locations and visible to all users is known as a **distributed database**.

Access levels and passwords Database software that can be used by more than one person at a time typically uses passwords and levels of access. This helps to protect the data from unauthorized viewing or change. A user is assigned a password and access levels by the system operator. Levels of access may include no access, the ability to view but not change, the ability to change, and the ability to create and delete.

The level of access given to a user is usually applied to individual tables, forms, and reports–not to the entire database. For example, one person may need to access student schedules but have no need for student grades; in that case, access can be selective. At times, a person should have access to only some of the fields in a given table. For those circumstances, a view or query is used for maintaining data security. A logical view or query can be set up especially for each employee or type of employee to make available only those fields that each should have access to. In other words, use of logical views is a method of making available to employees only those fields with which they should be concerned. This is in contrast to a physical view, which reflects the physical layout of the table, that is, a physical view makes available all of the columns and records that are contained in the table.

Record locking Databases to be accessed by more than one person also use **record locking**. This means that if someone else has a record open to make a change in it, you cannot access it at the same time to make a change. Depending on the decisions made by the designer of the database, you might be able to access a record for viewing only at the same time someone else is changing it. The necessity of locking records during changes is apparent if you consider an example. Suppose I have become aware that a student's phone number has changed, so I am in the process of updating it. At the same time, you realize that his middle name is misspelled, so you go in to change the name. Both of our computers have copied the record to the screen, and we both make our change. You get through first, so your modified record is written back to the database. (Note that the entire record is read and written during this process, not just certain fields.) I then finish my work and write the modified record back to the database. When I do that, the misspelled middle name that was displayed on my screen goes back to the database and overwrites the correction you made.

Record locking prevents this kind of error from happening. Record locking is usually handled automatically by the database application once the designer of the database tells the system to do so.

Database Administration

When just one individual is using a database on a microcomputer, that individual can do whatever is desired. When multiple users share a database, however, each of them cannot be allowed freedom to modify the structure and contents of the database at will. It is necessary that someone be charged with the job of administering the database. The database administrator decides what tables are in the database, what columns of data are in each table, and what access is permitted for each user. In discharging these duties, however, the database administrator works closely with other administrators, such as persons in accounting, personnel, and sales, who know more about their data needs than the database administrator does. In this respect, the database administrator is more like a traffic officer or an arbiter than a dictator.

Hardware Requirements

The power of the hardware required for databases is related to the power of the database software and the number of users. Simple database software with only one user can be operated on just about any entry-level microcomputer. More capable microcomputer database software requires as much as several million bytes of memory and a very fast processor, as well as a large hard-disk drive. The amount of disk storage required depends on the amount of data to be stored and on the size of the actual database software programs. The more powerful programs are rather large in terms of the disk space required.

Software designed for maintaining large databases and multiuser access can require a huge quantity of disk space to store the data and a very fast processor to make that data available to other users. Individual user computers under this circumstance, however, can usually be the typical ones found in most offices.

Do It!

1 Determine what database programs are available for your use. For each of them, write down the following, which you should be able to determine from the documentation:

- The name of the program.
- The computer hardware requirements for the program to run.
- Whether it is a flat file or relational database.
- The maximum number of records it can handle in a table.
- If relational, the maximum number of tables it can handle.
- The different kinds of data that can be stored in its fields.

Summary

A database is a collection of organized data whose elements in some way relate to one another.

- The functions of database management systems include creating the structure of the database, adding data to the database, editing data already in the database, selecting and retrieving data, designing reports, and modifying the structure of the database.
- In creating the structure of a database, you name the table and describe the columns (names, types of data, width) that the table is to contain.
- Adding data to an existing database is known as appending or loading, and it may be done with default or custom-designed screen forms.
- The ability to edit existing data makes it easy to update items, using either a default or custom-designed screen form.
- Querying and reporting of data may be done using criteria entered by you.
- Selecting and retrieving data from a relational database is done by using a query language.
- A report writer function is included with many database systems to make the design of reports easier.
- A database that consists of only one table is known as a flat file database.
- The use of a database may make data more accurate, because redundancy, the amount of labor necessary to maintain the data, and the amount of storage space needed on disk are all reduced.
- A set of computer programs known as a database system or database management system provides the functions necessary to operate a database.
- A relational database presents its data in the form of tables. The relationships between different data elements and different tables are not defined in the structure of the database.
- Common fields provide the connection between different tables of a relational database.
- Querying and reporting of data in a relational database are very flexible, because the relationships are defined at the time of need rather than when the database is created.
- It is easy to modify the structure of a relational database.

Summary

- Database software handles the storage and retrieval of data, relieving application programs of that burden.
- In designing a computerized database, it is common to start with the paperwork forms previously used for the application.
- When designing the tables of a relational database, replication of data should be limited to the number of fields required to connect a table with other tables.
- A relational database is created by specifying its name and defining its tables.
- Reports printed from a relational database are custom designed by means of report writer software.
- Structure of the tables and columns of a relational database can be modified without destroying already-entered data.
- Custom applications can be designed around relational databases without programming by using application generator software that either comes with or is available for many database management systems.
- Databases can be used by one person or one microcomputer, shared by multiple users or a computer system, or distributed.
- A distributed relational database stores various parts of its data on various computers, with data visible to you whenever needed.
- Passwords are used to control access to data stored in a database.
- Logical views may be defined to present data from several tables as if they were stored in one table or to present only some of a table's columns to you.
- A database administrator serves as arbiter of what is stored in a database and who has access to the data.
- The more powerful the database software is, the more powerful the hardware must be to use it.

The following key terms were defined in this module. For each of the following terms, write on a separate piece of paper the number of the definition followed by the letter of the appropriate term.

Terms

A. appending
B. Boolean logic
C. database
D. distributed database
E. field
F. first normal form
G. flat file database
H. loading
I. primary key
J. record
K. record locking
L. relational database
M. second normal form
N. third normal form

Definitions

1 the field whose value makes a record unique

2 an organized collection of data

3 the process of loading or adding new records into a database table

4 system of logic based on comparisons of data items

5 the level of refinement in a relational database that requires fields to be dependent only on the primary key

6 the information about one person, organization, or other entity; equivalent to a row in a table

7 another name for appending a database

8 the level of refinement of a database that requires no repeating fields in a table

9 the level of refinement of a database that requires each column be dependent on the primary key

10 the process by which records being modified by one user prevents simultaneous modification by other users

11 the equivalent of a column in a table

12 a database in which multiple tables may be used; common fields tie the different tables together

13 a database that is limited to one table

14 a database with data stored on several different computers, perhaps in different locations but transparently available to users

Matching

Review

1. What is a database? (Obj. 1)
2. What are some of the advantages of using a database system? (Obj. 1)
3. What functions are performed by a database management system? (Obj. 2)
4. What is the purpose of a query? (Obj. 2)
5. What is the purpose of report generation? (Obj. 2)
6. What are the characteristics of a flat file database? (Obj. 3)
7. Why is redundant data a problem? (Obj. 3)
8. What are the primary characteristics of a relational database? (Obj. 3)
9. What is meant by a distributed database? (Obj. 3)
10. What role do paper forms play in planning a database? (Obj. 4)
11. In planning the tables of a relational database, why should data be replicated as little as possible? (Obj. 4)
12. What information does database software need to define a table? (Obj. 4)
13. How do physical and logical views differ? (Obj. 6)
14. What does a database administrator do? (Obj. 7)
15. What is the relationship between database power and computer hardware requirements? (Obj. 8)
16. Under what circumstances is a flat file database appropriate for use? (Obj. 3)
17. The relational database is the standard for microcomputer database software. What are the most likely reasons for this? (Obj. 3)

Activities

1 *Speaking* Plan a simple, one-table database (using flat file or relational software) that will store the numbers, positions, and names of the members of a football team. Name the columns needed in that table, give the type of each column (alphanumeric or numeric), and give the length for each column. If you have a computer with database software, create the database on the computer, then enter data for several team members with whom you are acquainted. Display the data on players arranged alphabetically and then arranged by position. Describe to your classmates the way you organized the table.

2 *Math* Assume that you are the secretary/treasurer of a civic club. You need to keep records on members' names, addresses, phone numbers, original membership dates, and dates of dues payment for the current membership year. This can be kept in a database of only one table, using either flat file or relational software. Name the columns needed in that table, give the type of each column (alphanumeric or numeric), and give the length for each column. If you have a computer with database software available, create the database and perform the following functions:

A. Add member Sam Jones, 3987 Eighth St., Merrillville, IN 39873-6122, 320-9875, membership date 8/3/—, dues not yet paid.

B. Add member Marilyn Abel, 32 Gayle Drive, Merrillville, IN 39873-4380, 442-9873, membership date 2/6/78, dues paid 8/3/—.

C. Add member Jacki Sharon, 7643 Gulliver Trail, Valparaiso, IN 39874-1050, 234-9386, membership date 2/6/49, dues paid 1/2/—.

D. Display an alphabetic list of all members.

E. Display a list of all members who have not paid dues this year (only Sam Jones should appear).

F. Enter dues payment for Sam Jones on 8/7/—.

G. Display a list of all members who have not paid dues this year (no names should appear).

H. Delete member Jacki Sharon.

I. Display a list of all members to confirm that Jacki Sharon has been deleted.

(Continued on next page.)

Activities

3 *Teamwork, Speaking* Working in a group with two or three other students, do the following:

A. Decide on a kind of business the group would be interested in operating.

B. Using the self-adhesive note methodolgy discussed in the chapter, decide on the fields that would be required to manage the business' data. Place the fields in appropriate tables.

C. Subject all of your tables to the rules of normalization. Make any necessary changes by moving the self-adhesive notes to other tables.

D. Explain your business and your design to another group, and get their feedback. Make any needed modifications to the design.

E. Using a database program that is available to you, set up a database according to your design. Print out the structure of the database.

F. Design appropriate screens for entering and accessing data.

G. Enter sample data into your database.

H. Design appropriate reports for examining data in your database, and print them.

4 *Internet* Many Internet Web sites pull data from databases as you browse. Examples of these sites can show you the price of virtually any combination of new automobile with desired options or financial data about virtually any publicly owned company. Use your browser to explore the Web and locate at least three sites where the displayed data seems to be coming from a database. For each of the sites, design tables that you think could hold the data.

Additional Applications

Overview

In this module, you will learn about the main category of software, known as application software. In contrast to the functions of operating systems software, application software is designed to perform the particular functions needed to solve problems for the user.

Common types of application software include word-processing software, database software, spreadsheet software, graphics software, and communications software. These programs represent the bulk of the software used on personal computers today.

There are, however, combinations of these types of software as well as many other types of application software. In fact, software is available for almost any type of application imaginable. This module introduces some of the more commonly used applications in the areas of finance, productivity management, education, gaming, simulation, accessories, paint/draw, graph and chart presentations, CAD/CAM/CIM, and expert systems.

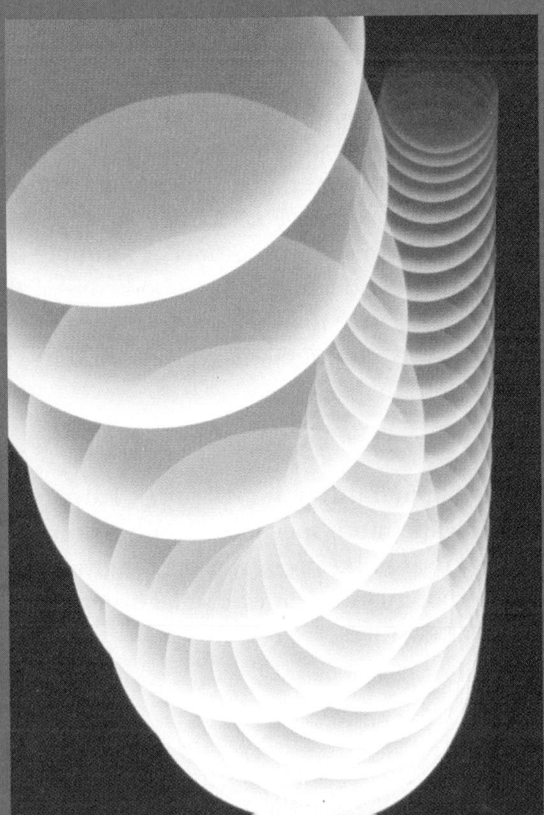

Objectives

1. State why application software is needed, describe the advantages/disadvantages of custom and commercial software, and list their sources.
2. List advantages/disadvantages of integrated software.
3. State the purpose of financial software.
4. State the purpose of productivity management software.
5. Identify how computers are used in education.
6. Identify applications for in-home computer usage.
7. Identify the characteristics of entertainment software.
8. Define and describe common desktop accessories.
9. Identify the purpose of draw and presentation software.
10. Define and describe the relationships in CAD/CAM/CIM.
11. State the purpose of expert systems.
12. Describe the guidelines for acquiring application software.

The Need for Application Software

Software designed to meet a particular computing need of the user is known as **application software**. A computing need represents a problem to be solved for the benefit of the user, and application software instructs the computer how to function to solve the problem. This is in contrast to the need for software to make the computer operate, which is met by operating system software. Software to handle word processing, to do financial processing, or to control an aircraft's flight all represent application software. Without application software, a computer is useless.

Application software may be either custom or commercial (also commonly referred to as off-the-shelf or generic software). **Custom application software** is written to meet the specific needs of an organization or individual. **Commercial software**, however, is written to meet the general needs of the public and business community.

Custom Application Software

In larger organizations, custom software is frequently written by an in-house staff of specialists. Smaller organizations sometimes employ independent consultants to write custom software. The fact that the software is written especially for the user leads to several advantages as well as disadvantages, as illustrated in figure 1.

Commercial Application Software

Many applications are relatively standard for most users. In these cases, commercial software is sufficient. Many programs related to word processing, financial processing, and spreadsheets fall into this category. As with custom software, commercial software has its advantages and disadvantages, as illustrated in figure 2.

Commercial software can be obtained from several sources. Some of these include computer stores, mail-order catalogs, software manufacturers, and vertical market sources.

Computer Store

For users of microcomputers, the local computer store or computer software store is an excellent source for ready-to-run software if the job to be done is a rather common one. These stores, however, generally stock only a limited variety of programs in each application area. For example, a store might stock three or four brands of word-processing programs or a couple of brands of database programs. An advantage of dealing with a good computer store is that advice, training, and assistance may be available through the store's staff. Organizations using larger computers will typically find little, if any, software available through computer stores.

Mail Order

Much application software can be obtained through mail order. Larger distributors carry many popular titles, while more specialized vendors carry programs for particular computers or kinds of businesses. A big disadvantage of mail order is that support is often not available; however, mail-order vendors may have lower prices than computer stores.

Manufacturers

Software manufacturers sometimes have direct sales forces that call on customers. This is most frequently the case with more complex, expensive software packages that run on more powerful computers. The larger the computer on which the package runs and the more expensive the software, the greater the likelihood the manufacturer will have a sales force working with customers. In-depth training in the use of the software is also usually available from such vendors.

Vertical Market Sources

Software products can be created to be sold across the board to a very wide range of users. Programs such as word processing and spreadsheets fall into this category. On the other hand, software may be constructed to meet the particular needs of one particular business or industry. In marketing lingo, a particular business or industry is known as a *vertical market.* For example, the insurance industry is a vertical market, and the banking industry is a vertical market. In many industries, consulting firms exist that assist the members of the industry in using computer software to help operate their businesses. In many vertical markets, there may also be trade associations that make software available; for example, an association of financial advisers might make programs available to help its members meet the needs of operating their businesses—needs that in some respects are rather unique. The primary value of software from vertical market sources is that the software is frequently tailored to meet the particular needs of the market being served.

Integrated Application Software

Integrated software combines the functions of two or more kinds of software. For example, it is very common to find word-processing, spreadsheet, database, graphing, and communication functions combined in the same package. There are two primary advantages of integrated packages. First, the user interface tends to be fairly consistent across all of the applications in the package. This makes the package easier to use than several different packages with different user interfaces. Secondly, data usually can be easily transferred from one portion of the package to another. For example, a spreadsheet or graph might be combined with text in a word-processing document.

Just as there are two main advantages, there are also two primary disadvantages to integrated software. One is that the components sometimes represent compromises. In other words, the process of merging the pieces into one product results in the individual components being less powerful or more difficult to use than equivalent stand-alone software packages. The second disadvantage is that integrated packages tend to require more computer memory to run than stand-alone packages with the same capability.

Today, data from most modern application software packages can be integrated into other application software via common user interfaces. This may be accomplished via dynamic data exchange or cut-and-paste methods.

Suite Application Software Products

Before graphic interface software (Macintosh, Windows, OS/2, and so on) was available, work was organized program by program: you had to purchase and learn separate applications, and sharing data between them was difficult if not impossible. Graphic interface software organizes work into directories or folders. The user can find a file, double-click on it, and the graphic user interface software launches the corresponding program for execution. The latest enhancement to the graphic user interface is called suite software. **Suite software** enables the user to use several applications to construct a single document. Instead of organizing the user's mind to fit the computer, suite software attempts to organize the computer to fit the user's mind.

Suite software consists of various software applications (word processor, database, spreadsheet, electronic mail [e-mail], accessories, network software,

figure 1

Advantages and disadvantages of custom application software.

Advantages and Disadvantages of Custom Application Software

Advantages	
Needs may be met more exactly	The output desired from the software may be defined exactly, and the processing required to produce the output can be specified as needed. The method of inputting data to the programs may be designed to suit the particular wishes of the user.
A strategic advantage may be gained	Businesses are beginning to use computers to develop strategic advantage, that is, to give them a competitive edge over businesses that do not have similar software. For example, an overnight air express company that completely computerized the tracking of packages, including having computers in its delivery trucks, gained an advantage over its competitors. To accomplish the continuous tracking of packages, a new concept in computer applications was required—one that was custom written. Once other companies copied the idea, however, it was no longer a strategic advantage, even though it was still required to remain competitive. Use of strategic software requires continual research and development of new ideas, because software to perform a particular function will remain unique for only a brief period of time after competitors find out about it.
System resources may be used more efficiently	Custom software is frequently more efficient in its use of system resources. It may require less memory and less disk space than commercial software. This is because the requirements that the program must meet are known upfront, and the program does not have to be written to handle contingencies that will not occur in the particular organization.
Programs may execute faster	The program can be written to address the situations it will encounter and the solutions it must provide in its particular environment. Alternatives that will never occur need not be addressed. For example, if a business will never have branch offices, its accounting programs need not be able to handle and consolidate financial figures from multiple locations.
Programs can be changed to meet changing conditions	When software has been custom written, it can be updated to meet changing needs of the user. Because it is custom written, the user has control over what will be done to the software and can make changes or upgrades as needed.

and so on) that are tightly integrated with each other. The software applications are modified to contain common toolbars, pull-down menus, and key dialog boxes that make it easier to operate and learn new applications.

Activities in suite software center around a customizable collection of application icons that you can place anywhere on your display screen (called the desktop). From the desktop, you can call up lists of tasks, such as create a letter (which launches a word-processor program and opens the letter template file), work on the budget (which launches a spreadsheet program and an associated template file), send an e-mail (which launches the communication software), and so on. If you are using suite software on a network, it will manage your e-mail, schedule meetings with colleagues, route voice-mail messages, maintain your calendar, and handle a host of other activities. It will also coordinate the work of circulating current versions of data, word-processing documents, and spreadsheet models.

Advantages and Disadvantages of Custom Application Software

Disadvantages	
Development time may be lengthy	Because custom software is written from scratch using a computer language chosen by the developer, it takes time to produce. The length of time depends on the language and development tools chosen as well as on the complexity of the task and the skill of the developers. The time required for writing a custom application may be anywhere from several days to several years.
Resources needed for development may not be available	Many businesses will not have the human resources needed to develop custom software. Development requires persons with excellent systems analysis and programming skills. Additionally, the financial resources necessary to do the job are considerable and may not be available in a company.
Expense of development may be much greater	When custom software is written, the organization for which it is developed may well be the only user. When this is the case, it is necessary for all development costs to be paid by that organization. Development costs may range into the millions of dollars depending on the complexity of the application.
Cost may be unknown upfront	Estimates for the cost of developing software are difficult to make with accuracy. Unknown or changing conditions as well as problems that may be encountered during development may make the costs of software much greater than originally anticipated.
Expense of upgrades and maintenance may be great	The same reasons that make original development of custom software expensive also tend to make upgrades and maintenance of the software very expensive. Maintenance refers to the resolution of problems that may occur during operation and refinement of the software. *Upgrades* refers to significant improvements in program function or performance. Upgrades and maintenance require much labor.

Advantages and Disadvantages of Commercial Software	
Advantages	
Availability is immediate	Commercial software can be purchased and put to work immediately. Only an installation process is necessary before it can start being productive for the organization. Depending on the complexity of the software, installation can take as little as a few minutes or as long as several months.
Cost is less	The cost of developing commercial software can be spread among a number of users who purchase the product. This can reduce the cost dramatically in relation to the expense of developing custom software.
Reliability may be greater	Usually, commercial software has been thoroughly tested before it is marketed. Additionally, many other users may have already used the software, adding their testing to that done by the developer. The testing to which commercial software is thus submitted may be much tougher than the testing designed to ensure the quality of custom software written for one user.
Updates and upgrades	Software updates (changes made to the software to correct a problem, update a tax table, and so on) are often made available from the developer. Software upgrades (new versions of the software or competitive updates) are often sold at a discount to owners of the previous versions by the developer or retail source.

figure 2

Advantages and disadvantages of commercial software.

Working from personal lists of people, events, projects, and so on enables the user to better understand how to organize this information in the computer. The computer keeps track of all these lists. For example, when there is something that needs to be done, it appears on your calendar. When you schedule a meeting, the system notifies everyone involved via e-mail and coordinates the schedules. Figure 3 illustrates a toolbar from a suite software package.

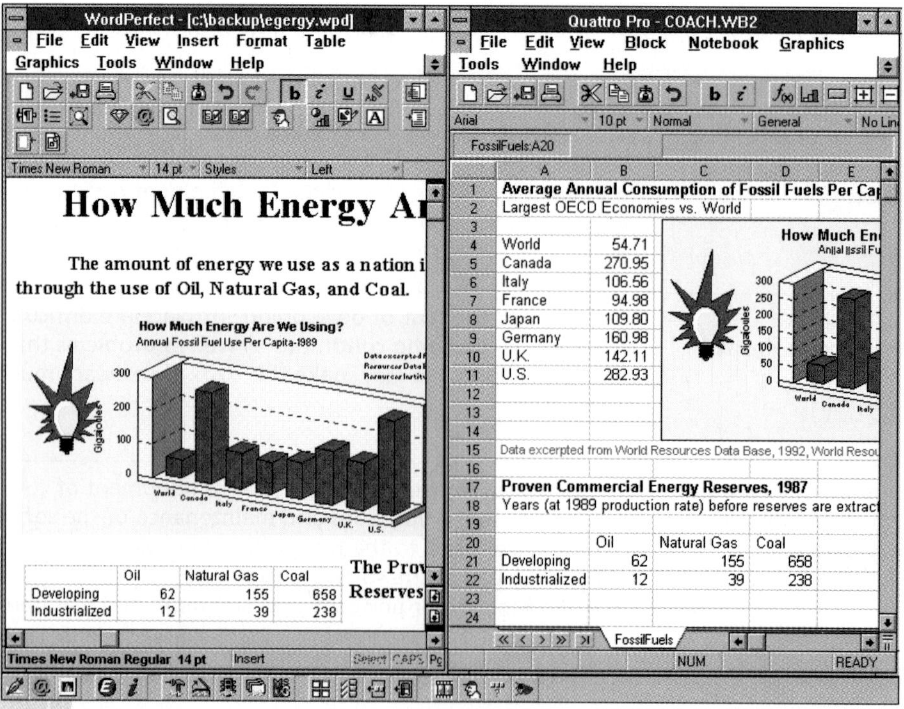

figure 3

All of the software applications used in a suite use a common toolbar to make the software easy to operate and learn.

Advantages and Disadvantages of Commercial Software	
Disadvantages	
May not be an exact match for user needs	The biggest disadvantage of commercial software is that it may not be an exact match for the needs of the organization. The more specialized the need, the less likely it will be that commercial software is capable of meeting that need.
May require more system resources	Commercial software must be written to handle the many possible conditions that may be required by various users. The capability to meet these conditions often results in less efficient use of system resources. Programs are frequently longer, requiring more memory and disk space.
May execute more slowly	Being able to handle many different conditions may result in commercial programs which will execute more slowly. This is caused by the necessity that the software continuously monitor the status of the various program options, many of which are never used by any one business.
May not be adaptable or responsive to changing needs	If the conditions of the business change, it may not be possible to adapt commercial software to the changing needs. This is because the program's code is under control of the developer, not the user. In such cases, it will be necessary either to select a different commercial software package or develop a custom package.

Financial Applications

Many businesses first began using computers to automate their financial (accounting) systems. **Financial software** is used to maintain the financial records of a business, for sending bills to customers and keeping records of what they owe, to assist management in decision-making, control inventory, prepare paychecks, pay bills, and many other purposes. Computers can save a tremendous amount of money and make the operation much more efficient.

Virtually all accounting in businesses of any size is done on the computer. Simple accounting systems can run on even the smallest microcomputer. Accounting systems for large businesses generally run on mainframe computers. Accounting systems can be purchased as an entire integrated package or as modules to meet the needs of the business.

Application software designed for individuals to use their own home computer systems to keep track of their finances is called **personal finance software**. Modern personal finance software will organize expenses, investments, earnings, bank accounts, loans, credit cards, and even project account balances. Figure 4 shows an example of a financial calendar from a financial software package that can be used by an individual for personal finance or by a small business for its financial needs.

Productivity Management

Productivity management software helps to plan and track the sequence of activities necessary to complete a complex project. Management of such projects has always been a challenge. A good example of this can be found in the construction of a building (figure 5). When construction is started, the foundation must be completed before work on the walls can begin.

Profile

Women in the Computer Industry

The computer industry started out as largely a men's club. Fortunately, there are signs that the business is becoming more inclusive, with more women assuming important roles in the world of computers and software.

How can the computer business attract and retain more women? One of the highest-ranking women in the software business, Carol Bartz, CEO of Autodesk, offers her solution: "To attract women to the industry, it is important the women in senior positions take the responsibility of mentoring other women. Women need to build a network." Heidi Roizen, cofounder and CEO of T/Maker, teaches two or three class sessions each year at Stanford's business school that focus on women's issues; she urges other successful women to serve as role models for others.

High-profile female role models are essential. Currently, the most notable software development companies in the United States report that 15% to 36% of their senior managers (vice-president and above) are women. This figure is slightly higher than the proportion at most noncomputer industry companies.

Companies with the most formalized efforts at attracting women and minorities to join their ranks are among the largest in the industry, such as Hewlett-Packard, IBM, Lotus, and Microsoft. Many of these companies are actively recruiting more women for technical positions and working directly with public schools, colleges, and universities to increase the number of women and minorities enrolled in math and science courses.

Less formal—but no less important—efforts are demonstrated by developers of entertainment software. By including more female role models in their games, these manufacturers report increased female participation—and that could ultimately lead to increased interest in computer careers for women.

Most women in the computer industry see increased opportunities for women. "There's a big improvement over the past ten years," says Karen Eriksson, who is head of the Interbase group and one of three female vice-presidents at Borland International. The future looks even brighter. There are strong feeder pools of younger women moving up the computer corporate ladder. The industry is quickly recognizing the talent that exists within a full 50% of the top talent pool in the United States.

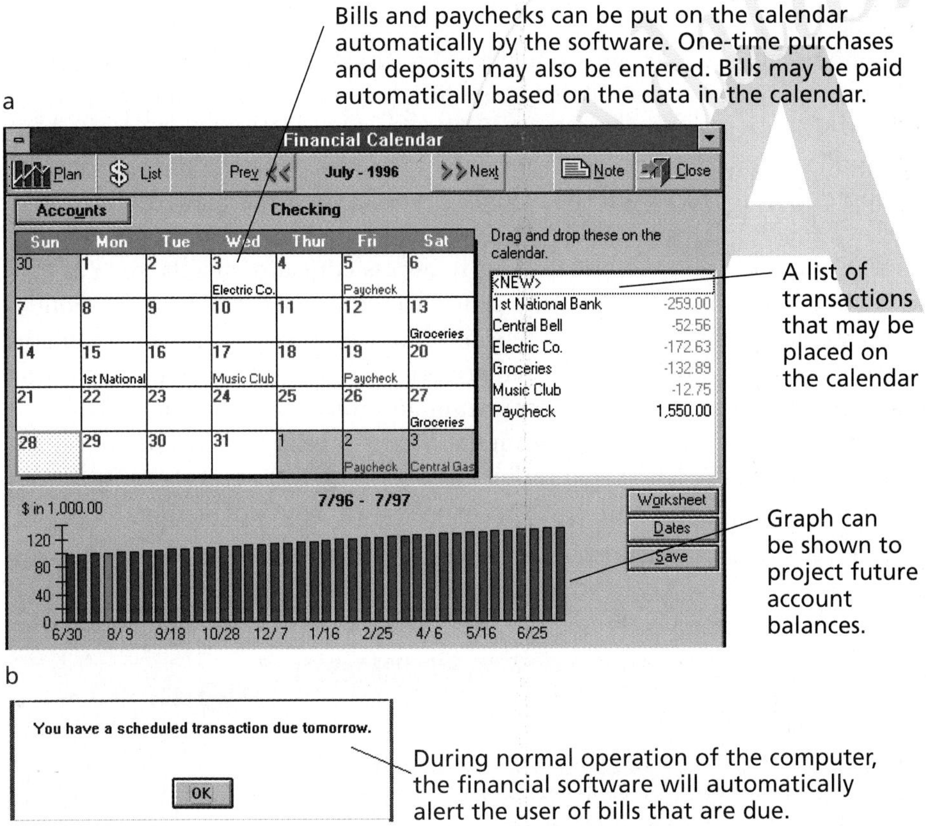

a

Bills and paychecks can be put on the calendar automatically by the software. One-time purchases and deposits may also be entered. Bills may be paid automatically based on the data in the calendar.

A list of transactions that may be placed on the calendar

Graph can be shown to project future account balances.

b

You have a scheduled transaction due tomorrow.

OK

During normal operation of the computer, the financial software will automatically alert the user of bills that are due.

figure 4

Financial calendar (panel A) *and reminder message* (panel B).

However, once the foundation is complete and the walls are roughed in, electrical and plumbing work can commence at the same time, but the finish wall cannot be put up until both the electrical and plumbing work are complete. The coordination of all these activities is difficult, and many persons often have waited around with no work until necessary prior steps were completed. In other cases, time was wasted after the completion of certain steps because workers were not available to begin the next step. Frequently, the estimated time necessary for completing a project would go by, and the project would not be finished because the estimates were just not accurate.

figure 5

Project management software can be used to coordinate the activities involved in completing a construction project.

Productivity management software can help schedule the various activities that must go into completion of a project. The software certainly does not make the job foolproof or relieve the human being of the burden of good judgment. It can, however, assist greatly by making the work of preparing complex charts that map activities and keep up with their progress much easier and more accurate.

Education

Computers have become a valuable educational tool. **Computer-assisted instruction** (CAI) has combined the fascination and excitement of a game with motivating lessons to teach virtually any subject. Computers are used in pre–grade school through graduate school to teach subjects from simple computer literacy to advanced calculus. CAI employs several methods of delivery, including simple drill and practice, interactive tutorials, and simulations. Computers also enable students to access educational aids, such as encyclopedias and other reference materials that are available via magnetic or laser disks or through various telecommunication networks. Many bulletin board systems are now available that are staffed by educators that offer tutoring services. Figure 6 shows a screen from an interactive educational software package that teaches trigonometry. Students read text, view examples and solve problems. The program includes a multimedia feature: at various intervals during instruction, students can view a video explanation.

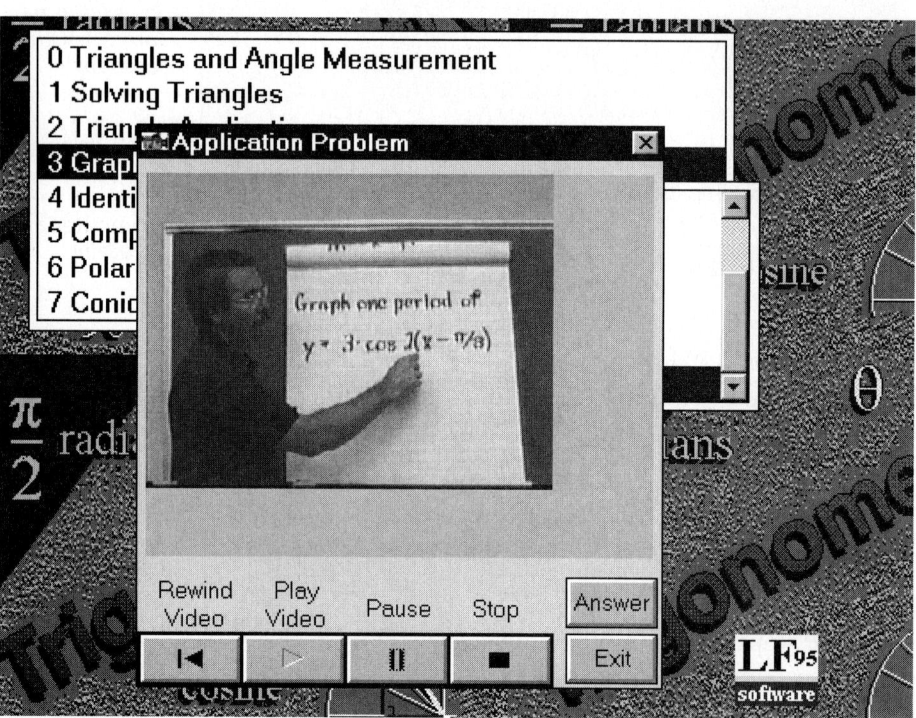

figure 6

Example of interactive educational software (trigonometry).

The Louvre (figure 7) is an educational art software product that explains concepts in art history while also providing computer graphic views of famous works of art that reside in the Louvre museum in Paris, France. Also included is a history and explanation of the physical structure of the Louvre building.

Microsoft Bookshelf (figure 8) provides access to several reference books on one CD-ROM. The example shows a selection from the encyclopedia. This educational reference product includes audio and video multimedia features.

Applications in the Home

Financial software (like that shown in figure 4) is available that will track an individual's earnings and spending, balance the checkbook, monitor investments, store tax information, and perform many other financial services. An abundance of computer games are used for entertainment (discussed later in this module). Software to help plan meals, plan a trip,

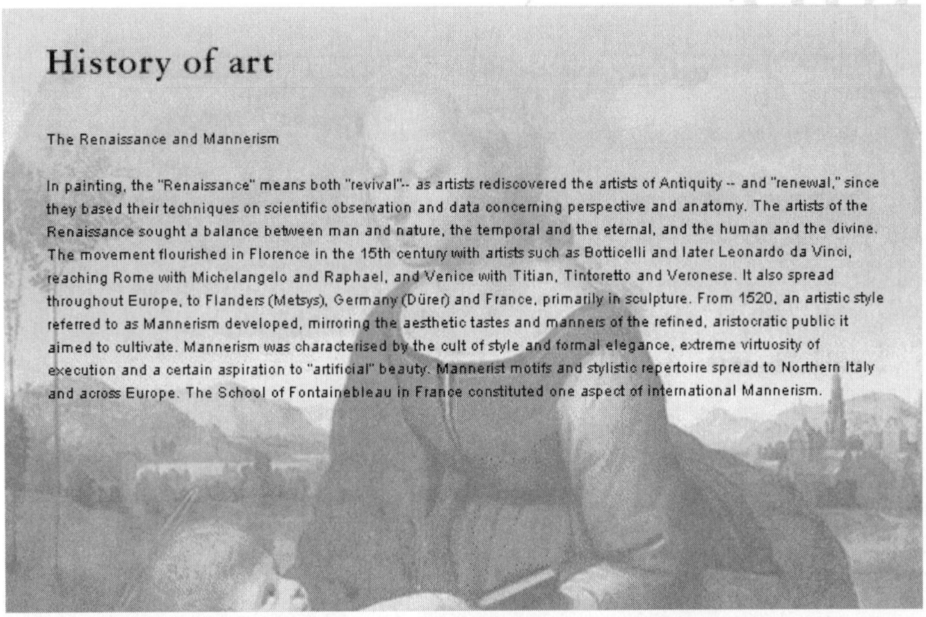

History of art

The Renaissance and Mannerism

In painting, the "Renaissance" means both "revival"-- as artists rediscovered the artists of Antiquity -- and "renewal," since they based their techniques on scientific observation and data concerning perspective and anatomy. The artists of the Renaissance sought a balance between man and nature, the temporal and the eternal, and the human and the divine. The movement flourished in Florence in the 15th century with artists such as Botticelli and later Leonardo da Vinci, reaching Rome with Michelangelo and Raphael, and Venice with Titian, Tintoretto and Veronese. It also spread throughout Europe, to Flanders (Metsys), Germany (Dürer) and France, primarily in sculpture. From 1520, an artistic style referred to as Mannerism developed, mirroring the aesthetic tastes and manners of the refined, aristocratic public it aimed to cultivate. Mannerism was characterised by the cult of style and formal elegance, extreme virtuosity of execution and a certain aspiration to "artificial" beauty. Mannerist motifs and stylistic repertoire spread to Northern Italy and across Europe. The School of Fontainebleau in France constituted one aspect of international Mannerism.

figure 7

Example of an educational art software.

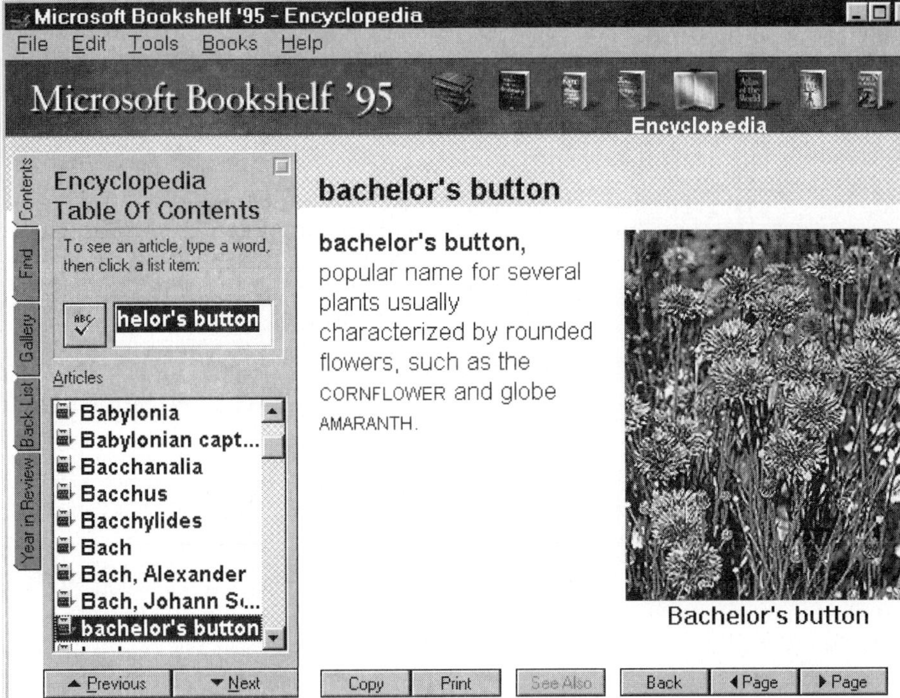

figure 8

Example of educational reference software.

arrange furniture, and personalize correspondence are but a few of the common applications of the modern home computer user. Figure 9 illustrates a travel-planner software package that has been used to plan a car trip from Cincinnati, Ohio, to Dallas, Texas. A graphic display shows the route, and a detailed display (that may be printed) specifies the time, distance, and cost of the trip. In addition, information can be accessed that shows the capital and major cities of each state, toll-free phone numbers of major hotels and car rental agencies, and weather conditions along the route.

Software used to create professional-looking signs, banners, greeting cards, calendars, and so on with graphic images is another common in-home computer application. Many of these software programs are taking advantage of the increased processing capabilities of powerful computers now

figure 9

Example of travel-planner software.

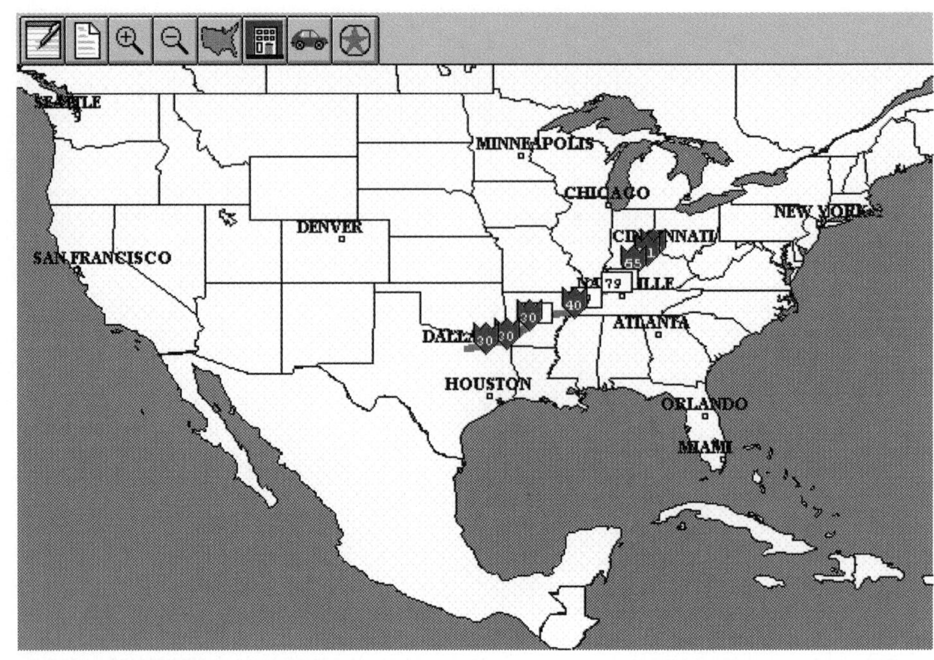


```
Starting City- CINCINNATI     , OH
Ending   City- DALLAS         , TX
Method- Shortest
-----------------------------------------------------------------------
Get On     I75/I71      GO SW 21 mi TO WALTON          for 0 hr 19 mn **
*** Leaving OH. ****
*** Entering KY. ****
Continue on I75/I71     towards WALTON
Exit onto I71           GO SW 43 mi TO CAMPBELLSBURG   for 0 hr 39 mn **
Stay on    I71          GO SW 30 mi TO LOUISVILLE      for 0 hr 27 mn **
Exit onto I65           GO SW 42 mi TO ELIZABETHTOWN   for 0 hr 38 mn **
Stay on    I65          GO SW 39 mi TO CAVE CITY       for 0 hr 35 mn **
Stay on    I65          GO SW  9 mi TO SMITHS GROVE    for 0 hr  7 mn **
Stay on    I65          GO SW 20 mi TO BOWLING GREEN   for 0 hr 17 mn **
Exit onto US68          GO SW 25 mi TO RUSSELLVILLE    for 0 hr 32 mn **
Exit onto US79          GO SW 31 mi TO JCT US79/I24    for 0 hr 40 mn **
*** Leaving KY. ****
*** Entering TN. ****
Continue on US79        towards JCT US79/I24
Stay on    US79         GO SW  6 mi TO CLARKSVILLE     for 0 hr  7 mn **
Stay on    US79         GO SW 37 mi TO DOVER           for 0 hr 49 mn **
Stay on    US79         GO SW 33 mi TO PARIS           for 0 hr 43 mn **
Stay on    US79         GO SW 38 mi TO MILAN           for 0 hr 50 mn **
Stay on    US79         GO SW 36 mi TO BROWNSVILLE     for 0 hr 47 mn **
Exit onto I40           GO SW 48 mi TO MEMPHIS         for 0 hr 43 mn **
Stay on    I40          GO  W 19 mi TO SHEAREVILLE     for 0 hr 17 mn **
*** Leaving TN. ****
*** Entering AR. ****
Continue on I40         towards SHEAREVILLE
Stay on    I40          GO SW 113 mi TO N LITTLE ROCK for 1 hr 43 mn **
Exit onto US65          GO  S   1 mi TO LITTLE ROCK   for 0 hr  0 mn **
Exit onto I30           GO SW  39 mi TO ROCKPORT      for 0 hr 35 mn **
Stay on    I30          GO SW  20 mi TO ARKADELPHIA   for 0 hr 17 mn **
Stay on    I30          GO SW  76 mi TO TEXARKANA     for 1 hr  9 mn **
Exit onto I30/US82      GO  E   1 mi TO TEXARKANA     for 0 hr  0 mn **
*** Leaving AR. ****
*** Entering TX. ****
Continue on I30/US82    towards TEXARKANA
Exit onto I30           GO SW 180 mi TO DALLAS        for 2 hr 45 mn **

**Arrived at Destination**
Total Distance- 907 mi        Total Time= 15 hrs 14 mn
Gas cost- 1.17
Highway Gas Mileage- 26
City Gas Mileage- 18
Total Gas Cost        - 44.87
Food + Hotel Cost     - 67.57
```

found in homes. These capabilities include full color, sophisticated graphics, highly readable fonts, designer layouts, high-resolution printouts, and many user customizing features. Figure 10 shows an example of the front of a personalized birthday card.

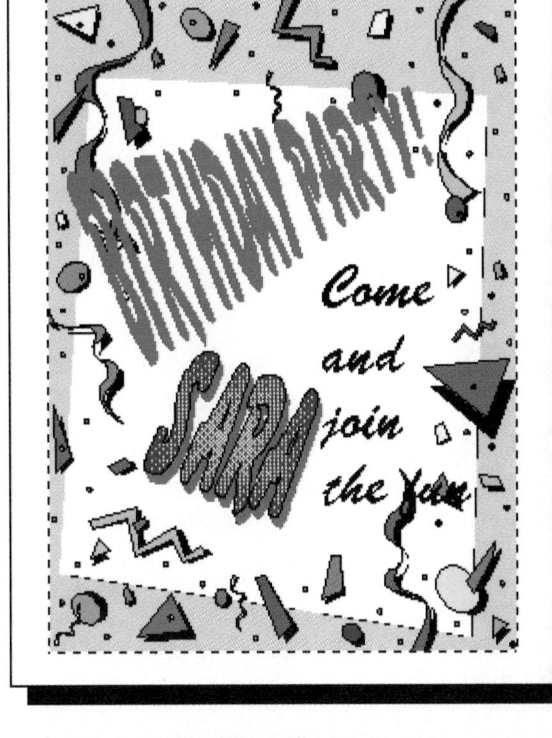

figure 10

Example of software used to create signs, banners, greeting cards, and calendars.

Entertainment

In 1982, there were approximately 10,000 game parlors in the United States. By the beginning of 1984, about 2000 had closed. This rapid decline was a direct result of the influx of home computers and video-game software. The advantage of the computer over the early machines in the arcade parlors is its ability to do more things than merely play games. As the market for home computers continued to expand, the cost also continued to fall because of mass production and increased competition.

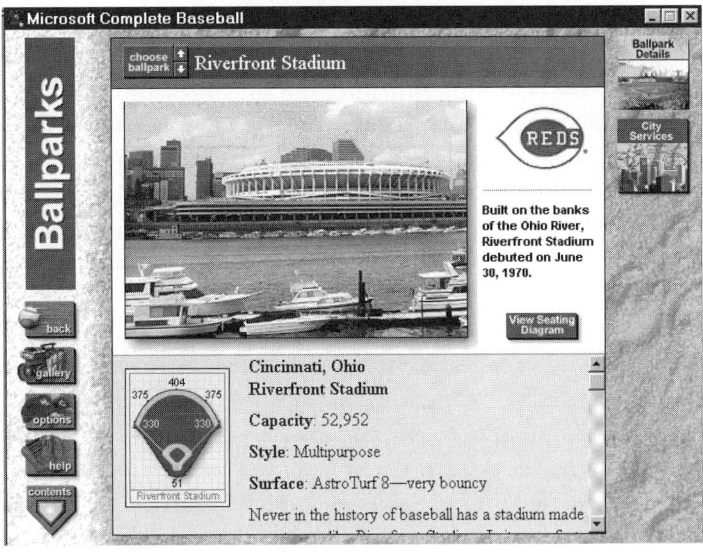

figure 11

Baseball entertainment software.

Entertainment software developers and manufacturers have turned to laser-disk technology to keep computer games interesting. The disk can be used to store large volumes of high-resolution graphics that can be projected and animated on the screen. Coupled with the player's ability to work controls to interact with the game-movie, this has greatly increased the realism and interest in modern home-entertainment software. Figure 11 illustrates an example of entertainment software.

Simulations

The purpose of **simulation software** is to duplicate or model conditions that are likely to occur in a real-world environment. Data is fed into a simulation, then the computer performs calculations based on the model that it

Trends

MPEG: Setting the (Compression) Standard

Personal computers with CD-ROM drives are a perfect medium for movies and interactive movie entertainment. The technology that enables CD-ROM drives to project video and sound through a personal computer comes from a compression standard called MPEG-1 (Motion Picture Experts Group). This technology is now available through inexpensive add-in computer boards that enable even the cheapest, single-speed CD-ROM disk drives to offer the same quality as a VHS videotape.

The MPEG-1 compression was developed specifically for CD-ROMs. What makes this technology unique is its ability to work with both video and audio by eliminating redundant data within each single picture frame and looking for redundant information *between* adjacent frames. MPEG-1 can do all this, with a video stream capable of playing at 30 frames per second (fps).

The MPEG-1 add-in cards have already hit the market and sell for around $400. The add-in card can play video at 30 fps at resolutions up to 1,024 x 768 in 32,000 colors. The add-in boards come bundled with a CD-based game that shows off its capabilities and colors.

The impressive MPEG-1 standard is about to be eclipsed by the upcoming MPEG-2 standard, which will be used for broadcasting to high-definition televisions (HDTV). This technology may be the key to squeezing 500 channels onto a single TV cable. While this is just a beginning, MPEG decoding chips are currently being licensed as an option for 3DO game machines and cable TV decoder boxes.

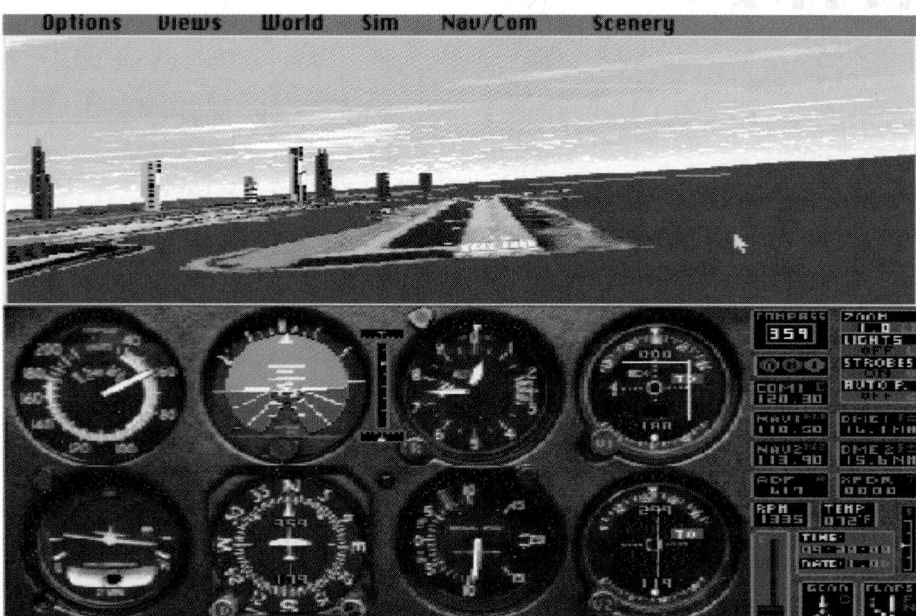

figure 12

Flight simulator applications allow users to practice flying various models of aircraft in realistic situations.

outputs to the user in turn. An example of a simulation is a flight simulator, as illustrated in figure 12. As the user inputs data to control the airplane, the software uses the model built in it to display the resulting action.

Desktop Accessories

Desktop accessories (also commonly called desktop tools) is a name applied to a classification of computer software designed to make day-to-day work and personal activities a little easier in a practical way. This software usually fulfills the most basic need for information or completion of a certain task. For example, common accessory software include maintaining a calendar, dialing the phone from numbers stored in its directory, providing a notepad for keeping track of miscellaneous information, and providing a calculator for quick computations. If more powerful and sophisticated features are required, then specific application software must be used.

A characteristic of desktop accessory programs is that they are ready to be used at a moment's notice. The exact method by which this is accomplished depends on the kind of computer system on which they are to run. Only a couple of keystrokes are usually required, however, to make the programs active, regardless of what other program may be running. When use of the accessory is completed, the other program is once again available for use, just as it was left.

For growing numbers of computer models, desktop tools software is included with the system. For others, the software is available from a variety of vendors.

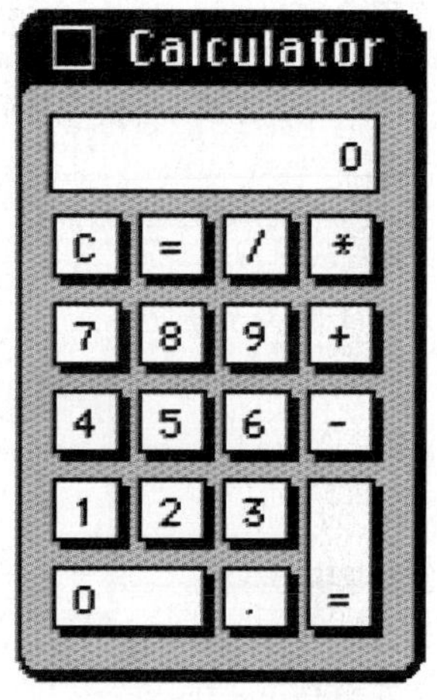

figure 13

Calculator.

Calculator As its name indicates, the calculator accessory displays what appears to be a calculator on the computer's screen, as illustrated in figure 13. By entering numbers on the keyboard or clicking on the appropriate keys with a mouse, a calculator can serve the same purpose as a desk calculator. With some programs, the

Do It!

1 Interview any acquaintance (relative, friend, neighbor) who is employed in the computer industry and works with computer software. Ask the interviewee if he or she prefers to work with custom or commercially developed software. Also, be sure to ask for an explanation of why one may be preferred over the other. Take notes during the interview, and share the information you obtain from your interview with your teacher and classmates.

2 Find out from an adult relative or friend who receives a paycheck prepared by a computer what types of data are shown on his or her paycheck stub (do not ask for specific amounts). What other data do you think the computer must store to prepare the paycheck and report tax information?

3 Find out if any of the educational software used on your computer(s) at school or any of the gaming or in-home software that you may have on a computer at home is integrated. That is, does it combine the functions of two or more kinds of software? Identify the software and the two or more integrated functions.

calculator can input numbers from another application currently running in the computer and send the results back to the application. Calculator programs are very useful for computations that are needed while another application program is in use.

Card file/phone directory/dialer Just as the calendar desktop accessory can take the place of a paper calendar, the card file/phone directory/dialer can take the place of a personal paper phone directory. Names, phone numbers, addresses, and any other desired information about each person can be entered. When the data is accessed, as shown in figure 14, the directory appears and the desired person is located. The computer can be instructed to dial the desired phone number. To use the dialing option, the computer must contain communication hardware and be connected through a modem to the phone system. In the absence of a modem, however, the directory portion can still be used to look up phone numbers, which can then be dialed manually.

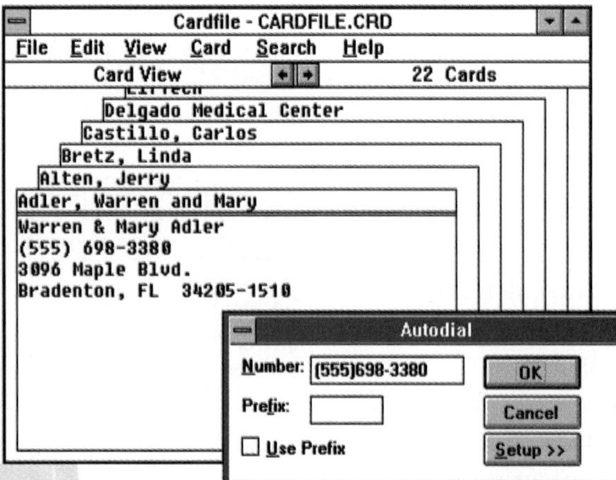

figure 14

Card file/phone directory/dialer accessory.

Calendar The basic function of calendar software is to computerize the functions of a paper desk calendar. As can be seen in figure 15, the calendar can hold entries of appointments and activities to be accomplished at specified times each day. Additionally, most calendar software can be set to alert the user when it is time for certain events. For example, if a user is working intently on a project but has a three-o'clock meeting, the computer can sound an alarm shortly before three-o'clock to signal the approaching time. A calendar program running on one computer can handle the calendars of several different persons.

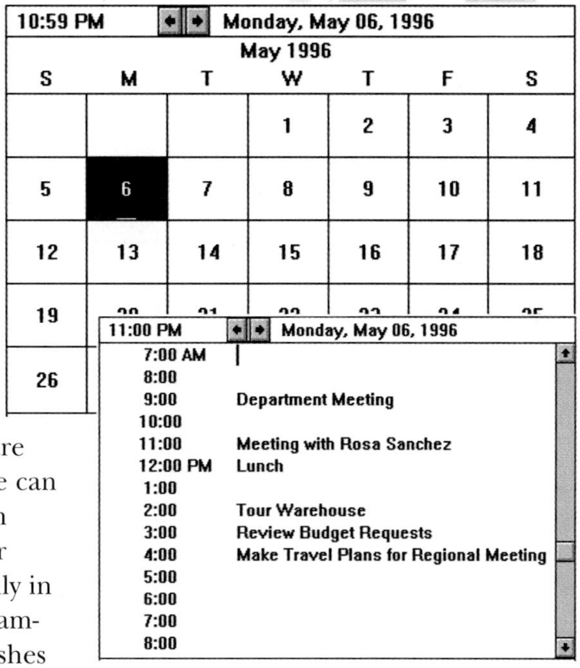

figure 15

Calendar accessory.

In network or time-share settings, where various computer workstations are connected, calendar software can become even more useful. In such circumstances, calendar software can help dramatically in scheduling meetings. For example, suppose an executive wishes to meet with four other employees sometime next week. By entering the names of the people who should attend the meeting along with the desired time frame for the meeting, the computer can examine the calendars of all the proposed participants and tell the executive the times when all are available. E-mail messages can then be sent automatically to those individuals, inviting them to the meeting. Obviously, this works nicely only if all persons in the organization faithfully use their computer calendars to keep up with their appointments. In a computer network or time-share system, it also is possible for the phone directory portion to contain some numbers from a central directory that is accessible to all users; additional personal numbers can then be added by each user.

Notepad The notepad capabilities of desktop accessory programs vary tremendously. The simplest programs are the equivalent of a stack of blank note cards on which anything desired can be written. Usually, the cards can be arranged and located by using a few designated keywords. More sophisticated software allows cards to be "linked" to other cards simply by pointing at the linkage point. For example, a main note card may contain the name and address for a customer, Helen Ayres. Other cards may contain notes related to her, such as the contents of phone conversations regarding her future purchase needs or her brand-name preferences of products. These related cards could be easily accessed from the main card. The most advanced software allows graphic images or sounds as well as text to be stored on the cards.

While sophisticated notepad capabilities come with some computers, they are available for virtually all computers via commercial software purchases. Figure 16 shows an example of a notepad accessory.

figure 16

Notepad accessory.

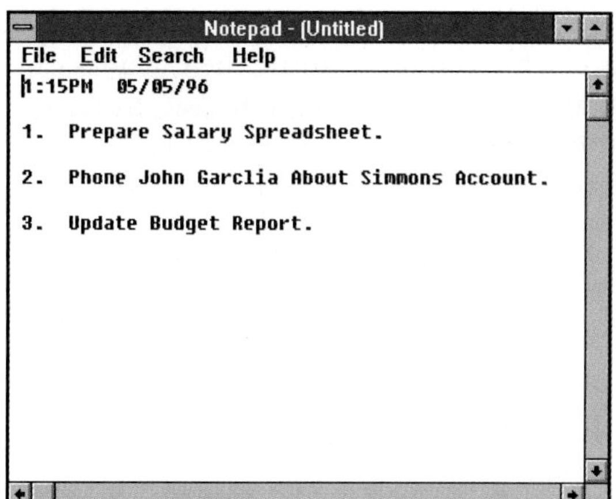
Notepad - (Untitled)
File Edit Search Help
1:15PM 05/05/96
1. Prepare Salary Spreadsheet.
2. Phone John Garclia About Simmons Account.
3. Update Budget Report.

Paint and Draw

Simple or elaborate color drawings may be created, edited, and printed with **paint and draw software**. Computer experience is not required to use paint and draw software. Simple mouse movements to use the features in the software's toolbox allow the user to easily create lines, curves, circles, boxes, and many other shapes and then add color. Additional features enable the user to reduce the drawing, enlarge the entire drawing or portions of it to perform finite work, rotate, flip, add text, and a host of other tasks. Users may use paint and draw programs for freehand drawings or to create elaborate, detailed drawings like those shown in figures 17 and 18.

Graph and Chart Presentation Applications

Many software programs available today have the capability to produce graphs and charts from the data they access. This capability is commonly referred to as **charting or graphing presentation software**. The terms *charting* and *graphing* refer to pictorial representation of data that can be produced by the computer and depicted on the display screen, printer, plotter, or other output device capable of producing the computer-generated output. For example, charts and graphs produced by spreadsheet software are used to clarify the meaning of the words and numbers that appear in the spreadsheet and thus improve communication. Graphs and charts are commonly

figure 17

Example of paint and draw software used to create artwork.

Paintbrush - SAMPLE1.BMP
File Edit View Text Pick Options Help
abc
Drawing area.
Linesize box. Contains the available drawing widths.
Toolbox. Contains the tools that are used to create the drawing.
Pallette. Contains the colors and patterns available for use in the background of the drawing area and with the drawing tools.

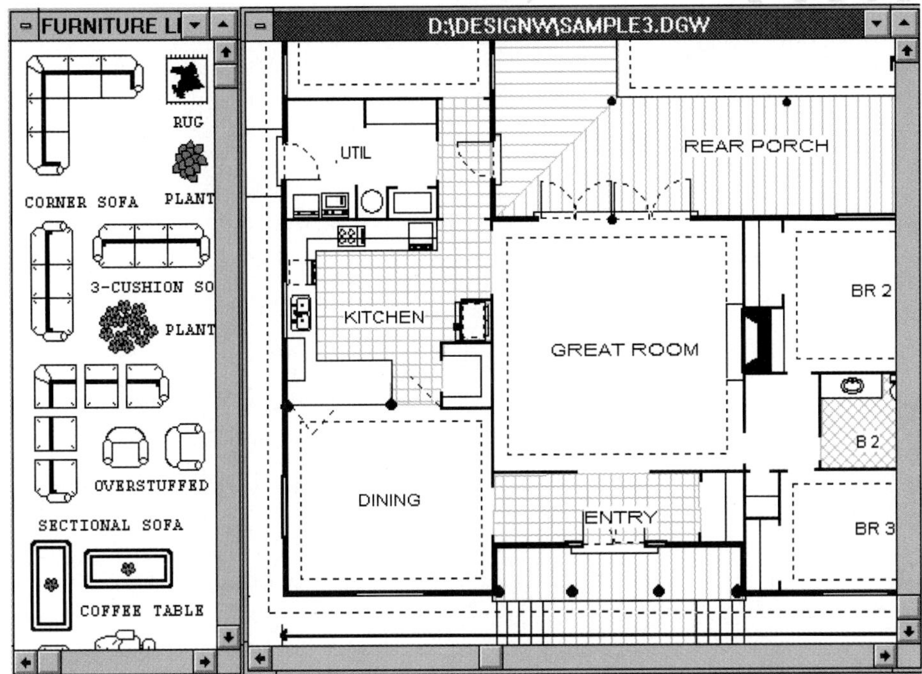

figure 18

Example of an application program that uses paint and draw–type software to design the interior of a home and arrange furnishings.

used to enhance presentations, track sales, monitor production, identify trends, and make forecasts for a wide variety of applications in many different industries. Figure 19 shows two examples—each depicting the same data—of charts produced by a spreadsheet program.

CAD/CAM/CIM

CAD/CAM stands for computer-aided (or -assisted) design (drafting)/computer-aided manufacturing. **CAD** refers to the process of using graphic computer programs to assist in the design of a product; the sophistication of CAD software can range from simple drafting programs to complex pro-

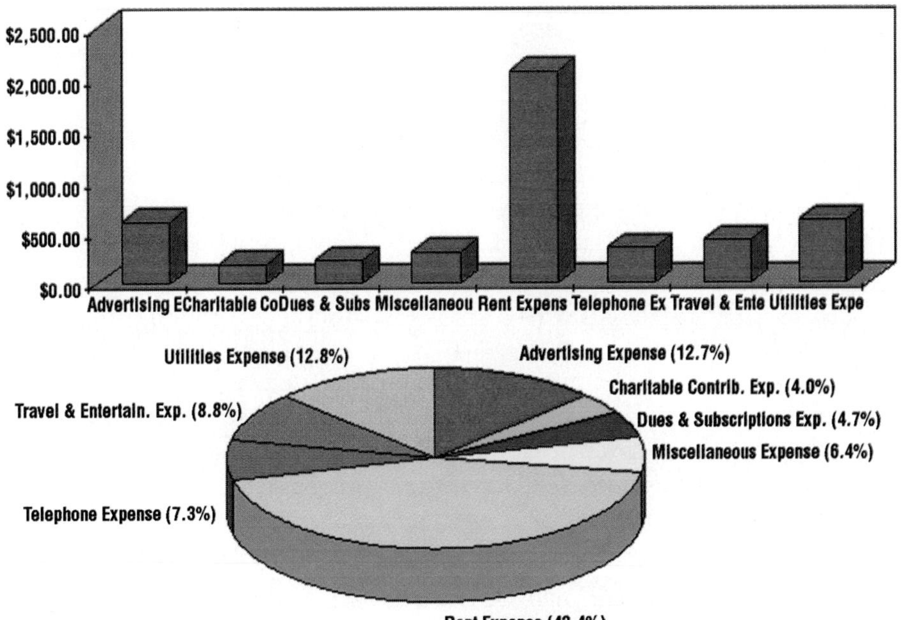

figure 19

Example of a three-dimensional bar chart and a three-dimensional pie chart.

Customer-Service Engineers

Who keeps computers and computer peripheral equipment up and running? Companies and individuals who purchase computer equipment do not usually make their own repairs, nor do they have people on staff who can fix an ailing motherboard or keyboard. Instead, they count on customer-service engineers employed by the manufacturer, retailer, or service provider.

Customer-service engineers are responsible for seeing that all equipment under warranty or service contract is running properly. This is a big responsibility, considering what the failure of just one machine can do to a network—and to an entire company. Businesses can lose customers or valuable data because of machine failure.

Customer-service engineers often repair equipment on site—that is, they go where the machines are. In the case of individual PCs and peripherals, however, owners are often encouraged to take their equipment to the repair shop where the service technician can make repairs. Whether at the shop or at a customer site, a customer-service engineer has an inventory of computer circuit boards and parts—along with test equipment—readily available. As each machine is repaired, the service engineer must maintain a log of what was done to repair the machine and the parts that were installed.

In addition to making repairs, many service engineers perform preventive maintenance—checking machines from time to time to make sure nothing is wrong. As part of this maintenance, the service engineer runs diagnostic software that checks various components of the computer, performs a visual check for worn parts, and cleans the printer and other equipment exposed to paper dust and other contaminants.

Ideally, customer-service engineers should have some mechanical or electronic aptitude. The job requires ongoing education to keep up with rapid changes and new equipment, but just as important are people skills. A service engineer must enjoy working with a diverse group of people.

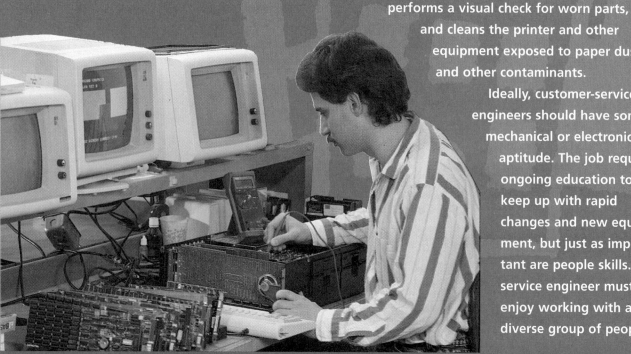

figure 20

CAD software is used to design items to be manufactured; CAM and CIM software automates the manufacturing processes based on the final design of the CAD system.

grams that make multitudes of computations related to product performance. **CAM** refers to the use of computer data to operate tools, such as drilling machines, to manufacturing a product. Although CAD and CAM may be used independently, they are frequently integrated so that the result of the design phase is used to automatically produce a part or product.

Recently, many of the obstacles to three-dimensional CAD have been overcome with new technologies. High-power, low-cost computers with special graphics processors have eliminated the performance problems in generating three-dimensional graphic designs. Soon, virtually all CAD software will be capable of generating dynamic and relational three-dimensional models.

As an example, consider the process of replacing a human hip joint with an artificial joint. Previously, artificial joints came in several standard sizes, with the surgeon selecting the size closest to the needs of the patient. With the use of CAD/CAM, the process has changed. Now, a designer working with CAD designs a joint tailored exactly to the needs of the patient—exactly the right size and with exactly the right direction and range of movement. Then, automated machines in the CAM phase take over, using the output of the CAD program to produce the joint exactly to the designer's dimensions (figure 20).

Computer-integrated manufacturing, or **CIM**, refers to the process of integrating computers throughout a manufacturing plant. Much pioneering work in this area has resulted in the development of a standard called the

Manufacturing Automation Protocol (MAP) that links all the computers together so they can communicate with each other. A factory may have many integrated computers being controlled by MAP communications.

Expert Systems

Software designed to assist in the application of a known body of knowledge is known as an expert system. For example, software exists that can help a doctor diagnose illnesses (figure 21). All expert systems operate in a similar fashion in that they quantify the knowledge of experts and make that knowledge available to help other persons solve problems. Great amounts of time are consumed in the development of expert systems, amassing the knowledge various persons have accumulated over years in the practice of their professions. Expert systems are software packages that enable the computer to make recommendations about courses of action to be taken. In some cases, the actions are taken automatically by the computer system; in others, the computer makes recommendations that humans can decide whether or not to follow.

Many persons use the terms *expert systems* and *artificial intelligence* interchangeably. The term **artificial intelligence**, for the most part, seems to give computers more credit than they presently deserve. It implies that computers can think. That is not the case, even though expert systems are the closest anyone has yet come to making computers think.

Rather than making computers think, however, expert systems software allows the computer to analyze complex conditions. That is, under certain combinations of conditions, one course of action will be recommended, while under other combinations of conditions, other courses of action will be recommended. This process is designed to accept numerous inputs of data and to produce the most logical recommendation as output. To prepare expert systems, developers glean everything they can from acknowledged experts in the field for which the system is being developed. The program then becomes an automated version of the experts' knowledge. Specialized programming languages have been designed to help in the development of expert systems.

figure 21

Expert systems can help a doctor diagnose a medical problem.

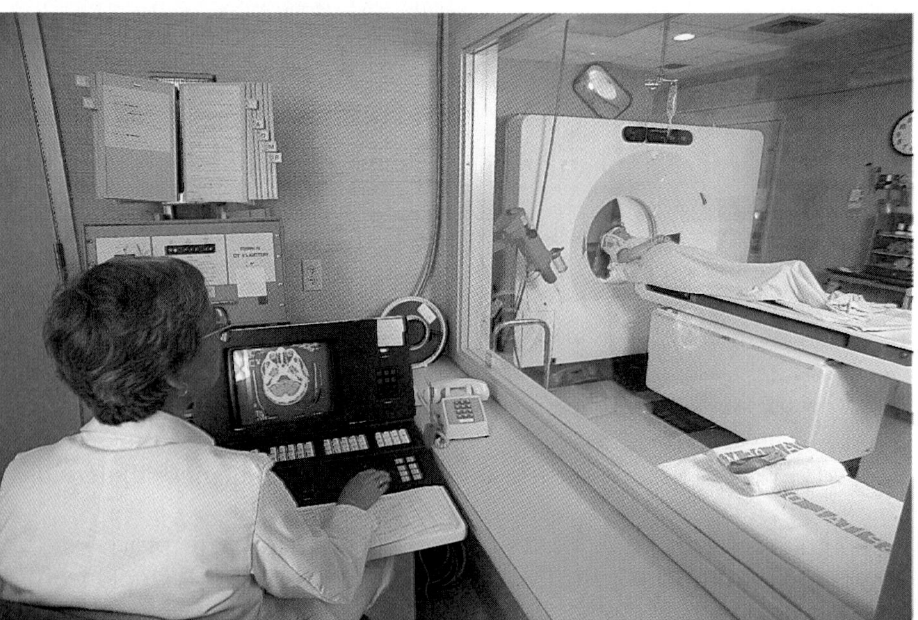

Expert systems have been developed for a wide range of applications. One of the earliest was a medical diagnosis program that suggested possible diseases after analyzing the patient's symptoms. Among many other systems are ones that suggest the most likely places to drill for oil, the kind of packaging to use for a new product, and the likely cause of problems in a computer system.

Guidelines for Acquiring Application Software

Many computer users purchase application software by the "seat-of-the-pants" method or on the recommendation of someone else who is using a particular program. However, there are several guidelines that can help make the selection and purchase more satisfactory.

Establishing Needs

The first step in selecting any software should be to establish the need to computerize the anticipated application. For example, scheduling the meeting room in a small restaurant can be done through the use of a paper calendar or computer software. In all likelihood, scheduling will be easier (as well as much less expensive) if the paper calendar is used. Thus, before looking for a computer program to perform a function, it is wise to examine the procedure itself. Then, if it appears that computerization is wise, the search for the ideal software should begin.

Once it is determined that computerization will improve the completion of a particular operating function of a business, the exact requirements to be met by the software can be planned. Typically, this will take the form of deciding what output the software has to produce, then determining the input and processing necessary to generate that output. When the required capabilities of the software have been determined, the search for the most suitable software can begin.

If the functions to be performed by the software are intended to create a strategic advantage for the business, it may be possible to develop the software around a commercially available piece of software, such as a database program or a project manager program. Frequently, however, there is no choice with strategic programs but to have them custom written.

Performance

Software performance primarily means two things. First, the software must be capable of doing all of the things expected of it. If the necessary functions cannot be handled, a software package should be avoided regardless of its price. Once it is verified that the desired functions are available in a piece of software, performance then refers to the speed and accuracy with which functions are performed. One package may perform functions slowly and clumsily, while another performs them with speed and grace. It is important to remember, however, that there can be many possible combinations of speed and accuracy (or the lack thereof). A program that performs some functions very nicely may perform others very poorly.

Documentation

If the user cannot figure out how to use a particular application program, that program has no value. Therefore, it is important that the chosen software be well documented. The software industry has come a long way from the days when users' manuals were vague, jargon-filled books written hurriedly by programmers. Most software now has readable, easily understood manuals; however, there are still wide variations in quality. In addition to well-written manuals, a variety of different help systems are available that can be referenced while the software is in use. For example, help screens that provide general information about the operation of the software from topical or indexed lists are commonly provided (figure 22). Content-sensitive help windows may be accessed while a specific menu command, data field, and so on is selected that provides detail information about the specific item(s) selected. Some software uses balloon help; where the user gets specific help on a feature or function from dialog that appears within a balloon shaped outline as the pointer is moved around the display screen. Readme files (files that can be accessed with any word processor) that include last-minute changes to printed documentation or specific installation instructions for different computer or network systems may also be provided on the software disk.

figure 22

Application help screens provide quick access to operating instructions.

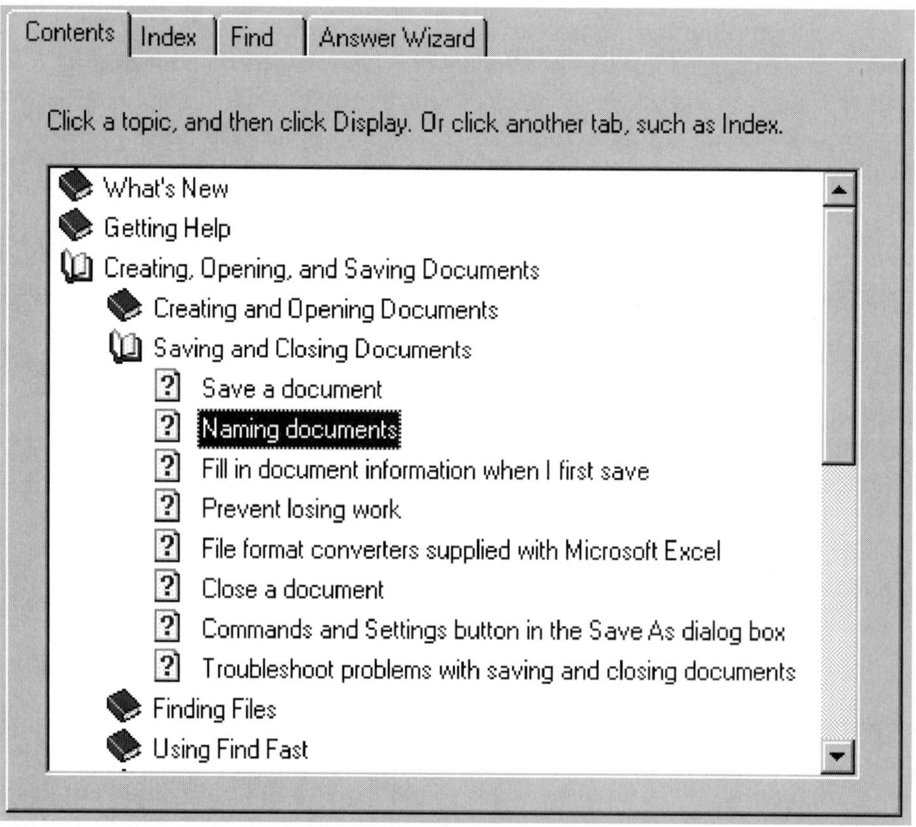

When evaluating the documentation of a program, several criteria can be examined. For example, the following items can help determine the quality of documentation:

1. Does the manual have a complete table of contents?
2. Does the manual have a complete index, or are topics missing? (For example, in word processing, moving a block of text is a common operation and should certainly be included in the index.)
3. Are there illustrations and accompanying explanation for each dialog box and menu?
4. Does the manual proceed from simple to complex?
5. If the manual is for an upgraded version of the software, does it include instructions that list new and modified features? (That way, users who upgrade to a newer version will not have to sift through the entire manual just to find what is new and different.)
6. Does the manual include a "troubleshooting" section or a section that lists frequently asked questions?
7. Are installation instructions included? Are they easy to follow?
8. Is the manual easy to read and understand by the person using the software?
9. Does the software provide help screens, windows, or balloons that can be viewed during program execution?

Ease of Learning

Time spent by employees learning to use new software is unproductive time. The faster they learn the program and return to active work, the more productive they will be. Therefore, the ease with which a new software package can be learned should be considered.

Do It!

1. Try using a desktop accessory program. Identify the capabilities of the software. Discuss with your classmates how this accessory software can make work easier, more productive, or more convenient.

2. Access a paint and draw, graphic presentation, or any other software capable of generating graphic images or charts. Use the software (and printer, if available) to display a graphic image produced by this software. The graphic image may be existing art or data or a simple drawing that you create.

3. If a friend asks your opinion about how to go about choosing a math tutoring program to buy for his or her computer at home, what advice would you offer?

Ethics

Software Copyright

The Software Act of 1980 made programs copyrightable as long as there is even a minimal amount of creativity. As a matter of fact, a program is also copyrightable if it is stored in the computer's memory rather than on paper.

Ideas cannot be copyrighted. Copyright law protects only the words, images, sounds, and so on that an author uses to express ideas. Authors are free to express the same ideas in their own way. That is why there are many different word processors, databases, and spreadsheets on the market. The idea of a word processor, database, and spreadsheet cannot be copyrighted. However, the courts have found the following elements to be copyrightable expressions of ideas: 1) source code and object code; 2) flowcharts; 3) sequence, structure, and organization of a program; 4) structure of a program's audiovisual displays; and 5) menu structure, including what appears in the menu.

Copyright is the right to prohibit other people from making copies. This is known as an exclusive right to reproduce the work. Copyright involves five exclusive rights: 1) the exclusive right to make copies, 2) the exclusive right to distribute copies to the public, 3) the exclusive right to prepare derivative works, 4) the exclusive right to perform the work in public (applies mainly to plays, dances, and so on), and 5) the exclusive right to display the work in public.

The Software Act allows the person who purchases a software product to make a backup copy—as long as it is for archival purposes only. The archive copy cannot be given to another person for his or her use. Only the original and backup (not subsequent sales or rental) can be given away, sold, lent, or rented to others as long as the original purchaser does not retain a copy. Although the copyright owner has the exclusive right to distribute copies of the software, that right only applies to the first sale of any particular copy. That is, if you buy a copyrighted book, you may give your book to a friend or sell it to someone else. The copyright owner does not have the right to control resales of the first copy.

Any program that comes into existence in a tangible medium (source and object code, flowchart, stored on a disk, and so on) are copyright protected. Programs do not have to be registrated to be copyright protected, although it is a good idea. The reason that programs are registered is for protection *before* infringements take place. The court can award up to $100,000 per infringed work, called statutory damages, and impose other actions to stop the illegal copyright activities.

Many software packages provide automated tutorials (also called coaches) to help the user learn specific tasks quickly. These tutorials often take the user on a "tour" of the program to teach operational tasks and illustrate what is available or new in upgrades. Software features called wizards may also be provided that enable the user to perform common tasks by simply responding to questions.

Training

If a software package is at all complex, training will be required. It is important, therefore, to determine before the purchase of a package what training is available. Are classes available from the vendor of the software? Does a local technical school or college conduct classes?

Many larger companies have in-house software trainers that conduct training seminars for their employees. Also, individuals or user groups familiar with the software may be contacted (within a company or through e-mail, bulletin board systems, and so on) who are willing to share helpful tips that are specific to the software package.

Availability When Needed

Many software packages are announced and even advertised before they are ready for delivery to customers. These software packages are sometimes referred to as vapor ware. At times, demonstration packages may be available before the product is finished. Though it seems an obvious point, it should be verified that the product will be available when needed.

Consider the reputation of the software company when waiting for announced software. Do you think the company will be around in the future and continue to support the product? Check to see if there may already be a product on the market that meets your needs or even outperforms the new product you are waiting for.

Value

After the items discussed previously have been considered, there may be several software packages still under consideration. At this point, price can become the determining factor. Simply put, which of the qualified programs offers the needed capabilities at the lowest cost?

Summary

Application software is software designed to meet a particular computing need of the user.

■ Application software specially written for the use of a designated organization or individual is known as custom application software.

■ Custom application software is developed in-house or under contract with an outside vendor.

■ Custom application software may meet user needs exactly, provide a strategic advantage, use system resources more efficiently, execute faster, and be changed to meet changing conditions.

■ Custom application software may require lengthy development time, require developmental resources that are not available, be expensive to develop, have cost overruns, and be expensive to upgrade and maintain.

■ Commercial application software is application software that is created by a developer for sale to various users.

■ Commercial application software is immediately available, costs less, and may be more reliable.

■ Commercial application software may not be an exact match for needs, require more system resources, execute more slowly, and not be adaptable to changing needs.

■ Commercial application software can be obtained from computer stores, mail-order distributors, manufacturers, or vertical market sources.

■ Integrated software combines the functions of two or more kinds of software.

■ Financial software is used to maintain the financial records of a business, to send bills to customers and keep records of what they owe, to assist management in decision-making, control inventory, prepare paychecks, pay bills, as well as many other purposes.

■ Productivity management software helps to plan the steps in a complex project and then track the completion of those steps according to the designated time schedule.

■ Computer-assisted instruction (CAI) has combined the fascination and excitement of a game with lessons to teach virtually any subject.

■ A wide array of software is available for the in-home computer user.

■ Entertainment software manufacturers have turned to laser-disk technology to greatly increase the player's involvement and keep gaming software interesting.

Summary

- Simulation software duplicates or models conditions that are likely to occur in a real-world environment.
- Desktop tools (accessories) refers to software designed to make day-to-day work and personal activities easier in a practical way.
- Common desktop accessory software includes calculators, card file/phone directory/dialers, calendars, and notepads.
- Paint and draw software is used to create and edit simple to elaborate drawings.
- Many software programs available today have the capability to produce graphs and charts from data they access.
- While computer-aided drafting (CAD) aids in the design or drafting of an object, computer-aided manufacturing (CAM) uses CAD's output to actually produce the product that was designed.
- Computer-integrated manufacturing (CIM) integrates computers into the manufacturing process.
- Computer-aided drafting/computer-aided manufacturing (CAD/CAM) software is used first to assist engineers in designing products and then to control machinery that manufactures the designed products.
- Expert systems assist in the application of a known body of knowledge to the solution of problems. Expert systems synthesize the knowledge from known experts in a field and apply that knowledge to computer solution of problems.
- The need to computerize an application should be established before beginning a software selection process.
- The most important criterion in selecting application software is performance—whether the product can do the job, and how well it can do it.
- Documentation, ease of learning, and availability of training should be considered when evaluating software.
- When choosing among several software packages that are satisfactory in all other respects, price becomes the determining factor.

The following key terms were defined in this module. For each of the following terms, write on a separate piece of paper the number of the definition followed by the letter of the appropriate term.

Terms

A. personal finance software

B. custom application software

C. expert system

D. commercial software

E. graphs and charts

F. productivity management

G. artificial intelligence

H. computer-aided design (CAD)

I. computer-aided manufacturing (CAM)

J. computer-integrated manufacturing (CIM)

K. desktop accessories

L. financial software

M. integrated software

N. computer-assisted instruction

O. simulation software

Definitions

1 software specially written to meet the needs of an organization or individual

2 software created by a developer for sale to various users

3 a term given to software that combines the functions of two or more kinds of software

4 software used to maintain the records of a business, for sending bills to customers and keeping records of what they owe, to assist management in decision-making, control inventory, prepare paychecks, pay bills, as well as many other purposes

5 software designed for individuals to use on their own home computer systems to keep track of their finances

6 software that is used to help plan and track the sequence of activities necessary to complete a complex project

Matching

7 a term given to educational software that is used to teach students

8 software that duplicates or models conditions that are likely to occur in a real-world environment

9 a name applied to a classification of computer software designed to make day-to-day work and personal activities a little easier in a practical way

10 a type of presentation that is commonly used to improve communications, track sales, monitor production, identify trends, and make forecasts for a wide variety of applications in many different industries

11 the process of using graphic computer programs to assist in the design of a product

12 the use of computer data to operate tools, such as drilling machines, to manufacture a product

13 the process of integrating computers throughout a manufacturing plant

14 a name given to software designed to assist in the application of a known body of knowledge

15 term(s) used interchangeably with expert systems that imply that computers can think

Review

1. Why is application software needed? (Obj. 1)
2. What is the primary difference between custom software and commercial software? (Obj. 1)
3. What are the advantages of custom application software? (Obj. 1)
4. What are the disadvantages of custom application software? (Obj. 1)
5. What are the advantages of commercial application software? (Obj 1)
6. What are the disadvantages of commercial application software? (Obj. 1)
7. What is an advantage of purchasing software from a computer store? (Obj. 1)
8. What is an advantage of purchasing software by mail order? What is a disadvantage? (Obj. 1)
9. What type of software is more likely to be sold by representatives employed by the manufacturer? (Obj. 1)
10. What is the primary advantage of software obtained through vertical market sources? (Obj. 1)
11. List and explain the advantages and disadvantages of integrated software. (Obj. 2)
12. List at least four uses of financial application software. (Obj. 3)
13. What is the purpose of productivity management software? (Obj. 4)
14. Explain why the computer has become a valuable educational tool. (Obj. 5)
15. What technologies have game software developers turned to in an effort to increase realism and keep the player's interest? (Obj. 7)
16. What is desktop tools (accessory) software? (Obj. 8)
17. What is the purpose of paint and draw software? (Obj. 9)
18. What is CAD/CAM/CIM software? (Obj. 10)
19. What is expert system software? (Obj. 11)
20. What is the first evaluation that should be made when selecting computer software for an application? (Obj. 12)

Activities

1 *Writing* A friend who has never used a desktop accessory program before has asked you to explain why this software is so popular. Open and load one of the desktop accessory programs discussed in this text, or use another desktop tool with which you are familiar. Use this program as an example, and point out several of the features that your friend should know about. Print any data that you may have entered into the desktop tool during your demonstration, and save the data to your data disk or directory/folder (recommend a file name of XXXAA-A, where *XXX* is your initials). Prepare a list highlighting what you demonstrated for your friend.

2 *Math* Choose a business, industry, or vocation that uses computers for mathematic applications. Research newspaper articles and journals, and check with your library to find information regarding the mathematic applications used by your chosen business, industry, or vocation. As an alternative, and if your school uses computer-assisted math software, find out what the software does and how it is used to help students learn mathematics. Report your findings.

3 *Science* The use of computers and electronic diagnostic instruments have provided physicians views of the human body that were not possible before. Computers are used to analyze x-rays and produce three-dimensional, animated views of the function of internal organs. Check with your library, newspaper, magazine, or other journals to obtain an article about a computer application in the field of medicine. As an alternative, interview a pharmacist, nurse, or anyone associated with the field of medicine to obtain this information. Report your findings.

4 *Global* Amassing large volumes of knowledge is an essential element of expert systems. Divide into teams with four students per team. Each team should identify at least two specific areas in which an expert system could have global implications. For example, explain how a vast amount of knowledge in a medical expert system could benefit medical-care facilities in countries that do not have a good health-care system. Present your team's results to the class.

5 *Teamwork* In this activity, you will participate in a team competition dealing with the use of card file/phone directory, calendar, or notepad desktop accessory software. The purpose of this activity is to find the best way(s) to use these accessories. Divide into teams with four students per team. Each team should choose one of the above desktop accessory programs that is currently available on a computer to which at least one member has access. The team members should agree on how their chosen accessory is to be used, then each team member should be responsible for a part of the project. One possible division of the responsibilities is as follows:

Activities

Student 1: Gather the data to be inputted into the chosen accessory software.

Student 2: Enter the data prepared by Student 1 into the computer.

Student 3: Run the accessory software, and generate output that illustrates how the team has chosen to use the accessory software. Save the data to a data disk or directory/folder (recommend a file name of XXXAA-B, where *XXX* is your initials).

Student 4: Present your team's accessory application to the class.

The winner of the competition is the team chosen by a majority vote of the other teams.

6 *Speaking* Visit a local computer installation, school computer laboratory, or computer store that has CD-ROM hardware and software available. Watch the CD-ROM–based software operate. Make notes describing the purpose of the application and what you observe when you watch it execute. Give a 2- to 4-minute presentation to your class based on the content of your notes. Have a printout generated by the application (if available) or literature regarding the application to pass around the class if possible.

7 *Ethics* A journalist, knowledgeable in the use of computer graphics, uses a paint and draw program to retouch a photograph of a suspected criminal to make the suspect appear mean and angry. The journalist then submits the altered photo to the editor to be included on the front page of the local newspaper. Do you think that what the journalist did was ethical, unethical, or an act that could be considered computer crime? Justify your choice.

8 *Internet* Access the Internet, and use your search engine to find out the current weather conditions of a major city in another country. Use terms such as WEATHER, LONDON, MOSCOW, and so on in your search. Report your findings.

Systems Analysis & Design

Overview

It is said that the human race's knowledge is doubling every 5 to 10 years, and that this rate of knowledge accumulation is accelerating. Coupled with the human race's thrust for new knowledge, increased research and development have contributed to this rate of expansion and fueled an accelerated pace of technologic improvement. One only needs to look around the environment (home, town or city, school) to see the many changes brought about by technology over the past few years. Rapid advances in technology have also affected how our country's businesses and industries function, causing them to become more complex and dependent on more information to be competitive.

This module discusses procedures and techniques that can help develop computer systems that address the changes in our environment, businesses, and industries. How computer systems are developed and how these systems must change to keep pace with their surroundings are also examined.

Objectives

1. Understand why systems must change to keep pace with our rapidly changing environment.
2. Describe a computer system's life cycle.
3. Explain and describe the tasks associated with systems analysis.
4. Explain and describe the tasks associated with systems design.
5. Explain and describe the tasks associated with software acquisition and testing.
6. Explain and describe the tasks associated with implementation.
7. Explain the purpose of evaluation and maintenance.
8. Identify the factors that cause systems to require updating or become obsolete.

Why Systems Must Change

The term **system**, as used in this module, can be defined as related devices or procedures that function together to achieve a common goal or objective (figure 1). For example, the picture tube, tuners, antenna, and electronic components of a TV all functioning together compose a system called a television set. The workers, machines, buildings, and materials of a factory that work together to produce goods that can be sold is a system. The procedures that an accountant performs when working with journals, ledgers, computers, and other people to produce financial reports for a company can be called an accounting system.

figure 1

Systems encompass such diverse areas as business and industry.

The television set has undergone many changes during the past four decades. It is a system that is constantly being perfected and changed to reflect technologic advances in the electronic industry. A factory may hire new employees, other employees may retire, newer and more sophisticated machines may be brought in to replace older machines, new buildings may be built or old ones renovated, and the materials that were once used to produce a product may be changed. All or any of these changes affect the way in which the factory must go about meeting its goal of producing a product. The procedures an accountant performs can also change drastically if the company for which he or she is working grows, acquires additional businesses, or provides additional services. External factors such as changes in tax laws may affect accounting rules, methods, and procedures.

In a world of accelerated accumulation of human knowledge, technologic improvement, and the human race's thrust to improve its work and personal environment, there is only one constant: change. No one can accurately predict what inventions will make our world and life better, but one can be assured that change will continue at an accelerated pace. Improved systems and procedures will be required to cope with these changes.

The computer is a device that can be used to help keep pace with the rapidly changing environment. As discussed in previous modules, there have been several advances in computer technology that enable the computer to handle more sophisticated applications and store more data than in the past. Despite recent advances in hardware and software, however there is still a lack of "brainware." That is, today's computers are capable of doing much more than humans have been able to program them to do. It is estimated that the capabilities of today's computers are 5 years ahead of our abilities to use them to their potential. Nonetheless, the computer is considered to be one of the most powerful tools of this century.

The System Life Cycle

Just as changes must be made to help humans keep pace with their environment, so must changes be made to computer systems for them to keep up with technologic advances. Once a computer program is written, it does not automatically change in accordance with the tasks it is expected to perform. Unless it is given new instructions, a computer will process data and produce reports in the same way, year after year. As the needs of businesses or industries change or technologic improvements are made, so must the software be changed to keep pace and avoid becoming obsolete. Therefore, computer systems have what is referred to as a system life cycle. A computer's **system life cycle** can be defined as the period of time in which a given computer system's usefulness to perform a given task is measured.

Most computer systems are developed with the recognition that change is constantly occurring and must be dealt with within the system life cycle to produce information that is current and useful. To accomplish this, a systematic, step-by-step procedure for system development can be established. This procedure can be broken into five different tasks or stages of development: analysis, design, acquisition and testing, implementation, and evaluation and maintenance. After all of the stages in the development process are complete and the system is up and running, the system must be updated as necessary to prolong its life cycle of usefulness. Figure 2 illustrates each stage of system development and the changes that require the system to be updated during its system life cycle.

In the remainder of this module, it will become evident how each stage of system development is performed and leads to a comprehensive computer system. Next, you will learn how a system, once developed, is periodically updated to increase its life cycle and remain an effective information resource for its users.

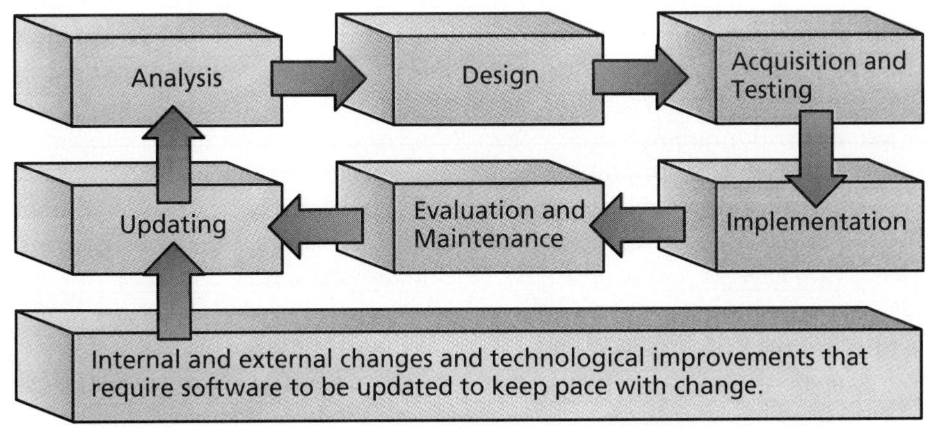

figure 2

The system life cycle can be broken into various stages of development.

Careers

Systems Analyst

Interested in the design and development of computer system software? Consider a career as a systems analyst—the link between the users of the computer system and the technical personnel who actually develop and install the system. The primary role of the systems analyst is the design and creation of an information-processing system. The systems analyst works under the supervision of the manager of the computer center (also commonly referred to as the manager of information processing) or a project leader.

Ideally, a systems analyst needs a strong background in business as well as in the technical aspects of computer systems and programming. A bachelor's degree is usually required; this degree may be in information systems, computer science, or in a related academic program that emphasizes a broad business-management background. The systems analyst should know at least one programming language and be familiar with database systems.

It takes more than the right academic background to succeed as a systems analyst. A keen interest in solving problems and an ability to think logically are mandatory. What's more, a creative mind is a must to see new ways of doing things. The ability to compare costs of several different options for solving problems—with and without a computer—is necessary.

In addition, the systems analyst must be able to communicate well with users to plan a successful system, and once the system is planned, additional communication is needed as the users become familiar with the system. The system analyst should be able to communicate effectively with others—both verbally and in writing—without resorting to computer jargon.

Opportunities for advancement are great. A systems analyst who wishes to advance into management positions within the company should acquire a solid foundation in business administration and a broad general knowledge of the operation of the company.

Stages of System Development

The five stages of analysis, design, acquisition and testing, implementation, and evaluation and maintenance comprise a model that can be used as a systematic approach to the development of computer systems. Because the operation of many organizations is so complex, the task of developing a new computer system must involve a carefully thought-out plan or approach. The five stages of the system development model can be used to break down such a task into meaningful and effective information flows; these effective information flows in turn can be used by management, decision-makers, and production personnel to more efficiently meet their company's objectives and goals. The individual who is responsible for the overall system development is called a systems analyst. The **systems analyst** acts as a link between the users of the system and the technical personnel who actually develop and install the system (figure 3). The systems analyst often has expertise in the area being considered for development as well as a technical knowledge of the computer industry.

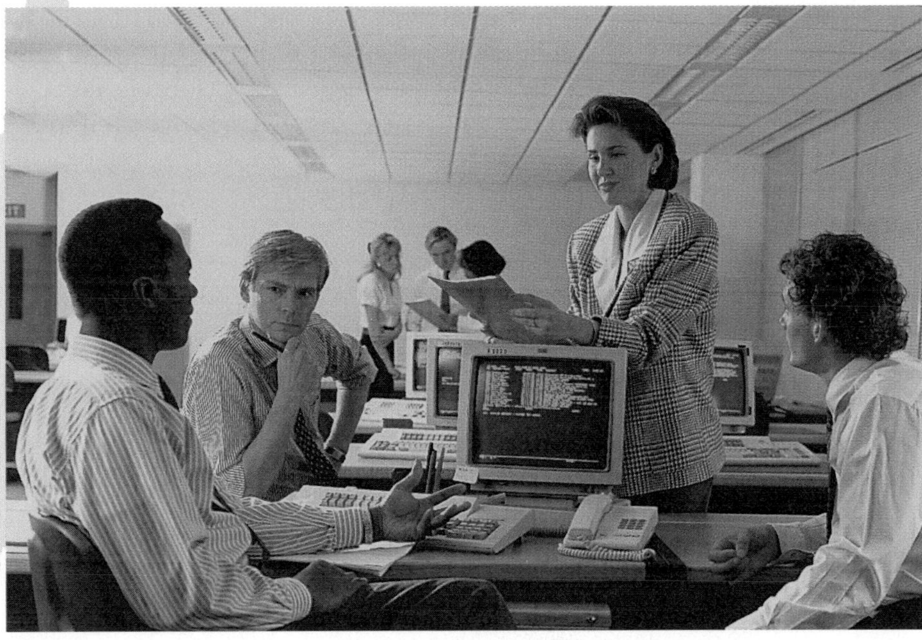

figure 3

The systems analyst acts as a link between the users of the system and the technical personnel who actually develop and install the system.

Analysis

The first stage of system development is the systems analysis stage. In this stage, the systems analyst must perform four separate tasks. First, a definitive and precise statement of the problem or reason for the development must be stated. Second, measurable objectives of what the system is to accomplish must be stated. Third, both the sources of information and the actual information that is needed to meet the system's objectives must be identified. Finally, an analysis report must be prepared that states the findings of this analysis stage to management.

Statement of the problem Often, the reason for developing a new computer system is to meet a specific need of the organization. For example, a business may have grown to a size where it is no longer efficient to produce its employees' payroll checks and records manually. At the same time, and because personnel records contain similar information about each employee, the personnel files could be integrated with the payroll files. The statement of the problem in this example could be as follows: "The purpose of the systems analysis study is to determine the feasibility of developing an integrated payroll/personnel information system."

Another reason for developing a new computer system occurs when an organization's existing computer system becomes obsolete from the availability of newer, faster, and less costly computer hardware. Management may decide to explore the possibility of replacing the old computer system with a newer system. Because the new system is not compatible with the existing system, the existing software must be rewritten. Therefore, the newly rewritten software should be developed to take advantage of the new system's capabilities while at the same time addressing additional user needs that the new hardware is capable of meeting. The statement of this problem could be expressed as follows: "The purpose of the systems analysis study is to determine the feasibility of upgrading the organization's existing hardware and information system software."

Measurable objectives Whether the system being developed is a new system or a replacement of an obsolete system, its objectives should be stated in measurable terms. The reason for doing this at this stage is to help define more precisely what the system is to do and how efficiently it is to perform its tasks. Later, during the review stage, these initial objectives will be compared with actual system performance; based on the results, the new system may be accepted for meeting the stated objectives, fine-tuned, or rejected for failure to perform as expected.

An example of measurable objectives for the company seeking an integrated payroll/personnel information system may include the following:

1. The integrated payroll/personnel information system must be able to produce and maintain internal and external government reporting information with at least a 97% accuracy rate.

2. The integrated payroll/personnel information system must be able to produce paychecks and complete payroll processing for 500 employees within 1 hour after all pay-period data has been entered into the system.

3. The integrated payroll/personnel information system must accurately maintain personnel and employee data on a random-access device capable of accessing any employee's record within 1 to 3 seconds.

4. The integrated payroll/personnel information system must be capable of producing personnel and payroll reports in various sequences based on the categories of employee name/number, department, classification, date, and pay history for 500 employees within 5 minutes of program execution.

Sources and information identification The individuals who will supply the data and use the informational output of the system being analyzed must be identified. It is from these individuals that existing and new data needed in the system will be obtained. Interviews should be conducted with individuals within as well as outside the organization (government agencies, suppliers, customers) to find out what their informational requirements are. In addition, existing reports and data files should be examined to make sure that the new system will meet existing information requirements.

A Data Element Identification form, similar to the one shown in figure 4, can be used to record the data fields (called data elements). This document acts as a form of control to ensure that all data elements required to meet the systems objectives have been identified. Also, it helps to ensure that no data elements are listed twice. Notice the two columns to the right side of the document (Maximum Size and Frequency). These columns indicate the maximum size of the element and the frequency of use (times per week). The purpose of the Maximum-Size-of-Element column is to assist in estimating the size of the record that must be stored for each employee and, in turn, the total storage capacity required of the system. The purpose of the frequency-of-use column is to assist in arranging the data items that are referenced the most frequently first. This consideration in the arrangement of the elements within the data file can significantly reduce the time (access time) it takes the computer to locate any given data element in a database system.

DATA ELEMENT IDENTIFICATION CONTROL FORM		
Data Element Name	Maximum Size	Frequency Per Week
Employee Number	6	60
Employee Name	25	32
Employee Classification (Exempt or Nonexempt)	1	15

figure 4

A Data Element Identification form helps to ensure that all data elements required to meet the system's informational objectives have been identified.

Analysis report After stating the problem, stating the measurable objectives, and identifying the sources and data elements required to meet the objectives and produce the desired information, the system analyst prepares the **analysis report**. This report should contain each of the items mentioned plus an explanation of the present system (whether automated or manual), the procedures used, and any problems that must be overcome in a new system. In addition, an estimate of the resources (equipment, personnel, money, time) required to develop the new system should be specified.

After the analysis report is prepared, it is presented to management by the systems analyst. If management decides to proceed after reviewing the analysis report, stage 2 of the system development procedure—design—can begin. If, however, management determines that the cost of the new system is too great for the benefits derived, or for some reason the system is no longer feasible, the system development project is stopped. Management's decision to continue or stop the process after the analysis stage is critical. If it is determined to continue, hundreds of thousands of dollars may be committed to the development of the new system.

Design

The second stage of systems development is the detailed design stage. In this stage, the systems analyst has four major tasks to perform. First, a systems design flowchart must be prepared; this flowchart shows each of the major components that comprise the system and how these components interact with each other. Second, several viable alternative designs that meet the stated objectives should be developed within the organizational constraints. Third, a feasibility analysis study weighing the costs to benefits derived, time, effort, and so on must be performed for each of the viable alternatives. Finally, the systems design report must be prepared, which among other things recommends the best alternative.

Systems design flowchart One of the most useful tools of the systems analyst is a flowchart template, similar to that shown in figure 5. Symbols on the flowchart template represent various input/output devices and processing

figure 5

A flowchart template contains symbols that represent various input/output and processing operations.

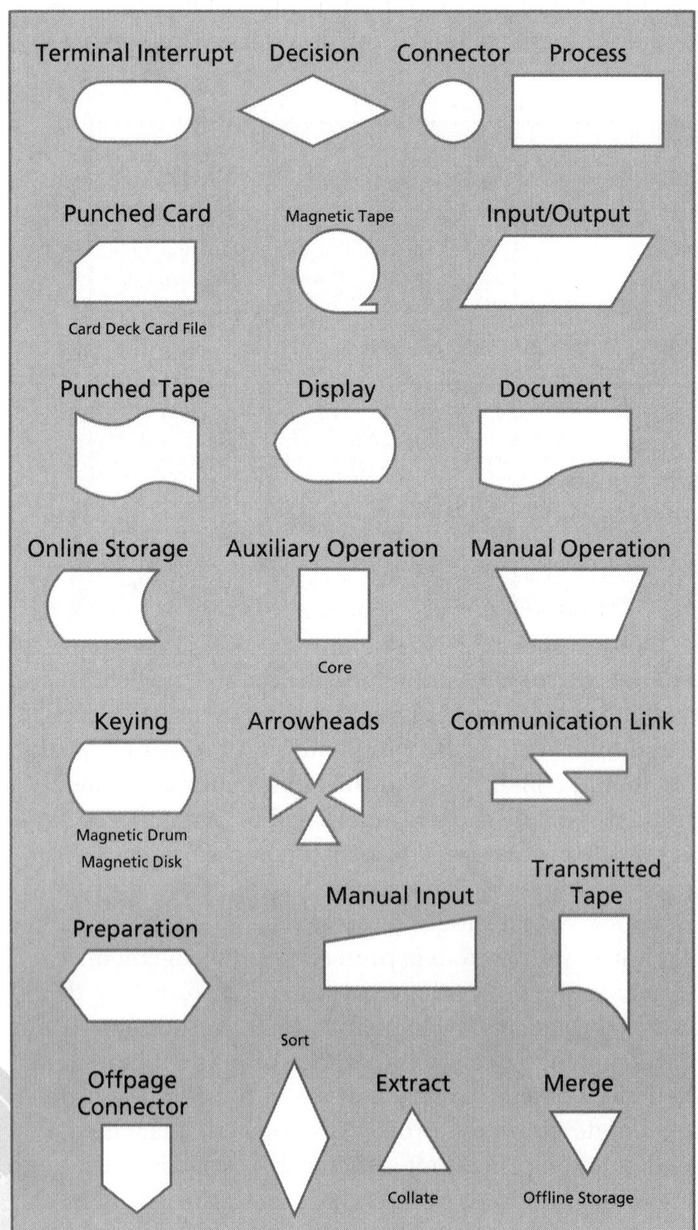

operations. The analyst uses the symbols on this tool to draw a diagram that depicts what components are involved in the system and how each of these components interact with each other. For example, the system flowchart for the integrated payroll/personnel system discussed previously may be depicted as shown in figure 6.

Note that both the personnel and payroll departments are the primary users of this system. Each department submits data to the computer, which in turn accesses and updates a database containing the payroll and personnel data stored on disk. From the data submitted and the data stored in the computer's database, each department can perform inquiries as needed to obtain valuable information about any employee in the organization. Also, each department can obtain the various reports that it requires. The analyst has used the appropriate symbols of the flowchart template to denote each component involved in the system and the directional flow of data and information.

After the **systems design flowchart** is complete, it becomes the model by which the analyst will develop the various ways, or alternatives, of achieving what is depicted. The general design of the entire system must be reflected in this model. The individuals (or departments) responsible for keeping the data up to date and the information the system must generate should be shown. The analyst must be careful not to overlook others, such as management and coworkers in other departments, who could also benefit from the system.

Alternative designs The way in which an organization is structured has a great influence on how the system is designed. For example, if all of the component parts (individuals, users, equipment, and so on) are located within the same building, the design will be different than if the component parts were spread across great distances. Also, the way in which the company is managed, the education and expertise of its employees, the type of business or products that are produced, and the technology of the computer equipment available all contribute to the system design. In most organizations, management will impose constraints that also affect the design. These constraints may include a fixed budget to which the new system must adhere, the number of personnel that can work on its development, or a time frame by which the new system must be operational.

There are often several ways to design a system to meet given objectives within established constraints. The analyst must use her or his creativity and knowledge to develop these alternative designs. In putting together each design, the analyst must consider many different variables. These variables include considerations such as:

1. Interactions of the personnel who will be the users of the system.
2. Capabilities and capacities of the computer hardware.
3. New technologic improvements in equipment.
4. Communications (if any) to be used.
5. Number of devices on a network.
6. Speed and types of input/output devices.
7. Capabilities and capacities of a database.

FLOWCHARTING TEMPLATE

Symbols are in three groups: (1) BASIC symbols; (2) processing and sequencing symbols related to programming; (3) input/output, communication link, and processing symbols related to systems.

BASIC Symbols

Process — Any processing function; defined operation(s) causing change in value, form, or location of information.

Comment, Annotation — Additional descriptive clarification, comment. (Dotted line extends to symbols as appropriate.)

Input/ Output — General i/o function; information available for processing (input), or recording of processed information (output).

CONNECTOR: Exit to, or entry from, another part of chart.

Special OFFPAGE CONNECTOR for entry to or exit from a page.

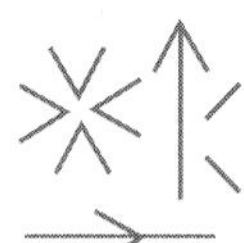

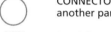

Arrowheads and flowlines: These show the order of operations and direction of data flow. Arrowheads required if path of any flowline is not left-to-right or top-to-bottom.

Symbols Related to PROGRAMMING

A decision operation that determines which of a number of alternative paths to follow.

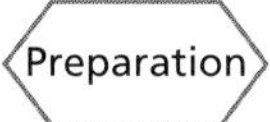

Instruction modification to change program — set a switch, modify an index register, initialize a routine.

Pre-Defined Process — One or more named operations or program steps specified in a subroutine or another set of flowcharts.

Terminal Interrupt — A terminal point in a flowchart — start, stop, halt, delay, or interrupt; may show exit from a closed subroutine.

Parallel Mode: Beginning or end of two or more simultaneous operations.

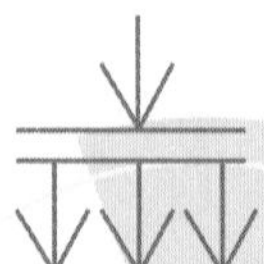

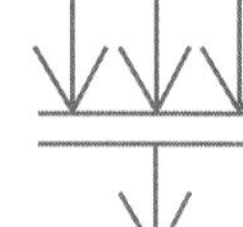

Symbols Related to SYSTEMS

Punched Card — Input/output function in card medium (all varieties):

A collection of punched cards.

Card File — A collection of related punched-card records.

Other specific media: Document

Punched Tape

TRANSMITTAL TAPE: Proof - or adding machine tape or other batch-control info.

Online Storage — Input/output using any kind of online storage — magnetic tape, drum, disk.

Keying — An operation using a key-driven device — such as punching, verifying, typing.

Other specific media for input/output functions:

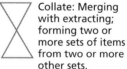

Core

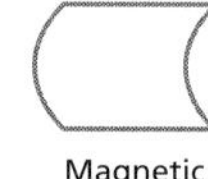

MERGE: Combining two or more sets of items into one set.

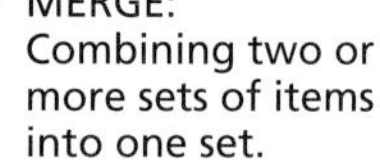

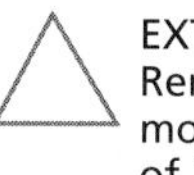

EXTRACT: Removal of one or more specific sets of items from a set.

Collate: Merging with extracting; forming two or more sets of items from two or more other sets.

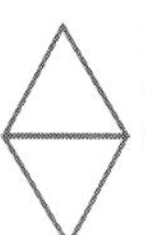

Sort: Arranging a set of items into sequence.

Offline Storage: Storing offline, regardless of recorded medium.

Display — Information display by online indicators, video devices, console printers, plotters, etc.

Manual Input — Information input by online keyboards, switch setting, pushbuttons.

Manual Operation — Any offline process ("at human speed") without mechanical aid.

AUXILIARY OPERATION: Offline performance on equipment not under direct control of central processing unit.

COMMUNICATION LINK: Function of transmitting information by a tele-communications link.

(Vertical, horizontal, or diagonal,with arrowheads for clarity; biderectional flow shown by two opposing arrowheads.)

figure 6

A system flowchart illustrates the interaction of the components involved in the system.

8 Method of collecting and inputting data into the system.

9 Method of processing.

10 Potential expansion of the system.

11 Ease of programming or availability of software.

From the alternatives designed, management will choose the one best-suited for the good of the organization. Therefore, each alternative must be able to meet the objectives established during the analysis stage. To determine if a design is worthy of being presented to management, however, the systems analyst must perform a feasibility analysis on each alternative.

Feasibility analysis A **feasibility analysis** study can be defined as an analysis that is performed on each design alternative to determine whether the alternative meets the given objectives while remaining within the constraints of the organization. Often, cost–benefit considerations are at the heart of the feasibility analysis study. The costs of the development, installation, and ongoing operation of each design must be weighed against the benefits that it could bring to the organization. The costs should include such things as additional personnel who may be required to set up, run, and maintain the system; new hardware; developing or purchasing new software; and educational expenses.

The benefits of each design must also be identified. Benefits, however, are not always as easy to measure as costs are. Benefits can be tangible (measurable) as well as intangible (not measurable). Measurable benefits may include an increase in the number of completed orders, a decrease in the time customers are put on hold, an increase in the percentage of accurately filled orders, more accurate and timely tracking of costs and profits, the reduction of equipment cost if the newer hardware is less expensive, or the reduction of maintenance cost if an obsolete system is replaced. Benefits that are considered intangible include the availability of better information, improved customer service, or more efficient use of employees' time.

In addition to cost–benefit considerations, the feasibility analysis must determine if each design is within the constraints the organization has established. Recall that these constraints may be a budget within which the new system must operate, the number of new employees who can be hired, or the time it will take to get the new system operational.

Systems design report After the feasibility analysis has been completed and the various alternative designs identified as worthy to present to management, the **systems design report** must be prepared. This report brings together the information created during each of the tasks described previously. The systems design report should include the following information:

I. Introduction.
   A. Review of the statement of the problem.
   B. Review of the objectives.
II. Identification of the components involved.
   A. The users.
   B. The computer hardware and software.
III. Systems design summary for each of the design alternatives.
   A. Flowchart and written documentation of the proposed design.
   B. Employees affected, hired, or reassigned.

Trends

Disktop Publishing

You've heard of desktop publishing. Now get ready for the next wave for books: *disktop* publishing. CD-ROM and the floppy disk are spawning a revolution in the publishing industry. Presently, there are currently more than 20 publishing companies producing books of all types on disk instead of paper. These publishers are targeting Macintosh and PC-compatible computer users as their primary markets.

The disktop market offers several unique advantages over a printed book. First, it is much cheaper to publish books on disk than to produce them through traditional print methods. Second, disks can be distributed more cheaply and get into the market faster. Third, disks can be updated in the field and, therefore, remain current much longer. Fourth, publishers can afford to produce material for small or specialized areas where there are a limited number of readers. And finally, this media opens up new avenues of distribution through already established shareware and bulletin board systems that permit downloading.

Disktop publishing is especially appealing for educational institutions. Putting textbooks and other scholarly works on disk lets teachers and students acquire material more quickly, and it makes the material more affordable. Disktop publishing products also contain indexes and text-search capabilities that are invaluable for research and student use.

C. Educational requirements.
D. Time schedule for implementation.
E. Cost–benefit considerations.
F. Other constraint considerations.
G. Conclusions.

IV. Recommendations of the first, second, and third best alternative.

It is from this information that management will make its decision to continue or stop the system development project. If the decision is to proceed, management will select the alternative it believes best meets the needs of the organization within the established constraints. Often, the systems analyst's recommendation is chosen. This is because the analyst has become so familiar with the project, management that realizes he or she is in the best position to recognize the alternative with the most potential.

Do It!

1 Think of an application (at home, school, work, and so on) that could be computerized. Write a definitive and precise one- or two-sentence statement of the problem or reason for the development of the application.

2 Interview a manager at a local company or an administrator at your school. Find out what information is used to make his or her decisions and where the information comes from.

3 If your school uses a computer for student reporting (report cards, attendance, class scheduling, and so on), identify the sources of the information (or individuals) who provide the data the computer needs to produce the various reporting output. If your school does not use a computer for student reporting, identify the individuals who could supply the data to this type of computer system.

Acquisition and Testing

After management has chosen the new system design, the new hardware (if needed) and software must be acquired. Software may be acquired by in-house programming, custom programming, off-the-shelf programs, or a combination of all three. Once the software is obtained (regardless of the method of acquisition), it must be tested to make sure that it works properly and produces accurate output. Finally, the software must be documented for its operational use for those responsible for its future maintenance and updating.

Software acquisition Organizations large enough to have their own programming staff often write their own software. In this environment, the design typically is unique to the organization's needs. Therefore, the software must be created specifically to meet the needs of the systems design that management has chosen. Often, these in-house programs will be written to interface with database or communications software provided by the manufacturer of the computer being used.

Custom programming is the term used when the design specifications are given to a professional programming resource outside of the organization for development (figure 7). It is called custom programming because the software is written specifically to meet the customer's design specifications. This method of software acquisition is used by organizations with either a limited technical staff or a small staff that can support only the operational and maintenance requirements of the system. Rather than hire additional personnel to write the software for a new system, which is a one-time task, the programming is contracted out-of-house to a company that specializes in this type of custom work.

Off-the-shelf software may be used by companies whose needs and objectives can be accomplished by software that already exists. The purchase and use of such software can save hundreds of thousands of dollars in personnel costs, time, and testing. However, users of off-the-shelf software must often adjust their requirements to what the software can or cannot do. Seldom will an organization find prewritten software that does everything according to the company's specifications. Some companies with a limited programming staff will select an off-the-shelf program and modify it to more closely meet their needs. Many small companies that use small computers can find off-the-shelf programs that enable them to effectively and efficiently do all of the processing they require. Because of the increased speed and power of personal computers, they are fast fulfilling the role of larger mainframe computers. Companies are therefore moving applications from the mainframe to the personal computer, thus fueling the development and abundance of personal-computer application software.

figure 7

Software is custom developed to the user's specific needs or acquired from outside sources, such as computer superstores.

Testing After the software is written or acquired from an outside source, it must be tested. The testing of the software must include checking for error-free execution of the software, the accuracy of the output, and the procedures that users must follow to communicate with the system.

After the software is installed in the computer, it must be debugged. (Errors that may cause the program to crash or operate incorrectly are called **bugs**. These bugs must be removed, which is called **debugging**.) In addition, input data must be validated, processing routines that interface with the software must be checked, and output must be checked to make sure that files are updated properly and reports appear in the correct format.

Once the software is operational, the output must be checked for accuracy. This can be accomplished by comparing similar output of the old system (whether computerized or manual) with that created by the new system. Manual calculations should also be performed and compared with that generated by the new software. Remember that a computer can generate incorrect output just as easily as it can generate correct output. It is essential that the new system reports correct and accurate information in which management, decision-makers, and production workers can have confidence.

The testing process must also consider how the entire system interacts and interfaces with its users. These processes include clerical tasks involving data collection and input, data storage, file access, backup, security, and operational procedures of both the users of the system and those operating the computer. To test the entire system, it may be necessary to run the new system in parallel (at the same time) with the existing system. By running the new system in parallel, programs can be debugged, procedures can be smoothed out, and all aspects of the system can be checked.

Documentation Before, during, and after software and hardware testing, documentation should be prepared. This should include two sets of documentation, each addressing a different audience: the users of the system, and the programmer who will be responsible for future updating and maintenance of the software. For example, a user may refer to the documentation when entering data into the system, while a programmer may use the documentation to determine where a program must be changed to reflect new data.

Documentation written for the user of the system should contain an overview of the entire system, a flowchart that shows how each of the component parts interact, and a description of how the system functions. In addition, input forms or screen illustrations, with an explanation of each data field to be entered, should be included. An example of each of the various outputs, with instructions on how to obtain this information, should also be provided.

Documentation written for the programmer who will be responsible for future updating and maintenance of the software should contain program listings, detailed program flowcharts, and key formulas or logic descriptions of each program. Layouts illustrating the data and its location in the input, database files, and printed reports should be included. Procedures for keeping documentation up to date as changes are made over time should also be a part of this documentation.

Implementation

The implementation stage involves two primary tasks: training and educating the personnel who will be the users of the system, and converting from the existing system to the new system (figure 8). The training and educating of personnel must address two different audiences: the users of the system, and the personnel responsible for operating the computer system. Once the personnel are ready to use and operate the system, the conversion from the old to the new system can take place.

Education The key component in any system is knowledgeable, cooperative employees. Even the best of systems is doomed to failure if the individuals who work with it do not know how to use it correctly. To make sure this does not happen, the training and educating of the individuals who will use and operate the system is given a high priority. The systems analyst is usually the

figure 8

Once the system has been installed, the new users of the system must be trained to use it.

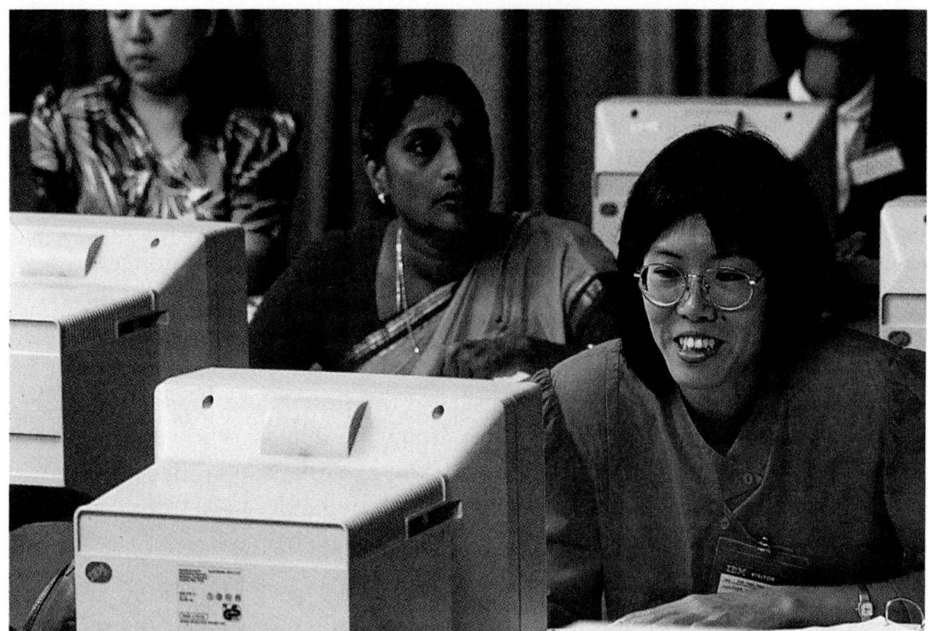

person responsible for training and educating personnel. The analyst must make sure that users of the system know what their individual responsibilities are and how to use the information the system provides. Likewise, the analyst must make sure the personnel who operate and maintain the system know what their responsibilities are and how to perform their jobs.

Education and training may be provided in-house, out-of-house, or both. For example, if new computer hardware is to be used, the computer programmers and operators may attend special classes at the computer manufacturer's educational center. After certain key personnel have completed these courses, they may in turn teach others what they have learned. Users of the system may be given a short, in-house, hands-on course that actually uses the new system during the parallel testing period to learn and become familiar with the new system.

Conversion After the new system has been fully tested and the personnel have been trained, the new system is ready to be installed. This process of installing a new system, or replacing an old system with a new one, is called **conversion**. Several different methods may be used to convert to a new system. One is a direct conversion. That is, at a given, convenient point, the old system is replaced with the new system, and the new one is used from that time on. A second method is to run the new system in parallel with the old system in much the same way that testing is performed. Some organizations prefer to simply extend the test period until it is deemed time to discontinue the old system. A third method is to phase-in the new system. For example, one branch office may be converted to the new system as a trial project before converting the rest of the branch offices. Another example of the phase-in method would be to convert one or several of the major components of the system at a time. In the example of the integrated payroll/personnel system, the payroll system could be implemented first, and the personnel system could follow at a later date.

Regardless of the conversion methods used, careful thought and planning must be given to this task. The personnel affected, how they are affected, and the best time to convert must be considered by the systems analyst to minimize effort and disruption. A smooth conversion can contribute greatly to the users' future cooperation and confidence in the system.

Evaluation and Maintenance

After the implementation stage is completed and the new system is operational, an evaluation of the system should be conducted. The purpose of the evaluation is to determine whether the system has met its stated objectives. The evaluation will also act as a summary of the system development project. An evaluation document to be presented to management should include the following:

1. Whether the new system has adequately addressed the statement of the problem.
2. How the implemented system meets each of the organization's stated objectives.
3. Whether the system has stayed within its given constraints.
4. Whether the costs versus benefits have been realized.
5. How personnel have adapted to the new system.
6. How new information is used.
7. Whether the new system has been accepted by its users.

As a result of this evaluation, minor alterations or modifications may be made to improve the system.

When the evaluation document has been prepared, it should be presented to management to recap the systems development project and to receive management's stamp of approval. Seldom at this stage will management decide to toss aside all of the resources that have been invested in the system, especially with all the checkpoints along the way. If for some reason the system turned out to be a total failure, however, it would be better to discontinue the system and acknowledge the losses than to continue investing in a bad system.

Finally, system updating, necessitated by change, should be an integral part of system design. A system must be designed to recognize change in the form of feedback. **Feedback** can be defined as a continuous monitoring of the system to ensure that its purpose and objectives are being met. Feedback from both within and outside the organization can help ensure the system's effectiveness over a long period of time. Therefore, systems should be designed in such a way that programming changes can be made with minimal effort. Flexible database software, for example, should permit data to be changed, added, and deleted from the system as required without adversely affecting the users of the system.

Changes that require a system to be updated occur both inside and outside of the organization. Both the number and the extent of these changes contribute to the length of a system's life cycle. Figure 9 illustrates several internal and external factors which require systems to be updated.

Over time, systems become obsolete and too costly to maintain for the benefits they provide. Eventually, a new system will need to be developed to take advantage of technologic improvements and to facilitate new requirements of the organization. The entire system development procedure of

Profile

Herman Hollerith

Familiar with punched cards used by early computers to record factual information? Herman Hollerith developed this system for processing data more than a century ago to help the U.S. Census Bureau count citizens. He adapted the punched paper tape and punched card technology that was first created to control weaving patterns as early as 1728 and had been perfected by Joseph Jacquard for his automatic loom in 1801.

Hollerith was an independent inventor who was contracted by the Census Bureau in 1880 to help speed up the sorting and tabulating of census data. (It had been estimated that it would take over 10 years to tabulate the next census figures.) By 1887, Hollerith had worked out a code to represent census information through a system of punched holes in paper strips. He later changed to a system of standard-sized cards because the paper strips did not work very well. Thus, Hollerith developed the first machine capable of processing statistical information from punched cards. The system included the cards, a card punch, a sorting box, and a tabulator equipped with electromagnetic counters. With this equipment, cards could be sorted at the rate of about 80 cards per minute. Data appearing in the cards could be tabulated and counted at the rate of 50 to 75 cards per minute.

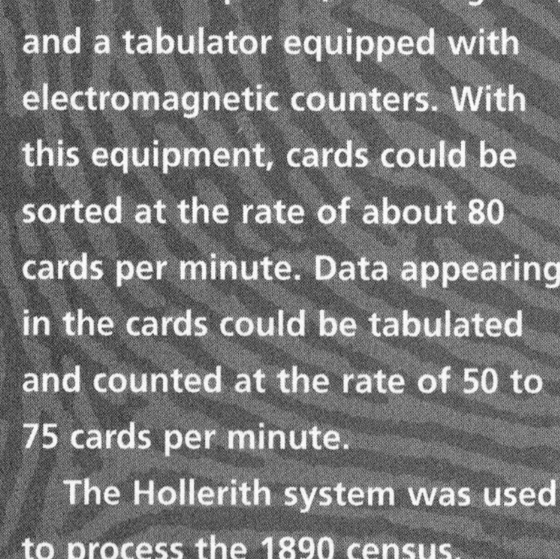

The Hollerith system was used to process the 1890 census, which was completed in one fourth of the time needed to compile the results of the 1880 census. Hollerith then organized a company to manufacture and market his system. The company later became known as the International Business Machines Corporation (IBM).

analysis, design, acquisition and testing, implementation, and evaluation and maintenance will again be used to develop the new replacement system. Once implemented, this system will also require updating during its life cycle to remain effective as long as possible—and so the cycle continues.

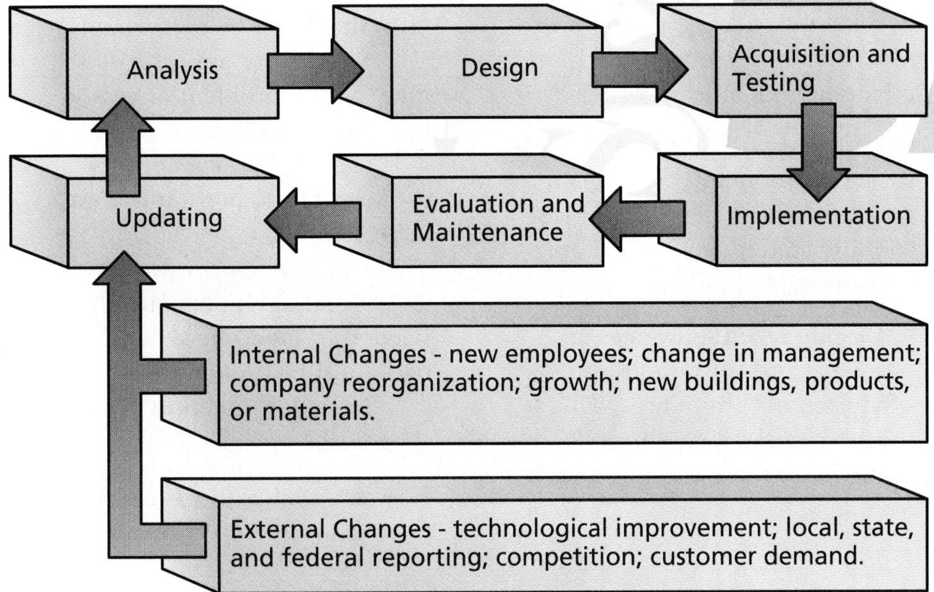

figure 9

Both internal and external factors influence a system's life cycle.

Do It!

1 Interview someone who uses output from a computer in his or her job. Identify the information that is used, and find out what information is not provided by the computer that would be helpful. Also, find out if this information could be provided by the system.

2 Prepare a flowchart diagram showing the procedure you followed to register for the classes you are taking. Document your diagram with copies of the forms, worksheets, and so on that you used during the registration process.

3 Describe the educational material(s) you used to operate a computer, software application, or video game. Was the material written with the user in mind? Was it filled with computer jargon? Could you understand it? What would you have done differently if you could have written the instructions?

Summary

Coupled with the human race's thrust for new knowledge, increased research and development have contributed to this rate of expansion and fueled an accelerated pace of technologic improvement.

- The term *system* can be defined as related devices or procedures that function together to achieve a common goal or objective.

- In a world of fast-paced technologic invention and the human race's thrust for better and more sophisticated tools, there is only one constant: change.

- Despite recent advances in hardware and software, there is still a lack of "brainware." That is, today's computers are capable of doing more than humans have been able to program them to do.

- Just as changes must be made to help us keep pace with our environment, so must changes be made to computer systems for them to keep up with technologic advances.

- Computer systems have a life cycle. A life cycle can be defined as the period of time in which a given computer system's usefulness to perform a given task is measured.

- The five stages of systems development are: analysis, design, acquisition and testing, implementation, and evaluation and maintenance. In addition, once the new system is operational, it must be updated as necessary to prolong its life cycle of usefulness.

- **Stage 1**—analysis—has four tasks that must be performed:
  1. A definitive and precise statement of the problem or reason for the development must be stated.
  2. Measurable objectives of what the system is to accomplish must be stated.
  3. The sources of information and the actual information needed to meet the system's objectives must be identified.
  4. The analysis report must be prepared.

- **Stage 2**—design—has four major tasks that must be performed:
  1. A systems design flowchart must be prepared.
  2. Several viable alternative designs that meet the stated objectives should be developed within the organizational constraints.
  3. A feasibility analysis study weighing costs to the benefits derived, time, effort, and so on must be performed for each of the viable alternatives.
  4. The detailed systems design report must be prepared.

■ **Stage 3**—acquisition and testing—has three tasks that must be performed:

1 Software must be acquired through in-house programming, custom programming, off-the-shelf programs, or a combination of all three.

2 Once the software is obtained, it must be tested to make sure it works properly and produces accurate output.

3 The software must be documented for the users of the system as well as those responsible for its future maintenance and updating.

■ **Stage 4**—implementation—involves two primary tasks:

1 Personnel who will be the users of the system must be trained and educated.

2 The old system must be converted to the new system.

■ **Stage 5**—evaluation and maintenance—is conducted after the implementation stage is completed and the new system is operational. The purpose of the evaluation is to determine whether the system has met the stated objectives and to act as a summary of the systems development project.

■ System updating necessitated by future change should be an integral part of system design. A system can be designed to recognize change in the form of feedback.

■ Feedback can be defined as a continuous monitoring of the system to ensure that its purpose and objectives are being met.

■ Feedback from both inside and outside the organization can help to ensure the system's effectiveness over a long period of time.

Summary

The following key terms were defined in this module. For each of the following terms, write on a separate piece of paper the number of the definition followed by the letter of the appropriate term.

Terms

A. analysis report

B. conversion

C. feasibility analysis

D. feedback

E. system

F. system life cycle

G. systems analyst

H. systems design flowchart

I. systems design report

Definitions

1 related devices or procedures that function together to achieve a common goal or objective

2 the period of time in which a given computer system's usefulness to perform a given task is measured

3 the person who acts as a link between the users of the system and the technical personnel who actually develop and install the system

4 a report that contains a statement of the problem, measurable objective, sources of information, and data elements required to meet the objectives of the new system

5 a model of the general design of the entire system that is developed by the systems analyst

6 an analysis that is performed on each design alternative to determine whether the alternative meets the given objectives while remaining within the constraints of the organization

7 a report that brings together the information created from each task involved in the first two stages (analysis and design) of the system development procedure

8 the process of installing a new system or replacing an old system with a new one

9 a continuous monitoring of the system to ensure that its purpose and objectives are being met

Matching

Review

1. What factors have fueled an accelerated pace of technologic improvement? (Obj. 1)
2. Identify two changes that technology has brought about in your home, town, or city within the past 5 years. (Obj. 1)
3. What is a system? Give examples of three different systems. (Obj. 1)
4. Why must computer systems be changed periodically? (Obj. 1)
5. Describe a computer system's life cycle. (Obj. 2)
6. What are the five stages of systems development? (Obj. 2)
7. Identify the four tasks that must be performed during the analysis stage of systems development. (Obj. 3)
8. Identify the four tasks that must be performed during the design stage of systems development. (Obj. 4)
9. What are the three tasks that are performed during the acquisition and testing stage of systems development? (Obj. 5)
10. Identify the two tasks involved in the implementation stage. (Obj. 6)
11. What is the purpose of the evaluation and maintenance stage of the systems development project? (Obj. 7)
12. Why should systems be developed for ease of future updating? (Obj. 8)
13. What is feedback? (Obj. 8)
14. Identify at least three internal factors that can require an existing system to be updated or become obsolete. (Obj. 8)
15. Identify at least three external factors that can require an existing system to be updated or become obsolete. (Obj. 8)

Activities

1 *Writing* Consult a computer magazine, local newspaper, computer store, library, or other source to obtain information about a new use of the computer that has resulted from technologic change over the past 5 years. Prepare a report describing the application.

2 *Math* One of the significant technologic changes in computer hardware is the increased speed at which the computer can perform its calculations. This capability has enabled new software to be developed and existing software to be revised—especially software with heavy computational processing. Consult a computer magazine, local newspaper, computer store, library, or other sources to obtain information regarding how the increased computational processing speed of modern computers is now being used in mathematical applications. As an alternative, and if your school uses computer-assisted math software, find out what changes have occurred in the software that is being used to take advantage of this increased computational processing. Report your findings.

3 *Presentation* Systems design flowcharts are often used for communication and discussion between system analysts, software developers, and system users. Study the system flowchart shown in figure 6. Translate the processing steps into a brief narrative that you would use to describe the system functions to a potential user. Be sure to identify the different computer components involved in the system and the direction of the data flow.

4 *Teamwork* Divide into teams of four or five students each. Each team is to explore the feasibility of developing a computerized textbook inventory system for the Terrace Park School District. The school district is made up of four elementary schools (grades 1 through 6), two middle schools (grades 7 and 8), and two high schools (grades 9 through 12).

The school district's business manager has recently noticed that more textbooks are being purchased than are needed because accurate records of the textbooks available at each of the different schools are not being kept. For example, one of the high schools may not have enough of a given textbook while the other may have a surplus. Under the current system, the high school that does not have enough books purchases the number of textbooks that are needed instead of obtaining them from the other high school. The business manager has estimated that excess textbook purchases cost the school district at least $8500 per year. This problem must be resolved before the end of the current school year, when textbooks for the next school year are ordered.

The business manager has hired your team (a team of system analysts) to analyze the feasibility of developing a textbook inventory system to run on one of the school's personal computers. On completion of this project, your team must justify its decision to proceed or not to proceed with development of the software for the computerized textbook inventory system.

(Continued on next page.)

Activities

Each team member should be responsible for a part of the project. Complete each of the following activities:

- **Step 1:** Specify the **statement of the problem**.
- **Step 2:** State the **measurable objectives**.
- **Step 3:** Identify the **sources of information**.
- **Step 4:** Prepare the **analysis report**. Based on the information you provided in the analysis report, make a decision to either proceed to the design stage or terminate the effort. If in your opinion the costs of developing the new system are greater than the benefits derived, justify your decision at this time and end this activity. If in your opinion the benefits outweigh the costs, continue to step 5.
- **Step 5:** Prepare a **systems design flowchart** of your proposed system.
- **Step 6:** Develop **alternative designs**.
- **Step 7:** Conduct a **feasibility analysis**.

5 *Speaking* Visit with a systems analyst, or invite him or her to your class. Ask the analyst to describe the procedures he or she follows when developing a new computer system. Find out what considerations are given during system development to anticipate changes and what proportion of work is devoted to maintaining existing systems rather than to devising new ones. After your interview (or after the analyst has spoken to your class), share the procedures and considerations identified by the analyst that you believe to be the most important with your classmates. Consolidate your comments into 2 to 4 minutes.

6 *Ethics* A self-employed programmer was hired by a small company to develop the software for a payroll/personnel system the company had designed. After completing the project, the programmer sells the software, with minor modification, to other companies. Do you think that what the programmer did was ethical, unethical, or an act that could be considered computer crime? Justify your choice.

7 *Internet* Access the Internet, and use your search engine to find information about presentation software that could be used to help present a systems design report to management. Identify features of the software you find that could be used to enhance and clarify information in such a presentation. Use terms such as PRESENTATION, SOFTWARE, PROJECT, POWERPOINT, MANAGEMENT, and so on to help narrow your search. Report your findings.

Software Design

Development & Implementation

SDI

Overview

Without software, a computer is absolutely useless. Software is the means by which the computer is directed to perform its given tasks. Software can be purchased, or it can be written by the user. In this module, you will learn the two general classifications of programs, take a look at the most commonly used programming languages, and find out how programs are developed.

Objectives

1. Describe the differences between low-level and high-level programming languages.
2. Identify the characteristics of commonly used programming languages.
3. Describe the procedures and methods used for program development.

Classification of Programs

All computer programs, whether they are manufacturer supplied, off-the-shelf, custom, or user written, are written in some language the computer can understand. There are more than 150 different programming languages that are available for a wide variety of computers.

Some of these languages are general purpose and have been designed for a wide variety of applications. Other languages have been designed for specific purposes, such as mathematics and engineering. Regardless of which language is chosen by the programmer or is required by the application, it can be classified as either a low-level or a high-level language.

Low-Level Programs

Programs written in the computer's native language, or in a language similar to the computer's native language, are said to be written in **low-level languages**. Originally, computers were programmed in **machine language**; instructions were written in the numeric code directly understood by the processor of the target machine. Each different type of processor has its own unique machine language. For example, because the processor in an IBM PC is different than the processor in an Apple Macintosh computer, the machine language of each computer is also different.

All data is represented inside the computer as binary numbers. The instructions that are understood by the computer's processor are also expressed as binary numbers. Therefore, computer instructions written in machine language are written as a string of binary numbers that are unique to that processor. For example, the instructions to tell the IBM PC processor to add 2 plus 2 can be represented as shown in figure 1.

Programming in machine language is very technical and time-consuming. Not only must the instructions be in binary numbers, the programmer must keep track of the exact memory locations where the data is stored. All programs must be translated (interpreted) into the machine language that the computer can understand regardless of what programming language is used. Therefore, each programming language provides a means for translating its language into the computer's native machine language code before execution.

High-Level Programs

Low-level language programs require that the programmer think in terms of the particular processor being used and the instructions that processor requires. That is, low-level languages are unique to the processor. **High-level languages**, however, are similar for all different processors. This allows the programmer to think in terms of solving the problem rather than how to use the processor to its fullest potential. The programmer is able to write instructions to the computer using English and English-like terms.

Because it is easier to use, a high-level language is used to write most application programs. Programs written in a high-level language must first be entered into the computer using a word processor or text editor, then translated into machine language before they can be understood by the processor. The translation is done by either an **interpreter program** or a **compiler program**. The interpreter or compiler is supplied by the computer manufacturer, language developer, or another vendor.

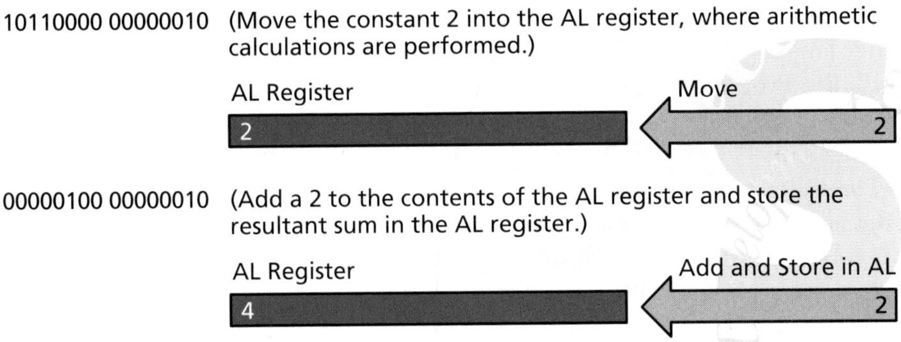

10110000 00000010 (Move the constant 2 into the AL register, where arithmetic calculations are performed.)

AL Register | Move
2 | 2

00000100 00000010 (Add a 2 to the contents of the AL register and store the resultant sum in the AL register.)

AL Register | Add and Store in AL
4 | 2

figure 1

Computer instructions are expressed in binary numbers.

The operation of an interpreter can be compared to an English-speaking person talking to a Spanish-speaking person through an interpreter. The English-speaking person says a sentence, then the interpreter repeats the sentence in Spanish. This process is repeated as long as the English-speaking person talks. In a similar fashion, an interpreter program for a computer looks at one instruction written in a high-level language, translates the instruction into machine language, and relays it to the processor. The processor immediately carries out the instruction, then the interpreter looks at the next instruction and translates it. The process is repeated until all instructions are carried out. Using an interpreter causes a program to operate more slowly, because each instruction must first be translated into machine language before it can be executed. The use of an interpreter makes it easy for a programmer to debug a program (find and correct the errors).

Compilers also translate high-level languages into machine language. A compiler operation is similar to that of a person who translates a book from English to French. After the entire book is translated and written in French, a person literate in French can read it. A compiler program similarly translates the entire high-level language program into machine language and stores the machine language version in RAM or on an auxiliary storage device. Once the compiled program is loaded in the CPU's RAM (the computer's memory), the processor executes the instructions that it provides. Programs that have been compiled operate faster than those translated with an interpreter; this is because all of the instructions have been converted into machine language before the program is executed. Debugging compiled programs, however, is more difficult and time-consuming than with interpreted programs, because it is often more difficult to isolate problems. Also, each time the program is changed, it must be recompiled before it can again be executed.

Characteristics of Commonly Used Programming Languages

You have already learned that programming languages are either general purpose or designed for specific applications. In addition, there may be several versions of the same language, each with different capabilities and slightly different instructions. For example, the BASIC programming languages used on a mainframe computer and a PC use different instructions to read and write data to/from disk. Therefore, a program written in BASIC for one computer will not necessarily run on another.

Programming languages also differ in structure. That is, their makeup, design, and degree of organization may vary greatly. Some are very structured and require the programmer to follow strict rules of organization. Other languages are freeform and give the programmer a great deal of flexibility. Programming languages also vary greatly in the ease with which they are learned. Some languages are very easy to learn, while others can be very difficult.

The following sections examine several of the commonly used programming languages. The purpose of briefly discussing these languages is to provide a brief outline of low- and high-level languages, their use for general purpose or specific applications, their varying structures, and their ease of learning and use.

Assembly Language

Assembly language is similar to machine language, but it is considered to be a step above machine language. An assembly language program is one that works intimately with the machine's hardware. It is a language for those programmers who want to communicate at the lowest level with the inter-workings of their computer. Also, assembly languages enable the programmer to interface with a computer's operating system.

When using high-level languages, compilers and interpreters read in a given language's commands and must convert them into machine language before the program can be executed. To do this, these compilers and interpreters must churn out a sequence of machine language instructions that enable the computer to perform the given task, handle a wide variety of error conditions, and include code that may not be used or needed. This means that there is often a large amount of overhead required for even a small program. For example, a compiled program may take at least 25K of RAM and disk storage to instruct the computer to display one character on the screen; however, an assembly language program that does the same thing can be written that uses fewer than 25 bytes. Because the computer does not have to execute all of the unnecessary instructions, it can execute the assembly language program much faster.

While assembly language programs are often faster and more efficient than compiled and interpreted programs, their greatest disadvantage is that *everything* must be coded by the programmer. For example, programs written in assembly languages make no provisions to permit the user to rekey incorrect data unless they have been specifically designed and coded to do so. Also, the user must provide instructions to make sure a given disk drive is available and ready, with the heads positioned at the proper location, when attempting to write or read data from/to disk.

Before programs written in assembly language can be understood by the computer, they must be translated into machine language. The translation is done by a program called an **assembler**, which is supplied by the computer manufacturer or another vendor. The assembler program simply reads the programmer's assembly language program, translates each instruction into its machine language equivalent, and creates a second executable version of the original.

Figure 2 contains a segment of an assembly language program that simply counts backward from 7 to 1 and outputs the contents of the counter each time through the loop. A loop is a break in the normal processing sequence so that previous instructions can be re-executed. Line numbers have been

```
Line    Program Code:

 1                  .
 .                  .
 .                  .
51              MOV  AL,7    ;set up the loop counter with the value 7
52      LOOP:
53              OUT  123,AL  ;send the contents of AL to port 123
54              DEC  AL      ;subtract 1 from the contents of AL
55              JNZ  LOOP    ;loop back unless AL has become 0
 .                  .
 .                  .

        The following output will be sent to port 123:
                             7
                             6
                             5
                             4
                             3
                             2
                             1
```

figure 2

Assembly languages are considered to be a step above machine languages.

placed in front of each program line to make reference to the program easier; however, line numbers are not used when entering assembly language programs.

Line 51 moves the constant value 7 into AL to establish the loop counter AL. Line 52 identifies the following instructions as those belonging to the routine LOOP. Line 53 sends the content of what is stored in AL to port 123 (output device). Line 54 deducts (subtracts) 1 from the contents of AL. Line 55 (Jump Not Zero) causes control to jump back to line 52 and the following instructions to be repeated until the contents of AL equal 0.

FORTRAN

FORTRAN was the first problem-oriented compiler language. *FORTRAN* is an acronym that stands for **FOR**mula **TRAN**slation. As its name implies, it was specifically designed for mathematic and scientific applications. FORTRAN statements resemble algebraic expressions that use a combination of variables (names assigned to data stored in memory that will be referenced by statements within the program), constants (fixed values, labels, numbers, letters, and so on), and operators (symbolic notations that specify what action is to occur). One of its greatest advantages is the extensive collection of scientific and mathematic subroutines available. Because these subroutines are a part of the FORTRAN language, complex calculations can automatically be performed without the need to code the formulas each time they are needed. Another advantage is that it is a relatively easy-to-learn, problem-oriented language. That is, it does not require a programmer familiar with the internal operation of the computer to use it. Instead, a mathematician, scientist, or engineer who understands mathematics could use FORTRAN most effectively. Thus, the programming effort can focus on the solution of the problem rather than on the hardware characteristics of the computer (figure 3).

The major disadvantage of the FORTRAN language is its limited ability to handle character data and input/output operations. Because it was designed to be a mathematic language used to solve problems that are numeric in nature, it does not lend itself for use in business applications.

Careers

Programmers

A computer programmer is the person who writes the instructions that make the programs (software) that actually tell the computer to do what the user wants. Once the job of the systems analyst is complete, the programmer breaks the job down into detailed steps depicted in a flowchart. Next, the programmer codes the program instructions into a language the machine can understand, such as Assembly Language, COBOL, BASIC, C, or Pascal. Once this coding is complete, the programmer must test his or her work. If the program does not work, it must be "debugged" of any coding or logic errors that may exist.

A programmer tends to work within a specific type of application—business, scientific, engineering, or systems applications. For that reason, programmers need to have knowledge in the specific area for which they are writing programs. Depending on the level of responsibility, a programmer can be a systems programmer, lead programmer, senior programmer, or a programmer trainee. Some programmers develop new software, while some maintain or enhance existing software programs. Still others evaluate or supervise other programmers.

There are no specific standard requirements for becoming a computer programmer. Some programmers are college graduates, while others have completed only a few courses in a community school or junior college. Vocational or technical schools also offer training for programmers. In the near future, as technology becomes increasingly complex, employers will require more formal education.

What kind of person is best suited for a programming career? Computer programmers must be self-motivated individuals who like to work independently. They should enjoy working with abstract problems and be able to organize their work and actions into logical sequences. Programmers must also have a lot of patience and be persistent in seeing a project through every detail until it is complete.

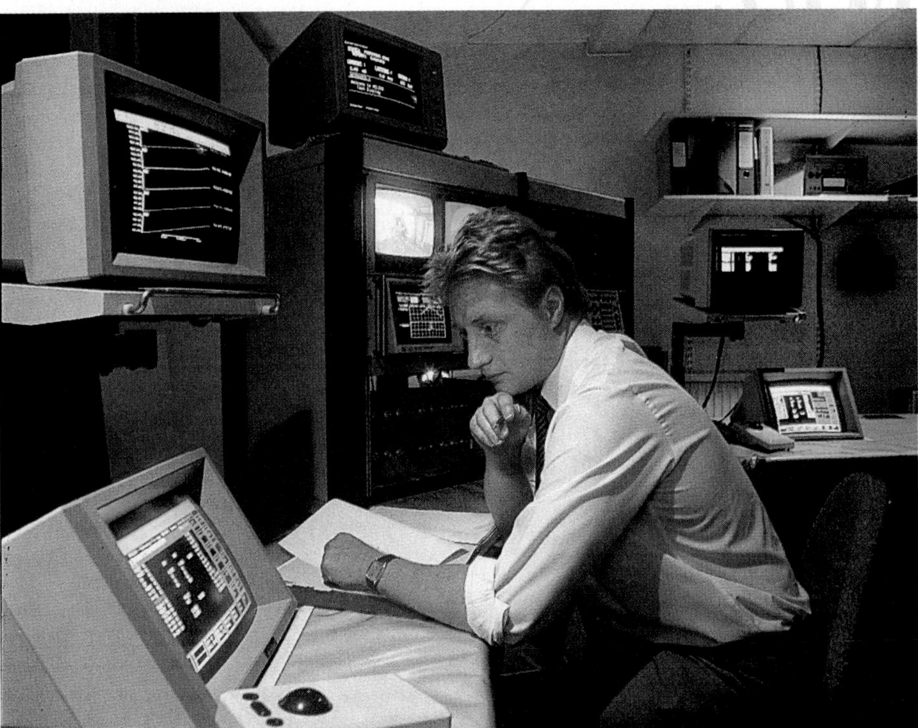

figure 3

The FORTRAN programming language is used for scientific applications that handle complex formulas.

The FORTRAN program in figure 4 calculates and then prints the area of a triangle given the base and height. Refer to this program as you study the following paragraph about how the program works.

The statement numbers under the column labeled Stmnt (statement) are used as references to instructions contained within other instructions in the program code. For example, the first statement in the program contains a statement number 100. Notice the third line from the end of the program contains a GOTO instruction that references this first program statement. The READ command instructs the computer to read input data and store this into the variables BASE and HEIGHT according to the parameters specified within parentheses. The first number within the parentheses (5) identifies the input device from which the data will be read. The second number (110) references the following FORMAT statement, which specifies the format of the input data. In this program, both input data fields can contain a maximum of seven numeric digits, two of which are decimal digits.

The IF statement compares the contents of the variable BASE to 0. If the BASE is less than or equal (LE) to 0, program execution will jump to (GOTO) statement 130, where the program will stop its execution and end. If the BASE is greater than 0, the

```
Stmnt: Program Code:

100    READ (5,110) BASE, HEIGHT
110    FORMAT (F7.2,F7.2)
       IF (BASE.LE.0) GOTO 130
          AREA = 0.5 * BASE * HEIGHT
          WRITE (6,120) BASE, HEIGHT, AREA
120       FORMAT (F7.2,3X,F7.2,3X,F8.3)
          GOTO 100
130    STOP
       END

       Results from the execution of the program:

         8.25      15.00        61.875
        (BASE)    (HEIGHT)      (AREA)
```

figure 4

The FORTRAN programming language is often used for mathematic or scientific applications.

next instruction will be performed. Note how the FORTRAN language permits the programmer to write the formula to find the area of a triangle in a format that closely resembles an algebraic expression. In this instruction, 0.5 will be multiplied by the contents of the variable BASE. The product of 0.5 multiplied by BASE will then be multiplied by the contents of the variable HEIGHT, and the result will be stored in the variable AREA.

The WRITE statement that follows has a format similar to the READ statement. The contents of BASE, HEIGHT, and AREA will be written to an output device according to the parameters specified within parentheses. The first number within the parentheses (6) identifies the output device to which the data will be written (display screen, printer, disk drive, and so on). The second number (120) references the following FORMAT statement, which specifies the format of the output data. In this program, BASE will be output as a seven-digit numeric field with two of the digits being decimal. The 3X instructs the computer to leave three spaces before outputting the second variable (HEIGHT), which also contains seven numeric digits, two of which are decimals. Another three spaces are left before outputting the content of the AREA variable, containing eight digits, three of which are decimal digits.

The GOTO 100 statement sends control back to statement number 100, and the entire process is repeated for a new set of input BASE and HEIGHT data. This process continues until a BASE data field containing a 0 or a negative value is read.

BASIC

BASIC is the acronym for **B**eginner's **A**ll-Purpose **S**ymbolic **I**nstruction **C**ode. The BASIC language was designed to be a high-level, interactive programming language. It is usually translated by an interpreter, which makes the identification and correction of program bugs easier than with most other languages. BASIC has always been considered to be an easy-to-learn language, partly because of its freeform structure and English-like instructions. Recent versions have enhanced its capabilities and made it suitable for writing application programs in virtually any area.

Like all high-level languages, BASIC translates English-like instructions into machine language for execution by the processor. Unlike most others, however, BASIC also includes the necessary software for entering a program into the computer's memory, editing the program, and saving it on an auxiliary storage device. Use of a separate word processor or text editor is not required.

The BASIC program in figure 5 calculates and then prints the area of a circle given the radius. Refer to this program as you study the comments in the following paragraph about how the program works.

Each numbered line of a BASIC program is known as a **BASIC statement**. In this program, statements have been assigned numbers beginning with 100 and incremented by 10. This type of numbering scheme allows additional statements to be added between

figure 5

BASIC programs make use of English-like instructions.

```
100 REM CALCULATE THE AREA OF A CIRCLE
110 INPUT "ENTER THE RADIUS OF A CIRCLE: ";RADIUS
120 AREA = 3.14 * RADIUS^2
130 PRINT "THE AREA OF THE CIRCLE EQUALS ";AREA
140 END

    Execution of the program:

    ENTER THE RADIUS OF A CIRCLE: 12
    THE AREA OF THE CIRCLE EQUALS 452.16
```

existing BASIC statements if required. Statement 100 is a Remark (REM) statement that is used to tell the reader what this program does. Remark statements are optional and used for documentation purposes only. Statement 110 prints the prompt message enclosed within quotes to the screen and waits for the user to enter a numeric value representing the radius of a circle from the keyboard. Once the radius is entered, statement 120 calculates the area of the circle by multiplying pi (3.14) times the radius squared. The result is stored in the variable named AREA. Statement 130 prints the message contained within quotes followed by the contents of AREA (the computed area of the circle) to the display screen. Finally, statement 140 ends the program.

Pascal

The Pascal language was named in honor of the mathematician Blaise Pascal, who lived in the seventeenth century. It was designed to be a high-level, general-purpose language useful for writing programs for nearly every application. Like all high-level languages, Pascal must be translated into machine language for execution by the computer. A Pascal program must first be entered into the computer with a word processor or text editor and stored on an auxiliary storage device. The program keyed into the computer is known as a **source program** because it is the source from which the translation is to be made.

After the source program is keyed into the computer and stored, the Pascal compiler is used to translate the program into an **object program**, which is the result or object of the translation. Depending on the implementation of Pascal, the translation may be directly into machine code or an intermediate type of code. If the translation is into machine code, the translated program can be executed directly and will run at a high speed. If the translation is into intermediate code, the source program is translated into "pseudo commands" (made-up processor commands that do not necessarily match the machine code commands of any processor). A special interpreter program, called a **run-time program**, translates these commands into machine code at the time the program is executed. The advantage of this procedure is that the same translated Pascal code can be used regardless of the processor on which the program is to run. It is only necessary to provide a different run-time interpreter program for each different model of processor. The disadvantages are slower program execution and the requirement that the run-time interpreter program always be available on the disk.

One of the primary advantages of the Pascal language is that it encourages the use of good programming techniques through an established structure that must be followed. For example, each program must be named, all variables must be specified before use, and all processing must be performed between the Begin and End statements. In addition, the code resembles English-like sentences, which makes learning the language and modifying the program easier than with most other languages.

As stated previously, a variable is a named storage location in the computer's memory. As a program is executed, various data may be stored in this location. One of Pascal's strong points is the many different types of data that may be stored in variables. In addition to the data types provided by the language, the programmer may define other types. For example, if a program is to be used by a bakery, a data type known as PIES could be defined. The programmer could then specify that this data type could have only the values APPLE, COCONUT, LEMON, and PECAN (figure 6). The program could contain a statement that says, in effect, "Print sales figures for all apple, coconut, lemon, and pecan pie sales."

figure 6

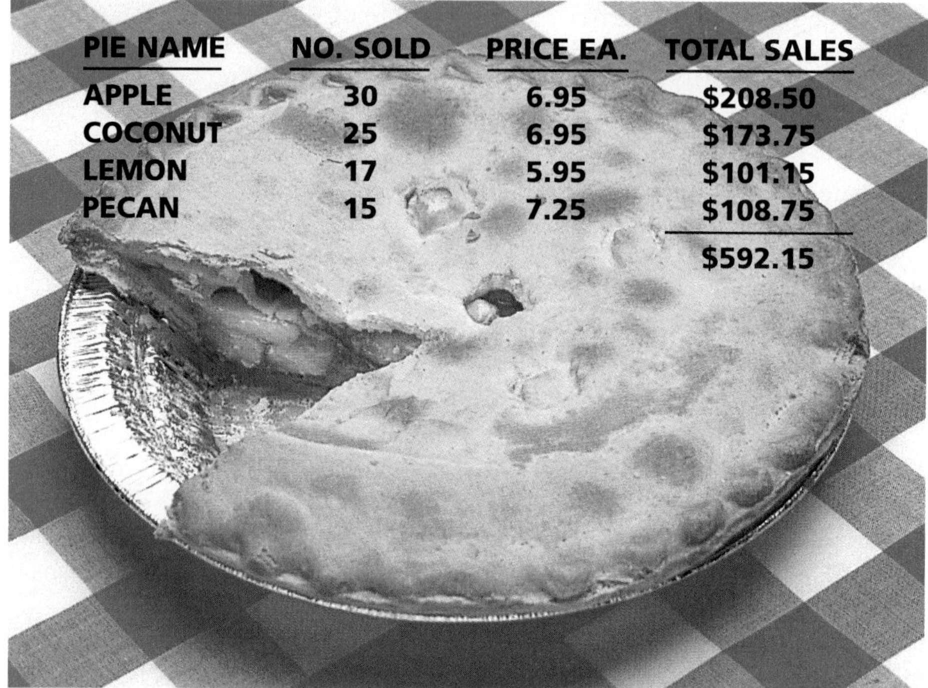

PIE NAME	NO. SOLD	PRICE EA.	TOTAL SALES
APPLE	30	6.95	$208.50
COCONUT	25	6.95	$173.75
LEMON	17	5.95	$101.15
PECAN	15	7.25	$108.75
			$592.15

The Pascal programming language is useful for writing programs to handle many different types of data. The programmer may define these data types as names and numbers.

The three most commonly used data types are character data, integer numbers, and real numbers. Character data consists of alphabetic, numeric, and special symbols, such as a street address (952 Creek Drive). An integer is a whole number, such as 10, while a real number is a number with a decimal point, such as 85.5. The variables that are used to store these various data types are given names known as **identifiers**.

The Pascal program shown in figure 7 calculates the amount of commission to pay a salesperson. If a salesperson sells less than $6000 worth of merchandise for the week, the commission will be computed at a rate of 7%. If the sales for the week are $6000 or greater, the commission will be computed at a rate of 9%. Refer to this program as you study the comments in the following paragraphs about how the program works. Note that line numbers have been placed in front of the statements to make reference to the program easier; however, line numbers are not used when entering Pascal programs.

Line 1 names the program PAY and indicates that the program will do both input and output operations. Lines 2 and 3 contain comments indicated by braces, { }, which are ignored by Pascal when the program is compiled; the comments are optional and for the benefit of those reading the program. In line 4, the variables that are used in the program are declared. This program is using only real variables. The program instructions begin with line 5. Line 6 prints a prompt message, followed on line 7 by the READLN procedure to get a sales amount from the keyboard and place it in the variable SALES.

Once the input is received from the keyboard, line 8 prints a blank line. Next, a decision must be made on whether the commission rate to be used

```
Line: Program Code:

 1    PROGRAM PAY (INPUT,OUTPUT);
 2      (Written by Juan Vazquez, 10/15/--)
 3      (This program calculates commissions)
 4    VAR SALES, COMMISSION, RATE: REAL;
 5    BEGIN
 6      WRITE(`Enter the amount of sales: `);
 7      READLN(SALES);
 8      WRITELN;
 9      IF SALES<6000 THEN RATE:=0.07
                      ELSE RATE:=0.09
10      COMMISSION:=SALES*RATE;
11      WRITELN(`RATE: `,RATE:3:2,´  Commission:   `,COMMISSION: 7:2);
12    END.

      Execution of the program with less than $6,000.00:

      Enter the amount of sales: 5250.00

      Rate:  0.07   Commission: 367.50

      Execution of the program with sales greater than $6,000.00:

      Enter the amount of sales: 7218.50

      Rate:  0.09   Commission:  649.67
```

figure 7

Pascal programs can be used for a wide variety of computer applications.

should be 7% or 9%. This is done in line 9 by using the IF . . . THEN . . . ELSE statement. Here, one of two alternative actions may be taken. As stated, if the amount stored in SALES is less than (<) 6000, store 0.07 in the variable named RATE, else store 0.09 in RATE. Line 10 multiplies this rate times the sales amount and places the product into the variable that holds the amount of commission. On line 11, the WRITELN procedure is then used to print the result. Finally, line 12 ends the program.

COBOL

COBOL was the first high-level language written for use in business applications. Its name is an acronym derived from **CO**mmon **B**usiness **O**riented **L**anguage. It was developed through the efforts of the U.S. Department of Defense working in conjunction with representatives from the computer industry, government, and computer user groups. By 1960, the first commercial versions of COBOL were made available. Several revisions of the COBOL language have occurred since then.

COBOL is still a commonly used language for business applications, especially with minicomputers and mainframes. Its strong point is the handling of large amounts of data stored on auxiliary storage devices (figure 8). It is also one of the wordiest languages and one that uses a great deal of RAM. While some programmers object to the large number of words required or the amount of memory it consumes, its English-like sentences make COBOL programs easier to understand than those written in some other languages. Therefore, they are also easy to modify and maintain. COBOL is most often translated by a compiler; however, interpreted versions are also available on mainframe computers.

COBOL is generally considered to be a standard language. A COBOL compiler must contain certain standard capabilities. With some exceptions (the reference manual for the version of COBOL being used will point out variations from the standard), the COBOL program that runs on one computer can be easily changed to run on another. For this reason, COBOL is said to be a machine-independent language.

All COBOL programs are written in four parts, known as divisions. These divisions and their titles must appear in every program in the following order:

1. Identification Division. This division is used to identify the name of the program, the author, and the date the program was written.
2. Environment Division. This division specifies the type of computer on which the program is to run. It also names the input and output files and may specify the input and output devices to be used.
3. Data Division. This division describes the data files and structures to be used by the program.
4. Procedure Division. This division specifies the actual steps the computer is to follow in processing data to solve a problem. This part of a COBOL program is the part most like a BASIC program.

figure 8

COBOL is often used in business applications to handle large amounts of data.

Each of these four divisions can be subdivided into several SECTIONS. These sections are used to categorize related information and define files, data, or processing steps.

The English-like words used in writing a COBOL program are of two types: those on a reserved word list, and those supplied by the programmer. A **reserved word** is a word that has a specific meaning to a COBOL compiler. The compiler reserves such words for given purposes, such as ADD, SUBTRACT, MOVE, and WRITE. **Programmer-supplied words** are any nonreserved words used in a program; these words must be defined in the Data Division of the program.

The COBOL program shown in figure 9 has been written to record student data in a student-scores file on disk. A record containing the name, class code, and three test scores are recorded to disk for each student keyed into the computer. Lines 1, 5, 12, and 26 identify the four divisions of the program.

Notice how lines 2 through 4 of the Identification Division are used to identify the name of the program (STSCORE), the name of the author (JANICE MATTHEWS), and the date the program was written (NOVEMBER 21, 19--).

figure 9

COBOL programs are written in four parts, known as divisions.

```
Line:   Program Code:

 1      IDENTIFICATION DIVISION.
 2      PROGRAM-ID.    STSCORE.
 3      AUTHOR.        JANICE MATTHEWS.
 4      DATE-WRITTEN. NOVEMBER 21, 19--.
 5      ENVIRONMENT DIVISION.
 6      CONFIGURATION SECTION.
 7      SOURCE-COMPUTER. IBM-PC.
 8      OBJECT-COMPUTER. IBM-PC.
 9      INPUT-OUTPUT SECTION.
10      FILE-CONTROL.
11          SELECT SCORES-FILE, ASSIGN TO DISK.
12      DATA DIVISION.
13      FILE SECTION.
14      FD  SCORES-FILE.
15          LABEL RECORDS STANDARD
16          VALUE OF FILE-ID IS "A:SCORES".
17      01  STUDENT.
18          05  STUDENT-NAME   PIC A(20).
19          05  CLASS-CODE     PIC 9.
20          05  SCORE-1 PIC 999.
21          05  SCORE-2 PIC 999.
22          05  SCORE-3 PIC 999.
23      WORKING-STORAGE SECTION.
24      77  CONTINUE-OPTION    PIC X.
25          88  FINISHED VALUE IS `N´.
26      PROCEDURE DIVISION.
27      MAIN-MODULE.
28          OPEN OUTPUT SCORES-FILES.
29          PERFORM DETAIL-PROCESSING-MODULE UNTIL FINISHED.
30          CLOSE SCORES-FILE.
31          STOP RUN.
32      DETAIL-PROCESSING-MODULE.
33          DISPLAY `ENTER STUDENT NAME:´.
34          ACCEPT STUDENT-NAME.
35          DISPLAY `ENTER CLASS CODE (1,3,3, OR 4):´.
36          ACCEPT CLASS-CODE.
37          DISPLAY `ENTER THE FIRST SCORE:´.
38          ACCEPT SCORE-1.
39          DISPLAY `ENTER THE SECOND SCORE:´.
40          ACCEPT SCORE-2.
41          DISPLAY `ENTER THE THIRD SCORE:´.
42          ACCEPT SCORE-3.
43          WRITE STUDENT.
44          DISPLAY `ANY MORE SCORES (Y/N)?´.
45          ACCEPT CONTINUE-OPTION.
```

Lines 6 through 11 of the Environment Division contain two sections: line 6 identifies the Configuration Section, and line 9 identifies the Input–Output Section. The Source-Computer (line 7) identifies the computer that the COBOL program will be compiled on, while the Object-Computer (line 8) identifies the computer that will execute the compiled program. In this case, both the source and object computers are the same (IBM-PC). Lines 9 through 11 of the Input-Output Section identify the file called SCORES-FILE as the file that will be written to disk.

Lines 13 through 25 of the Data Division are used to describe the file and data fields used in the program. Two sections are also contained in this division: the File-Section (line 13), and the Working-Storage Section (line 23).

Lines 27 through 45 make up the Procedure Division. Notice that this division is broken into two modules: a main module, which controls the processing; and a submodule, which does the detailed processing.

PL/1

PL/1 (**P**rogramming **L**anguage/**1**) was designed to be a general-purpose language that combined the business processing features of COBOL with the mathematic and scientific features of FORTRAN. The language can be easily learned, because it can be written in a freeform or structured format, uses English-like sentences, and is self-documenting. Like FORTRAN, it contains many features that permit solutions to complex mathematic problems. Like COBOL, it contains many features that permit a high level of input/output operations and efficient handling of large amounts of both character and numeric data. PL/1 has not enjoyed the popularity of many of the languages already discussed, however, primarily because users of the FORTRAN and COBOL languages have such a large investment in the development of their software that they have been reluctant to change. As a result, the potential of PL/1 has appealed to relatively new computer users or those companies without heavy investments in a particular language.

C Programming Language

The C language was developed in the early 1970s by Dennis Ritchie at Bell Laboratories for rewriting the company's Unix operating system. Today, after several revisions, it is considered to be a general-purpose programming language. The C programming language enables programmers to code their programs using a high level-type symbolic code, yet it offers low-level control over the hardware. C is considered to be a low-level language that makes extensive use of prewritten routines (called library routines) that can be used in different programs for a variety of applications. Its greatest use is by programmers who need (or like) to work at machine level to get the best possible performance from their computers. C is also considered to be a very transportable language. That is, it can execute on a wide variety of different computers with minor modification. For these reasons, C is becoming a popular language among programmers writing software for PCs.

Today, a successor to C, called C++, is an object-oriented programming language that allows data to be more active in the running of a program. Through its object-oriented nature, C++ allows codes to be reused from program to program. C++ is replacing C as the dominant programming language in many commercial and research institutions.

Java Programming Language

The Java language was initially developed to provide software for consumer electronic devices. In the late 1980s, devices such as toasters, ovens, and personal digital assistants were being produced with tiny computer chips that needed to be programmed to instruct the devices to perform various tasks. The programs used by these devices had to work on the vast array of different computer chips used by the manufacturers, and be extremely reliable.

In 1990, a small team headed by James Gosling at Sun Microsystems, Inc., realized that existing programming languages could not do the job of providing the architecture-independent, reliable software that was needed to program these consumer devices. Each time a new computer chip came out, the program had to be recompiled or changed to execute correctly on the new chip. Also, the complexity of many of the existing languages made it difficult to write reliable code.

In 1993, as the team continued to work on the design of a new language, public access to the Internet was mushrooming. The team realized that their new language, called Java, was ideally suited for programming on the Internet. A program generated from Java could run on all of the different computers connected to the Internet.

Java is often described as an easy-to-learn programming language. This statement, however, is only true from a C or C++ programmer's point of view because Java's syntax (coding rules and format) is similar to C and C++ syntax. Java is a full-blown, high-level programming language that requires the programmer to learn its syntax before it can be used effectively. The special appeal of Java is in its ability to allow the Internet (or any network) to serve as a repository for software that would otherwise have to be loaded onto a computer. In effect, the network is the computer. Software that is developed at one site—using a variety of computers—can be accessed and executed by any computer that is on the network.

One of Java's key features is the ability to create small programs called "applets," which can be included in other Java programs or inserted in Web pages downloaded from the Internet. When applets are downloaded into an Internet user's computer, they are automatically executed. These applets may display text and graphics, animate a company logo, produce an eye-catching title, play audio files, or enable the user to perform interactive activities. To run a Java applet, the user must use a Java-enabled Web browser. At the time of this writing, Netscape Navigator (version 2.0 and up) supported Java. The increased interest in Java has prompted IBM®, SGI, and Oracle® to license the Java technology from Sun Microsystems. Microsoft® also has announced its intention to license Java. Many additional software and hardware products likely will be using the Java technology in the near future.

Figure 10 shows a simple example of a Java program.

```
Public class HelloJava {
    public static void main (String[] args) {
        System.out.println("Hello from Java!");
    }
}
```

figure 10

A simple Java program that prints out the message: Hello from Java!

Perl Interpreted Language

Perl is an interpreted language that is designed to collect information for the purpose of managing systems. Perl can scan text files (such as system logs or other system monitoring files), extract information from the files, and print reports based on the information extracted. The name "Perl" is an acronym for **P**ractical **E**xtraction and **R**eport **L**anguage. It was developed by Larry Wall in the late 1980s and has since grown in its language functionality and user base. The language, though not a full-blown programming language, is similar to C and includes some of the characteristics of BASIC and Pascal.

Perl is considered to be one of the most popular programs on the Internet. It is widespread and will run on most computer systems. In addition, it is free! Perl's text processing, report generation, and system-management capabilities make it an excellent choice for Web server management. For example,

Profile

Grace Murray Hopper

The late Navy Rear Admiral, Grace Murray Hopper, has been called the "Grand Old Lady of Software" and the "Grandmother of the Computer Age." Dr. Hopper was a mathematician and distinguished Navy career woman who was a pioneer contributor to modern-day computer science.

In 1951, Hopper conceived of a new type of internal program, called a *compiler,* that could scan a programmer's coded instructions and produce the equivalent binary machine language used by the computer to carry out the user's commands. The compiler had the ability to understand ordinary English letters, words, phrases, and mathematic expressions. It could perform certain operations automatically (such as those involved in multiplying fractions by a power or using floating point numbers), thus eliminating the need to write lengthy code detailing how to perform such common operations.

In the late 1950s, Hopper was appointed as a member of the CODASYL (COnference of DAta SYstem Languages) committee. This committee was assembled by the Department of Defense to develop a language that could solve business problems. One of committee's main objectives was to design a machine-independent language—a language that could be used with *any* computer. By 1960, the committee had established the specifications for the COBOL language. Later that year, the first commercial version of COBOL was ready. In 1968, guidelines for a standardized COBOL (called ANSI COBOL) were established, and the CODASYL committee continued to examine and incorporate new features into the language.

In addition to these accomplishments, Grace Hopper has also been credited as the first person to use the term *bug* to describe an error in a computer system or program. In 1947, while working for the U.S. Navy, Hopper tried to determine why one of the computers was not working properly. She discovered a moth had gotten inside the computer and been crushed to death in one of the machine's relays. When the moth was removed, the problem cleared up. Hopper taped the moth into her logbook and next to it wrote, "First actual case of bug being found." When an officer came into the computer room to ask how things were going, Hopper told him that she and her colleagues were debugging the program. That is how the commonly used phrases "bugs in the program" and "debugging the program" came to describe programming errors.

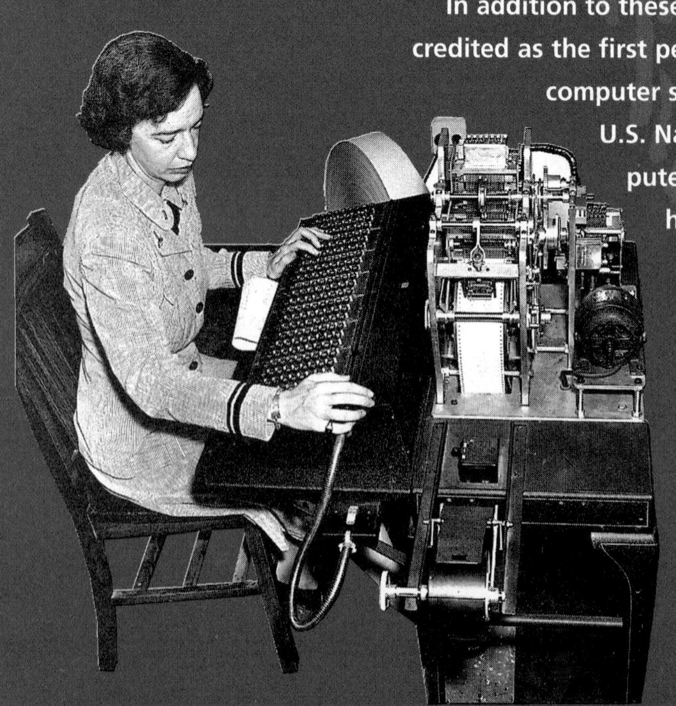

Perl can be used to process log files containing information about on-line activities that have occurred over a given period of time. In addition, Perl can be used to evaluate data from forms or to interface with existing databases.

Fourth-Generation Languages

Fourth-generation languages, such as FOCUS, RAMIS, and NOMAD, are the highest level of high-level programming languages. Several fourth-generation languages have been developed as a result of the recent advancements in computer technology. New high-speed computers with vast amounts of storage and sophisticated auxiliary storage devices have been developed because of a demand for additional processing capabilities (figure 11). More users of computers have also contributed to this rapid growth of technology and the applications for which the computer is used. As a result, new languages have been developed to take advantage of this technology and to improve application services to the users.

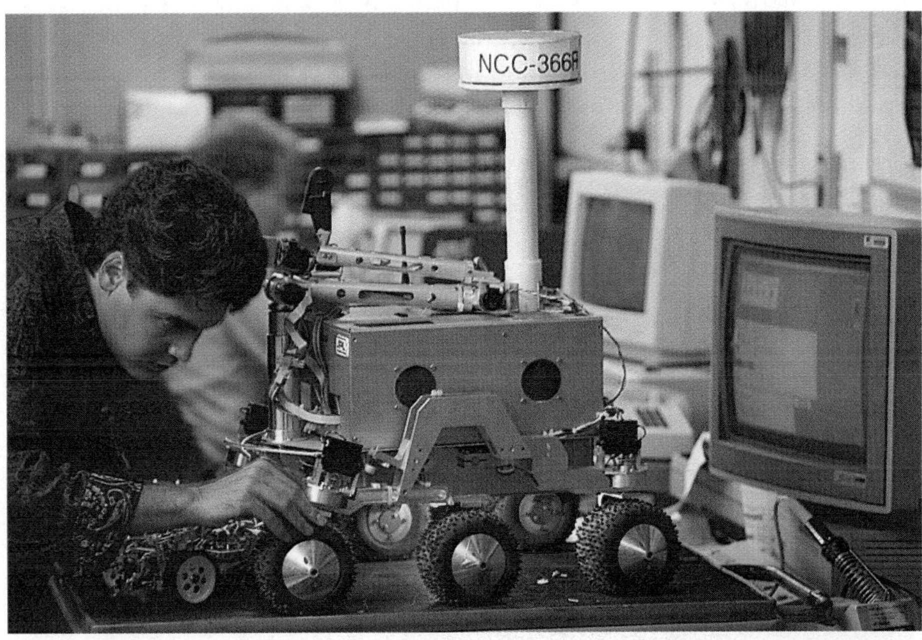

figure 11

Advancements in computer technology require more advanced programming languages.

Fourth-generation languages have been designed to be general purpose in nature and to be used by both programmers and computer users. They can be learned with a minimum amount of training. Most require the user to respond to a series of questions that request information about the tasks to be performed. After all of the needed information is supplied, a program is automatically generated by the language itself. Once the program is generated, it can be compiled and executed. This procedure can be completed in a fraction of the time it would take a programmer to write a program in any of the languages previously discussed.

The speed with which programs can be written and the ease with which fourth-generation languages can be used hold great potential for permitting users who are not computer programmers to satisfy their own information needs. These languages remove the technical concerns of using the computer and emphasize the applications to be performed.

Event-Driven Programming Concepts

During the past few years, versions of the most commonly used programming languages (BASIC, Pascal, C) have become available that permit programming in event-driven (also called interrupt) environments. These environments include software that run on the Macintosh, IBM, and compatible computers using graphic interfaces (System 7, OS/2 Warp, Microsoft Windows, and so on). **Event-driven software** is software designed to check for a user action (pointing and clicking a mouse, keyboard entry) at frequent intervals during program execution (figure 12). For example, at any time during the execution of a program, a user may want to choose a menu command, select an item from a list, display a report, generate a graph, or a host of other activities. The program must be able to sense and respond to these events.

The new generation of event-driven software is very structured. Typically, tasks are broken down into small subroutines that are easy to write, test, maintain, reuse, and comprehend. These small subroutines may be tested independently from the rest of the program, and they are saved as separate files on disk. When programming is completed, the subroutines are compiled together into one complete, executable program.

To assist the programmer, prewritten software, called software tools, are used to help simplify the coding and minimize program coding errors. **Software tools** consist of routines that have been written to perform common tasks. For example, a routine may be used to draw a window on the display screen. The programmer specifies the size of the window in a statement that is passed along to the software tool subroutine that then draws the window. Software tools are said to be in the toolbox. The **toolbox** (also commonly referred to as a toolkit) is a collection of commonly used, prewritten software tools that can be used by the programmer. Toolboxes are provided by the computer manufacturer or many software developers. Also, many programmers share software tools they develop by placing copies of their work in bulletin board and online service systems.

Programmers who write programs in event-driven environments are strongly encouraged to follow standard programming conventions set forth by the operating system of the object computer. For example, programs written for the Macintosh computer should use menus, dialog message boxes, list windows, scrolling, selection procedures, and other features commonly found in Macintosh software. Likewise, programs written to operate in the Microsoft Windows environment should use its programming conventions. The reason programmers are encouraged to follow these standards is to keep the appearance and operation of all software similar to help the user more quickly learn how to use the software.

Figure 13 illustrates portions of an event-driven program written in BASIC for the Macintosh computer. Note the structure of the program. The first window shows GOSUB statements that direct processing to routines designed to handle main events, menu actions, mouse button detection, and so on. The second

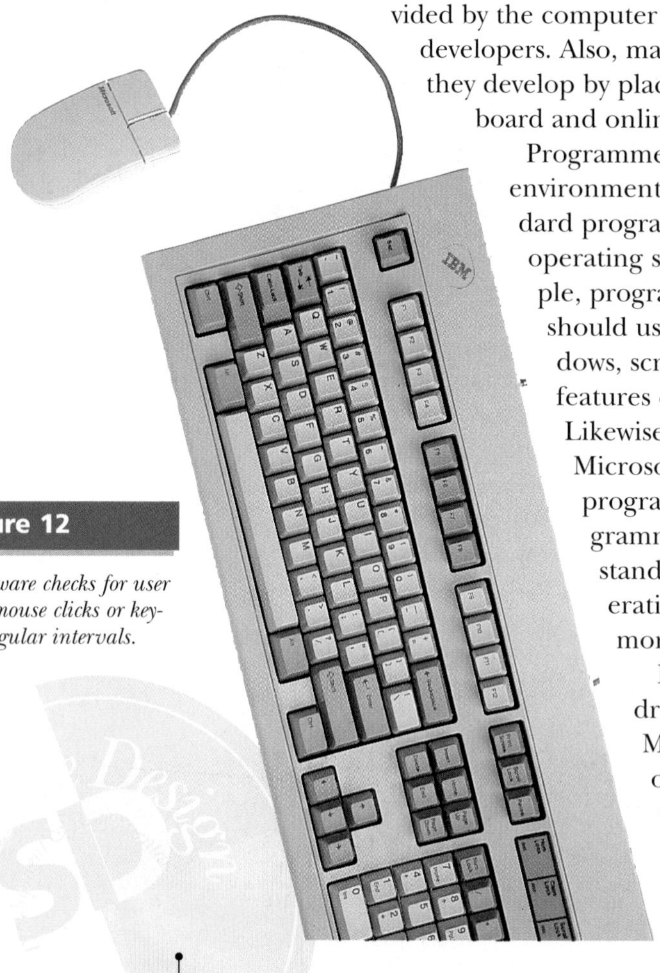

figure 12

Event-driven software checks for user actions, such as mouse clicks or keyboard entry, at regular intervals.

window shows the Main, Menu, and Button routines program code. The window located on the upper-right side labeled Project contains a list of all subroutines comprising this program that have been written and stored on disk. Each of these subroutines is compiled and, together, make up the completed program. If an error is detected and fixed in one of the subroutines, then only that subroutine need be recompiled, thus saving testing and developmental time. The window located on the lower-right side titled Labels contains a list of the labels used to identify routines within the module currently displayed (Checker.Main).

figure 13

Event-driven programs are very structured and often use prewritten software tools from vendor-supplied toolboxes. The first screen shows the main part of the program, and the second screen shows the coding of some of the subroutines.

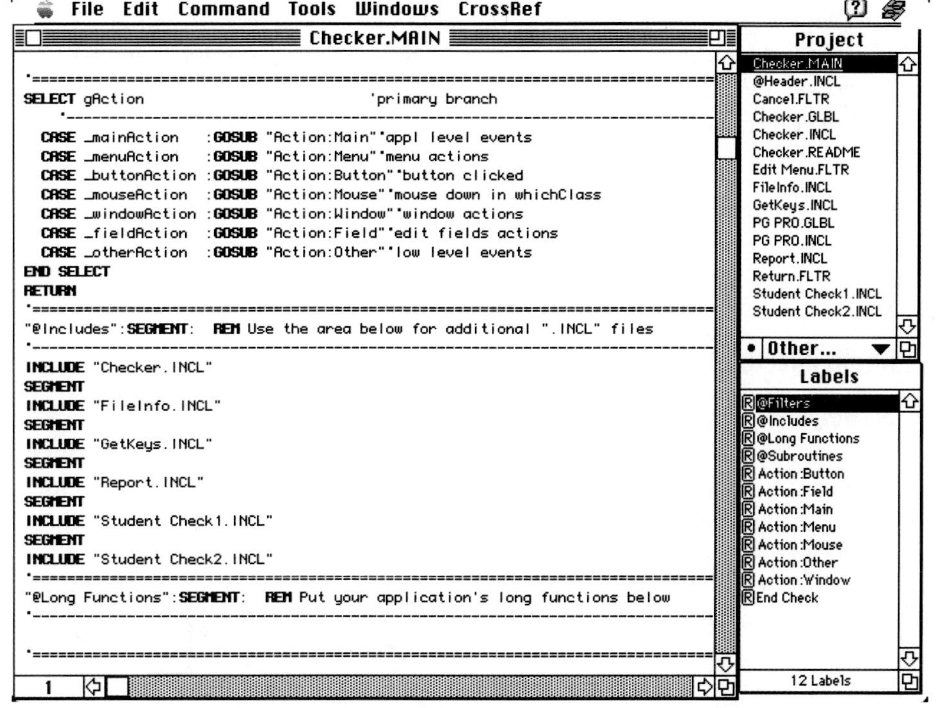

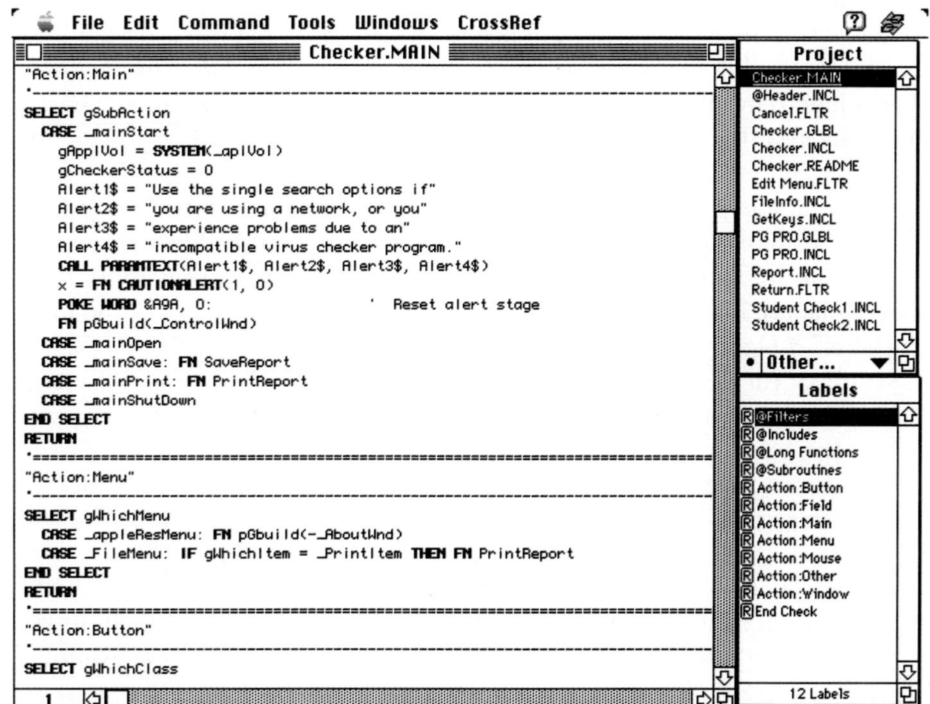

Do It!

1 Why do you think so many different programming languages have been developed? Explain your response.

2 Some programmers believe that a low-level language should be used so that the code is written in as few instructions as possible and as efficiently as possible. Other programmers believe that a high-level language should be used so that the code can be easy to write and understand by others. If you were asked to learn a new programming language, would you choose a low-level or a high-level language? Justify your choice.

3 Find out what language was used to program one of your school's computer applications (such as an educational software package, class scheduler, student reporting system, accounting, inventory, and so on) and why it was chosen.

Program Development

Structured programming is a method used to write programs from logically organized, detailed plans that define the steps that must be performed. Some persons separate the process into **structured design** (the planning of the program) and **structured programming** (the actual writing of the program). This section discusses the methods used in structured programming. These steps can be used regardless of which high-level language is used. Writing structured programs is easier in some languages, however, than in others.

Top-Down Design/Hierarchy Charts

Top-down design of a program begins by defining what the program is to do and then gradually increases the level of detail in the plan. This begins with a hierarchy chart. A **hierarchy chart** looks like an organizational chart for a business that shows the boss at the top and the workers below. The following example will help clarify this concept.

The example program to be developed will be a mailing labels program. It must be able to perform four functions: add names and addresses, make corrections in names and addresses, delete names and addresses, and print mailing labels. Figure 14 depicts the completed hierarchy chart for the mailing labels program.

Think of each box as being a functional component of a computer program. The top box (labeled Mailing Labels) is the boss part of the program. Under the boss, there are four workers; each worker knows how to perform one of the four functions of the program. Each worker performs its duty when instructed to do so by the boss.

Output Design

The output to be produced by the program must also be designed. In this example, the output is mailing labels. A report spacing chart, as shown in figure 15, is used to illustrate what the output should look like. Note that the

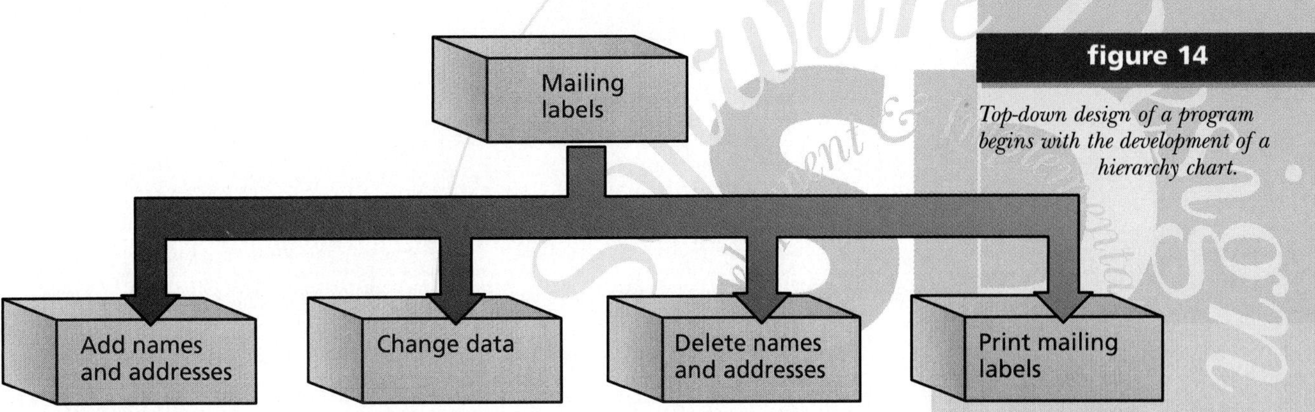

figure 14

Top-down design of a program begins with the development of a hierarchy chart.

report spacing chart is a form arranged in rows and columns, with space for each position in which a character can be printed. When completed, it shows the maximum length of each data item that is to appear on the output as well as its location. The spacing for this example shows two labels to indicate that the layout is repeated down a page of labels.

Program Design

One of the main concepts of structured programming is that any program can be written using only four kinds of instructions. These four kinds of instructions are described below:

1. **Sequential instructions** are simply steps that are performed one after another. For example, clear the display screen, list the four functions on the screen, or obtain the user's choice of functions.
2. **Case instructions** provide a way for executing one set of instructions out of numerous possibilities included in the program. For example, depending on the user's choice, perform one of the four functions.
3. **Loop control instructions** are those that are used to make the computer repeat certain instructions. Instructions may be repeated until some condition becomes true, or they may be repeated as long as some condition remains true. For example, while the user wants to add more people, get name from keyboard, and check to see if name is already stored.
4. **IF . . . THEN . . . ELSE instructions** instruct the computer to perform one task if a statement is true or another if the statement is false. For example, IF name is already stored, THEN inform the user, ELSE get street address, city, state, and ZIP code data from the keyboard and store it on disk.

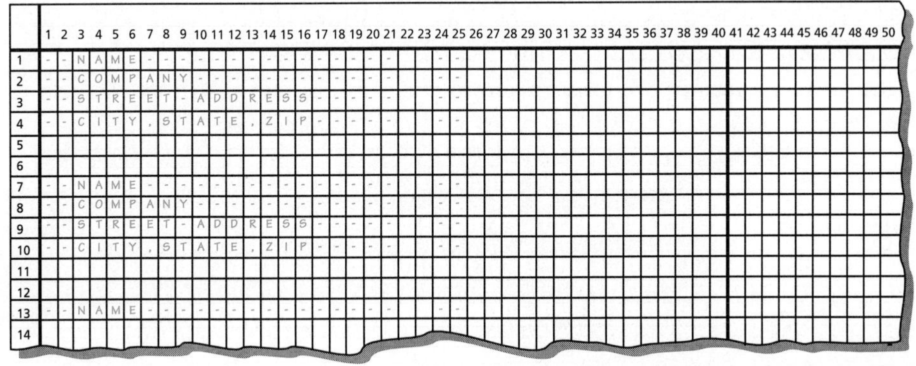

figure 15

Program output is designed on a report spacing chart.

Issues
In Technology

Computer Viruses: Spreading Trouble

A computer virus is similar to the viruses that cause a cold or the flu. Like a human virus, a computer virus can disrupt an individual computer—and can be spread from one computer to another.

A computer virus is a small program, usually no more than 1 to 20 lines of code, that is intentionally designed to do some type of damage. It may delete data, turn existing files into garbage, or even destroy hardware. Planting a computer virus is a form of software sabotage that is especially damaging, because the virus is able to procreate and makes no distinction among its victims.

The virus program buries itself deep within the computer's operating system program. Because the operating system program is run each time the computer is used, the virus can execute itself and issue commands to make room for a copy of itself on every data disk or every program stored to disk. Every time a new disk is used, the virus attaches itself. Then, when an infected disk is used on another computer system, the virus goes along and spreads to that operating system. Thus, the virus spreads, much like a common cold.

Often, virus programs are designed to activate themselves based on a certain event, time, or date. As a result, they are likely to inflict their damage and spread among several other programs and users before they are detected.

With today's trend toward connecting computers and sharing information over electronic bulletin boards, virus programs can become even more contagious. Corporations are also threatened, especially when employees take work home, where a disk could be infected. For this reason, many companies now require employees to use only specific software monitored by the company.

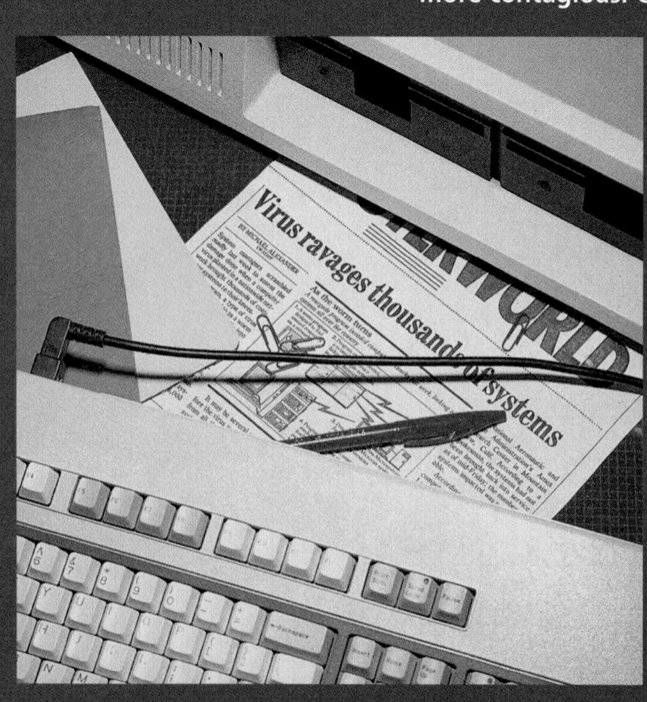

Software is also being developed and marketed to detect a virus. This type of software is known as inoculation or anti-virus software. One type of inoculation software—called a vaccine—has been developed that when run, warns the computer user if a self-executing file attempts to attach itself into the system. It then blocks the file so that the suspect file cannot attach itself. Another method being used to control the spread of viruses is to download or copy only original source code programs, examine the code, and then compile the program. Thus, a new, executable object program is created.

With these kinds of instructions in mind, a program design is written on a Module Documentation form for each of the boxes from the hierarchy chart shown in figure 14. Each box, which represents a function or task the program must perform, is known as a **module**. A **program design** (also known as **pseudocode**) consists of the detailed steps that must be performed by each module within a program. The program design is written in ordinary English. By consolidating the steps given in the example and adding a few more instructions, the program design for the **main module** (the top box) is created. The program designs for the main module and the Names and Addresses Module are shown in figure 16. Note that what is written in figure 16 is really a detailed outline of the instructions that the computer must perform to accomplish its tasks. In addition, and in a similar fashion, program designs must be written onto Module Documentation forms for each of the remaining three modules.

Some programmers prefer to draw a flowchart to identify the detailed steps that must be performed rather than use pseudocode and module documentation forms. A **flowchart** is a method of using graphic representations to illustrate the detailed steps of a hierarchy chart. To illustrate the design of a program in flowchart form, each detailed step of the program is placed inside a symbol that indicates what kind of action is taking place at each step. Arrows, called **flowlines**, are used to connect the different steps and show the direction of data flow. The flowline usually proceeds from top-to-bottom and left-to-right, although there can be exceptions.

MODULE DOCUMENTATION	Program: MAILING LIST	Module: MAIN

Module Function (Program Design):

```
1.  Clear the CRT screen.
2.  List the possible functions on the CRT.
3.  Obtain the user's choice of functions.
4.  Depending on user's choice, perform one of the four
    functions.
5.  If user does not want to quit, go back to Step 1.
6.  End.
```

MODULE DOCUMENTATION	Program: MAILING LIST	Module: NAMES AND ADDRESSES

Module Function (Program Design):

```
1.  While user wants to add more people:
      Get name from keyboard.
      Check to see if name is already stored.
      If name is already stored, then inform user
             Else get street address from keyboard
                  get city, state, ZIP from keyboard
                  store data on disk.

2.  Return to Main Module.
```

figure 16

Program design consists of listing the program steps in English.

A template is used to draw the flowchart. There are many symbols that can be used in flowcharting; however, the logic of most programs can be illustrated adequately by using only the symbols shown in figure 17.

Figure 18 illustrates how our example Mailing Labels program could be flowcharted from the hierarchy chart shown in figure 14. Note the flowlines and how each of the common flowchart symbols have been used to illustrate the detailed logic of the program.

figure 17

Most programs can be depicted using these flowchart symbols.

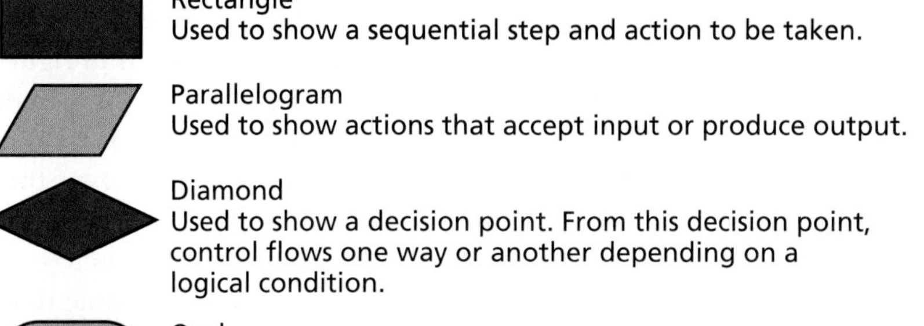

Rectangle
Used to show a sequential step and action to be taken.
Parallelogram
Used to show actions that accept input or produce output.
Diamond
Used to show a decision point. From this decision point, control flows one way or another depending on a logical condition.

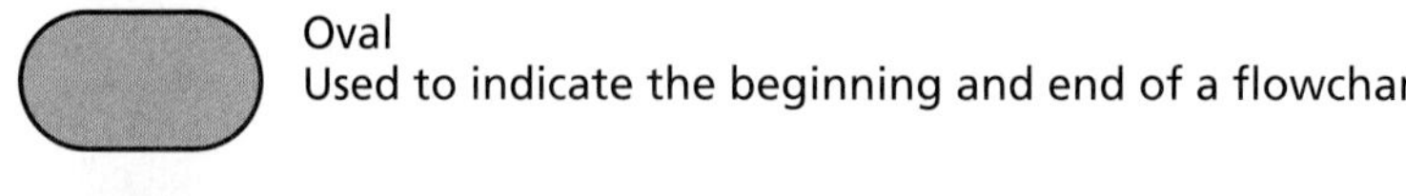

Coding and Testing

Writing the instructions of a computer program in a computer language is known as **coding** the program. To this point in the program development process, the language in which the program is ultimately to be coded has not been considered. This is because the program design (pseudocode) or flowchart that was developed can be converted to assembly language, FORTRAN, BASIC, Pascal, COBOL, or virtually any other language. For each statement in the program design or each step in the flowchart, one or more statements (or subroutines) are written in the chosen programming language.

When using structured design, the main module is coded and tested first, then all other modules are coded and tested. To illustrate the process, figure 19 shows the main module of the Mailing Labels program coded in a version of BASIC used by the IBM PC and many other popular microcomputers. Remark statements are included to help explain the program.

After the program has been coded, it must be tested. Errors in a program are called *bugs*. Programs with errors either will not execute properly or will produce incorrect results. To determine if bugs exist, the newly coded program must be tested. **Testing** is the process of finding and correcting errors and is commonly known as *debugging*. The process typically involves inputting data similar to the actual input that the program has been designed to process, then checking the output produced against the expected results. The testing process also involves inputting a wide assortment of data (including data with errors) to make sure the program can adequately deal with a variety of situations.

Two different types of bugs are checked for during the testing process: syntax bugs and logic bugs. Syntax bugs are errors that occur when the rules of the language the program is coded in are violated. These types of bugs often cause the program to stop execution when they are encountered. Logic bugs are those that occur when poor decisions, incorrect formulas, or incorrect conclusions have been coded in the program. These bugs are the most difficult to find because they do not cause program execution to stop

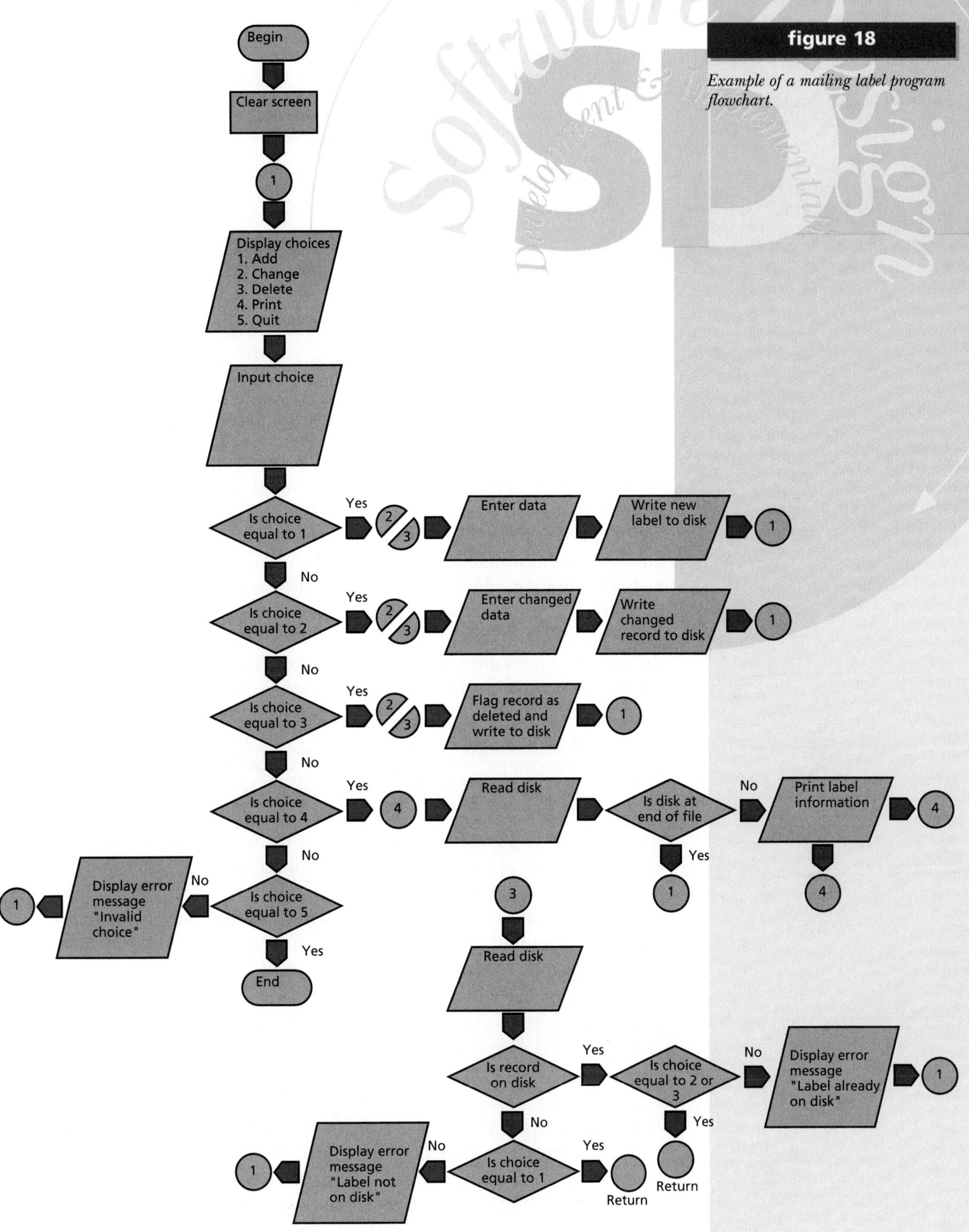

figure 18

Example of a mailing label program flowchart.

figure 19

The instructions of a computer program must be coded in a computer language, such as BASIC.

```
100 REM MAILING LABELS PROGRAM
110 REM WRITTEN BY SUSAN WILLIAMS, 10/12/--
120 REM THIS PROGRAM MAINTAINS MAILING LABELS
130 CLS: REM CLEAR THE DISPLAY SCREEN
140 PRINT "1. ADD NAMES AND ADDRESSES"
150 PRINT "2. CHANGE DATA"
160 PRINT "3. DELETE NAMES AND ADDRESSES"
170 PRINT "4. PRINT LABELS"
180 PRINT "5. QUIT"
190 PRINT
200 INPUT "ENTER THE NUMBER OF THE DESIRED ACTION: ";C
210 ON C GOSUB 1000,2000,3000,4000
220 IF C <> 5 THEN GOTO 130
230 END
```

and are often the most serious as they frequently cause incorrect output to be generated.

"Alpha" and "beta" are two terms commonly associated with the testing process. Alpha (meaning one, or the first) testing is usually conducted by the developer in a very controlled environment. Beta (meaning two, or the second) testing occurs after bugs and other short-comings detected in the alpha test have been fixed. It is usually conducted by the end user(s) in the environment in which the software will be used.

In this module, you have learned that programming languages vary greatly in structure, purpose, and usage. Languages are tools that when used properly, help the programmer to accomplish his or her job. Similar to choosing the right tool for a given job, the proper programming language must be chosen to complete a given task. Each language has unique features that must be considered during the selection process. These considerations include the type of problem to be solved, the personnel that will be using the language, the ease of use, and the type of computer system that will be used.

Each programming language is unique in its syntax, function, and capabilities. Because of these differences, there is little, if any, compatibility among them. The greatest compatibility exists in data-file sharing. That is, files created by a program written in one programming language can usually be read by a program written in another language. There are commercial software programs available that claim to convert a program written in one language to another; however, additional manual conversion efforts are often required.

Do It!

1 Using figure 18 as a guide, draw a flowchart showing the program logic to maintain a student data file (add, change, and delete students). The program should also be able to print a report showing all students in the file.

2 Transpose the flowchart you just developed into pseudocode or module documentation.

3 Of the programming languages discussed in this module, which would you use to code the program described here? Justify your choice.

Summary

Without software, a computer is useless.

- All computer programs, whether they are manufacturer supplied, utilities, off-the-shelf, custom, or user written, are written in some language the computer can understand.

- Some languages are general purpose and have been designed for a wide variety of applications. Other languages have been designed for a specific purpose, such as mathematics or engineering.

- Low-level programs with instructions written in the numeric code that is directly understood by the processor of the target machine are known as machine language programs.

- High-level programs are written in a language that allows the programmer to think in terms of solving the problem rather than how to use the processor to its fullest potential.

- High-level languages are translated into machine language by either an interpreter program or a compiler program.

- An interpreter program looks at one instruction written in a high-level language, translates the instruction into machine language, and relays it to the processor for execution.

- A compiler translates the entire high-level language program into machine language and stores the machine language version in RAM or an auxiliary storage device ready for execution.

- Assembly language is a low-level programming language used by programmers who want to communicate at the lowest level with the interworkings of their computer. Assembly language programs usually consume less RAM and execute faster than high-level programs.

- An assembler is a program that translates assembly language programs into machine language.

- FORTRAN (**FOR**mula **TRAN**slation) was the first problem-oriented compiler language. It was specifically designed for mathematic and scientific applications. One of its greatest advantages is the extensive collection of scientific and mathematic subroutines that are available.

- BASIC is the acronym for **B**eginner's **A**ll-Purpose **S**ymbolic **I**nstruction **C**ode. The BASIC language was designed to be a high-level, interactive programming language. BASIC is easy to learn, partly because of its free-form structure and English-like instructions.

- The Pascal language was designed to be a high-level, general-purpose language useful in writing programs for nearly every application. It can be compiled and executed directly, or it can be translated into intermediate code and executed with a run-time program. The advantage of the run-time method is that the same translated Pascal code can be run on many different computers.

Summary

- COBOL (**CO**mmon **B**usiness **O**riented **L**anguage) was the first high-level language written for use in business applications. Its strong point is the handling of large amounts of data stored on auxiliary storage devices. It is also one of the wordiest languages and one that uses a great deal of RAM. COBOL is written in English-like sentences that make its programs easier to understand than those written in some other languages.

- PL/1 (**P**rogramming **L**anguage/**1**) was designed to be a general-purpose language combining the business processing features of COBOL with the mathematic and scientific features of FORTRAN. The language can be easily learned, because it can be written in a freeform or structured format, uses English-like sentences, and is self-documenting.

- The C programming language is considered to be a low-level programming language that enables the programmer to code programs using a high-level type of symbolic code, yet it offers low-level control over the hardware. C++ improves upon C through its object-oriented nature.

- Java is a full-blown, high-level programming language that offers the potential of making the Internet (or any network) the computer itself. It will permit software to be developed at one site (using one or a variety of different computers) and be executed on any computer, anywhere on the Internet.

- Perl is an interpreted language designed for system management, scanning text files, extracting information from those files, and printing reports based on the information extracted. The name Perl is an acronym for **P**ractical **E**xtraction and **R**eport **L**anguage. It is a popular program for use on the Internet.

- Fourth-generation languages are the highest level of high-level programming languages. Most fourth-generation languages require the user to respond to a series of questions that request information about the tasks to be performed. After all of the needed information is supplied, a program is automatically generated by the language itself. Once the program is generated, it can be compiled and executed.

- Event-driven software is software designed to check for a user action at frequent intervals during program execution.

- Software tools are routines that have been prewritten and designed to perform common tasks. A collection of software tools are said to be in a toolbox.

- Structured programming is a method used to write programs from organized, detailed plans defining the steps that must be performed.

Summary

■ Top-down design of a program begins by defining what the program is to do and then gradually increases the level of detail in the plan.

■ A hierarchy chart is similar to an organizational chart and is used to graphically illustrate the top-down design.

■ Before a program can be coded, the output to be produced must be designed. The report spacing chart is a form arranged in rows and columns with space for each position in which a character can be printed. When completed, it shows the length as well as the location of each data item that is to appear on the output.

■ One of the main concepts of structured programming is that any program can be written using only four kinds of instructions: sequential, case, loop control, and IF . . . THEN . . . ELSE instructions.

■ Each function or task the program must perform is known as a module.

■ A program design (also known as pseudocode) consists of the detailed steps that must be performed by each module within a program.

■ A flowchart is a method of using graphic representations to illustrate the detailed steps of a hierarchy chart.

■ Arrows, which are called flow-lines, are used in a flowchart to connect the different steps and show the direction of data flow.

■ For each of the statements in the program design or flowchart, one or more statements are written in the chosen programming language. When using structured design, the main module is coded and tested first, then all other modules are coded and tested.

■ The testing process involves inputting a wide assortment of data (including data with errors) to make sure the program can adequately deal with a variety of situations and yield the correct output. Two different types of bugs are checked for during the testing process: syntax bugs and logic bugs. Alpha testing is usually conducted by the developer in a very controlled environment. Beta testing is usually conducted by the end user after bugs and other short-comings detected in the alpha test have been fixed.

■ There is little compatibility among the various programming languages.

The following key terms were defined in this module. For each of the following terms, write on a separate piece of paper the number of the definition followed by the letter of the appropriate term.

Terms

A. assembler

B. assembly language

C. BASIC

D. C programming language

E. COBOL

F. coding

G. compiler program

H. flowchart

I. FORTRAN

J. fourth-generation language

K. hierarchy chart

L. high-level language

M. interpreter program

N. low-level program

O. machine language

P. module

Q. object program

R. Pascal

S. PL/1

T. event-driven software

U. pseudocode

V. Java

W. run-time program

X. source program

Y. structured programming

Z. testing

Definitions

1 programs written in the computer's native language or in a language similar to the computer's native language

2 instructions written in the numeric code directly understood by the processor of the target machine

3 programs in which the programmer is able to write instructions to the computer using English and English-like terms

4 a program that translates each instruction of a high-level language into machine language before it can be executed

5 a program that translates an entire high-level language into machine language

6 a low-level language similar to machine language but considered to be a step above machine language

7 a program that translates the instructions of an assembly language program into its machine language equivalent and creates a second, executable version of the original

8 a programming language that is specifically designed for mathematic and scientific applications and whose acronym stands for formula translation

9 a programming language designed to be a high-level, interactive programming language whose acronym stands for beginner's all-purpose symbolic instruction code

10 a programming language designed to be a high-level, general-purpose language useful for writing programs for nearly every application

Matching

11 the term used to describe the program that is keyed into the computer from which translation is to be made

12 the term used to describe a translated, executable program

13 a special interpreter program that translates intermediate code (pseudocommands) into machine code at the time the program is executed

14 a high-level programming language designed for use in business applications whose acronym is derived from common business-oriented language

15 a high-level programming language designed to be general-purpose language combining the business processing features of COBOL with the mathematic and scientific features of FORTRAN

16 a programming language that can be used to create executable content, called applets, that can be inserted in pages downloaded from the Internet. Applets that are downloaded into an Internet user's computer are automatically executed to display text and graphics, provide animation, produce titles, play audio files, or enable the user to perform interactive activities.

17 a programming language that is considered to be a general-purpose language that enables programmers to code their programs using a high-level type symbolic code while providing low-level control over the hardware

18 the highest level of high-level programming languages

19 software designed to check for a user action at frequent intervals during program execution and that often uses prewritten routines designed to perform common tasks

20 a method used to write programs from logical, organized, detailed plans that define the steps that must be performed

21 a top-down design of a program that gradually increases in level of detail

22 the term used to describe each function or task the program must perform

23 detailed steps written in ordinary English that detail the steps to be performed by each module within a program

24 a graphic representation that illustrates the design of a program by using symbols to indicate tasks that must be completed and flowlines that show the direction of data flow

25 the process of writing the instructions of a computer program in a computer language

26 the process of finding and correcting errors, which is commonly known as "debugging"

Review

1. Why is a computer useless unless it has software? (Obj. 1)
2. Identify two characteristics of an assembly language. (Obj. 2)
3. Identify two characteristics of the FORTRAN language. (Obj. 2)
4. Identify at least two characteristics of the BASIC language. (Obj. 2)
5. Identify at least two characteristics of the Pascal language. (Obj. 2)
6. What is the advantage of using a run-time program when using the Pascal language? What is the disadvantage? (Obj. 2)
7. Identify at least two characteristics of the COBOL language. (Obj. 2)
8. What is the difference between a reserved word and a programmer-supplied word? (Obj. 2)
9. Identify at least two characteristics of the PL/1 language. (Obj. 2)
10. For what purpose was the Java programming language initially designed? (Obj. 2)
11. What is the purpose of the Perl programming language? (Obj. 2)
12. Why is the C programming language so popular among programmers writing software for PCs? (Obj. 2)
13. Briefly describe how most fourth-generation languages work. (Obj. 2)
14. What is meant by top-down design? (Obj. 3)
15. For what purpose is a report spacing chart used? (Obj. 3)
16. Identify the four general kinds of instructions used when writing any program. (Obj. 3)
17. What is a main module? (Obj. 3)
18. What are flowlines? (Obj. 3)
19. What is the difference between alpha and beta testing? (Obj. 3)

Activities

1 *Writing* Visit a local business, industry, governmental agency, your school's administration computer center, or other computer user. Find out what programming language is being used, why that language was chosen, and how new programs are developed. Prepare a report summarizing what you learned.

2 *Research* Consult the Help Wanted section of a computer magazine or your local newspaper to find employment advertisements for computer programmers. List the number of programming positions advertised. For each programming position, list the type of application, the kind of computer, the programming language used, and any other information provided.

3 *Speaking* Choose one of the languages discussed in this module. Give a short presentation to your class explaining the applications for which it is most commonly used. During your presentation, show an example of a program written in the language you have chosen, and briefly explain how the code is written.

4 *Teamwork* Divide into teams of approximately six students each. Each team is to develop a structured flowchart that can be used to code a program to update an existing student data file (that is already stored on your school's computer) with quarter or semester report-card information. A Report Card (containing the same information shown on your report card) should be printed to an attached printer as each student's record is updated. Be sure to include error-handling conditions in your design.

Each team should appoint a project leader. The project leader is to assign each team member one of the following tasks (add to and modify the tasks as necessary):

- Project Leader: Manages the team and combines each of the different modules into the finished program design.
- Team Member 1: Designs the report card output.
- Team Member 2: Designs the routine to handle the input (inputting the student's report card information and locating the matching student data file stored on the school's computer system).
- Team Member 3: Designs the routine to handle updating the student's data file.
- Team Member 4: Designs the routine to print the report card in the format designed by Team Member 1.
- Team Member 5: Designs the routine to handle the output (updating of the appropriate student's data file).

(Continued on next page.)

Activities

5 *Math* You are employed by an engineering company that uses computers for mathematic applications. To date, the company has used commercial, off-the-shelf software to satisfy its computer needs, but it now needs to write several of its own engineering application programs. You have been asked to submit a list of the criteria that should be considered when choosing the programming language best suited for the company. Justify your suggestions.

6 *Ethics* A programmer is given a detailed design from a systems analyst to develop a program that will produce a report for investors showing the financial condition of the company. While coding the program, the programmer discovers that the output will incorrectly produce a report showing that the finances of the company are better than they really are. When the programmer tells the analyst of this discovery, the programmer is told to follow the specifications or be fired. What would you do if you were the programmer? Do you think what the programmer was asked to do was ethical or unethical? Could it be considered a computer crime? Explain your responses.

7 *Internet* Access the Internet, and use your search engine to find information about a programming language not discussed in this module. Identify the language's primary purpose, advantages, and any disadvantages that may be provided. Popular programming languages you could search for include: ADA, RPG, ALGOL, APL, FORTH, LISP, LOGO, PILOT, or PROLOG. Use terms such as PROGRAMMING, LANGUAGE, COMPILER, and so on to help narrow your search. Report your findings.

Absolute Cell Reference
Cell address that remains the same no matter where the formula is copied.

Access Privilege
Each directory on a network can be set to read/write, read-only, or no access; individual users' access may be similarly controlled.

Access Time
The time it takes the computer to load a desired record from the auxiliary storage device into memory.

Accessories
Small applications that provide special needs (examples: clock, calculator, games).

Alphanumeric
Term that refers to both alphabetic and numeric characters.

Alpha Test
The first major test of developed software, usually conducted by the developer in a controlled environment.

Analysis Report
Report prepared by a systems analyst that states the problem, lists measurable objectives, and identifies data elements and sources required to meet the objectives and produce the desired information.

Anchor
The capability of attaching a figure to a point in text so that it stays with the appropriate text if other surrounding material is lengthened or shortened.

Appending
See Loading.

Application Program
A program that instructs the computer to perform a specific, user-defined task.

Archie
A utility on the Internet that searches for files available to be copied (transferred) by the network user.

Area Chart
A chart on which is displayed both the total and sum of each of the parts over time (example: total sales and sales of each item individually).

Artificial Intelligence
Systems that analyze complex conditions (though they are not able to think). Also called Expert Systems.

Ascender/Descender
The portion of a letter that rises above the x height or falls below the baseline.

ASCII (American Standard Code for Information Interchange)
Pronounced "as-key." The standardized code by which each letter, digit, punctuation mark, and special character is represented by seven or eight bits (ones and zeros).

Assembler
A program that translates assembly language programs into machine language.

Assembly Language
A low-level language that allows the programmer to communicate at the lowest level with the inner workings of the computer; considered a step above machine language.

Auxiliary Storage Device
A device that stores data and programs.

Background Task
When two or more applications are running simultaneously, the task that has a lower priority.

Backing Up
The process of copying the data to another medium (examples: floppy, tape) so that a duplicate is available. *See* Backup.

Backup
A copy of stored data; to copy such data. Backups are made to protect data from being damaged or destroyed.

Band Printer
A printer that uses a moving band or belt containing all printable characters. Tiny hammers strike the desired characters through an inked ribbon after they are correctly positioned against the paper.

Bandwidth
The volume or speed at which a communication channel operates.

Bar Graph
A graph on which each item is shown by a bar, either vertical or horizontal; generally used to show comparison.

Bar-Code Scanner
An input device that reads bars (lines) printed on a product. *See* Universal Product Code (UPC).

Baseline
The imaginary line on which the letters of type rest.

BASIC (Beginner's All-Purpose Symbolic Instruction code)
High-level interactive computer programming language; easy to learn because of its English-like instructions.

BASIC Statement
A single instruction of a BASIC program. *See* BASIC.

Baud Rate
The speed at which data can be transmitted, measured in number of bits (or signal events) per second.

BBS (Bulletin Board System)
With this system, any computer may be called by other computers to exchange messages and upload or download files; this requires a modem and BBS software.

Beta Test
The second major test of developed software, usually conducted at a customer site.

Boilerplate Text
Standard paragraphs or sentences stored on an auxiliary storage device that can be combined with custom text to produce a desired document.

Booting Up
Turning on, or activating, the computer's operating system and associated software programs.

Bridge
A connection between two similar networks.

Bugs
Errors in the program that may cause it to crash or operate incorrectly.

Bulletin Board System
See BBS.

Bus Topology
The arrangement of signal flow in a computer network where each computer is linked to a single communication channel by a terminator cable; signals travel the entire length of the channel, moving down each terminator cable and bouncing back.

Button
A screen area on which the user can click to select an action.

C Programming Language
A low-level language used mostly by programmers who want to get the best possible performance from their computers.

C++ Programming Language
An object-oriented successor to the C language that allows data to play an active role in the running of a program.

Cache Memory
Very high-speed RAM, generally available in small amounts, that is used to increase the speed of the processing cycle.

CAD/CAM
Computer-aided design and computer-aided manufacturing.

CAI
See Computer-Assisted Instruction.

Case Instructions
In program design, a way of executing one set of instructions out of numerous possibilities (example: Depending on [in case of] this user's choice, perform one of four functions...).

Cathode-Ray Tube (CRT)
The display device used in a monitor; it consists of an electron gun and a phosphorescent display screen. When the electrons hit the screen, they cause the screen's coating to glow, creating images.

CD-ROM (Compact Disk/Read-Only Medium)
A disk, similar in appearance to an audio CD, that is a random-access device with immense storage capacity (example: an encyclopedia) that can output text, graphics, and sound through the computer system.

Cell
The space on a spreadsheet where a single item is stored (examples: a value, a formula).

Cell Address
The location of a given spreadsheet cell, such as F17 (row F, column 27).

Cell Pointer
The cursor on a spreadsheet.

Central Processing Unit (CPU)
A hardware device that stores data and programs, executes program instructions, and performs arithmetic and logic operations.

Chain Printer
A printer that uses a rotating chain containing several sets of printable characters. Tiny hammers strike the desired characters through an inked ribbon after they are correctly positioned against the paper.

Chapter
In some publishing programs, a document or a file.

Character
A single letter, symbol, or number.

Character Data
In spreadsheets, alphanumeric data not used for computation but to identify the numeric values that appear in rows and columns (example: column heads).

Charting/Graphing Presentation Software
Software that enables the user to present numeric data in pictorial form as a graph or chart.

Chat Mode
An electronic means of sharing conversations with other selected users of a computer network.

CIM
Computer-integrated manufacturing.

Client-Server Computing
The process by which the user (client) is sent only a portion of a database through a computer network (example: only students who have an A average).

Clipboard
A temporary storage location in memory.

Coaxial Cable
High-quality communication cable that is heavily shielded and thus protected from outside interference; able to carry signals over distances up to 1000 feet.

COBOL (COmmon Business-Oriented Language)
First high-level language written for business applications; written in English-like sentences for ease of use.

CODASYL (COnference of Data System Languages)
Committee, assembled by the Department of Defense to design a machine-independent language, that laid down the specifications for COBOL.

Coding
Writing instructions for a computer program.

Color Models
Ways of replicating color in differing media (examples: printed paper, computer screen).

Color Separations
The pieces of film—most often four—that are required to print color on a press; each piece is burned onto a printing plate, and the paper passes over four plates while being printed. *See* Process Color.

Column
A single vertical area extending down a spreadsheet.

COM
See Computer Output Microfilm.

COM1
The modem connection on a PC; there may be more than one (COM2, COM3, etc.). *See also* Serial Port, Modem Port.

Command Line Entry
A method in which commands are entered by typing them on a keyboard.

Commercial Application Software
Application software available commercially because it is standard for most users.

Compiler Program
A program that at one time converts all of a program's English-like statements written by a programmer into the binary code understood by the computer.

Component Libraries
Computer files that contain mathematically defined shapes that may be used to build an image.

Compression
The reduction in size of a file by recognizing repeating patterns in the data.

Computer
An electronic device that accepts data, performs computations, and makes logical decisions to produce information in a form useful to humans.

Computer Graphics
Any pictorial representation produced by the computer, either on the display screen or another output device.

Computer Output Microfilm (COM)
This output device uses a photographic process to record computer data on film in greatly reduced size.

Computer System
A combination of hardware and software that interacts to accomplish a task.

Computer-Assisted Instruction (CAI)
The use of computers to enhance classroom learning.

Configuring
The process of matching logical and physical computer devices, done through a utility program (examples: setting up a particular brand of printer, setting the number of colors on the screen).

Contention Standard
The usual transmission standard for bus topology, in which data can be transmitted on the network any time there is no other computer already on the wire (examples: Ethernet, FDDI, CDDI, Apple's LocalTalk). *See* CSMA/CD.

Contents Box
A box on-screen where a label appears as it is being keyed; sometimes a separate stroke is required to enter it on a spreadsheet.

Controller
See Joystick.

Conversion
Replacing an old system with a new one; also, changing the data on a disk from one program or operating system to another.

Copy and Paste
A procedure that copies selected material without deleting it and inserts the material at another location in the document.

CPU
See Central Processing Unit.

Cross-References
An entry that refers to another page in the publication; many programs now automatically update the page number as the publication changes length during its creation.

CSMA/CD (Carrier-Sensing Multiple Access with Collision Detection)
The process by which the networked computer "listens" and responds to signals about the availability of the network for transmission. *See* Contention Standard.

Current Cell(s)
One or more selected cells, which will be affected by the next data entered.

Cursor
A marker that can be moved about the screen (using the keyboard, a mouse, or a joystick) to indicate where input will appear.

Custom Application Software
Application software written to meet the specific needs of an organization or individual.

Custom Programming
Programming done to specification by a professional resource outside of the organization.

Cut and Paste
Used in editing a document, these commands allow material to be deleted from one position and inserted at another.

D

Data
Facts in the form of alphabetic characters, numbers, special symbols, or words.

Data Communication
Communication of data from one location to another by using hardware, software, and transmission carriers.

Data Elements
See Data Fields.

Data Fields
Individual categories or types of data (for example, name and address). Also known as Data Elements.

Data Processing
See Information Processing.

Data Transfer Rate
The rate at which desired data is transferred from the auxiliary storage device into primary memory.

Database
A collection of organized data whose elements are related to each other.

Debugging
Removing errors (bugs) in a program that may cause it to crash or operate incorrectly.

Decompression
Restoration of a file to its full character status when retrieving it from storage.

Decorative Typeface
See Display Typeface.

Decryption
The decoding of data; unreadable code is turned into readable data.

Dedicated Communication Connection
A continuous connection to a Wide Area Network, used when the need for communication is constant.

Descender
See Ascender/Descender.

Desk Accessories
See Accessories.

Desktop Publishing
The use of a computer to produce an original layout of material that is to be printed.

Device Driver
Portion of the operating system that makes the connection between the logical device (such as the idea of a printer) and the physical device (the printer itself).

Digitally Recorded Sound
A method of recording sound wherein thousands of "slices" of the sound are recorded each second.

Digitizer Scanner
An input device used to convert shapes, pictures, or graphic images into numbers for storage by a computer.

Direct Access
See Random Access.

Disk Cartridge
A removable container holding a hard disk or disks.

Disk Pack
A group of hard disks.

Diskette
See Floppy Disk.

Disktop Publishing
The process of publishing on CD-ROM rather than on paper. *See* CD-ROM.

Display Typeface
A typeface with obvious design features that is used to create a decorative or attention-grabbing effect.

Distributed Database
A database where data is stored in more than one location and available to all users.

Document Construction
Combining various previously written and saved paragraphs and/or images to produce a finished document.

Document Templates
Feature of a word-processing program that presents formats for commonly used documents (examples: fax cover sheets, memos).

DOS (Disk Operating System)
Operating system developed by Microsoft and used on IBM PCs and clones since 1981. Character-based, it is often modified by shells that make it easier to use. *See* Shells.

Dot-Matrix Printer
An impact printer that produces images through rows and columns of dots.

Drawing Programs
Graphics programs that enable you to draw images that are then stored in mathematically defined objects.

Driver
PC term for software that enhances the computer's communications capability (examples: better sound, speech recognition). Called Extensions in the Macintosh environment.

Dumb Terminal
A terminal with no memory that is totally dependent on the stored program to which it is connected in the computer.

Dynamic Data Exchange
See Linking.

E

e-mail
Messages or files sent over a network to another user.

Electronic Mail
See e-mail.

Em Spaces and Dashes
These are the width of the letter *M* in the font being used; an em dash is typically used to set off a part of a sentence (example: You will—in time—learn to use dashes correctly).

En Spaces and Dashes
These are the width of the letter *N* in the font being used; an en dash is typically used to connect numerals (example: 1920–1939).

Encryption
The coding of data; readable data is turned into unreadable code, generally for efficiency of transmission.

Event-Driven Software
Software designed to check for a user action at frequent intervals during program execution and use prewritten routines to perform common tasks (example: automatic saving).

Executive
Portion of the operating system that controls or manages all other operating functions; sorts commands entered by user and determines which components are necessary to carry out the command.

Executive Information System
A system designed to allow business managers easy access to information from large data systems.

Expert Systems
See Artificial Intelligence.

Extensions
Macintosh term for software that enhances the computer's communications capability (examples: better sound, speech recognition). Called Drivers in the PC environment.

F

Feasibility Analysis Study
An analysis performed on each systems design alternative to test whether the alternative meets the objectives and is within the constraints of the organization. *See* Analysis Report.

Feedback
Continuous monitoring of a system to ensure that its purpose and objectives are being met.

Fiber Optics
The technology of passing light images over tiny strands of conductive material; used for high-speed transmission of data.

Fiber-Optic Cable
Cable made of very fine glass fibers that transmits laser light instead of electricity and can carry more data faster and farther than any other known transmission medium; used in WANs.

Field
One piece of data about an individual, organization, or other entity; all fields together make up a record. *See* Record.

File
A collection of related records.

File Library
An electronic source where users of a computer information service can both upload and download programs to share with other users.

File Manager
Windows application that presents a screen listing disk directories for user selection; clicking on the desired file opens it.

File Server
The main computer on a network; its function is to allow access to shared files.

Financial Software
Software designed to maintain financial records.

Finder
Shell used by Macintosh to launch programs, show contents of disks, and manage files. Clicking on the desired icon opens that file. *See* Shells.

First Normal Form
The level of refinement of a database that requires no repeating fields in a table. *See* Field.

Flat File Database
A database limited to only one table.

Flexible Disk
See Floppy Disk.

Floppy Disk
A small (5 1/4 or 3 1/2 inch) pliable magnetic disk commonly used for data storage. Also known as a Flexible Disk or a Diskette.

Flowchart
A graphic representation of a hierarchy chart that indicates what kind of action is taking place at each step. *See* Hierarchy Chart.

Flowlines
The arrows that connect the steps of a flowchart and show the direction of flow.

Font
In typefaces, a specific combination of size, style, and weight (example: 10-point Times Roman boldface and 10-point Times Roman italic are separate fonts).

Foreground Task
When two or more applications are running simultaneously, the task that has priority.

Formatting
The process by which a new disk or tape is prepared for storing data in a particular operating system.

Formulas
Mathematic equations used to compute spreadsheet values; the formula may appear in the contents box.

FORTRAN (FORmula TRANslation)
The first problem-oriented compiler language; specifically designed for math and science applications.

Forums
A resource for users of computer networks where questions may be posted and answered and information may be debated.

Frame
The designated area of each individual element on a text page (examples: a photo, some text, a graph). Material within the frame can be worked on without affecting the other elements on the page.

Function
A calculation or procedure that is built into the spreadsheet software (example: summing).

Function Keys
Keys on the computer keyboard that activate stored software programs to perform specific tasks.

G

General-Purpose Computers
Computers where both computation and input/output processing capabilities support a wide array of applications.

Gigabyte
One billion bytes (actually 1,024,000,000).

Gopher
A utility on the Internet that provides access to information on a server.

Graphic User Interface
Program such as Windows (for PCs) or System 7 (for Macintosh) that presents icons on screen for ease of selection by the user.

Graphics Tablet
An input device consisting of a flat surface and a stylus for creating drawings that are stored in the computer's memory.

Graphing
See Charting/Graphing Presentation Software.

Graphing Software
Software that translates textual and numeric data into charts or graphs (examples: pie chart, line graph).

GUI (Graphic User Interface)
Program that substitutes on-screen icons for alphabetic commands to make the computer easier to use.

H

Hard Copy
Data on paper.

Hard Disk
A rigid magnetic disk with high density and speed that is used within the computer to store data.

Hardware
The tangible, physical equipment of a computer, which includes input, processing, storage, and output devices.

Hierarchic Directory Structure (Tree Structure Directory)
A method by which the operating system appears to organize disk storage space into directories and subdirectories; it is patterned on a file cabinet, where drawers contain folders and folders contain documents.

Hierarchy Chart
A way of planning a top-down program design that depicts the gradually increasing level of detail.

High-Level Languages
Similar for all processors, these computer languages allow the programmer to focus on problem-solving rather than on fully utilizing the processor (example: they may use English or English-like terms).

HTML
Hypertext Markup Language—a set of markup codes for creating Web pages.

Hypermedia
An application that connects a multimedia front end to a number of data sources for retrieval of information.

Icon
An image that conveys information quickly (example: a scissors that allows the user to cut text).

Identifiers
In Pascal, the variables used to store various data types (characters, integer numbers, real numbers). *See* Variable.

IF...THEN...ELSE Instructions
Instructions to the computer to perform one task if a statement is true or another if the statement is false.

Image Libraries
Computer files that contain predrawn art for use with painting and drawing programs.

Impact Printer
A printer that physically strikes the paper to form images.

Index
A reference typically found at the end of a publication that lists items and page numbers for readers seeking specific information; indexes may now be done automatically by a program if items are specially marked by the writer as the publication is created.

Information
Data in a form that humans can understand and use.

Information Processing (Data Processing)
The process of sharing information between humans and computers. It includes sorting, classifying, calculating, summarizing, and comparing data.

Information Superhighway
A global network of computers that provides access through digital, voice, and video communication to information resources anywhere in the world.

Information Utilities
Businesses or universities that use large computers to store huge amounts of information about many subjects and make it available to the public.

Ink-Jet Printer
A nonimpact printer that produces high-quality images by spraying liquid ink onto the paper. Some can print in color.

Input
Data that enters the computer system via an input or storage device.

Input Device
A hardware device that enables the computer to accept data (example: a keyboard).

Insertion Point
A blinking, on-screen bar that indicates where text will be inserted when keyed. Also called a Cursor.

Integrated Software
Software that combines the functions of two or more applications (example: word processing/spreadsheet/database).

Interactivity
The operation of a program under which the user controls the progression of events (example: a program to teach typing is interactive).

Internet
The world's largest Wide Area Network. Begun by the U.S. Defense Department, it is now worldwide and includes governmental, educational, commercial, and personal users.

Interpreter Program
A program that translates high-level language into machine language as a user runs the program (as opposed to translating all of the program statements at the same time upon completion of the program writing activity).

Intranet
A variation of the Internet that is internal to a company and protected against outside access.

ISDN (Integrated Services Digital Network)
Digital phone technology where conversation is converted to digital signals before being transmitted and converted back to analog form to produce sound at the receiving end.

J

Java Programming Language
A high-level language that permits software developed at one site to be executed on a variety of different computers on a network or the Internet.

Joystick
A metal or plastic rod that moves both horizontally and vertically which is used to locate a position on the screen. Also called a Controller.

K

Kerning
The process of adjusting the spaces between letters so that all combinations of letters appear to be spaced equally.

Keyboard
The most common input device. When a computer key is pressed, the computer converts the stroke into a specific code and stores it in memory. A typical computer keyboard is divided into four sections: function keys, typewriter keyboard, numeric pad, and directional keys.

Kilobyte
One thousand bytes (actually 1,024).

L

Labels
Alphanumeric characters entered into spreadsheet cells to identify them (example: column heads) and on which no calculations may be done. *See* Alphanumeric.

LAN
See Local Area Networks.

Landscape Orientation
A text page that prints wider than it is tall.

Laser Printer
A nonimpact printer that produces a high-quality image, sometimes in color, by an electrophotographic process in which a beam of light creates an electrically charged figure on a metal drum receptive to photographic images. Tiny ink particles (called toner) stick to the image, which the drum rolls onto the paper.

Latency
The time it takes the desired data to pass under the reading mechanism while it is being read.

Leading
A printing term that indicates the amount of space between lines of type; when typesetters used hot metal to set type, they literally inserted a strip of lead between each line.

Line Graph
A graph where the values of an item are plotted over time and then the nodes are connected to form a horizontal line; generally used for ease of understanding changes over time.

Line-Based Graphics
Graphics created through a drawing program where the elements are stored as shapes represented by mathematical formulas.

Linking
A process of connecting two programs so that they can share data (example: a letter that contains a chart).

Liquid Crystal Display (LCD)
A screen made of two layers of clear material between which is a fluid that changes color when electricity is applied in a pattern to create characters.

Loading (Appending)
Entering data into a table or database.

Local Area Networks (LANs)
Computer networks limited to a small area such as a school or an office building and generally connected with cables.

Local Terminal
A device, usually a display screen and keyboard, located near the computer and directly cabled into the computer's processor.

Logging On (Login)
Entering your user name and password to gain access to a network.

Logging Out (Logout)
Disconnecting from the network; this frees network space for other users.

Logical Device
The intangible set of instructions used by the operating system to control physical devices (examples: mouse, printer).

Loop Control
Instructions used to make the computer repeat what it is doing until some new condition exists.

Low-Level (Machine) Languages
Programs with instructions written in numeric code directly understood by the processor that require the programmer to think in terms of the particular processor being used.

Machine Languages
See Low-Level Languages.

Macro
A recorded sequence of strokes or mouse-click instructions that can be easily "replayed" upon demand.

Magnetic Disk
A disk that is an input, output, and storage medium. It uses magnetic spots to record data.

Magnetic Ink Character Recognition (MICR)
An input process (used by banks) whereby numbers and symbols printed with magnetic ink on checks, deposits, and withdrawals are recognized by the computer.

Magnetic Scanner
An input device to read encoded information from magnetic strips, generally those on the back of credit or bank cards; operates similar to a videotape player.

Magnetic Tape
A long strip of flexible plastic that is coated with microscopic bars of a material that can be magnetized; may be on reels or contained in a cartridge.

Magneto-Optical Drive
A drive, using removable media capable of large storage capacity, where data are stored by a magnetic reversal induced by a laser beam.

Mailbox
The electronic location in the server where messages are held for the user and displayed at the time the user logs on. *See* e-mail, Logging On.

Main Storage
See Memory.

Mainframes
The largest computer systems, gradually being replaced by microprocessor-based systems.

Mapping
A way of making any directory or subdirectory look like a separate disk drive so that it will appear on startup.

MAUs (Multistation Access Units)
Connector boxes to which the cables of a token ring network are attached.

Megabyte
One million bytes (actually 1,024,000).

Megahertz
One million cycles, or pulses, per second; this measurement is used to state the internal clock speed of a computer.

Membrane Keyboard
A computer keyboard with a protective flexible cover that is designed to withstand a hazardous environment.

Memory
The location within the CPU where electronic data is stored. Also known as Main Storage or Primary Storage.

Menu
An on-screen list of commands available to the user in preparing a document.

Metalanguage
A programming language or set of codes used to create other programming languages or sets of codes.

Microfiche
Small rectangular sheets of photographic transparencies containing miniature text and graphics that can be viewed with a magnifying reader. Can be produced as computer output or through photographic means.

Microminiaturization
The ongoing technological process of size reduction that has enabled an entire microprocessor to occupy the space of a tiny chip.

Microprocessor
A miniaturized processor, made possible by the development of the silicon chip, that led to the creation of the microcomputer (personal computer).

Microsecond
One millionth of a second (1/1,000,000).

Microwave Carriers
Transmitters of communication over distance on a straight-line path from one station to another; "dishes" and satellites are microwave carriers.

Minicomputers
Mid-size computers, smaller than mainframes and larger than microcomputers.

Modem
A device that modulates the digital signals from a computer into analog signals for the phone system and then demodulates the analog signals back into digital signals for the receiving computer; the word *modem* is taken from the terms "modulator/demodulator."

Modem Commands
Signals from software to the modem that tell it to do something (example: dial a telephone).

Modem Port
The modem connection on a Macintosh. *See also* Serial Port, COM1.

Module
A segment of a program design; the main module is the top box in the hierarchy chart. *See* Program Design, Hierarchy Chart.

Monochromatic Screen
A video display screen that is limited to one color, usually green, amber, or white.

Mouse
A palm-sized device with one or more push buttons that has a ball housed in the undercarriage; used to move the cursor or tell the computer to take a specific action.

Multimedia
The use of several mediums, such as sound, graphics, text, animation, and video.

Multitasking
Characteristic of an operating system that can juggle more than one task at a time; commonplace today.

Nanosecond
One billionth of a second (1/1,000,000,000).

Network
A group of computers connected together so they can communicate with each other.

Network Operating System
Software that controls the communication between the different components of a computer network. May be dedicated to network operation (such as Novell NetWare) or may be included as a portion of a general purpose operating system (such as Windows NT or OS/2).

Node
A single computer attached to a network.

Nodes
Reference points indicating the boundaries of an object; moving the nodes can change the size, shape, or position of the object.

Nonimpact Printer
A printer that produces images through mechanical or electronic action other than physically striking the paper.

Numeric Pad
The arrangement of numeric keys on the computer keyboard that is like a calculator, where numeric data can be quickly keyed.

O

Object Program
In Pascal, the result of using the Pascal compiler to translate the source program.

OCR
See Optical Character Reader.

Off-the-Shelf Software
Software available commercially that is not customized and may thus require some adjusting of the users' requirements.

On-Demand Connection
A connection to a Wide Area Network through a phone line that is accessed as needed.

On-line Banking
Access to a bank's services using a personal computer and modem.

Operating System 2
See OS/2.

Operating System
The software that controls operation of the computer and enables communication between components.

Optical Character Reader (OCR)
An input device that "reads" numbers, letters, and symbols directly from a typed, printed, or handwritten page.

Optical Mark Reader
An input device that scans a form and records whether a mark (usually a rectangle or circle) is present or absent (example: the scoring of a standardized test).

Original Data
See Raw Data.

OS/2 (Operating System 2)
Originated as a joint venture of Microsoft and IBM, later retained by IBM when Microsoft developed Windows NT. Similar to Windows; runs on chips in the Intel microprocessors and the clones.

Output
Data that leaves the computer system via any output or storage device.

Output Device
A hardware device that reports information in an understandable form (examples: a monitor, a printer).

P

Paint and Draw Software
Software that can be used to create, edit, and print color drawings.

Paint Programs
Graphics programs that enable the user to change the colors of pixels on the display.

Pascal
A high-level, general-purpose programming language named for Blaise Pascal; its advantage is that the same Pascal code can run on many different computers.

Passive-Matrix Color Display
A flat-panel color screen used on portable computers. Still in development, these screens are slow and shadowy.

Password
The secret word that must be input by the user before being allowed access to a program or network.

PC-CD Drive
Combines the ability to read a standard CD-ROM with the abilities to both read and write an optical disk.

Peer-to-Peer Networking
Characteristic of a network on which the users are all equals, or peers, and can open each others' files (with permission); all the computers are connected to all the other computers.

PERL
An interpreted language designed for system management, scanning text files, extracting information from those files, and printing reports based on the information extracted.

Personal Computer
A small, desk-sized microcomputer designed for individual use in homes and offices.

Personal Finance Software
Software designed to maintain financial records for an individual or family.

Physical Device
The actual, physical equipment attached to a computer (examples: mouse, printer).

Pica
A measurement used in printing; 12 points make a pica, and 6 picas (72 points) make an inch.

Pie Chart
A chart in the form of a circle with each item taking its appropriate portion (slice) of the pie; generally used to show proportions or a division of the whole into its parts.

Pixel-Based Graphics
Graphics that are stored in the computer as a pattern of dots. *See* Pixels.

Pixels
PICture ELements, or tiny particles of phosphorescence activated by electrons to produce images on a screen (the more pixels, the greater clarity—resolution—of the screen image).

PL/1 (Programming Language/1)
Program that combines the business features of COBOL with the mathematical and scientific features of FORTRAN.

Plotter
A graphics output device that can produce maps, artwork, or any type of line (no shades of gray) illustration. It consists of one or more pens that either move over the surface of a sheet of paper (flat-bed plotter) or are fixed while the paper moves under them (drum plotter).

Points
A measurement used in printing; 12 points make a pica, and 6 picas (72 points) make an inch.

Portable Computer
A lightweight (15 ounces to 15 pounds) computer designed to be easily carried from place to place. Also called laptops, notebooks, powerbooks, or PDAs (personal digital assistants).

Portrait Orientation
A text page that prints taller than it is wide.

Predefined Styles
Selections of available page designs that are part of publishing programs; may be called tags, styles, or templates.

Presentation Software
Software that organizes graphic images for use as visual aids (examples: sales presentations, classroom instruction).

Primary Key
A field or combination of fields that makes each row or record unique (example: a social security number).

Primary Storage.
See Memory.

Printer
An output device that produces a printed paper record.

Printhead
A device that moves across the paper firing tiny pins or wires that tap the paper through an inked ribbon and form the desired images.

Process Color
The full range of colors that becomes available when the four basic printing colors—magenta (red), cyan (blue), yellow, and black—are combined. *See* Color Separations.

Processing
Activity within the computer's processor where detailed instructions, called software programs, tell the computer what to do to produce the desired information.

Processor
A hardware device that processes data into meaningful information.

Program
A series of detailed, step-by-step instructions that tell the computer what to do.

Program Manager
Windows application that presents a screen showing icons for the programs available to the user; clicking on an icon opens the program.

Programmer-Supplied Words
In COBOL, words used in the program that are not reserved; they must be defined in the data division of the program. *See* Reserved Word.

Pseudocode
The steps a computer program must perform, expressed in plain English as opposed to a computer language; a program design.

Public Message Service
Messages and announcements are placed in a special mailbox for all valid users on the network.

Publication
An entire work that may be a collection of chapters or sections made up of text and graphics.

Q

Queue
The intangible printer "waiting line" where jobs are placed until the printer is available.

R

RAM (Random Access Memory)
Memory where stored data can be retrieved for review and further processing. This data can be stored and retrieved in whatever order is desired (randomly).

Random Access
A system for going directly to the location of specific data without having to read through all other data (as with a CD player).

Random Access Memory
See RAM.

Range
Any contiguous (adjoining) group of cells.

Raw Data
Data fed into the computer for processing. Also called Original Data.

Read-Only Memory
See ROM.

Real-Time Sensors
Input devices that monitor processes (example: air conditioning equipment) or events and transmit findings to a computer at regular intervals without human assistance.

Record
A collection of related data fields.

Record Locking
A safeguard where only one user at a time can access a field to change it.

Reference Points
See Nodes.

Relational Database
A database that consists of more than one table where the tables are related to one another (example: names/addresses with records of contributions).

Relative Cell Reference
Cell address that automatically changes or is updated when the formula is copied to another cell.

Remote Networks
See Wide Area Networks.

Remote Terminal
A device, usually a display screen and keyboard, located at a geographical distance and connected to the computer by a telephone line.

Research Services
Large databases from a wide array of sources that may be accessed through a computer that is part of a network.

Reserved Word
A word that has specific meaning to a COBOL compiler (examples: ADD, MOVE) and is used only in that context.

Resolution
The clarity of an image, which in printing derives from the number of dots per inch (dpi) and on a monitor derives from the number of pixels per inch.

Restoring
The process of copying data from backup media to the hard disk after a failure has been rectified. *See* Backing Up.

Ribbon
An area of a graphic user interface screen that contains "buttons" that can be "pressed" to change the appearance of text (examples: italic, bold, left justified, right justified).

Ring Topology
The arrangement of signal flow in a computer network where data travels around an unbroken loop, bypassing others until it reaches the device for which it is intended. *See also* Token Passing.

ROM (Read-Only Memory)
Memory where data can be "read" but not changed. It is used to tell the computer how to start up and how to perform the tasks for which it was designed.

Router
A processor that connects a network to a dissimilar network (example: a LAN to a mainframe) and is also able to translate one protocol (language) to another.

Row
A single horizontal area extending across a spreadsheet.

RPG (Report Program Generator)
High-level programming language initially designed to generate business reports.

Ruler
An on-screen measuring device that allows the user to change paragraph indents and tabs or margin settings.

Run-Time Program
In Pascal, an interpreter program that translates commands into machine code as the program is executed; a specific run-time program for each model of computer allows Pascal code to run on each of them.

S

Sampling Rate
The number of times per second the computer records an image of the sound being recorded.

Sans Serif Typeface
A typeface with no horizontal embellishments; its simpler look is often used where ease of reading is not paramount (example: newspaper headlines). *See* Serif Typeface.

Scanners
Input devices that can recognize printed characters, symbols, and graphic images and store them in memory.

Screen
A presentation of a color or black that is less that 100% and thus achieves shades of gray or tints of a color. Screens are measured in grid lines ("a 133-line screen") because, before computers, printers overlaid actual screens on photographs to achieve a printable dot pattern.

Scroll Bars
Vertical and horizontal on-screen bars that are used to move a document through the text area for viewing.

Search Engine
An navigation device that lets you look up information based on entry of key words.

Search Time
See Seek Time.

Second Normal Form
The level of refinement in a database where each field (column) must be dependent on the primary key. *See* Primary Key.

Seek Time
The time it takes to position the access mechanism over the desired data. Also known as Search Time.

Sequential Access
A system for recording and reading data only in one-after-the-other sequence (as with an audio tape).

Sequential Instructions
Steps to be performed one after another; used in program design.

Serial Port
A connection on the computer through which bits travel in single file. Typically used for a modem or mouse.

Serif Typeface
A typeface that has small horizontal embellishments at the ends of the strokes to guide the eye across the line of type for ease of reading.

SGML
Standard Generalized Markup Language—a metalanguage that can be used to create different markup schemes.

Shells
User-interface programs that present menus to make the operating system easier to access; Windows is such a shell. *See* Windows.

Simulation Software
Software designed to duplicate or model conditions in the real world (example: a flight simulator).

Single-Program Execution
Characteristic of an operating system that can execute just one application program at a time.

Smart Terminal
A terminal with memory that can be programmed to perform tasks.

Software
The nonphysical, electronic instructions that tell a computer what to do; software includes system and application programs.

Software Tools
Routines that have been written to perform common tasks (example: drawing a window on the display screen).

Sound Boards
Devices that mimic sounds (including human voices and musical instruments) and can be installed in the computer. Also called Sound Cards.

Sound Cards.
See Sound Boards.

Source Documents
Paper forms on which data may be written before being entered into the computer.

Source Program
The English-like version of a computer program that can be read and understood by humans; it is translated into computer binary code by either a compiler or interpreter program.

Special-Purpose Computers
Computers of varying sizes designed to perform specialized tasks, from running a microwave oven or an automobile's ignition system to controlling traffic lights or space vehicles.

Speech Recognition Device
An input device that is voice-controlled.

Spelling Checker
A feature of a word-processing program that compares the words of a document to an internal dictionary and calls attention to any words that may need correction—often suggesting corrected spelling as well as alternate choices in case of a typographical error. Sometimes simply called a Spell Checker.

Spindle
A vertical shaft on which several hard disks may be stacked.

Spot Color
Limited areas of color on publications printed with various colored ink as opposed to using process color.

Spreading
See Trapping/Spreading.

Spreadsheet
An arrangement of data in rows and columns, allowing ease of comprehension as well as the computing of values through formulas.

Status Bar
An on-screen bar that displays such information as current page number, number of pages in the document, and whether the CAPS and NUM keys are engaged.

Stop Bits
Bits that come after the seven or eight bits that designate a character in ASCII code; they designate the end of the character. *See also* ASCII.

Storage Device
A hardware device that permits storage of data.

Structured Design
See Structured Programming.

Structured Programming
The writing of programs from logically organized, detailed plans that define steps to be performed; based on structured design (the planning of the program).

Suite Software
Software applications that are tightly integrated so that the user can access all available functions easily (example: by using a common tool bar).

Supercomputer
The fastest and most expensive mainframes. They are used for highly complex tasks such as advanced research and mathematical calculations that cannot be performed on smaller systems.

Synthesizer
A device connected to a computer that can generate sound and combine elements of different sounds into a complex whole.

System 7
Popular version of Apple's operating system for the Macintosh.

System
Related devices or procedures that function together to achieve a common objective.

System Design Report
A report submitted to management after completing feasibility analysis of all design alternatives.

System Life Cycle
The period of time in which a given computer system's usefulness to perform a given task is measured.

System Program
A program that controls the computer's circuitry and hardware devices.

Systems Analyst
The person who acts as a link between users of a system and the technical personnel who actually develop and install the system.

Systems Design Flowchart
A chart showing each of the major components of a system and how they interact with each other.

Table of Contents
A listing of the sections and chapters within a publication, sometimes including the major headings as well.

Tape Cartridge
A device used primarily with personal computers to provide backup for hard disks.

Tape Reel
A flexible magnetic tape on a spool that is used primarily by mainframes and minicomputers for processing sequential applications or backup of data stored on disk.

Telnet
A utility on the Internet that allows a user to log on to another computer network (LAN) as if actually present at the network location.

Template
A spreadsheet format that has no labels or values and can be easily utilized for certain common tasks by simply entering current data.

Terminal
Any device that inputs or outputs data to or from a computer system. Though they vary, terminals often consist of a display screen and a keyboard that are connected in some way to a computer.

Terminal Emulation
A way in which software allows your microcomputer to act like a dumb terminal in relation to a mainframe.

Terminate-and-Stay-Resident (TSR) **Program**
Used in single-program systems to run accessories; TSRs temporarily take the place of the application program—it does not run simultaneously.

Testing
See Debugging.

Text Area
The large empty portion of the screen where text appears when it is keyed.

Text Formatting
Controlling the characteristics that affect the appearance of a document when it is printed.

Thermal Printer
A nonimpact printer that produces images on heat-sensitive paper. A matrix arrangement of tiny, heated rods fires against the heat-sensitive paper, burning the images onto it.

Thesaurus Software
A resource within a word-processing program where the user can find a selection of synonyms for a word used in a document.

Third Normal Form
The level of refinement in a database requiring that all fields (columns) in a table be dependent ONLY on the primary key.

Time Slicing
A technique by which the computer allots processing time to two or more tasks simultaneously.

Token Passing (Token Ring)
In ring topology, the token is a packet of data that carries an electronic address; the token is delivered before another token is accepted on the network.

Token Ring
See Ring Topology and Token Passing.

Toolbar
A row of on-screen icons (sometimes called "buttons") that allow commands to be chosen quickly.

Toolbox
A collection of commonly used, prewritten software tools available to the programmer.

Toolkit
See Toolbox.

Tools
See Desktop Accessories.

Top-Down Design
A program design that proceeds from defining the program to more and more complex levels of detail.

Topology
The logical arrangement of signal flow in a computer network.

Touch Screen
A screen that allows input by direct touch of the finger.

Trackball
Performs the same functions as a mouse, but from a stationary housing; some trackballs are extensions of standard keyboards.

Transmission Carriers
The kinds of cable or other media that connect computers to a network.

Transmission Standards
The "rules of the road" that govern the flow of traffic on a computer network.

Trapping/Spreading
In printing, slightly shrinking the "holes" or slightly enlarging the "top" objects in a multicolored layout to make the finished product look better when the different colored inks are not applied in perfect registration or alignment with each other.

Tree Structure Directory
A directory in the form of an inverted tree with branching subdirectories. *See* Hierarchic Directory Structure.

TSR Program
See Terminate-and-Stay-Resident Program.

Twisted-Pair Wire
Similar to telephone wire, it is used to connect computers in networks; pairs of wires are twisted to reduce electrical noise.

Typeface
A set of letters, digits, and symbols that share a particular design.

Typeface Styles
Variations on a typeface that can be used for special effects (examples: italics, boldface).

U

Universal Product Code (UPC)
A product-identification code consisting of a series of vertical bars of varying widths that are "read" by the laser of a bar-code scanner. Each product has a bar code assigned by the manufacturer.

Unix
Multiprocessing operating system originated by Bell Labs to control telephone switching computers; subsequently popular as an operating system for minicomputers and microcomputers; now owned by Novell.

UPC
See Universal Product Code.

User Name
A name designated by the network administrator for each person who can legitimately use the network; frequently some combination of the user's name, such as a first initial and last name combined.

Utility Programs
Software that is loaded from disk whenever needed to perform housekeeping functions for the computer (examples: formatting disks, backing up data).

V

Values
Numbers (measurements) entered into a spreadsheet on which calculations may be performed (examples: prices, expenses).

Variable
A named storage location in the computer's memory.

Veronica
A utility on the Internet that uses Boolean searching (AND and OR) to look at all available gopher menus.

Video Display Screens
The most common output devices, they display images and thus are well suited for both input and output.

Video Graphics Controller
A separate board inside the CPU that contains its own memory and greatly increases the computer's graphic and color capabilities.

Virtual Memory
The use of disk space to simulate memory.

W

WAIS (Wide Area Information System)
A utility on the Internet that allows the network user access to entire texts, all available topics, and complete mailing lists.

WAN
See Wide Area Network.

Web Browser
Software installed on user's computer that allows the user to connect to and navigate the Internet.

Wide Area Information System
See WAIS.

Wide Area Network (WAN)
Computer network not limited geographically (examples: across a state, a country, the world). Such networks use carriers such as telephone lines, satellites, and microwave stations to transmit data. Also called Remote Networks. Several LANs may be part of a WAN. *See* Local Area Network.

Windows
Graphic user interface (GUI) for DOS operating system that presents icons (pictures) on screen for user selection; double-clicking on the icon starts up the desired application.

Word Processing
The preparation of documents.

Word Processing Software
Complex software program that allows the preparation of documents and provides an array of supportive features such as revising, spelling and grammar checks, and graphics.

Worldwide Web (WWW)
A service on the Internet that allows the user to locate and read documents that include typefaces and graphics.

WORM (Write Once/Read Many Times)
Disk storage devices that use laser beams and precision opticals to serve as high-volume backup for permanent archives of information (example: a library).

WYSIWYG
Pronounced "wizzy wig," it stands for What You See Is What You Get and indicates the degree to which the screen shows what will be output by the printer. Today's word processing programs achieve a high degree of WYSIWYG.

x-height
The vertical measurement of the letter *x* in a given typeface.

Photo Acknowledgments

Openers

IN 1 © Marjory Dressler
IP 1 © Marjory Dressler
OS 1 © 1995 PhotoDisc, Inc.
NT 1 © 1995 PhotoDisc, Inc.
TE 1 © 1995 PhotoDisc, Inc.
WP 1 © 1995 PhotoDisc, Inc.
SP 1 © 1995 PhotoDisc, Inc.
PB 1 © 1995 PhotoDisc, Inc.
GP 1 © 1995 PhotoDisc, Inc.
MH 1 © 1995 PhotoDisc, Inc.
DB 1 © 1995 PhotoDisc, Inc.
AP 1 © 1995 PhotoDisc, Inc.
SA 1 © 1995 PhotoDisc, Inc.
SD 1 © 1995 PhotoDisc, Inc.

Module IN

3 © 1995 PhotoDisc, Inc.
© Robert Copeland/Westlight.
4 Photo courtesy of Apple Computer, Inc.
6 Photography by Alan Brown.
6 © Robert Landau/Westlight.
6 © Robert Menzel/Stock, Boston.
6 © Joseph Nettis/Stock, Boston.
7 (r) Reprinted with permission of Compaq Computer Corporation. All Rights Reserved.
7 © P. M. Grecco/Stock, Boston.
9 Photo courtesy of International Business Machines.
10 © R. Ian Lloyd/Westlight.
12 © 1995 PhotoDisc, Inc.
14 Photo courtesy of Sperry Corporation.
14 John Greenleigh/Apple Computer, Inc.
15 Photo courtesy of International Business Machines.
16 Photo courtesy of Apple Computer, Inc.
17 © John Coletti/Stock, Boston.
18 Photo courtesy of Hewlett-Packard Company, Convex Division.
19 © Stock, Boston.
20 © H. Morgan/Rainbow.
22 Photo courtesy of Dial One Security, Inc.
23 © Peter Menzel/Stock, Boston.
24 © Bob Daemmrich/Stock, Boston.
25 © Spencer Grant/Stock, Boston.

Module IP

2 Photo courtesy of NCR Corporation.
3 (a) © Guennadi Maslou/Photonics.
3 (b) Photography by Eric Von Fischer/Photonics.
4 © William McCoy/Rainbow.
4 © Hank Morgan/Rainbow.
5 © Hank Morgan/Rainbow.
6 © Charles Gupton/Stock, Boston.
8 © Drew Jimsan/Tony Stone Worldwide.
8 Photo courtesy of International Business Machines.
12 © William McCoy/Rainbow.
13 Photo courtesy of Apple Computer, Inc.
17 Photo courtesy of International Business Machines Corporation. Unauthorized use not permitted.
20 Photo courtesy of Hewlett Packard.
20 Photo courtesy of Hewlett Packard.
23 © 1995 PhotoDisc, Inc.

23 © John Abbott.
26 (a) Photo courtesy of International Business Machines Corporation.
27 Photo courtesy of Plus Development Corporation.
29 Photo courtesy of SyQuest Technology, Inc.
32 © Stone/Neurath/Stock, Boston.

Module OS

4 © Nick Dolding/Tony Stone Images.
7 Photo courtesy of Hewlett Packard Company.
18 © Ralph Mercer/Tony Stone Images.
22 Photo courtesy of International Business Machines.
24 Reprinted with permission from Microsoft Corp., 1996.

Module NT

2 Photo courtesy of International Business Machines Corporation. Unauthorized use not permitted.
16 Courtesy Optical Cable Corporation.
18 Photo courtesy of International Business Machines Corporation. Unauthorized use not permitted.
32 © Jeff Greenberg/d/MR.

Module TE

2 © Bob Daemmrich/Stock, Boston.
4 © Ron Lowery/Tony Stone Worldwide.
6 Photo courtesy of Supra Corporation.
8 © Michael Simpson/FPG International.
19 © Lawrence Manning/Westlight.
20 © Peter Poulides/Tony Stone Worldwide.
21 © Dallas & John Weston/Westlight.
23 Photo courtesy of AT&T Archives.
24 © Rob Brandall/Rainbow.

Module WP

20 © 1995 PhotoDisc, Inc.

Module SP

8 © 1992 Seth Resnick. All rights reserved.
12 Photo courtesy of Minolta Corporation.
12 Photo courtesy of International Business Machines.
26 © Phil Matt.

Module PB

2 © Richard Pasley/Stock, Boston.
6 © Kim Heacox/Tony Stone Images.
9 © Richard Pasley/Stock, Boston.
12 © Stan Fellerman/Tony Stone Worldwide.
13 © Tom Walker/Stock, Boston.
23 © Richard Pasley/Stock, Boston.
25 Courtesy of Association of American Railroads.

Module GP

6 (a) © 1995 PhotoDisc, Inc.
6 (b) © 1995 PhotoDisc, Inc.
6 (c) © 1995 PhotoDisc, Inc.
6 (d) © 1995 PhotoDisc, Inc.
10 © Miro Vintoniv/Stock, Boston.
11 © Michael Rosenfield/Tony Stone Images.
14 Courtesy of Corel Corporation.

Module MH

2 Photo courtesy of International Business Machines Corporation. Unauthorized use not permitted.
4 Photo courtesy of Canter Technology.
6 © Randy Beck, courtesy of Indianapolis Children's Museum.
12 Photo courtesy of International Business Machines.
16 The Bettmann Archive.
17 Photo courtesy of Digital Vision, Inc.
18 © Francoise/Science Library.

Module DB

11 © 1995 PhotoDisc, Inc.
20 © Matthew Borkoski/Stock, Boston.

Module AP

8 Photo courtesy of Autodesk.
9 © Stephen Agricola.
20 © Phil Matt.
22 © Jim Pickerell/Stock Connection.
22 © Jim Pickerell/Stock Connection.
23 © Larry Mulvehill/Science Source.

Module SA

2 © Richard Pasley/Stock, Boston.
5 © Tim Brown/Tony Stone Worldwide.
12 © Phil Matt.
14 Photo courtesy of CompUSA, the computer superstore.
16 Photo courtesy of International Business Machines Corporation. Unauthorized use not permitted.

Module SD

7 James Holmes, Oxford Instruments LTD/ Science Photo Library.
12 © Jim Pickerell/Stock Connection.
16 UPI/Bettmann.
17 © Peter Menzel/Stock, Boston.

Index

A

B

C

D

E

F

I

J

K

L

M

N

O

P

Q

R

S

T

U

V

W

X